Lecture Notes in Artificial Intelligence 4511

Edited by J. G. Carbonell and J. Siekmann

Subseries of Lecture Notes in Computer Science

T0241847

Cristina Conati   Kathleen McCoy
Georgios Paliouras (Eds.)

User Modeling 2007

11th International Conference, UM 2007
Corfu, Greece, June 25-29, 2007
Proceedings

 Springer

Series Editors

Jaime G. Carbonell, Carnegie Mellon University, Pittsburgh, PA, USA
Jörg Siekmann, University of Saarland, Saarbrücken, Germany

Volume Editors

Cristina Conati
University of British Columbia
Vancouver, BC, Canada
E-mail: conati@cs.ubc.ca

Kathleen McCoy
University of Delaware
Newark, DE, USA
E-mail: mccoy@cis.udel.edu

Georgios Paliouras
Institute of Informatics and Telecommunications
National Centre of Scientific Research (NCSR) "Demokritos"
PO Box 60228, Ag. Paraskevi, Attiki, 15310, Greece
Email: paliourg@iit.demokritos.gr

Library of Congress Control Number: 2007928795

CR Subject Classification (1998): H.5.2, I.2, H.5, H.4, I.6, J.4, J.5, K.4, K.6

LNCS Sublibrary: SL 7 – Artificial Intelligence

ISSN   0302-9743
ISBN-10   3-540-73077-X Springer Berlin Heidelberg New York
ISBN-13   978-3-540-73077-4 Springer Berlin Heidelberg New York

This work is subject to copyright. All rights are reserved, whether the whole or part of the material is
concerned, specifically the rights of translation, reprinting, re-use of illustrations, recitation, broadcasting,
reproduction on microfilms or in any other way, and storage in data banks. Duplication of this publication
or parts thereof is permitted only under the provisions of the German Copyright Law of September 9, 1965,
in its current version, and permission for use must always be obtained from Springer. Violations are liable
to prosecution under the German Copyright Law.

Springer is a part of Springer Science+Business Media

springer.com

© Springer-Verlag Berlin Heidelberg 2007
Printed in Germany

Typesetting: Camera-ready by author, data conversion by Scientific Publishing Services, Chennai, India
Printed on acid-free paper   SPIN: 12077441   06/3180   5 4 3 2 1 0

Preface

As the variety and complexity of interactive systems increase, understanding how a system can dynamically capture relevant user needs and traits, and automatically adapting its interaction to this information, has become critical for devising effective advanced services and interfaces. The International User Modeling Conference represents the central forum for presenting the advances in the research and development of personalized, user-adaptive systems. Bi-annual scientific meetings of the user modeling community started in 1986 as a small invitational workshop held in Maria Laach, Germany, with 24 participants. The workshops continued with an open format, and grew into an international conference with 74 submissions in 1994. While maintaining its feel as a highly engaged and intimate community, the conference has continued to grow, reaching the record number of 169 submissions (153 full papers and 16 posters) in this current edition, held in Corfu, Greece.

With an acceptance rate of 19.6% for long papers and 38% for posters, selected by a team of reviewers who proved to be exceptionally thorough and thoughtful in their reviewers, this year's program followed the high standards set by the previous editions, and presented an exciting range of interdisciplinary work covering topics such as cognitive modeling, modeling of user affect and meta-cognition, empirical evaluations of novel techniques, user modeling for mobile computing and recommender systems, user adaptivity and usability. In addition to 30 long paper presentations and 32 posters, this year's program featured 3 invited lectures, a doctoral consortium session with 5 student presentations, a demo program with 5 demos, 4 tutorials and 8 workshops. We continued the UM tradition of being a truly international event by having the first invited speaker from Asia (Yasuyoki Sumi from Japan), along with an invited speaker from North America (Martha Pollack from the USA) and one from Europe (Norbert Streitz from Germany). The international diversity was also reflected in the conference papers and posters with the geographical distribution of papers (posters) as follows: Europe 15 (14), Asia 3 (2), North America 10 (10), Australia/New Zealand 1 (3), Middle East 1 (2), South America 0 (1).

This volume includes the abstracts of the invited lectures and the texts of the papers, posters and doctoral consortium submissions presented at the conference. Separate notes and proceedings were generated for the four tutorials and eight workshops associated with the main program:

- Affective Natural Language Generation, by Fiorella de Rosis and Chris Mellish
- Modeling, Discovering and Using User Communities, by Myra Spiliopoulou, Dimitrios Pierrakos and Tanja Falkowski
- Evaluation 1: Fundamental Empirical Techniques and Caveats, by David Chin

- Evaluation 2: Formative Evaluation Methods for Adaptive Systems by Stephan Weibelzahl, Alexandros Paramythis, Judith Masthoff

W1: A3H: Fifth International Workshop on Authoring of Adaptive and Adaptable Hypermedia, by Alexandra Cristea and Rosa M. Carro

W2: Personalization in E-Learning Environments at Individual and Group Level, by Peter Brusilovsky, Maria Grigoriadou and Kyparisia Papanikolaou

W3: Personalization-Enhanced Access to Cultural Heritage, by Lora M. Aroyo, Tsvi Kuflik, Oliviero Stock and Massimo Zancanaro

W4: Data Mining for User Modeling, by Ryan S.J.D. Baker, Joseph E. Beck, Bettina Berendt, Alexander Kroener, Ernestina Menasalvas and Stephan Weibelzahl

W5: Towards User Modeling and Adaptive Systems for All, by Martyn Cooper, Carlos Velasco, Jesus G. Boticario and Olga Santos

W6: SociUM: Adaptation and Personalization in Social Systems: Groups, Teams, Communities, by Julita Vassileva, Manolis Tzagarakis and Vania Dimitrova

W7: 2nd Workshop on Personalization for E-Health, by Floriana Grasso, Alison Cawsey, Cecile Paris, Silvana Quaglini and Ross Wilkinson

W8: UbiDeUM: Ubiquitous and Decentralized User Modeling, by Shlomo Berkovsky, Keith Cheverst, Peter Dolog, Dominik Heckmann, Tsvi Kuflik, Phivos Mylonas, Jerome Picault, Julita Vassileva

UM 2007 was co-organized by the National Center for Scientific Research "Demokritos" and the Ionian University, under the auspices of User Modeling, Inc. Many people worked hard to make this event a success, and they deserve our most heartfelt acknowledgments. The UM 2007 Program Committee members gave invaluable contributions at several stages of the conference organization, including the selection of the invited speakers and of additional reviewers, and the nomination of the best papers. But most importantly, together with the additional reviewers they did an outstanding job at providing careful and insightful reviews on all submissions. Susan Bull and Antonio Krüger were the minds behind our excellent tutorial and workshop programs, while Kurt Van-Lehn and George Magoulas organized the Doctoral Consortium. We would also like to thank Christos Papatheodorou (Organizing Chair), Constantine D. Spyropoulos and Tasos Anastasakos (Sponsorship Co-chairs), Yannis Ioannidis and Alexandros Paramythis (Demos Co-chairs), Nikolaos Avouris and Michalis Vazirgiannis (Publicity Co-chairs). Last but not least, we would like to thank Giannis Tsakonas and Dimitris Gavrilis for the design of our publicity material and the maintenance of the Web site, as well as Spyros Veronikis, Dimitris Pierrakos, Hara Zarvala and Pantelis Lilis for helping with the organization of the conference.

June 2007   Cristina Conati
                                                                         Kathleen F. McCoy
                                                                        Georgios Paliouras

Organization

The 11th International Conference on User Modeling (UM 2007) was co-organized by the National Center for Scientific Research "Demokritos" and the Ionian University, under the auspices of User Modeling, Inc..

Committees

Conference Chair	Georgios Paliouras (National Center for Scientific Research "Demokritos," Greece)
Program Co-chairs	Cristina Conati (University of British Columbia, Vancouver, BC, Canada)
	Kathleen F. McCoy (University of Delaware, Newark, DE, USA)
Organizing Chair	Christos Papatheodorou (Ionian University, Greece)
Doctoral Consortium Co-chairs	George D. Magoulas (University of London, UK)
	Kurt VanLehn (University of Pittsburgh, USA)
Workshop/Tutorials Co-chairs	Susan Bull (University of Birmingham, UK)
	Antonio Krüger (University of Muenster, Germany)
Sponsorship Co-chairs	Constantine D. Spyropoulos (National Center for Scientific Research "Demokritos," Greece)
	Tasos Anastasakos (Yahoo Inc., USA)
Demo Co-chairs	Yannis Ioannidis (National and Kapodistrian University of Athens, Greece)
	Alexandros Paramythis (Johannes Kepler University, Austria)
Publicity Co-chairs	Nikolaos Avouris (University of Patras, Greece)
	Michalis Vazirgiannis (Athens University of Economics and Business, Greece)

Program Committee

Elisabeth Andre	University of Augsburg, Germany
Liliana Ardissono	University of Turin, Italy
Lora M. Aroyo	Eindhoven University of Technology and Free University Amsterdam, The Netherlands
Ryan Baker	University of Nottingham, UK

Mathias Bauer	mineway GmbH, Germany
Joseph Beck	Carnegie Mellon University, USA
Nadia Bianchi-Berthouze	University College London, UK
Peter Brusilovsky	University of Pittsburgh, USA
Susan Bull	University of Birmingham, UK
Sandra Carberry	University of Delaware, USA
Giuseppe Carenini	University of British Columbia, Canada
David N. Chin	University of Hawaii, USA
Stavros Christodoulakis	Technical University of Crete, Greece
Albert Corbett	Carnegie Mellon University, USA
Fiorella de Rosis	University of Bari, Italy
Vania Dimitrova	University of Leeds, UK
Stephanie Elzer	Millersville University, USA
Cristina Gena	University of Turin, Italy
Brad Goodman	The MITRE Corporation, USA
Jim Greer	University of Saskatchewan, Canada
Jon Herlocker	Oregon State University, USA
Eric Horvitz	Microsoft Research, USA
Anthony Jameson	DFKI and International University in Germany
Vangelis Karkaletsis	National Centre for Scientific Research "Demokritos," Greece
Judy Kay	University of Sydney, Australia
Alfred Kobsa	University of California, Irvine, USA
Joseph Konstan	University of Minnesota, USA
Frank Linton	The MITRE Corporation, USA
Diane Litman	University of Pittsburgh, USA
Alessandro Micarelli	University of Rome 3, Italy
Lisa Michaud	Wheaton College, USA
Eva Millan	Universidad de Malaga, Spain
Tanja Mitrovic	University of Canterbury, New Zealand
Bamshad Mobasher	DePaul University, USA
Chas Murray	Carnegie Learning, USA
Jon Oberlander	University of Edinburgh, UK
Helen Pain	University of Edinburgh, UK
Cecile Paris	CSIRO, Australia
Daniela Petrelli	University of Sheffield, UK
Pearl Pu	Swiss Federal Institute of Technology in Lausanne, Switzerland
Barry Smyth	University College Dublin, Ireland
Constantine Stephanidis	ICS-FORTH, Greece
Julita Vassileva	University of Saskatchewan, Canada
Maria Virvou	University of Piraeus, Greece
Frank Wittig	SAP AG, Germany
Massimo Zancanaro	ITC-irst, Italy
Ingrid Zukerman	Monash University, Australia

Organizing Committee

Dimitris Gavrilis   University of Patras, Greece
Dimitrios Pierrakos   National Centre for Scientific Research
                            "Demokritos," Greece
Hara Zarvala   Ionian University, Greece
Spyros Veronikis   Ionian University, Greece
Pantelis Lilis   Ionian University, Greece
Giannis Tsakonas   Ionian University, Greece

Additional Reviewers

Sarabjot Singh Anand   Jill Freyne   Nikolaos Nanas
Margherita Antona   Susan Gauch   Pantelis Nasikas
Jim Arvo   Abigail Gertner   Hien Nguyen
Bettina Berendt   Anna Goy   Elena Not
Dan Bohus   Nancy Green   Michael O'Mahony
Andrea Bunt   Seda Guerses   Fabio Pianesi
Robin Burke   Eduardo Guzmàn   Dimitrios Pierrakos
Valeria Carofiglio   Dominik Heckmann   Symeon Retalis
Li Chen   Shamsi Iqbal   Jöerg Schreck
Nathalie Colineau   Katerina Kabassi   Eric Schwarzkopf
Berardina Nadja De   Stasinos   Erin Shaw
  Carolis   Konstantopoulos   Christoph Stahl
Peter Dolog   Alexander Kröener   Carlo Strapparava
Doug Downey   Daniel Kudenko   Pramuditha Suraweera
Jon Dron   Vitaveska Lanfranchi   Michael Yudelson
Kate Forbes-Riley   Heather Maclaren   Diego Zapata-Rivera
Paulina Fragou   Rob McArthur   Jiyong Zhang

Sponsoring Institutions

 Microsoft Corporation

 Springer - Academic Journals, Books and Online Media

 PASCAL - Network of Excellence for Multimodal Interfaces

 InterOptics SA - Information Services

 SWETS SA - Subscription Services

 National Science Foundation

 Prefecture of Corfu

 DELOS - Network of Excellence on Digital Libraries

Table of Contents

Collaborative Filtering and Recommender Systems

Cognitive Modeling

User Adaptation and Usability

Modeling Affect and Meta-cognition

Mobile, Ubiquitous, and Context Aware User Modeling

Intelligent Information Retrieval, Information Filtering, and Content Personalization

Poster Papers

Doctoral Consortium Papers

The Disappearing Computer:
User-Centered Interaction Design for Smart Artefacts

Norbert Streitz

Fraunhofer IPSI, Darmstadt, Germany
streitz@ipsi.fraunhofer.de

The increasing trend of embedding computation in everyday objects creating *smart artefacts* (Streitz et al., 2005 b) and the associated concept of the *disappearing computer* (Streitz, 2001, Streitz et al, 2007) raises new challenges for designing interactive systems. The unobtrusive character of this development is illustrated in this statement by Streitz and Nixon (2005): "It seems like a paradox but it will soon become reality: The rate at which computers disappear will be matched by the rate at which information technology will increasingly permeate our environment and our lives".

Computers used to be primary artefacts, now they become "secondary" artefacts moving in the background in several ways. We distinguish here between "physical" and "mental" disappearance (Streitz, 2001). Human-*Computer* Interaction is being transformed to Human-*Artefact* and Human-*Environment* Interaction (Streitz et al, 2001). While "disappearance" is a major aspect, smart artefacts are also characterized by sensors collecting data about the environment, the devices and humans in this context. User models, profiles, and preferences will be more and more based on sensor data obtained by observing and analysing users' behavior in the real world. They are also the starting point for discussing issues as privacy due to comprehensive activity monitoring and recording of personal data. This creates a new set of challenges for designing the interaction of humans with computers embedded in everyday objects resulting in smart artefacts. Smart environments are becoming a major application area for the deployment of adaptive and personalized systems in "real-world" applications when integrating mobile, ubiquitous and context-aware computing. This keynote will present examples from different applications domains based on a discussion of ubiquitous computing and ambient intelligence.

The integration of information, communication and sensing technology into everyday objects results in augmenting the standard functionality of artefacts thus enabling a new quality of interaction and "behavior" (of artefacts). Without entering into the philosophical discussion of when you might call an artefact "smart", the following distinction seems useful (Streitz et al., 2005b).

System-Oriented, Importunate Smartness
An environment is called "smart" if it enables certain self-directed (re)actions of individual artefacts (or by the environment as a whole) based on previously and continuously collected information. In this version of 'smartness', the environment would be active (in many cases even proactive) and in control of the situation by making decisions on what to do next, and actually take action and execute them automatically (without a human in the loop).

C. Conati, K. McCoy, and G. Paliouras (Eds.): UM 2007, LNAI 4511, pp. 1–2, 2007.
© Springer-Verlag Berlin Heidelberg 2007

People-Oriented, Empowering Smartness

The above view can be contrasted by another perspective where the empowering function is in the foreground and which can be summarized as "smart spaces make people smarter". This is achieved by keeping "the human in the loop", thus empowering people to be in control, making informed decisions and taking actions. In this case, the environment also collects data about what is going on and aggregates the data, but provides and communicates the resulting information for guidance and subsequent actions determined by the people.

Another important aspect of our work is to go beyond traditional support for productivity-oriented tasks, e.g., in the office, and focus on designing "experiences" with the help of smart or augmented spaces (Streitz et al. 2005a). The goal is to design smart artefacts that enable us to interact with them and the overall environment in a simple and intuitive way or just being exposed to it perceiving indicators in the environment that indicate events and changes. This includes extending the awareness about our physical and social environment by providing observation data and parameters that – in many cases – are "invisible" to our human senses and therefore enable new experiences. Examples are taken from our Ambient Agoras project (Streitz et al, 2007). When using smart artefacts for designing experiences, one has to reflect also on the role of "affordances" that are associated with "traditional" real-world objects and how the mental model and associated metaphors (Streitz, 1988) of its previous use are being extended by making it smart. The affordances of a well established object can help to focus on interacting with the hidden affordances of the digital application. Examples are being reported in the keynote presentation.

References

Streitz, N.: Mental Models and Metaphors: Implications for the design of adaptive user-system interfaces. In: Mandl, H., Lesgold, A. (eds.) Learning Issues for Intelligent Tutoring Systems. Cognitive Science Series, pp. 164–186. Springer, New York (1988)

Streitz, N.: Augmented Reality and the Disappearing Computer. In: Smith, M., Salvendy, G., Harris, D., Koubek, R. (eds.) Cognitive Engineering, Intelligent Agents and Virtual Reality, pp. 738–742. Lawrence Erlbaum Associates, Mahwah (2001)

Streitz, N., Kameas, A., Mavrommati, I. (eds.): The Disappearing Computer. LNCS, vol. 4500. Springer, Heidelberg (2007)

Streitz, N., Magerkurth, C., Prante, T., Röcker, C.: From Information Design to Experience Design: Smart Artefacts and the Disappearing Computer. ACM Interactions, Special Issue on Ambient Intelligence 12(4), 21–25 (July and August 2005)

Streitz, N., Nixon, P.: The Disappearing Computer. Communications of the ACM 48(3), 33–35 (2005)

Streitz, N., Röcker, C., Prante, T., van Alphen, D., Stenzel, R., Magerkurth, C.: Designing Smart Artifacts for Smart Environments. IEEE Computer, March 2005, pp. 41–49 (2005b)

Streitz, N., Tandler, P., Müller-Tomfelde, C., Konomi, S.: Roomware: Towards the Next Generation of Human-Computer Interaction based on an Integrated Design of Real and Virtual Worlds. In: Carroll, J. (ed.) Human-Computer Interaction in the New Millennium, pp. 553–578. Addison-Wesley, Reading (2001)

Experience Medium: Toward a New Medium for Exchanging Experiences

Yasuyuki Sumi

Graduate School of Infomatics, Kyoto University,
Yoshida-Honmachi, Sakyo-ku, Kyoto 606-8501, Japan
sumi@acm.org
http://www.ii.ist.i.kyoto-u.ac.jp/~sumi

In this talk, I will propose a notion of "experience medium" in which we can exchange our experiences in museum touring, daily meetings, collaborative work, etc. The experience medium is a medium for capturing, interpreting, and creating our experiences, i.e., not only verbalized representations of our experiences but also their contextual information (awareness, common sense, atmosphere). I will show our previous and ongoing projects as follows:

- Building a context-aware mobile assistant for guiding museum visitors and facilitating communications among the users by casual chats between the users' guide characters and comic-like diaries based on their visiting records;
- Collaborative capturing and interpretation of experiences like conversations, staying together, and gazing something by ubiquitous and wearable sensors; and
- Supporting systems of casual communications by facilitating to share photos and comments among community members.

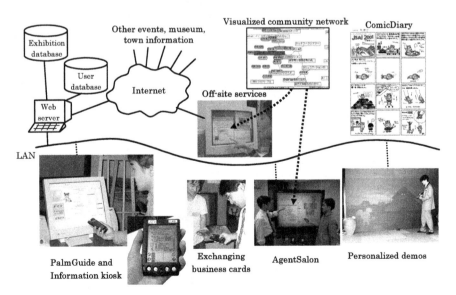

C. Conati, K. McCoy, and G. Paliouras (Eds.): UM 2007, LNAI 4511, pp. 3–4, 2007.
© Springer-Verlag Berlin Heidelberg 2007

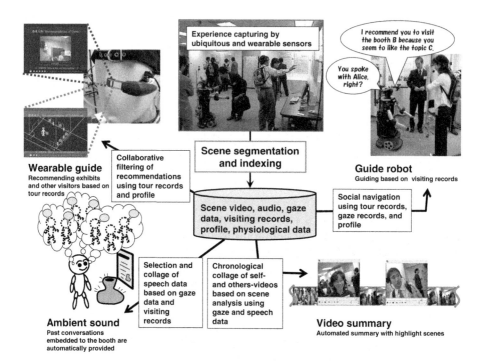

Intelligent Assistive Technology: The Present and the Future

Martha E. Pollack

Computer Science and Engineering, University of Michigan, Ann Arbor, MI 48109 USA
pollackm@eecs.umich.edu

Abstract. Recent advances in two areas of computer science—wireless sensor networks and AI inference strategies—have made it possible to envision a wide range of technologies that can improve the lives of people with physical, cognitive, and/or psycho-social impairments. To be effective, these systems must perform extensive user modeling in order to adapt to the changing needs and capabilities of their users. This invited talk provides a survey of current projects aimed at the development of intelligent assistive technology and describes further design challenges and opportunities.

Keywords: Assistive technology.

1 Intelligent Assistive Technology

The world's population is rapidly aging: by 2050, the percentage of people worldwide over the age of 60 is expected to double (to 21.4%), and the percentage of those over the age of 85 will quadruple (to 4.2%) [1]. While many adults will remain healthy and active for their whole lives, older adults have higher rates of disabilities—physical, cognitive, and/or psycho-social—than do younger people. There has thus been growing interest in developing assistive technology that can help older adults and others with impairments to remain more autonomous for longer periods of time. Recent advances in two areas of computer science—wireless sensor networks and AI inference strategies—have been particularly important in the development of such technology. This talk surveys intelligent assistive technology, focusing on technology targeted to people with cognitive impairment. Such systems must perform extensive user modeling to adapt to their users' changing needs and abilities, and the hope is that UM researchers will be interested in contributing to their design.

In general, current assistive technology for cognition (ATC) has three main goals: providing *assurance* to a user and her caregiver of her safety and well-being; helping a user *compensate* for her impairment; and/or providing continual *assessment* of a user's level of functioning. To achieve these goals, most ATC systems use sensors to monitor a user and obtain information about her location, level of activity, performance of daily activities, etc. Because the information provided by such sensors is noisy, methods of reasoning under uncertainty, such as Hidden Markov Models or Dynamic Bayes Nets are employed to interpret the sensor data. Examples of this work include [2,3,4].

C. Conati, K. McCoy, and G. Paliouras (Eds.): UM 2007, LNAI 4511, pp. 5–6, 2007.
© Springer-Verlag Berlin Heidelberg 2007

Sensed information can be used in assurance systems, to provide alerts when deviations from normal patterns of activity are detected (e.g., [5]), or it can be subject to further analysis and inference within compensation or assessment systems. The former assist people in navigating, managing a daily schedule, completing multi-step tasks, locating objects, and so on. Examples include Autominder [6], which uses AI planning technology to track the activities that a user is expected to perform, and then uses machine learning to induce strategies for interacting with a user when the expected activities have not been performed on time, and Coach [7], which models plan-tracking and reminding as a Markov Decision Process. Less work has been done to date on assessment systems, but an interesting example uses variations in walking speed as an early indicator of potential cognitive decline [8].

Obviously, this is just an extremely brief introduction, highlighting a handful of systems as illustration of ATC. More complete surveys can be found in [9,10].

References

1. United Nations Dept. of Economic and Social Affairs Population Division http://www.un.org/esa/population/unpop.htm
2. Liao, L., Fox, D., Kautz, H.: Location-based activity recognition using relational Markov networks. In: Proc. of the Intl. Joint Conf. on Artificial Intelligence, pp. 773–778 (2005)
3. Philipose, M., Fishkin, K.P., Perkowitz, M., Patterson, D.J., Fox, D., Kautz, H., Hahnel, D.: Inferring activities from interactions with objects. In: IEEE Pervasive Computing 3(4), 50–57 (2004)
4. Munguia-Tapia, E., Intille, S.S., Larson, K.: Activity recognition in the home setting using simple and ubiquitous sensors. In: Ganzinger, H. (ed.) ESOP 1988. LNCS, vol. 300, pp. 158–175. Springer, Heidelberg (1988)
5. Glascock, A.P., Kutzik, D.M.: The impact of behavioral monitoring technology on the provision of health care in the home. Journal of Universal Computer Science 12(1), 80–98 (2006)
6. Pollack, M.E., Brown, L., Colbry, D., et al.: Autominder: An intelligent cognitive orthotic system for people with memory impairment. Robotics and Autonomous Systems 44, 273–282 (2003)
7. Boger, J., Poupart, P.l., Hoey, J., Boutilier, C., Fernie, G., Mihailidis, A.: A planning system based on Markov decision processes to guide people with dementia through activities of daily living. In: IEEE Transactions on Info. Tech. in Biomedicine 10(2), 323–333 (2006)
8. Jimison, H., Pavel, M., McKanna, J., Pavel, J.: Unobtrusive monitoring of computer interactions to detect cognitive status in elders. In: IEEE Trans. On Inf. Tech. in Biomedicine 8(3), 248–252 (2004)
9. Pollack, M.E.: Intelligent technology for an aging population: The uses of AI to assist elders with cognitive impairment. In: AI Magazine 26(2), 9–24 (2005)
10. LoPresti, E., Mihailidis, A., Kirsch, N.L.: Assistive technology for cognitive rehabilitation: State of the art. In: Neuropsychological Rehabilitation 14(1-2), 5–29 (2004)

Exploiting Evidence Analysis
in Plan Recognition[*]

Sandra Carberry[1] and Stephanie Elzer[2]

[1] Dept. of Computer Science, University of Delaware, Newark, DE 19716 USA
carberry@cis.udel.edu
[2] Dept. of Computer Science, Millersville University, Millersville, PA 17551 USA
elzer@cs.millersville.edu

Abstract. Information graphics, such as bar charts and line graphs, that appear in popular media generally have a message that they are intended to convey. We have developed a novel plan inference system that uses evidence in the form of communicative signals from the graphic to recognize the graphic designer's intended message. We contend that plan inference research would benefit from examining how each of its evidence sources impacts the system's success. This paper presents such an evidence analysis for the communicative signals that are captured in our plan inference system, and the paper shows how the results of this evidence analysis are informing our research on plan recognition and application systems.

1 Introduction

Plan recognition systems develop a model of an agent's plans and goals by analyzing the agent's actions. We contend that plan recognition research and its applications would be strengthened by focusing not only on the success of the overall system but also on the impact of the different evidence sources on the system's ability to form a correct hypothesis. This paper describes a novel use of plan recognition — namely, to hypothesize the intended message of an information graphic. The paper presents an analysis of the impact of different communicative signals on the system's success, and it discusses how our research has benefited from this evidence analysis.

Section 2 introduces plan recognition from information graphics. Section 3 presents our Bayesian model of plan recognition, with emphasis on the cues available to a graphic designer. Section 4 presents an analysis of the various types of cues on the system's recognition of a graphic's message; Section 5 discusses the impact of this evidence analysis on our work and argues that other plan recognition research would benefit from evaluating the contributions of their various evidence sources.

---

[*] This material is based upon work supported by the National Science Foundation under Grant No. IIS-0534948.

C. Conati, K. McCoy, and G. Paliouras (Eds.): UM 2007, LNAI 4511, pp. 7–16, 2007.
© Springer-Verlag Berlin Heidelberg 2007

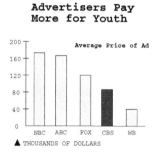
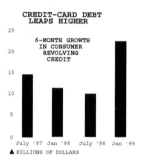

Fig. 1. Two Graphics from Business Week

2   Plan Inference and Information Graphics

Our research is concerned with information graphics (non-pictorial graphs such as bar charts and line graphs). Most information graphics that appear in popular media such as magazines, newspapers, and formal reports, have a message that they are intended to convey. Consider for example the information graphics displayed in Figure 1. The intended message of the left graphic is ostensibly that CBS ranks fourth in terms of the average price of Ad compared with NBC, ABC, FOX, and WB, and the intended message of the right graphic is ostensibly that consumer revolving credit grew in Jan '99 in contrast with the previously decreasing trend from July '97 to July '98.

We have developed a novel application of plan inference techniques to information graphics. In the context of our work, the designer of the graphic is treated as the user whose plan is being modeled, and plan inference hypothesizes this plan that the graphic designer intends for the viewer of the graphic to infer in recognizing the intended message of the graphic. This correlates with plan inference in language understanding, where the speaker intends for the listener to infer the speaker's plan and thereby recognize the intended meaning of the speaker's utterance. And as with language understanding, identifying the intended message of an information graphic will enable our system to exhibit behavior appropriate to the recognized message.

3   Bayesian Plan Recognition from Information Graphics

We have designed a Bayesian system for inferring the plan that the graphic designer intends for the viewer to pursue in recognizing the graphic's message which is captured by the plan's top-level communicative goal. Although we believe that our methodology is extendible to other kinds of information graphics, our implemented system currently handles only simple bar charts such as the ones shown in Figure 1. Input to our plan inference system is an xml representation of a graphic, produced by a computer vision module[1] that specifies the graph's axes, the individual bars (including their heights, labels, color, etc.), and

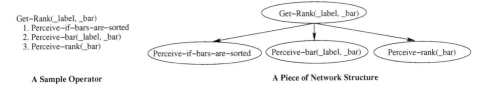

Get-Rank(_label, _bar)
  1. Perceive-if-bars-are-sorted
  2. Perceive-bar(_label, _bar)
  3. Perceive-rank(_bar)

A Sample Operator   **A Piece of Network Structure**

Fig. 2. A Sample Operator and its Associated Piece of Network Structure

the graph's caption. The plan inference system outputs a logical representation of the intended message of the graphic which is then realized in English.

3.1   Constructing the Network

The top level of our Bayesian network captures the twelve categories of communicative goals (or categories of messages) that we identified for simple bar charts, such as *getting the rank of an entity, comparing two entities, contrasting a point with a trend*, etc. As with previous plan recognition work[2], we use operators to decompose high-level goals into a set of subgoals; since we are working with information graphics, subgoals eventually decompose into perceptual or cognitive tasks[3], where a perceptual task is one that can be performed by viewing the graphic (such as determining which of two bars is taller in a bar chart) and a cognitive task is one that requires a mental computation (such as interpolating between two values). The operators determine the structure of the Bayesian network, in that the subgoals in an operator become children of their goal node in the Bayesian network. Figure 2 displays a plan operator for getting the rank of a bar given its label and the piece of network structure derived from it. However, memory limitations restrict the size of the network. Our solution is to start with only the ten easiest perceptual tasks as identified by our effort estimation rules[4] (limited to one instantiation per task type) and with perceptual tasks whose parameters are salient entities (such as a bar that is colored differently from other bars, as in Figure 1). The network is then built by both 1) chaining backwards from these primitive perceptual tasks to higher-level goals, and 2) chaining forwards from each newly entered node to primitive tasks.

3.2   Evidence Nodes

Bayesian networks need evidence for guiding the construction of a hypothesis. We have identified eight kinds of communicative signals that can appear in information graphics: effort, highlighting, annotation, most-recent-date, salient-height, noun-matching-bar-label, verb, and adjective.

The AutoBrief project was concerned with generating information graphics[3]. We have adopted their hypothesis that the graphic designer constructs a graphic that makes intended tasks as easy as possible. Thus the relative difficulty of different perceptual tasks serves as a communicative signal about which tasks the viewer was intended to perform in deciphering the graphic's intended message.

For example, identifying the taller of two bars in a bar chart will be much easier if the bars are adjacent and significantly different in height than if they are widely separated and only slightly different in height. We constructed a set of effort estimation rules for estimating the effort involved in performing different perceptual tasks on simple bar charts. These rules have been validated by eyetracking experiments and are presented in [4].

Coloring one bar differently from other bars in the bar chart, or annotating it with a special mark, draws attention to the bar and provides highlighting or annotation evidence. The presence of a bar associated most closely (via its label) with the date of the publication is used as most-recent-date evidence, since we hypothesize that it is mutually believed that the viewer will notice events that are current. A bar that is significantly taller than other bars "stands out" in the graphic, and provides salient-height evidence. The presence of a noun in the caption that matches the label of a bar in the graphic is a communicative signal that the referenced entity is important to the graphic designer's message.

Nodes capturing these six types of evidence are attached to each primitive perceptual task in the network, since effort evidence captures the difficulty of a perceptual task and the other five kinds of evidence capture the presence/absence of some feature of a bar serving as a parameter of the perceptual task.

The presence of certain verbs (such as *lag* or *rise*) and adjectives (such as *more* or *largest*) in the caption can signal the category of the intended message, such as conveying the rank of an entity or conveying a rising trend. (Adjectives derived from verbs, such as *rising*, are treated as verbs.) We use a part-of-speech tagger and a stemmer to identify the presence of one of our identified verb or adjective classes in the caption; nodes capturing this evidence are attached to the top-level node in the network since they suggest a general category of message.

3.3 Implementation

The conditional probability tables in our Bayesian network are obtained from our corpus of 110 bar charts. To facilitate leave-one-out cross validation of results (and also re-training under different sets of evidence, as discussed in the next section), we automated the construction of a spreadsheet containing the information needed from each graphic to compute the necessary probabilities. System performance was measured using leave-one-out cross validation. The system's hypothesis for a graphic was viewed as correct if it matched the intended message assigned to the graphic by the human annotators and the probability that the system assigned to the hypothesis exceeded 50%. Overall success was computed as the average success over the 110 graphics in the corpus.

4 Analyzing How Evidence Impacts Plan Recognition

Research in many areas, including dialogue act tagging[6], emotion recognition [7], and question answering[8], have analyzed their knowledge sources to identify to what extent each affects the system's hypothesis. In many cases, this has consisted of examining the features in the resulting decision tree or comparing performance results of decision trees constructed from different sets of features; in the work on question answering by Moldovan et. al., the system is prevented from accessing various resources such as WordNet, and system performance is compared to a baseline system with all resources accessible. However, in the domain of plan recognition, evaluation has focused on the overall success of the system and has given little attention to how much each evidence source contributes to recognizing the user's plans and goals. We contend that an analysis of the impact of the various sources of evidence can inform subsequent research directed at improving the system and can be used in the development of applications utilizing plan inference. This section provides an analysis of the contribution of each of our evidence sources to recognizing the intended message of an information graphic, and Section 5 discusses how this analysis has impacted our subsequent research.

We wanted to evaluate how each kind of evidence impacted system performance by 1) examining system performance with only one kind of evidence, and 2) examining the degradation in system performance when a particular kind of evidence is disabled. It is important to note that disabling an evidence source means that we effectively remove this kind of evidence node from the network by eliminating its ability to contribute to the network probabilities. This is different from recording that the particular cue, such as highlighting, is absent, since the absence, as well as the presence, of a cue is evidence.

To provide baselines for our experiments, we ran the system first without any evidence sources enabled and then with all eight evidence sources enabled. Even without any evidence sources, the system still has certain basic information, such as the ten easiest perceptual tasks (limited to one instantiation per task type) from which the Bayesian net is constructed and whether the independent axis is ordinal (such as consecutive dates, age groups, etc.). The system without any evidence sources enabled had a success rate of only 6% at identifying the intended message of a bar chart, while the system with all evidence sources enabled had a success rate of 79%.

We then ran eight experiments in which only one kind of evidence (such as the presence/absence of highlighting in a graphic) was enabled, and compared the improvement in performance with the baseline system with no evidence sources enabled. Similarly, we ran eight experiments in which one kind of evidence was disabled, and analyzed the degradation in performance (if any) that resulted from omission of this evidence source. We used a one-tailed McNemar test for the significance of changes in related samples[9,5]. McNemar is a non-parametric test that is appropriate when the samples are related. For our experiments, the samples are related since one sample is obtained from a baseline system and the other sample is obtained after some perturbation of the system (by adding or removing an evidence source). The results of these experiments are shown in Tables 1 and 2. In Table 1, the hypothesis H_1 is that adding the particular evidence source produces better performance than the system with no evidence; in Table 2, H_1 is that removing an evidence source results in worse performance.

Table 1. Improvement in Performance with Addition of Evidence Source

Baseline: System Without Any Evidence	6% success rate		
TYPE OF EVIDENCE ADDED	**SUCCESS RATE**	**McNEMAR STATISTIC**	**p VALUE**
Only effort evidence	57%	52.155	.0001
Only current-date evidence	49%	45.021	.0001
Only annotation evidence	35%	29.032	.0001
Only verb evidence	24%	17.053	.0001
Only highlighting evidence	21%	14.063	.0001
Only evidence about salient-height	19%	12.071	.0005
Only evidence about noun-matching-bar-label	18%	9.600	.001
Adjective	14%	6.125	.01

The rightmost column of each table gives the p value — that is, the significance level at which the null hypothesis is rejected and H_1 is accepted.

Table 1 shows that addition of every evidence source produces improved performance that is statistically significant at the .01 level or better. The three evidence sources producing the largest improvement in performance were *effort*, *current-date*, and *annotation*. On the other hand, Table 2 shows that *noun-matching-bar-label*, *effort*, and *current-date* are the only evidence sources whose removal caused degradation in performance that was statistically significant at the .01 level or better.[1] Moreover, the degradation in performance was much less than the contribution of each of these evidence sources when they are the only source used. Thus it is clear that the evidence sources compensate for one another: when one source of evidence is disabled, cues from other sources generally provide evidence that still enables recognition of the intended message.

We will discuss the *effort* and *noun-matching-bar-label* evidence sources since their removal has the greatest impact on system performance. *Effort* both has the greatest impact on system performance when it is the only source of evidence and results in major degradation in performance when it is removed. Although we did not expect this, in retrospect it is not surprising since *effort* evidence reflects how the organization of data in the graphic facilitates different perceptual tasks; thus it affects the message of every graphic whereas other signals, such as *highlighting*, only occur in some graphs. However, *effort* by itself is insufficient for recognizing some kinds of messages, such as that a graph is conveying the rank of a particular bar. (The rules for estimating *effort* do not take salience into account; thus a bar being highlighted does not affect the *effort* computation, but the highlighting is captured by the *highlighting* evidence node.) We also find that, when *effort* is the only evidence source, the average probability attached to the correct hypotheses is 70% whereas the average probability assigned to hypotheses about these same graphs with all evidence is 98%. Thus we conclude that although *effort* has a strong impact on system performance, not only is it

---

[1] Note that disabling the *adjective* evidence source improved performance, although this change was not statistically significant.

Table 2. Degradation in Performance with Omission of Evidence Source

Baseline: System With All Evidence	79% success rate		
TYPE OF EVIDENCE OMITTED	**SUCCESS RATE**	**McNEMAR STATISTIC**	**p VALUE**
Noun-matching-bar-label evidence	70%	8.100	.005
Effort evidence	71%	5.818	.01
Current-date evidence	72%	6.125^2	.01
Highlighting evidence	74%	3.125	.05
Salient-height evidence	74%	3.125	.05
Annotation evidence	75%	2.250	*
Verb evidence	78%	0.500	*
Adjective evidence	81%	0.500	*

* Not statistically significant

insufficient by itself for recognizing certain categories of intention but it results in less confidence assigned to the correct hypotheses that it does produce.

Noun-matching-bar-label is another evidence source whose omission results in large degradation in system performance. We examined the graphs whose captions contained a noun matching a bar label and whose intended message was correctly identified using all evidence. Without *noun-matching-bar-label* evidence, the system failed to identify the correct message when there was no other evidence that made the bar salient, such as highlighting of the bar or the bar being significantly taller than other bars. However, in ten graphs, such additional evidence enabled the system to recognize the intended message even when *noun-matching bar-label* evidence was disabled. Thus we see that the absence of *noun-matching-bar-label* evidence degrades system performance, but this degradation is sometimes alleviated by the presence of other compensating evidence.

5   Lessons Learned

We contend that research on plan recognition and its use in adaptive systems would benefit from examining the impact of the individual evidence sources on the system's performance. In this section, we support this contention by showing how our evidence analysis has informed our research.

5.1   Applications of Plan Recognition from Information Graphics

We are applying plan inference from information graphics to several projects. In the area of digital libraries, the graphic's intended message will be used as the basis for the graphic's summarization, indexing, and retrieval; furthermore,

---

[2] The McNemar statistic is based on 1) the number correct by System-1 and wrong by System-2, and 2) the number wrong by System-1 and correct by System-2. Thus although a greater difference in success rates usually correlates with greater statistical significance, this is not always the case.

the graphic's summary will be integrated into an overall summary of the multimodal document. In the area of assistive technology, we have built a system, SIGHT, that infers the graphic's intended message and conveys it via speech to individuals with sight-impairments. A third project is a graph design assistant that will compare the message inferred for a graphic with the designer's intentions and help the designer improve the graphic so that it better conveys his desired message. And lastly, we are investigating a system for tutoring individuals with disabilities in the analysis, understanding, and construction of information graphics.

5.2   Implications of Evidence Analysis for Plan Recognition

Recognizing a graphic's intended message is an integral part of each of our projects; consequently, improving our system's success at plan recognition and extending our methodology to more complex graphics, such as grouped bar charts, is important. *Effort* evidence requires the construction of effort estimation rules and their validation via eyetracking experiments with human subjects; thus it requires substantial research, particularly in the case of grouped bar charts since there is little prior work by cognitive psychologists to draw on. Contrary to our expectations prior to our evidence analysis, *effort* evidence has the strongest overall impact on system performance, (in terms of its contribution when it is the only evidence source and the degradation in system performance when *effort* evidence is disabled). Thus our evidence analysis has caused us to give high priority to devising very good effort estimates for complex graphics.

Disabling *noun-matching-bar-label* evidence also had a major impact on system performance. This suggested that we examine our graphics to determine whether any similar forms of evidence were overlooked in our implementation. We found that mutual beliefs by the graphic designer and the intended viewer about implicitly salient entities seems to play a role in the intended message of a graphic. These implicitly salient entities are a function of the intended audience of a publication. For example, *Canadian Business* is directed toward Canadians. Thus, implicitly salient entities are those associated with Canada, such as *Canada*, *Toronto*, any Canadian company, etc. We hypothesize that if only one bar in a bar chart is labelled with an implicitly salient entity, this salience is similar to mentioning the bar's label in the caption. This conjecture is supported by an analysis of the accompanying articles of such graphics, where it is clear from the article that the graphic designer intended that the implicitly salient entity play a major role in the graphic's message. Thus we are adding such implicitly salient entities as a new evidence source.

We expected *verb* evidence to be a major factor in system success, and had begun to study WordNet similarity metrics that might improve system performance by identifying when new verbs in captions were related to our identified verb classes. However, our evidence analysis (particularly Table 2) suggests that additional verb evidence will not have much of an impact on system performance. Upon reviewing our graphics, we found that there is too much contradictory evidence provided by verbs; for example, the caption on a recent graphic conveying a rising trend in revenue from water parks was entitled *Slip Slidin' Away* — the verb *slide* would be most associated with falling trends and thus hamper recognition of the graphic's intended message. Thus our evidence analysis has led us to conclude that additional work on verb evidence would not be a productive use of research resources.

Our evidence analysis also motivated an addition to our system's message categories. When we gave our system a new bar chart containing a large number of bars and with the bar for Canada highlighted, it failed to infer that the graph was conveying the rank of *Canada*. Since our evidence analysis indicated that *effort* evidence has the strongest impact on system performance, we looked at the effort estimates for the perceptual tasks involved in the plan for the Get-rank message, and we found that identifying the exact rank (14th) of *Canada* required considerable effort given the large number of bars. Upon further reflection and discussion with viewers of the graphic, we realized that the graphic was not conveying the *exact* rank of Canada, but rather its *relative* rank (low, middle, high); estimating *relative rank* is a much easier perceptual task than computing *exact rank*. Thus we are adding *Get-relative-rank* as a new message category.

5.3   Exploiting Evidence Analysis in Applications

In addition to influencing plan inference research, evidence analysis can guide application projects by suggesting which sources of evidence will be most useful. Our graph design assistant will use the results of the evidence analysis to suggest ways in which a graphic might be improved so that it better conveys the designer's intended message. Evidence that has the strongest impact on plan inference, both overall (such as *effort* evidence) and with respect to the specific desired message category, will be considered first in deciding how the graph might be improved.

Our graph retrieval system for digital libraries will respond to requests for a particular kind of graphic. If the library does not contain a graphic whose intended message matches the request, we anticipate using the relative contribution of the different evidence sources to rank other graphics from which the desired information can be inferred. For example, suppose that the system is unable to satisfy a request for a graphic whose intended message is the rank of the CBS network in terms of revenue, but the system does have two alternative graphs from which the desired information could be inferred: 1) a graph conveying the rank of the NBC network (with the bar for NBC highlighted and the bar for CBS not distinguished in any way), and 2) a graph with the bars for network revenue ordered alphabetically by network rather than ordered by bar height. Since highlighting a bar has less impact on plan inference than does perceptual effort, the first alternative would be ranked higher than the second. Furthermore, the ranking of the different evidence sources will be used to explain why this graphic was selected.

Our SIGHT system provides blind individuals with access to information graphics by conveying the graphic's intended message via speech. The system should be able to justify its inferred message upon request, rather than forcing a blind individual to accept without question what the system has produced. The results of our evidence analysis will affect which evidence sources are considered first in constructing the justification. And lastly, our system for tutoring individuals with learning disabilities will use the results of our evidence analysis to order the kinds of evidence that students are taught to consider in inferring the graphic's message and for teaching students to construct graphs that effectively convey their desired message.

6   Conclusion

This paper presented our implemented system for extending plan recognition techniques to inferring the intended message of one kind of information graphic, simple bar charts. Prior work on plan recognition has focused on the success of the overall system, without considering the impact of different evidence sources. We have analyzed the individual evidence sources in our system, both in terms of their contribution to system performance when they are the only enabled evidence source and in terms of degradation in system performance when they are disabled. We contend that the results of such evidence analysis should be taken into account in further research, and we have shown the impact that our evidence analysis has had (and is having) on our plan inference in the domain of information graphics and on our application projects.

References

1. Chester, D., Elzer, S.: Getting computers to see information graphics so users do not have to. In: Proc. of 15th Int. Symp. on Methodologies for Intelligent Systems (2005)
2. Perrault, R., Allen, J.: A Plan-Based Analysis of Indirect Speech Acts. American Journal of Computational Linguistics 6(3-4), 167–182 (1980)
3. Kerpedjiev, S., Roth, S.: Mapping communicative goals into conceptual tasks to generate graphics in discourse. In: Proc. of Intelligent User Interfaces, pp. 60–67 (2000)
4. Elzer, S., Green, N., Carberry, S., Hoffman, J.: A model of perceptual task effort for bar charts and its role in recognizing intention. User Modeling and User-Adapted Interaction, pp. 1–30 (2006)
5. GraphPad Software. QuickCalcs: Online Calculators for Scientists (2002) http://www.graphpad.com/quickcalcs/McNemarEx.cfm
6. Shriberg, E., Bates, R., Stolcke, A., Taylor, P., Jurafsky, D., Ries, K., Coccaro, N., Martin, R., Meteer, M., Van Ess-Dykema, C.: Can prosody aid the automatic classification of dialog acts in conversational speech? Language and Speech (1998)
7. Forbes-Riley, K., Litman, D.: Predicting emotion in spoken dialogue from multiple knowledge sources. In: Proceedings of the HLT/NAACL, pp. 201–208 (2004)
8. Moldovan, D., Pasca, M., Harabagiu, S., Surdeanu, M.: Performance issues and error analysis in an open-domain question answering system. In: Proc. of the 40th Annual Meeting of the Assocation for Computational Linguistics, pp. 33–40 (2002)
9. Daniel, W.: Applied Nonparametric Statistics. Houghton Mifflin (1978)
10. Kennel, A.: Audiograf: A diagram-reader for the blind. In: Second Annual ACM Conference on Assistive Technologies, pp. 51–56 (1996)

Modeling the Acquisition of Fluent Skill in Educational Action Games

Ryan S.J.D. Baker[1], M.P. Jacob Habgood[1], Shaaron E. Ainsworth[1],
and Albert T. Corbett[2]

[1] Learning Sciences Research Institute, University of Nottingham, Nottingham, UK
[2] Human-Computer Interaction Institute, Carnegie Mellon University, Pittsburgh, PA, USA
ryan@educationaldatamining.org, jake@gamelearning.net,
Shaaron.Ainsworth@nottingham.ac.uk, corbett@cmu.edu

Abstract. There has been increasing interest in using games for education, but little investigation of how to model student learning within games [cf. 6]. We investigate how existing techniques for modeling the acquisition of fluent skill can be adapted to the context of an educational action game, Zombie Division. We discuss why this adaptation is necessarily different for educational action games than for other types of games, such as turn-based games. We demonstrate that gain in accuracy over time is straightforward to model using exponential learning curves, but that models of gain in speed over time must also take gameplay learning into account.

1 Introduction

Over the last decades, a number of very effective techniques have been developed for modeling student learning within interactive learning environments. Bayesian Knowledge-Tracing [3] and Bayes Nets [6] have proven to be very effective at modeling student knowledge at a specific point in time. Another technique, empirical learning curves [cf. 1,5] have proven successful for assessing students' gains in both accuracy and speed over time, as they use a learning environment.

These techniques have been generally very successful at modeling knowledge and learning within the environments where they have been used, and have contributed to making these environments more educationally effective. However, there are many types of environments where these techniques are underused – in particular educational games [6]. Almost since the advent of the personal computer, educational games have been an important part of many students' educational experiences. It has been hypothesized by many researchers that games have the potential to make education more fun, and to improve student learning by improving student engagement [cf. 7]. Yet the development of educational games has generally not benefited from the analytical tools that have been used to study and improve the educational effectiveness of other types of learning environments, such as intelligent tutoring systems [cf. 1,2,3,5].

One important and popular type of educational game is the educational action game. Educational action games incorporate educational material into fast-paced

C. Conati, K. McCoy, and G. Paliouras (Eds.): UM 2007, LNAI 4511, pp. 17–26, 2007.
© Springer-Verlag Berlin Heidelberg 2007

game environments where the student must respond quickly to continual challenges. Unlike many other forms of interactive learning environments, and turn-based educational games (studied in [6]), educational action games offer little time for reflection, at least during main gameplay. Because educational action games do not offer time for reflection, it has been suggested that they are more appropriate for building skill fluency (i.e. speed and accuracy at exercising a skill) than for the acquisition of new and complex concepts [cf. 9].

In intelligent tutoring systems, empirical learning curves have been found to be an appropriate method for assessing gain in speed and accuracy [cf. 1,2,5]. Two challenges will need to be surmounted, however, in order to use exponential learning curves for fluency assessment in educational action games.

The first challenge is that the relationship between performance and knowledge is more complex in games than tutors. Unlike tutors, educational games generally do not attempt to explicitly make student thinking visible and communicate domain goal structure [cf. 1], design goals which result in environments where it is comparatively easy to assess student knowledge. However, Manske and Conati [6] have successfully developed Bayes Nets which can make appropriate assessments of knowledge in turn-based educational games. In this paper, we will discuss what additional challenges to assessing knowledge are present within educational action games.

A second challenge, particularly important within educational action games, is that some portion of students' gain in speed is likely due to learning how to play the game, rather than domain learning. In this paper, we will investigate how gameplay learning affects our ability to assess the development of fluent skill.

Within this paper, we will investigate how these challenges can be addressed, so that student fluency gain can be accurately modeled within an educational action game, Zombie Division.

1.1 Zombie Division

Zombie Division, shown in Figure 1, is an educational game designed to help elementary school students learn about division [cf. 4]. Zombie Division is at its core a third-person action game, though it also has adventure-game elements.

Within Zombie Division, the player is a hero from Ancient Greece, who must defeat skeletal enemies in hand-to-hand combat in order to progress. Each skeleton has a number on its chest. The player has a set of weapons, each of which corresponds to a divisor number. Each weapon is linked to a key on the keyboard – the 2 weapon is used by pressing the "F2" key, the 3 weapon is used by pressing the "F3" key, and so on. If the player attacks (attempts to divide) a skeleton by a number which divides that skeleton's number (i.e. skeleton modulus weapon = 0), the skeleton dies. If the player attacks (attempts to divide) a skeleton using a number which is not a divisor of the skeleton's number, the skeleton counter-attacks, causing the player to lose health.

As the player proceeds from level to level of the game, his or her weapons (set of potential divisors) change, requiring the player to use different divisors to divide the same skeleton at different times (for example, needing to use 2 or 4 on different levels to divide a 32 skeleton). Some skeletons are not divisible by any of the student's weapons and must be avoided. The mathematical skills involved in Zombie Division (and which a student will hopefully know more about after playing Zombie Division) are, therefore, being able to determine whether a number is divisible by 2 (e.g. even), 3, or 5, and being able to determine whether a number is divisible by 4, 6, 8, or 10 when small divisors are not available.

Beyond the mathematical features of the gameplay, there are also aspects to the game which are included purely to support enjoyable and challenging gameplay: some skeletons move from place to place, other skeletons hold special keys that enable the student to move on to new game regions, some skeletons pursue the student, and some skeletons (increasingly on higher levels) attack spontaneously if the player delays. Hence, Zombie Division is designed for the joint purposes of teaching mathematics and providing the student with a fun experience.

Later in the paper, we will also discuss data from an alternate ("extrinsic") version of Zombie Division. In the "intrinsic" version discussed above, the mathematical content of Zombie Division is integrated into the gameplay. The "extrinsic" version, has the same mathematical content and the same gameplay, but these two components of the student's experience are separated. Mathematical problems are given at the completion of each game level, and the student plays a game which is identical to the intrinsic version of the game described above, but where the mathematical content has been removed. The same keys on the keyboard are used to kill skeletons, but no divisors are associated with those keys. Instead of having numbers on their chests, the skeletons have pictures of the weapons that can kill them. The student encounters exactly the same skeletons at the same times and locations in each version of Zombie Division; the only difference is the conceptual meaning of the key the student must press to kill each skeleton.

In this paper, we will focus predominantly on studying learning and gameplay in the intrinsic condition of Zombie Division, where these two components are mixed (as in most educational action games) – however, we will in some cases consider evidence from the extrinsic condition in order to better understand the pattern of student performance in the intrinsic condition.

Fig. 1. Zombie Division (intrinsic version)

The data we will discuss is drawn from four classes in a large primary school in a low-income area on the outskirts of a medium-size city in northern England. The school has an average number of students with special educational needs, but with significantly below-average scores on national assessments. 17 students used the intrinsic condition of Zombie Division; 18 students used the extrinsic condition of Zombie Division – two additional students were removed from each condition for missing the post-test. Each student used Zombie Division for 135 total minutes of class-time, across 6 class days spread across 4 weeks. Log files were used to distill measures of students' learning and performance as they used Zombie Division.

2 Accuracy-Based Models of Student Learning Within Zombie Division

In this section, we will study how to adapt empirical learning curves [cf. 1,2,5] to the context of Zombie Division in order to study students' gain in accuracy over time.

2.1 Mapping Game Actions to Evidence on Learning

In order to plot learning curves, we need to map the student actions and their consequences within Zombie Division to a conceptual framework which allows us to define opportunities to practice a mathematical skill and whether a student has correctly demonstrated the skill or not. Such a conceptual framework has been created for intelligent tutoring systems [1] and, more recently, for turn-based educational games [6].

One challenge that does not occur in intelligent tutoring systems and is substantially less common in turn-based educational games is that not all "errors" from the perspective of the game give evidence about the student's mathematical skill. For example, if a student walks into a skeleton and does not attack, the skeleton attacks the student and the student loses health; though this is an error in gameplay (and results in negative consequences within the game), it gives little evidence on the student's mathematical knowledge.

However, many events within the game do give information on the student's mathematical knowledge. Attacking a skeleton and killing it (for example, using the "2" weapon to divide a "26" skeleton), is evidence that the student knows how to determine whether a number is divisible by 2. Correspondingly, unsuccessfully attacking a specific skeleton (for example, trying to use the "2" weapon to divide a "15" skeleton), is evidence that the student does not know how to determine whether a number is divisible by 2. In addition, avoiding certain actions may also give information about the student's knowledge. If a student flees from a skeleton (defined as leaving the room the skeleton is in) which he/she could not have killed (the student has "2", "3", and "5" weapons but the skeleton is "49"), there is evidence that the student knows how to determine if a number is divisible by 2,3, and 5; if a student flees from a skeleton which he/she could have killed, on the other hand (the student has a "2" weapon and flees from a "16" skeleton), there is evidence that the student does not know how to determine if a number is divisible by 2.

In the analyses that follow, we consider any given skeleton as a single opportunity for a student to demonstrate a skill [cf. 3]: multiple attempts to kill a skeleton with different weapons may indicate process of elimination rather than mathematical knowledge.

2.2 Details of Analysis

In the analyses that will follow, we focus on four mathematical skills: the student's ability to determine if a number is divisible by 2, 3, 4, and 5. 2, 3, and 5 are all prime numbers, introduced as weapons/divisors early in the game, and are thus reasonably straightforward to analyze. 10 is also introduced as a weapon/divisor early in the game, but 10 is co-present with 2 or 5 in all early opportunities to use 10. This creates considerable risk of bias: with both 2 and 10 available, a student having difficulty deciding if an even number was divisible by 10 can automatically revert to using 2 – hence, a number of situations where the student did not know how to divide by 10 could be missed during analysis. 4, on the other hand, is introduced as a weapon/divisor later in the game, when 2 has been removed as a weapon/divisor. Hence, students' ability to determining if a number is divisible by 4 is not occluded by the presence of 2. 6, 8, and 9 also occur in the game as divisors, but only on later levels and thus with insufficient frequency to analyze.

Since time was controlled in this study, some students are able to complete more of Zombie Division than others. Hence, some students will encounter more skeletons than others. Since students who get further in Zombie Division and encounter more skeletons are likely to be better at mathematics, it would introduce bias to use all data from all student actions in our analyses. Hence, we set a cut-off, and do not analyze opportunities to practice a mathematical skill which were reached by less than half of the students (in practice, this gives us from 50 actions per student for the divisible-by-2 skill, to 19 actions per student for the divisible-by-4 skill).

2.3 Results

Graphs showing students' accuracy over time at using some of the mathematical skills needed to play Zombie Division are shown in Figure 2. Each of these graphs shows the average performance at each opportunity to practice each skill, with the best-fitting exponential curve overlaid on each graph. An exponential learning curve will fit the data if students have a fairly high error rate at the beginning, improve fairly rapidly, and show slowing improvement over time.

The skill of determining whether a number is divisible by 2, shown in the top-left graph of Figure 2, appears to fit this pattern very well. The best-fitting exponential function to this data achieves a very healthy r^2 of 0.52. The skill of determining whether a number is divisible by 5, shown in the top-right graph of Figure 2, also appears to fit this pattern very well. The best-fitting exponential function to this data achieves a respectable r^2 of 0.32. The skill of determining whether a number is divisible by 4, shown in the bottom-right graph of Figure 2, also appears to fit this pattern, though the best-fitting exponential function to this data achieves a relatively low r^2 of 0.09. At first glance, it appears that the leap in difficulty at the seventh opportunity to divide by 4 may indicate that two different skills are being combined together. However, many skeletons can be killed by multiple weapons and students often encounter skeletons in different orders, so it is not immediately possible to interpret a spike in difficulty as a second skill being encountered, unlike in learning curve analyses of intelligent tutors [cf. 1]. In fact, that point represents 12 different skeletons encountered by 19 students, with no two errors made on the same skeleton.

The skill of determining whether a number is divisible by 3, shown in the bottom-left graph of Figure 2, does not appear to fit an exponential curve. The best-fitting exponential function to this data achieves an r^2 under 0.01, and even points in the wrong direction, going very slightly up over time. This suggests that students are having more difficulty determining if a number is divisible by 3 than if a number is divisible by 2,4, and 5 – interestingly, division by 3 had not yet been discussed in class before the students used Zombie Division, whereas the other divisors had been. This serves as a valuable reminder that fluency-building learning environments will probably be most effective if used after appropriate conceptual instruction.

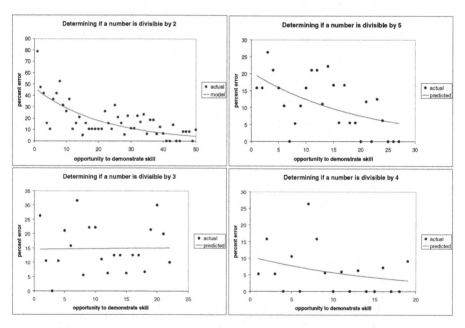

Fig. 2. Students' change in percent correct over time, for specific mathematical skills

3   Time-Based Learning Models of Student Learning Within Zombie Division

In this section, we investigate whether students learn to use mathematical skills with greater speed during the time they use Zombie Division, again using empirical learning curves. Empirical learning curves have been used successfully to model gain in speed in intelligent tutoring systems [cf. 1,5]. However, the relationship between speed and learning is different in educational action games than in intelligent tutors. Intelligent tutors generally involve interface actions which are common to most computer applications (such as clicking on a blank and typing a number, or pointing and clicking). It is reasonable to assume that most students will have experience applying these basic interface skills; and therefore most of the speed gains a student has while using an intelligent tutor should involve the relevant domain skills, not gains in speed in interacting with the user interface.

By contrast, an educational action game like Zombie Division involves several novel interface skills which must be learned, such as how to move the correct distance away from a skeleton, and how to use each divisor. While many students will have had considerable prior gaming experience, Zombie Division's gameplay will be subtly different from games students have played in the past (for example: how much movement is obtained by pressing a movement key, and which keys correspond to different divisors). Therefore, some of each student's speed gains while using Zombie Division may be attributable to learning gameplay skills instead of domain skills.

In this section, we will first present an analysis which ignores interface and gameplay learning. We will then explicitly account for interface and gameplay learning, and show how accounting for gameplay learning affects the results.

3.1 Details of Analysis

In the analyses which follow, we will consider only a subset of actions within Zombie Division. Specifically, we will analyze the time a student takes to attack a skeleton with an appropriate weapon, on their first attempt to respond to that skeleton. We eliminate errors (attacking with the wrong number) from consideration, since these actions will not be representative of the student's gain in efficiency at using correct knowledge over time. We also eliminate second and subsequent attempts to respond to a skeleton, since they are likely to involve error-correction instead of simply exercising a known skill. Finally, we eliminate fleeing actions from consideration, since the amount of time required to flee may be governed primarily by the size of the room and presence of other skeletons in the room.

In addition, as in the previous section, we do not analyze opportunities to practice a mathematical skill which were reached by less than half of the students. For brevity, we will focus on the skill of determining whether a number is divisible by 2; however, the pattern we will show in this section is the same pattern as is found when the skills of dividing by 4 and 5 are analyzed.

3.2 Results

A graph showing students' accuracy over time at determining whether a number is divisible by 2 is shown on the left of Figure 3. This graph shows the average time taken at each opportunity to practice each skill, with the best-fitting exponential curve overlaid. An exponential learning curve will fit the data if students work fairly slowly at the beginning, improve fairly rapidly, and show slowing improvement over time.

The skill of determining whether a number is divisible by 2, shown in the left graph of Figure 3, appears to fit this pattern very well. The best-fitting exponential function to this data achieves a reasonably high r^2 of 0.23. Hence, using this approach suggests that students are getting faster at dividing by 2 over time, and therefore that they are gaining fluency in this skill.

However, it is not clear from this approach whether the students' gain in fluency is a gain in fluency with mathematics or a gain in fluency at playing Zombie Division. In many cases, this distinction would be difficult to tease apart. However, in this case, data from the extrinsic condition can be used. As discussed earlier, the two conditions have identical gameplay but in the extrinsic condition the mathematics is given separately. The extrinsic condition data can therefore be used to determine how much of the speed-up seen in the intrinsic condition is explained by gameplay learning, and therefore how much domain learning occurred. This will in turn give evidence on the appropriateness of computing time learning curves which do not account for gameplay.

A graph showing students' accuracy over time at killing the skeletons using F2 in the extrinsic condition (equivalent to dividing by 2 in the intrinsic condition) is shown on the right of Figure 3. This graph shows the average time at each opportunity to practice each skill, with the best-fitting exponential curve overlaid. The best-fitting exponential function to this data achieves only a modest r^2 of 0.05, but interestingly, the best-fitting functions have a fairly similar appearance between conditions.

We can now use this gameplay-only curve to calculate whether there is mathematics learning occurring in the intrinsic condition. If there is both gameplay and mathematics learning in the intrinsic condition, the learning curve in the intrinsic condition should actually be a composite of two curves: a gameplay learning curve, and a mathematics learning curve. The gameplay learning curve derived in the

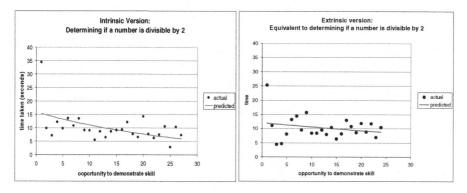

Fig. 3. Students' change in speed at exercising a skill over time

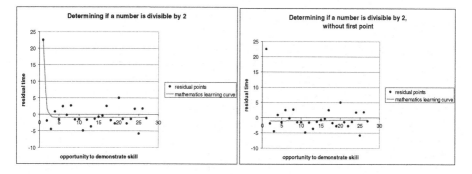

Fig. 4. Students' mathematics learning in the intrinsic condition, with gameplay factored out. The graph on the left includes the first point in curve calculation; the graph on the right omits that point.

extrinsic condition should be a reasonably accurate estimate of the gameplay learning curve in the intrinsic condition, since gameplay is identical across conditions. Hence, we subtract the extrinsic gameplay learning curve from the data in the intrinsic condition. If the resultant points still fit an exponential learning curve, we can be certain that mathematics learning actually was occurring in the intrinsic condition.

The resultant residual data points, and learning curve, are shown on the left side of Figure 4. This curve achieves a spectacular r^2 of 0.77 – at first glance suggesting that considerable domain learning is indeed occurring. However, note that the curve is completely flat after the earliest opportunities to practice the skill, and that the first point is a major outlier. If we eliminate the first point from consideration when fitting the curve, the slope flips around (see the right side of Figure 4), going upwards (though with r^2 under 0.01). Hence, it appears that non-gameplay learning is occurring in the intrinsic condition, but only between the first and second opportunities to practice the skill. The additional learning does not appear to be a gain in mathematics fluency over time. It may instead be the student learning to apply his or her existing mathematical knowledge within Zombie Division.

Hence, when we look at the overall picture, it does not appear that students are gaining fluency, at least in terms of speed, at deciding if a number is divisible by 2, while playing Zombie Division. At minimum, if the students are gaining fluency, the effect is much smaller and more variable than the effects of gameplay learning. This suggests that plotting learning curves of student speed, without taking gameplay into account, is not an appropriate way to model fluency gain in educational action games.

4   Conclusions

In this paper, we have analyzed two ways of studying student gains in fluency over time, within an educational action game: studying gains in accuracy over time, and studying gains in speed over time. We have found that studying gains in speed over time is not straightforward to do correctly; in particular, different results are obtained, depending on whether or not gameplay is explicitly accounted for. Because of this, simply computing gain in speed over time, without accounting for gameplay, does not appear to be an appropriate way to model learning in educational action games. In the absence of a measure of gameplay, an alternate and probably more reliable way to assess whether students gain speed at applying a skill is to time students' responses on the pre-test and post-test.

It does appear, though, that existing methods for modeling gain in accuracy over time are appropriate for use in educational action games, with only minor modifications. This will make it possible to quickly and effectively determine which skills students gain and fail to gain while using an educational action game, solely from their behavior within the system. In the case of Zombie Division, we see that students successfully gained fluency in determining if a number is divisible by 2,4, or 5, but that students did not gain fluency in determining if a number is divisible by 3; in developing future versions of Zombie Division, we now know that this skill will require extra support and scaffolding. Generally, analysis of accuracy learning curves has been found to be a useful technique for making formative assessments which can be used to drive rapid re-design and improvement of intelligent tutoring systems [cf. 2]. The results presented here suggest that, properly used, this technique will be useful for formative assessment in educational action games as well.

Acknowledgements. We would like to thank Jenny Habgood, Lucy Button and Lizzie Evans for their assistance in organizing and conducting the studies reported here. The work presented in this paper was funded by research fellowships from the Learning Sciences Research Institute, at the University of Nottingham.

References

1. Anderson, J.R., Conrad, F.G., Corbett, A.T.: Skill Acquisition and the LISP Tutor. Cognitive Science 13, 467–505 (1989)
2. Beck, J.E.: Using learning decomposition to analyze student fluency development. Proceedings of the workshop on Educational Data Mining at the 8th International Conference on Intelligent Tutoring Systems, pp. 21–28 (2006)
3. Corbett, A.T., Anderson, J.R.: Knowledge Tracing: Modeling the Acquisition of Procedural Knowledge. User Modeling and User-Adapted Interaction 4, 253–278 (1995)
4. Habgood, M.P.J.: Zombie Division: Intrinsic Integration in Digital Learning Games. In: Proceedings of the Human Centered Technology Workshop (2005)
5. Martin, B., Koedinger, K., Mitrovic, A., Mathan, S.: On Using Learning Curves to Evaluate ITS. In: Proceedings of the 12th International Conference on Artificial Intelligence in Education (AIED-2005), pp. 419–426 (2005)
6. Manske, M., Conati, C.: Modeling Learning in Educational Games. In: Proceedings of the 12th International Conference on Artificial Intelligence in Education (AIED-2005), pp. 411–418 (2005)
7. Prensky, M.: Digital game-based learning. Computers in Entertainment 1(1), 1–4 (2003)
8. Repenning, A., Clayton, L.: Playing a game: the ecology of designing, building, and testing games as educational activities. In: Proceedings of ED-MEDIA: World Conference on Educational Multimedia, Hypermedia, and Telecommunications (2005)

A User Modeling Server for Contemporary Adaptive Hypermedia: An Evaluation of the Push Approach to Evidence Propagation

Michael Yudelson, Peter Brusilovsky, and Vladimir Zadorozhny

School of Information Science, University of Pittsburgh
135 N. Bellefield Ave. Pittsburgh, PA 15232, USA
mvy3@pitt.edu,{peterb,vladimir}@sis.pitt.edu

Abstract. Despite the growing popularity of user modeling servers, little attention has been paid to optimizing and evaluating the performance of these servers. We argue that implementation issues and their influence on server performance should become the central focus of the user modeling community, since there is a sharply increasing real-life load on user modeling servers, This paper focuses on a specific implementation-level aspect of user modeling servers – the choice of *push* or *pull* approaches to evidence propagation. We present a new push-based implementation of our user modeling server CUMULATE and compare its performance with the performance of the original pull-based CUMULATE server.

1 Introduction

User modeling servers are becoming more and more popular in the field of user modeling and personalization. The predecessors of the present user modeling servers, known as generic user modeling systems [9; 10], were developed to distill the user modeling functionality of the user models within adaptive systems and to simplify the work of future developers of these systems. Modern Web-based user modeling servers [1; 4; 8; 11; 12; 14] added another important function: to serve as a central point for user modeling and the provision of information about a user in a distributed environment, where several adaptive systems may simultaneously communicate with the same server to report or request information about the user.

Typical usage of a user modeling server follows: an adaptive system interacts with the user and sends the results of that interaction to the user modeling server. In some cases, the user modeling server simply stores the information provided by the adaptive system. For example, the adaptive system can report user age, as provided by the user herself, which will be stored by the server for future use. In other cases, the user modeling server has to make inferences based on the evidence it receives. Typically, inferences are formed when the adaptive system reports some meaningful interaction event (i.e., the user just read a specific news article or solved a specific educational problem), which is then distilled into meaningful user parameters such as user knowledge or interest. The information about the user accumulated by the server

C. Conati, K. McCoy, and G. Paliouras (Eds.): UM 2007, LNAI 4511, pp. 27–36, 2007.
© Springer-Verlag Berlin Heidelberg 2007

can further be requested by various adaptive systems that are also working with this user. While the main function of a modeling server is to answer requests about stored or derived user parameters (such as age, knowledge, or interests) some modern servers such as Personis [8] and CUMULATE [4] are also able to respond to different requests about the history of the user's interactions.

With an increasing number of adaptive systems accessing the same server and the increasing complexity of user model inferences, the performance of a user modeling server is becoming an important factor. However, with the exception of the pioneer work of Kobsa and Fink [11], the literature on user model servers focuses solely on the conceptual architectures and functionality without paying any attention to implementation details and real-life performance. We argue that these issues should receive more serious attention from the user modeling community. As our experience shows, a range of implementation details may dramatically affect the server performance. A specific implementation aspect that is discussed in this paper is the balance between the *push* and *pull* styles of inference that is chosen within user model servers. A server with *pull* inference deduces user parameters (such as knowledge or interests) from collected observations "on demand" – i.e., when requested. A server with *push* inference updates user parameters after each reported observation, thus keeping them instantly available. While both approaches may be used to implement the same conceptual architecture, the choice of approach may determine the ultimate productivity of the server, depending on the individually required balance of reports and requests to the server.

Historically, in several kinds of adaptive systems that build a model of user knowledge (such as intelligent tutoring systems), event reports are frequent while user model requests are rare. For example, after a good number of reported user events, created during the process of solving a problem or the exploration of a virtual lab, the system comes to a decision point, where information about a user is required, such as to choose the next task to solve. Hence, the issue of response delay to read requests hasn't been considered as a critical issue. Read request response time becomes crucial when the following conditions are met:

- user models become more complex,
- more users start using the adaptive systems more frequently, hence increasing the volume of data sent to the user model, and
- the user model is queried for updated information about the user more often.

When these three conditions are met, the propagation of evidence starts to cost a lot more when it's done only upon read request as opposed to being done right after the arrival of new evidence.

Recently, we have witnessed the above situation arise in our research. Our pull-propagation user modeling server CUMULATE [4] was originally able to accommodate a small set of adaptive educational activities, which was used by a small group of students (20-30 people). Over the years, with the growth of the number of adaptive applications, the number of users, and the frequency of their work with the system [3] we started to experience noticeable delays when querying user parameters. After several semesters, the delays had become unacceptable (up to 5-7 seconds per each request). We have attempted to introduce a pseudo-optimization to reduce the inference load caused by the user model read requests by introducing the concept of query precision. Precision became an additional parameter in a read request to the user model. It specified how 'fresh' the user model was required to be. If the last state of the user model was calculated less than the specified amount of time ago, then the current state of the user model was considered acceptable and was reported without additional inference. This pseudo-optimization didn't help. As it turned out, each of our adaptive applications demanded 'fresh' data from the user model *after each reported event*. For example, QuizGuide and NavEx [5], two adaptive hypermedia services, attempted to update the state of link annotation after every user action (such as answering a question or accessing an example line of code). Since a fresh read of the user model was required after every click of every user, this resulted in a large volume of user model requests, which caused unacceptable delays. Our analysis of contemporary work on adaptive hypermedia demonstrated that the same need to regenerate adaptive annotations after each click is shared by many systems which use adaptive link annotation and this caused us to design a new version of CUMULATE that can support a large number of users working with contemporary adaptive hypermedia.

Given the increased volume of read requests, we decided that one of the main reasons for the original CUMULATE performance problems was the use of pull evidence propagation on the implementation level. To resolve these problems we developed a new version of our user modeling server – CUMULATE 2 – which introduced push evidence propagation. The CUMULATE 2 server was successfully used for two semesters and its performance evaluation returned positive results. This paper reports our work on CUMULATE 2 and is organized in the following way. Section 2 presents the conceptual architecture implemented by both the original CUMULATE and CUMLATE 2 user modeling servers. Section 3 provides details about the implementation of the evidence propagation in each of these servers. Section 4 reports the comparative evaluation of the two servers. Finally, we conclude with section 5.

2   The Conceptual Architecture of a User Modeling Server

How does a typical user modeling server (UMS) works? It receives reports of the user's activities from external applications (i.e., links the user has followed, pages read, questions answered, etc.). From these reported activities, the UMS infers user parameters such as knowledge or interests. The inference is typically based on some kind of knowledge about how each user action contributes to the change in user knowledge, interests, or other parameters. Inference is done using various approaches, ranging from simple ad hoc math to Bayesian Networks [6] and ontology reasoning [7].

A typical approach to connecting actions with user model parameters in educational adaptive hypermedia is called 'indexing.' Educational content is indexed with metadata created beforehand (ontology, taxonomy or flat list) or extracted from content itself using machine learning methods. The indexing is done manually by teacher or semi-automatically with the help of an intelligent parser. Chunks of domain knowledge are referred to as keywords, concepts or topics, depending on the granularity and method of extraction. In simple cases, each piece of content is connected to one chunk of domain knowledge. For example, in QuizGuide [3] – a system that serves parameterized in the domain of the C- programming language – each quiz is assigned to one topic. In other cases, each piece of content is assigned to a set of chunks. For instance, in the system NavEx [13], which provides dissected code examples, each example is indexed with a set of domain concepts.

The two UMS discussed in this paper – the original CUMULATE (which we will call *legacy* CUMULATE, to avoid confusion) and the newer CUMULATE 2 – are typical representatives of a large class of centralized educational user modeling systems. Both of them implement the same conceptual architecture for centralized user modeling that we summarize below.

A user modeling server stores or uses information about the following data objects:

- users,
- groups of users,
- learning objects, and
- domain concepts.

The corpus of learning objects is comprised of several sets of learning objects that are supplied by external applications. For example, learning objects could be parameterized online quizzes or dissected program examples. Domain concepts, contained in the *metadata* corpus, consist of a number of domain ontologies (represented as hierarchies, networks, or flat lists) that are called upon to describe learning objects in terms of knowledge components (often referred to as concepts or sometimes topics). For instance, in the domain of programming language knowledge, components might include such concepts as 'arithmetic operations,' 'addition,' 'data structure,' 'array,' etc. Listed objects are linked by the following relations:

- Group-user membership links. User groups consist of several users and users can be members of several groups.
- Links between learning objects allow learning objects to aggregate subordinates. Leaf objects do not necessary have to be invoke-able but user activity can be attributed to them. For instance, a learning object 'quiz' could consist of several 'questions.'. Both quiz and question can be invoked. A learning object, such as 'code example,' could consist of several 'lines of code.'. In this case, lines are only invoked as a part of the whole code example. These links are optional.
- Links of diverse types connect knowledge components within domain ontologies. For example, 'arithmetic operations' and 'data structure' would be parents to 'addition' and 'array.' These links are optional as well.
- 'Indexing' links between knowledge components and learning objects. These links are crucial for the user modeling process, since they allow the user model to 'propagate' the results of user activity with learning objects, in order to create knowledge components and make assertions about the user mastery of those components. For instance, the line of code 'for(int i=0; i<10; i++)' (as part of a code example or part of question of a quiz on C - programming language) could be associated with the knowledge components 'loops,' 'for-loop,' 'declaration of a variable,' 'arithmetic expressions,' 'post-increment,' etc.

There are two more special types of relationships in our user model. The first one is evidence links, which describe the results of user activity. They link learning objects to users and groups (because users interact with learning objects as members of some group). Evidence links are assigned timestamps and contain results of such interaction. Usually, the result is expressed in the form of a decimal value between 0 and 1, with 0 denoting an unsuccessful result and 1, the opposite.

The second special type of link, assertions about user knowledge – represent the user model's probabilistic hypotheses about the user knowledge level of some knowledge components. Assertions are modeled with respect to the cognitive levels of Bloom's Taxonomy [2].

Propagation of evidence about user knowledge is driven by reports of user activity from external applications. These reports are generated when a user, for example, clicks on one line of a dissected code example or answers one question of an online quiz. A set of inference agents [4] are configured to aggregate incoming evidence and infer the user's knowledge of concepts belonging to domains stored in the user model based on evidence of user work with various sets of learning objects supplied by specific external application(s). Agents propagate evidence from events to knowledge components of the user model by using indexing links between the learning objects that generated the evidence and knowledge components. The path that evidence travels is shown in Fig. 1. It is important to note that the presented framework is relatively universal. While in our case it was applied to user knowledge modeling, similar approaches have been used for modeling user interests and other features.

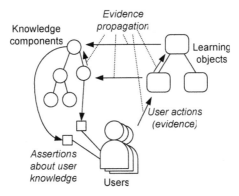

Fig. 1. The structure of the user model, showing the path of evidence propagation

The conceptual description above gives a structural framework and doesn't suggest any particular implementation of the user modeling server's internal inference mechanisms. The inference agents can be implemented using Bayesian Networks, machine learning, or information retrieval methods. One aspect of inference implementation is considering when such inference happens. Possible options include the *pull* approach, where inference is done 'just-in-time,' after a request for inferred information has been received. In other words, external applications *pull* assertions about the user out of the UMS. An alternative to *pull* is the *push* approach, where the computation of user knowledge is done upon arrival of new evidence that *pushes* itself through the user model from the learning objects to the knowledge components.

In this paper, we draw a comparison of two user modeling servers: one implementing pure pull strategy of inference, and the other implementing the push strategy. The following sections describe implementation details for both of them.

3   User Modeling in Legacy CUMULATE and CUMULATE 2

Legacy CUMULATE [4] is a centralized user modeling server that implements pure pull approach. Here, inference agents are not activated by the arrival of new evidence (such as a write operation to the user model). As new evidence arrives, it is constantly recorded in the event history and is not aggregated until an external application requests information about the user's knowledge (a read query to the user model).

Inference in legacy CUMULATE is performed by a set of SQL queries to the UMS database. The process of evidence aggregation is implemented by nesting queries. Because of the just-in-time nature of evidence propagation in the legacy CUMULATE, as our evidence store size increased we began to experience proportionate delays in response to user model read requests. In addition to the growth of evidence, storing new adaptive applications demanded more complex models. Instead of indexing learning objects with a single domain topic (a rather coarse-grained chunk of the domain), we have switched to indexing them with a set of finer -grained concepts. The increased knowledge -component -to -learning -object - ratio, in addition to growth of the event base has slowed the inference process.

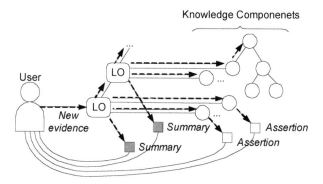

Fig. 2. Propagation of evidence in CUMULATE 2

In our second attempt to implement the conceptual architecture described above, we decided to switch from pull to push inference of user knowledge, in order to improve performance of the user modeling server. Our new UMS CUMULATE 2 performs the inference of user knowledge immediately after arrival of new evidence. The evidence log is used as a backup in case of server failure, when upon restart, CUMULATE 2 sequentially propagates all evidence cached in the log in the same fashion evidence is propagated in the working mode. The CUMULATE 2 propagation architecture can be used with a range of *incremental* user modeling approaches (i.e., where new values for knowledge, interests or other features can be determined by combining old values with new evidence). The current inference agents in

CUMULATE 2 use a set of threshold, averaging and asymptotic formulas for evidence propagation. For example, user knowledge of the concept grows asymptotically (on a transposed cubic curve) each time a user successfully answers one question of a quiz which is related to this concept. However, the architecture allows the use of Bayesian inference approaches such as used in SMODEL [14] and other Bayesian user modeling systems.

CUMULATE 2 is implemented as a network of interactive Java objects. A single entry point to the server API is created in the form of an instance singleton class. Java servlets further abstract the server's API via an HTTP interface. External applications can send a write request to the servlet that is responsible for UMS updates with parameters of a single piece of evidence about its user. When a new piece of evidence arrives, it is first checked for consistency of server settings (existence of the user and user group with such user, identity of a reporting application, existence of the learning object that the user is reported to be interacting with). Second, evidence is stored in the database. Third, the piece of evidence is propagated throughout the user model.

Results of evidence propagation in the form of summaries and assertions are cached for faster access (Fig. 2). Each learning object summarizes evidence that 'passes' through it by counting the total number of pieces of evidence, mean result value (i.e., number of correctly answered questions over all question attempts). Then the learning object passes the evidence to its superiors (e.g., question to quiz, or individual code line to a full dissection) and to the knowledge components it has been indexed with. Superior learning objects aggregate the 'count' of pieces of evidence by summing the counts of their subordinates, and find the mean interaction result by taking the average of the mean interaction results of subordinates.

Each knowledge component aggregates evidence by computing the probability of a user mastering it. The formulas for computing these probabilities are configured individually for external adaptive applications. For instance, knowledge components aggregate evidence coming from users browsing dissected code examples [13] by applying an ad hoc step function that sets the threshold of 10 'clicks' on annotated lines of code that connect to the knowledge component as the amount of interaction which will enable the user to master this knowledge component. If the user has made less than 10 clicks, then the probability is taken as the number of clicks made over 10, and 1 otherwise. These probabilities are recorded in the slot that corresponds to Bloom's 'comprehension' cognitive level.

Evidence from learning objects that represent questions of online quizzes [3] are aggregated using a sigmoid asymptotic function. Probability of the user mastering a knowledge component grows with each successful answer to the quiz question. The first two to three attempts to successfully apply the knowledge components result in the slow growth of the probability of mastery (a warm-up period), further success results in the linear growth of probability and as probability approaches 1, the increments asymptotically decrease.

Queries to CUMULATE 2 for the snapshot of an individual user model are handled by another servlet – the report manager. At this point, CUMULATE 2 performs a simple lookup operation and responds with an XML document that describes the requested information.

4   A Preliminary Evaluation

Over the several years that we have been using the legacy CUMULATE as our primary UMS, we have accumulated a large number of records. Records of our most heavily used and researched application, QuizPACK, contain about 19,000 pieces of evidence obtained in more than 13,000 sessions. In a typical session, users answered 28 questions. On average, users generated a single piece of evidence within a session once every 102 seconds.

Using these figures as a 'realistic' baseline, we compared the performance of the legacy CUMULATE to the performance of CUMULATE 2 to see whether the shift from pull to push evidence propagation strategy made any difference. Since our main reason behind the strategy switch was to overcome large read request delays, we were primarily interested in whether the situation improved in CUMULATE 2 (i.e., whether the delay became smaller). Our secondary point of interest was whether the write request delay grew larger for CUMULATE 2, since CUMULATE 2 performs more computations when updating the user model, while legacy CUMULATE doesn't compute anything at that point.

A small experiment was setup, where we subjected both versions of the user modeling server to various types of loads. Both servers were configured identically. The size of the learning objects corpus was 1000, while the metadata corpus was 500. The ratio of knowledge concepts to each learning object ranged from 5 to 100. Servers were running on the same software/hardware.

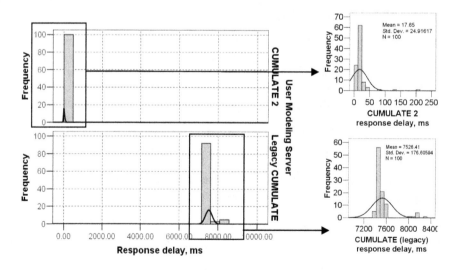

Fig. 3. Comparing the read request delays of CUMULATE (bottom) and CUMULATE 2 (top)

To quantitatively compare the servers' ability to handle read requests from external applications we sent 100 consecutive queries to each of them. Fig. 3 shows that CUMULATE 2 wins a convincing victory with 18 milliseconds average response time over the legacy CUMULATE, which delays responses to read requests for 7526 milliseconds. The left side shows histograms of the read request delays for legacy CUMULATE (bottom) and CUMULATE 2 (top) placed on one scale. Call-outs on the right show the histograms in greater detail.

We have also investigated the ability of the servers to handle write requests. We varied server loads from 1 second to 80 milliseconds between requests for a duration of 3,000 milliseconds. At the peak load of 80 milliseconds between write requests, legacy CUMULATE was able to complete 90% of the requests within 32 milliseconds. Under these conditions, CUMULATE 2 was only able to complete 90% of requests within 126 milliseconds.

As we have mentioned above, when users employ our tools for an introductory programming course, they typically answer one quiz question per 102 seconds during a learning session. For each update of the user mode, the user expects an update of the user model (expressed as changed annotations for quizzes and questions).

In this situation, CUMULATE 2 is able to support roughly 700 users working simultaneously, namely, 126 milliseconds per write request and 18 milliseconds per read, giving us 144 milliseconds for the write-read cycle. Knowing that user answers come once in 102 seconds we have $102 * 1000 / 144 = 708 \approx 700$. This is more than enough, given that the size of the class is rarely over 20 students. Taking into account that at any moment no more than 25% of students' sessions overlap, CUMULATE 2 could easily support a user population that is 4 times as large. The legacy CUMULATE is quite slow because of read requests' delays, even when only one student is working with the adaptive applications that use the server.

This shows us that moving from pull to push propagation did in fact pay off and the improvement is quite significant.

5   Conclusions

In this paper we have described our user modeling server CUMULATE 2, which implements the push approach to evidence propagation. We have drawn initial comparisons between CUMULATE 2 and our legacy user modeling server CUMULATE, which implements the pull evidence propagation strategy.

Results of the comparison show that switching from pull to push propagation has dramatically decreased query delays to the user modeling server (from 7526 to 18 milliseconds). The fact that the propagation strategy was the only tangible difference between the two servers allows us to conclude that it is the push propagation that has caused the performance leap. However, it is only a preliminary result. Both write and read requests to the user modeling servers were quite simple, namely, 'update with one piece of evidence' and 'read full user model.'. Detailed investigation is needed to understand how environment and internal conditions as well as parameters of the requests influence the performance of the servers. We intend to continue analysis of the proposed method with the twin goals of understanding underlying factors that influence its performance and building a detailed cost model of the evidence propagation process.

Acknowledgments. This material is partially based upon work supported by the National Science Foundation under Grants No. 0310576 and 0426021.

References

1. Agostini, A., Bettini, C., Cesa-Bianchi, N., Maggiorini, D., Riboni, D.: Integrated Profile Management for Mobile Computing. In: Proc. of Workshop on Artificial Intelligence, Information Access, and Mobile Computing at IJCAI' 2003, Acapulco, Mexico (2003) http://www.dimi.uniud.it/workshop/ai2ia/cameraready/agostini.pdf
2. Bloom, B.S.: Taxonomy of Educational Objectives, Handbook I: The Cognitive Domain. David McKay Co Inc., New York
3. Brusilovsky, P., Sosnovsky, S.: Engaging students to work with self-assessment questions: A study of two approaches. In: Proc. of 10th Annual Conference on Innovation and Technology in Computer Science Education, ITiCSE'2005, Monte de Caparica, Portugal, pp. 251–255. ACM Press, New York (2005)
4. Brusilovsky, P., Sosnovsky, S., Shcherbinina, O.: User Modeling in a Distributed E-Learning Architecture. In: Ardissono, L., Brna, P., Mitrovic, A. (eds.) Proc. of 10th International User Modeling Conference, pp. 387–391. Springer-Verlag, Berlin, Heidelberg (2005)
5. Brusilovsky, P., Sosnovsky, S., Yudelson, M.: Addictive links: The motivational value of adaptive link annotation in educational hypermedia. In: Wade, V., Ashman, H., Smyth, B. (eds.) (AH' 2006). Proc. of 4th International Conference on Adaptive Hypermedia and Adaptive Web-Based Systems, Dublin, Ireland, pp. 51–60. Springer, Heidelberg (2006) http://dx.doi.org/10.1007/11768012_7
6. Bunt, A., Conati, C.: Probabilistic student modelling to improve exploratory behaviour. User Modeling and User Adapted Interaction 13(3), 269–309 (2003)
7. Conlan, O., O'Keeffe, I., Tallon, S.: Combining adaptive hypermedia techniques and ontology reasoning to produce dynamic personalized news services. In: Wade, V., Ashman, H., Smyth, B. (eds.) (AH'2006). Proc. of 4th International Conference on Adaptive Hypermedia and Adaptive Web-Based Systems, Dublin, Ireland, pp. 81–90. Springer, Heidelberg (2006)
8. Kay, J., Kummerfeld, B., Lauder, P.: Personis: A server for user modeling. In: De Bra, P., Brusilovsky, P., Conejo, R. (eds.) (AH'2002). Proc. of Second International Conference on Adaptive Hypermedia and Adaptive Web-Based Systems, pp. 201–212. Málaga, Spain (2002)
9. Kobsa, A.: Generic user modeling systems. User Modeling and User Adapted Interaction 11(1-2), 49–63 (2001)
10. Kobsa, A.: Generic user modeling systems. In: Brusilovsky, P., Kobsa, A., Neidl, W. (eds.) The Adaptive Web: Methods and Strategies of Web Personalization. LNCS, vol. 4321, Springer-Verlag, Berlin Heidelberg New York (2007)
11. Kobsa, A., Fink, J.: An LDAP-based User Modeling Server and its Evaluation. User Modeling and User-Adapted Interaction 16(2), 129–169 (2006)
12. van der Sluijs, K., Houben, G.-J.: Towards a Generic User Model Component. In: Proc. of PerSWeb'05, Workshop on Personalization on the Semantic Web at 10th International User Modeling Conference (2005) available online at http://www.win.tue.nl/persweb/Camera-ready/13-Sluijs-full.pdf
13. Yudelson, M., Brusilovsky, P.: NavEx: Providing Navigation Support for Adaptive Browsing of Annotated Code Examples. In: Looi, C.-K., McCalla, G., Bredeweg, B., Breuker, J. (eds.) Artificial Intelligence in Education: Supporting Learning through Intelligent and Socially Informed Technology, pp. 710–717. IOS Press, Amsterdam (2005)
14. Zapata-Rivera, J.-D., Greer, J.E.: SMODEL Server: Student modeling in distributed multi-agent tutoring systems. In: Moore, J.D., Redfield, C.L., Johnson, W.L. (eds.) Artificial Intelligence in Education: AI-ED in the Wired and Wireless Future, pp. 446–455. IOS Press, Amsterdam (2001)

Principles of Lifelong Learning for Predictive User Modeling

Ashish Kapoor and Eric Horvitz

Microsoft Research,
Redmond WA 98052, USA
{akapoor,horvitz}@microsoft.com

Abstract. Predictive user models often require a phase of effortful supervised training where cases are tagged with labels that represent the status of unobservable variables. We formulate and study principles of *lifelong learning* where training is ongoing over a prolonged period. In lifelong learning, decisions about extending a case library are made continuously by balancing the cost of acquiring values of hidden states with the long-term benefits of acquiring new labels. We highlight key principles by extending BusyBody, an application that learns to predict the cost of interrupting a user. We transform the prior BusyBody system into a lifelong learner and then review experiments that highlight the promise of the methods.

1 Introduction

Probabilistic user models have been generated via a process of applying a statistical machine-learning procedure to a library of training cases. The process typically relies on supervised learning to acquire labels for variables that are not directly observed in the collection of activity or sensor data. Supervised training often requires an effortful phase of labeling hidden user states such as a user's current or future intention, affective state, or interruptability.

Some user modeling applications bypass manual supervised learning by performing *in-stream supervision*, where tagging occurs in the course of normal activity. For example, in the mixed-initiative Lookout system for calendaring and scheduling [3], a probabilistic user model is used in real-time to infer a user's intention to perform scheduling, based on the content of email messages at the user's focus of attention. To build a case library, the system watches users working with email and assigns labels of a scheduling intention by noticing if calendaring actions occur within some time horizon of the reading of email at the focus of the user's attention. The Priorities system [6], which uses machine learning to assign incoming email messages a measure of urgency, makes available an in-stream supervision capability. A set of policies, communicated to users, is used to label messages with urgency values and made available for review as draft case libraries. For example, messages that are deleted without being read are labeled as non-urgent.

Unfortunately many applications may not be amenable to in-stream supervision as labels for hidden states are not available. In such cases, the construction of predictive user models depends on either manual training sessions or the use of an *experience-sampling* methodology, where users are periodically asked for feedback that is used

© Springer-Verlag Berlin Heidelberg 2007

to label a situation or state of interest. To date, experience-sampling probes have been guided by random probe policies and such heuristics as seeking labels for states that a system is most uncertain about.

We formulate and study a decision-theoretic approach to guide experience sampling, centering on taking a value-of-information perspective. The methods address the challenge of building user-modeling systems that have the ability to perform lifelong learning, by continuing to use the current user model to make decisions about if and when to probe users for feedback, and considering the long-term value associated with such feedback. Beyond the use of the methods for learning predictive models in an efficient manner, the techniques have value for the ongoing updating of a user model given potential changes in users, tasks, and challenges.

We first introduce the legacy BusyBody system [5] as a motivating example. Busy-Body employs experience sampling to learn a user model that provides inferences about the cost of interrupting users. We discuss the core challenges of extending BusyBody with machinery that can guide its experience sampling. After laying out core concepts of lifelong learning, we discuss the specialization of the concepts for an alert mediation application. Finally, we discuss experiments with an implementation.

2   Motivating Application: Context-Sensitive Mediation of Alerts

Interest has blossomed in the construction of models that can predict the cost of interrupting computer users. To our knowledge, methods and opportunities with the use of probabilistic models to predict the cost of interrupting users, based on the ongoing sensing of a stream of activity, were first described in [6]. The work explored a cost-benefit analysis to controlling the flow of alerts to users, where the inferred urgency of incoming messages is balanced with the inferred cost of interruption, as computed by a Bayesian model. Several studies in the spirit [6] have

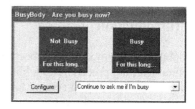

Fig. 1. BusyBody probe for user feedback, running in a binary modality

explored the learning of predictive models for interruptability based on observations of user activity [4,1]. Efforts in this realm include methods for seeking training from users in an ongoing manner. The BusyBody system employs experience sampling to construct personalized models for real-time predictions of the expected cost of interruption [5]. When BusyBody is in a training mode, the system intermittently probes users with a pop-up query requesting an assessment of their current or recent interruptability. The initial version of the system probed users at random times, constrained to an overall rate set by users. Figure 1 shows a request by BusyBody for input, used when the system is running in a binary hypothesis modality. In other modalities, the system inquires about finer-grained states of the cost of interruption. BusyBody contains an event infrastructure that logs desktop activities including such activities as typing, mouse movements, windows in focus, recent sequences of applications and window titles, and high-level statistics about the rates of switching among applications and windows. The system also considers several kinds of contextual variables, including the

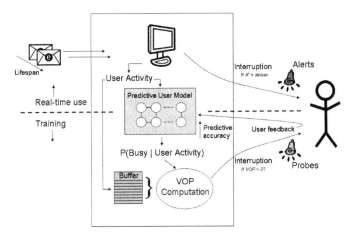

Fig. 2. Lifelong learning framework for training an alert mediation system

time of day and day of week, the name of the computer being used, the presence and properties meetings drawn from an electronic calendar, and wireless signals. The system employs a conversation-detection system, using a module that detects signals in the human-voice range of the audio spectrum. Responses to probes about interruptability are stored, along with the sensed evidence. Bayesian structure search is employed to build predictive models that are then used in real-time to provide predictions about the cost of interruption from the stream of sensed data.

BusyBody and the models it constructs are typically deployed in larger systems that reason about whether to relay incoming alerts and provides the current cost of interruption to these information triaging systems, which continue to balance the cost of interruption with the inferred urgency of incoming messages [4].

3   Lifelong Learning for User Modeling

We now revisit the experience-sampling challenge in BusyBody to highlight key aspects of a lifelong learning methodology. Assume that BusyBody is used, per its design to continually provide the current cost of interruption within an alert mediation system, based on sensed events and states. The model can become better with additional cases, obtained via experience sampling, where "better" is defined in terms of the performance of the mediation system.

The lifelong-learning challenge is to use the current predictive model within a value-of-information framework to control probes for new cases in an ideal manner, and to incorporate the cost of probing in different contexts into the overall long-term optimization of the use of the system. Figure 2 highlights the lifelong learning framework in a schematic manner. At the core of the framework is the predictive user model that plays a critical role in determining how to handle the incoming alerts. The predictive user model needs to adapt and to learn continuously from the user, and this is done with requests to the user. As shown in the figure, we divide the approach into two interrelated components of analysis: the real-time usage component and the learning component. These components can run simultaneously, each relying on the other.

3.1   Real-Time Usage

Over its lifespan, the alert mediation system encounters many incoming messages and
the aim is to take appropriate actions when they arrive. Alerting a user about an incoming message that may be urgent comes at the cost of an interruption, which in turn is
a function of the user state. Upon receiving a message, the system can either instantly
relay it to the user, defer its delivery, or store it for later review, and each of the different
actions is associated with a utility. The system aims to maximize the expected value (or
equivalently minimize the expected cost) of the handling of messages.

   We shall use $U(A, m)$ to refer to the utility of taking a message alerting action A
given the arrival of message m. We use $C(A, s)$ to refer to the cost of interruption
when the system takes action A given that the user is in state of interruptability s.
Upon seeing a message, the optimal action, A^*, is the action associated with maximum
expected utility. Assuming decomposability of costs and benefits, A^* is computed as:

$$A^* = \arg \max_A U(A, m) - \int_s C(A, s) p(s|E) \tag{1}$$

We cannot directly observe the user's state of interruptability s. We only have access to
the evidence E about the user's context and activity from BusyBody's event system. The
user model constructed with available data is used to predict the probability distribution
$p(s|E)$ over states of interruptability. The fidelity of the computation of the best action
for the system during usage depends upon the accuracy of the user model.

3.2   Training and Probing

Several statistical machine-learning procedures can be employed to construct a user
model that computes $p(s|E)$. These methods associate patterns of evidence with states
of the user. Candidate learning procedures include Bayesian structure search, support
vector machines (SVMs), decision trees etc. As the posterior probability $p(s|E)$ plays
a key role in the lifelong learning methodology, we seek to use a probabilistic methodology such as Bayesian structure search or Gaussian Process (GP) classification.

   The goal of the training cycle is to learn and to refine the user model by seeking
labeled cases from the user. Increasing the number and representativeness of cases may
increase the accuracy of the user model on future cases. Unfortunately requesting feedback from the user in experience sampling results in an interruption; hence, a context-
dependent cost of probing must be considered. We shall now review the computation
of the *value of probing* (VOP) for a label, which is the expected gain in the long-term
utility of a system given a probe.

3.3   Computing the Value of Probing

The computation of the value of probing at any moment is based on (1) the available
labeled training set, (2) the current set of observations, (3) a characterization of the
instances facing the system over time, and (4) a specified period of time of system
usage being considered. The latter duration of usage can range from a specific period
of time to the expected lifetime of the system.

   Let us assume that the system already has n training cases $\mathcal{E}_L = \{E_1, .., E_n\}$, with
labels $\mathcal{S}_L = \{s_1, .., s_n\}$. Each E_i denotes evidence capturing desktop activities and

context and s_i again denotes the state of the user. Most learning methods focus on minimizing such metrics as classification accuracy. However, a more comprehensive aim is to construct a lifelong learning process that is sensitive to both the predictive accuracy as well as the cost of interrupting the user with probes.

Consider the decision about whether to seek information from users about their state given E_{new}, a vector of observed evidence with relevance to the hidden state. The decision about whether to proceed with a probe is determined according to a maximization of the expected value of information (VOI) [7]. To embark on the computation of the VOP, we first consider a default situation where no triaging system is available to handle incoming messages. In the absence of a mediation system, the user would be alerted by all messages, $(A = A_{deliver})$. The mediation system is introduced to increase the expected utility of messaging to the user. For each message m, the utility of messaging in the absence of the alert mediation system is:

$$V^0(m, s) = U(A_{deliver}, m) - C(A_{deliver}, s) \tag{2}$$

Let A^* be the action selected according to the policy described in (1). Then, for a user state $\hat{s}$ predicted by the current user model, the utility achieved by the system is:

$$V^*(m, \hat{s}) = U(A^*, m) - C(A^*, \hat{s}) \tag{3}$$

The value that the system provides for an incoming message m is the marginal increase in utility over the default situation:

$$V^*(m, \hat{s}) - V^0(m, s) \tag{4}$$

We need to compute the expected gain in utility for future alerts. Assuming stationarity, we approximate this quantity using the mean utility gained over the labeled $\mathcal{E}_L$ and the unlabeled $\mathcal{E}_U$ cases. We note that a user's pattern of activity may not be stationary over time; as time progresses, a user might acquire new behaviors. A system should have the ability to adapt to these potential dynamics. Nonstationarity in users is addressed by using a moving buffer $\mathcal{E}_U$ that summarizes recent user activity and provides a means for modeling the current underlying distribution of a user's behavior. Given the labeled data points $\mathcal{E}_L$ and the buffer of unlabeled data points $\mathcal{E}_U = \{E_{n+1}, .., E_{n+m}\}$ that represents the recent distribution of data points, we can compute the total gain in utility with the use of the system as:

$$J_{all} = \sum_{E_i \in \mathcal{E}_L \cup \mathcal{E}_U} \int_{m_i} \int_s (V^*(m_i, \hat{s}) - V^0(m_i, s)) p(s|E_i) p(m_i) \tag{5}$$

Note, that we do not know the state of the user s for all $E_i \in \mathcal{E}_U$; thus, we need to marginalize over s by considering the conditional posterior $p(s|E_i)$. We must rely on our current predictive user model to provide us a good estimate of $p(s|E_i)$. We also need to learn a model of the future stream of messages m_i associated with each situation E_i. Such a model provides the likelihood of different messages, $p(m_i)$, allowing us to marginalize over m_i. We can simply use probability distributions compiled via observation of incoming messages m_i as approximations of future streams of messages. We can alternately model $p(m_i)$ via over time via updating of Beta or Dirichlet distributions. Let us consider the use of a Beta distribution for the case where there are only two kinds of messages, $m = 0$ and $m = 1$. Specifically, if $P(m = 1) = q$, the system models the distribution of future messages as:

$$P(q) = \text{Beta}(\alpha, \beta) = \frac{1}{\mathbf{B}(\alpha, \beta)} q^{\alpha-1} (1-q)^{\beta-1} \tag{6}$$

Here, $q \in [0, 1]$, $\mathbf{B}(\cdot)$ is the Beta function with α and β as parameters. Intuitively, α and β correspond to the number of messages encountered so far where $m = 1$ and $m = 0$ respectively. At the start, we have no information about the proportions of messages, so we have $\alpha = 0$ and $\beta = 0$. Note, that these values of α and β lead $P(q)$ to be a uniform distribution, representing an uninformative prior. As the system encounters more messages, it updates α and β, thus, maintaining an up-to-date belief about the proportions of urgent messages that the system might encounter.

Given the gains in utility computed by considering the labeled points and the unlabeled points, we can compute the *expected value of a system (EVS)* associated with each incoming message as the average gain per message:

$$EVS = \frac{J_{all}}{|\mathcal{E}_L| + |\mathcal{E}_U|} \tag{7}$$

The EVS per incoming message can be converted into an EVS per second, representing the rate at which value is being delivered by the system, given the expected rate of incoming messages.

Following a user response to a probe for a label, we update the predictive user model and may see a gain in the expected value that the system would be delivering per message. However, we must consider the cost of the probe. The difference in the gain and the cost guides the selection of cases to label. Let C_{new}^{probe} be the cost that will be incurred when the user is interrupted by a probe. For simplicity, we shall assume that the cost of interruption for the probe, like the cost of interruption for incoming messages, only depends upon the user state.

We introduce an optimization horizon, k that defines the duration of system usage considered in the learning optimization. k refers to the number of future alerts that will be handled. This value is selected according to the time frame that the user wishes to optimize over. For example, a user may wish to have the system probe so as to optimize the value of the system over two weeks. k determines the tradeoff between the acute cost of a probe and the long-term benefits associated with the expected improvements of system performance by refining the model using the additional case. A large k will tend to push the system to probe the user a great deal early on, while a small k would make the system reluctant to ask for supervision. Formally, we define the value of probing (VOP_k) for the new point E_{new} as the gain in the total expected value that the system is expected to deliver for the k alerts subtracted by the cost of probing:

$$VOP_k(E_{new}) = k \cdot (EVS_{new} - EVS) - C_{new}^{probe} \tag{8}$$

Here, EVS_{new} denotes the total expected value of the system delivered per alert should a label for E_{new} be acquired from the user. The VOP_k quantifies the gain in utility that can be obtained by interrupting the user. Thus, our strategy is to probe the user when $VOP_k \geq 0$. This approach differs from the earlier methods in active learning where the focus has been to minimize the classification error. Note, that this formulation of VOP_k assumes stationarity in the distribution of cases and associated patterns of evidences.

We need to compute VOP_k *before* we know the label for E_{new}. Note that J_{all}^{new} and EVS_{new} cannot be computed before we know the actual label s_{new}. Similarly, C_{new}^{probe} cannot be computed as the costs of labels are different for different classes. Thus, we must approximate J_{all}^{new} with an expectation of the empirical gain:

$$J_{all}^{new} \approx \int_s J_{all}^{new,s} p(s|E_{new}) \tag{9}$$

Here $J_{all}^{new,s}$ is the gain in utility when E_{new} is considered labeled as s and to calculate $J_{all}^{new,s}$, we retrain the predictive model by considering E_{new} labeled as s in the training set. Similarly, we can use the expectation of C_{new}^{probe} as the costs of labeling vary with the user state. Thus, given the VOP_k for the new point E_{new}, our strategy is to interrupt the user if $VOP_k \geq 0$. This strategy ensures that the system learns continuously while working to minimize interruptions to the user.

4   Implementation and Experiments

We now describe experiments with a sample instantiation of the lifelong learning methodology for an alert mediation system. Let us assume that there are two kinds of incoming messages: urgent ($m = 1$) and non-urgent ($m = 0$). Next, we assume that there are two kinds of actions the system can take: either deliver the message ($A = 1$) or postpone the delivery ($A = 0$). We shall consider the utility of outcomes in terms of the cost of delayed review of messages [6]. For simplicity, we shall assume that a fixed cost C_u is incurred if an urgent message is not delivered immediately and that this cost is greater than the cost of deferring delivery of a non-urgent message, $C_{\neg u}$. Note, this requires that we know if the message received by the system is urgent or not. Prior work has applied machine learning to infer the urgency of the messages [6]. We are interested in building a predictive user model that detects whether the user is busy or not, and have $s \in \{1, 2\}$, where $s = 1$ ($s = 2$) correspond to the state that the user is busy (not busy).

Next, we define the cost of interruption $C(A, s)$ by taking an action A. When we hold back ($A = 0$), there is no interruption so ($C(A = 0, m) = 0$). However, the cost of interruption is different when we relay the message to the user in different states:

$$C(A = 1, s) = \begin{bmatrix} C_b & \text{if the user is busy} \\ C_{\neg b} & \text{if the user is not busy} \end{bmatrix} \tag{10}$$

In cases where $C_u \geq C_b \geq C_{\neg u} \geq C_{\neg b}$, the optimal policy is to withhold delivery of the alert if the user is busy, unless the alert is urgent. We shall assume this policy.

We shall use a binary classifier as the predictive user model to detect the state of busy ($s = 1$) and not busy ($s = 2$). We use the GP classification to generate the probability distribution, $p(s|E)$. Details of the GP classification and its implementation can be found in [7] and [12].

If an incoming message is non-urgent and the system correctly detects that the user is busy, then per the policy described above, the message will not be sent to the user and the user will incur the cost of delayed review of non-urgent information ($C_{\neg u}$). However, in absence of the alert mediation system, the non-urgent message would be sent to the user who would incur the cost of interruption should they be busy (C_b). Thus, the net gain of the system is $G_{11}^{\neg u} = C_b - C_{\neg u}$. Here, $G_{ij}^{\neg u}$ denote the reduction in cost when classifying the user state belonging to class i as j while handling a non-urgent message. Similarly, consider the scenario when a non-urgent message is received and the system misclassifies the user state as busy. The system will not deliver the message immediately; consequently, we have $G_{21}^{\neg u} = C_{\neg b} - C_{\neg u}$. Note that the cost of interruption when the user is not busy is low; thus, $C_{\neg b} \leq C_{\neg u}$ suggesting that $G_{21}^{\neg u} \leq 0$. Further, the system relays all messages when the user is not busy and relays all the urgent messages regardless of the user state; consequently, there is no net gain in utilities for the rest of the cases. Note, that the system provides gain in utilities only via suppressing the delivery of non-urgent messages. The system maintains the Beta distribution over the set of urgent and non-urgent messages. Thus, Equation 5 reduces to:

$$J_{all} = \frac{\beta}{\alpha + \beta} \cdot [\sum_{i \in L_1} G_{11}^{\neg u} p_i + G_{21}^{\neg u} (1 - p_i)] \tag{11}$$

Here $p_i = p(s_i = 1|E_i)$, the probability that the user is busy, given the evidence E_i and L_1 is the indices of points labeled by the current predictive user model as class 1 (busy). The term $\frac{\beta}{\alpha + \beta}$ appears in the equation as gains only occur for the non-urgent alerts; consequently, the term enables us to consider the likelihood of receiving a non-urgent alert while computing the total gain J_{all}.

The lifelong learning policy guides the BusyBody probe for assessments. Let us consider the cost C_{new}^{probe} incurred when the user is interrupted to label the current instance E_{new}. We assume that the cost of probing depends upon the user state, that is:

$$C_{new}^{probe} = \begin{bmatrix} C_b^{probe} & \text{if the user is busy} \\ C_{\neg b}^{probe} & \text{if the user is not busy} \end{bmatrix} \tag{12}$$

We employ the concepts in Section 3.3 to guide requests for labels based on a computation of the value of probing.

We studied the value of the methods with simulations on data collected previously by the BusyBody system for two subjects. The first user is a program manager and the other a developer at our organization. The data for each contains two weeks of desktop activity as well as the busy/not-busy tags collected by the legacy BusyBody system, using a random probe policy. We only consider data points in the sequence for which the label for the user state was available, rather than all labeled and unlabeled cases. Thus, the results described can be considered as providing lower-bounds on performance. We expect the value to be greater in usage settings where the system monitors users continuously and can make decisions about all cases. We performed hold-out cross validation, randomly holding out 20% of the data for testing. For evaluation, the system employs the predictive model trained using the data seen *up to* the point being tested. Thus, we can observe and characterize the performance of the system as it is evolving.

In the experiments, we assigned utilities of different outcomes as follows: $C_u = 16$, $C_{\neg u} = 4$, $C_b = 8$, $C_{\neg b} = 1$, $C_b^{probe} = 8$, $C_{\neg b}^{probe} = 1$. We assumed that all of the incoming alerts are non-urgent, *i.e.*, $\frac{\beta}{\alpha + \beta} = 1.0$. Also, we chose k to be the length of the whole sequence. We employed a GP classifier using a polynomial kernel of degree 2 as the core machine-learning methodology for constructing the predictive model. We compare the lifelong learning scheme, both with and without a case buffer, with two alternate policies. First, we consider the policy of randomly selecting cases with a probability of 0.5 to query the user. The other scheme selects cases on which the predictive user model is most uncertain. Specifically, the system probes for labels if $0.3 \leq p(s_{new}|E_{new}) \leq 0.7$.

Table 1 shows the recognition accuracy on the test points and net gain in utilities over the hold-out set. The net gain in utilities includes the gain associated with the system usage and the cost of interruptions from the probes themselves. The lifelong learning method (VOP) outperformed the heuristic policies in accuracy as well as gain in utilities. We found that the buffer helps to improve the performance of the system as

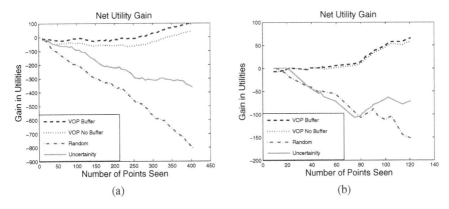

Fig. 3. The net gain in utilities by the system on the test points as it encounters data instances from the case libraries of the (a) program manager and (b) developer

it enables the system to exploit the additional available data in computing the expected gain in utility. The lifelong learning scheme with the use of a buffer resulted in overall accuracies of 67.90% for the program manager and 92.31% for developer. The program manager was queried 6 times and the developer was queried 3 times. We compared the accuracy achieved for the same number of labels with the random probe policy used in the legacy BusyBody system. Drawing the same numbers of cases for each subject randomly led to models with accuracies of 59.26% and 50%, respectively, a significant drop in accuracy for both. Figure 3 shows the gain in utilities over the hold-out set as the system sees progressively more labels. The graph highlights the ability of the lifelong learning methodology to provide an efficient means of learning predictive user models continuously over time.

5   Related Work

Most research on statistical models considers training and usage phases separately. Training data is used to generate predictive models and these models are analyzed. Exceptions include the paradigm of active and online learning where the model is continuously updated as the system collects data from the environment. In active learning, the aim is to probe a human/oracle about the label of the points as they arrive. Numerous heuristics and schemes have been proposed for choosing unlabeled points for tagging. For example, Freund *et al.* [2] propose as a criterion for active learning the disagreement among a committee of classifiers. Tong and Koller [11] propose to choose unlabeled points to query that minimize the version space for SVMs. Within the Gaussian Process framework, the method of choice has been to look at the expected informativeness of unlabeled data points [8,9]. All of these methods inherently focus on minimizing the misclassification rate. Key aspects of the work presented here build upon our earlier work on *selective supervision* [7], employing decision-theoretic principles.

Table 1. Performance on the test set. Left: program manager data. Right: developer data.

Strategy	Accuracy	# of Probes	Utility Gain
VOP (Buffer)	67.90%	6	100
VOP (No Buffer)	62.96%	12	42
Most Uncertain	66.67%	88	-371
Random (p = 0.5)	59.26%	169	-812

Strategy	Accuracy	# of Probes	Utility Gain
VOP (Buffer)	92.31%	3	66
VOP (No Buffer)	84.62%	3	59
Most Uncertain	80.77%	24	-79
Random (p = 0.5)	69.23%	36	-200

6   Conclusion

We reviewed principles of lifelong learning where the costs and benefits of acquiring and learning from additional cases are considered over the lifetime of a system. We focused on the use of lifelong learning to guide supervision in experience sampling. The method harnesses the value of information to make decisions about probing users for states that are not available to the system. Concepts were illustrated in the context of the BusyBody system, applied on the challenge of balancing the costs and benefits of alerting users to potentially urgent messages. We reviewed the use of a comprehensive measure of the expected value of a system that incorporates both the cost of acquiring additional cases for learning and the net gains associated with real-world use of refined predictive models. In ongoing work, we are pursuing the use of principles of lifelong learning in multiple applications as well as working to extend the methods. Our current research includes investigating the modeling of non-stationary distributions and methods for caching, forgetting, and reusing cases.

References

1. Fogarty, J., Hudson, S.E., Lai, J.: Examining the Robustness of Sensor-Based Statistical Models of Human Interruptability. In: Proceedings of CHI (2004)
2. Freund, Y., Seung, H.S., Shamir, E., Tishby, N.: Selective Sampling Using the Query by Committee Algorithm. Machine Learning, vol. 28 (1997)
3. Horvitz, E.: Principles of Mixed-Initiative User Interfaces. In: ACM SIGCHI Conference on Human Factors in Computing Systems (1999)
4. Horvitz, E., Apacible, J.: Learning and Reasoning about Interruption. In: Intl. Conference on Multimodal Interfaces (2003)
5. Horvitz, E., Apacible, J., Koch, P.: BusyBody: Creating and Fielding Personalized Models of the Cost of Interruption. In: Conference on Computer Supported Cooperative Work (2004)
6. Horvitz, E., Jacobs, A., Hovel, D.: Attention-Sensitive Alerting. Uncertainty in Artificial Intelligence (1999)
7. Kapoor, A., Horvitz, E., Basu, S.: Selective Supervision: Guiding Supervised Learning with Decision-Theoretic Active Learning. In: Intl. Joint Conference on Artificial Intelligence (2007)
8. Lawrence, N., Seeger, M., Herbrich, R.: Fast Sparse Gaussian Process Method: Informative Vector Machines. Neural Information Processing Systems, vol. 15 (2002)
9. MacKay, D.: Information-Based Objective Functions for Active Data Selection. Neural Computation, vol. 4(4) (1992)
10. Platt, J.: Probabilities for support vector machines. Adv. in Large Margin Classifiers (2000)
11. Tong, S., Koller, D.: Support Vector Machine Active Learning with Applications to Text Classification. In: Intl. Conference on Machine Learning (2000)
12. Williams, C.K.I., Barber, D.: Bayesian Classification with Gaussian Processes. IEEE Transactions on Pattern Analysis and Machine Intelligence (1998)

Users in Volatile Communities: Studying Active Participation and Community Evolution

Tanja Falkowski and Myra Spiliopoulou

Otto-von-Guericke-Universität Magdeburg, Faculty of Computer Science, Universitätsplatz 2, 39106 Magdeburg, Germany
{falkowski,myra}@iti.cs.uni-magdeburg.de

Abstract. Active participation of a person in a community is a powerful indicator of the person's interests, preferences, beliefs and (often) social and demographic context. Community membership is part of a user's model and can contribute to tasks like personalized services, assistance and recommendations. However, a community member can be active or inactive. To what extend is a community still representative of the interests of an inactive participant? To gain insights to this question, we observe a community as an evolving social structure and study the effects of member fluctuation. We define a community as a high-level temporal structure composed of "community instances" that are defined conventionally through observable active participation and are captured at distinct timepoints. Thus, we capture community volatility, as evolution and discontinuation. This delivers us clues about the role of the community for its members, both for active and inactive ones. We have applied our model on a community exhibiting large fluctuation of members and acquired insights on the community-member interplay.

Keywords: user communities, community evolution, community participation.

1 Introduction

A community is traditionally defined as a group of persons characterized by common interests, preferences or expertise and/or by mutual interaction. Knowledge about community membership is valuable for the design of personalized assistance or the formulation of recommendations: First, the topics dominant inside the community can be assumed to be of interest to each community member. Second, the community members with which one person interacts can be assumed to reflect or even influence the interests of that person, so that their interests can be used for recommendations.

However, this definition of a community oversees that participation can also be passive. Does a community still reflect the interests of an inactive user? This is particularly important for communities that exhibit high fluctuation of active members: Active participants influence and shape the interests of their community [2], so that the community's relevance for inactive participants may fade.

We address this issue by modeling a community as an evolving structure: Its instances are communities in the traditional sense (we call them *community instances*), i.e. dense graphs of interactions among the users under observation. Two

C. Conati, K. McCoy, and G. Paliouras (Eds.): UM 2007, LNAI 4511, pp. 47–56, 2007.
© Springer-Verlag Berlin Heidelberg 2007

community instances are similar if they share a minimum number of active members. This notion of similarity allows for continuity inside the evolving community, even if some participants become inactive. If the similarity between past and current community instances becomes marginal, though, this signals that the old community is dissolved and the new one does not reflect the interests of past members.

Our method is based on our previous work on community dynamics [5]. In [5], we have proposed a temporal model for communities that captures the evolutionary aspect of human interactions, a two-step clustering process for the discovery of community instances at each timepoint and for the discovery of similar instances across the time axis, and a visualization utility for the inspection of community evolution. In this study, we extend [5] by modeling user membership to a community and studying the evolving relevance of a community towards its members.

The remainder of the paper is organized as follows: In Section 2, we discuss related work on communities and their evolution. Section 3 describes our three-step method for the formation of evolving communities and introduces the model of user membership to an evolving community. Section 4 contains our preliminary experimental results on the members of a small community inside a larger social structure that exhibits seasonal fluctuations. We conclude in Section 5.

2 Related Work

Communities as clusters of interacting agents (humans or processes) are of interest in many research fields, including: Citations networks in social sciences [10, 15], genetic networks [19] and food webs [4] in biology, user communities in the Web [7, 11] and user communities manifesting themselves through other types of Internet-based interaction, e.g. mail exchange [18]. Research advances encompass (a) a variety of definitions for the concept "community", taking the interaction medium and the form of the interaction graph into account and (b) mining algorithms for the discovery of *static*, densely connected subgraphs, i.e. of participants that interact with each other more intensively than with the rest of the network.

The temporal perspective is studied by Leskovec et al., who study evolution in graphs [12]. Their methodology delivers insights to changes and trends concerning the graph properties, such as average vertex degree, with some emphasis on large networks (e.g. the Internet). Cortes et al. propose a data structure that captures a dynamic graph over time [3]: The authors introduce the notion of communities of interest upon this structure, where a community is the neighborhood of a chosen vertex, subject to the vertex's connectivity to other vertices. A method for the discovery of human communities in data streams has been proposed by Aggarwal and Yu [1]: They focus on indicators of a given community's evolution and use to this purpose the increase, resp. decrease of interaction within a dense subgraph.

The research on Web communities is strongly influenced by the seminal work of Kleinberg et al. [7] on the discovery of hubs and authorities by studying link topology. The roles of *hub* and *authority* are of major importance for the understanding of groups of semantically related documents (e.g. hyperlinked Web pages). However, user communities can take more elaborate forms than captured by these two roles.

Research on communities poses large demands on visualization. Software tools like SoNIA [14] and TeCFlow [9] support visualization of social networks across time. However, these tools depict the changing behavior between single actors rather than the evolution of the community they belong to. We take a different perspective here, because community evolution influences community membership and the relevance of a community's manifested interests for its individual participants, especially for the inactive ones.

3   The Community Discovery Process

We first describe briefly our approach of [5] for modeling and discovering communities as clusters of community instances[1]: Community instances discovered at different timepoints are linked on similarity across the time axis, thus building a *community evolution graph*. On this graph, a *community* is a dense subgraph of linked instances. Then, we model the relevance of a community to a user, taking into account the intensity and recency of her active participation to the instances constituting the evolving community.

3.1   Clustering Users into Community Instances

We observe a stream of user interactions. We partition the stream into time periods and discover the community instances manifested at each period. The challenges to be dealt with are (a) the specification of a *proximity* notion for interacting users and (b) the importance assigned to old vs. new interactions.

User *proximity* is modeled as interaction, e.g. exchange of messages. Although proximity can be used to assess similarity among users, it is stressed that proximity-by-interaction does not imply that the users are conceptually similar: Indeed, users with very different properties or original preferences may interact and influence each other, to the effect that their preferences coerce.

We capture user proximity by connecting interacting users with undirected edges. Each edge is weighted by the *intensity* of the interaction, defined as the number of exchanges between the two users. To prevent the prevalence of "old" users that have performed many interactions over "new" ones that have not yet interacted with many people, we use a sliding window of n periods, beyond which interactions are forgotten. Hence, for a period t and two users u, u', the intensity of their interaction *intensity(u, u', t)* is the number of exchanges between them for the last n periods.

Using this notion of intensity, we build at each t the graph of interactions G_t and extract community instances from it by hierarchical divisive clustering: The algorithm partitions the graph iteratively into denser subgraphs by deleting edges that do not belong to the dense subgraphs but rather serve to separate them. The edges to be deleted are those with the highest "edge betweenness", as proposed by Girvan and Newman [8]:

---

[1] Hereafter we use the symbol C for a community instance or for the cluster corresponding to a community instance, unless otherwise specified.

Definition 3.1. *The edge betweenness of an edge e in a graph G(V,E) is defined as the number of shortest paths between pairs of vertices that run along it.*

The method is based on the assumption, that the few edges between communities have more "traffic", as, e.g., an information flow between vertices in two communities has to travel along these edges. The hierarchical clustering algorithm iteratively removes these edges with the highest edge betweenness score.

The output of the hierarchical divisive algorithm is a dendrogram; the root is the whole graph, the leaf nodes are individual vertices. A cluster $C \subseteq V$ is a subset of vertices. A *clustering* $\zeta = \{C_1,...,C_t\}$ of G is a partition of all vertices into clusters. We select the clustering with the highest modularity $Q(\zeta)$ as proposed by Newman and Girvan [16]:

$$Q(\zeta) = \sum_{C \in \zeta} \left[\frac{|E(C)|}{m} - \left(\frac{\sum_{v \in C} \deg(v)}{2m} \right)^2 \right] \tag{1}$$

$m = |E|$ and the *degree* $\deg(v)$ of a vertex v is the number of directly connected vertices (direct neighbors). The function Q compares the fraction of edges within a community to those that lead to vertices outside the community. Q favors graph clusterings that consist of modular dense subgraphs and is thus a measure of graph modularity: Values close to $Q = 1$ indicate strong community structure. According to [16], values greater than 0.3 already indicate significant community structure. We thus set 0.3 as threshold for Q, to detect community instances composed of intensively interacting individuals [5].

3.2 Evolution of Community Instances

Given a community instance found in period t, we are interested in its survival in subsequent periods. For the conceptual definition of "survival", we assume that a community instance is characterized by the people participating in it. However, we tolerate a fluctuation of the community members [5].

Following our MONIC framework for cluster evolution over a data stream [17], we juxtapose each cluster/community instance C discovered in period t with each candidate cluster of the next period t': A *match* of C is a cluster C' that overlaps with C for more than a threshold. For the comparison of community instances, the overlap of two clusters is a set of users (rather than: interactions) found in both of them. The threshold τ_{match} is set to 0.5, so that, there is at most one match per cluster. If match C' exists, we state that C has survived into C' ($C \rightarrow C'$) [17].

In [17], we have limited the notion of cluster survival to adjacent time periods. For community evolution, we allow for matching between community instances that are more than one period apart from each other: We introduce an upper boundary $\tau_{periods}$ to the number of periods that may separate two matching community instances; instances that are more than $\tau_{periods}$ apart have zero similarity by default.

Active users contribute to the similarity of community instances, because they launch interactions with other users and thus increase their proximity to them. This agrees with the findings of [2], where it is stated that active participants of the studied community shape "its" topics of interest. Moreover, this extended notion of "survival" for a community instance allows us to tolerate short times of inactivity within the stream of user interactions: Indeed, even the most active users inside a community may be temporarily inactive for arbitrary external reasons.

3.3   Communities in the Survival Graph

Within each time window of $\tau_{periods}$, we compare community instances and connected matching instances with an edge, thus establishing a "time-folded survival graph". This graph is similar to the "evolution graph" of [13]: In both cases, the nodes are clusters found in different time periods, while edges denote that the nodes match. However, Mei & Zhai perform soft clustering upon documents and study matching cluster labels rather than the clusters themselves; the graph is used to predict label evolution [13]. We are rather interested in discovering superordinate community structures in the time-folded survival graph and relate them to their members.

Formally, let $G = (V, E)$ be the time-folded survival graph. A vertex v has the form (C, t), where C is a community instance discovered at period t. An edge $e = (v, v') = ((C, t), (C', t'))$ denotes that cluster C has survived into C', i.e. $t < t'$ and $overlap(C, C') > \tau_{match}$. The threshold value $\tau_{periods}$ ensures that $|t' - t| < \tau_{periods}$ for all pairs (t, t') that appear in edges of E. An edge is further associated with a weight, again defined as the *edge betweenness* of the connected vertices (cf. DEF. 3.1). To discover groups of community instances upon the survival graph, we again use hierarchical divisive clustering: It uses the edge betweenness of the edges to eliminate edges which separate subgraphs that are denser than their surroundings.

Definition 3.2. *A "k-community" upon a time-folded survival graph $G(V, E)$ is a connected subgraph retained after k iterations.*

Definition 3.3. *Let $G(k, V, E_k)$ be a time-folded survival graph after k iterations, let $t_1, ..., t_n$ be the periods encountered in V and let χ be a k-community found in G. Community χ dissolves in t_g, iff there is no edge $e = (v, v')$ in E_k with $v = (C, t)$ and $v' = (C', t')$ with $t < t_g$ and $t' \geq t_g$. The timepoint t_g is the "dissolution point" or "gap" for community χ.*

According to this definition, a gap separates two clusters of community instances in the sense that no instance observed before the gap has edges that cross the gap. In practice, the demand that no edge "crosses" the gap is too restrictive: We relax it by requiring that the number of retained edges belonging to an instance of χ is minimal. Then, the "lifetime" of k-community is the *timespan* $[t_{min}, t_{max}]$ between the first point it was encountered and the gap at which it has disappeared.

3.4   Users Within Evolving Communities

In each time period a user u belongs to one community instance. Within a community, i.e. a cluster of community instances upon the time-folded graph, a user may appear more than once, as the result of interactions at different times. Obviously, a user may belong to more than one community. For each community χ and user u, the relevance of χ for u is reflected in the ratio of her activity inside the community towards her overall activity. To compute this ratio, we first define the *involvement* of a user within a community instance:

Definition 3.4. *Let u be a user and C be a community instance discovered in time period t. The "involvement" of u in C is the number of interactions that the user has performed inside this community instance in period t:*

$$involvement(u,C) = \left| \{ e \in E_t \cap C : e = (u,v) \vee e = (v,u) \} \right| \qquad (2)$$

Similarly to the intensity of interaction specified in Section 3.1, user involvement is also based on the number of exchanges performed. However, the intensity is used to discover the community instances upon the graph of interactions $G_t(V_t, E_t)$, while the involvement is computed upon already derived instances.

On the basis of the involvement value for community instances, we can compute the following indicators of a user's behavior towards communities:

Definition 3.5. *The participation of user u in a community χ with lifetime $[t_{min}, t_{max}]$ is defined as*

$$participation(u, \chi) = \frac{\sum_{C \in \chi} involvement(u,C)}{\sum_{C \in \Xi} involvement(u,C)} \qquad (3)$$

the fraction of the involvement in community instance χ divided by the involvement of the user in other community instances during the lifetime of the community.

User participation may be active or inactive, since the user may have non-zero involvement in some community instances and zero involvement value on other instances of the same community.

Definition 3.6. *For a given time period T, the relevance of a community χ for a user u is defined as:*

$$rscore(u, \chi, T) = \frac{\sum_{C \in \chi \; \wedge \; C \in \Xi_T} involvement(u,C)}{\sum_{C \in \Xi_T} involvement(u,C)} \qquad (4)$$

where Ξ_T are all community instances during T. Thus, the relevance score is the fraction of the involvement of user u in community χ during the given time period T divided by the involvement in other community instances during T. By this, the relevance of communities with lifetime outside T is zero.

The representative community for a user u in a period T is the community for which the $rscore()$ value is maximum. We denote this community as $community(u, T)$. This definition allows us to identify a representative community for each user during a time period, even if the user was not active during the whole time period.

3.5 A Tool for Monitoring Community Dynamics

We have implemented the model described thus far into a tool for the discovery of community instances, the clustering of instances across the time axis into communities and the visualization of their evolution. The tool offers a control panel by which the human expert can specify the similarity threshold $\tau_{overlap}$ for the linking of communities into the evolution graph, the threshold $\tau_{periods}$ for the clustering of linked instances over time and the number of iterations k to discover k-communities. The tool delivers statistics and a visualization panel for the static community structure (cf. [6]). It further highlights community discontinuations by drawing a vertical bar at each structural gap and depicting the communities at both sides of the gap in different colors [5]. The figures of the communities depicted for our experiments in the next section have been drawn with this tool.

4 Experiments

We have performed a preliminary set of proof-of-concept experiments on a social network that exhibits membership fluctuation. We have observed this network over several time periods, discovering community instances and grouping them into evolving communities according to the model above. We have selected one small community and studied the behavior of its users during its lifetime, using the measures as proposed in Section 3.4. We analyzed a social network of about 1,000 members over a time period of 18 months. We observed around 250,000 interactions between these users during this time period. Using the method described above we clustered users in community instances and determined sets of similar community instances along the time axis.

In Fig. 1 (left side) the k-communities of our social network are shown after $k = 48$ iterations. We observe four communities that are depicted in the visualization in four different colors. To enhance visibility, the borders of the communities are also indicated by vertical bars. After further iterations we determine a small community of five community instances that is separated from the other communities (the respective instances are encircled in the upper part of the right side of Fig. 1; $\chi = blue$). The community *blue* has a lifetime of four periods ($t_{start} = 38$, $t_{end} = 41$).

The first instance of *blue* in t = 38 consists of eleven members. The second instance consists of eight members: Five of the eight users where already participating in the first instance and three members are new to the community. The third instance in $t = 40$ consists of seven members. All of them participated in $t = 38$ and/or in $t = 39$. In $t = 41$ two instances are assigned to *blue*. Both instances have three members and all members have already been participating in previous instances.

To assess the relevance of a community to a given user we observe the interaction behavior of the community members inside the community as well as interaction with members from other communities during the lifetime of the community under observation. We thus fix the time period T to the lifetime of *blue*, i.e. to the period 38-41, and measure the *involvement* and the *participation* for a subset of six members of the community. Since our observation period equals the lifetime of χ, the measure for the *participation* equals the *rscore* measure. We can therefore use the *participation* measure to assess the relevance of a community to a user.

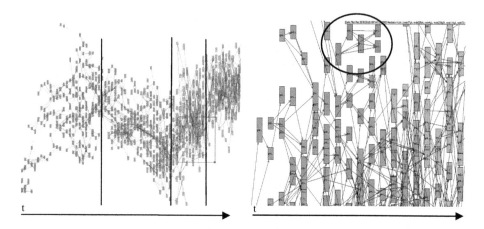

Fig. 1. Left side: k-communities after 48 iterations. Right side: Separated k-community after further iterations (encircled community instances in the upper part named in the following community *blue*)

Table 1. Involvement and participation of six community members of the *blue* community

user u	involvement(u, C)		participation(u, χ)	Remark
v_{695}	t=38	13	0.57	no assignment to other
	t=39	0		community instance in T
	t=40	0		
	t=41	0		
v_{685}	t=38	4	0.33	no assignment to other
	t=39	0		community instance in T
	t=40	0		
	t=41	0		
v_{700}	t=38	8	0.32	no assignment to other
	t=39	1		community instance in T
	t=40	0		
	t=41	0		
v_{525}	t=38	5	0.45	no assignment to other
	t=39	1		community instance in T
	t=40	0		
	t=41	1		
v_{368}	t=38	57	0.17	no assignment to other
	t=39	53		community instance in T
	t=40	1		
	t=41	0		
v_{58}	t=38	10	0.28	in T *also* assigned to
	t=39	9		community ϕ :
	t=40	0		
	t=41	0		participation(u, ϕ)=0.38

A user, who is assigned to a community, is most likely represented by this community; at least during the lifetime of the community she is assigned to. However, the involvement in the assigned community may vary over the lifetime of the community as shown in Table 1. No user is involved in community *blue* in all periods. Some users are only involved once (see v_{695}, v_{685}). Since we used an overlapping sliding window to partition the time axis, to smooth out gaps in the interaction behavior between periods, members might be assigned to a community instances, even though they had no interaction in the respective period because of former interactions. Thus, it is of interest to consider the involvement in other community instances. In our case both users are not involved in other community instances, therefore it can be assumed, that they are still represented by community *blue* even in periods they are not active.

Users who are assigned to different community instances during the lifetime of the community *blue* might be still best represented by this community in the periods they are involved in *blue*; however users may not be represented best by this community over the whole period of their interaction. As shown in Table 1, users may change their interaction behavior during the lifetime of a community and switch to another community (see user v_{58}). Thus, the participation in the assigned community is not maximal in all periods. User v_{58} was assigned to the community *blue* but shows in the last period of the community's lifetime higher involvement in another community instance. This is reflected in the *participation* of the user for both communities: It is higher for community ϕ (0.38 compared to 0.28 in χ). Thus, the respective time period should be considered when making a decision which community best represents a user. The relevance of a community for a user in a certain time period can therefore be assed by determining the highest relevance score.

5 Conclusions and Outlook

We have studied the issue of community relevance for a user participating in multiple communities, whereupon periods of active participation may be followed by inactivity. We have modeled communities as dynamic structures comprised of static "community instances", each of them characterized by its *active* users. From the viewpoint of community evolution, this allows us to detect "structural gaps", i.e. the discontinuation of a community's lifetime span. From the viewpoint of community membership, the model allows us to assign for a certain period users to a most relevant community.

We have experimented with a real community that exhibits membership fluctuation and has known structural gaps. The experiment delivered some first insights on the number of clusters (dense subgraphs of similar community instances) to which users participate actively or inactively. As a next step, the preferences, interests or other type of semantics captured by an evolving community should be captured and juxtaposed to those of their individual members.

Acknowledgments. We are grateful to Jörg Bartelheimer who has implemented the mining and visualization tool and collected the data for the analysis during his diploma thesis at the Otto-von-Guericke-Universität Magdeburg.

References

1. Aggarwal, C.C., Yu, P.S.: Online Analysis of Community Evolution in Data Streams. In: Proceedings of SIAM International Data Mining Conference (2005)
2. Backstrom, L., Huttenlocher, D., Kleinberg, J., Lan, X.: Group Formation in Large Social Networks: Membership, Growth, and Evolution. In: Proc. of KDD'06 (2006)
3. Cortes, C., Pregibon, D., Volinsky, C.: Communities of Interest. In: Proceedings of the 4th International Conference on Advances in Intelligent Data Analysis, pp. 105–114 (2001)
4. Dunne, J.A., Williams, R.J., Martinez, N.D.: Food-web structure and network theory: The role of connectance and size. PNAS 99(20), 12917–12922 (2002)
5. Falkowski, T., Bartelheimer, J., Spiliopoulou, M.: Mining and Visualizing the Evolution of Subgroups in Social Networks. In: Proc. of IEEE/WIC/ACM International Conference on Web Intelligence (WI-06) (2006)
6. Falkowski, T., Spiliopoulou, M.: Observing Dynamics in Community Structures. In: Proc. of Adaptation in Artificial and Biological Systems (AISB'06), pp. 102–105 (2006)
7. Gibson, D., Kleinberg, J., Raghavan, P.: Inferring Web Communities from Link Topology. In: Proceedings of the 9th ACM Conference on Hypertext and Hypermedia (1998)
8. Girvan, M., Newman, M.E.J.: Community structure in social and biological networks. PNAS 99(12), 7821–7826 (2002)
9. Gloor, P.A., Zhao, Y.: TeCFlow- A Temporal Communication Flow Visualizer for Social Networks Analysis. In: CSCW'04 Workshop on Social Networks, ACM (2004)
10. Jeong, H., Néda, Z., Barabási, A.-L.: Measuring preferential attachment in evolving networks. Europhysics Letters 61(4), 567–572 (2003)
11. Kleinberg, J., Lawrence, S.: The Structure of the Web. Science 294, 1849–1850 (2001)
12. Leskovec, J., Kleinberg, J., Faloutsos, C.: Graphs over Time: Densification Laws, Shrinking Diameters and Possible Explanations. In: Proc. of KDD'05 (2005)
13. Mei, Q., Zhai, C.: Discovering evolutionary theme patterns from text: An exploration of temporal text mining. In: Proc. of KDD'05, pp. 198–207 (2005)
14. Moody, J., Mc Farland, D., Bender-deMoll, S.: Dynamic Network Visualization. American Journal of Sociology 110(4), 1206–1241 (2005)
15. Newman, M.: The structure of scientific collaboration networks, PNAS, vol. 98(2) (2001)
16. Newman, M., Girvan, M.: Finding and evaluating community structure in networks, Physical Review, E 69(026113) (2004)
17. Spiliopoulou, M., Ntoutsi, I., Theodoridis, Y., Schult, R.: MONIC - Modeling and Monitoring Cluster Transitions. In: Proc. of KDD'06, pp. 706–711 (2006)
18. Tyler, J.R., Wilkinson, D.M., Huberman, B.A.: Email as Spectroscopy: Automated Discovery of Community Structure within Organizations. In: Huysman, M., Wenger, E., Wulf, V. (eds.) Communities and Technologies, Kluwer, Dordrecht (2003)
19. Wilkinson, D.M., Huberman, B.A.: A method for finding communities of related genes. In: Proc. National Academy of Sciences U.S.A., vol. 10(1073) (2004)

Learning from What Others Know: Privacy Preserving Cross System Personalization

Bhaskar Mehta

L3S Researchzentrum/University of Hannover, Hannover 30177, Germany
mehta@l3s.de

Abstract. Recommender systems have been steadily gaining popularity and have been deployed by several service providers. Large scalable deployment has however highlighted one of the design problems of recommender systems: *lack of interoperability*. Users today often use multiple electronic systems offering recommendations, which cannot learn from one another. The result is that the end user has to often provide similar information and in some cases disjoint information. Intuitively, it seems that much can be improved with this situation: information learnt by one system could potentially be reused by another, to offer an overall improved personalization experience. In this paper, we provide an effective solution to this problem using Latent Semantic Models by learning a user model across multiple systems. A privacy preserving distributed framework is added around the traditional *Probabilistic Latent Semantic Analysis* framework, and practical aspects such as addition of new systems and items are also dealt with in this work.

1 Introduction

The World Wide Web provides access to a wealth of information and services to a huge and heterogeneous user population on a global scale. As the web becomes the source for commercial businesses to reach a large number of people, service providers are looking for ways to extend electronic systems to provide more effective services to their customers. Since the last decade, commercial providers have identified *personalization* as a key driver of business growth and repeat customers. This has led to a wide scale deployment of personalization engines which provide scalable personalization, examples being Amazon and Netflix.

However, benefiting from these personalized web sites requires both explicit and implicit involvement of the end-users over a long period of time. Each system independently builds up user profiles and may then use this information to personalize the system's content and service offering. Today, users often use multiple electronic systems offering personalization, which cannot *interoperate*, or share user information with one another. The end result is that a user has to often provide similar information and in some cases disjoint information to different systems. Such isolated approaches have two major drawbacks: firstly, investments of users in personalizing a system either through explicit provision of information or through long and regular use are not transferable to other systems. Secondly, users have little or no control over the information that defines their profile, since user data are deeply buried in personalization engines running on the server side.

C. Conati, K. McCoy, and G. Paliouras (Eds.): UM 2007, LNAI 4511, pp. 57–66, 2007.
© Springer-Verlag Berlin Heidelberg 2007

Cross system personalization(CSP) [7] allows for sharinge information across different information systems in a user-centric way and can overcome the afore-mentioned problems. Information about users, which is originally scattered across multiple systems, is combined to obtain maximum leverage and reuse of information. Previous approaches to cross system personalization[9] relied on each user having a *unified profile* which different systems can understand. The basis of 'understanding' in this approach is of a semantic nature, i.e. a user pro-file can be semantically interpreted by another system. The main challenge in this approach is to establish some common and globally accepted vocabulary and to create a standard every system will comply with.

Machine learning techniques provide a promising alternative by using example data to learn mappings between profile formats to enable cross system person-alization without the need to rely on accepted semantic standards or ontologies. The key idea is that one can try to learn dependencies between profiles main-tained within one system and profiles maintained within a second system based on data provided by users who use both systems and who are willing to share their profiles across systems – which we assume is in the interest of the user. Here, instead of requiring a common semantic framework, it is only required that a sufficient number of users cross between systems and that there is enough regularity among users that one can learn within a user population, a fact that is commonly exploited in social or *collaborative filtering*.

2   Automatic Cross System Personalization

For simplicity, we consider a two system scenario in which there are only two sites or systems denoted by A and B that perform some sort of personalization and maintain separate profiles of their users; generalization to an arbitrary number of systems is relatively straightforward. For simplification, we assume that the complete user profiles for a user u_i are represented as vectors $\mathbf{x}_i^A \in \mathcal{X} \subseteq \mathbb{R}^m$ and $\mathbf{x}_i^B \in \mathcal{Y} \subseteq \mathbb{R}^p$ for systems A and B, respectively. Given the profile $\mathbf{x}_i^A$ of a user in system A, the objective is then to find the corresponding profile $\mathbf{x}_i^B$ of the same user in system B. Formally we are looking to find a mapping

$$F_{AB} : \mathbb{R}^m \to \mathbb{R}^p, \quad \text{s.t.} \quad F_{AB}(\mathbf{x}_i^A) \approx \mathbf{x}_i^B \tag{1}$$

for users u_i. The situation may be further complicated by the fact that for some users, $\mathbf{x}_i^A$ may be known partially, and that some aspects or values of $\mathbf{x}_i^B$ may be directly observable only at system B. In the latter case, the goal is to exploit the information available at system A in order to improve the inference about unknown values of $\mathbf{x}_i^B$. Such a mapping is the crux of the CSP problem: given a profile at one system, find the profile at another system.

2.1   Requirements from a CSP Solution

The above stated problem maps well to the *machine learning* area, where a program learns from a set of examples given as input. The aim of the learning program is learn a function which can best mimic the pattern learnt in input data. The CSP problem has a similar setting, where users using two systems have one profile for each system, which can be used as input for learning a mapping. Since our input and output values are both vectors, this problem requires a vector valued learning method. Besides the obvious learning capability required from a candidate method, there are additional constraints form the problem itself. These include:

a) Perform vector-valued regression *en bloc* and not independently,
b) Exploit correlations between different output dimensions,
c) Scalability of the method to large user populations and many systems/sites,
d) Capability to deal with missing and incomplete data,
e) Preserve the privacy of the end users,
f) Capability to deal with addition of new variables without explicit retraining.
g) Capability to take unlabeled data into account (semi-supervised learning)

Few methods can provide principled support for all the above requirements, dealign either with sparsity, or with vector valued learning, but not both(see [7,8] for a more detailed analysis). In this work, we use PLSA[6] as a method of choice after transforming the CSP task into a missing value problem, similar to traditional collaborative filtering. However, privacy preservation is not built into PLSA; thus we introduce a distributed version of PLSA in this paper, which can be used in a privacy preserving manner by using encryption homomorphisms similar to [2]. Further, we also extend the PLSA model to support addition of new items. The next subsection explains how we transform CSP into a missing value problem; section 3 explains our extended Distributed PLSA model.

2.2   Cross System Personalization as a Matrix Completion Problem

Two basic assumptions help us in casting the CSP task as a missing value problem: *first*, that users have their profiles for multiple systems available to them, and *second*, that users are willing to provide their multiple profiles for computing a mapping between the profile formats of these systems. In this section, we use these basic assumptions to cast CSP as a missing value problem.

In a two system scenario, we have two sites A and B, containing user profiles for their users represented as vectors. A user u_i has a profile $\mathbf{x}_i^A \in \mathbb{R}^m$ at site A, and a profile $\mathbf{x}_i^B \in \mathbb{R}^p$ at site B. Let matrices $\mathbf{X}^A$ and $\mathbf{X}^B$ represent all user profiles (with each user representing a column) at systems A and B and further assume that c users are common to both sites and that the data matrices can be partitioned as:

$$\mathbf{X}^A = \left[\mathbf{X}_c^A \ \mathbf{X}_s^A\right], \qquad \mathbf{X}^B = \left[\mathbf{X}_c^B \ \mathbf{X}_s^B\right], \tag{2}$$

where $\mathbf{X}_c^A$ and $\mathbf{X}_c^B$ represent the sub-matrices of $\mathbf{X}^A$ and $\mathbf{X}^B$ corresponding to the common users and $\mathbf{X}_s^A$ and $\mathbf{X}_s^B$ the sub-matrices for users that are unique to A and B.

One way of looking at the CSP problem in the context of latent semantics is to relate the profiles in both (or multiple) systems by assuming that the user profiles are likely to be consistent in terms of the basic factors, i.e. that they can be explained by latent factors common to both systems.

A simple manner of enforcing this constraint is to construct a new combined vector $\mathbf{x} = [\mathbf{x}^A \ \mathbf{x}^B]$ and to perform a joint analysis over the combined profile space of system A and B. This means we effectively generate a data matrix

$$\mathbf{X} = \begin{bmatrix} \mathbf{X}_c^A \ \mathbf{X}_s^A \ ? \\ \mathbf{X}_c^B \ ? \ \mathbf{X}_s^B \end{bmatrix}, \tag{3}$$

where '?' denotes matrices of appropriate size with unobserved values. Note that the other submatrices of $\mathbf{X}$ may also contain (many) missing entries. Also note that a column of this matrix $\mathbf{X}$ effectively contains a unified user profile of the user across two systems, adding more systems can be done in a similar fashion. It is interesting to make a further simplification by restricting the data matrix to users that are known to both systems

$$\mathbf{X}_c = \begin{bmatrix} \mathbf{X}_c^A \ \mathbf{X}_c^B \end{bmatrix}, \tag{4}$$

and to ignore the data concerning users only known to one system. Obviously, this will accelerate the model fitting compared to working with the full matrix $\mathbf{X}$.

Related Work. Recently, a few techniques have been suggested for the purposes for Cross System Personalization which deal with the vector valued learning problem that CSP entails. The earliest technique for CSP is Manifold Alignment [7], which performs satisfactorily in the test scenarios evaluated, but does not deal well with incomplete data.Manifold alignment uses non linear dimensionality reduction techniques like Locally Linear Embedding(LLE) and Laplacian Eigenmaps, which have previously not been applied to Collaborative filtering, and do not scale very well. The next technique to emerge is using Sparse Factor Analysis(SFA)[3,8], which performs very well even on large datasets. SFA was originally proposed by [3] in the context of privacy preserving collaborative filtering. The advantage of PLSA over the above methods is better performance for the collaborative filtering domain, and ease of updation in case new items are added. While SFA is a fast method for collaborative filtering, it does not offer any easy mechanism to add new items without a complete re-computation of the model.

3   Distributed PLSA for Cross System Personalization

Introduction to PLSA: PLSA is a probabilistic variant of Latent Semantic Analysis(LSA), which is an approach to identify hidden semantic associations from co-occurrence data. The core of PLSA is a latent variable model(also known as the aspect model) for general co-occurrence data which associates a hidden variable $\mathbf{z} \in Z = \{z_1, z_2, ..., z_K\}$ with each observation. In the context of collaborative filtering, each observation corresponds to a vote by a user to a item. The space of observations is normally represented as an $M \times N$ co-occurrence matrix (in our case, of M items $\mathcal{Y} = \{y_1, y_2, .., y_M\}$ and N users $\mathcal{X} = \{x_1, x_2, .., x_N\}$. The aspect model can be described as a generative model:

- select a data item y from $\mathcal{Y}$ with probability $P(y)$,
- pick a latent factor **z** with probability $P(z|y)$,
- generate a data item x from $\mathcal{X}$ with probability $P(x|z)$.

Since in collaborative filtering we are usually interested in predicting the vote for an item for a given user, we are interested in the following conditional model:

$$P(y|x, z) = \sum_z P(y|z)P(z|x) \tag{5}$$

The process of building a model that *explain* a set of observations $(\mathcal{X}, \mathcal{Y})$ is reduced to the problem of finding values for $P(z), P(y|z), P(x|z)$ that can maximize the (log)likelihood $L(\mathcal{X}, \mathcal{Y})$ of the observations. The model parameters $P(z|u)$ and $P(y|z)$ are learnt using the *Expectation Maximization* [4] algorithm which is a standard procedure for latent variable methods. The EM equations for Gaussian PLSA have been derived in [6] and are as follows:

E-Step:
$$p(z|u, y, v) = \frac{p(z|u)p(v|z, y)}{\sum_{z'} p(z|u)p(v|z, y)} \tag{6}$$

M-Step 1:
$$p(z|u) = \frac{\sum_{(u',y,v):u=u'} p(z|u, y, v)}{\sum_{(u',y,v):u=u'} 1} . \tag{7}$$

M-Step 2:
$$\mu_{z,y} = \frac{\sum_{(u,y',v):y'=y} p(z|u, y, v)\, v}{\sum_{(u,y',v):y'=y} p(z|u, y, v)} \tag{8}$$

$$\sigma_{z,y}^2 = \frac{\sum_{(u,y',v):y'=y} p(z|u, y, v)\, (v - \mu_{y,z})^2}{\sum_{(u,y',v):y'=y} p(z|u, y, v)} \tag{9}$$

3.1   Privacy Preserving Distributed PLSA

We assume that each user accesses the recommendation system via a client which can communicate with other clients. We assume a completely distributed setting where each client can interact with every other client like in a peer to peer environment. The main goal behind distributed PLSA is that private user data is not shared with other users or with a central server. However the PLSA model is known to everyone, and can be used to by a user's client to compute recommendations for the user. Therefore, a new user only needs to know the probability distribution over the user communities z, i.e. $(p(z|u)$ and the values of PLSA parameters μ and σ. The probability distribution can be computed by Eq. (8), given the model parameters.

Initially, given the first n users, the initial model has to be constructed. For Gaussian PLSA, this requires the repeated iteration of the EM equations. To maintain our goals of privacy, the EM equations have to be computed in a distributed fashion, with contributions from each user made available in the encrypted format.

Our communication protocol between the clients has two phases: in the first phase, the model parameters are computed by iterating the EM equations; the second phase is the normal recommendation phase where a trained model is available and is available to everyone for computing their own recommendations. Similar protocols based on shared Elgamal encryption[5] have also been used in [2].

Phase 1: Training the dPLSA Model

In the first version of the protocol, we assume all users to be honest. We assume that the set of items $\mathbf{y}$ and the set of users $\mathbf{u}$ remains fixed during the entire protocol, and have a size of M items and N users. Note that we refer to the combined user profile in this protocol ($\mathbf{x} = [\mathbf{x}^A \ \mathbf{x}^B]$, with a combined dimensionality of M), and build a model for the matrix $\mathbf{X}$. The protocol proceeds in the following fashion:

1. At first, the number of communities is fixed, and this parameter K is communicated to every client.
2. The first set of model parameters are initiated as $\mu_{z,y} = \{\mathbf{0}\}^{K \times M}$ and $\sigma_{z,y} = \{\mathbf{1}\}^{K \times M}$. Further, each client initiates the probability distribution of belonging to a user community to a random distribution.

$$\mathbf{P}_{z|u} = [p(z|u)]^{K \times N} \ , \quad \text{such that} \sum_z p(z|u = i) = 1 , \ \forall i$$

3. Each client receives the unencrypted values of μ and σ.
4. Each client computes the prior probabilities using given values for μ and σ

$$p(v|z,y) = e^{-\frac{(\mu_{z,y} - v_{u,y})^2}{2\sigma_{z,y}}}/\sigma_{z,y} \tag{10}$$

5. Using $p(z|u)$ and $p(v|z,y)$ calculated in the previous step, each client computes the posterior probabilities of each of its votes:

$$p(z|u = i, y, v) = \frac{p(z|u = i)p(v|z,y)}{\sum_{z'} p(z|u = i)p(v|z,y)} \tag{11}$$

6. Each user also updates their probability distribution over the user communities.

$$p(z|u = i) = \frac{\sum_{(u,y,v):u=i} p(z|u = i, y, v)}{\sum_{(u',y,v):u=i} 1} . \tag{12}$$

7. Each client computes two matrices of fixed point numbers

$$\mathbf{F}_i^{k \times m}, \text{ where } \mathbf{F}_i(z,y) = \sum_{(u=i,y',v):y'=y} p(z|u = i, y, v)\,v \tag{13}$$

$$\mathbf{G}_i^{k \times m}, \text{ where } \mathbf{G}_i(z,y) = \sum_{(u=i,y',v):y'=y} p(z|u = i, y, v) \tag{14}$$

Notice that the overall mean $\mu_{z,y}$ (see Eq. (9))can be written as

$$\mu^{k \times m}, \text{ s.t. } \mu_{z,y} = \frac{\mathbf{F}_1(z,y) + \mathbf{F}_2(z,y) + ... + \mathbf{F}_n(z,y)}{\mathbf{G}_1(z,y) + \mathbf{G}_2(z,y) + ... + \mathbf{G}_n(z,y)} \tag{15}$$

where $\mathbf{F}_i$ and $\mathbf{G}_i$ are contributions from user i.

8. Vector addition can be be done in an encrypted format using the scheme discussed in [3] where an El-Gamal public key[5] is known to everyone, and the private key is shared by some d users. The key generation protocol of Pederson[10] does exactly this: it enables each user to have a share s_i of the private key s, which can be reconstructed from given sufficient number of shares. The advantage of the El-Gamal encryption process is that multiplicative homomorphism is preserved.

$$E(M_1 + M_2) = E(M_1)E(M_2)$$

Thus an addition of two numbers can be performed even if only their encrypted values are available. Using this property, addition of vectors and matrices can be simulated by doing piecewise encryption of each matrix value. Each client therefore uses the public key to encrypt each value of their matrix F, and create a vector of the encrypted values $\Gamma_i^{1 \times km}$, such that $\Gamma_i(l) = Enc(\mathbf{F}_1(div(l, m), mod(l, m) + 1))$ (concatenating rows to make one large row). Here $Enc()$ is an encryption function. Similarly, another vector $\mathbf{\Omega}_i^{1 \times km}$ is created from the encryption of the matrix G.

9. Each client sends its encrypted values Γ and Ω to all the *tallier* nodes. Tallier nodes are a subset of the user population which are trusted to perform the vector additions. On receiving the contributions of each user, the talliers compute the addition of the $\mathbf{F}$ and $\mathbf{G}$ matrices.

10. Since homomorphic properties for division do not exist, one needs to decrypt the totals $\sum_i Enc(\mathbf{F}_i)$, and $\sum_i Enc(\mathbf{G}_i)$. To decrypt, the encrypted sums are broadcast to every client which then decrypt these totals using their portions of the keys. The decrypted values are then sent back to the talliers, who them perform an element-wise division of $\sum_i \mathbf{F}_i$ and $\sum_i \mathbf{G}_i$ to compute $\mu_{z,y}$

$$\mu_{z,y} = \frac{\sum_i \mathbf{F}_i(z, y)}{\sum_i \mathbf{G}_i(z, y)} \tag{16}$$

11. The newly computed $\mu_{z,y}$ is broadcast to all clients, which is then used to calculate a new matrix $\mathbf{S}$

$$\mathbf{S}_i^{k \times m}, \text{ where } \mathbf{S}_i(z, y) = \sum_{(u=i, y', v): y' = y} p(z|u = i, y, v)(v - \mu_{y,z})^2 \tag{17}$$

This matrix is encrypted and converted to a vector $\mathbf{\Lambda}$ which is send to the talliers. There, an encrypted sum is calculated, which is then sent back to clients for encryption (see the two previous steps). Finally, a new value of sigma is computed using the following element-wise division.

$$\sigma_{z,y} = \frac{\sum_i \mathbf{S}_i(z, y)}{\sum_i \mathbf{G}_i(z, y)} \tag{18}$$

12. Repeat from step 3, till the values of μ and σ converge. 30-100 iterations maybe required. To simulate hold out data, talliers may decide to hold back their own data, and compute their predicted values from the model. By judging the performance of the model in these values, a tallier can make a recommendation to perform another iteration, so to stop. If the majority of the talliers recommend stopping the EM updates, the training phase is over, otherwise the protocol is repeated step 3 onwards.

Phase 2: Recommendation Mode

For a new user, the precomputed model is enough to compute recommendations.

1. Each client initiates the probability distribution of belonging to a user community to a random distribution. (See Step 2 of Training phase)
2. Repeat steps 3-6 twice.
3. Compute predicted votes using the equations: $p(v|u,y) = \sum_z p(z|u)p(v|z,y)$. Note that the original profile will renumber the item order due to concatenation of profiles form multiple systems.

3.2   Update and Synchronize

When a new item is added to one of the systems (say A), the profile representing the user on that system changes. After the profiles for this system has been updated for all users, the model over A and B also has to be updated. We do this by adding one more dimension to $\mu_{z,y}$ and $\sigma_{z,y}$ each, and initializing it to zero. After that, 2-3 iterations from step 3 onwards of the training phase can be run to update the values of σ and μ.

To add update the model using data from new users, a similar procedure has to be followed. Not that in this case, the size of matrices σ and μ, remains the same. Therefore, the model simply has to be training in a manner similar to using held out data. To do it in our distributed setting, a new client should simply broadcast its availability, and participate from step 2 onwards. This protocol adjustment however opens the door for malicious users to insert arbitrary data to manipulate the system, which has to be dealt with in the algorithm itself. Robust collaborative filtering extensions are required to take this into account.

4   Data and Evaluation

We choose the EachMovie data with ratings from 72,916 users for 1,682 movies. Ratings are given on a numeric six point scale (0.0, 0.2, 0.4, 0.6, 0.8, 1.0). The entire dataset consists of around 2.8 million votes, however around 1.8 million of these votes are by the first 21835 users. We chose this dense subset of 21835 users and 1682 movies and we scale these ratings on a scale of 5, which is also the scale in other datasets like *MovieLens* and lately *Netflix*.

To simulate two systems A and B, we divide this data set into two parts by splitting the item set of the entire data. In our experiments, we have used 15,000 users for both A and B, with 8,000 users being common between the two systems. We allow a random 5% of items to overlap between the datasets. The overlap is not explicitly maintained. In our test runs, we build a PLSA model using the matrix $\mathbf{X}$ (see eq. (2)) varying c from 1000 users to 8000 users. For the users not in correspondance, we randomly rearrange their order. We refer to this case as the *full* data case. In our setting, it is vital that we can build an effective predictive model with as few users crossing over from one system to another which works effectively for a large number of new users. We use 5000 users as test (randomly from the 7000 users not common to the systems). In addition, we also performed the model building step using only the users common to both systems using $\mathbf{X}_c$. We refer to this case as the *common* data case.

4.1 Metrics Used

1. Mean Average Error $= \frac{1}{m} \sum |p_v - a_v|$, where p_v is the predicted vote and a_v is the actual vote.
2. Ranking score of top-20 items. $R_{score} = \frac{100*\sum R}{\sum R_{max}}$. This metric gives a values between 0 and 100. Higher values indicate a ranking with top items as the most highly rated ones.(see [1] for details)

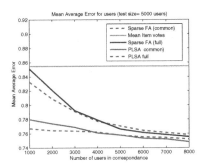 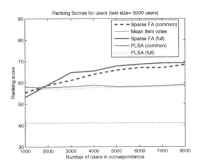

Fig. 1. MAE and Ranking scores for 5000 test users (with 5 fold validation). "*'common'*' refers to the use of only common users (eq. 3) for training the model.

Our evaluation is aimed at testing the following hypotheses:

1. CSP using *PLSA* offers an advantage over mean item voting for a large number of first time users,
2. CSP using *PLSA* offers an advantage over existing methods like SparseFA.

4.2 Results

The experimental bench described above sets the scene: PLSA models and SparseFA models are trained over identical datasets, and MAE and Ranking Scores are measured. Results are then averaged over 5 runs and plotted in Figure 1. For the SparseFA model training, we use an improved implementation (w.r.t [8]) which is optimized w.r.t. model parameters and reports better results than previously. SparseFA remains a fast and effective model; however, we expect PLSA to outperform SparseFA.

Figiure 1 provides experimental proof: PLSA has a distinct advantage with smaller training data and provides highly accurate recommendations for 5000 test users *even* when only 1000 users have crossed over. While SparseFA also outperforms the baseline *most popular* method, it catches up with PLSA only after more than 7000 users have crossed over: even then PLSA maintains a slight lead. The results in the ranking score experiment show an advantage for Sparse FA over PLSA: this means that while PLSA is an overall more accurate method, Sparse FA is able to pick the top 20 relevant items and rank them better than PLSA. A lower *Mean Average Error* for PLSA shows that the complete profile predicted by PLSA is closer to the original profile than the one predicted by

SparseFA. One more important observation is that the models trained with only common data(supervised) outperform the models trained with full data (semi-supervised). However, this trend is observable only when a small number of users are common to both systems. Once around 4000 users have crossed over, the semi supervised methods have a small lead. In a practical situation, we might use only the common users, since the overhead of training this model is much smaller than the full data.

5 Conclusion

This paper outlines a novel approach to leverage user data distributed across various electronic systems to provide a better personalization experience. One major benefit of this approach is dealing with the new user problem: a new user of a collaborative filtering system can usually be provided only the non-personalized recommendation based on popular items. Our approach allows systems to make better recommendations using the user's profile in other systems. The contribution of this paper is in describing and comparing methods which offers a satisfactory improvement over status quo for a potentially important application scenario. In addition, the highly popular PLSA method has been extended to add privacy and distributively. Future work includes using recent advances in the Expectation Maximization technique to reduce the number of iterations required and consequently simplify the protocol described in this paper.

Acknowlegements. The author would like to thank Thomas Hofmann and Peter Fankhauser for various discussions fundamental to this work.

References

1. Breese, J.S., Heckerman, D., Kadie, C.M.: Empirical analysis of predictive algorithms for collaborative filtering. In: UAI, pp. 43–52 (1998)
2. Canny, J.F.: Collaborative filtering with privacy. In: IEEE Symposium on Security and Privacy, pp. 45–57 (2002)
3. Canny, J.F.: Collaborative filtering with privacy via factor analysis. In: SIGIR, pp. 238–245 (2002)
4. Dempster, A., Laird, N., Rubin, D.: Maximum likelihood from incomplete data via the em algorithm. Journal of the Royal Statistical Society 39(1), 1–38 (1977)
5. Elgamal, T.: A public key cryptosystem and a signature scheme based on discrete logarithms. Information Theory, IEEE Transactions on 31(4), 469–472 (1985)
6. Hofmann, T.: Collaborative filtering via gaussian probabilistic latent semantic analysis. In: SIGIR, pp. 259–266 (2003)
7. Mehta, B., Hofmann, T.: Cross system personalization by learning manifold alignment. In: KI (2006)
8. Mehta, B., Hofmann, T., Fankhauser, P.: Cross system personalization by sparse factor analysis. ITWP Workshop at AAAI (2006)
9. Mehta, B., Niederée, C., Stewart, A., Degemmis, M., Lops, P., Semeraro, G.: Ontologically-enriched unified user modeling for cross-system personalization. In: User Modeling (2005)
10. Pedersen, T.: A threshold cryptosystem without a trusted party, Advances in Cryptology. In: Davies, D.W. (ed.) EUROCRYPT 1991. LNCS, vol. 547, pp. 522–526. Springer, Heidelberg (1991)

Construction of Ontology-Based User Model for Web Personalization

Hui Zhang[1], Yu Song[2], and Han-tao Song[1]

[1] Department of Computer Science and Engineering
Beijing Institute of Technology 100081, Beijing, China
jackyzhang@bit.edu.cn
[2] Asia Technology Development Center
100027, Beijing, China
sporty_gir615@hotmail.com

Abstract. Personalized Web browsing and search hope to provide Web information that matches a user's personal interests. A key feature in developing successful personalized Web applications is to build user model that accurately represents a user's interests. This paper deals with the problem of modeling Web users by means of personal ontology. A Web log preparation system discovering user's semantic navigation sessions is presented first. Such semantic sessions could be used as the input of constructing ontology-based user model. Our construction of user model is based on a semantic representation of the user activity. We build the user model without user interaction, automatically monitoring the user's browsing habits, constructing the user ontology from semantic sessions. Each semantic session updates the user model in such a way that the conceptual behavior history of the user is recorded in user ontology. After building the initial model from visited Web pages, techniques are investigated to estimate model convergence. In particular, the overall performance of our ontology-based user model is also presented and favorably compared to other model using a flat, unstructured list of topics in the experimental systems.

1 Introduction

With the explosive growth of information available on the World Wide Web, it has become more difficult to access relevant information from the Web. One possible approach to solve this problem is Web personalization [1].These systems often require some form of representation for user interest model in order to provide a backbone for information recommending and reasoning. An accurate representation of a users interests, generally stored in some form of user model, is crucial to the performance of personalized search or browsing agents. User model is often represented by keyword/concept vectors or concept hierarchy. The acquired model can then be used for analyzing and predicting the future user access behavior. User model may be built explicitly, by asking users questions, or implicitly, by observing their activity.

C. Conati, K. McCoy, and G. Paliouras (Eds.): UM 2007, LNAI 4511, pp. 67–76, 2007.
© Springer-Verlag Berlin Heidelberg 2007

An ontology is defined by [2] as "an explicit specification of a conceptualization". A conceptualization consists of a set of entities (such as objects and concepts) that may be used to express knowledge and relationships. Ontology provides a common framework that allows data to be shared and reused across application, enterprise and community boundaries [3]. User access behavior models can be represented as ontology.

Ontology-based user modeling is the use of ontology to structure user models. We examine the roles that ontology plays in user modeling as well as the requirements that user modeling imposes on ontology. Some of these roles are identical to the broader uses of ontology, such as supporting reasoning across granularities, providing a common understanding of the domain to facilitate reuse, and harmonization of different terminologies. There are also some requirements specific to user modeling such as scrutability and the ability to support a reasoning layer specific to user evidence.

The user models are constructed using a variety of learning techniques including the vector space model [4], genetic algorithms [5], or clustering [6]. Many systems require user feedback for this, e.g., Persona [7]. Others, such as OBIWAN [8] adapt autonomously. Lexical and syntactic (i.e., structural) information are not taken into account for building user models in these cases, thus, they are not capable of capturing the semantics underlying each concept as well as semantic relationships among concepts. However, there are more proposals in the context of conceptual user model construction recently [9][10][11][12][13]. Concept rating or filtering algorithms are often employed to improve the user models.

In this paper, we propose an approach for constructing ontology-based user model. Firstly we present the architecture of SWULPM (Semantic Web Usage Log Preparation Model), which is capable of both creating and managing ontology as well as of exploiting it for discovering users semantic navigation sessions. Web usage mining [14], which aims to discover interesting and frequent user access patterns from Web usage data in the SWULPM, can get semantic access behavior of users as the input of ontology-based user modeling. Secondly we show capability of the ontology-based user models representation, which involves user-behavior dependent relationships among concepts and, importantly, deals with structural and semantic heterogeneity of Web sources. A conceptual model, called concept-graph (c-graph, for short), is defined for the representation. Finally the construction of the user model is done by taking into account users semantic navigation sessions, encoding such a new knowledge into the ontology, and updating the user ontology. During the navigation of a personalized Web site, user model could provide a set of recommendations based on user interests.

This section discusses our chosen problem domain and our general approach to construction of ontology-based user model, along with related work. The rest of this paper is organized as follows. In Section 2, an overview of the research efforts on SWULPM architecture is given. Section 3 describes the representation of user model based on the concept-graph. Section 4 illustrates technical details of ontology-based user model constructing. We put forward an experiment to show how ontology can improve user modeling and hence recommendation accuracy in Section 5.Future enhancements of the system and conclusions are presented in Section 6.

2   SWULPM Architecture

In this section we present the architecture of SWULPM (Semantic Web Usage Log Preparation Model), a Web log preparation system that integrates site semantics and ontology with usage data. The Web usage Logs are inputted to the semantic Web usage log preparation process, resulting in a semantical set of user sessions that include thematic categories, except for pages with URLs. Such semantic sessions, which combine both the semantic of visited sites and the way the user navigates them, could be used as the input of constructing ontology-based user model. The block diagram representing SWULPM's architecture appears in Fig.1.

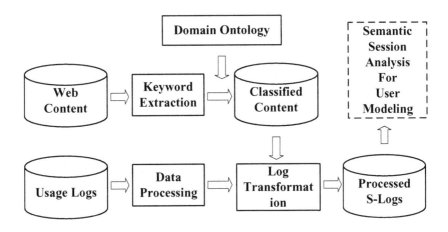

Fig. 1. Architecture of SWULPM

One of the systems innovative features is that the Web documents are classified based on the domain ontology; therefore the recommended categories are further expanded to contain the documents that fall under them. The ontology is either a domain-independent ontology or the result of the integration of existing ontology; the category is presented by entity classes (Concepts). A fuzzy related classification approach for Web document based on ontology concept semantic measurement is presented in our project [15]. Based on the semantic similarity and the fuzzy characteristics of the Web document, the fuzzy related technology combined with VSM in classifying Web documents into a predefined set of ontology categories is adopted.

Another innovative feature of this system is the creation of S-log (Semantic-log) from the original Web logs and their use for extraction of usage patterns.

S-Log is an extended form of the Web server log. Each record of the Web server logs is enhanced with relevant keywords and concept (from the ontology) representing the semantics of the respective URL. All possible categorical and ordered paths for the requested URL, above all, are obtained, after conceptualizing this URL by domain ontology.

Additionally, session analysis algorithms are then applied to this enriched version of Web logs. In order to detect the candidate sets of session identifiers, semantic factors like semantic mean, deviation, and distance matrix are established. Eventually, each semantic session is obtained based on nested repetition of top-down partitioning and evaluation process. The outcome of this phase is a set of semantic sessions that include thematic categories, except for Web pages or URLs. The way these sessions enhance the user model of the Web personalization process is depicted in the following sections.

3 Ontology-Based User Model Representation

In this section we describe the representation of ontology-based user model. This is based on the capability of the ontology model (a graph of concepts called c-graph with labeled arcs). The c-graph is used for representing the user model. The concept-graph is defined for a given user and a given set of concepts with different names. It contains an explicit representation of membership of instances to such concepts, as well as the semantic relationships among them. Labels encode knowledge about both structure and semantics of visited sites and past user behavior. Moreover, information about accesses of the user is included.

A concept is a pair $< c, name(c) >$ where c is a set of instances and $name(c)$ is a string (with prefixed maximum length). We define now the *concept-graph* (*c-graph*, for short). Given a subset of concepts N such that no two concepts with same name occur in it and an instance may belong only to one concept, and a user u, a *c-graph* is a rooted labeled direct graph $C\_Graph(N, u) = < N, A >$, where N is the set of nodes and $A \subseteq N \times N$ is the set of arcs. Informally, N represents the set of concepts of interest for the user u. Arcs encode semantic relationships among concepts. Their labels define a number of properties associated to relationships of $C\_Graph(N, u)$ containing also the dependency of the model on the user u.

More precisely, an *arc (s, t)* is provided with $label(s,t) = < d_{st}, r_{st}, h_{st}, \tau_{st} >$, where both d_{st} and r_{st} are real numbers ranging from 0 to 1, h_{st} is a non negative integer, and τ_{st} is a non negative real number. The four label coefficients above encode different properties, and their definition, which we next provide, clarifies why our graph is directed. In particular:

- d_{st} is the semantic independence coefficient. It is inversely related to the contribution given by the concept t in characterizing the concept s.

- r_{st} is the semantic relevance coefficient, indicating the fraction of instances of the concept s whose complete definition requires at least one instance of the concept t.

- h_{st} is the hit coefficient, counting the number of hits which u carries out on t (i.e., on some instance of t) coming from s (i.e., coming from some instance of s).

- τ_{st} is time coefficient, defined as $\sum_{i=1}^{h_{st}} \frac{t_i}{q_i}$, where t_i is the effective total time spent by u at the i-th hit for consulting the concept t coming from s and q_i is the size of the relative accessed page.

The construction and management of the user ontology is a task of our agent and will be explained in detail in Section 4.

4 Ontology-Based User Model Representation

4.1 Session C-Graph Updating

Each new semantic session updates the user model in such a way that the conceptual behavior history of the user is recorded in user ontology. For updating the user ontology, the user dynamically builds a c-graph $B(IS)$ during the visit and, at the end, incorporates the knowledge encoded in $B(IS)$ into the user global ontology O by integrating the session c-graph and global c-graph. Suppose now the user's new session is represented by IS, and the c-graph $S(IS)$, representing the structure of the site, is automatically built.

At the beginning of the visit, $B(IS)$ is empty. During the visit $B(IS)$ changes, both concepts accessed by u and their neighborhoods in $S(IS)$, are recorded in $B(IS)$ by inserting new nodes and new arcs. Moreover, hit and time coefficients are recomputed at each step according to their definition. Independence and relevance coefficients are taken from corresponding arcs in $S(IS)$. At the end of the visit, $B(IS)$ is a representation of the portion of IS, visited by u in this session, containing also information about the user behavior, with hit and time coefficients.

By considering also neighborhoods (in $S(IS)$) of visited concepts, the agent autonomously discovers potentially interesting concepts for the user and includes them in $B(IS)$. More formally, given a concept s, we denote by $nbh(s)$ its k-neighborhood.

In obvious way, we define as $arcs(nbh(s))$ the set of arcs induced by the k-neighborhood of a concept s. Thus, for each access a to an instance t of a concept s:

- if a is the first access of the visit, then the node s is inserted into $B(IS)$ with only the instance t belonging to it. h_{st} and τ_{st} are updated (in this case h_{st} is set to 1).

- if s is accessed for the first time, a is not the first access, and, thus, the user comes from an instance of another concept, say s', then the node s is inserted into $B(IS)$ with only the instance t belonging to it, and an arc (s', s) is also added. h_{st} and $h_{s's}$ are set to 1, τ_{st} and $\tau_{s's}$ are set to the same measured value. Independence and relevance coefficients of the arc (s', s) are set to the corresponding values occurring in $S(IS)$.

- if a is an access coming from a concept s' but s was already accessed, then the arc (s', s) is added in $B(IS)$ if not already present. h_{st} and $h_{s's}$ are increased of 1; τ_{st} and $\tau_{s's}$ are equally updated.

- if a is an access and it is not the first one, then h_{st} is increased and τ_{st} is updated.

- for every kind of access a, nodes of $nbh(s)$ and arcs of $arcs(nbh(s))$ are inserted into $B(IS)$, if not already occurring in it. Independence and relevance coefficients of inserted arcs are taken from the corresponding arcs of $S(IS)$. Hit and time coefficients are set to 0. At this point, before handling the choice of a new information source, the knowledge encoded in $B(IS)$ has to be incorporated into the ontology O, updating it.

4.2 Session C-Graph Updating

In this section we describe how session c-graphs can be incorporated to the global c-graph. This problem could be solved by the integration of two c-graphs. Informally, this merge consists of a "union" of the two c-graphs executed after that synonymies and homonymies are eliminated: by computing the similarity coefficients between all possible pairs of nodes (a node belonging to the first c-graph, the other belonging to the second c-graph), synonyms and homonyms are first detected, and then, synonymy nodes are renamed giving the same name and homonym nodes are renamed in such a way that they assume distinct names. The union of the two "normalized" c-graphs is done by suitably averaging labels of arcs.

Let $B_1 =< N_1, A_1 >$ and $B_2 =< N_2, A_2 >$ be two c-graphs. The union of B_1 and B_2, denoted by $U(B_1, B_2)$, is a directed labeled graph with set of nodes:

$$N =\{s|s \in N_1 \wedge \neg(\exists t)(t \in N_2 \wedge name(s) = name(t))\}\cap$$
$$\{t|t \in N_2 \wedge \neg(\exists s)(s \in N_1 \wedge name(s) = name(t))\}\cap \qquad (1)$$
$$\{x|x = s \cup t, s \in N_1 \wedge t \in N_2 \wedge name(s) = name(t) = name(x)\}$$

And set of arcs

$$A =\{(s,t)|(s_1,t_1) \in A_1 \wedge name(s) = name(s_1) \wedge name(t) = name(t_1)\}\cap$$
$$\{(s,t)|(s_1,t_1) \in A_2 \wedge name(s) = name(s_1) \wedge name(t) = name(t_1)\} \qquad (2)$$

Nodes are obtained by copying nodes of each c-graph with name not appearing in the other c-graph, and by merging nodes with common name into a node with equal name including all the instances of the original nodes. Arcs are obtained in obvious way. Now we define how labels are determined. Let (s, t) be an arc belonging to A. Its label is the 4-tuple $label(s,t) =< d_{st}, r_{st}, h_{st}, \tau_{st} >$ defined as follows:

(a) $d_{st} = d_{s1t1}, r_{st} = r_{s1t1}, h_{st} = h_{s1t1}, \tau_{st} = \tau_{s1t1}$

$$if \exists (s_1,t_1)((s_1,t_1) \in A_i \wedge name(s) = name(s_1) \wedge name(t) = name(t_1)\wedge$$
$$\neg(\exists s_2)(s_2 \in N_j \wedge name(s) = name(s_2)) \qquad (3)$$

(b) $d_{st} = d_{s1t1}, r_{st} = f(r_{s1t1}, |s_2|), h_{st} = h_{s1t1}, \tau_{st} = \tau_{s1t1}$

$$if \exists (s_1, t_1)((s_1, t_1) \in A_i \wedge name(s) = name(s_1) \wedge name(t) = name(t_1) \wedge$$
$$\exists s_2(s_2 \in N_j \wedge name(s) = name(s_2)) \wedge \qquad (4)$$
$$\neg(\exists (s_2, t_2))((s_2, t_2) \in A_j) \wedge (name(t_1) = name(t_2)))$$

(c)$d_{st} = \frac{|s_1| \times d_{s1t1} + |s_2| \times d_{s2t2}}{|s_1| + |s_2|}, r_{st} = f(r_{s1t1}, |s_2|), h_{st} = h_{s1t1} + h_{s2t2}, \tau_{st} = \tau_{s1t1} + \tau_{s2t2}$

$$if \exists (s_1, t_1)((s_1, t_1) \in A_i \wedge name(s) = name(s_1) \wedge name(t) = name(t_1) \wedge$$
$$\exists s_2(s_2 \in N_j \wedge name(s) = name(s_2)) \wedge \qquad (5)$$
$$\exists (s_2, t_2)((s_2, t_2) \in A_j) \wedge (name(t_1) = name(t_2)))$$

where $i = 1, 2, j = 1, 2, i \neq j$, and by f($r_{s1t1}, |s_2|$) we denote the function for recomputing the relevance coefficient of the *arc (s1, t1)* when the cardinality of the node s1 is increased by $|s_2|$ (recall that the relevance coefficient depends on the number of instances of the source node). With a little abuse, we assume that $U(B_1, B_2)$ is a c-graph. Note that this is not necessarily true since $U(B_1, B_2)$ might not to be rooted. However, in this case, a dummy root can be added to make $U(B_1, B_2)$ a c-graph. After the integration of O, $B(IS)$ is not useful anymore, since the memory of such a visit of IS is kept into the ontology. Now, O must be pruned, in order to eliminate all concepts and instances with low interest for the user u. O now can be exploited for supporting next user visits.

4.3   Model Convergence

Every time a new Web page is classified, it either adds a new concept to the user profile or it gets assigned to an existing concept whose weight and number of documents are increased. Our expectation is that although the number of concepts in the user model will monotonically increase, eventually the highest weighted concepts should become relatively stable, reflecting the users major interests. In order to determine how much of the users browsing history we need to obtain a relatively stable profile, we evaluated the metrics based on time and number of visited URLs. In both cases, we measured the total number of non-zero concepts and the similarity between top 50% of the concepts over time to see if we could determine when (and if) profiles become stable.

5   Experiment and Results

We built an experimental personalized Web system to compare subjects whose user interest was computed using ontological user model with subjects whose models did not. The overall performance of ontological user model were presented and favorably compared to others.

Experiments data sets had 24 topics collected from China National Library (CNL, www.nlc.gov.cn). The experimental trial had been conducted for 50 days.

Topics were divided into two groups, one using an ontological approach to construct user model and the other using a flat, unstructured list of topics. Both groups had their own separate training set of examples. The system interface and the classifier used by both groups algorithm were identical.

The system recorded each time the user declared an interest in a topic by selecting it "interesting" or "not interesting", jumped to a recommended paper or corrected the topic of a recommended paper. These feedback events were date stamped and recorded in a log file for later analysis, along with a log of all recommendations made. Good topics were defined as either "no comment" or "interesting" topics. The cumulative frequency figures for good topics are presented in figure 2 as a ratio of the total number of topics recommended.

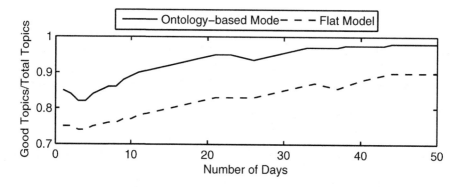

Fig. 2. Ratio of good topics/total topics

From the experimental data of the trial, several suggestive trends are apparent. The ontological group has a 10% higher topic acceptance. The initial ratios of good topics are lower than the final ratios, reflecting the time it takes for enough log information to be accumulated to let the models settle down.

Recommendation accuracy is the ratio of good jumps to recommendations, and is an indication of the quality of the recommendations being made as well as the accuracy of the user model. The jump is where the user jumps to a recommended paper by opening it via the Web browser. Jumps are correlated with topic interest feedback. Figure 3 shows the recommendation accuracy results.

The experiment shows between 12-16% of recommendations leading to good jumps. Since 100 recommendations are given to the users at a time, on average 12-16 good jumps are made from each set of recommendations received. As with the topic feedback, the ontology group again is marginally superior but only by a 5% margin when the model gets convergent; this trend is promising but not statistically significant. This smaller difference is probably due to people having time to follow only one or two recommendations. Thus, although the ontology group had more good topics, only the top topic of the three recommended was really be looked at; the result was a smaller difference between the good jumps made and the good topics seen.

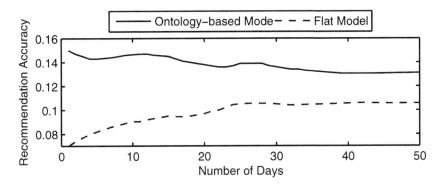

Fig. 3. Recommendation accuracy

A hypothesis for the ontology group's apparently superior performance was that the hierarchy produced a rounder, more complete ontology by including general super class topics when a specific topic was browsed by a user. This in turn helped the model to acquire a broader range of interests, rather than just latching onto one correct topic, therefore the initial recommendation accuracy ratios might be higher than the final ratios for the range of interest.

6 Conclusions

The main goal of this research is to investigate techniques that implicitly build ontology-based user models. Many ways in which ontology can be useful for user modeling have been discussed in this paper. Our approach is based on a semantic representation of the user activity, which takes into account both the structure of visited sites and the way the user navigates them. We build the user model without user interaction; automatically monitoring the user's browsing habits. After building the initial model from visited Web pages, we focus on how quickly we can achieve model stability. Since user model tends to have the problem of structural and semantic heterogeneity in cross-system personalization, we will be absorbed in providing the model with the capability of representing structural properties of information sources with different formats and dealing with inter-source heterogeneity in the future work.

References

1. Eirinaki, M., Vazirgiannis, M.: Web Mining for Web Personalization. ACM Transactions on Internet Technology 3(1), 1–27 (2003)
2. Gruber, T.: Toward Principles for the Design of Ontologies Used for Knowledge Sharing. Formal Ontology in Conceptual Analysis and Knowledge Representation (1993)
3. Maedche, A., Staab, S.: Ontology Learning for the Semantic Web. IEEE Intelligent Systems 16(2), 72–79 (2001)

4. Pretschner, A.: Ontology based personalized search.Master's thesis. The University of Kansas, Lawrence, KS (1999)
5. Mitchell, M.: An Introduction to Genetic Algorithms. In: A Bradford Book, MIT Press, Cambridge, MA (1996) ISBN 0-262-63185-7
6. Mladenic, D.: Text-learning and related intelligent agents.Revised versio. In: IEEE Expert special issue on Applications of Intelligent Information Retrieval (1999)
7. Tanudjaja, F., Persona, M.L.: A contextualized and personalized Web search. In: Proceedings of the 35th Annual Hawaii International Conference on System Sciences (HICSS'02), Big Island, Hawaii, vol. 3(53) (2002)
8. Gauch, S., Chaffee, J., Pretschner, A.: Ontology Based Personalized Search.Web Intelligence and Agent Systems (2003)
9. Yudelson, M., Gavrilova, T., Brusilovsky, P.: Towards User Modeling Meta-ontology. In: Ardissono, L., Brna, P., Mitrović, A. (eds.) UM 2005. LNCS (LNAI), vol. 3538, pp. 448–452. Springer, Heidelberg (2005)
10. Denaux, R., Dimitrova, V., Aroyo, L.: Integrating Open User Modeling and Learning Content Management for the Semantic Web. In: Ardissono, L., Brna, P., Mitrović, A. (eds.) UM 2005. LNCS (LNAI), vol. 3538, pp. 9–18. Springer, Heidelberg (2005)
11. Zhu, T., Greiner, R., aubl, G.H.: Learning a Model of a Web User's Interests. In: Brusilovsky, P., Corbett, A.T., de Rosis, F. (eds.) UM 2003. LNCS, vol. 2702, pp. 65–75. Springer, Heidelberg (2003)
12. Chaffee, J., Pretschner, A.: Ontology-based personalized search and browsing.Web Intelligence and Agent Systems 1(3-4), 219–234 (2003)
13. Li, Y., Zhong, N.: Ontology-based Web mining model: representations of user profiles. In: Proceedings IEEE/WIC International Conference on Web Intelligence, pp. 96–103 (2003)
14. Kosala, R., Blockeel, H.: Web Mining Research: A Survey ACM SIGKDD Explorations (2000)
15. Zhang, H., Song, H.-t.: Fuzzy Related Classification Approach Based on Semantic Measurement for Web Document. In: The International Conference on Data Mining, HongKong (2006)
16. Choi, K.-S., Lee, C.-H.: Document ontology based personalized filtering system. In: Proceedings ACM Multimedia 2000, pp. 362–364 (2000)

Preference-Based Organization Interfaces: Aiding User Critiques in Recommender Systems

Li Chen and Pearl Pu

Human Computer Interaction Group, School of Computer and Communication Sciences
Swiss Federal Institute of Technology in Lausanne (EPFL)
CH-1015, Lausanne, Switzerland
{li.chen,pearl.pu}@epfl.ch

Abstract. Users' critiques to the current recommendation form a crucial feedback mechanism for refining their preference models and improving a system's accuracy in recommendations that may better interest the user. In this paper, we present a novel approach to assist users in making critiques according to their stated and potentially hidden preferences. This approach is derived from our previous work on critique generation and organization techniques. Based on a collection of real user data, we conducted an experiment to compare our approach with three existing critique generation systems. Results show that our preference-based organization interface achieves the highest level of prediction accuracy in suggesting users' intended critiques and recommendation accuracy in locating users' target choices. In addition, it can potentially most efficiently save real users' interaction effort in decision making.

Keywords: Recommender systems, user preference models, critique generation, organization, decision support, experiment.

1 Introduction

Recommender systems propose items that may interest a user. When it comes to suggesting decisions, such as which camera to buy, the ability to accurately recommend items that users truly want and reduce their effort in identifying the best choice is important. Decision accuracy and user effort are indeed two of the main factors influencing the design of product recommenders [8].

Many highly interactive recommender systems engage users in a conversational dialog in order to learn their preferences and use their feedback to improve the system's recommendation accuracy. Such interaction models have been referred as conversational recommenders, using both natural language models [14] and graphical user interfaces [2,12]. The main component of the interaction is that of example-and-critique. The system simulates an artificial salesperson that recommends example options based on a user's current preferences and then elicits his/her feedback in the form of critiques such as "I would like something cheaper" or "with faster processor speed". These critiques form the critical feedback mechanism to help the system improve its accuracy in predicting the user's needs in the next recommendation cycle.

C. Conati, K. McCoy, and G. Paliouras (Eds.): UM 2007, LNAI 4511, pp. 77–86, 2007.
© Springer-Verlag Berlin Heidelberg 2007

Our previous work proved that intelligent critiquing support allows users to more effectively refine the quality of their preferences and improve their decision accuracy up to a higher degree, compared to the non critiquing-based system such as a ranked list [8,10]. We have also investigated and compared two approaches to help users adopt such critiquing support tools. One is the system-proposed critique generation technique that aims at proposing a set of critiques for users to choose, and another is the user self-motivated critiquing support which stimulates users to freely compose and combine critiques on their own [3]. A comparative user evaluation shows that users on average achieved higher confidence in choice and decision accuracy while being self-motivated to make critiques. However, some users still preferred the system-proposed critiques since they found it intuitive to use and potentially their decision process could be accelerated if the critiques closely matched the critiques they were prepared to make.

Motivated by these findings, we have been engaged in improving the critiquing-based recommender system mainly from two aspects. On the one hand, we have developed a hybrid critiquing system with the purpose of combining the two types of critiquing assistances and making them compensate for each other. The hybrid system was empirically shown to have potential to both effectively improve users' objective decision performance and promote their subjective perceptions [4].

On the other hand, given the limitation of traditional system-proposed critique generation approaches in predicting users' intended critiques (due to their purely data-driven selection mechanism), we have designed and implemented computation algorithms focusing on users' preferences. The critique generation method based on multi-attribute utility theory (MAUT) [5] was shown to more effectively stimulate users to apply the proposed critiques [16]. After testing different concrete interface designs with real users, we have further proposed the preference-based organization interface aimed at organizing the individual MAUT-based critiques into different categories and using the category titles (i.e. frequent critique patterns) as upper-level critique suggestions. This interface was demonstrated to more effectively promote users' trust in recommendations and increase their trusting intentions to return and save effort [9].

In this paper, we attempt to further evaluate the preference-based organization interface in terms of its actual accuracy in predicting critiques matching real users' intended criteria and in recommending products that are in fact users' target choices. Based on a collection of 54 real users' data, we compared our approach with three primary existing critique generation methods: the FindMe [2], dynamic critiquing system [11,12], and MAUT-based compound critiques [16].

2 Related Work

FindMe systems generate critiques according to their knowledge of the product domain. For example, the tweak application (also called assisted browsing) developed in one FindMe system (i.e. RentMe) allows users to critique the current recommended apartment by selecting one of the proposed simple tweaks (e.g. "cheaper", "bigger" and "nicer") [2]. However, since the critiques are pre-designed by the system, they may not reflect the current status of available products.

Table 1. Main differences between four system-proposed critique generation methods

	Dynamic critiques	Critiques typical of the remaining products	Critiques adaptive to user preferences	Diversity among critiques and their contained products
Preference-based organization	✓	✓	✓	✓
MAUT-based compound critiques	✓	✗	✓	✗
Dynamic critiquing	✓	✓	✗	Partially (only critiques)
FindMe	✗	✗	✗	Partially (only critiques)

The dynamic critiquing method [11] and its successor, incremental critiquing [12], have been proposed mainly to automatically and dynamically generate compound critiques (e.g. "Different Manufacture, Lower Resolution and Cheaper" that can operate over multiple features simultaneously), by discovering the frequent sets of value differences between the current recommendation and remaining products based on Apriori algorithm [1]. Since a potentially large number of compound critiques would be produced by Apriori, they further filter all critiques using a threshold value favoring those critiques with lower support values ("support value" refers to the percentage of products that satisfy the critique). The dynamically generated critiques can also perform as explanations explaining to users the recommendation opportunities that exist in the remaining products [13].

However, the critique selection process purely based on support values indeed does not take into account users' preferences. It can only reveal "what the system can provide". For instance, the critique "Different Manufacture, Lower Resolution and Cheaper" is proposed if only there is a fewer percentage of products satisfying this critique. Even though the incremental dynamic critiquing method keeps a history of user previous critiques [12], the history only influences the computation of recommended products (i.e. requiring them compatible with the previous critique history as well as the current critique), not the process of critique generation.

In order to respect user preferences in the proposed critiques, Zhang and Pu [16] have proposed an approach to adapting the generation of compound critiques to user preference models based on the multi-attribute utility theory (MAUT) [5]. During each recommendation cycle, several products best matching a user's current preferences will be computed and the detailed comparison of each of them with the top candidate will be presented as a compound critique. These preference-based compound critiques were shown to more likely match users' intended critiquing criteria. However, relative to the dynamic critiquing approach, this method is limited in exposing remaining recommendation opportunities since each MAUT-based compound critique only corresponds to one product. In addition, it does not provide diversity among critiques. From real users' point of view, each critique also contains too many attributes so as to likely cause information overload.

With the aim of keeping these approaches' advantages while compensating for their limitations, we have further developed the preference-based organization interface. It was designed not only dynamically generating critiques adaptive to users' current preferences and potential needs, but also applying the data mining technique to produce representative compound critiques typical of the remaining data set. In addition, the critiques and their contained products are diversified so as to potentially assist users in refining and accumulating their preferences more effectively. Table 1 summarizes the main differences between the preference-based organization technique and other system-proposed critique generation methods.

3 Preference-Based Organization Interface

To derive effective design principles for the preference-based organization interface, we previously designed more than 13 paper prototypes and tested them with real users in form of pilot studies and interviews (see details in [9]). Four primary principles were derived covering almost all design dimensions, such as proposing improvements and compromises in the critique using conversational language (principle 1), keeping the number of tradeoff attributes in the critique under five to avoid information overload (principle 2), including actual products (up to six) under the critique (principle 3), and diversifying the proposed critiques and their contained products (principle 4) (the critique was termed as "category title" in [9]).

Manufacturer	Price	MegaPixels	Optical zoom	Memory type	Flash memory	LCD screen size	Depth	Weight	
The top candidate according to your preferences									
Canon	$242.00	5.0 MP	3x	CompactFlash Card	32 MB	1.8 in	1.37 in	8.3 oz	choose
We have more products with the following									
they are cheaper and lighter, but have fewer megapixels									
Nikon	$167.95	4 MP	3x	SD Memory Card	14 MB	1.6 in	1.4 in	4.6 oz	choose
Canon	$230.00	4.1 MP	3x	CompactFlash Card	32 MB	1.5 in	1.09 in	6.53 oz	choose
Canon	$180.00	3.3 MP	3x	SD Memory Card	16 MB	2 in	0.83 in	4.06 oz	choose
Canon	$219.18	4.2 MP	4x	MultiMedia Card	16 MB	1.8 in	1.51 in	6.35 oz	choose
Canon	$163.50	3.2 MP	4x	MultiMedia Card	16 MB	1.8 in	1.5 in	6.3 oz	choose
Canon	$199.40	3.2 MP	2.2x	SD Memory Card	16 MB	1.5 in	1.4 in	5.8 oz	choose
they have more megapixels and bigger screens, but are more expensive									
Sony	$365.00	7.2 MP	3x	Internal Memory	32 MB	2.5 in	1.5 in	6.9 oz	choose
Canon	$439.99	7.1 MP	3x	SD Memory Card	32 MB	2 in	1.04 in	6 oz	choose
Fuji	$253.00	6.3 MP	4x	XD-Picture Card	16 MB	2 in	1.4 in	7.1 oz	choose
Sony	$336.00	7.2 MP	3x	Internal Memory	32 MB	2 in	1 in	5 oz	choose
Nikon	$304.18	7.1 MP	3x	Internal Memory	13.5 MB	2 in	1.4 in	5.3 oz	choose
Olympus	$334.00	7.4 MP	5x	XD-Picture Card	32 MB	2.0 in	1.7 in	7.1 oz	choose
they are lighter and thinner, but have less flash memory									
Pentax	$238.99	5.3 MP	3x	Internal Memory	10 MB	1.8 in	0.8 in	3.7 oz	choose
Canon	$273.18	4.0 MP	3x	SD Memory Card	16 MB	2 in	0.82 in	4.59 oz	choose
Nikon	$329.95	5.1 MP	3x	Internal Memory	12 MB	2.5 in	0.9 in	4.2 oz	choose
Canon	$316.18	5.3 MP	3x	SD Memory Card	16 MB	2 in	0.81 in	4.59 oz	choose
Casio	$386.00	7.2 MP	3x	Internal Memory	8.3 MB	2.5 in	0.68 in	4.48 oz	choose
Fuji	$309.18	6.3 MP	3x	XD-Picture Card	16 MB	2.5 in	1.1 in	5.5 oz	choose
they have more optical zoom with different memory type, but are thicker and heavier									
Panasonic	$386.00	5.0 MP	12x	SD Memory Card	16 MB	1.8 in	3.34 in	11.52 oz	choose
Konica Minolta	$349.99	5.0 MP	12x	SD Memory Card	16 MB	2 in	3.3 in	12 oz	choose
Fuji	$259.18	4.23 MP	10x	XD-Picture Card	16 MB	1.5 in	3.1 in	11.9 oz	choose
Olympus	$253.00	4.0 MP	10x	XD-Picture Card	16 MB	1.8 in	2.7 in	9.9 oz	choose
Olympus	$284.99	4.0 MP	10x	XD-Picture Card	16 MB	1.8 in	2.7 in	10.6 oz	choose
Nikon	$259.18	4.2 MP	8.3x	Internal Memory	13.5 MB	1.8 in	2.2 in	9 oz	choose

Fig. 1. The preference-based organization interface

We have accordingly developed an algorithm to optimize the objectives corresponding to these principles (see Fig. 1 of a resulting interface). Note that in our interface design, multiple products that satisfy the proposed critique are recommended simultaneously, rather than only one product returned (once a critique is picked) in the traditional system-proposed critiquing interfaces [2,12,16]. This interface was in fact favored by most of interviewed users since it could potentially save their interaction effort and give them higher control over the process of choice making. The following lists the main characteristics of our algorithm as how it models and incrementally refines user preferences, and how critiques are generated typical of the remaining products and selected adaptive to user preferences and potential needs.

Model user preferences based on MAUT. We represent the user preferences over all products as a weighted additive form of value functions according to the multi-attribute utility theory (MAUT) [5,16]. This MAUT-based user model is inherently in accordance with the most normal and compensatory decision strategy, the weighted additive rule (WADD) that resolves conflicting values explicitly by considering tradeoffs [7]. Formally, the preference model is a pair $(\{V_1,...,V_n\}, \{w_1,...,w_n\})$ where V_i is the value function for each attribute A_i, and w_i is the relative importance (i.e. weight) of A_i. The utility of each product ($\langle a_1,a_2,...,a_n \rangle$) can be hence calculated as:

$$U(\langle a_1,a_2,...,a_n \rangle) = \sum_{i=1}^{n} w_i V_i(a_i) \tag{1}$$

Suggest unstated preferences in critiques. Giving user suggestions on unstated preferences was demonstrated to likely stimulate preferences expression and improve users' decision accuracy [15]. Thus, while generating the critique pattern of each remaining product by comparing it with the current recommendation (i.e. the top candidate), we assign default tradeoff properties (i.e. *improved* or *compromised*) to these features without explicit stated preferences. For example, if a user does not specify any preference on the notebook's processor speed, we will assign *improved* (if faster) or *compromised* (if slower) to the compared product's processor speed. We believe that the proposed critiques with suggested preferences could help users learn more knowledge about the product domain and potentially stimulate them to expose more hidden preferences.

Produce critiques typical of the remaining products. In our algorithm, each product (except the top candidate) will be turned into a tradeoff vector (i.e. critique pattern) comprising a set of (*attribute, tradeoff*) pairs. The *tradeoff* property is determined by the user's stated preference or our suggested direction. More concretely, it indicates whether the *attribute* of the product is *improved* (denoted as ↑) or *compromised* (denoted as ↓) compared to the same *attribute* of the top candidate. For example, a notebook's tradeoff vector can be represented as {(price, ↓), (processor speed, ↑), (hard drive size, ↑), (display size, ↓), (weight, ↑)}.

We then apply the Apriori algorithm to discover the recurring and representative subsets of (*attribute, tradeoff*) pairs within these tradeoff vectors (the discovered subset is called a "compound critique" or "category title" [9]). The reason of applying Apriori is due to its efficiency and popularity in mining associate rules among features [1]. Additionally, it provides various parameters enabling us to control the number of attributes involved in each critique and the percentage of products each critique contains so as to satisfy our design principles (principle 2 and 3).

Thus, at this point, all remaining products can be organized into different categories and each category be represented by a compound critique (e.g. "cheaper and lighter but lower processor speed") indicating the similar tradeoff properties of products that this category contains (principle 1).

Favor critiques with higher tradeoff utilities. The Apriori algorithm will potentially produce a large amount of critiques since a product can belong to more than one category given that it has different subsets of tradeoff properties shared by other groups of products. It then comes to the problem of how to select the most prominent critiques presented to users. In stead of simply selecting critiques with lower support values as the dynamic critiquing method does [11,12], we focus on using users' preferences and their potential needs to choose critiques. More specifically, all critiques are ranked according to their tradeoff utilities (i.e. gains vs. losses relative to the top candidate) in terms of both the critiques themselves and their contained products:

$$TradeoffUtility(C) = (\sum_{i=1}^{|C|} w(attribute_i) \times tradeoff_i) \times (\frac{1}{|SR(C)|} \sum_{r \in SR(C)}^{|SR(C)|} U(r)) \qquad (2)$$

where C denotes the critique as a set of (*attribute, tradeoff*) pairs, and $SR(C)$ denotes the set of products that satisfy C. Therefore, according to the user's stated preferences and our suggestions on his/her potential needs, $\sum_{i=1}^{|C|} w(attribute_i) \times tradeoff_i$ computes the weighted sum of tradeoff properties represented by C ($w(attribute_i)$ is the weight of $attribute_i$; $tradeoff_i$ is default set as 0.75 if *improved*, or 0.25 if *compromised*, since *improved* attributes are in nature more valuable than *compromised* ones). $\frac{1}{|SR(C)|} \sum_{r \in SR(C)}^{|SR(C)|} U(r)$ is the average utility (see formula (1)) of all the products contained by C.

Diversify proposed critiques and their contained products. To further diversify the proposed critiques to increase their suggestion power since similar items are limited to add much useful values to users [6] (principle 4), we multiply the tradeoff utility of each critique by a diversity degree:

$$F(C) = TradeoffUtility(C) \times Diversity(C, SC) \qquad (3)$$

where SC denotes the set of critiques so far selected. The first proposed critique is hence the critique with the highest tradeoff utility, and the subsequent critique is selected if it has the highest value of $F(C)$ in the remaining non-selected critiques. The selection process ends when the desired k critiques have been determined.

The diversity degree of C is concretely calculated as the minimal local diversity of C with each critique C_i in the SC set. The local diversity of two critiques is defined by two factors: the diversity between critiques themselves (i.e. C and C_i) and the diversity between their contained products (i.e. $SR(C)$ and $SR(C_i)$):

$$Diversity(C, SC) = \min_{C_i \in SC} ((1 - \frac{|C \cap C_i|}{|C|}) \times (1 - \frac{|SR(C) \cap SR(C_i)|}{|SR(C)|})) \qquad (4)$$

Incrementally refine user preferences. After a user has selected one of the proposed critiques and a new reference product from the set of products that satisfy the selected critique, his/her preferences will be accordingly refined for the computation of critiques in the next cycle. More concretely, the weight (i.e. relative importance) of *improved* attribute(s) that appears in the selected critique will be increased by β, and the weight of *compromised* one(s) will be decreased by β (β = 0.25). All attributes' preferred values will be also updated based on the new reference product's values.

4 Experimental Results

4.1 Materials and Procedure

The goal of this experiment is to evaluate the performance of the preference-based organization interface in terms of its accuracy in predicting critiques that users are likely to make and in recommending products that are targeted by users. We particularly compared our system with three primary existing critique generation approaches: MAUT-based compound critiques [16], dynamic critiquing [11,12], and FindMe [2].

As a matter of fact, few earlier works have empirically measured the prediction accuracy of their algorithms in suggesting critiques. In respect of their simulation experiments, a product randomly chosen from the database was used to determine a simulated user's target choice and his/her initial preferences [11,12,16].

The difference of our experiment is that it was based on a collection of real users' data so that it can potentially more realistically and accurately reveal the system's actual critique prediction accuracy and recommendation accuracy. The data has been concretely collected from a series of previous user studies where users were instructed to identify their truly intended critiquing criteria in the user self-motivated critiquing interface [3]. So far, 54 real users' records have been accumulated (with around 1500 data points), half of them asked to find a favorite digital camera (64 products, 8 main features) and the other half for a tablet PC (55 products, 10 main features). Each record includes the real user's initial preferences (i.e. a set of <attribute preferred value, attribute weight> pairs), the product he/she selected for critiquing and his/her self-motivated critiquing criteria (i.e. attributes to be *improved* or *compromised*) during each critiquing cycle, the total interaction cycles he/she consumed, and his/her target choice which was determined after he/she reviewed all products in an offline setting.

In the beginning of our experiment, each real user's initial preferences were first entered in the evaluated system. The system then proposed k critiques (k = 4), and the critique most matching the real user's intended critiquing criteria during that cycle was selected. Then, among the set of n recommended products (n = 6) that satisfy the selected critique, the product most similar to the actual product picked in that cycle was used for the next round of critique generation. This process ended when the corresponding real user stopped. That is, if a real user took three critiquing cycles to locate his/her final choice, he/she would also end after three cycles in our experiment.

4.2 Measured Variables and Results

4.2.1 Critique Prediction Accuracy

The critique prediction accuracy for each user is defined as the average matching degree between his/her self-motivated critiquing criteria and the most matching system-proposed critique of each cycle (see formula (5)). A higher matching degree infers that the corresponding critique generation algorithm can likely be more accurately predicting the critiques that real users intend to make.

$$PredictionRate(user_i) = \frac{1}{NumCycle} \sum_{j=1}^{NumCycle} \max_{c \in C_j} (\frac{\alpha \times NumImproveMatch(c) + (1-\alpha) \times NumCompromiseMatch(c)}{\alpha \times NumImprove(t) + (1-\alpha) \times NumCompromise(t)}) \quad (5)$$

where C_j represents the set of system-proposed critiques during the jth cycle, *NumImprove(t)* is the number of improved attributes in the real user's critique (denoted as *t*) during that cycle, and *NumCompromise(t)* is the number of compromised attributes. *NumImproveMatch(c)* denotes the number of improved attributes that appear in both the proposed critique (i.e. *c*) and the user's actual critique, and *NumCompromiseMatch(c)* is the number of matched compromised attributes ($\alpha=$ 0.75, since users likely want more accurate matching on the improved attributes).

The experimental results show that both the user preferences based critique generation approaches, the preference-based organization (henceforth PB-ORG) and MAUT-based compound critiques (henceforth MAUT-COM), achieve relatively higher success rate (respectively 66.9% and 63.7%) in predicting the critiques users actually made, compared to the dynamic critiquing method (henceforth DC) and FindMe approach ($F = 94.620$, $p < 0.001$; see Fig. 2 (a)). The PB-ORG is even slightly better than MAUT-COM. It therefore implies that when the proposed critiques can be well adaptive to the user's changing preferences and his/her potential needs, the user will likely more frequently apply them in the real situation.

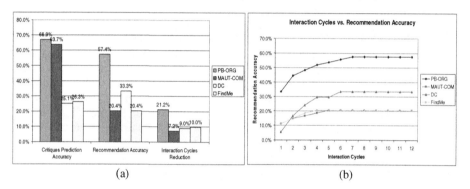

(a)   (b)

Fig. 2. Experimental comparison of four critique generation algorithms

4.2.2 Recommendation Accuracy

In addition to evaluate the system's ability in predicting critiques, we also measured its recommendation accuracy as how likely users' target choices could have been located in the recommended products once the critique was made.

$$RecommendationAccuracy = \frac{1}{NumUsers} \sum_{i=1}^{NumUsers} FindTarget(target_i, \sum_{j=1}^{NumCycle(u_i)} RC_j(u_i)) \qquad (6)$$

In this formula, $RC_j(u_i)$ denotes the set of recommended products that satisfy the selected critique during the jth cycle for the user u_i. If the user's target choice (denoted as $target_i$) appears in any $RC_j(u_i)$ set, *FindTarget* is equal to 1, otherwise *FindTarget* is 0. The higher overall recommendation accuracy hence represents the larger proportion of users whose target choice appeared at least in one recommendation cycle, inferring that the corresponding system can likely more effectively recommend the target choice to real users during their acceptable critiquing cycles.

The experiment indicates that PB-ORG achieves the highest recommendation accuracy (57.4%) compared to the other systems ($F = 8.171$, $p < 0.001$; see Fig. 2 (a)). Fig. 2 (b) further illustrates the comparison of recommendation accuracy on a per cycle basis in an accumulated way (the maximal number of interaction cycles is 12). It is worth noting that although MAUT-COM obtains relatively higher critique prediction accuracy compared to DC and FindMe, it is rather limited to recommend accurate products. In fact, regarding the recommendation accuracy, the best two approaches (PB-ORG and DC) are both based on the organization technique, and PB-ORG performs much better than DC likely due to its user preferences based selection mechanism. Therefore, PB-ORG is proven not only being most accurate at suggesting critiques that real users intended to make, but also most accurate at recommending products that were targeted by real users.

4.2.3 Interaction Effort Reduction

It is then interesting to know how effectively the system could potentially reduce real users' objective effort in locating their target choice. This was concretely measured as the percentage of cycles the average user could have saved to make the choice relative to the cycles he/she actually consumed in the self-motivated critiquing condition:

$$EffortReduction = \frac{1}{NumUsers}(\sum_{i=1}^{NumUsers} \frac{actualCycle_i - targetCycle_i}{actualCycle_i}) \qquad (7)$$

where $actualCycle_i$ denotes the number of cycles the corresponding real user consumed and $targetCycle_i$ denotes the number of cycles until his/her target choice first appeared in the products recommended by the system. For the user whose target choice did not appear in any recommendations, his/her effort reduction is 0.

In terms of this aspect, PB-ORG again shows the best result ($F = 4.506, p < 0.01$; see Fig. 2 (a)). More specifically, the simulated user can on average save over 21.2% of their critiquing cycles while using the preference-based organization algorithm (vs. 7.2% with MAUT-COM, 8.95% with DC and 9.96% with FindMe). This finding implies that the preference-based organization interface can potentially enable real users to more efficiently target their best choice, not only relative to the user self-motivated critiquing system (where the $actualCycle$ was consumed), but also compared to the other system-proposed critiquing systems.

5 Conclusion

In this paper, we described a new approach to generating proposed critiques based on users' preferences. The preference-based organization method computes critiques not only with MAUT-based user preference models but also with additional considerations such as classification and diversification. It organizes the critiques so as to identify the most prominent and representative critiques in the set of eligible critiques. To understand the new approach's accuracy in predicting critiques that users are likely to make and furthermore its accuracy in recommending products that are targeted by real users, we conducted an experiment to compare it with three primary existing critique generation approaches based on a collection of 54 real users' data. The experimental results show that both preference-based critique generation algorithms (PB-ORG and MAUT-based compound critiques [16]) achieve significantly higher critique prediction accuracy (above 60%), compared to the dynamic critiquing method (purely data-driven critique selection) [11,12] and the FindMe approach (pre-designed critiques) [2]. In addition, PB-ORG is most accurate at recommending users' target choice (57.4%), while potentially requiring users to consume the least amount of interaction effort (by saving up to 22% critiquing cycles).

Thus, as a conclusion of our previous and current work, we believe that the preference-based organization interface can be well combined with the user self-motivated critiquing support [4] to maximally improve users' decision accuracy while demanding a low amount of users' objective and subjective effort. In addition, such hybrid critiquing system is likely to promote users' high subject opinions (i.e. trust and decision confidence) given that users can not only feel in control of their preference refinement process with the aid of user self-motivated critiquing support, but also have the opportunity to learn the remaining recommendation opportunities and accelerate their decision process in the preference-based organization interface. In the future, we will further verify these results via real user trials. We will also establish a more consolidated and sharable set of ground truth with more real users' data for the performance measurements of various recommender systems.

References

1. Agrawal, R., Imielinski, T., Swami, A.: Mining Association Rules between Sets of Items in Large Databases. In: Proc. ACM SIGMOD, pp. 207–216 (1993)
2. Burke, R.D., Hammond, K.J., Young, B.C.: The FindMe Approach to Assisted Browsing. IEEE Expert: Intelligent Systems and Their Applications 12(4), 32–40 (1997)
3. Chen, L., Pu, P.: Evaluating Critiquing-based Recommender Agents. In: Proc. 21st AAAI, pp. 157–162 (2006)
4. Chen, L., Pu, P.: Hybrid Critiquing-based Recommender Systems. In: Proc. IUI, pp. 22–31 (2007)
5. Keeney, R., Raiffa, H.: Decisions with Multiple Objectives: Preferences and Value Tradeoffs. Cambridge University Press, Cambridge (1976)
6. McGinty, L., Smyth, B.: On the Role of Diversity in Conversational Recommender Systems. In: Proc. 5th ICCBR, pp. 276–290 (2003)
7. Payne, J.W., Bettman, J.R., Johnson, E.J.: The Adaptive Decision Maker. Cambridge University Press, Cambridge (1993)
8. Pu, P., Chen, L.: Integrating Tradeoff Support in Product Search Tools for e-commerce Sites. In: Proc. 6th ACM EC, pp. 269–278 (2005)
9. Pu, P., Chen, L.: Trust Building with Explanation Interfaces. In: Proc. IUI, pp. 93–100 (2006)
10. Pu, P., Kumar, P.: Evaluating Example-Based Search Tools. In: Proc. 5th ACM EC, pp. 208–217 (2004)
11. Reilly, J., McCarthy, K., McGinty, L., Smyth, B.: Dynamic Critiquing. In: Proc. 7th ECCBR, pp. 763–777 (2004)
12. Reilly, J., McCarthy, K., McGinty, L., Smyth, B.: Incremental Critiquing. In: Proc. 24th SGAI International Conference on Innovative Techniques and Applications of Artificial Intelligence, pp. 101–114 (2004)
13. Reilly, J., McCarthy, K., McGinty, L., Smyth, B.: Explaining Compound Critiques. Artificial Intelligence Review, vol. 24(2) (2005)
14. Thompson, C.A., Goker, M.H., Langley, P.: A Personalized System for Conversational Recommendations. Journal of Artificial Intelligence Research 21, 393–428 (2004)
15. Viappiani, P., Faltings, B., Pu, P.: Preference-based Search using Example-Critiquing with Suggestions. To appear in Journal of Artificial Intelligence Research (2007)
16. Zhang, J., Pu, P.: A Comparative Study of Compound Critique Generation in Conversational Recommender Systems. In: Proc. AH, pp. 234–243 (2006)

"More Like This" or "Not for Me": Delivering Personalised Recommendations in Multi-user Environments

David Bonnefoy[1], Makram Bouzid[1], Nicolas Lhuillier[1], and Kevin Mercer[2]

[1] Motorola Labs, Parc des Algorithmes, 91193 Gif-sur-Yvette cedex, France
[2] Motorola Labs, Jays Close, Viables Industrial Estate, Basingstoke, UK
{David.Bonnefoy, Makram.Bouzid, Nicolas.Lhuillier,
Kevin.Mercer}@motorola.com

Abstract. The television as a multi-user device presents some specificities with respect to personalisation. Recommendations should be provided both per-viewers as well as for a group. Recognising the inadequacy of traditional user modelling techniques with the constraint of television's lazy watching usage patterns, this paper presents a new recommendation mechanism based on anonymous user preferences and dynamic filtering of recommendations. Results from an initial user study indicate this mechanism was able to provide content recommendations to individual users within a multi-user environment with a high level of user satisfaction and without the need for user authentication or individual preference profile creation.

Keywords: Personalisation, recommendation, preference, user model, group.

1 Context and Motivation

Watching television is one of the most popular activities. As a consequence of that ubiquity, hundreds of channels are now available, and thus thousands of programmes each day. This, with the emergence of content available on the Internet, makes it more and more difficult for viewers to find suitable content to watch. Cotter and Smyth, for instance, estimated a typical Electronic Programme Guide (EPG) may require more than 200 screens to cover each day [4]. Within many domains when such a case arises, recommender systems have been developed. An example of this is the book recommendations on the Amazon web site. As such, the earliest attempt to personalise the EPG as a way to help users find unknown content of interest dates from 1998 with Das & Horst's "TV Advisor" [5]. But personalisation of television presents some particular challenges.

The television at home is a multi-user device: the whole family uses it. But not all the family members watch television with the same frequency, at the same time and with the same motivations. Children and parents for instance have very different watching schedules and programme tastes. Thus, the system must be able to cope with individual preferences. Besides, as Masthoff pointed out [9], though this may be

C. Conati, K. McCoy, and G. Paliouras (Eds.): UM 2007, LNAI 4511, pp. 87–96, 2007.
© Springer-Verlag Berlin Heidelberg 2007

culturally dependent, watching television is also a social activity and therefore the system should also deal with situations where several family members watch television as a group.

Watching television is additionally a casual and passive activity. This aspect has been studied by Taylor and Harper [12], who found that generally television is an unplanned activity and viewers turn first to the search strategies requiring the least possible effort when seeking programmes. A television is not a computer, it requires lower effort to operate and conversely many of the interaction paradigms people associate with computers, such as logging-in prior to use, are alien within this context. It is also common for the television to be switched on just for background whilst other activities are carried out. This could make implicit feedback (e.g. inferring user preferences by tracking channel selections) rather noisy and ineffective.

These challenges particular to television viewing put strong constraints on a recommendation system. To better understand the user needs, we have carried out a user study that helped us understand the particular needs of television users. Consideration of these constraints and the results of our user study led us to the requirements below.

Not surprisingly, the first user requirement is to be able to get individual recommendations. However, the second one is to also get group recommendations, as the optimum recommendations for a group are often different from those of any one individual user within that group.

More remarkable are users' requests to provide explicit feedback to the system. Users seem neither to trust nor like a system that would silently learn preferences on their behalf. Rating programmes is therefore seen as a key tool to putting the system back on track after spurious recommendations. In addition, users asked for the ability to benefit from other household members' preferences: as they may watch programmes in groups, they would like the possibility for a rating provided by one member of the group or family to be used by another member. This had been mentioned in [7] and would avoid the entire family having to rate the same programme separately and multiple times if all are interested in it.

This paper presents a new personalisation mechanism addressing these requirements. Section two starts by reviewing some existing solutions for television personalisation. Section three then introduces our new concept and section four provides the details of its implementation as a prototype. Finally, section five presents the results of an evaluation of this concept with some users.

2   Current Personalisation Solutions for Television

The characteristics of television viewing put particular requirements on a personalisation system that aims at helping home viewers find the most suitable content to watch. These requirements are not met by existing personalisation systems.

Some personalisation systems available today are designed mostly for a unique user. For instance Yahoo! Movies (http://movies.yahoo.com) and MyBestBet.com (http://mybestbets.com), powered by ChoiceStream (http://www.choicestream.com) technology, deliver recommendations the former for movies and the latter for television programmes. Both however require each individual to provide ratings to build a user profile. Thus, users always need to sign up in order to supply ratings or to get personal recommendations. As observed in the previous section, such authentication mechanisms are not suited to television viewing habits. Alternate authentication mechanisms based on fingerprint [8] or on automatic user detection via face recognition [15] have also been investigated. In addition to the lack of reliability or the privacy issues inherent to such technologies, which could probably be improved in the future, the main drawback with automatic authentication comes from ambiguity and inaccuracy in the user preferences being inferred, mainly due to the inherent social usage aspects of television. For instance if the fingerprint detector is placed on the remote, the user who holds it may not be the only one who is watching the television. Neither may this user have chosen the programme being watched. With automatic user detection, some users may be sitting in front of the television set but not actively watching television or not even enjoying the programme, as discovered during our user study. Another proposed solution was to analyse channel surfing behaviour to identify which user is in front of the TV [13] and use the corresponding profile to make recommendations, but it requires to preliminary build individual user profiles associated to channel surfing patterns and it is not suitable for group recommendations.

On the other hand, popular television programme recommender TiVo (http://www.tivo.com) solved the user logging issue by simply managing a single profile for the entire household. Though this may be acceptable for all single-member households, TiVo's recommendations are often criticised by users for being biased towards the tastes of the family member who provides the highest number of ratings to the system. Some other research prototypes aim to alleviate this issue by providing stereotypes in order for users to quickly build an individual profile in addition to the default family profile [2], but these systems still require the user to log in to update their profiles.

Finally, very few personalisation systems support a multi-user functionality. Web-based movie recommender MovieLens included a group feature with PolyLens [10]. Masthoff [9], Jameson [7] or Yu et al. [14] also described different strategies or techniques to combine preferences for members of a group, but again these require users to build individual user models and to provide the recommender with the list of members forming the group.

In conclusion, no recommendation system for television programmes currently succeeds in combining the multi-user requirements to deliver individualised and group recommendations, whilst remaining simple and effortless to use.

3 The "Preference Cluster Activation" Mechanism

Considering the requirements and pitfalls from the above sections, a new mechanism, dubbed "Preference Cluster Activation" (PCA), has been designed to deliver individualised recommendations in the context of television, bearing in mind the constraints of its unengaged usage pattern. TV viewers are passive and they tend to choose sources that require less effort [3]. This is the main reason why this mechanism primarily aims at minimizing the number of steps required to get the recommendations.

The first requisite for any personalisation system are the user preferences. No effective reasoning is possible without accurate user data. However, users almost always consider entering preferences as a tedious task [7]. Additionally taking into consideration the fact that television sets, unlike computers, do not have a notion of "user", it is unlikely that requiring viewers to authenticate in order to provide their preferences will motivate them to create and maintain a user profile.

In the domain we consider, user preferences are expressed as ratings of television programmes. This input is done anonymously: users can rate a programme at any time without authenticating. This decision may seem contradictory with the stated objective of delivering individualised recommendations. Indeed, as shown in Figure 1, the rationale behind the PCA mechanism is that the ratings of the different users can be grouped by similarities. Later, when browsing the recommendations, users will be able to bias the recommendations towards those that have been inferred from ratings they agree with.

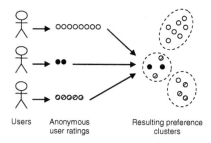

Users   Anonymous   Resulting preference
          user ratings   clusters

Fig. 1. Creation of preference groups from anonymous preference inputs. Note that for clarity, preference inputs have been tagged differently for each user, but they are not distinguishable in the actual mechanism.

The actual details of the PCA are illustrated in Figure 2: The process starts by a user, for instance a family member, asking for a list of recommendations. The recommendations are determined by first predicting ratings for upcoming programmes. The system regroups the ratings that have been previously (and anonymously) provided by all users. In order to compute a rating prediction for a given programme, the system first looks for the cluster which this programme is the closest to, then the prediction is performed only using the ratings contained within this cluster. If the predicted user appreciation is satisfactory, the prediction becomes a recommendation which is said to "come" from this cluster. The system therefore initially returns a first list which roughly contains an equivalent amount of recommendations originating from the different clusters.

Using an input mechanism such as the TV remote control, the user is able to browse the list and provide feedback on the different recommendations, which will automatically and dynamically update the recommendation list. Two types of feedback are available:

-   *"More like this"* means the recommendation suits the user wishes or needs. Consequently, the cluster associated with this recommendation will be promoted so that the updated list contains more content coming from this cluster.

- *"Not for me"* means such recommendations do not satisfy the user. Therefore the updated list will no longer contain recommendations coming from this cluster. This action allows the banning of preference inputs entered by users who have very different tastes compared to the current one (e.g. young children versus parents).

The user may continue the recommendation filtering process, by repeating such feedback actions, until the resulting list is seen as satisfactory.

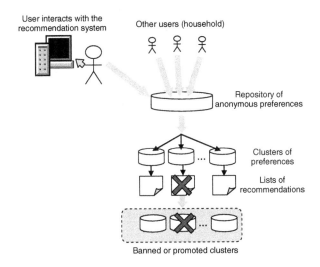

Fig. 2. Overview of the "Preference Cluster Activation" mechanism. User first gets a list of recommendations built using the preferences from all users. Then based on feedback actions, recommendations associated with some clusters are banned whilst some others get promoted.

Comparing the PCA mechanism with the list of requirements drawn from the first section, this new process should allow the delivery of individual recommendations by dynamically adapting the list to the current user needs. Within a multi-user context such as a family, this obviously applies to a single member, but this may also apply to a set of members who will carry out the feedback process all together to get a group recommendation. The process can even allow a single user to get different lists of recommendations for different contexts (e.g. weekend afternoons versus weekday evenings). Additionally, due to the anonymity of preferences, this mechanism also naturally fulfils the requirement to allow an individual user to benefit from the ratings of other household members.

Critically, the claimed advantages of the PCA mechanism only remain valid if the filtering by feedback step is not seen as tedious nor complicated by users. Due to the finite number of preference clusters, this process is short. No matter, great care needs to be taken in the design of the user interface and the implementation of the mechanism to ensure that the filtering converges within about two actions.

In order to validate the feasibility and the user acceptance for this new concept, a prototype has been built which is described in the next section.

4 Design of the PCA Prototype

The PCA prototype, implemented in Java, consists primarily of an Electronic Programme Guide (EPG) which allows users to anonymously rate programmes. A recommendation page allows users to access and perform feedback actions to the recommendation list. The content of the EPG is retrieved in XMLTV (http://xmltv.org/wiki) format. The descriptive metadata vary depending on the content source but generally include information such as: title, channel, time, genre, description, etc. As mentioned in the previous section, users enter their preferences as programme ratings. A preference input P_i therefore consists of a set of metadata C_j for a piece of content and a rating R defined on a 5-point bipolar scale (from -2 to +2): $P_i(C) = (C_1,...,C_j,...,C_n, R_i)$.

The overall architecture of the PCA mechanism used to generate the recommendation is depicted in Figure 3 and consists of three main components: a clustering algorithm, a prediction algorithm and a recommender engine.

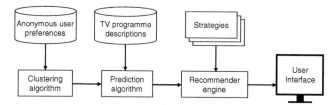

Fig. 3. Functional architecture of the PCA prototype with its three main components

As explained in the previous section, the clustering algorithm is used to regroup anonymous preferences based on their similarity. In our prototype we developed a modified version of K-means. This algorithm first requires a function to compute similarity between two items C and D. In the prototype, this function returns a float between 0 (very similar) and 1 (very dissimilar) and has been defined as the normalised weighted sum over different similarity functions for the various description metadata:

$$sim(C,D) = \frac{1}{\sum a_i} \sum_{i=1}^{n} a_i . sim(C_i, D_i) \qquad (1)$$

K-means is known to suffer from two main drawbacks: a) the number of clusters needs to be set in advance and b) the resulting configuration may depend on the initial selection of the centroids. In order to solve these issues and to dynamically adapt the number of clusters, a mechanism similar to X-means [11] has been used. Starting from one cluster, the cost of splitting an existing cluster is evaluated using the Akaike Information Criterion [1]. This criterion, like the Schwartz criterion, aims at balancing the fitness of the model in relation to its complexity (e.g. degrees of freedom). Additionally, in order to simplify the computation of the clusters' centroids, which is difficult when data are not numeric, a method inspired from K-median [6] has been applied. The centroid therefore corresponds to the cluster element which is the closest to all other elements in the cluster.

The prediction algorithm is a mere naïve Bayes classifier. In order to predict a rating for a new piece of content, the similarity function is first used to identify the cluster which the piece of content should belong to. Then, using the ratings from this cluster as training set, the most probable rating for the content piece is returned.

Finally, the recommender engine is responsible for assembling a list of recommendations from the content pieces that have been positively predicted. The expected size for this list is frequently much smaller than the number of programmes which received a positive prediction. Different filtering strategies are therefore used to reduce the size of this list. At first, the strategy used to create the initial list L_0 consists of ensuring there is the same proportion of recommendations from each cluster.

In a second step, the recommender engine takes user feedback actions ("More like this" and "Not for me") into account to dynamically update the recommendation list. These feedback actions have also been implemented as strategies. Considering that the user selects a recommendation R in the list L_i, the former ensures, for example, that at least half of the recommendations in list L_{i+1} come from the same cluster as R. On the other hand, the latter removes in L_{i+1} all recommendation coming from the same cluster as R. Note that depending on the number of preferences, we realised that clusters may not always be homogeneous, therefore a similarity threshold allows us not to ban or promote all recommendations from a cluster but only those which are similar enough to the recommendation under consideration. Note that as users may never precisely control the effect of their feedback actions to the list, an "undo" function always allows them to return to the previous list. This prototype has then been used in an initial trial to evaluate the efficiency and acceptability of the PCA mechanism with users.

5 Experimental Results

For the purposes of the initial investigative study, six users were recruited consisting of three couples. Each couple lived in the same household and regularly watched TV both individually and together as part of a family group.

Each user was asked to rate a total of twenty television programmes from the EPG of the PCA prototype using the rating feature provided within the application. These ratings were saved as six separate profiles based on individual user preferences. Additionally for each couple their two separate profiles were duplicated and then merged together to form a joint profile. This action mimics the expected profile generation where two users provide anonymous ratings to a single shared profile.

Users were then asked to review recommendation lists within the PCA prototype and to employ the filtering actions to modify these lists. This task was executed using either each of the couple's individual profiles or the joint profile over a range of different viewing contexts and times. Situations when one individual was searching for content alone and when the couple were searching for content to watch together were also investigated. Task success was reported only in situations where users had been able to find something of interest to watch. Additionally, the reported user satisfaction in relation to the overall quality of the recommendation accuracy, time to find and level of effort expended were also documented. This data was collected through an investigator-administered questionnaire which allowed responses on a five point Likert scale ranging from "extremely satisfied" through to "extremely dissatisfied".

The focus of the study was to investigate if improvements could be perceived (both by individuals and groups) within recommendation lists that had been based upon a shared repository of ratings from that group of users in contrast to when ratings had come only from the individual. Therefore the two areas of particular interest to the investigators during the study were: task success and satisfaction when users searched for content in the context of watching TV alone but recommendations had been built using the shared anonymous rating profile, in contrast to when they had been built from the user's individual preferences only; and task success and satisfaction when users searched for content as a couple in the context of watching TV together when the profile recommendations had been built using the shared anonymous rating profile.

User responses for this study are presented in Figure 4 and consist of the following main findings: when searching for interesting content to watch individually, users reported higher levels of satisfaction and achieved greater task success when the recommendations were based upon the couple's combined profile compared to when they were based upon the user's own individual preference ratings. Using the shared anonymous profiles, users achieved 100% overall task success in relation to finding content of interest to watch. Using their own individual profiles this figure was 94%. For the same tasks the overall level of reported user satisfaction in relation to the accuracy of the content discovered with the PCA controls when using the shared profiles was 78% extremely or somewhat satisfied[1] in contrast to 50% when using their own individual profiles[2].

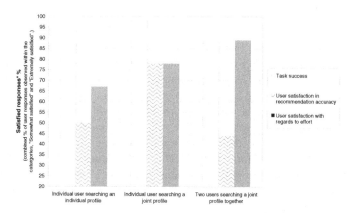

Fig. 4. User responses with respect to task success, satisfaction in recommendation accuracy and satisfaction in the amount of effort expended to find content. These metrics were all higher when an individual user utilised an anonymous preference profile containing ratings from all family members.

---

[1] Corresponding levels of extremely or somewhat dissatisfied responses for this task was 6%.

[2] Corresponding levels of extremely or somewhat dissatisfied responses for this task was 22%.

When searching for interesting content to watch as a couple using the shared anonymous rating profile, users achieved an overall task success rate of 89%. For the same tasks the overall level of user satisfaction recorded in relation to the accuracy of the content discovered was 44% extremely or somewhat satisfied[2].

Although this investigation was conducted with a very small sample of users the initial results appear favourable. In the case of individual users, the levels of user satisfaction in content recommendations that could be discovered through the use of the PCA prototype appear to have actually benefited from the presence of more than one user's preference ratings within the profile (i.e. the shared anonymous profile is richer than individual ones even when users have only few joint tastes). This is positive in respect to the possibility of the system to offer recommendations to individuals within a multi-user environment without the need for any form of user authentication or personal profile.

The prototype appears to have also been reasonably successful in allowing multiple users to locate content of interest to watch together within this same environment, though not to the same extent as when searching as an individual. However the levels of satisfaction in the accuracy of the recommendations was only 6% lower in this instance than the observed comparable figure for individual users when searching a profile consisting solely of their own ratings, and overall task success for couples searching for content of interest remained high at 89%. Further user evaluation work would now be required with larger sample sizes to verify these formative findings.

6 Conclusion and Future Work

The primary objective of Preference Cluster Activation mechanism was to deliver per user recommendations on a multi-user device, with a quality as close as possible to what a dedicated user model would allow, whilst excluding the cost for users to authenticate and build individual profiles. Surprisingly, in our study, user satisfaction was greater with the anonymous profile, when preferences from all users were combined, compared to recommendations computed with the proper user preferences only. This is definite evidence of the positive effect for one user to benefit from the preferences of another user. As experienced by one couple in our experiment, this positive effect is strengthened when users have close tastes. Though the negative effect of combining preferences from users with very different tastes has not been encountered, further work would be required to test the system in a wider multi-user environment such as a whole family to measure the performance of the system when the shared profile is built by more than two users and also includes perhaps more diverse viewing preferences such as those of both children and adults.

User experience can likely be further improved by enhancing the quality of the recommendations, for instance combining a collaborative filtering algorithm with our naïve Bayes classifier. However, the main challenge remains to ensure that the filtering step is seen as less tedious for users than the creation of an individual user profile. This is partly a user interaction design issue, though a technical improvement could be to allow users to save configurations (i.e. banned and promoted clusters) so that these can be easily retrieved, for instance using a button on the remote, without users going each time through the whole process of filtering the recommendation list.

References

1. Akaike, H.: A new look at the statistical model identification. IEEE Transactions on Automatic Control 19(6), 716–723 (1974)
2. Barbieri, M., Ceccarelli, M., Mekenkamp, G., Nesvadba, J.: A Personal TV Receiver with Storage and Retrieval Capabilities. In: Proceedings of workshop on personalization in future TV, 8th Conference on User Modeling (2001)
3. Bonnici, S.: Which Channel Is That On? A Design Model for Electronic Programme Guides. In: Proceedings of the 1st European Conference on Interactive Television: from Viewers to Actors? pp. 49–57 (2003)
4. Cotter, P., Smyth, B.: Personalised Electronic Programme Guides - Enabling Technologies for Digital T. Kunstliche Intelligenz, pp. 37–40 (2001)
5. Das, D., Horst, H.: Recommender Systems for TV. In: Proceedings of 15th AAAI Conference (1998)
6. Gómez-Ballester, E., Micó, L., Oncina, J.: A Fast Approximated k-Median Algorithm. In: Caelli, T., Amin, A., Duin, R.P., Kamel, M.S., de Ridder, D. (eds.) SPR 2002 and SSPR 2002. LNCS, vol. 2396, pp. 725–733. Springer, Heidelberg (2002)
7. Jameson, A.: More than the sum of its members: Challenges for group recommender systems. In: Proceedings of the International Working Conference on Advanced Visual Interfaces, pp. 48–54 (2004)
8. Krumm, J., Shafer, S., Wilson, A.: How a Smart Environment Can Use Perception. Workshop on Sensing and Perception for Ubiquitous Computing, part of UbiComp conference (2001)
9. Masthoff, J.: Group Modeling: Selecting a Sequence of Television Items to Suit a Group of Viewers. User Modeling and User-Adapted Interaction 14(1), 37–85 (2004)
10. O'Connor, M., Cosley, D., Konstan, J.A., Riedl, J.: PolyLens: A Recommender System for Groups of Users. In: Proceedings of the seventh European Conference on Computer Supported Cooperative Work, pp. 199–218 (2001)
11. Pelleg, D., Moore, A.: X-means: Extending K-means with Efficient Estimation of the Number of Clusters. In: Proceedings of the Seventeenth International Conference on Machine Learning, pp. 727–734 (2000)
12. Taylor, A., Harper, R.: Switching on to switch off: An analysis of routine TV watching habits and their implications for electronic program guide design. UsableiTV, pp. 7–13 (2001)
13. Thawani, A., Gopalan, S., Sridhar, V.: Viewing characteristics based personalized ad streaming in an interactive TV environment. In: First IEEE Consumer Communications and Networking Conference, pp. 483–488 (2004)
14. Zhiwen, Y., Xingshe, Z., Yanbin, H., Jianhua, G.: TV Program Recommendation for Multiple Viewers Based on user Profile Merging. Journal User Modeling and User-Adapted Interaction 16(1), 63–82 (2006)
15. Zuo, F., de With, P.H.N.: Real-time Embedded Face Recognition for Smart Home. In: IEEE Transactions on Consumer Electronics (2005)

Feature-Weighted User Model for Recommender Systems⋆

Panagiotis Symeonidis, Alexandros Nanopoulos, and Yannis Manolopoulos

Aristotle University, Department of Informatics, Thessaloniki 54124, Greece
{symeon, alex, manolopo}@csd.auth.gr

Abstract. Recommender systems are gaining widespread acceptance in e-commerce applications to confront the "information overload" problem. Collaborative Filtering (CF) is a successful recommendation technique, which is based on past ratings of users with similar preferences. In contrast, Content-Based filtering (CB) assumes that each user operates independently. As a result, it exploits only information derived from document or item features. Both approaches have been extensively combined to improve the recommendation procedure. Most of these systems are hybrid: they run CF on the results of CB and vice versa. CF exploits information from the users and their ratings. CB exploits information from items and their features. In this paper, we construct a feature-weighted user profile to disclose the duality between users and features. Exploiting the correlation between users and features we reveal the real reasons of their rating behavior. We perform experimental comparison of the proposed method against the well-known CF, CB and a hybrid algorithm with a real data set. Our results show significant improvements, in terms of effectiveness.

1 Introduction

Recommender systems are gaining widespread acceptance in e-commerce and other world wide web applications to confront the "information overload" problem. It is recognized that user modeling plays the main role in the success of these systems [2]. A robust user model should handle several real life problems such as, the sparsity of data, the over-specialization, the shallow analysis of content, the unwillingness of users to fill in their profile and so on.

Collaborative Filtering (CF) and memory-based (nearest-neighbor) algorithms in particular, are successful recommendation techniques. They are based on past ratings of users with similar preferences, to provide recommendations [5]. However, this technique introduces certain shortcomings. If a new item appears in the database, there is no way to be recommended before it is rated. On the other hand, if a user's taste is unusual, he can not find neighbors, and gets inaccurate recommendations.

In contrast, Content-Based filtering (CB) assumes that each user operates independently. As a result, CB exploits only information derived from document or

---

⋆ This paper is supported by a national GSRT PABET-NE project.

C. Conati, K. McCoy, and G. Paliouras (Eds.): UM 2007, LNAI 4511, pp. 97–106, 2007.
© Springer-Verlag Berlin Heidelberg 2007

item features (e.g., terms or attributes). A pure content-based system faces the problem of over-specialization [2], where a user is restricted to seeing items similar to those already rated. It also suffers from possible shallow analysis of content.

Recently, CB and CF have been combined to improve the recommendation procedure. Most of these hybrid systems are process-oriented: they run CF on the results of CB and vice versa. CF exploits information from the users and their ratings. CB exploits information from items and their features. However being hybrid systems, they miss the interaction between user ratings and item features. In this paper, we construct a feature-weighted user profile to disclose the duality between users and features. Moreover, exploiting the correlation between users and features we reveal the actual reasons of their rating behavior. For instance, in a movie recommender system, a user prefers a movie for various reasons, such as the actors, the director or the genre of the movie. All these features affect differently the choice of each user. Our approach correlates user ratings with item features bringing to surface the actual reasons of user preferences.

Our contribution is summarized as follows: (i) We construct a novel feature-weighted user model, which discloses the duality between users and features, (ii) based on Information Retrieval, we include the Term Frequency Inverse Document Frequency (TFIDF) weighting scheme in CF, (iii) we propose a new top-N generation list algorithm based on features frequency and (iv) we perform extensive experimental results with the internet movies database (imdb) and MoviesLens data sets, which demonstrate the superiority of the proposed approach.

The rest of this paper is organized as follows: Section 2 summarizes the related work, whereas Section 3 contains the analysis of the examined factors. The proposed approach is described in Section 4. Experimental results are given in Section 5. Finally, Section 6 concludes this paper.

2   Related Work

In 1994, the GroupLens system [5] implemented a CF algorithm based on common users preferences. Nowadays, this algorithm is known as user-based CF, because it employs users' similarities for the formation of the neighborhood of nearest users. In 2001, another CF algorithm was proposed. It is based on the items' similarities for neighborhood generation [7]. This algorithm is denoted as item-based or item-item CF, because it employs items' similarities for the formation of the neighborhood of nearest users.

The content-based approach has been studied in the information retrieval (IR) community. It assumes that each user operates independently. It exploits only information derived from documents or item features (eg. terms or attributes). There are two basic subproblems in designing a content filtering system: (i) It is the user profile construction and (ii) the document representation. In 1994, Yan et al. [8] implemented a simple content-based filtering system for internet news articles (SIFT).

There have been several attempts to combine CB with CF. The Fab System [2], measures similarity between users after first computing a profile for each user. This process reverses the CinemaScreen System [6] which runs CB on the results of CF. Melville et al. [4] used a content-based predictor to enhance existing user data, and then to provide personalized suggestions though collaborative filtering. Finally, Xin Jin et al. [3] proposed a Web recommendation system in which collaborative and content features are integrated under the maximum entropy principle.

All the aforementioned approaches are hybrid: they either run CF on the results of CB or vice versa. CF considers the dependency between user ratings, but misses the dependency between item features. CB considers the latter, but not the former. Since hybrid approaches run CB and CF separately, they miss the existed dependency between user ratings and item features. Our model, discloses the duality between user ratings and item features, to reveal the actual reasons of their rating behavior. Moreover, we introduce a scheme to weight features, according to their impact on users preferences. Thus, similarity between users is measured with respect to the dominant features in their profiles.

3 Examined Factors

In this section, we provide details for the examined factors that are involved in CF algorithms. Table 1 summarizes the symbols that are used in the sequel.

Table 1. Symbols and definitions

Symbol	Definition	Symbol	Definition
k	number of nearest neighbors	N	size of recommendation list
P_τ	threshold for positive ratings	$\mathcal{F}_u$	set of features correlated with user u
$\mathcal{U}$	domain of all users	$W(u,f)$	the correlation of user u on feature f
$\mathcal{F}$	domain of all features	$R(u,i)$	the rating of user u on item i
$\mathcal{I}$	domain of all items	W	the weighted user-feature matrix
u, v	some users	R	the user-item ratings matrix
i	some items	P	the user-feature matrix
f	some features	F	the item-feature matrix

Neighborhood size: The number, k, of nearest neighbors used for the neighborhood formation is important because it can affect substantially the system's accuracy. In most related works, k has been examined in the range of values between 10 and 100. The optimum k depends on the data characteristics (e.g., sparsity). Therefore, CF and CB algorithms should be evaluated against varying k, in order to tune it.

Positive rating threshold: It is evident that recommendations should be "positive", as it is not success to recommend an item that will be rated with, e.g., 1 in 1-5 scale. Thus, "negatively" rated items should not contribute to the increase of accuracy. We use a rating-threshold, P_τ, to recommended items whose rating is not less than this value. If we do not use a P_τ value, then the results become misleading.

Train/Test data size: There is a clear dependence between the training set's size and the accuracy of CF and CB algorithms [7]. Therefore, these algorithms should be evaluated against varying training data sizes.

Recommendation list's size: The size, N, of the recommendation list corresponds to a tradeoff: With increasing N, the absolute number of relevant items (i.e., recall) is expected to increase, but their ratio to the total size of the recommendation list (i.e., precision) is expected to decrease. In related work [7], N usually takes values between 10 and 50.

Evaluation Metrics: Several metrics have been used for the evaluation of CF and CB algorithms. We focus on widely accepted metrics from information retrieval. For a test user that receives a top-N recommendation list, let R denote the number of *relevant recommended items* (the items of the top-N list that are rated higher than P_τ by the test user). We define the following:

- *Precision* is the ratio of R to N.
- *Recall* is the ratio of R to the total number of relevant items for the test user (all items rated higher than P_τ by him).

Notice that with the previous definitions, when an item in the top-N list is not rated at all by the test user, we consider it as *irrelevant* and it counts negatively to precision (as we divide by N). In the following we also use $F_1 = 2 \cdot$ recall $\cdot$ precision$/($recall $+$ precision$)$. F_1 is used because it combines both the previous metrics.

4   Proposed Methodology

The outline of our approach consists of four steps:

1. The content-based user profile construction step: It constructs a content-based user profile from both collaborative and content features.
2. The feature-weighting step: We quantify the affect of each feature inside the user's profile(find important intra-user features) and among the users (find important inter-users features).
3. The formation of user's neighborhood algorithm: To provide recommendations, we create the user's neighborhood, calculating the similarity between each user.
4. The top-N list generation algorithm: We provide for each test user a Top-N recommendation list based on the most frequent features in his neighborhood.

In the following, we analyze each step in detail. To ease the discussion, we will use the running example illustrated in Figure 1a, where I_{1-6} are items and U_{1-4} are users. The null (not rated) cells are presented with dash. Moreover, in Figure 1b, for each item we have four features that describe its characteristics.

4.1   The Content-Based User Profile Construction

We construct a feature profile for a user from both user ratings and item features. In particular, for a user u who rated positively (above P_τ) some items, we build a feature profile to find his favorite features.

In particular, matrix $R(u,i)$ denotes the ratings of user u on each item i. We use a boolean matrix F, where $F(i,f)$ element is one, if item i contains feature

	I_1	I_2	I_3	I_4	I_5	I_6
U_1	-	4	-	-	5	-
U_2	-	3	-	4	-	-
U_3	-	-	-	-	-	4
U_4	5	-	3	-	-	-

	F_1	F_2	F_3	F_4
I_1	0	1	0	0
I_2	1	1	0	0
I_3	0	1	1	0
I_4	0	1	0	0
I_5	1	1	1	0
I_6	0	0	0	1

	F_1	F_2	F_3	F_4
U_1	2	2	1	0
U_2	1	2	0	0
U_3	0	0	0	1
U_4	0	2	1	0

(a)   (b)   (c)

Fig. 1. (a) User-Item matrix R, (b) Boolean Item-Feature matrix F (c) User-Feature matrix P

f and zero otherwise. In our running example, matrices R and F are illustrated in Figures 1a and 1b, respectively. For a user u, his profile is constructed with matrix $P(u,f)$, with elements given as follows:

$$P(u, f) = \sum_{\forall R(u,i) > P_\tau} F(i, f) \qquad (1)$$

Therefore, $P(u,f)$ denotes the correlation between user u and feature f. Notice that we use only the positively rated items i (i.e., $R(u,i) > P_\tau$) by user u.

In our running example (with $P_\tau = 2$), we construct the P matrix by combining information from R and F matrices. As we can see in Figure 1c, the new matrix P reveals a strong similarity (same feature preferences) between users U_1 and U_4. This similarity could not be derived from the corresponding user ratings in the R matrix.

4.2   The Feature-Weighting of the User Profile

Let $\mathcal{U}$ be the domain of all users and $\mathcal{F}_u$ the set of features that are correlated with user u, i.e., $\mathcal{F}_u = \{f \in \mathcal{F} \mid P(u,f) > 0\}$. Henceforth, user u and feature f are correlated when $P(u,f) > 0$.

We will weight the features of matrix P, in order to find (i) those features which better describe user u (describe the $\mathcal{F}_u$ set) and (ii) those features which better distinguish him from the others (distinguishing him from the remaining users in the $\mathcal{U}$ domain). The first set of features provides quantification of intra-user similarity, while the second set of features provides quantification of inter-user dissimilarity.

In our model, motivated from the information retrieval field and the TFIDF scheme [1], intra-user similarity is quantified by measuring the frequency of each feature f for a user u. Henceforth, this factor is referred as *Feature Frequency* (FF) factor. Furthermore, inter-user dissimilarity is quantified by measuring the inverse of the frequency of a feature f among all users. Henceforth, this factor is referred as *Inverse User Frequency*(IUF) factor.

Thus, *Feature Frequency* $FF(u,f)$ is the number of times feature f occurs in the profile of user u. In our model, it holds that $FF(u,f) = P(u,f)$. The *User*

Frequency $UF(f)$ is the number of users in which feature f occurs at least once. Finally, the *Inverse User Frequency* $IUF(f)$ can be calculated from $UF(f)$ as follows:

$$IUF(f) = \log \frac{|\mathcal{U}|}{UF(f)}. \tag{2}$$

In Equation 2, $|\mathcal{U}|$ is the total number of users. The *Inverse User Frequency* of a feature is low, if it occurs in many users' profiles, whereas it is high, if the feature occurs in few users profiles. Finally, the new weighted value of feature f for user u is calculated as following:

$$W(u, f) = FF(u, f) * IUF(f) \tag{3}$$

This feature weighting scheme represents that a feature f is an important indexing element for user u, if it occurs frequently in it. On the other hand, features which occur in many users' profiles are rated as less important indexing elements due to the low inverse user frequency.

In our running example, the matrix P of Figure 1c is transformed into the matrix W in Figure 2a. As it can be noticed in matrix P, features F_1 and F_2 for user U_1 have the same value, equal to two. In contrast, in matrix W, the same features are weighted differently (0.60 and 0.24). It is obvious now that feature F_1 for user U_1 is an important discriminating feature, whereas this could not be noticed in matrix P.

	F_1	F_2	F_3	F_4
U_1	0.60	0.24	0.30	-
U_2	0.30	0.24	0	-
U_3	-	-	-	0.60
U_4	0	0.24	0.30	-

(a)

	U_1	U_2	U_3	U_4
U_1	-	0.96	0	1
U_2	0.96	-	0	1
U_3	0	0	-	0
U_4	1	1	0	-

(b)

Fig. 2. (a) weighted User-Feature matrix W (b) User-User similarity matrix

4.3   The User's Neighborhood Formation

To provide recommendations, we need to find similar users. In our model, as it is expressed by equation 4, we apply cosine similarity in the weighted user-feature W matrix. We adapt cosine similarity to take into account only the set of features, that are correlated with both users. Thus, in our model the similarity between two users is measured as follows:

$$sim(u, v) = \frac{\sum_{\forall f \in X} W(u, f)W(v, f)}{\sqrt{\sum_{\forall f \in X} W(u, f)^2} \sqrt{\sum_{\forall f \in X} W(v, f)^2}}, X = \mathcal{F}_u \cap \mathcal{F}_v. \tag{4}$$

In our running example, we create a user-user matrix according to equation 4, where we can find the neighbors of each user (those which have the higher value, are the nearest ones). In Figure 2b, we can see that the nearest neighbor of user U_2 is U_4 with similarity 1, and U_1 follows with similarity value 0.96.

4.4   The Top-N List Generation

The most often used technique for the generation of the top-N list, is the one that counts the frequency of each positively rated item inside the found neighborhood, and recommends the N most frequent ones. Our approach differentiates from this technique by exploiting the item features. In particular, for each feature f inside the found neighborhood, we add its frequency. Then, based on the features that an item consists of, we count its weight in the neighborhood. Our method, takes into account the fact that, each user has his own reasons for rating an item.

In our running example, assuming that we recommend a $top - 1$ list for U_2 (with k=2 nearest neighbors), we work as follows:

1. We get the nearest neighbors of U_2: $\{U_4, U_1\}$
2. We get the items in the neighborhood: $\{I_1, I_3, I_5\}$
3. We get the features of each item: I_1: $\{F_2\}$, I_3: $\{F_2, F_3\}$, I_5: $\{F_1, F_2, F_3\}$
4. We find their frequency in the neighborhood: $fr(F_1)$=1, $fr(F_2)$=3, $fr(F_3)$=2
5. For each item, we add its features frequency finding its weight in the neighborhood: $w(I_1) = 3$, $w(I_3) = 5$, $w(I_5) = 6$.

Thus, I_5 is recommended, meaning that it consists of features that are prevalent in the feature profiles of U_2's neighbors.

5   Performance Study

In this section, we study the performance of our feature-weighted user model against the well-known CF, CB and a hybrid algorithm, by means of a thorough experimental evaluation. For the experiments, the Featured-Weighted User Model is denoted as FWUM, the collaborative filtering algorithm as CF and the content-based algorithm as CB. Finally, as representative of the hybrid algorithms, we have implemented a state-of-the-art algorithm, the Cinemascreen Recommender Agent [6], denoted as CFCB. Factors that are treated as parameters, are the following: the neighborhood size (k, default value 10), the size of the recommendation list (N, default value 20) and the size of train set (default value 75%). The metrics we use are recall, precision, and F$_1$. P_τ threshold is set to 3. Finally, we consider the division between not hidden and hidden data. For each transaction of a test user we keep the 75% as hidden data (the data we want to predict) and use the rest 25% as not hidden data (the data for modeling new users).

The extraction of the content features has been done through the well-known internet movie database (imdb). We downloaded the plain imdb database (ftp.fu-berlin.de - October 2006) and selected 4 different classes of features (genres, actors, directors, keywords). In the imdb database there are 28 different movie genres (Action, Film-Noir, Western etc.), 32882 different keywords referring to movie characteristics, 121821 directors and 1182476 actors and actresses (a movie can be classified to more genres or keywords). We joined the aforementioned data with one real data set that has been used as benchmark in prior work. In particular, we used the 100K MovieLens [5] data set with 100,000 ratings assigned by 943 users on 1,682 movies. The range of ratings is between 1(bad)-5(excellent) of the numerical scale. The joining process lead to 23 different genres, 9847 keywords, 1050 directors and 2640 different actors and actresses (we selected only the 3 most paid actors or actresses for each movie). Finally, notice that we have validated the presented results with other real data sets (Movielens 1M and EachMovie). Due to lack of space, these results will be presented in a extended version of this work.

5.1   Comparative Results for CF Algorithms

Firstly, we compare the two main CF algorithms, denoted as user-based (UB) and item-based (IB) algorithms. The basic difference between these two CF algorithms is that, the former constructs a user-user similarity matrix while the latter, builds an item-item similarity matrix. Both of them, exploit the user ratings information(user-item R matrix). Figure 3 demonstrates that item-based CF compares favorably against user-based CF for small values of k. For large values of k, both algorithms converge, but never exceed the limit of 40% in terms of precision. The reason is that as the k values increase, both algorithms tend to recommend the most popular items. In the sequel, we will use the IB algorithm as a representative of CF algorithms.

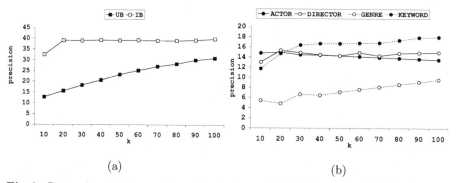

(a)   (b)

Fig. 3. Comparison in terms of precision between (a) CF algorithms (b) CB classes of features

5.2   Comparative Results of Feature Classes for CB Algorithm

As it is already discussed, we have extracted 4 different classes of features from the imdb database. We test them using the pure content-based CB algorithm to reveal the most effective in terms of accuracy. Pure CB algorithm exploits information derived only from document or item features. Thus, we create an item-item similarity matrix based on cosine similarity applied on features of items (by exploiting information only from the item-feature F matrix). In Figure 3b, we see results in terms of precision for the four different classes of extracted features. As it is shown, the best performance is attained for the "keyword" class of content features.

5.3 Comparative Results for CF, CB, CFCB and FWUM Algorithms

We test the FWUM algorithm against CF, CB and CFCB algorithms using the best options as they have resulted from the previous measurements. In Figures 4a and 4b, we see results for precision and recall. FWUM presents the best performance in terms of precision (above 60%) and recall(above 20%). The reason is two-fold:(i) the sparsity has been downsized through the features and (ii) the applied weighting-schema reveals the actual user preferences.

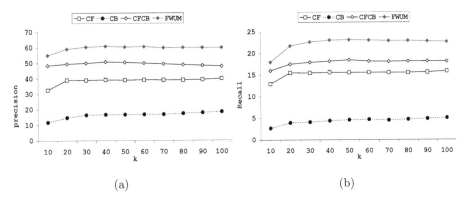

(a)   (b)

Fig. 4. Comparison between CF, CB and CFCB with FWUM in terms of (a) precision (b) recall

5.4 Examination of Additional Factors

Recommendation list's size: We examine the impact of N. The results of our experiments are depicted in Figures 5a and 5b. As expected, with increasing N, recall increases and precision decreases. Notice that the FWUM outperforms CF, CB and CFCB in all cases. The relative differences between the algorithms are coherent with those in our previous measurements.

Training/Test data size: Now we test the impact of the size of the training set. The results for the F_1 metric are given in Figure 5c. As expected, when the training set is small, performance downgrades for all algorithms. Similar to the previous measurements, in all cases FWUM algorithm is better than CF, CB and CFCB cases and low training set sizes do not affect determinatively the FWUM accuracy.

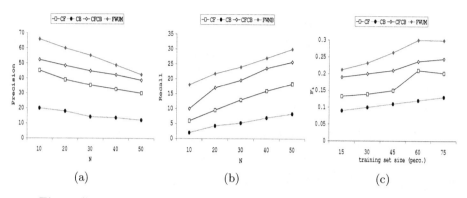

Fig. 5. Comparison vs.: (a) N precision, (b) N recall, (c) training set size

6   Conclusions

We proposed a feature-weighted user model for recommender systems. We perform experimental comparison of our method against well known CF, CB and a hybrid algorithm with a real data set. Our approach shows significant improvements in accuracy of recommendations over existing algorithms. The reason is that our approach reveals the favorite features of a user and recommends those items that are composed of these features. Summarizing the aforementioned conclusions, our feature-weighted user model is a promising approach for getting more robust recommender systems. In our future work, we will consider the fusion of different classes of features in a multivariate user model for getting more precise recommendations.

References

1. Baeza-Yates, R.A., Ribeiro-Neto, B.A.: Modern Information Retrieval. ACM Press / Addison-Wesley (1999)
2. Balabanovic, M., Y, S.: Fab: Content-based, collaborative recommendation. ACM Communications 40(3), 66–72 (1997)
3. Jin, X., Zhou, Y., Mobasher, B.: A maximum entropy web recommendation system: Combining collaborative and content features. In: Proc. ACM SIGKDD Conf., pp. 612–617 (2005)
4. Melville, P., Mooney, R.J., Nagarajan, R.: In: Proc. AAAI conf. In Content-Boosted Collaborative Filtering for improved Recommendations, pp. 187–192 (2002)
5. Resnick, P., Iacovou, N., Suchak, M., Bergstrom, P., Riedl, J.: Grouplens: An open architecture for collaborative filtering on netnews. In: Proc. Conf. Computer Supported Collaborative Work, pp. 175–186 (1994)
6. Salter, J., Antonopoulos, N.: Cinemascreen recommender agent: Combining collaborative and content-based filtering. Intelligent Systems Magazine 21(1), 35–41 (2006)
7. Sarwar, B., Karypis, G., Konstan, J., Riedl, J.: Item-based collaborative filtering recommendation algorithms. In: Proc. WWW Conf., pp. 285–295 (2001)
8. Yan, W.T., Molina, H.G.: Sift: A tool for wide-area information dissemination. In: Proc. UNSENIX Conf., pp. 177–186 (1995)

Evaluating a Simulated Student Using Real Students Data for Training and Testing*

Noboru Matsuda[1], William W. Cohen[2], Jonathan Sewall[1],
Gustavo Lacerda[2], and Kenneth R. Koedinger[1]

[1] Human-Computer Interaction Institute,
[2] Machine Learning Department,
Carnegie Mellon University
5000 Forbes Ave., Pittsburgh PA, 15217
[mazda,wcohen,sewall,gusl,koedinger]@cs.cmu.edu

Abstract. SimStudent is a machine-learning agent that learns cognitive skills by demonstration. It was originally developed as a building block of the Cognitive Tutor Authoring Tools (CTAT), so that the authors do not have to build a cognitive model by hand, but instead simply demonstrate solutions for SimStudent to automatically generate a cognitive model. The SimStudent technology could then be used to model human students' performance as well. To evaluate the applicability of SimStudent as a tool for modeling real students, we applied SimStudent to a genuine learning log gathered from classroom experiments with the Algebra I Cognitive Tutor. Such data can be seen as the human students' "demonstrations" of how to solve problems. The results from an empirical study show that SimStudent can indeed model human students' performance. After training on 20 problems solved by a group of human students, a cognitive model generated by SimStudent explained 82% of the problem-solving steps performed correctly by another group of human students.

1 Introduction

Modeling students' cognitive skills is one of the most important research issues for Cognitive Tutors, a.k.a. Intelligent Tutoring Systems [1]. Such a model, often called a *cognitive model*, is used to assess students' performance and to provide feedback (model-tracing), to monitor progress in students' learning over the course of problem-solving, to plan instructional strategies adaptively (knowledge tracing), or simply to give a hint on what to do next [2]. Yet, developing a cognitive model is a labor-intensive task that forces even a skilled expert to work for hundreds of hours.

   We have developed a machine learning agent – called *SimStudent* – that learns cognitive skills from demonstration. SimStudent is designed to be used as an intelligent building block of a suite of authoring tools for Cognitive Tutors, called the Cognitive Tutor Authoring Tools, or CTAT [3]. Using the SimStudent technology, an author can simply demonstrate a few solutions. SimStudent generalizes those

---

* The research presented in this paper is supported by National Science Foundation Award No. REC-0537198.

C. Conati, K. McCoy, and G. Paliouras (Eds.): UM 2007, LNAI 4511, pp. 107–116, 2007.
© Springer-Verlag Berlin Heidelberg 2007

solutions and generates a cognitive model that is sufficient to explain the solutions. This cognitive model is then plugged into a Cognitive Tutor as the knowledge base for model-tracing. This way, the authors are relieved from the burden of building a cognitive model by hand.

The goal of the SimStudent project is twofold: on the engineering side, we investigate whether SimStudent facilitates the authoring of Cognitive Tutors. On the user modeling side, we explore whether the SimStudent helps us advance studies in human and machine learning.

As a step towards the first goal, we have tested SimStudent on several domains including algebra equation solving, long division, multi-column multiplication, fraction addition, Stoichiometry (chemistry), and Tic-Tac-Toe. So far, SimStudent showed a reasonable and stable performance on those test domains [4].

The goal of this paper, as an attempt to address the second goal mentioned above, is to see whether SimStudent actually models cognitive skills acquired by human students during learning by solving problems. To address this issue, we apply SimStudent to the student-tutor interaction log data (i.e., the record of activities collected while human students were learning with a computer tutor) to see whether SimStudent is able to learn the same cognitive skills that the human students learn. In other words, we consider the human students' learning log as the "demonstrations" performed by individual human students. We then train SimStudent with these demonstrations and have it learn cognitive skills. If SimStudent indeed learns cognitive skills in this way, then we would further be able to use SimStudent to investigate human students' learning by analyzing cognitive models generated by SimStudent as well as their learning processes.

The fundamental technology that supports SimStudent is inductive logic programming [5] and programming by demonstration [6]. There are studies on using a machine-learning technique for cognitive modeling and educational tools. Some studies use a machine-learning agent to learn domain principles, e.g., [7]. Some applied a machine-learning technique to model human students' behavior [8, 9], or to assess instructions [10]. Probably the most distinctive aspect of SimStudent developed for the current study is that it generates human-readable (hence editable) production rules that model cognitive skills performed by humans.

The outline of the paper is as follows. We first introduce the Cognitive Tutor that the human students used in the classroom. This gives a flavor of how human students "demonstrated" their skills to the Cognitive Tutor. We then explain how SimStudent learns cognitive skills from such demonstrations. Finally, we show results from an evaluation study on the applicability of SimStudent to the genuine student-tutor interaction log data.

2   Algebra I Cognitive Tutor

The Algebra I Tutor is a Cognitive Tutor developed by Carnegie Learning Inc. This tutor is used in real classroom situations for high school algebra at about 2000 schools nationwide in the United States [11]. For the current study, we use human students' log data collected from a study conducted in a high school in an urban area of Pittsburgh. There were 81 students involved in the study. The students used the Cognitive Tutor individually to learn algebra equation solving. There were 15 sections taught by the tutor, which covered most of the skills necessary to solve linear equations. In this paper, we only use the log data collected through the first four sections. The equations in these introductory sections only contain one unknown and the form of equation is A+B=C+D where A, B, C, and D are monomial terms (e.g., a constant R or Rx where R is a rational number).

The tutor logged the students' activities in great detail. For the current study, however, we only focus on the *problem-solving steps*, which are slightly different from *equation-transformation steps*. Explanations follow.

There are two types of problem-solving steps: (1) an *action step* is to select an algebraic operation to transform an equation into another (e.g., "to declare to add 3x to the both sides of the equation"), and (2) a *type-in step* is to do a real arithmetic calculation (e.g., "to enter –4 as a result of adding 3x to –4–3x"). By performing these problem-solving steps, a given equation is transformed as follows: a student first selects an action and then applies it to both sides of the equation. For example, for an equation shown in Fig. 1 (a), the student first selected "Add to both sides" from the pull down menu (b), which in turn prompts the student to specify a value to add (c). This completes the first problem-solving step, which by definition is an action step. The student then enters the left- and right-hand sides separately. The Fig. 1 (d) shows a moment at which the student had just typed-in the left-hand side. Thus, entering a new equation is completed in two problem-solving steps, which are both type-in steps. In sum, three problem-solving steps correspond to a single equation-transformation step that transforms an equation into another. Sometimes, however, the tutor carries out the type-in steps for the student, especially when new skills have just been introduced.

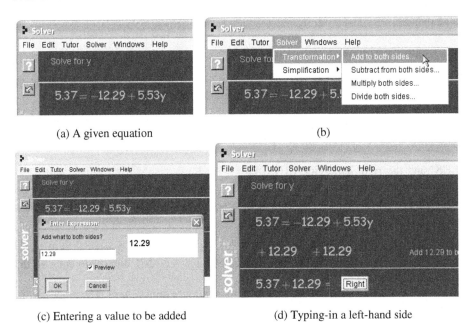

(a) A given equation   (b)

(c) Entering a value to be added   (d) Typing-in a left-hand side

Fig. 1. Screen shot from the Algebra I tutor

As mentioned above, when a student performs a problem-solving step, the tutor provides immediate feedback on it. This is possible because the tutor has a *cognitive model* of the target cognitive skills, represented as a set of production rules. Since a cognitive model usually contains production rules not only for correct steps, but also for incorrect steps, the tutor can provide situated feedback on typical errors. The student can also ask for a hint (by pressing the [?] button on the left side of the tutor window) when he/she gets stuck.

Every time a student performs a step, the tutor logs it. The log contains, among other things, (1) the equation on which the step was made, (2) the action taken (either the name of the algebraic operation selected from the menu for an action step, or the symbol "type-in" for a type-in step), (3) the value entered (e.g., the value specified to be added to the both sides for the "add" action mentioned above, or the left- and right-hand side entered for the type-in steps), and (4) the "correctness" of the step, which is either "correct" (in case the student's steps is correct), "error" (the student's steps is incorrect), or "hint" (when the student asked a hint).

3   Overview of SimStudent

This section is a brief overview of SimStudent. We first explain how SimStudent learns cognitive skills from demonstration. The double meaning of "demonstration" in the current context will then be explained – a demonstration by an author who is building a Cognitive Tutor, and a "demonstration" in a learning log made by human students. We then explain briefly how SimStudent learns a cognitive model. Due to the space limitation, we do not provide details of the learning algorithms. See [12] for more details.

3.1   Cognitive Modeling with SimStudent

Fig. 2 shows a sample interface for a Cognitive Tutor to teach algebra equation solving. In this particular tutor, equation-solving steps are represented in a simple table with three columns. The first two columns represent the left-hand side (LHS) and the right-hand side (RHS) of an equation (e.g., 41.72y + 87 = 34.57). The third column represents the name of a *skill* applied to transform an equation into another. In this tutor, an equation is

Student Interface		
Student		
LHS	RHS	Skill Operand
41.72y+87	34.57	subtract 87
41.72y	34.57-87	clt

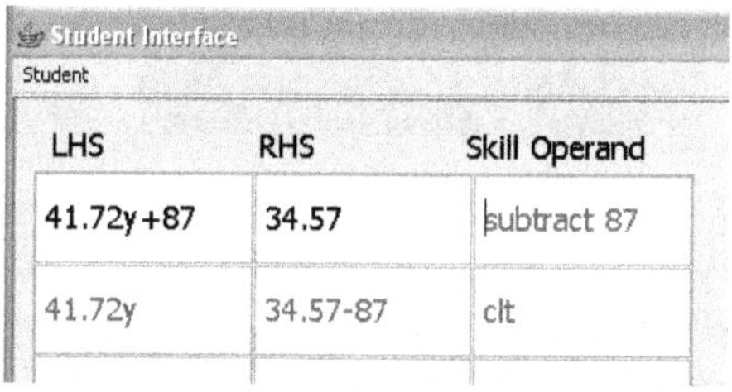

Fig. 2. A tutor interface for algebra equation solving

transformed with three *problem-solving steps* that are (1) to specify a skill, e.g., "subtract 87" from both sides, (2) to enter LHS, e.g., "41.72y", and (3) to enter RHS, e.g., "34.57–87."

A step is modeled with a tuple representing *what* was done *where*. The what-part is further decomposed into an *action* taken and a value *input* by the action. The where part is called *selection* because it is an element of the user interface that the demonstrator selected to do some action on. In summary, a problem-solving step is represented with a tuple <selection, action, input>. For example, when the demonstrator inputs "41.72y" into the LHS on the 2nd row, the tuple reads <C1R2, 41.72y, Fill_in_cell> where C1R2 represents a cell at the 1st column in the 2nd row.

SimStudent learns a single production rule for each of the problem-solving steps demonstrated. The demonstrator must specify two things when demonstrating a problem-solving step; (1) the *focus of attention*, and (2) the *skill name*. The focus of attention is a set of previous selections or the given equation. For example, in Fig. 2, the first problem-solving step, which is to enter "subtract 87," requires two elements, "41.72y+87" and "34.57," as the focus of attention. The *skill name* must be unique for unique steps and consistent throughout the demonstration. In the above example, the skill to enter "subtract 87" is called "subtract," and the skill to enter "41.72y" and "34.57-87" is "subtract-typein." The actual value entered (e.g., "subtract 87") is called an "input."

3.2 Learning Algorithm

Production rules are represented in the Jess production rules description language [13]. A production rule used in the Cognitive Tutors consists of three major parts: (1) WME-paths, (2) feature conditions, and (3) an operator sequence. The first two components construct the left-hand side of a production rule, which specifies which elements of the interface are involved in the production rule, and what conditions should hold about those elements in order for the production rule to be fired. The operator sequence constitutes the right-hand side actions of the production rule, which specifies what should be done with the interface elements to make the "input" value of the step (see the definition of the tuple in section 3.1).

SimStudent utilizes three different learning algorithms to learn three components (the WME-path, the feature conditions, and the operator sequence) separately. An example would best explain how. Suppose a step is demonstrated and named as N. Also suppose that this is the k-th *instance* of demonstration for the skill N. Let's denote this as $I(N,k)$. Let's assume that the skill N requires two elements as focus of attention, and we denote them as $<F^{N,k}_1, F^{N,k}_2>$, the elements of focus of attention for the k-th instance of the skill N.

The WME-path is a straightforward generalization of the focus of attention. The elements specified in the focus of attention are elements on the tutor interface. They can thus be uniquely identified in terms of their "location" in the interface. Suppose, for example, that the first element of focus of attention in the j-th instance of the skill N, $F^{N,j}_1$ is "a cell in the 1st column on the 2nd row." If the first element of focus of attention in the $(j+1)$-th instance $F^{N,j+1}_1$ is "a cell in the 1st column on the 3rd row," then the WME-path for the 1st element of focus of attention for the skill N would be "a cell in the 1st column at any row."

SimStudent uses FOIL [14] to learn feature conditions. The target concept is the "applicability" of the skill N given the focus of attention $<F^N_1, F^N_2>$, or in a prolog-like form $N(F^N_1, F^N_2)$. When a step $I(N,k)$ is demonstrated, it serves as a positive example for the skill N, and a negative example for all other skills. Basically, as the demonstration proceeds, the skill N has all $<F^{N,k}_1, F^{N,k}_2>$ as positive examples, and $<F^{X,k}_1, F^{X,k}_2>$ as negative examples, where X is all the other skills demonstrated. We provide FOIL with a set of *feature predicates* as the background knowledge with which to compose hypotheses for the target concept. Some examples of such feature predicates are isPolynomial(A), isNumeratorOf(A,B), isConstant(A). Once a hypothesis is found for the target concept, the body of the hypothesis becomes the feature condition in the left-hand side of the production rule. Suppose, for example, that FOIL found a hypothesis $N(F^N_1, F^N_2)$:- isPolynomial(F^N_1), isConstant(F^N_2). The left-hand side feature condition for this production rule would then say that "the value of the first focus of attention must be a polynomial and the second value must be a constant."

SimStudent applies iterative-deepening depth-first search to learn an operator sequence for the right-hand side of the production rules. When a new instance of demonstration on skill N is provided, SimStudent searches for the shortest operator sequence that derives the "input" from the focus of attention for the all instances demonstrated. Those *operators* are provided prior to learning as background knowledge.

4   Evaluation

To evaluate the applicability of the SimStudent technology to genuine real students' learning log, we conducted an evaluation study to see (1) whether SimStudent can generate cognitive models for the real students' performance, and if so (2) how accurate such models are.

The tutor interface shown in Fig. 2 is also used in the current study as a tutor interface for SimStudent to be demonstrated. It is a simple but straightforward realization of the human students' performances in a SimStudent-readable form. There is an issue on focus of attention to be mentioned here. When the human students were using the Algebra I Tutor, they did not indicate their focus of attention, and hence no information of focus of attention is stored in the log. We have presumed that both LHS and RHS are used as the focus of attention for the action steps. Likewise, for the type-in steps, we presume that the Skill Operand and the cell immediately above the cell to be typed-in are the focus of attention. So, for example in Fig. 2, if "34.57-87" is entered, which is a skill "subtract-typein", the elements "34.57" and "subtract 87" are used as the focus of attention.

4.1   Data

The students' learning log was converted into *problem files* that SimStudent can read. Each problem file contains the sequence of problem-solving steps made by a single student to solve a single problem. There were 13451 problem-solving steps performed by 81 human students. These problem-solving steps were converted into 989 problem files.

4.2   Method

We applied the following validation technique. The 81 students were randomly split into 14 groups. Each of those 14 groups were used exactly once for training and once for testing. More precisely, for the n-th validation, the n-th group is used for training and the $(n+1)$-th group is used for testing. A total of 14 validation sessions were then run.

During training, SimStudent learned cognitive skills only on those steps that were correctly performed by the human students. In other words, SimStudent learned only the correct skill applications "demonstrated" by the human students.

Because of memory limitations, we could use only as many as 20 training and 30 test problems in each of the validation sessions. To select those problems, a human student was randomly selected in a given group. If the selected human student did not have enough problem files, then more human students were selected randomly. A total of 280 training and the 420 test problems were used across the 14 validation sessions.

In a validation session, the 30 test problems were tested. The validation took place after *each* training problem on which SimStudent was trained. Since there were 20 training problems, a total of 600 tests were carried out for validation. There were 32 operators and 12 feature predicates used as the background knowledge.

4.3 Results

In two out of 14 validation sessions, we identified corrupted data and could not complete runs on these. In one validation session, not all cognitive skills discussed below appeared in the training problems. Hence there are 11 validation sessions (220 training and 330 test problems) used for the analysis discussed in the rest of the section.

Table 1. Frequency of learning for each skill appearing in the training problems. The numbers on the first row are the IDs for the validation sessions. The validation sessions and the skills are sorted by the total number.

Skill	014	010	009	004	008	011	006	003	001	005	007	Total	Ave.
divide	22	21	22	20	22	19	20	21	20	21	20	228	20.73
divide-typein	20	16	18	18	14	12	12	10	10	10	12	152	13.82
subtract	15	18	12	14	13	11	16	9	6	11	7	132	12.00
add	7	4	10	6	10	8	5	12	14	10	13	99	9.00
subtract-typein	14	16	8	12	10	6	10	4	2	4	6	92	8.36
multiply	9	10	9	6	8	11	9	10	8	6	6	92	8.36
add-typein	6	2	10	6	8	6	2	6	8	6	6	66	6.00
multiply-typein	6	8	4	6	2	6	4	4	6	6	2	54	4.91
Total	99	95	93	88	87	79	78	76	74	74	72	915	83.18

4.3.1 Learning Opportunities

There were 12 skills involved in the training problems. Eight of them are action skills and another four are type-in skills. Four out of the eight action skills were learned in only a very few training problems and they did not appear in all validation sessions. Therefore, we have excluded those skills from the analysis. In sum, there are four action skills and four type-in skills included in the current analysis. Table 1 shows the frequency of learning for each of those skills. The skills add, subtract, multiply, and divide are action skills. The skill add, for example, is to add a term to both sides. The skill add-typein is for a type-in step that follows the step "add." Note that those eight skills are the most basic skills used to solve simple equations.

4.3.2 Learning Curve Analysis

To analyze how SimStudent's learning improved over the time, we measured the "accuracy" of production rules on the test problems. Each time learning was completed on a training problem, each of the steps in the 30 test problems were model-traced using the production rules available at that moment. An attempt at model-tracing is defined to be *successful* when there is a production rule with the LHS conditions that hold and the RHS operator sequence generates an "input" that matches the step.

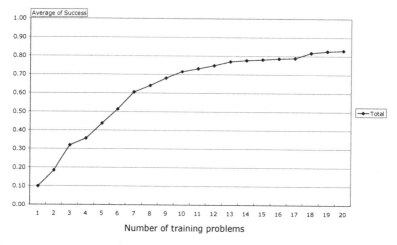

Fig. 3. Overall performance improvement in terms of the average ratio of successful model-tracing aggregated across all validation sessions and the (eight) skills. The x-axis shows the number of training problems.

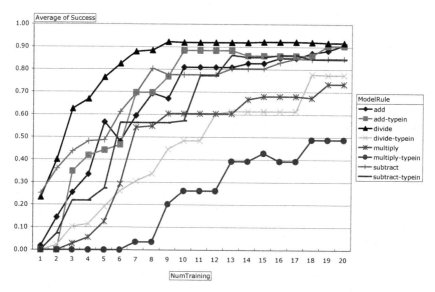

Fig. 4. Learning curve on individual skills. The learning curve shown in Fig. 3 is decomposed into individual skills.

Fig. 3 shows the learning curves aggregated across all eight skills and averaged across the 11 validation sessions. Fig. 4 shows the learning curve for the individual skills. Overall, SimStudent learned skills quite well. After training on 20 problems, the ratio of successful model-tracing reached at least 73% on most of the skills. However, some skills were not exactly learned as well as the other skills – it seems to be difficult to learn the skill "multiply-typein." It turned out that not all skills had the same number of opportunities to be learned. Different training problems have different solution steps, and hence contain a different number of instances for each of the skills to be demonstrated.

Fig. 5 shows how the accuracy of model-tracing grew as SimStudent had more and more opportunities to learn individual skills. The x-axis shows the *frequency of learning* (in contrast to the number of problems demonstrated). The y-axis shows the *overall average of the average ratio* of successful model-tracing aggregated from the beginning when a certain number of instances of learning occurred. That is, this graph shows how quickly (or slowly) the learning occurred. For example, even when two skills ended up with having the same performance rate (e.g., the skills "add" and "add-typein" shown in Fig. 4), it can be read from Fig. 5 that the skill "add-typein" reached its final performance quickly within only 5 instances of demonstration.

The four action skills, add, subtract, multiply, and divide, were learned at the same rate. Different type-in skills had different rates and the quality of the production rules (i.e., the accuracy of model-tracing) varied significantly. We have yet to investigate the reason for the variation in the learning rate of these skills.

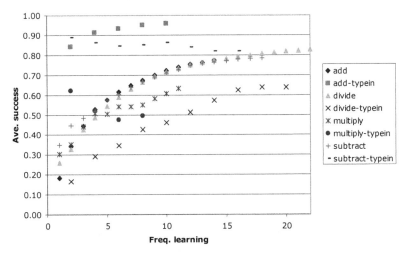

Fig. 5. Average of the average ratio of successful model-tracing in the first *x* opportunities for learning. For example, for the skill "add," the average success ratio for the first 3 learning opportunities were .18, .50, and .64. Therefore, on the above graph, the value for the 3rd plot for add is .44.

5   Conclusion

We have shown that SimStudent can indeed model human students' performances from their learning activity log. The accuracy of model-tracing based on the cognitive model generated by SimStudent reached 83% after training on 20 problems performed by human students.

As long as the human students exhibit correct performances (i.e., the performances are consistent), even when they have variations in strategy and representations, SimStudent can generate a cognitive model that is consistent with the human students' (correct) performances. We have yet to improve the learning ability of

SimStudent so that the human students' incorrect behaviors can be modeled. This is one of the important issues to be addressed in the future.

The above finding on the ability of SimStudent to model real students' performance suggests potential ways to expand the applicability of SimStudent. For example, if we can model human students' erroneous performances as well, then it might be possible to predict human students' performance on novel problems. Technically speaking, modeling "incorrect" performances does not differ greatly from modeling a "correct" performance, as long as the human student makes a systematic error (based on a stable misconception). The real challenge would then be how to deal with the inconsistent behaviors (e.g., guess, slip, or even gaming).

References

1. Greer, J.E., McCalla, G.: Student modelling: the key to individualized knowledge-based instruction, vol. x, p. 383. Springer-Verlag, Berlin, New York (1994)
2. Anderson, J.R., et al.: Cognitive tutors: Lessons learned. Journal of the Learning Sciences 4(2), 167–207 (1995)
3. Aleven, V., et al.: The Cognitive Tutor Authoring Tools (CTAT): Preliminary evaluation of efficiency gains. In: Ikeda, M., Ashley, K.D., Chan, T.W. (eds.) Proceedings of the 8th International Conference on Intelligent Tutoring Systems, pp. 61–70. Springer Verlag, Berlin (2006)
4. Matsuda, N., et al.: Applying Machine Learning to Cognitive Modeling for Cognitive Tutors, in Machine Learning Department Technical Report (CMU-ML-06-105), School of Computer Science, Carnegie Mellon University: Pittsburgh, PA (2006)
5. Muggleton, S., de Raedt, L.: Inductive Logic Programming: Theory and methods. Journal of Logic Programming 19-20(Suppl.1), 629–679 (1994)
6. Lau, T.A., Weld, D.S.: Programming by demonstration: an inductive learning formulation. In: Proceedings of the 4th international conference on Intelligent user interfaces, pp. 145–152. ACM Press, New York, NY (1998)
7. Johnson, W.L., et al.: Integrating pedagogical agents into virtual environments. Presence 7(6), 523–546 (1998)
8. Baffes, P., Mooney, R.: Refinement-Based Student Modeling and Automated Bug Library Construction. Journal of Artificial Intelligence in Education 7(1), 75–116 (1996)
9. Merceron, A., Yacef, K.: A web-based tutoring tool with mining facilities to improve learning and teaching. In: Proceedings of the 11th International Conference on Artificial Intelligence in Education, Hoppe, U., Verdejo, F., Kay, J.(eds.), pp. 201–208 (2003)
10. Mertz, J.S.: Using A Simulated Student for Instructional Design. International Journal of Artificial Intelligence in Education 8, 116–141 (1997)
11. Koedinger, K.R., Corbett, A.: Cognitive Tutors: Technology Bringing Learning Sciences to the Classroom. In: Sawyer, R.K. (ed.) The Cambridge Handbook of the Learning Sciences, pp. 61–78. Cambridge University Press, New York, NY (2006)
12. Matsuda, N., Cohen, W.W., Koedinger, K.R.: Applying Programming by Demonstration in an Intelligent Authoring Tool for Cognitive Tutors. In: AAAI Workshop on Human Comprehensible Machine Learning (Technical Report WS-05-04), AAAI association: Menlo Park, CA, pp. 1–8 (2005)
13. Friedman-Hill, E.: Jess in Action: Java Rule-based Systems, Greenwich, CT: Manning (2003)
14. Quinlan, J.R.: Learning Logical Definitions from Relations. Machine Learning 5(3), 239–266 (1990)

Modeling Students' Natural Language Explanations

Albert Corbett, Angela Wagner, Sharon Lesgold, Harry Ulrich, and Scott Stevens

Human-Computer Interaction Institute, Carnegie Mellon University, Pittsburgh, PA, USA
{corbett,awagner,slesgold}@cmu.edu, {hgu,sms}@cs.cmu.edu

Abstract. Intelligent tutoring systems have achieved demonstrable success in supporting formal problem solving. More recently such systems have begun incorporating student explanations of problem solutions. Typically, these natural language explanations are entered with menus, but some ITSs accept open-ended typed inputs. Typed inputs require more work by both developers and students and evaluations of the added value for learning outcomes has been mixed. This paper examines whether typed input can yield more accurate student modeling than menu-based input. This paper examines the application of Knowledge Tracing student modeling to natural language inputs and examines the standard Knowledge Tracing definition of errors. The analyses indicate that typed explanations can yield more predictive models of student test performance than menu-based explanations and that focusing on semantic errors can further improve predictive accuracy.

1 Introduction

Intelligent tutoring systems that support problem solving activities in math, science and programming have been shown to yield large achievement gains in real world classrooms [1], [2], [3]. More recently, intelligent tutoring systems have emerged that provide feedback and advice on student self-explanations in problem solving. These systems reflect extensive cognitive science research showing that self-explanation is a highly effective learning strategy [4], [5]. Intelligent tutors have been developed that support student explanations of worked problem-solving examples [6] and student explanations of their problem solving steps [7]. These environments employ menu-based input of student explanations, but intelligent tutoring environments are emerging that employ open-ended type-in interfaces for natural language input [8], [9], [10], [11] and one system has emerged that supports student's typed explanations of geometry problem solving steps [12].

Students' self-explanations not only improve learning outcomes, but hold the promise of improved student modeling. Student modeling algorithms have been developed for problem solving intelligent tutors that can track student learning and accurately predict learning outcomes [13], [14], [15], [16]. Student explanations may provide the grist to achieve greater predictive accuracy, since they are similar to "talk aloud" protocols employed to analyze human reasoning in cognitive science research. This paper reports an initial study of student knowledge modeling based on student explanations. The study employs an Algebra Model Analysis task that is employed in several Cognitive Math Tutors [17]. In this task students are given worked algebraic

C. Conati, K. McCoy, and G. Paliouras (Eds.): UM 2007, LNAI 4511, pp. 117–126, 2007.
© Springer-Verlag Berlin Heidelberg 2007

models of real-world problem situations and are asked to describe what each hierarchical component of the symbolic model represents in the real world. We recently reported a summative evaluation that compared two versions of this task, one in which students select their descriptions from a menu and one in which they type their descriptions [18]. That study examined the impact of menu-based vs. typed explanations on learning time and learning outcomes. The two tutor versions provided step-by-step feedback and advice upon request in both conditions, but did not monitor the students' changing knowledge state as they worked through the fixed problem set. In this paper we retroactively examine the tutor logfiles that were generated in the study to ask two questions about modeling student knowledge based on student explanations: (1) Do the two interfaces lead to comparable student modeling accuracy? (2) Can we achieve greater modeling accuracy by focusing on semantic errors and ignoring more superficial errors. In the following sections, we describe the algebra model analysis task, briefly describe the Knowledge Tracing student modeling algorithm employed in Cognitive Tutors and describe the study itself.

2 Algebra Modeling

The Algebra Model Analysis Tool is employed in Cognitive Tutor Algebra and Pre-Algebra courses. A major objective in these courses is to introduce students to algebraic modeling of real-world problem situations. An example situation is:

> The Pine Mountain Resort is expanding. The main lodge holds 50 guests.
> The management is planning to build cabins that each hold 6 guests.

This situation can be represented as a linear function with two co-varying quantities, the number of cabins and the total number of guests in the resort. Many Cognitive Tutor units in the Pre-Algebra and Algebra courses engage students in generating Algebraic expressions to model situations, in this example, $Y = 6X + 50$. The Model Analysis Tool is a tutor unit that essentially provides worked examples of such modeling problems. The tutor presents both the problem situation and an algebraic model of it and asks the student to describe the mapping from the hierarchical components of the algebra model to the components of the situation.

Fig. 1 displays the menu-based Model Analysis Tool near the end of the Pine Mountain problem. The tutor was seeded with the problem description and algebra model at the top of the screen and with the six hierarchical components of the algebra model down the left side of the screen (50, 6, X, 6X, 6X+50, Y). The six text fields were initially blank and the student filled them with menu selections. For instance, the student selected "The number of guests in all the cabins" to describe 6X. Students receive immediate accuracy feedback on the menu entries they select and can ask for help on selecting the menu entries.

The Model Analysis Tool has proven effective in both Algebra and Pre-Algebra courses [17]. It yields large student learning gains both in describing model components, and more importantly, in generating algebraic models of problem situations. In a recent study we compared two versions of the Model Analysis Tool. One condition employed the basic Model Analysis Tool with menu-based entry and the second condition employed a new ALPS (Active Learning in Problem Solving) version that is designed to more closely simulate an interaction with a human tutor. In the ALPS version of the tutor unit, students type their descriptions instead of selecting them from a menu and receive feedback and hints via a video tutor window, as displayed on the right in Fig. 1. In the study, [18] students completed a pretest, a fixed set of tutor problems, a posttest and a transfer test. This summative evaluation yielded three main results: (a) students finished the fixed problem set faster in the menu-based condition than in the ALPS condition; (b) there were no reliable differences between the two conditions in pretest-posttest learning gains; and (c) students in the ALPS condition performed better than students in the menu condition on the transfer task in which students described algebraic models of problem situations with novel structures.

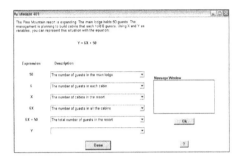 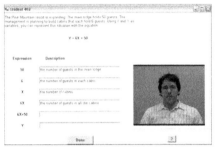

Fig. 1. The menu-based Model Analysis Tool (left) and Type-in Model Analysis Tool (right)

In this paper we retroactively apply the Cognitive Tutor Knowledge Tracing algorithm to the logfiles of students' problem-solving performance in the two tutor versions, to estimate individual differences in students' knowledge based on their explanations and to examine how accurately the model predicts individual differences in students' test performance.

3 Knowledge Tracing

The cognitive modeling framework underlying Cognitive Tutors assumes that knowledge can be represented as a set of independent production rules. Knowledge Tracing assumes a simple two-state learning model. Each production rule is either in the learned state or the unlearned state and a rule can make the transition from the unlearned to the learned state at each opportunity to apply the rule in problem solving. Each time the student has the opportunity to apply one of the cognitive rules during problem solving, the tutor employs a simple Bayesian algorithm to update an estimate of the probability that the student knows the rule, contingent on whether the student's action is correct or incorrect. The learning and performance assumptions that underlie Knowledge Tracing also predict the probability that a student will apply a production rule successfully, and Knowledge Tracing has been shown to accurately predict individual differences in test performance across students [15].

In this paper we compare two variations on Knowledge Tracing. First, we apply the standard Knowledge Tracing algorithm to student explanations in the menu-based interface and the ALPS type-in interface and compare how well the student knowledge estimates predict student test performance. In a second comparison, we modify the operational definitions of a "correct response" and "error" in student modeling. Standard Knowledge Tracing tracks whether the student's first action at each problem solving step is correct or an error (with a hint request being equivalent to an error). The student may make multiple errors at a step before generating a correct action, but only the first action at a problem solving step is traced. However, in the current Model Analysis unit, student self-explanation errors include relatively minor surface form errors as well as serious semantic errors. As a result, we examined whether we can obtain more accurate student modeling predictions from student explanations by tracking not just the student's first explanation action at each step, but by tracking whether or not the student makes any substantial semantic error in the course of generating a correct description.

4 Study Design

Fifty-three students enrolled in the 7th, 8th or 9th grade completed this study for pay. Students completed six problems in a Model Analysis Tutor unit. Each problem presented a real-world problem situation and corresponding slope-intercept form algebraic model ($Y = MX+B$) and students entered descriptions of what each of the hierarchical components of the equation represented in the real-world situation. Twenty-eight students completed these problems with a menu-based tutor, and 25 typed descriptions in their own words in the ALPS tutor. Students received accuracy feedback on each explanation and could request hints on entering each description.

   Three comparable paper-and-pencil tests were constructed, each containing two problems. The first problem presented a statement of a real-world situation and students were asked to both solve three arithmetic questions and to generate a symbolic model of the situation. The second problem was analogous to the tutor problems. It presented a problem statement and slope-intercept form symbolic model of the situation and students wrote descriptions what each of the symbolic components represented in the situation. Students completed one test as a pretest, one as a midtest after three tutor problems and one as a posttest after finishing the tutor problems. The order in which these three test forms were presented was counterbalanced across students.

   A paper-and-pencil transfer test with four problems was designed to examine whether students' skill in describing equation components generalizes to novel problem structures. For example, one problem presented a problem situation that was modeled with a distributive form Algebraic model, $Y = 4(X - 1) + 10$.

   Six canonical component descriptions for the Pine Mountain Resort problem are:

50	The number of guests in the main lodge.
6	The number of guests in each cabin.
X	The number of cabins.
6X	The number of guests in all the cabins.
6X+50	The total number of guests in the main lodge and all the cabins.
Y	The total number of guests in the resort.

In the ALPS self-generation condition, students were not required to type canonical descriptions, but were required to type descriptions that unambiguously referenced the appropriate component of the problem situation. The ALPS tutor employed a key-word matching algorithm to process student entries and observed these principles: (a) synonyms were accepted (e.g., people for guests); (b) syntax was not enforced if the meaning could be inferred; (c) the description of the rate constant M (6 in the example) required a synonym of "each," as shown above; (d) the description of the MX product (6X in the example) required a variation of "all" as shown above; (e) the description of Y required some synonym of "total," as in "total guests"; and (f) the MX+B expression could be described in the same way as Y or as the sum of MX and B, as shown above. The ALPS version of each problem distinguished among an average of 47 error categories. Each error category was associated with a feedback messages, except for an "uninterpretable" error category. In the menu-based version of the Model Analysis Tool, the menu was seeded with three incorrect entries along with the six correct entries. The three incorrect entries for each problem were selected from common errors that had been observed previously, for example, the ambiguous description "the number of guests in cabins."

5   Results

Two human judges categorized the descriptions students typed in the ALPS condition and met to resolve disagreements in their coding. The tutor accurately categorized 90% of the descriptions as either correct or incorrect. More specifically, it correctly accepted 84% of the students' correct descriptions and correctly rejected 98% of the incorrect descriptions. Among the incorrect descriptions the tutor accurately rejected, 82% were assigned to the correct error category, while 18% were assigned to the wrong error category. We briefly examine the raw descriptions students enter in the menu-based and type-in conditions, then examine the success of knowledge tracing in predicting student test performance.

5.1   Error Patterns and Error Coding

Each student entered 36 descriptions in the curriculum (6 descriptions in each of 6 problems). In these analyses a hint request is counted as equivalent to an error. Average student accuracy was almost identical in the two conditions, by two measures. Students in the menu-based condition entered 25.1 descriptions correctly on their first attempt, while students in the type-in condition entered 25.4 descriptions correct on their first attempt. Student in the menu-based condition averaged 28.3 total mistakes in entering the 36 descriptions and students in the type-in condition averaged 27.1 total mistakes.

For purposes of analysis, we can group the multiple error types into the following broader categories:

- Applying a correct description of a symbolic model component to the wrong component of the model, e.g., describing 6x as "the number of guests in each cabin";
- Entering a component description that might be clear in a real-life conversation, but is ambiguous out of context. Specifically, the description "The number of guests in cabins" is ambiguous with respect to 6 (the rate constant) and 6X";

- Entering a description in which the quantity was omitted, e.g., "The total amount";
- Entering a description which only referenced a quantity noun, e.g., "the guests";
- Entering a description of a mathematical term rather than its mapping to the problem situation, e.g., describing X as "a variable";
- Entering a mapping description that employed mathematics, e.g., describing 6X as "the number of guests in each cabin times the number of cabins";
- Othr errors, for instance referring to a component that would exist in the problem situation but is irrelevant to the problem, for instance, a reference to "rooms".

Several patterns in the raw data suggest that students in the menu-based condition are thinking less deeply about the descriptions, as discussed in the following three sections.

Confusing the Independent and Dependent Quantity. The X variable represents the independent quantity, e.g., the number of cabins. Four of the other five descriptions describe the dependent quantity, e.g., the total number of guests, or an additive component (e.g., the number of guests in the main lodge). Confusing these two quantities, i.e., applying the X description "number of cabins" to any of these four components, or vice versa, is a fundamental semantic error. Students in the ALPS condition averaged 1.5 such errors across the six problems, while students in the menu condition averaged 3.9.

Ambiguity. The description "The number of guests in the cabins" is ambiguous between the rate constant M (the number of guests in each cabin) and MX product (the number of guests in all cabins). In the ALPS condition, students generated this error an average of 3.6 times across the six problems. These students were attempting to describe either M or MX 91% of the time. In the menu condition, students entered this error an average of 5.8 times, but only 54% of these errors were actually attempts to describe either M or MX.

Hints. The previous results could suggest that students in the menu-based condition are more deeply confused about the mappings between the symbolic model and the problem situation, but students in the ALPS condition were far more likely to ask for help. Students in the ALPS condition averaged 8.2 help requests while students in the menu condition only averaged 1.0 help requests.

This overall pattern of errors and hint requests suggests that students are more likely to "game the system" in the menu condition and simply try one menu entry after another until finding a correct one. So there is a preliminary reason to suspect that student performance with menu-based explanations may be less predictive of test performance than student performance in the ALPS type-in condition.

5.2 Knowledge Tracing and Predicting Test Performance

We fit two versions of the Knowledge Tracing model that varied in their definitions of an error to both the menu-based and type-in tutor, for a total of four fits. In the first, "standard" Knowledge Tracing version, we strictly coded whether the student made any type of error or asked for help on the first attempt at a description and ignored subsequent errors or help requests on that step. In the second "semantic" Knowledge Tracing version, we monitored all errors at each step and traced whether the student made any substantial semantic error or asked for a hint before generating a correct description, while ignoring other errors. Our definition of semantic errors included just the first two categories in the list of seven above. These are complete descriptions that either are wrong or blur an essential distinction among model components. We excluded the other error categories as superficial form errors, addressing the wrong goal (e.g., describing X as a variable), or too incomplete to draw a strong conclusion about the student's intended meaning.

The cognitive model consisted of six production rules, one for each of the six types of component descriptions. Each student had six opportunities to apply each of the rules, one opportunity per problem. The Knowledge Tracing model assumes two learning parameters (the probability students already know the rule before the first opportunity to apply it and the probability of learning the rule at each opportunity to apply it) and two performance parameters (the probability of a slip in applying a known rule and the probability of guessing correctly if the rule is not known). We employed a curve fitting program to generate a set of best-fitting group estimates of these learning and performance parameters for each of the six rules in each of the four fits (two interface conditions crossed with two error definitions). We used the best-fitting estimates to trace each student's data and generate a probability estimate that the student knew each of the six rules in the cognitive model at the conclusion of problem solving. We computed the product of these probabilities to obtain a single measure of a student's knowledge across the six rules, by analogy with [15]. Finally, we correlated this estimate of each student's knowledge of linear algebraic models with (a) the student's average post-test performance, (b) the student's performance on each of the three post-test questions (numeric, model generation and model description), (c) the students average transfer test performance and (d) the student's performance on each of the four problems on the transfer test.

Standard Knowledge Tracing: Type-In Vs. Menu. Table 1 displays the predictive validity of the standard Knowledge Tracing model in the ALPs type-in condition and menu-based condition. Each cell contains the correlation coefficient (r) obtained in correlating the model's estimate of each student's knowledge with four measures of the student's posttest performance (accuracy on each of the three separate questions and mean accuracy across the questions) and five measures of the student's transfer test performance (accuracy on each of the four separate problems and mean accuracy across the problems). For the Type-in group, correlation coefficients ≥ 0.40 are significant at the 0.05 level, as are menu group correlation coefficients ≥ 0.37 in Tables 1 and 2. As can be seen, the fit is better (higher correlation coefficient) in the ALPS type-in condition than in the menu-entry condition for all the comparisons except transfer problem 2. We computed a t-test across just the seven individual questions and this difference is reliable, $t = 2.38$, $p = 0.05$. We computed pairwise tests for the significance of the difference in correlation coefficients for independent samples across all nine measures. For the posttest question which asks students to generate a symbolic model of a problem situation, the difference in correlations coefficients, 0.61 vs. 0.21 is marginally reliable $z = 1.70$, $p < 0.1$.

Table 1. Predictive Validity of the Standard Knowledge Tracing model based on the student's first description at a problem solving step. Each cell shows the correlation coefficient (r) for predicted test accuracxy and actual test accuracy across students.

	Post Test				Transfer Test				
	Mean	Num	Gen	Desc	Mean	1	2	3	4
Type-in	0.67	0.66	0.61	0.42	0.61	0.51	0.19	0.46	0.65
Menu	0.41	0.33	0.21	0.41	0.38	0.39	0.34	0.25	0.33

Semantic Knowledge Tracing: Type-In Vs. Menu. Table 2 displays the predictive validity of the semantic Knowledge Tracing model in the ALPS type-in condition and menu-based condition. Again, each cell contains the correlation coefficient (r) obtained in correlating the model's estimate of each student's knowledge with four measures of the student's posttest performance (accuracy on each of the three separate questions and mean accuracy across the questions) and five measures of the student's transfer test performance (accuracy on each of the four separate problems and mean accuracy across the problems). Again, the fit is better in the ALPS type-in condition than in the menu-entry condition for all the comparisons except transfer problem 2. We computed a t-test across just the seven individual questions and this difference is significant, $t = 2.40$, $p = 0.05$. We again computed pairwise tests for the significance of the difference in correlation coefficients for independent samples across all nine measures. For the posttest question in which students are asked to generate a symbolic model of a problem situation, the difference in correlations coefficients, 0.73 vs. 0.27 is reliable $z = 2.23$, $p < 0.05$.

Table 2. Predictive Validity of the Knowledge Tracing model based on whether a student makes any substantial semantic error at a problem solving step. Each cell shows the correlation coefficient (r) for predicted test acuracy and actual test accuracy across students.

	Post Test				Transfer Test				
	Mean	Num	Gen	Desc	Mean	1	2	3	4
Type-in	0.76	0.67	0.73	0.52	0.73	0.54	0.36	0.57	0.70
Menu	0.51	0.41	0.27	0.50	0.52	0.49	0.44	0.40	0.39

Student Modeling Error Definition. The first rows of Table 1 and Table 2 display the correlation coefficients for the ALPS condition under the two error definitions. As can be seen, the correlation coefficient is higher for the semantic Knowledge Tracing model than for the standard Knowledge tracing model for all nine correlations. This small but consistent difference is reliable in a t-test across just the seven individual questions, $t = 3.95$, $p < 0.01$. We computed pairwise tests for the significance of the difference in correlation coefficients for correlated samples across all nine measures and none is reliable. The second rows of the tables display the correlation coefficients for the menu condition under the two error definitions. Again, the correlation coefficient is higher for the semantic model than for the standard model for all nine correlations. This consistent difference is reliable in a t-test across the seven individual questions, $t = 7.86$, $p < 0.01$. We computed pairwise tests for the significance of the difference in correlation coefficients for correlated samples across all nine measures. The difference for mean transfer test performance, 0.73 vs. 0.52 is marginally reliable, t = 2.00, p < .10 as is the difference in correlation coefficients for transfer problem 3, 0.57 vs. 0.40, t = 2.02 p < .10.

6 Conclusion

The analysis of raw error patterns suggested that there is a tendency for students in the menu-based condition, to game the system, trying one menu entry after another until finding a correct description. This pattern raises suspicions that the menu-based interface may yield less accurate predictions of student test performance. The results of the Knowledge Tracing analysis confirmed these suspicions. Each of the two Knowledge Tracing versions predicted test performance more accurately in the ALPS type-in condition than in the menu-based condition. There is a further interesting trend in the data. The difference in predictive accuracy between the two interface conditions is almost non-existent for the posttest model-description questions, which are identical to the tutor task. Instead, the differences emerge most strongly for parts of the transfer test and for the posttest model generation question, which is itself a type of transfer task. This suggests that the ALPS interface is tapping students' deep semantic knowledge that supports such transfer. These results suggest that the substantial extra effort required to develop type-in interfaces and the additional effort required of students in typing rather than selecting explanations can pay off in better modeling and consequently more valid individualization by the tutor.

The second analysis revealed that in both interface conditions, the semantic Knowledge Tracing model that tracks whether a student makes any substantial semantic error in generating a correct description yields consistently better predictive accuracy than the standard Knowledge Tracing model that tracks whether a student makes any kind of error on the first attempt at generating a description. This study employs a fairly simple model of deep and superficial errors and suggests that additional research in defining the content of student errors could yield additional improvements in predictive accuracy. Student explanations should be particularly useful for examining this issue, since the student's behavior is intended to be a direct report of what the student is thinking.

Acknowledgement. This research was supported by National Science Foundation Grant EIA0205301 "ITR: Collaborative Research: Putting a Face on Cognitive Tutors: Bringing Active Inquiry into Active Problem Solving."

References

1. Anderson, J.R., Corbett, A.T., Koedinger, K.R., Pelletier, R.: Cognitive tutors: Lessons learned. The Journal of the Learning Sciences 4, 167–207 (1995)
2. Koedinger, K., Anderson, J., Hadley, W., Mark, M.: Intelligent tutoring goes to school in the big city. International Journal of Artificial Intelligence in Education 8, 30–43 (1997)

3. VanLehn, K., Lynch, C., Schulze, K., Shapiro, J.A., Shelby, R., Taylor, L., Treacy, D., Weinstein, A., Wintersfill, M.: The Andes Physics Tutoring System: Five years of evaluations. In: Proceedings of AIED 2005: The 12th International Conference on Artificial Intelligence and Education, pp. 678–685 (2005)

4. Atkinson, R., Derry, S., Renkl, A., Worthman, D.: Learning from examples: Instructional principles from the worked examples research. Review of Educational Research 70, 181–214 (2000)

5. Chi, M.T.H., Bassok, M., Lewis, M., Reimann, P., Glaser, R.: Self-explanations: How students study and use examples in learning to solve problems. Cognitive Science 13, 145–182 (1989)

6. Conati, C., VanLehn, K.: Toward computer-based support for meta-cognitive skills: A computational framework to coach self-explanation. International Journal of Artificial Intelligence in Education 11, 398–415 (2000)

7. Aleven, V.A., Koedinger, K.R.: An effective metacognitive strategy: Learning by doing and explaining with a computer-based Cognitive Tutor. Cognitive Science 26, 147–179 (2002)

8. Graesser, A.C., Person, N., Harter, D.: The TRG: Teaching tactics and dialog in AutoTutor. International Journal of Artificial Intelligence in Education, 12, 257–279 (2001)

9. Rose, C.P., Jordan, P.W., Ringenberg, M., Siler, S., Vanlehn, K., Weinstein, A.: Interactive conceptual tutoring in Atlas-Andes. In: Proceedings of AIED 2001: The 10th International Conference on Aritifical Intelligence and Education, pp. 256–266 (2001)

10. Khuwaja, R.A., Evens, M.W., Michael, J.A., Rovick, A.A.: Architecture of CIRCSIM-tutor. In: Proceedings of the 7th Annual IEEE Computer-Based Medical Systems Symposium, vol. 3, pp. 158–163 (1994)

11. Zinn, C., Moore, J., Core, M.: A three-tier planning architecture for managing tutorial dialogue. In: Proceedings of the 6th International Intelligent Tutoring Systems Conference, pp. 574–584 (2002)

12. Aleven, V., Koedinger, K.R., Popescu, O.: A tutorial dialogue system to support self-explanation: Evaluation and open questions. In: Proceedings of AIED 2003: The 11th International Conference on Artificial Intelligence and Education, pp. 39–46 (2003)

13. Arroyo, I., Woolf, B.P.: Inferring learning and attitudes from a Bayesian Network of log file data. In: Proceedings of AIED 2005: The 12th International Conference on Artificial Intelligence and Education, pp. 33–40 (2005)

14. Conati, C., Gertner, A., VanLehn, K.: Using Bayesian networks to manage uncertainly in student modeling. User Modeling and User-Adapted Interaction 12(4), 371–417 (2002)

15. Corbett, A.T., Anderson, J.R.: Knowledge Tracing: Modeling the Acquisition of Procedural Knowledge. User Modeling and User-Adapted Interaction 4, 253–278 (1995)

16. Shute, V.: SMART Evaluation: Cognitive diagnosis, mastery learning & remediation. In: Proceedings of AIED 1995: The 7th World Conference on Artificial Intelligence and Education, pp. 125–130 (1995)

17. Corbett, A., Wagner, A., Raspat, J.: The Impact of analysing example solutions on problem solving in a pre-algebra tutor. In: Proceedings of AIED 2003: The 11th International Conference on Artificial Intelligence and Education, pp.133–140 (2003)

18. Corbett, A.T., Wagner, A., Lesgold, S., Ulrich, H., Stevens, S.: The impact on learning of generating vs. selecting descriptions in analyzing algebra example solutions. In: Proceedings of the 7th International Conference of the Learning Sciences, pp. 99–105 (2006)

Applications for Cognitive User Modeling

Marcus Heinath, Jeronimo Dzaack, Andre Wiesner, and Leon Urbas

Center of Human-Machine-Systems - Technische Universität Berlin
{marcus.heinath,jeronimo.dzaack,andre.wiesner}@zmms.tu-berlin.de
Institute of Automation - Technische Universität Dresden
leon.urbas@tu-dresden.de

Abstract. Usability of complex dynamic human computer interfaces can be evaluated by cognitive modeling to investigate cognitive processes and their underlying structures. Even though the prediction of human behavior can help to detect errors in the interaction design and cognitive demands of the future user the method is not widely applied. The time-consuming transformation of a problem "in the world" into a "computational model" and the lack of fine-grained simulation data analysis are mainly responsible for this. Having realized these drawbacks we developed HTAmap and SimTrA to simplify the development and analysis of cognitive models. HTAmap, a high-level framework for cognitive modeling, aims to reduce the modeling effort. SimTrA supports the analysis of cognitive model data on an overall and microstructure level and enables the comparison of simulated data with empirical data. This paper describes both concepts and shows their practicability on an example in the domain of process control.

Keywords: usability evaluation, human computer interaction, cognitive modeling, high-level description, analysis.

1 Introduction

Recent introductions of new information technologies in the range of dynamic human-machine systems (e.g. process control systems in the chemical industry or airplane cockpits) have led to increasing cognitive requirements caused by a shift from operation of processes to the management of processes. This calls for user interfaces which are characterized by a high complexity and a high degree of dynamics. Because of the integrated functionality and the complex data structures, these interfaces require more cognitive information processing. One aim is to design systems which support the cognitive demands of users.

Cognitive modeling seems to be a good candidate for this purpose and makes it possible to understand cognitive aspects of human behavior in a more specific way than empirical or heuristic methods. But despite the promising potential, this method is still rarely used in industrial research departments. The main reasons are time and cost efforts for developing and analyzing cognitive models caused by a lack of support tools and by sophisticated knowledge in both cognitive psychology as well as artificial intelligence programming [9].

C. Conati, K. McCoy, and G. Paliouras (Eds.): UM 2007, LNAI 4511, pp. 127–136, 2007.
© Springer-Verlag Berlin Heidelberg 2007

Having realized this drawback we present HTAmap (Hierarchical Task Mapper) and SimTrA (Simulation Trace Analyzer), two new approaches to simplify the development and analysis of cognitive models and thereby reducing costs and time. HTAmap provides two key features: firstly, it uses a plain high-level description based on appropriate task analysis methods. Secondly, it supports the reuse of cognitive model components based on cognitive activity pattern. SimTrA provides applications to extract and process cognitive model data on an overall and microstructure level. It allows to analyze cognitive model data and to compare the data with empirical data afterwards. Both are part of a series of software tools within an integrated modeling environment for analyzing, implementing, and validating cognitive models.

2 Potentials and Constraints of Cognitive Modeling

Cognitive architectures incorporate psychological theories (e.g. visual information processing, decision making, motor commands) and empirically based representations about aspects of human cognition. There is general agreement that these cognitive aspects are relatively constant over time and relatively task-independent [11]. Therefore, cognitive architectures present these aspects in a software framework to explain and predict human behavior in a detailed manner. In this context, a cognitive model can be seen as an application of a cognitive architecture to a specific problem domain with a particular knowledge set.

Building a cognitive model, the modeler must describe cognitive mechanisms in a highly-detailed and human-like way. Two levels of cognitive architectures can be differentiated [17]. High-level architectures (e.g., [3]) describe behavior on a basic level and define interactions as a static sequence of human actions. Low-level architectures (e.g. ACT-R, SOAR or EPIC, for an overview see [2]) describe human behavior on an atomic level. They allow a more detailed insight into cognitive processes than high-level architectures. Most low-level architectures use production systems to simulate human processing and cognition. The use of independent production rules allows cognitive models to react on external stimuli (bottom-up processes) and to model interruption and resumption of cognitive processes in contrast to high-level architectures which are usually controlled top-down. The research presented in this paper uses the cognitive architecture ACT-R [1].

In a practical application cognitive models can be used to evaluate the usability of prototypes. This helps to detect errors in the interaction design of interfaces and gives indications about the cognitive demands of the future user. Cognitive models extend classical usability methods and expand the repertoire by cognitive aspects. However, this method is seldom employed in usability research and development because of a lack of support tools for creating and analyzing cognitive models.

2.1 Development Effort for Cognitive Models

Various authors (e.g. [4], [9], [17]) analyzed the cognitive modeling process in detail, together with the necessary subtasks and requirements. Transformation of task knowledge into the computational description of the cognitive architecture is challenging and requires extensive programming experience. The resulting high cost/benefit ratio is an important constraint on the practical application. The real bottleneck lies in the preliminary task analysis process and is caused by the differential level of task decomposition and formalization. Task analysis methods formalize knowledge about cognitive processes with a greater degree of abstraction and formalization compared to low-level modeling approaches such as ACT-R. For example, an operator "read button" at the level of task analysis corresponds to a complex sequence of production rules in ACT-R (e.g. retrieve-position, find-position, attend-position, read and store results). It is up to the cognitive modeler to fill the "transformation-gap" between the high-level task description and low-level cognitive modeling implementation. A current topic in the cognitive research community is to minimize this gap with the development of high-level languages to model human cognition based on low-level cognitive architecture (for an overview of current approaches see [15]). The main objectives are to simplify the model-building process and to improve concepts for sharing and reusing model components [4].

2.2 Analyzing Effort for Simulation Data

Most low-level simulation experiments use global information to analyze the model and its fit to empirical data (e.g. errors or times). Two problems are connected with this procedure. Firstly, in order to validate that a current cognitive model acts like a human, not only the results of a cognitive model and the human have to be the same, but also the kind of computations to achieve the results [19]. Secondly, cognitive models can predict the same behavior but can differ in underlying sub-processes. With the psychological theories implemented in low-level cognitive architectures a more detailed analysis of cognitive model data is possible to enrich the explanatory power of cognitive models. This makes it possible to analyze the kind of computations that lead to a result and to determine the level of correctness of the cognitive model. For this purpose fine-grained patterns can be detected in the simulation data to enrich the explanatory power of cognitive models (e.g., sequence of actions). For example, the arrangement and the appearance of elements of an interface can be evaluated with respect to theories of eye-movement or signal detection. But using cognitive models reveals some problems. Cognitive architectures and models are incomplete and describe only a small part of the processes that are responsible for human cognition. Reasons for this are the partial knowledge of internal cognitive processes in cognitive science and the insufficient implementation of all cognitive aspects that are needed to handle a task. Aspects like esthetics, boredom, fun or personal preferences which can be observed in empirical settings are not implemented [2]. When analyzing and comparing cognitive model data with empirical data, these difference have to be taken into account. So far, no tools exist for the extraction of fine-grained information from model data for the evaluation of user interfaces.

3 Integrated Environment for Cognitive Modeling and Analysis

To reduce the effort for developing cognitive models in ACT-R and to support the analysis of simulation and empirical data in a systematic way, HTAmap (Hierarchical

Task Mapper) and SimTrA (Simulation Trace Analyzer) were developed. The placement of HTAmap and SimTrA within the general cognitive modeling process (consisting of the four steps: task analysis, empirical data collection, model implementation and validation) is shown in Figure 1. On the following pages the concepts, paradigms and first implementations of HTAmap and SimTrA are described in detail.

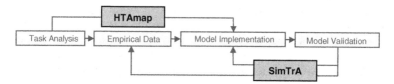

Fig. 1. Placement of HTAmap and SimTrA within the general cognitive modeling process

3.1 HTAmap

Building cognitive models is not easy and involves a strong process of synthesis, i.e. building a new solution by putting parts together in a logical way. For developing cognitive models in ACT-R this implies programming in a "cognitive assembly language". Behavior is expressed in terms of production-rules that manipulate knowledge expressed in declarative memory elements. To open cognitive modeling for a wider user group and make the developing task easier and more accessible, HTAmap addresses (1) a structured formalization method to minimize the "transformation-gap" between the high-level and low-level approaches of cognitive modeling, and (2) programming paradigms with more immediate results. These can be achieved by model reuse, domain-oriented paradigms and model adaptation.

3.1.1 Pattern-Oriented Cognitive Modeling

HTAmap provides cognitive modeling based on predefined and modifiable "cognitive activity patterns" (CAP) so that much of the cognitive model building process is transformed to a pattern-oriented modification task. A CAP represents a generally valid solution for execution of a task using cognitive resources to tackle a recurrent problem in a specific context. Building cognitive models composed of CAPs require a preliminary structured task analysis. For this purpose the "sub-goal template (SGT)" method [13] is used. The SGT method extends the "hierarchical task analysis (HTA)" method [18] by providing a nomenclature for stereotypical operator tasks. Four steps are essential (see Figure 2 left): the (1) initial task/subtask decomposition to the point where (2) "information-handling operations" (IHO) are recognized, followed by the (3) strategic decomposition and the (4) redescription in terms of sub-goal templates. Information handling operations are divided into three classes: receiving (IHO_R), evaluating (IHO_E) and acting on information (IHO_A). The identified IHOs are redescribed as predefined operator tasks regarding one of the four sub-goal templates: (A)ct, (E)xchange, (N)avigate and (M)onitor. In addition, the SGT method defines the plan in which IHOs are sequenced relative to each other (i.e. fixed, free, parallel or contingent sequence) and specifies information requirements needed by an operator needs to carry out tasks during operation of a technical system.

The redescription to the level of SGTs is the starting point for the HTAmap approach (see Figure 2 left). "Cognitive activity patterns" (CAP) were used to solve the high to low level mapping-problem. Within HTAmap, CAPs add a layer between a higher-level behavior specification in terms of SGTs and the lower-level behavior specification in terms of ACT-R. Examples of CAPs are scan, observe, monitor, execute or regulate (for an overview and a definition of operator activities see [10]). Compound CAPs (cCAP) are composed by setting relations between elementary CAPs (eCAP). In general, the presented CAP approach allows the transition of IHOs into the less abstract level of ACT-R. In detail, a CAP comprises the necessary ACT-R declarative and procedural structures and provides interfaces for parameterization regarding various task environments and flows of execution. To summarize, with HTAmap cognitive models are described at a meta description level and composed by parameterized CAPs and relations between them.

3.1.2 Formalization and Implementation

The CAPs are implemented using a specific notation based on the "Extensible Markup Language (XML)" standard. The notation specifies semantic information about the pattern, descriptions of functionality in terms of ACT-R primitives, the relations to other CAPs and a structured documentation. The CAP implementation concept provides reusable and task independent components, i.e. generic cognitive behavior blocks in the form of associated production rules and the specification of domain dependent components within one structure. The latter offers possibilities to parameterize the CAPs regarding particular task situations. The HTAmap-model represents the meta-description of an ACT-R model concerning its associated high-level task model defined by elementary and compound cognitive activity patterns (eCAP/cCAP), a description of the used tasks interface elements (GUI element) and required strategies that handle the perception and action of models.

To build a cognitive model within HTAmap, the modeler selects one of the predefined CAPs stored in the CAP repository. In addition, compound CAPs are composed by their associated elementary CAPs and their relations to each other (e.g., sequencing information). Afterwards, the CAPs are parameterized on the basis of the predefined GUI elements and their associated strategies using the AGImap [20] approach. The high-level task is now specified as HTAmap-model in terms of the low-level cognitive architecture ACT-R relating to a specific task environment. The resulting HTAmap-model is transformed into specific ACT-R constructs and is executable within the cognitive framework.

3.2 SimTrA

For the analysis of cognitive model data the simulation data has to be preprocessed and provided conveniently. For this reason the simulation data of cognitive models in ACT-R is transferred into a general-purpose format for complex, hierarchically structured data (XML). This forms the basis for a general algorithm-based analysis of the interaction processes. Two levels of abstraction have to be observed in order to analyze the model's performance on the basis of the integrated psychological theories (e.g. visual perception and processing): the global structure and the microstructure level to identify the underlying processes [7]. For the global structure, aspects of the model's overall performance are analyzed (e.g. times, errors, and transition-matrices

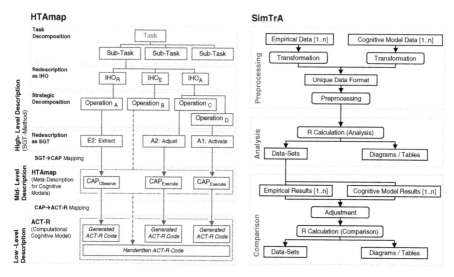

Fig. 2. Overview of the implementation concept of HTAmap (left) and SimTrA (right)

of areas of interest). The microstructure can be characterized by the sub-processes of the cognitive model, i.e. repeated short sequences of action such as control-loops, or scanpaths. For the automated simulation data analysis, algorithms are implemented and integrated in a software tool. The results are plotted as in classical usability-evaluation methods. Finally, applicability of the implemented algorithms is validated by empirical data. The model data is compared with human data regarding the quality of the underlying parameters.

3.2.1 Analyzing Cognitive Model Data

The important role of eye-movement studies in psychological and cognitive research shows that eye movement data is able to give an insight into human behavior and its underlying cognitive processes ([12], [14], [16]). Cognitive models with ACT-R can process visual information, providing spatial and temporal information of the simulated eye movement as in empirical studies. The extraction of this information provides a way to analyze and compare cognitive model data with empirical data on an global (e.g., number of fixations) and microstructure level (e.g., scanpaths). That is the reason for the implementation of SimTrA for eye-movement data (empirical and simulated). The process is divided into three steps: the (1) preprocessing of the raw data, the (2) analysis of the preprocessed data and the (3) comparison with further models or empirical data (see Figure 2 right). This allows the independent development of each module and an easy extension of its functionality in the future. The tool SimTrA enables the user to apply basal applications regarding the process of analyzing and comparing. After each step the processed data is stored in a general-purpose format and is usable with external tools (e.g. MatLab, R, SPSS). It is possible to import empirical data into SimTrA for comparison with cognitive model data.

3.2.2 Preprocessing

For the preprocessing of the raw data the empirical data and the cognitive model data are transferred into a general-purpose format (see Figure 2 right). The transformation allows processing of the data with different quality and origin (e.g. different cognitive architectures, empirical study) with the same algorithms afterwards. In this step the data is scaled to a similar resolution to ensure that it is comparable. In the cognitive data, as well in the empirical data, two similar interpolation points have to be set before the experiment and identified by the user in the plotted data to allow the algorithm to calculate the scaling-factor. After the transformation, the data is enriched by additional information that is needed for the analysis. This is done by using the preprocessing interface. The first step is finished by choosing the desired analysis methods.

3.2.3 Analysis

This module enables the analysis of the preprocessed data (see Figure 2 right). The algorithms for the analysis are implemented in R, a free tool for statistical computing. The data is analyzed and saved in datasets and as graphical plots. For example, in this step algorithms are implemented to analyze the transition frequencies [6] and the local scanpaths [8].

3.2.4 Comparison

The process ends with the comparison between the analyzed data from cognitive models or empirical studies (see Figure 2 right). This allows the rating of the simulation experiment and the simulated behavior with respect to empirical findings and psychological theories. This last step enables the iterative adjustment of cognitive models (see Figure 1). Therefore the analyzed data is revised by the user in the provided interface (e.g. missing data, insufficient data points) and compared by algorithms implemented in the software R. The evaluation is done by descriptive methods because cognitive model data do not have a high variance and statistical interference methods are not applicable.

4 Practical Application: Process Control System

The use of HTAmap and SimTrA can be illustrated by considering a user's interaction with a complex dynamic interface of a process control system (see Figure 3). The aim is to stabilize the level of liquid in a container which is moderated by inflow, outflow and evaporation.

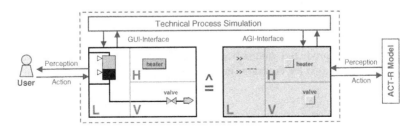

Fig. 3. Schematic representation of the empirical study and the simulation experiment with the areas of interest (AOI) for the human and the models interface

4.1 Pattern Based Modeling of the Task

In dynamic human-machine systems, the human-machine dialogue is normally based on different levels of manual and supervisory control actions. Using the SGT method the regulation task is broken down into the IHOs: get a general idea of the system state (IHO_R), evaluate the system state (especially the level of the container) (IHO_E) and, as necessary, make adjustments to control the level (IHO_A). The identified IHO_R is mapped within the HTAmap-model to the compound CAP "scan" (see Table 1). The compound CAP "scan" is composed of a sequence of elementary "observe" CAPs, executed in turn. Required task information for the "observe" CAPs are the interface elements and their values. Within the HTAmap-model the predefined "observe" CAPs are parameterized in the task environment by choosing the relevant GUI elements (i.e. valve, heater and level) and their associated perception strategies (i.e. read-button and read-level) from the particular repositories (see Figure 3). With the compound CAP "scan" two types of sequencing the "observe" CAPs have been implemented: a predefined order (fixed sequence: state-based/top-down control) and a non-defined order (free sequence: reactive/bottom-up control).

4.2 Analysis of the Simulation Trace

After simulating the user behavior by the constructed model the simulation data was analyzed by the tool SimTrA. To analyze the microstructure behavior, the local scanpaths (consistent patterns of consecutive fixations) [8] of actual perceptions were analyzed. They represent stimuli-driven bottom-up processes. Therefore the stimuli were divided in suitable areas of interest (AOI) in the first step (preprocessing): heater: H, valve: V and level: L (see Figure 3). All theoretical triples of AOIs were determined by the algorithm in the second step (analysis) whereas any sequence of fixations falling into the same AOI is treated as a single gaze fixation and the number of occurrence in the whole sequence of AOIs is assigned to them (e.g. AOIs: 1, 2 - Sequence: 2122112 - triple: 121: 1, 212: 2). Ordering these by frequency shows the most important local scanpaths. Comparing the outcomes with empirical data of a previous experiment in the last step (comparison) reveals that the important local scanpaths in model and empirical data are almost congruent [5]. Therefore local scanpaths with a frequency 3% were excluded and the remaining five important scanpaths that cover 90% of the model data were used for the comparison human - model. These scanpaths are found to be important for the subjects as well (all five scanpaths cover 80% of the subject's data) and the rank order of the first 3 empirical and predicted scanpaths is the same. The mean relative frequencies of 3 model's scanpaths are within one standard deviation of the subject's data. The mean deviation between the frequency of all scanpaths in the model and human data is about 4%. The mean deviation of predicted interaction behavior and human interaction behavior around 5 % is acceptable for decisions concerning theoretical and practical aspects.

5 Outlook

We designed HTAmap, a pattern-oriented approach for high-level description of cognitive models. Within this approach the cognitive activity patterns (CAP) are the central elements that specify a generic solution for a stereotypical operator task on the description level of ACT-R. Currently, only a selection of CAPs is specified. To transfer more "associated" production rules into CAPs, further work on verification and validation is required. An editor for building HTAmap-models is being implemented and an usability evaluation will be conducted. Further work is needed on the extension of the analysis tool SimTrA. It has to be found which additional usability related analysis algorithms can be integrated for this purpose. Subsequently a second experiment is planned where different interface designs for the task described above are tested with humans and with a cognitive model. HTAmap and SimTrA are being integrated in a cognitive modeling environment which strives to implement and analyze cognitive models. We believe that building cognitive models with the help of HTAmap makes the modeling process more accessible for a wider user group, simplifies the reuse of model fragments and improves the model communication. SimTrA enables the comparison of cognitive model behavior with human behavior on a global and a microstructure level. Both together could lead to an increased application of cognitive models in the usability evaluation of human-machine systems.

Acknowledgments. The project has been funded by Deutsche Forschungsgemeinschaft (Research Training Group 1013 prometei) and VolkswagenStiftung.

References

1. Anderson, J.R., Bothell, D., Byrne, M.D., Douglass, S., Lebiere, C., Qin, Y.: An integrated theory of the mind. Psychological Review 111, 1036–1060 (2004)
2. Byrne, M.D.: Cognitive Architectures. In: Jacko, J., Sears, A. (eds.) Handbook of Human-Computer Interaction, pp. 97–117. Lawrence Erlbaum Associates, Hillsdale, NJ (2003)
3. Card, S.K., Moran, T.P., Newell, A.: The Psychology of Human-Computer Interaction. Lawrence Erlbaum Associates, Hillsdale, NJ (1983)
4. Crossman, J., Wray, R.E., Jones, R.M., Lebiere, C.A.: High Level Symbolic Representation for Behaviour Modeling. In: Proceedings of the Conference on Behavior Representation. Arlington (2004)
5. Dzaack, J., Urbas, L.: Kognitive Modelle zur Evaluation der Gebrauchstauglichkeit von Mensch-Maschine Systemen. In: Grandt, M., Bauch, A. (eds.): Cognitive Systems Engineering in der Fahrzeug- und Prozessführung. pp. 305–318, DGLR, Bonn, (2006)
6. Ellis, S.R., Smith, J.D.: Patterns of Statistical Dependency in Visual Scanning. In: Groner, R., McConkie, G.W., Menz, C. (eds.) Eye Movement and Human Information Processing, pp. 221–238. Elsevier, Amsterdam (1985)
7. Gray, W.D., Sims, C.R., Schoelles, M.J.: Musings on Models of Integrated Cognition: What Are They? What Do They Tell Us that Simpler Approaches Cannot? How Do We Evaluate Them? In: Proceedings of the 7th ICCM, pp. 12–13, LEA, Hillsdale, NJ, (2006)
8. Groner, R., Walder, F., Groner, M.: Looking at faces: local and global aspects of scanpaths. In: Gale, A.G., Johnson, F. (eds.) Theoretical and Applied Aspects of Eye Movement Research, pp. 523–533. Elsevier, North-Holland (1984)
9. Heffernan, N.T., Koedinger, K.R., Aleven, V.A.: Tools Towards Reducing the Costs of Designing, Building, and Testing Cognitive Models. In: Proceedings of the Conference on Behavior Representation in Modeling and Simulation (2003)

10. Hollnagel, E.: Cognitive Reliability and Error Analysis Method (CREAM). Elsevier, Oxford (1998)
11. Howes, A., Young, R.M.: The role of cognitive architecture in modeling the user: Soar's learning mechanism. Human-Computer Interaction 12(4), 311–343 (1997)
12. Just, M.A., Carpenter, P.A.: Using eye fixations to study reading comprehension: Individual differences in working memory. Psychological Review 99, 122–149 (1984)
13. Ormerod, T.C., Shepherd, A.: Using Task Analysis for Information Requirements Specification: The Sub-Goal Template (SGT) Method. In: Diaper, D., Stanton, N.A. (eds.) The handbook of task analysis for human-computer interaction, pp. 347–365. Lawrence Erlbaum Associates, Mahwah, NJ (2004)
14. Rayner, K.: Do eye movements reflect higher order processes in reading? In: Groner, R., d'Ydewalle, G., Parham, R. (eds.) From Eye to Mind: Information Acquisition in Perception, Search, and Reading, pp. 179–190. Elsevier, New York (1999)
15. Ritter, F.R., Haynes, S.R., Cohen, M., Howes, A., John, B., Best, B., et al.: High-level Behavior Representation Languages Revisited. In: Proceedings of the ICCM '06. Edizioni Goliardiche, pp. 404– 407 (2006)
16. Rötting, M.: Parametersystematik der Augen- und Blickbewegungen für arbeitswissenschaftliche Untersuchungen. Shaker, Aachen (2001)
17. Salvucci, D.D., Lee, F.J.: Simple Cognitive Modeling in a Complex Cognitive Architecture. In: Proceedings of the CHI '03, pp. 265–272. ACM Press, New York (2003)
18. Shepherd, A.: Hierarchical task analysis. Taylor & friends, New York (2001)
19. Strube, G.: Cognitive Modeling: Research Logic in Cognitive Science. In: Smelser, N.J., Baltes, P.B. (eds.) International encyclopedia of the social and behavioral sciences, pp. 2124–2128. Elsevier, Oxford (2001)
20. Urbas, L., Leuchter, S.: Model Based Analysis and Design of Human-Machine Dialogues through Displays. KI – Künstliche Intelligenz, vol. 4, pp. 45–51 (2005)

Identifiability: A Fundamental Problem of Student Modeling

Joseph E. Beck and Kai-min Chang

School of Computer Science
Carnegie Mellon University
Pittsburgh, PA 15213. USA
joseph.beck@gmail.com
http://www.andrew.cmu.edu/~jb8n

Abstract. In this paper we show how model identifiability is an issue for student modeling: observed student performance corresponds to an infinite family of possible model parameter estimates, all of which make identical predictions about student performance. However, these parameter estimates make different claims, some of which are clearly incorrect, about the student's unobservable internal knowledge. We propose methods for evaluating these models to find ones that are more plausible. Specifically, we present an approach using Dirichlet priors to bias model search that results in a statistically reliable improvement in predictive accuracy (AUC of 0.620 ± 0.002 vs. 0.614 ± 0.002). Furthermore, the parameters associated with this model provide more plausible estimates of student learning, and better track with known properties of students' background knowledge. The main conclusion is that prior beliefs are necessary to bias the student modeling search, and even large quantities of performance data alone are insufficient to properly estimate the model.

1 Introduction and Motivation

The problem of student modeling, using observations of learner behavior to infer his knowledge, is a well studied one. However, the problem of accurately inferring the student's (not directly observable) mental state is challenging. Although knowledge tracing [1] claims to enable such inference, there are statistical difficulties that restrict how can we can interpret its claims. In this paper we identify this difficulty, then propose and validate a method for correcting it. First, we will provide a brief overview of knowledge tracing and identify a crucial shortcoming with the approach.

1.1 Description of Knowledge Tracing

The goal of knowledge tracing is to map student performance (observable) to an estimate of the student's knowledge (unobservable). For example, Figure 1 shows hypothetical student performance (on the left) and learning (on the right) curves. In both graphs, the x-axis represents the number of practice opportunities a student has with a particular skill. For the performance graph, the y-axis is the probability a student with that amount of practice will respond correctly. Since student performance

C. Conati, K. McCoy, and G. Paliouras (Eds.): UM 2007, LNAI 4511, pp. 137–146, 2007.
© Springer-Verlag Berlin Heidelberg 2007

is observable, this value can be directly estimated from the data. For the learning curve, the y-axis is student knowledge, which cannot be directly observed from the data. Instead, we rely on knowledge tracing to provide an estimate of the student's knowledge. Knowledge tracing infers student knowledge by first estimating four model parameters for each skill:

- K0: P(student knows the skill when he starts using the tutor)
- T: P(student learns the skill as a result of a practice opportunity)
- Slip: P(incorrect response | student knows the skill)
- Guess: P(correct response | student doesn't know the skill)

The first two parameters, *K0* and *T*, are called the learning parameters of the model and represent the student's knowledge of the skill. The final two parameters, *slip* and *guess*, are called the performance parameters in the model. They are the reason that student performance cannot be directly mapped to knowledge. Perhaps the student generated a correct response because he knew the skill, or perhaps he made a lucky guess? The *slip* and *guess* parameters account for several aspects in student performance, including lucky guesses, baseline performance for some testing formats (e.g. multiple choice tests), using partial knowledge to answer a question, using a weaker version of the correct rule to solve a problem, or even the inaccuracy from using a speech recognizer to score the student's performance [2]. All of these factors serve to blur the connection between student performance and actual knowledge.

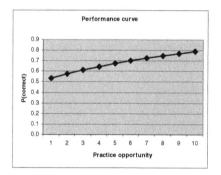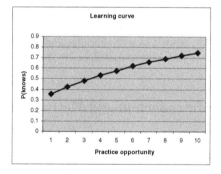

Fig. 1. Hypothetical performance and learning curves

1.2 Problems of Knowledge Tracing

Although the student performance curve can be obtained directly from the data, the learning curve must be inferred statistically. This inference would not be a problem if there were a unique, best fitting model. Unfortunately, such is not the case. Consider the three sets of hypothetical knowledge tracing parameters shown in Table 1. The *knowledge* model reflects a set of model parameters where students rarely guess, the *guess* model assumes that 30% of correct responses are due to randomness. This limit of 30% is the maximum allowed in the knowledge tracing code[1] used by the Cognitive Tutors [3]. The third model is similar to those used by Project Listen's Reading Tutor [4] for performing knowledge tracing on speech input [2]. This model's *guess* parameter is very high because of inaccuracies in the speech recognition signal. As seen in Figure 2, the three models have identical student performance[2]—somewhat surprising given that the models appear so different. The much larger surprise is that in spite of having identical performance, their estimates of student knowledge (right graph in Figure 2) are very different.

Table 1. Parameters for three hypothetical knowledge tracing models

Parameter	Model		
	Knowledge	Guess	Reading Tutor
K0	0.56	0.36	0.01
T	0.1	0.1	0.1
Guess	0.00	0.30	0.53
Slip	0.05	0.05	0.05

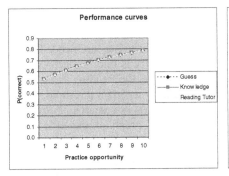
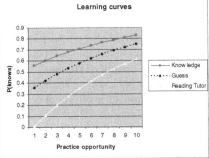

Fig. 2. Three knowledge tracing models illustrating the identifiability problem

Given the same set of performance data, we have presented three knowledge tracing models that fit the data equally well. Even if the *guess* parameter is capped at 0.3, there are still two competing models that perform equally well. In fact, the situation is considerably worse since there is an infinite family of curves that fit the data of which we are presenting three examples. Without loss of generality we will restrict the discussion to the three presented learning curves. One natural question is, given the ambiguity of the performance data in estimating the student's knowledge, which of three curves is correct? Unfortunately, the situation is more bleak: the question of which model is "correct" is not a meaningful one to ponder. All three of the sets of parameters instantiate a knowledge tracing model that fit the observed data equally

---

[1] Source code is courtesy of Albert Corbett and Ryan Baker and is available at http://www.cs.cmu.edu/~rsbaker/curvefit.tar.gz

[2] Technically the three curves are not perfectly identical, however they are equivalent under finite precision arithmetic.

well; statistically there is no justification for preferring one model over another. This problem of multiple (differing) sets of parameter values that make identical predictions is known as identifiability.

In general, researchers are not hand generating models and selecting which one fits the data. Instead we use optimization software that finds parameters that best fit our data. The optimization software's optimization method will drive which set of parameters it returns for a particular skill, and consequently the ensuing estimates of the student's knowledge—a rather odd dependency. This problem is not one of getting stuck in a local (rather than global) maximum. Rather, the space has several global maxima (for example, the three presented knowledge tracing parameter sets) all of which make different assertions about student knowledge.

1.3 Motivation

One reasonable question is why we should care about the randomness in how knowledge tracing maps observations of student performance to student internal knowledge. After all, all of the models have the same degree of model fit and make identical predictions, so what does it matter which one we select? The difficulty is that we do not train models to fit the data well, we train models to use them in actual adaptive systems. For example, the *knowledge* model predicts students will need 24 practice opportunities to master (have a greater than 95% chance of knowing) a skill, while the *Reading Tutor* model predicts 32 practice opportunities are needed. Which model's predictions should we believe? Another difficulty is tutorial decisions made on the basis of estimated student knowledge. For example, the Reading Tutor displays instruction if it believes the student's knowledge is below a certain threshold.

Another rationale is efforts at conducting learning sciences research or educational data mining. Imagine if the desired end product is a graph of the efficacy of a particular treatment when the student's knowledge is low, medium, or high. If some skills are modeled with parameters similar to *knowledge* while others are modeled with parameters similar to *guess*, the graph will not show the sharp contrast desired.

Generally, we have two desired outcomes for our student models: to accurately describe the student's knowledge and to make predictions about his behavior. In the past, some researchers have used accuracy in predicting student performance as evidence that the model was an accurate model of the student [2]. Unfortunately, given Figure 2, such claims are unwarranted as very different estimates of knowledge can predict the same performance.

2 Approach

The goal of this work is to address the identifiability problem by finding metrics that let us determine which of two equally accurate models is better, and finding a way to bias the search process to make it more likely to find such better models. Our approach is first to instantiate knowledge tracing in a graphical modeling framework. The Bayes Net Toolkit for Student Models (BNT-SM) [5] provides a framework for replicating knowledge tracing with a Bayesian network [6]. The reason for using graphical models is that they may provide a way out of our dilemma. We have more knowledge about student learning than the data we use to train our models. As cognitive scientists, we have some notion of what learning "looks like." For example, if a model suggest that a skill gets worse with practice, it is likely the problem is with the modeling approach, not that the students are actually getting less knowledgeable. The question is how can we encode these prior beliefs about learning?

2.1 Encoding Prior Beliefs as Dirichlets

Graphical models provide a means of encoding prior probabilities of the parameters in the model. A common method for representing such priors is to use the Dirichlet distribution [7]. To determine the Dirichlet priors for each parameter, we first examined histograms from our previous knowledge tracing experiments to see what values each parameter took on. We did not attempt to create Dirichlet distributions that perfectly mimicked those histograms or that minimized the sum-squared error. Our reasoning is that some of the parameter estimates were clearly nonsense. For example, approximately 10% of words had a T parameter that would result in students mastering the word after a single exposure, while 10% of the words would never be mastered. So we used the histograms as a starting point for the prior probabilities, but tempered them with our knowledge of student learning.

Figure 3 shows the prior probabilities we selected for our experiments. The x-axis is each possible value the four knowledge tracing parameters can take and the y-axis is the density of the distribution at that point. For example, the most likely value of the $K0$ parameter is 0.6; it is only about half as likely that $K0$ will take on a value of 0.45. The T parameter peaks at around 0.1, and has a long positive tail; most skills are learned relatively slowly but perhaps some are easier to acquire.

Our Dirichlets take as input two parameters that correspond to the number of positive and number of negative examples seen. The curve represents the likelihood of each possible probability value for P(positive). For example, the $K0$ curve was generated with 9 positive and 6 negative examples, which can be thought of as 9 cases of knowing the skill initially and 6 cases of not knowing the skill initially. The mean of this distribution is $9/(6+9) = 0.6$. The odds that P(knows the skill initially) (i.e. the $K0$ parameter) is 0.3 is quite low, as can be seen from the graph. If instead of 9 positive and 6 negative, we had instead created the distribution with 90 positive and 60 negative examples, the mean would still be 0.6. However, the distribution would have a much sharper peak at 0.6 and consequently a much lower variance. Thus, we control not only the mean of the distribution but also our confidence in how close most skills are to that value. For the T parameter we used 2 and 9 positive and negative examples, for the *guess* parameter 19 and 9, and for the *slip* parameter 1 and 15. The reason for the high guess rate is that we are using a speech recognizer to score student input, and is has a tendency to score incorrect reading as correct [2].

A plausible objection is there is no objective basis for preferring the numbers we used to generate these distributions and therefore this entire step should be omitted. However, skipping the step of creating a distribution is the same as asserting that the distribution is flat across the entire range of [0,1] and all possible values of the parameter are equally likely. Such an assertion seems questionable at best.

2.2   Using Dirichlets to Initialize Conditional Probability Tables

Once we have constructed a set of distributions for *K0*, *T*, *slip*, and *guess*, we use their associated parameters to initialize the conditional probability tables (CPT) in the graphical network. The CPTs keep track of counts of different types of events. For example, the Dirichlet distributions for *slip* and *guess* would be used to instantiate the CPT shown in Table 2 that maps student knowledge to expected performance.

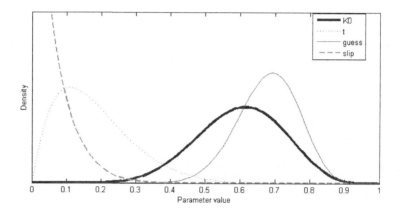

Fig. 3. Prior probabilities for knowledge tracing parameters

Table 2. Using Dirichlet priors to initialize conditional probability tables

		Knowledge	
		Doesn't know	Knows
Correct	Incorrect	9	1
	Correct	19	15

The mental model of this process is the Dirichlets are used to seed the CPT, then as actual observations accumulate those are added to the values in the CPT. Thus, if a skill has little training data available it will be biased towards the average distribution. If there are many training data, then that skill's parameters can deviate substantially from the mean. Thus the initialization step does not force parameters to have a particular value, but simply provides a bias. As mentioned previously, the number of positive and negative instances affects the shape of the distribution and consequently the amount of bias. Higher counts provide stronger bias.

3   Experimental Design and Results

The goal of our experiment is to validate whether our approach of using Dirichlet priors results in a better student model. We operationalize "better" as providing more believable estimates of the student's knowledge, without loss in predictive accuracy compared to a baseline model. Our approach is to use the BNT-SM to construct two knowledge tracing models. We constructed the first model using Dirichlet priors with the parameter values described previously. We did not examine the testing data when constructing the Dirichlet priors, and these results are for our first attempt at creating such priors (so they have not been tuned, and represent a lower bound on improvement). We constructed the second, baseline, model by initializing each parameter to be the mean value that parameter had in a previous experiment (the same data we examined to generate the Dirichlets). Note that our comparison condition is with knowledge tracing, the closest thing the student modeling community has to a standard statistical model. Furthermore, prior research with knowledge tracing estimated model parameters using conjugate gradient descent. Instead, we estimate parameters with expectation-maximization which we have found produces better parameter estimates [5]. So our baseline condition is far from a strawman.

Our data came from 360 children who were mostly between six and eight years old and who used Project LISTEN's Reading Tutor in the 2002-2003 school year. Over the course of the school year, these students read approximately 1.95 million words (as heard by the automatic speech recognizer). On average, students used the tutor for 8.5 hours. For modeling purposes, this paper treats each of the 3532 distinct English words that occurred that year as a separate skill. We had three hypotheses:

1.   The approach of using Dirichlet priors would result in a poorer model fit for the training data since the priors provide bias. We were not sure if the Dirichlet approach would better predict the testing data than the baseline.
2.   The student learning curves for the models constructed using Dirichlet priors will look more believable.
3.   The knowledge tracing parameter values obtained by the Dirichlet priors approach will better fit what is known about the domain.

To test our hypotheses, we randomly assigned students to either the train or to the test set with an approximately equal number of data in each set. To test the first hypothesis, we measured each approach's predictive accuracy using the Area Under Curve (AUC) metric for Receiver Operator Characteristic (ROC) curves. AUC is used for binary classification tasks when the true cost of each type of misclassification is unknown [8]. For the training set, both the Dirichlet and baseline had an AUC of 0.653 ± 0.002. This result contradicts our hypothesis; apparently the Dirichlet priors did not interfere with fitting the training data. For the testing set, the Dirichlet approach had an AUC of 0.620 ± 0.002 while the baseline approach had an AUC of 0.614 ± 0.002. Thus, Dirichlets resulted in a small but detectable improvement in model accuracy on unseen test data.

To test the second hypothesis, whether using Dirichlet priors would result in more plausible learning curves, we randomly selected three words that were at the 25th ("twist"), 50th ("Rome"), and 75th ("bought") percentiles for amount of training data. We then plotted the learning curves (see Figure 4) for the models derived using the Dirichlet and baseline approaches. The learning curves associated with Dirichlet priors look reasonable, while the three curves from the baseline approach do not show evidence that students learn. The Dirichlet approach asserts that students would require 24, 16, and 15 practice opportunities to master the words "bought," "Rome" and "twist," respectively. The baseline model believes those numbers should instead be 302, 5306, and 22313 practice opportunities. Reasonable people can disagree over how much practice is required for the average student to learn a word, but few people would assert that over 5000 exposures to a single word are necessary.

Perhaps these randomly selected three learning curves are not representative? These three words had an average T parameter of 0.14 in the Dirichlet approach vs. only 0.002 in the baseline approach. Across all 3532 words, both the Dirichlet and baseline approaches had an average T parameter of 0.11. However, 918 skills had a T parameter of 0.002 or lower in the baseline, compared to 0 such skills for the Dirichlet approach. Thus, roughly ¼ of words with the baseline approach were learned as slowly as those shown in the right graph compared to none with the Dirichlet.

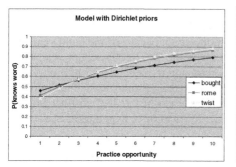 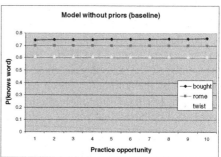

Fig. 4. Comparing learning curves for Dirichlet vs. baseline approach

Testing the third hypothesis, whether Dirichlet priors enabled knowledge tracing parameter estimates that better fit with domain knowledge, was more problematic. What do "better" parameter values look like? Except in gross circumstances, such as Figure 4, it is hard to distinguish what makes one set of parameters better than another. However, it is possible to take advantage of the domain we are studying, reading, by using known properties of how students learn words. The *K0* parameter represents the knowledge students have when they first start using the tutor. Unfortunately, we do not have a history of all of the words the student encountered before using the Reading Tutor. However, we do have word frequency tables of English text. These tables are not perfect at telling us which words a student has seen, since students will naturally read different material and thus see somewhat different sets of words, but the tables provide a starting point. Specifically, students should be more knowledgeable about words they encounter more frequently. Therefore, there should be a positive correlation between a word's frequency and its *K0* parameter.

The percent of text made up by the most frequent word, "the," is approximately 7.1%, while the least frequent word (of words occurring in both our training data and our word frequency table) was "shear" which only makes up 0.000085% of text. Since the most frequent word is over 80,000 times more frequent than the least frequent, we performed a log-transform on the percentages before attempting to find a relation. Figure 5 shows the plot of log-percent vs. the *K0* parameter for both the Dirichlet priors and the baseline approaches. A linear regression for each approach results in an R^2 of 1% for the baseline and 16% for using Dirichlets. Thus, using the Dirichlet approach produces the expected lawful relationship between prior knowledge and exposure to English text, while parameters estimated with the baseline approach exhibit almost no such relation. Interestingly, the Dirichlet priors were not tuned based on word frequency, nor did the priors assigned to a word vary based on its frequency. Simply providing the underlying distribution for the various parameters (as per Section 2.1) enabled it to correctly assign parameters that track with word frequency.

4   Future Work, Contributions, and Conclusions

The largest limitation of this work is that it has only been evaluated on one (rather large) data set from Project Listen's Reading Tutor, so it is possible the results may not transfer to other tutoring domains. However, the problem of knowledge tracing sometimes returning parameter values that "just don't look right" is well known. In fact, this work was motivated by the difficulties a researcher (Hao Cen) had with applying knowledge tracing to some Cognitive Geometry Tutor data. Furthermore, the Cognitive Tutor knowledge tracing code's caps on the *slip* and *guess* parameters strongly suggest this problem occurred sufficiently often in the past that it was worth modifying the code. However, validating our approach on another tutor's data set is much needed and high on our priority list.

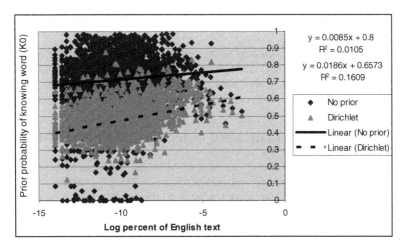

Fig. 5. Word frequency vs. estimated prior knowledge

The second big open question is how the Dirichlets should be generated. One possible critique is that our method of findings parameters isn't replicable across domains. While we acknowledge this argument may have merit, it is not obvious to us whether it is a serious flaw. Encoding the beliefs of domain experts is something that must be done on a case by case basis. If researchers working on the Geometry Tutor wish to apply our approach of using Dirichlets, they would need to think about what is a reasonable prior distribution for their data. That said, it would be nice to have some guidelines about what reasonable means and variances tend to be, and the best way to use existing data to guide the selection of priors.

This paper makes several basic contributions to student modeling. First, it shows how identifiability is a problem for knowledge tracing. Given a set of performance data, there is an infinite family of knowledge tracing models that can mimic student performance. Unfortunately, those models all make different claims about the student's knowledge. Although capping the performance parameters alleviates this issue somewhat, it is still a problem. We have not proven it, but we suspect identifiability affects not just knowledge tracing but any modeling approach that acknowledges student performance is a noisy reflection of his knowledge.

Second, we have shown that predictive accuracy is severely lacking as an evaluation metric for student models. We do not have a strong alternative, but have illustrated that two other techniques, examination of learning curves and inspection of model parameter estimates, can be used to evaluate models.

Third, this paper has proposed and validated a solution to the identifiability problem. The use of Dirichlet priors is a graceful way of biasing the model search process to result in more sensible models that (in this case) are slightly more accurate.

The main conclusion of this paper is that, as system developers and learning science researchers, we must take the assertions of our student model about the student's knowledge with a large grain of salt. Furthermore, acquiring additional training data is not a solution to this problem. Even with an order of magnitude more data, there are still many sets of parameters that will fit the student data equally well. We need to encode prior beliefs in order to do a satisfactory job of modeling student knowledge; performance data are not enough.

Acknowledgements. This work was supported by the National Science Foundation, ITR/IERI Grant No. REC-0326153. Any opinions, findings, and conclusions or recommendations expressed in this publication are those of the authors and do not necessarily reflect the views of the National Science Foundation.

References (see www.cs.cmu.edu/~listen for LISTEN publications)

1. Corbett, A., Anderson, J.: Knowledge tracing: Modeling the acquisition of procedural knowledge. User modeling and user-adapted interaction 4, 253–278 (1995)
2. Beck, J.E., Sison, J.: Using knowledge tracing in a noisy environment to measure student reading proficiencies. International Journal of Artificial Intelligence in Education 16, 129–143 (2006)
3. Anderson, J.R., Corbett, A.T., Koedinger, K.R., Pelletier, R.: Cognitive tutors:Lessons learned. The Journal of the Learning Sciences 4, 167–207 (1995)
4. Mostow, J., Aist, G.: Evaluating tutors that listen: An overview of Project LISTEN, in Smart Machines in Education, Forbus, K., Feltovich, P.(eds.) MIT/AAAI Press: Menlo Park, CA, pp. 169–234 (2001)
5. Chang, K.-m., Beck, J., Mostow, J.,Corbett, A.: A Bayes Net Toolkit for Student Modeling in Intelligent Tutoring Systems. In: Proceedings of the 8th International Conference on Intelligent Tutoring Systems, p. Jhongli, Taiwan (2006)
6. Reye, J.: Student Modelling based on Belief Networks. International Journal of Artificial Intelligence in Education 14, 1–33 (2004)
7. Heckerman, D.: A Tutorial on Learning With Bayesian Networks, Microsoft Research Technical Report (MSR-TR-95-06) (1995)
8. Hand, D., Mannila, H., Smyth, P.: Principles of Data Mining. MIT Press, Cambridge, Massachusetts (2001)

Understanding the Utility of Rationale in a Mixed-Initiative System for GUI Customization

Andrea Bunt, Joanna McGrenere, and Cristina Conati

Computer Science Department, University of British Columbia
2366 Main Mall, Vancouver, BC, V6T 1Z4
{bunt,joanna,conati}@cs.ubc.ca

Abstract. In this paper, we investigate the utility of providing users with the system's rationale in a mixed-initiative system for GUI customization. An evaluation comparing a version of the system with and without the rationale suggested that rationale is wanted by many users, leading to increased trust, understandability and predictability, but that not all users want or need the information.

1 Introduction

In recent years, substantial research efforts have been dedicated to finding ways to provide users with customized graphical user interfaces (GUIs) as a means of coping with the problem of increasing GUI complexity (e.g., [5, 14]). Solutions can be divided into three categories: i) *adaptive*: the system customizes the interface (e.g., [6]), ii) *adaptable*: the user customizes the interface (e.g. [14]), or iii) *mixed-initiative [10]*: the system and user cooperate to customize the interface through a combination of automation and direct manipulation (e.g., [2], [5, 15]). In combining aspects of adaptive and adaptable interfaces, mixed-initiative approaches address a number of their common disadvantages. In particular, by automatically generating customization recommendations, a mixed-initiative approach addresses concerns with adaptable interfaces related to the fact that they require additional user effort [13] and that not all users make good customization decisions [1]. By letting users make the final decision on when and how to customize, the mixed-initiative approach addresses one of the main drawbacks in purely adaptive approaches – lack of user control [9].

With a mixed-initiative approach, however, if users don't understand why and how the customization suggestions are generated, two potential disadvantages of adaptive interfaces remain: 1) lack of transparency, and 2) lack of predictability [9]. In this paper we explore whether both issues can be partially addressed by providing the user with access to the rationale underlying the customization suggestions. We investigate this concept within the MICA (Mixed-Initiative Customization Assistance) system, which provides support for GUI customization in Microsoft Word (MSWord) [2]. One of MICA's distinguishing traits is that its customization recommendations rely on a formal assessment of the performance savings, based on information on user expertise, task, and interface layout. MICA also includes an interface mechanism to

C. Conati, K. McCoy, and G. Paliouras (Eds.): UM 2007, LNAI 4511, pp. 147–156, 2007.
© Springer-Verlag Berlin Heidelberg 2007

explain its decision-making process to the user. A previous evaluation provided evidence that MICA's suggestions have a positive impact on task performance and that its mixed-initiative support is preferred to the purely-adaptable alternative [2]. The main contribution of this paper is a formal evaluation of MICA's rationale, which provides insight into the qualitative impact of including rationale within a mixed-initiative system for GUI customization.

There are numerous examples of adaptive or mixed-initiative systems that provide access to all or part of their rationale (e.g., [4, 16]), but none that do so in the context of GUI customization. For example, inspectable student models allow users to view and sometimes edit their student model, which in turn gives them a sense of what causes the particular adaptive behaviour to occur (e.g., [4, 16]). Provision of rationale has also been explored in recommender systems (e.g., [8]) and in expert systems (e.g., see [11]). Evaluations provide encouraging evidence that the rationale can increase transparency [16], promote reflection [16], and improve users' reactions to system recommendations [8]. If not properly designed, however, rationale can be difficult to use [4], and can even lead to less favourable responses towards the system [8].

Since, to our knowledge, there has been no work investigating rationale utility within mixed-initiative GUI customization systems, little is known about what information to include in the rationale, whether users want access to it, or how it will affect users' impressions of the system. We show that providing access to system rationale in this context has the potential to be beneficial for many users, but that impressions of its utility vary widely from user to user.

2   The MICA System

We begin by outlining MICA's mixed-initiative customization support. A more complete description can be found in [2].

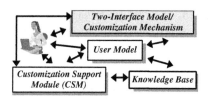

Fig. 1. MICA's architecture

MICA, whose architecture is depicted in Fig. 1, helps users customize within a two-interface version for Microsoft Word (MSWord) [14]. The two interfaces are: 1) the Full Interface (FI), which is the default full MSWord interface (Fig. 2, right), and 2) the Personal Interface (PI), a feature-reduced version, containing only features that the user has chosen to add (Fig. 2, left). A toggle button (circled in Fig. 2) allows the user to switch between interfaces.

MICA tries to identify the user's optimal PI by evaluating which features should be included in the PI and which should reside solely in the FI. The Customization Support Module (CSM) is responsible for determining this optimal PI and generating

Fig. 2. The two-interface model. The PI is only the left; the FI on the right.

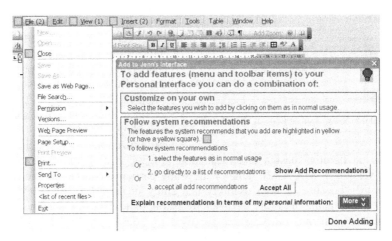

Fig. 3. MICA's customization interface

corresponding customization suggestions. To do so, the CSM relies on the User Model, which assesses the user's time performance given a particular PI. This assessment is done in cooperation with the Knowledge Base using a novel extension of a cognitive modelling technique known as GOMS analysis [3]. The performance assessment relies primarily on three factors. 1) *Expected Usages:* how often the user is expected to access each feature. 2) *Expertise:* the amount of time the user takes to locate each feature in the interface (users with lower expertise are likely to be more negatively impacted by excess functionality [1]). 3) *Interface Characteristics:* detailed layout information on the FI and the PI currently under consideration, including the number of features present and where they are located.

It should be noted that Expected Usages and Expertise are not yet assessed on-line. Although there are techniques that could guide both types of assessments (e.g., [7],[12]), we felt that giving priority to investigating rationale utility would provide the most benefit to GUI customization research, despite a user model with some "black box" components.

Fig. 3 shows MICA's mixed-initiative customization interface for adding features to the PI (a direct extension of the adaptable mechanism proposed in [14]). The central part of Fig. 3 shows the dialogue box that pops up when the user initiates customization. MICA's recommended additions are made visually distinct within the menus and toolbars (by yellow highlighting or a yellow square). Users can accept the recommendations using any combination of three methods: 1) selecting features as in normal usage, 2) selecting from a list accessible through the "Show Add Recommendations" button, and 3) using the "Accept All" button.

3   MICA's Rationale

MICA's rationale component describes why the system is making recommendations and the relevant user- and interface-specific factors impacting its decision-making process. Presenting this rationale has the potential to provide valuable insight into

Fig. 4. The "Why" component of the rationale

how the system works; however, effectively communicating the information to the average user is a challenging design task, particularly since MICA's algorithm is relatively complex.

Since this is the first attempt at providing rationale in GUI customization research, we undertook an iterative design and evaluation process. During the evaluation of a previous version of MICA [2], none of the study participants accessed the rationale spontaneously because of both usability and study methodology issues. We were, however, able to gather usability feedback by asking participants to view the rationale during post-session interviews, which we used to redesign the interface. Next, we pilot tested the new design with eight computer science graduate students. The pilot evaluation consisted of 30-minute interviews targeting issues such as: 1) wording clarity, 2) missing/unnecessary information, and 3) whether it was clear where to access, and how to navigate through the rationale. The pilot testing led to a number of improvements to the interface. One worth mentioning here is stressing that the rationale contains personalized information as opposed to canned text, because the pilot participants found this information most compelling.

In the final interface resulting from the aforementioned iterative design process, users can access the rationale by clicking on the "More" button next to the line "Explain recommendations in terms of my personal information" (Fig. 3, bottom). Once clicked, the dialogue box in Fig. 3 expands to include information on why and how the system makes recommendations. The "Why" component, displayed in Fig. 4, indicates that the recommendations are based on time savings and provides an estimated savings per feature invocation (based on the User Model's performance assessment) should the user choose to accept all recommendations.

The "How" component is a simplified explanation of MICA's decision-making. The first screen, "How: Recommendations Factors," explains that MICA balances the three factors described in Section 2, with their names altered based on pilot feedback:

1) Usage Frequencies (i.e., Expected Usages), 2) Expertise, and 3) Interface Size (i.e., Interface Characteristics). Next, three screens describe each factor in greater detail (two are in Fig. 5). The Usage Frequencies and Expertise screens also display the recommendations ranked according to the User Model assessments for that factor (e.g., Fig. 5, top).

4 Evaluation

Fig. 5. Usage Frequencies and Interface Size factors, excluding the navigation bar (see Fig. 4)

To understand the utility of the rationale, we compared two versions of the MICA system: one with and one without the rationale. The goal was to better understand the qualitative impact of the rationale on users' attitudes toward the system. Based on user feedback from the previous informal studies, we anticipated large individual differences along this dimension. We did not, however, expect rationale to significantly impact customization decisions, since in our earlier study, participants already followed most of the system's recommendations (96%) for additions to the PI without accessing the rationale [2]. While there would be room for improvement in terms of following recommendations for deletion, previous work has shown users to be very reluctant to do so [2], [14]. Therefore, we anticipated the most interesting findings to come from the qualitative data on user attitudes and preferences. Based on previous feedback, we expected that some users would appreciate the rationale and find it useful, while others would find it unnecessary. We wanted to better understand the reasons underlying different reactions, and the qualitative advantages and disadvantages of providing access to rationale information.

4.1 Method

Sixteen participants, recruited throughout the University of British Columbia campus, completed the experiment. The experiment was within subjects with two conditions: 1) *Rationale*, the MICA system with the rationale accessible (see Fig. 3) and 2) *No-Rationale*, the system without the rationale. A within-subjects design was chosen to elicit direct comparative statements. To account for carry-over effects, version order (*Rationale* vs. *No-Rationale*) and task order (described below) were counterbalanced.

In this section we briefly describe the experiment methodology, a direct extension of our previous methodology [2]. With this methodology, interacting with the rationale is not an explicit experimental task. Instead, the majority of the session is spent performing pre-assigned word-processing tasks with the target application, MSWord. Alternatively, we could have required users to interact with the rationale for a period of time, for example, by having them complete a worksheet or questionnaire based on information in the rationale (e.g., [4, 16]). We chose to build on our previous methodology, as opposed to designing tasks specific to the rationale, because we felt that it would generate more realistic feedback about when and why users may access the system's rationale.

The experimental procedure was as follows. First, participants completed a detailed questionnaire designed to assess their expertise for each interface feature used in the experiment. The questionnaire results were used to initialize the "Expertise" portion of the User Model since, as discussed earlier, it cannot yet assess expertise on line. Participants then performed two tasks, one with each version of the system (*Rationale* and *No-Rationale*). Prior to each task, the appropriate system version was briefly demonstrated. After finishing the tasks, participants completed a post-questionnaire and were interviewed by the first author using a semi-structured interview format. A session typically lasted 3 hours, but ranged from 2 hours 45 minutes to 4 hours.

We used a *guided task* structure [2], where users were provided with a list of step-by-step instructions and a target final document. The guided tasks served two purposes: 1) they required a large number of menu selections (necessary for customization to be beneficial) while still being of reasonable length, and 2) they provided "Expected Usage" information for the User Model. We further motivated customization through task repetition and a small amount of deception. Each task was actually repeated three times, however, participants were told that the tasks would be repeated up to five times. If at the end of the second task repetition the participant had yet to customize, the experimenter asked her do so at a point of her own choosing during the third repetition. We did so in hopes of achieving a higher customization rate than in our previous experiment, which was 66% without prompting.

Our goal was to give participants as much autonomy as possible with respect to rationale usage; however, we did want participants to look at it. To balance these two objectives, we showed participants where to access the rationale during the initial interface demonstration and requested that the participants "look through the information at some point." Apart from this request, no prompting to look at the rationale was done during the experiment.

4.2 Main Measures

Our emphasis in the evaluation was on qualitative measures. The questionnaire gathered preference information. In particular, participants who viewed the rationale during the study were asked which version of the system they would choose to install (Overall Preference). The post questionnaire also asked participants to state which version they preferred, or whether they found the two equal, for the following five criteria: 1) agreeing with the system recommendations (Agreement); 2) trusting the system to make good recommendations (Trust); 3) understanding why the system was making *specific* recommendations (Specific Understandability); 4) understanding why the system was making recommendations in *general* (General Understandability), and 5) ability to predict future recommendations (Predictability). The interview gathered more detailed qualitative data on topics such as: 1) influence of study methodology on rationale viewing, 2) additional reasons for viewing (or not viewing) the rationale, 3) the impact of the "Why" component on motivation to accept recommendations, and 4) impressions of the utility of the "How" component.

In addition to qualitative measures, we report the time spent viewing the rationale and the percentage of add and delete recommendations followed in both conditions.

4.3 Results

Similar to our last experiment, 69% of participants (11/16) customized in both conditions without any prompting. Once prompted, the remaining 5 participants customized. Since separate analysis of those who were prompted versus those who were not failed to reveal any substantial differences, the remainder of the analysis includes data from all participants.

In the *Rationale* condition, 94% (15/16) of participants accessed the rationale. Of these participants, 47% (7/15) accessed the "Why" component only, with an average viewing time of 15.1 seconds (sd: 9.6 seconds). The remaining 53% (8/15) accessed all of the rationale, with an average viewing time of 63.4 seconds (sd: 30.4 seconds).

To analyze the qualitative data, the interviews were first transcribed. Next, detailed coding was done by the first author, based on thorough analysis of the interviews and

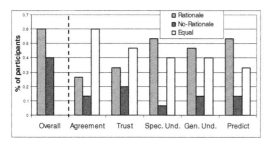

Fig. 6. Preference overall and on individual criteria

questionnaires. We report themes and trends that emerged from this analysis, along with the number of participants whose statements matched the given theme or trend. Our intention was not to prove or disprove hypotheses through statistical analysis, which, given the anticipated diversity of opinions, would have required a much larger number of participants.

Preference. Fig. 6 depicts the preference data both overall and for each of the individual criteria, and indicates that, in general, the preference data was mixed. When forced to choose, the majority of participants indicated that they would prefer to install the *Rationale* version (60%); however, the *No-Rationale* also had reasonable support (40%). For the individual criteria, participants were given the option of rating the two conditions "Equal." Having the rationale appeared to have the largest impact on both Specific and General Understandability, as well as the Predictability of the recommendations. While the *Rationale* version was preferred by some users for Agreement and Trust, the most popular response for these criteria was "Equal."

Influence of Study Methodology on Rationale Viewing. To understand whether users looked at the rationale solely because of the request during interface demonstration, users were asked i) why they looked at the rationale, and ii) to comment on the role of the request. Out of the 15 users who viewed the rationale, 33% (5/15) said they were not influenced by the request. Another 20% (3/15) indicated that they were partially influenced by the request, but had additional reasons for accessing the rationale. The remaining 47% (7/15) said the request during interface demonstration was their sole reason for accessing the rationale. Just over half of these users (4/7) said that there would be circumstances where they would want the information, but that our particular study methodology did not provide the right motivating conditions. Finally, three users indicated that they had no interest in the rationale. Therefore, 80% (12/15) of the participants either i) viewed the rationale for reasons other than our particular study methodology or ii) could see circumstances outside of the study where they would want to view the rationale.

Additional Reasons for Viewing or Not Viewing the Rationale. Three reasons were given for viewing the rationale by the 53% (8/15) that accessed it for reasons other than the request during interface demonstration. The first was general curiosity (3/8). The second was to have the recommendations explained (3/8), e.g., *"if something is customizing it for you [...] I want to have an understanding of why it is doing things."* The third reason was to have an aspect of the interface explained, such as an explanation of how the PI works (2/8).

The three users who were not interested in the rationale gave unique reasons for why not. One felt that the rationale is unnecessary in a mixed-initiative system, since she could follow the recommendations if she found them useful or customize on her own if she didn't. Another pointed to the fact that the rationale is embedded within a

Table 1. Reasons for finding the "How" component useful or not useful

"How" Useful (10/16)	"How" Not Useful (6/16)
• Gained a better understanding (or confirmed) (5/10) • Recommendations more trustworthy/believable (3/10) • Simple explanation (1/10) • Could use knowledge to become more efficient (1/10)	• Unnecessary or common sense (4/6) • Too technical (1/6) • Didn't influence customization decisions (1/6)

productivity application: *"...when it comes to a program like Microsoft Word most of the time you only care about getting the job done. You don't really care about why."* The final participant expressed trust in the system: *"I just assume recommendations are because they are useful for you. That's all really I need to know."*

Effectiveness of Rationale: Impact of "Why" on Recommendation Acceptance. Out of those who accessed the rationale, 93% (14/15) indicated that they actually read the "Why" component. Since its purpose is to illustrate the potential time savings that could result from accepting recommendations, we asked users to discuss whether or not this information was, in fact, motivating. Of these users, 43% (6/14) felt that the "Why" component motivated them to accept recommendations. Another 43% (6/14) were generally interested in having a PI that would save time, but were not motivated by the particular amount of time savings listed. They either felt that the amount of time savings was too small, or that its expression was unintuitive: *"I couldn't relate it to the real world. It was like saying how fast you are driving in meters per second..."*

In this study, three users did delete features and did so after having viewed the rationale. For two of the three users, the time savings was a motivating factor.

Effectiveness of Rationale: Usefulness of the "How" Information. Only 47% (7/15) of those who accessed the rationale indicated that they read the "How" component. To obtain as much feedback as possible, during the interview we asked all 16 users to read through the information and comment on its usefulness. After reading the information 62% (10/16) found it useful, including six of the seven users who read the information while customizing, however, 38% did not (6/16). Table 1 summarizes their reasons. The most popular reason for finding the information useful was gaining a better understanding of how the system makes recommendations or confirming their existing understanding. For those who didn't find the information useful, the majority indicated that it was unnecessary or "just common sense."

We also asked users to indicate which pieces of information, if any, were most or least useful. While participants responded favourably to the Expertise and Usage Frequencies factors, 50% (8/16) disliked the Interface Size factor. Many commented correctly that this factor wasn't as personalized, or that having a small interface was the point of customization. Participants didn't seem to understand that MICA balances this factor with both usage frequencies and expertise. This result is consistent with our pilot feedback, which indicated that users respond most favourably to information that is personalized.

Impact on Recommendations Followed. To analyze the impact of the rationale on the percentage of recommendations followed, we ran repeated-measures ANOVA with Version (*Rationale* or *No-Rationale*) as the within-subjects factor. Version Order and Task Order were included as between-subjects controls.

As anticipated, the percentage of Add recommendations followed was similar in both conditions, with participants following 94.2% (sd: 21.6%) of the Add Recommendations in the *Rationale* condition, compared to 93.5% (sd: 9.0%) in the *No-Rationale* condition (F(1, 11) = 0.001, p = 0.982). In terms of Delete recommendations, three users did delete, leading to an average of 14.2% (sd: 34.3%) Delete recommendations followed in the *Rationale* condition compared to 7.2% (sd: 24.8%) in the *No-Rationale*, a difference which was also not statistically significant (F(1, 11) = 0.978, p = 0.334).

Another result of interest was a marginally-significant between-subjects order effect for the percentage of Add recommendations followed (F(1,11) = 3.990, p = 0.071). Participants who completed the *Rationale* condition first followed more Add recommendations overall (average: 99.1%, sd: 2.5%) than those who completed the *Rationale* condition second (average: 87.9%, sd: 14.3%). This order effect was anticipated; we expected knowledge that the system would make principled recommendations in the first condition to transfer to the second. This result suggests that the rationale may be most effective when viewed earlier rather than later and that frequent viewing isn't necessary.

4.4 Discussion

Our findings indicate that the majority of users prefer to have the rationale present, but that a non-insignificant group of users do not need or want the information. For some users, the rationale led to increased trust, understanding, predictability, and motivation to accept recommendations. Some users, however, felt that the rationale was just common sense, or was unnecessary in a mixed-initiative system or productivity application. Others expressed an inherent trust in the system. These findings may suggest that, contrary to previously stated guidelines [9], transparency and predictability may not, in fact, be important to all users in all contexts. However, since some users found the rationale to be just common sense, it may be that our particular design did not always succeed in improving transparency and predictability.

In terms of rationale design, feedback from our iterative design and evaluation process suggests that the personalized aspects of the rationale should be emphasized when possible. In addition, since reactions to the rationale are mixed, the information should clearly visible for those who want it without disrupting those who don't, which was the approach taken here. Finally, we might see different reactions to more lightweight graphical representations of the rationale.

While the rationale was a motivating factor for two of the three users who deleted, and participants who viewed the information in the first condition tended to accept more add recommendations overall, the rationale had limited quantitative impact. Understanding whether the rationale could have a larger quantitative impact may require finding a target application where users are less likely to accept recommendations without the rationale, for reasons such as recommendations being contrary to expectations or a higher cost associated with accepting recommendations. Alternatively, it may be the laboratory environment that led to such high acceptance of recommendations. The rationale may have a larger impact in the field, where users might have lower levels of trust in the system.

5 Summary and Future Work

This paper described the iterative design and the formal evaluation of rationale provision within a mixed-initiative system for GUI customization. Qualitative reactions to having this information varied across individuals. While the evaluation revealed aspects of our rationale that could be improved, the most promising avenue of future research would be to gain a more global understanding of when and why rationale is useful. In particular, we are interested in evaluating how user variability, the target application's complexity, and the division of control between the system and the user affect the qualitative and quantitative utility of a system's rationale.

References

1. Bunt, A., Conati, C., McGrenere, J.: What Role Can Adaptive Support Play in an Adaptable System? In: Proc. of IUI, pp. 117–124 (2004)
2. Bunt, A., Conati, C., McGrenere, J.: Supporting Interface Customization Using a Mixed-Initiative Approach. In: Proc. of IUI, pp. 92–101 (2007)
3. Card, S.K., Newell, A., Moran, T.P.: The Psychology of Human-Computer Interaction. Lawrence Erlbaum Associates, Inc., Mahwah, NJ (1983)
4. Czarkowski, M., Kay, J.: How to Give the User a Sense of Control over the Personalization of Adaptive Hypertext? In: Proc. of Adaptive Hypermedia and Adaptive Web-Based Systems (in conjunction with UM'03), pp.121–131 (2003)
5. Debevc, M., Meyer, B., Donlagic, D., Svecko, R.: Design and Evaluation of an Adaptive Icon Toolbar. User Modeling and User-Adapted Interaction 6(1), 1–21 (1996)
6. Gajos, K., Weld, D.S.: Supple: Automatically Generating User Interfaces. In: Proc. of IUI, pp. 93–100 (2004)
7. Greenberg, S., Witten, I.H.: How Users Repeat Their Actions on Computers: Principles for Design of History Mechanisms. In: Proc. of CHI, pp. 171–178 (1988)
8. Herlocker, J., Konstan, J.A., Riedl, J.: Explaining Collaborative Filtering Recommendations. In: Proc. of CSCW, pp. 241–250 (2000)
9. Hook, K.: Steps to Take before Intelligent User Interfaces Become Real. Interacting with Computers 12, 409–426 (2000)
10. Horvitz, E.: Principles of Mixed-Initiative User Interfaces. In: Proc. of CHI, pp. 159–166 (1999)
11. Horvitz, E., Breese, J., Henrion, M.: Decision Theory in Expert Systems and Artificial Intelligence. Journal of Approximate Reasoning 2, 247–302 (1988)
12. Horvitz, E., Herckerman, D., Hovel, D., Rommelse, R.: The Lumiere Project: Bayesian User Modeling for Inferring the Goals and Needs of Software Users. In: Proc. of UAI, pp. 256–265 (1998)
13. Mackay, W.E.: Triggers and Barriers to Customizing Software. In: Proc. of CHI, pp. 153–160 (1991)
14. McGrenere, J., Baecker, R.M., Booth, K.S.: An Evaluation of a Multiple Interface Design Solution for Bloated Software. In: Proc. of CHI, pp. 163–170 (2002)
15. Oppermann, R.: Adaptively Supported Adaptability. International Journal of Human-Computer Studies 40, 455–472 (1994)
16. Zapata-Rivera, J.D., Greer, J.E.: Interacting with Inspectable Bayesian Student Models. International Journal of AI in Education 14, 127–163 (2003)

Respecting Users' Individual Privacy Constraints in Web Personalization*

Yang Wang and Alfred Kobsa

Donald Bren School of Information and Computer Sciences
University of California, Irvine, U.S.A.
{yangwang,kobsa}@ics.uci.edu

Abstract. Web personalization has demonstrated to be advantageous for both online customers and vendors. However, its benefits may be severely counteracted by privacy constraints. Personalized systems need to take users' privacy concerns into account, as well as privacy laws and industry self-regulation that may be in effect. In this paper, we first discuss how these constraints may affect web-based personalized systems. We then explain in what way current approaches to this problem fall short of their aims, specifically regarding the need to tailor privacy to the constraints of each individual user. We present a dynamic privacy-enhancing user modeling framework as a superior alternative, which is based on a software product line architecture. Our system dynamically selects personalization methods during runtime that respect users' current privacy concerns as well as the privacy laws and regulations that apply to them.

1 Introduction

Numerous consumer studies and lab experiments (see [17, 22] for an overview) suggest that privacy concerns may prompt people to withhold information about themselves when interacting with personalized systems, thereby preventing users to fully benefit from the potential of personalization. These studies also show that people's privacy preferences differ to some extent. Since personalized websites collect personal data, they are also subject to prevailing privacy laws and regulations if the respective individuals are in principle identifiable. As we will show below, such laws often not only affect the data that are collected by the website, but also the personalization methods that may be used for processing them.

In this paper, we will investigate how personalized web-based systems can be compliant with the privacy constraints that are currently in effect for each individual user (namely privacy laws, industry and company regulations, and privacy preferences of every user). We propose a novel approach based on software product lines that allow the configuration of the employed personalization methods to be tailored to each user's privacy constraints. We will first analyze how such privacy constraints may affect the admissibility of personalization methods, both with regard to individual privacy concerns and privacy laws. We then review existing approaches

* This research has been supported through NSF grant IIS 0308277. We would like to thank André van der Hoek, Eric Dashofy and the UM07 reviewers for their helpful comments.

C. Conati, K. McCoy, and G. Paliouras (Eds.): UM 2007, LNAI 4511, pp. 157–166, 2007.
© Springer-Verlag Berlin Heidelberg 2007

for handling the differences in privacy constraints that apply to different users, and analyze their shortcomings. Thereafter we present our software product line approach in Section 4, an illustrative example for its operation in Section 5, and conclusions and future work in Section 6.

2 Impacts of Privacy Constraints on Web Personalization

2.1 Impacts of Users' Privacy Concerns

Numerous opinion polls and empirical studies have revealed that Internet users harbor considerable privacy concerns regarding the disclosure of their personal data to websites, and the monitoring of their Internet activities. These studies were primarily conducted between 1998 and 2003, mostly in the United States. In the following, we summarize a number of important findings (the percentage figures indicate the ratio of respondents from multiple studies who endorsed the respective view). For more detailed discussions we refer to [17, 22].

Personal Data
1. Internet users who are concerned about the privacy or security of their personal information online: 70% - 89.5%;
2. People who have refused to give personal information to a web site at one time or another: 82% - 95%;
3. Internet users who would never provide personal information to a web site: 27%;
4. Internet users who supplied false or fictitious information to a web site when asked to register: 6% - 40% always, 7% often, 17% sometimes;
5. People who are concerned if a business shares their data for a different than the original purpose: 89% - 90%.

Significant concern over the use of personal data is visible in these results, which may cause problems for all personalized systems that depend on users disclosing data about themselves. False or fictitious entries when asked to register at a website make all personalization based on such data dubious, and may also jeopardize cross-session identification of users as well as all personalization based thereon. The fact that 80-90% of respondents are concerned if a business shares their information for a different than the original purpose may have impacts on central user modeling servers (UMSs) [16] that collect data from, and share them with, different user-adaptive applications.

User Tracking and Cookies
1. People concerned about being tracked on the Internet: 54% - 63%;
2. People concerned that someone might know their browsing history: 31%;
3. Users who feel uncomfortable being tracked across multiple web sites: 91%;
4. Internet users who generally accept cookies: 62%;
5. Internet users who set their computers to reject cookies: 10% - 25%;
6. Internet users who delete cookies periodically: 53%.

These results reveal significant user concerns about tracking and cookies, which may have effects on the acceptance of personalization that is based on usage logs.

Observations 4–6 directly affect machine-learning methods that operate on user log data since without cookies or registration, different sessions of the same user can no longer be linked. Observation 3 may again affect the acceptance of the central user modeling systems which collect user information from several websites.

Kobsa [17] suggests that developers of personalized system should however not feel discouraged by the abundance of stated privacy concerns and their potential adverse impact on personalized systems. Rather, they should incorporate a number of mitigating factors into their designs that have been shown to encourage users' disclosure of personal data. Such factors include perceived value of personalization, previous positive experience, the presence of a privacy seal, catering to individuals' privacy concern, etc. The approach proposed here addresses this last factor.

2.2 Impacts of Privacy Laws and Regulations

Privacy Laws. Legal privacy requirements lay out organizational and technical requirements for information systems that store and/or process personal data, in order to ensure the protection of these data. Those requirements include proper data acquisition, notification about the purpose of use, permissible data transfer (e.g., to third parties and/or across national borders) and permissible data processing (e.g., organization, modification and destruction). Other provisions specify user opt-ins (e.g., asking for their consent before collecting their data), opt-out, users' rights (e.g., regarding the disclosure of the processed data), adequate security mechanisms (e.g., access control), and the supervision and audit of personal data processing.

Our review of over 40 international privacy laws [24] shows that if such laws apply to a personalized website, they often not only affect the data that is collected by the website and the way in which data is transferred, but also the personalization methods that may be used for processing them. The following are some example codes:

1. *Value-added* (e.g. personalized) *services based on traffic or location data require the anonymization of such data or the user's consent* [9]. This clause clearly requires the user's consent for any personalization based on interaction logs if the user can be identified.
2. *The service provider must inform the user of the type of data which will be processed, of the purposes and duration of the processing and whether the data will be transmitted to a third party, prior to obtaining her consent* [9]. It is sometimes fairly difficult for personalized service providers to specify beforehand the particular personalized services that an individual user would receive. The common practice is to collect as much data about the user as possible, to lay them in stock, and then to apply those personalization methods that "fire" based on the existing data.
3. *Users must be able to withdraw their consent to the processing of traffic and location data at any time* [9]. In a strict interpretation, this stipulation requires personalized systems to terminate all traffic or location based personalization immediately when asked, i.e. even during the current service. A case can probably be made that users should not only be able to make all-or-none decisions, but also decisions on individual aspects of traffic or location based personalization.

4. *Personal data must be collected for specified, explicit and legitimate purposes and not further processed in a way incompatible with those purposes* [8]. This limitation would impact central UMSs, which store user information from, and supply the data to, different personalized applications. A UMS must not supply data to personalized applications if they intend to use those data for different purposes than the one for which the data was originally collected.

5. *Usage data must be erased immediately after each session* (except for very limited purposes) [7]. This provision could affect the use of machine learning methods when the learning takes place over several sessions.

Company and Industry Regulations. Many companies have internal guidelines in place for dealing with personal data. There also exist a number of voluntary privacy standards to which companies can subject themselves (e.g., of the Direct Marketing Association, the Online Privacy Alliance, the U.S. Network Advertising Initiative, the Personalization Consortium, and increasingly the TRUSTe privacy seal program).

3 Existing Approaches to Address the Variability of Privacy Constraints

No systematic approach has so far existed for building websites that cater to the different privacy constraints of different users. Sites that aimed at addressing this problem had to use simple escape strategies, which we list below.

Pseudonymous Personalization. Basically, this approach allows users to remain anonymous with regard to the personalized system and the whole network infrastructure, whilst enabling the system to still recognize the same user in different sessions and cater to her individually [19]. At first sight, this seems to be a panacea because in most cases privacy laws do not apply any more when the interaction is anonymous. However, anonymity is currently difficult and/or tedious to preserve when payments, physical goods and non-electronic services are being exchanged. It harbors the risk of misuse, and it hinders vendors from cross-channel marketing (e.g. sending a product catalog to a web customer by mail). Moreover, users may still have additional privacy preferences such as not wanting to be profiled even when this is done merely pseudonymously, to which personalized systems need to adjust.

Largest Permissible Dominator. Ideally, this approach means that only those personalization methods that meet all privacy laws and regulations of all website visitors are used. The Disney website, for instance, meets the European Union Data Protection Directive [8] as well as the U.S. Children's Online Privacy Protection Act (COPPA) [1]. This solution is likely to run into problems if more than a very few jurisdictions are involved, since the largest permissible denominator may then become very small. Individual user privacy concerns are also not taken into account.

Different Country/Region Versions. In this approach, personalized systems have different country versions, with personalization methods only that are admissible in the respective country. If countries have similar privacy laws, combined versions can be built for them using the above-described largest permissible denominator approach. For example, IBM's German-language pages meet the privacy laws of Germany, Austria and Switzerland [2], while IBM's U.S. site meets the legal constraints of the U.S. only. This approach is also likely to become infeasible as soon as the number of countries/regions, and hence the number of different versions of the personalized system, increases. Individual user privacy concerns are also not taken into account.

P3P. The Platform for Privacy Preferences (P3P) [25] enables websites to express their privacy policies in a standard machine-readable format that can be retrieved automatically and interpreted by user agents. Client-side agents can then inform users about the sites' privacy policies and warn them when those deviate from previously-specified preferences. P3P does not enforce privacy policies nor does it support different policies for different users. By itself, it is therefore not an answer to the need for privacy tailored to different user constraints. However, several proposals for individual negotiation of P3P policies have been made [5, 20]. The results of such negotiations could become the input to our own approach.

4   A Dynamic Privacy-Enhancing User Modeling Framework

User Modeling Servers (UMSs) store and represent user characteristics and behavior, integrate external user-related information, apply user modeling methods to derive additional assumptions about the user, and allow multiple external user adaptive applications to retrieve user information from the server in parallel [16]. UMSs are widely used for supporting user-adaptive applications. Our solution enhances a regular UMS by a new dimension of personalization, namely adaptation to each user's potentially different privacy constraints.

For many personalization goals, more than one method can often be used that differ in their data and privacy requirements and their anticipated accuracy and reliability. For example, a personalized website could use incremental machine learning to provide personalization to visitors from Germany (where user logs must be discarded at the end of a session to comply with Code 5 in Section 2.2), while it can use possibly better one-time machine learning with user data from several sessions to provide personalization to web visitors from the U.S. who are not subject to this constraint.

We propose a software architecture that encapsulates different personalization methods in individual components and, at any point during runtime, ascertains that only those components can be operational that are in compliance with the currently prevailing privacy constraints. Moreover, the architecture can also dynamically select the component with the optimal anticipated personalization effects among those that are currently permissible [15]. To implement this design, we utilize a product line approach from software architecture research and, simplistically speaking, give every user their own UMS instance which incorporates those user modeling methods only that meet the user's current privacy constraints [23].

Product Line Architectures (PLAs) have been successfully used in industrial software development [4]. A PLA represents the architectural structure for a set of related products by defining core elements that are present in all product architectures, and variation points where differences between individual product architectures may occur. Each variation point is guarded with a Boolean expression that represents the conditions under which an optional component should be included in a particular product instance. A product instance can be selected out of a product line architecture by resolving the Boolean guards of each variation point at design-time, invocation-time or run-time [13].

Figure 1 shows an overview of our PLA-based user modeling framework. It consists of external user-adaptive applications, the Selector, and the LDAP-based UMS of Kobsa and Fink [18] which includes the Directory Component and a pool of user modeling components (UMCs). External personalized applications can query the UMS for existing user information, so as to provide personalized services to their end users, and can supply additional user information to the UMS. The Directory Component is essentially a repository of user models, each of which stores and represents not only users' characteristics, behavior and inferences, but also their potentially different individual privacy constraints. The UMC Pool contains a set of UMCs, each of which encapsulates one or more user modeling methods (e.g., collaborative filtering) that make inferences about users based on existing user data.

The novel privacy enhancement consists in every user having their own instance of the UMC Pool, each containing only those user modeling components that meet the privacy requirements for the respective user (users with identical UMC Pool instances share the same instance). To realize this, the above framework has been implemented as a PLA, with the UMCs as optional elements [14] guarded by a Boolean expression that represents privacy conditions under which the respective UMC may operate (e.g. "(CombineProfile == allowed) && (TrackUser == allowed)").

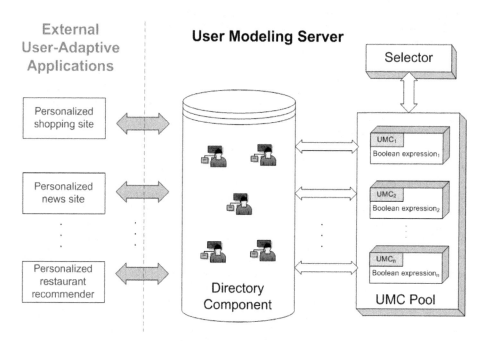

Fig. 1. A Dynamic Privacy-Enabling User Modeling Framework

At the beginning of the interaction with a user, the Selector verifies for every UMC whether it may operate under the privacy constraints that apply to the specific user, and creates an architectural instance with these permissible UMCs (or lets the user share this instance if one already exists). Moreover, in order to maximize the benefits of personalization, the Selector can further select the UMCs with the optimal anticipated personalization effects among those that are currently permissible based on a designer-specified preference order. The PLA management environment that we employ [3] supports dynamic runtime (re-)configuration, which allows the Selector to react immediately, e.g., users change their privacy preferences during the current session. The framework therefore allows a personalized website to adjust its data practices to the user's preferences in a nuanced and highly dynamic manner. The fact that if two or more users have the same set of privacy constraints they will share a single personalization architecture is key to the scalability of our solution.

5   An Illustrative Example

Assume that MyTaste is a mobile web service that provides restaurant recommendations worldwide based on customers' current location (collected from their GPS-embedded mobile devices), their food preferences and demographics as well as the proximity of nearby restaurants and their ratings by other customers. Upon registration, users will be asked to disclose their identities and optionally disclose some information about themselves (e.g., their food preferences). The system will then automatically retrieve their demographics from commercial databases or credit bureaus. The system also encourages users to rate places they have patronized, by offering discounts for restaurants that will be recommended to them in the future. The processing of all personal data is described in a privacy statement, i.e. the disclosure duties of Code 2 in Section 2.2 are being met.

The MyTaste web server relies on our privacy-enabling user modeling framework to infer information about users to provide recommendations. Table 1 summarizes the usage of data and inference methods for each user modeling component. For example, UMC_1 can recommend restaurants based on ratings of people in the same nationality cluster. If a user indicates a high interest in a specific type of food, UMC_2 can recommend nearby restaurants that have good ratings in this category.

We have three hypothetical adult users, Alice from Germany, Cheng from China, and Bob from the U.S. Cheng dislikes being tracked online, while Alice and Bob do not express any privacy preferences. MyTaste.com can tailor its provided personalization to the different privacy constraints of these users in the following manner:

1. When users log into the website, the system gathers their current privacy constraints, namely those imposed by privacy laws and regulations as well as their personal privacy preferences. Users can specify their privacy preferences and change them anytime during the interaction with the personalized system.

2. Our framework determines which UMCs may operate for each user given their privacy constraints. For example, the German Teleservices Data Protection Act [7] and the EU Directive on Electronic Communications [9] apply to Alice, with the following consequences:

Table 1. The UMC pool of MyTaste

UMC	Data used	Method used
UMC_1	– Demographic (such as age, gender, profession, nationality)	– Clustering techniques
UMC_2	– Food preferences	– Rule-based reasoning
UMC_3	– Demographic – Food preferences	– Rule-based reasoning
UMC_4	– Food preferences – Current session log (MyTaste pages that the user visited in the current session)	– Incremental machine learning
UMC_5	– Food preferences – Last n session log (MyTaste pages that the user visited across sessions)	– One-time machine learning across several sessions
UMC_6	– Demographic – Food preferences – Location data – Last n session log	– One-time machine learning across several sessions

- In the light of Code 4 in Section 2.2, UMC_1, UMC_3 and UMC_6 are illegal without Alice's consent because the demographic data that the website retrieves from commercial databases and credit bureaus had not been originally collected for personalization or recommendation purposes.
- In the light of Code 5, UMC_5 and UMC_6 are illegal because they both use cross-session log data.
- In the light of Code 1, UMC_6 is illegal without Alice's consent because it uses location data without anonymizing it.

Hence UMC_1, UMC_3, UMC_5 and UMC_6 cannot be used for Alice without her explicit consent.

3. With similar analyses, the system can determine that UMC_4, UMC_5 and UMC_6 cannot be used for Cheng who does not like to be logged. No privacy restrictions apply to Bob.
4. The system will thus instantiate three different UMCs pools for these three users, i.e. each user will have his own instance of the personalized system that meets her current privacy constraints.

6   Conclusions and Future Work

Privacy constraints in the domain of web personalization derive from users' personal privacy preferences, privacy laws and regulations. These privacy constraints have substantial impacts on the ways in which web-based personalized systems may operate internally, and indirectly on how much personalization they are consequently able to provide. Existing approaches fall short of a flexible, systematic and scalable solution to respecting privacy constraints that may differ among users. Our proposed

PLA-based user modeling framework allows personalized websites to address the combinatorial complexity of privacy constraints in a systematic and flexible manner, which builds on state-of-the-art industry practice for managing software variants at runtime. It should however not be misunderstood as a complete solution to all privacy issues in personalized web-based systems. Our approach focuses on the architectural aspects of user-tailored privacy provisioning but does not control (let alone enforce) what and how user data are or may be collected.

While we currently use Boolean variables to express identified privacy constraints [23], ultimately these constraints should be expressed in a privacy constraint specification language such as APPEL [6] or EPAL [21], or with semantic web technologies [10]. Unfortunately though none of these proposals has gained much impact so far. Future plans of P3P [25] include the support of privacy policy negotiation, whose results can be used as privacy constraints input to our system.

Conditions on the applicability of our constraints (e.g. the user's country) are currently fully "factored out", and nuances in the meanings of the same constraints in different contexts (e.g. countries) are currently represented by using different Boolean variables. It would be worthwhile to study the applicability of conditional constraints [11] and context-sensitive constraints [12], which allow for more compact representations and are also closer to the original legal phrasing.

Performance and scalability are of critical interest in practice, specifically if systems are expected to provide personalization services to hundreds of thousands of users from all over the world. We ran some basic performance experiments based on our current prototype [23]. The results imply that the overhead incurred by product line architecture is not negligible. We are currently experimenting with different ways of optimizing the architectural selection process. Fortunately though, since the number of privacy jurisdictions is limited (currently to about 40 countries and 100 states), we assume that many of our users will share the same architecture. The resource-intensive architecture selection and instantiation process is therefore likely not to be invoked too often. This reusability is key to performance and scalability, but its effects will need to be more thoroughly tested.

References

1. Personal Communication, Chief Privacy Officer, Disney Corporation (2002)
2. Personal Communication, Chief Privacy Officer, IBM Zurich (2003)
3. ArchStudio: ArchStudio 3.0 (2005) http://www.isr.uci.edu/projects/archstudio/
4. Bosch, J.: Design and Use of Software Architectures: Adopting and Evolving a Product-Line Approach. Addison-Wesley, New York (2000)
5. Buffett, S., Jia, K., Liu, S., Spencer, B., Wang, F.: Negotiating Exchanges of P3P-Labeled Information for Compensation. Computational Intelligence 20, 663–677 (2004)
6. Cranor, L., Langheinrich, M., Marchiori, M.: A P3P Preference Exchange Language 1.0 (APPEL1.0): W3C Working Draft (April 15, 2002)
7. German Teleservices Data Protection Act 1997, as amended on (December 14, 2001)
8. Directive 95/46/EC of the European Parliament and of the Council of 24 October, on the Protection of Individuals with Regard to the Processing of Personal Data and on the Free Movement of such Data. Official Journal of the European Communities, p. 31ff (1995)

9. Directive 2002/58/EC of the European Parliament and of the Council Concerning the Processing of Personal Data and the Protection of Privacy in the Electronic Communications Sector (2002)

10. Gandon, F.L., Sadeh, N.M.: Semantic Web Technologies to Reconcile Privacy and Context Awareness. Journal of Web Semantics 1, 241–260 (2004)

11. Gelle, E., Sabin, M.: Solving Methods for Conditional Constraint Satisfaction. In: The Eighteenth International Joint Conference on Artificial Intelligence, Workshop on Configuration, (IJCAI-03) Acapulco, Mexico, pp. 7–12 (2003)

12. Gray, J., Bapty, T., Neema, S., Tuck, J.: Handling crosscutting constraints in domain-specific modeling. Communications of the ACM 44, 87–93 (2001)

13. Hoek, A.v.d.: Design-Time Product Line Architectures for Any-Time Variability. Science of Computer Programming, special issue on Software Variability Management 53, 285–304 (2004)

14. Hoek, A.v.d., Mikic-Rakic, M., Roshandel, R., Medvidovic, N.: Taming Architectural Evolution. In: The Sixth European Software Engineering Conference (ESEC) and the Ninth ACM SIGSOFT Symposium on the Foundations of Software Engineering (FSE-9), Vienna, Austria, pp. 1–10 (2001)

15. Kobsa, A.: A Component Architecture for Dynamically Managing Privacy in Personalized Web-based Systems. In: Privacy Enhancing Technologies: Third International Workshop, pp. 177–188. Dresden, Germany (2003)

16. Kobsa, A.: Generic User Modeling Systems. In: Brusilovsky, P., Kobsa, A., Nejdl, W. (eds.) The Adaptive Web: Methods and Strategies of Web Personalization, Springer-Verlag, Heidelberg, Germany, pp. 136–154 (2007)

17. Kobsa, A.: Privacy-Enhanced Web Personalization. In: Brusilovsky, P., Kobsa, A., Nejdl, W. (eds.) The Adaptive Web: Methods and Strategies of Web Personalization, Springer-Verlag, Heidelberg, Germany, pp. 628–670 (2007)

18. Kobsa, A., Fink, J.: An LDAP-Based User Modeling Server and its Evaluation. User Modeling and User-Adapted Interaction: The Journal of Personalization Research 16, 129–169 (2006)

19. Kobsa, A., Schreck, J.: Privacy through Pseudonymity in User-Adaptive Systems. ACM Transactions on Internet Technology 3, 149–183 (2003)

20. Preibusch, S.: Personalized Services with Negotiable Privacy Policies. PEP06, CHI 2006 Workshop on Privacy-Enhanced Personalization, Montreal, Canada, pp. 29–38 (2006)

21. Schunter, M., Powers, C.: The Enterprise Privacy Authorization Language (EPAL 1.1): Reader's Guide to the Documentation. IBM Research Laboratory (2003)

22. Teltzrow, M., Kobsa, A.: Impacts of User Privacy Preferences on Personalized Systems: a Comparative Study. In: Karat, C.-M., Blom, J., Karat, J. (eds.) Designing Personalized User Experiences for eCommerce, pp. 315–332. Kluwer Academic Publishers, Dordrecht, Netherlands (2004)

23. Wang, Y., Kobsa, A., van der Hoek, A., White, J.: PLA-based Runtime Dynamism in Support of Privacy-Enhanced Web Personalization. In: The 10th International Software Product Line Conference, Baltimore, MD, pp. 151–162 (2006)

24. Wang, Y., Zhaoqi, C., Kobsa, A.: A Collection and Systematization of International Privacy Laws, with Special Consideration of Internationally Operating Personalized Websites (2006) http://www.ics.uci.edu/kobsa/privacy

25. Wenning, R., Schunter, M.(eds.): The Platform for Privacy Preferences 1.1 (P3P1.1) Specification: W3C Working Group Note (2006)

Personalized Previews of Alternative Routes in Virtual Environments

Mehmed Kantardzic and Pedram Sadeghian

CECS Department, Univeristy of Louisville
Louisville, KY 40292 USA
{mmkant01,p0sade01}@louisville.edu

Abstract. In virtual environments (VEs) there are often many routes available to a destination and each route has its own unique characteristics. At the same time, each VE user has unique preferences when selecting a route. In this paper, we present a new methodology for developing a personalized route preview interface, which provides a preview of several routes to a destination that closely match the user's preferences. The user's preferences are modeled by an automatically generated user profile that does not require any explicit input from the user. Simulation experiments have shown the potential of this approach in both accurately learning the user's preferences and personalizing the preview interface.

Keywords: Virtual Environments, Route Selection, Previews, Personalization.

1 Introduction

Virtual environments (VEs) provide a computer-synthesized world in which users can interact with objects, perform various activities, and navigate the environment. In some VEs, there are often several alternative routes available to a destination. Each one of these routes has its own unique characteristics that make it more or less preferable to different users. For example, one user may prefer to take a longer scenic route to a certain destination, while another user may prefer to take the shortest route to the same destination. In VEs with multiple routes to a destination, selecting an appropriate route is an important factor in determining the quality of the overall VE experience. This paper discusses a personalized route preview interface to help VE users with the route selection process.

In our previous research, we introduced the Frequent Wayfinding-Sequence (FWS) methodology to find "preferable" routes of travel in a VE [6]. In this methodology, the routes taken by the experienced users of a VE are recorded as a set of coordinates and pre-processed to form Wayfinding-sequences (W-sequences). A W-sequence is a formalized symbolic representation of a route in a VE from one landmark (i.e. memorable and distinctive object) to another landmark.

Once a W-sequence database is established, a sequence mining algorithm is executed to find all W-sequences for each landmark pair L_i-L_j. All sub W-sequences are counted in the mining process. The W-sequences found for a landmark pair L_i-L_j,

C. Conati, K. McCoy, and G. Paliouras (Eds.): UM 2007, LNAI 4511, pp. 167–176, 2007.
© Springer-Verlag Berlin Heidelberg 2007

correspond to the different routes taken by the experienced users while traveling between landmark L_i and landmark L_j. Frequent W-sequences for a landmark pair L_i-L_j are those W-sequences with a frequency of occurrence above a statistical confidence threshold. The frequent W-sequences are equated as the "preferred" routes of travel between the landmark pairs. Our present goal is to develop a personalized route preview interface so that VE users can select a suitable route out of a pool of FWS routes to a destination.

2 Related Research

Wayfinding is a difficult task for users of large virtual environments. Users often feel lost, disoriented, and lack the spatial knowledge needed to pick an appropriate route to a destination. To alleviate these problems, navigation aids such as maps have been introduced as part of the VE interface [2, 6].

Personalization systems create user profiles (i.e. model of user's preferences) and make recommendations based on data that is either implicitly or explicitly acquired. The advantage of explicit knowledge acquisition (e.g. asking users questions about their interests) is that it directly gathers data from the source, thus reducing the amount of ambiguity in the data collection process. On the other hand, the main disadvantage is that extra time and effort is required from the user. The main advantage of gathering data in an implicit manner (e.g. unobtrusive observation of the user's behavior) is that it does not impact the user's regular activities. The disadvantage to this approach is that it requires some interpretation to understand the user's preferences since the data is acquired indirectly [4].

Previews have been utilized in various domains, such the Web, digital libraries, music, and movies, to help users determine the relevance of contents retrieved or recommended by a system (e.g. [1]). In the domain of VEs, the *Worlds in Miniature* (WIM) approach can be used to preview an immersive VE [7]. *Worldlets* provide a 3-D preview of landmarks in VEs [3].

3 Route Selection Factors

Route selection in VEs is defined as the process of choosing a route of travel from one location to another location out of several alternative routes. There are many different factors (F) that influence the route selection process in VEs. These factors can be categorized as being quantitative factors or qualitative factors. Examples of quantitative factors include time to travel the route, the length of the route, and the number of intersections encountered along the route. Qualitative factors correspond to the 3-D models that are rendered in the virtual environment ALONG routes. A model *m* ALONG a route *r* means that the model *m* is accessible to the VE user from the route *r*. For example, the user can enter the virtual building from the route. Different users prefer the presence or absence of different models ALONG a route, and thus these models are also factors that influence the route selection process.

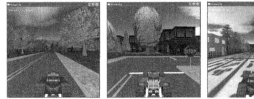

a) Scenic static   b) Interactive static   c) Scenic dynamic d) Interactive dynamic

Fig. 1. Examples of models

These 3-D models can be categorized as being static models or dynamic models (See Fig. 1). Static models are those models that will always be rendered in a fixed location within the VE. These static models can further be categorized as scenic or interactive. Scenic static models are models that primarily have only an aesthetic value associated with them (e.g. trees). Interactive static models are models that the user can interact with in some way (e.g. stop sign). Dynamic models are those models that will be rendered on a conditional basis, and they may also be rendered in different locations each time. Dynamic models can also be scenic (e.g. snow) or interactive (e.g. avatars of other users).

4   Route Preview Interface

A route preview interface has both a text component and an image component that provide information about alternative routes to a destination. The text component highlights the quantitative attributes of each route. The image component consists of n representative image snapshots of each one of the routes. Fig 2 shows an example of such an interface that provides a preview of four alternative routes to each destination. Users can view snapshots of each route and get directions by clicking on the appropriate button.

Fig. 2. Route preview interface

Our previous research explains how to capture n informative image snapshots of each route [5]. In short, a uniqueness value is assigned to each candidate snapshot of a route, and this value is a function of the saliency of the static models that are ALONG the route and clearly visible in the snapshot. Those n snapshots of a route with the highest uniqueness value are featured as the image component in the route's preview. Our experiments showed that this approach leads to the selection of informative, descriptive, and salient snapshots [5].

4.1 Route Preview Design: An Average-User Approach

Our initial route preview interface offered a preview of the top four routes to the destination with the highest statistical confidence as found by the FWS approach [5]. These routes are not optimized for any particular route selection factor, instead they serve as good *general* recommendations since they were taken by a significant number of previous experienced users. Limiting the number of routes displayed in the preview interface to four per destination ensures that the user is not overburdened by the interface and can use the interface to make a quick yet informative route selection decision. Therefore, the approach is scalable no matter how complex the environment, because only four routes per destination are previewed.

Although the average-user route preview interface is beneficial to the user, the approach is rigid. That is, all users regardless of their route preferences are offered the same four alternative routes to a destination. Other routes found to the destination besides the top four FWS routes are not considered, and this is problematic since such routes may actually be preferable to some users. Therefore, our goal is to consider the entire pool of FWS routes found to a destination, and offer each individual user a preview of routes determined to be preferable to the unique user.

4.2 Route Preview Design: A Personalized Approach

Our goal is to personalize the route preview interface for each user by offering four alternative routes to the destination that are the closest to the user's actual unique route preferences (Π). The proposed design requires no additional explicit input as compared to the average-user approach. Therefore, any improvements will not be at the cost of requiring extra effort from the user.

For each route in a VE, it is possible to develop a route profile (rP_i) as a comprehensive summary of the characteristics of the route, r_i. The structure of the route profile can be conceptualize as a n x 1 table with a numeric value in each of the n cells that represents one qualitative or quantitative route factor. For quantitative route factors the numeric value represents the actual value of the quantitative factor (e.g. 50 distance units, 25 units of time), while for qualitative route factors the numeric value represents the number of occurrences of the model ALONG the route (e.g. 40 trees, 4 stop signs). In order to implement the personalized route preview interface, the system develops and centrally stores the profile of all FWS routes of travel between a landmark L_i to landmark L_j. Each profile is normalized (i.e. range of [0, 1]) to avoid overweighting those features that usually have large values.

The user profile (uP) is a representation of the user's actual route preferences (Π). The route preferences of the user are not known to the system, therefore the system unobtrusively observes the normal process of using the route preview to select a route to learn and model the user's preferences. Each time a user selects a route, the user profile is updated to reflect the new bit of knowledge gained about the user's preferences.

The structure of the user profile (uP) is identical to the structure of the route profile (rP), where each normalized numeric value in the $n \times 1$ cells represents the system's estimation of the user's preference level for the particular route selection factor. For each new user, an initial normalized user profile consisting of .5 preference level is assumed for all factors. Each time the user selects a new route, the user profile is updated with the following learning function:

$$uP(F_i)_{New\_Value} = uP(F_i)_{Old\_Value} + \alpha \, (rP(F_i)_{Selected\_Route} - uP(F_i)_{Old\_Value}) . \qquad (1)$$

where:

- α is the learning factor which is $1/(k+1)$ and k is the kth route selection by the user

The routes displayed in the route preview interface are dependant on the user profile. Each time a user selects a new destination, the system examines all available routes to the destination found by the FWS methodology, and displays the top four that are the most similar to the user profile. The measure of similarity used is the Euclidean distance measure (D) for n-dimensional space, where n is the number of factors considered.

$$D(uP, rP) = \sqrt{\sum_{i}^{n} (uP(F_i) - rP(F_i))^2} . \qquad (2)$$

Table 1. Profile of all FWS routes to a destination sorted based on confidence

Factor ID	rP_1	rP_2	rP_3	rP_4	rP_5	rP_6	rP_7	rP_8
F_1	0.25	0.51	0.13	0.51	0.29	0.55	0.79	0.37
F_2	0.65	0.28	0.23	0.11	0.65	0.25	0.41	0.35
F_3	0.66	0.22	0.84	0.73	0.43	0.65	0.48	0.79
F_4	0.46	0.54	0.30	0.34	0.95	0.75	0.65	0.65
F_5	0.64	0.71	0.69	0.31	0.16	0.39	0.75	0.40
Confidence	*.25*	*.20*	*.15*	*.12*	*.10*	*.8*	*.5*	*.5*

Table 2. Demonstration of selecting routes to display in the preview based on the user profile

a) User profile

	Current uP
$uP(F_1)$	0.50
$uP(F_2)$	0.20
$uP(F_3)$	0.60
$uP(F_4)$	0.80
$uP(F_5)$	0.30

b) Distance between uP and rPs

	Distance
$D(uP, rP_1)$	0.71
$D(uP, rP_2)$	0.62
$D(uP, rP_3)$	0.77
$D(uP, rP_4)$	0.49
$D(uP, rP_5)$	0.56
$D(uP, rP_6)$	0.13
$D(uP, rP_7)$	0.61
$D(uP, rP_8)$	0.33

As an example, assume that there is a pool of 8 routes found by the FWS methodology to a destination. The normalized profiles of these routes are listed in Table 1. The routes are sorted according to the confidence level as established by the FWS methodology. That is, route 1 has the highest confidence; route 2 has the second highest confidence, and so forth. Table 2a has the current user profile of a hypothetical user, and Table 2b shows the distance between the user profile and the eight route profiles using Equation 2.

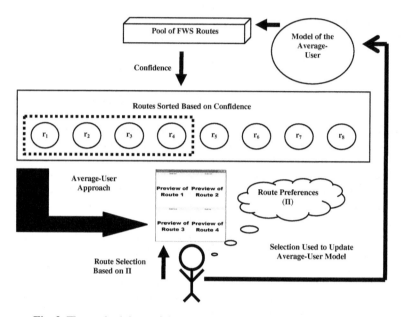

Fig. 3. The methodology of the average-user route preview approach

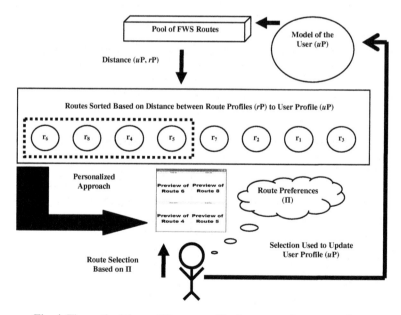

Fig. 4. The methodology of the personalized route preview approach

Based on the similarity analysis, rP_4, rP_5, rP_6, and rP_8 are the most similar to the user profile (i.e. smallest distance). Therefore, in the enhanced personalized version of the route preview interface, these four routes would be displayed to the user. Fig. 3 and Fig. 4 show the difference between the average-user approach and the personalized approach for this example. The average-user approach would automatically display previews of Route 1, Route 2, Route 3, and Route 4 to all users since they are the top four FWS routes based on confidence levels. However, the personalized version of the route preview interface would display previews of Route 6, Route 8, Route 4, and Route 5 (i.e. ordered based on similarity) for a user with the user profile in Table 2a. Of course if the user profile was different, then it is highly likely that the routes featured in the preview would also be different.

5 Experiments and Discussion

The goal of the simulation experiments was to compare the average-user approach to the personalized approach. A large-scale VE (200 landmarks) was simulated with 10 FWS routes of travel between any landmark pair, L_i-L_j. The FWS routes for each landmark pair, L_i-L_j, were sorted based on confidence levels. For this simulation, 10 route selection factors were considered. Normalized route profiles were generated for each FWS route. As an example, Table 3 shows the normalized route profiles of the 10 FWS routes found for a hypothetical landmark pair, L_i-L_j.

Table 3. Ten sample FWS routes sorted based on confidence levels

Factor ID	rP_1	rP_2	rP_3	rP_4	rP_5	rP_6	rP_7	rP_8	rP_9	rP_{10}
F_1	0.26	0.04	0.93	0.29	0.80	0.77	0.76	0.14	0.54	0.48
F_2	0.45	0.29	0.46	0.08	0.98	0.46	0.13	0.13	0.66	0.43
F_3	0.19	0.23	0.89	0.43	0.43	0.66	0.74	0.94	0.84	0.76
F_4	0.34	0.51	0.65	0.14	0.66	0.76	0.35	0.30	0.46	0.97
F_5	0.65	0.71	0.98	0.17	0.76	0.72	0.33	0.92	0.70	0.56
F_6	0.80	0.84	0.14	0.22	0.23	0.32	0.34	0.11	0.78	0.77
F_7	0.18	0.09	0.44	0.84	0.23	0.95	0.53	0.57	0.25	0.29
F_8	0.24	0.69	0.64	0.22	0.68	0.63	0.57	0.23	0.24	0.60
F_9	0.17	0.12	0.69	0.54	0.96	0.09	0.53	0.36	0.15	0.44
F_{10}	0.85	0.37	0.86	0.02	0.69	0.80	1.00	0.71	0.75	0.69
Confidence	.20	.16	.15	.12	.8	.8	.6	.5	.5	.5

Table 4. The route preferences (Π) of a hypothetical user

	Π
Π (F_1)	0.5
Π (F_2)	0.2
Π (F_3)	0.6
Π (F_4)	0.8
Π (F_5)	0.3
Π (F_6)	0.25
Π (F_7)	0.75
Π (F_8)	0.4
Π (F_9)	0.4
Π (F_{10})	0.9

Fifty VE users were simulated. Each user was randomly assigned a unique set of route preferences, and these preferences were not provided as input to the navigation system. As an example, Table 4 shows the route preferences (Π) of one hypothetical user.

A two-stage experiment was performed. The first stage simulated users using the route preview interface designed by the average-user approach. Each route selection case involved simulating the process of presenting the top four FWS routes with the highest confidence to a destination, and the user selecting one of the four routes. In each route selection simulation, the route most similar to the user's actual preferences (Π) out of the four alternatives was selected. Equation 3 shows the measure of similarity used.

$$D(\Pi, rP) = \sqrt{\sum_{i=1}^{10} (\Pi(F_i) - rP(F_i))^2}. \tag{3}$$

Table 5 shows the distance between the hypothetical user preferences in Table 4 and the profiles of the top four FWS routes from Table 3. Since the distance between Π and rP_3 is the smallest, Routes 3 would be the selection of the user in this simulated route selection case.

Table 5. A sample route selection case of the average-user approach

$D(\Pi, rP_1)$	$D(\Pi, rP_2)$	$D(\Pi, rP_3)$	$D(\Pi, rP_4)$
1.15	1.35	*1.04*	1.17

The second stage of the experiment simulated the same users using the route preview interface designed by the personalized approach. Each route selection case involved simulating the process of presenting the four routes out of the ten available FWS routes to a destination that are the most similar to the user's current profile, and the user selecting one of the four routes. In order to determine which route choices to offer to the user in each selection case, the distance between the user's current profile (uP) and the ten available FWS routes were computed. As an example, Table 6b shows the distance (see Equation 2) between the hypothetical user profile shown in Table 6a and the ten FWS routes in Table 3. The four routes with profiles that are the closest to the user's profile are offered to the user in the route preview interface as available personalized routes to the destination. In this example, previews of Route 7, Route 6, Route 10, and Route 8 (i.e. sorted based on similarity level) are offered to the user.

Table 6. Demonstration of distance computation between the uP and all ten route pofiles

a) Sample user profile

	uP
$uP (F_1)$	0.45
$uP (F_2)$	0.3
$uP (F_3)$	0.75
$uP (F_4)$	0.62
$uP (F_5)$	0.25
$uP (F_6)$	0.33
$uP (F_7)$	0.69
$uP (F_8)$	0.48
$uP (F_9)$	0.31
$uP (F_{10})$	0.7

b) Distance analysis

	Distance
$D(uP, rP_1)$	1.09
$D(uP, rP_2)$	1.21
$D(uP, rP_3)$	1.05
$D(uP, rP_4)$	1.02
$D(uP, rP_5)$	1.28
$D(uP, rP_6)$	0.72
$D(uP, rP_7)$	0.61
$D(uP, rP_8)$	0.92
$D(uP, rP_9)$	0.93
$D(uP, rP_{10})$	0.79

In the simulation, the route that was selected for a user in each route selection case was the one route out of the four personalized routes that was the most similar to the user's actual preferences (Π). Table 7 shows the distance (see Equation 3) between the hypothetical preferences (Π) from Table 4 and the route profiles of Route 7, Route 6,

Route 10, and Route 8 (i.e. the personalized recommendations for this route selection case). Since the distance between Π and rP_7 is the smallest, Routes 7 would be the selection of the user in this simulated route selection case. After each selection, the route profile of the selected route is used to update the user's profile as described by Equation 1.

Table 7. A sample route selection case of the personalized approach

D(Π, rP_7)	D(Π, rP_6)	D(Π, rP_{10})	D(Π, rP_8)
0.64	0.73	0.86	1.00

For each of the fifty users, 100 route selection cases were simulated using the average-user approach, and 100 route selection cases were simulated using the personalized approach. Fig. 5 shows the average distance between the users' profiles (uP) and the users' preferences (Π) for the fifty users in the 100 route selection cases of the personalized approach. As can be seen from the graph, as the number of route selection cases increases, the user profile becomes more accurate since there are more learning opportunities.

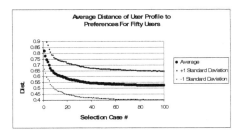

Fig. 5. Average distance between the users' profiles (uP) and preferences (Π) of the fifty users

The average distance between the 100 selected routes and Π in each approach was also calculated for each user. Figure 6a shows the distribution of these average values of the fifty users for the average-user approach, and Figure 6b shows this data for the personalized approach. Analysis revealed that for all fifty users, the average distance is always less when the personalized approach is used instead of the average-user approach. In fact, a t-test analysis (H_0: $\mu_{A\text{-}uA} = \mu_{PA}$ (reject null), H_a: $\mu_{A\text{-}uA} > \mu_{PA}$, t=7.491, p<.001, α =0.01) showed a statistically significant difference between the average-user approach ($\mu_{A\text{-}uA} = 1.02$, standard deviation =.08) and the personalized approach ($\mu_{PA} = .90$, standard deviation =.08). In other words, the use of the personalized approach provides users with route choices that are closer to the user's actual preferences.

Although, only a modest 12% improvement is gained by the use of the personalized approach, this level of improvement should be analyzed while keeping in mind two considerations. First, this improvement is gained without requiring any extra efforts, tasks, or time from the user. The second consideration is that the limiting factor on the improvement level and the learning process is the size of the pool of route choices (e.g. 10) available to a destination and the number of VEs used by the user. Better results can be expected by not limiting the pool to only FWS routes and analyzing the data from the user in multiple VEs instead of just one.

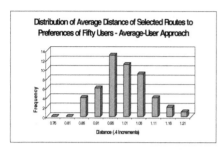
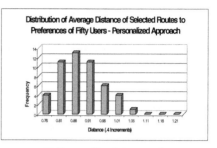

a) Average-user Approach   b) Personalized Approach

Fig. 6. Route selection results for all fifty users

6 Conclusions

In this paper, we introduced a route preview tool that can be used by VE users to select personalized routes. The system automatically creates a user profile and updates this profile based on the user's route selections. The user profile serves as a model of the user's actual preferences, and is used to recommend several routes to a desired destination that would be deemed as preferable to the specific user. Simulation experiments demonstrated the potential of this approach over a general route preview interface that makes route recommendations that are of common interest to all users and not personalized to specific users. Future work will be directed at modifying the approach to detect and adapt to changing preferences, and conducting real-world experiments.

References

1. Chen, L., Su, C., Liao, H., Shih, C.: On Preview of Digital Movies. Journal of Visual Communication and Image Representation 14(3), 358–368 (2003)
2. Darken, R., Sibert, J.: Navigating Large Virtual Spaces. The International Journal of Human-Computer Interaction 8(1), 49–72 (1996)
3. Elvins, T., Nadeau, D., Kirsh, D.: Worldlets: 3D Thumbnails for Wayfinding in Large Virtual Worlds. Presence 10(6), 565–582 (2001)
4. Godoy, D., Amandi, A.: User Profiling in Personal Information Agents: A Survey. The Knowledge Engineering Review 20(4), 329–361 (2006)
5. Sadeghian, P., Kantardzic, M., Lozitskiy, O., Lozitskiy, Y.: Preview of Recommended Routes in Large-Scale Virtual Environments. In: Proceedings of the ACM International Conference on Virtual Reality Continuum and Its Applications (VRCIA), Hong Kong, China, pp. 35–42 (2006)
6. Sadeghian, P., Kantardzic, M., Lozitskiy, O., Sheta, W.: The Frequent Wayfinding-Sequence (FWS) Methodology: Finding Preferred Routes in Complex Virtual Environments. The International Journal of Human-Computer Studies 64(4), 356–374 (2006)
7. Stoakley, R., Conway, M., Pausch, R.: Virtual Reality on a WIM: Interactive Worlds in Miniature. In: Proceedings of the 1995 Conference on Human Factors in Computing Systems (CHI'95), Denver, CO, pp. 265–272 (1995)

Visual Attention in Open Learner Model Presentations: An Eye-Tracking Investigation

Susan Bull, Neil Cooke, and Andrew Mabbott

Electronic, Electrical and Computer Engineering, University of Birmingham,
Edgbaston, Birmingham, B15 2TT, U.K.
{s.bull,n.j.cooke,axm891}@bham.ac.uk

Abstract. Using an eye-tracker, this paper investigates the information that learners visually attend to in their open learner model, and the degree to which this is related to the method of displaying the model to the learner. Participants were fourteen final year undergraduate students using six views of their learner model data. Results suggest some views of the learner model information may be more likely to encourage learners to inspect information about their level of knowledge, whereas in other views attention is directed more towards scanning the view, resulting in a lower proportion of time focussed on knowledge-related data. In some views there was a difference according to whether the learner model view was one of the participants' preferred formats for accessing their learner model information, while in other views there was little difference. This has implications for the design of open learner model views in systems opening the learner model to the learner for different purposes.

I Introduction

Open learner models - learner models that are accessible to users - are becoming more common in adaptive learning environments. Examples include simple presentations of the learner model data such as skill meters [1,2,3,4,5,6]; or more complex presentations such as a textual description of knowledge and misconceptions [7]; a text explanation of a fuzzy logic model [8]; a hierarchical tree structure [9]; a conceptual graph [10]; a graphical representation of a Bayesian model [11]. Reasons for opening the learner model to the user are varied (see [12]), but those particularly relevant to our current discussion include promoting learner reflection on their knowledge, facilitating planning, self-monitoring or navigation, and allowing the user to contribute information about their knowledge to improve the accuracy of their learner model in order to improve system adaptation.

While multiple representations to support learning or problem-solving have been investigated (e.g. [13,14]), the use of alternative presentations of the open learner model within a system has received less attention. However, in systems which do offer a choice of learner model presentations, it has been found that users have different preferences for how to access their model both when simple formats are used [15], and when more complex presentations are available [16]. Furthermore, students sometimes prefer or reject model presentation formats for what seem like similar

C. Conati, K. McCoy, and G. Paliouras (Eds.): UM 2007, LNAI 4511, pp. 177–186, 2007.
© Springer-Verlag Berlin Heidelberg 2007

reasons, as illustrated by the following excerpts from open-ended questionnaire responses: "The concept map was the most useful as it shows the relationship between all subject areas and where my weaknesses lie"; "Concept map is a bit complex compared to the others, making it a bit difficult to understand". We therefore do not intend to recommend a single presentation or a specific set of presentation methods for open learner models based only on the type of information and level of detail that the learner model externalisations display. Rather, the purpose of this paper is to investigate the information that learners look at in their open learner model, taking into consideration whether the particular view is one of the user's preferred methods for accessing their model, and the structure of the model view. Based on this information we will consider requirements for the design of presentation formats for open learner models, which also allow for individual differences amongst users.

In line with previous studies of use of educational environments employing eye-trackers to record gaze, for example to help detect motivational factors [17] or enhance the interaction between a learner and software agent [18], we here describe a study of students' attention to the various components of the Flexi-OLM open learner model [19] revealed by use of an eye-tracker following students' inspection of six learner model views. While eye-tracking to determine gaze direction has been questioned as a way of identifying attention because it is often based on visual search (which is only one of the tasks a user may be undertaking) [20], here it is precisely visual search or scanning of the learner model that we are interested in measuring.

2   What Do Students Attend to in Their Open Learner Model?

In this section we investigate students' use of an open learner model with multiple views using the 'EyeLink 2' head-mounted binocular eye-tracking device which measured their gaze position to an accuracy of 0.5°-0.1° visual angle with a sample rate of 500 Hz, relative to a 22 inch computer monitor screen. The fact that the learner model information for an individual student was identical across learner model views (as these were representing the same underlying model), allows us to make comparisons between what learners visually attended to in the various views.

2.1   Participants, Materials and Methods

The Flexi-OLM open learner model was implemented for the domain of C programming. Participants were 14 final year undergraduate students who had completed a C programming course, and who had knowledge of what an open learner model represents, all having previously used a simple open learner model [1] in two of their courses. Students had not yet used more complex open learner model views as offered by Flexi-OLM, in any of their courses. However, they had participated in a two-hour lab session where their Flexi-OLM learner models were constructed, and their preferences for the learner model views investigated using questionnaires (data which was used in the current study). The eye-tracking study was therefore measuring their gaze in a learner model with which they were familiar.

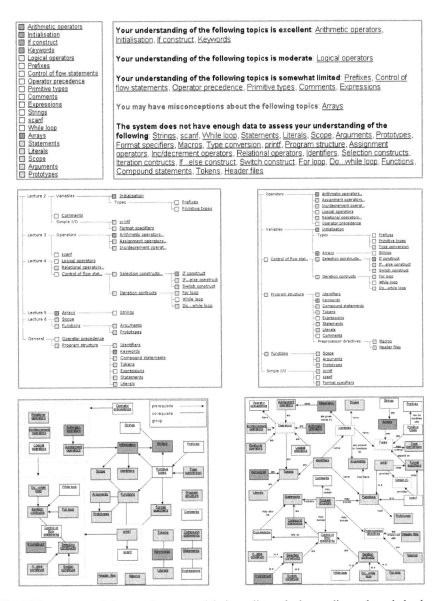

Fig. 1. The structure of the open learner model views: list ranked according to knowledge level, text summary, hierarchical lecture structure, hierarchical topic/concepts structure, prerequisite relationships, concept map

Flexi-OLM aims to help learners identify their learning needs for themselves, by permitting them access to the contents of their learner model constructed according to their answers to multiple choice and short answer questions. Flexi-OLM has seven views of the learner model data which are accessible at any time, to allow students to view the information about their understanding in the format or formats that suit them best: alphabetical index, list ranked according to knowledge level, text summary, lecture structure (i.e. structured according to the lecture course in which Flexi-OLM is deployed), related topics/concepts hierarchical structure, concept map, and prerequisite relationships. Previous studies have demonstrated that students differ in their preferences for the Flexi-OLM learner model views [16,19]. The eye-tracking was insufficiently accurate to determine the focus of visual attention confidently for the alphabetical index, so we here consider visual attention in the remaining six views. The differing layouts of these learner model views are illustrated in Figure 1.

In all but the text summary, coloured boxes or nodes indicate knowledge level (shades of green - for high levels of knowledge, through yellow, to white - representing low knowledge; and red for topics with misconceptions). Text statements of probable misconceptions are also given in each view, accessed by clicking on the links associated with the red nodes. In this study, given the size of the learner model and the fact that the previous lab session in which the learner models were constructed, lasted two hours only, all participants had more grey (insufficient data) areas in their learner models than coloured nodes. However, all data included here is from users who interacted sufficiently to allow a learner model with a variety of instantiated nodes to be built. This allowed investigation of visual attention in the context of a mix of instantiated and incomplete learner model information, potentially relevant to open learner model settings where students are encouraged to view their learner model to prompt self-monitoring or reflection, facilitate planning or navigation, or where they may contribute information directly to the model to increase its accuracy - thereby leading to improved adaptation.

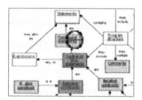

Fig. 2. Video excerpt showing part of screen illustrating visual attention

Figure 2 illustrates an excerpt from an eye-tracking video, showing the user's focus of visual attention. The 'EyeLink 2' system consists of a head-mounted camera system and two PCs for processing data and running experiments. On the head-mounted device, both left and right eye pupil position and the head position relative to computer monitor, were tracked. Combining the position of the head with the pupil movement relative to the screen, enabled recording of the gaze direction. Eye tracking data for both eyes was captured at a sample rate of 500Hz (2ms samples) with a resolution of 0.01° visual angle. The effective resolution, however, was limited by the calibration process, which provided an accuracy of typically 0.5° - 1.0° visual angle.

In addition to recording gaze direction, the eye tracker also detected eye movement types such as saccades, fixations and blinking. Fixation events, assigned to their nearest visual focus (i.e. nodes in the learner model), were used as the unit of analysis.

Sessions commenced by calibrating the eye tracker. This took 5-15 minutes. In 5 sessions, eye movement recordings showed poor calibration, so these have been omitted from this study. Rejection criteria were horizontal and/or vertical offsets in gaze direction, loss of gaze altogether, and general corruption in the eye signal, making the eye movement unintelligible. There are a number of causes for calibration failure. Overt indications of errors during recording occurred if a subject inadvertently moved the eye tracker when coughing, gesticulating or touching his or her face. As the human scalp is elastic, the head mounted device was also liable to moving. The eye tracker was also sensitive to the ambient light levels in its environment.

Once comfortable with the eye-tracker, students logged on to Flexi-OLM, accessing the learner model created in the previous lab session (see above). While students could move freely, they were requested to restrict their head movements as far as possible. They were instructed to continue using Flexi-OLM as they had previously, in order to avoid potentially biasing their choice of learner model views to access, and their behaviour within a view. Interaction may have involved answering additional questions, editing the learner model, or attempting to persuade the system to change the learner model contents (see [19]). This allowed the interaction to proceed as naturally as possible, observing attention in the context of using the system as a whole. The eye-tracking sessions lasted around 10 minutes to ensure that the calibration remained sufficiently accurate for the whole interaction. The eye-tracking data for each view was analysed from the videos, and compared against the data for the other learner model views and against the learner's preference for the view as indicated in their questionnaire responses (on a 5 point scale) in the previous lab session. As the participant numbers are relatively low, the figures were checked to ensure that they were not biased by unusual behaviour by a small minority of users.

2.2 Results

12 of the 14 participants stated in the questionnaire that the open learner model was useful (giving a score of 4 or 5 on a 5 point scale); 1 gave a neutral response (3); and 1 gave a negative response (2). 13 stated that they understood their learner model; the remaining student gave a neutral response. 4 students stated that they would regularly use 1 of the views only; 5 would use 2 views; 2 would use 3 views; 1 would use 4 views; and 2 would use 5 views.

During the 10 minute eye-tracking period, students spent an average of 145 seconds in their learner model (median - 143; range 70-261 seconds), spending up to 30 seconds in their learner model at any one viewing. The rest of the time was spent answering questions (all students), editing the model (7 students) and attempting to persuade the system that the learner model was incorrect (8 students). 5 students attempted to both persuade the learner model, and edit it directly.

Figure 3 shows the breakdown of visual attention to information in the learner model according to whether students were using one of their preferred views, as indicated in their questionnaire responses. 'High' indicates gaze focused on nodes showing a high level of knowledge for a topic or concept; 'medium' indicates a medium level of knowledge; 'low' indicates a low level of knowledge; and 'unknown' indicates that there is insufficient data on knowledge of that topic or concept for it to be modelled. The numbers in brackets show participants who claimed to be either users or non-users of a view (total = 84: 14 users x 6 views).

Figure 3 suggests that there is little difference in the distribution of visual attention according simply to whether a student is using one of their preferred views. However, there was a slight tendency for misconceptions to be accessed relatively more frequently in views that participants would be more likely to use.

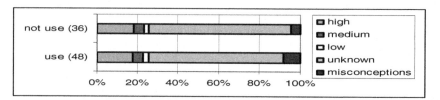

Fig. 3. Visual attention according to whether participants were users/non-users of the views

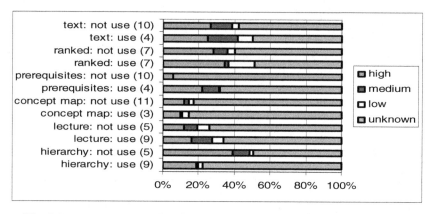

Fig. 4. Visual attention according to learner model view, and view users/non-users

Figure 4 gives the breakdown of the proportion of time participants spent viewing the various components of each of the learner model views according to whether they claimed that they would use the particular view in their questionnaire responses. As found previously [16,19], participants had different preferences for which views to use. Because not all participants had misconceptions, resulting in some of the categories in Figure 4 having no misconceptions to view, in order to compare the relative percentage of time directed to viewing knowledge level versus lack of data the figures for viewing misconceptions have been omitted. (In all but one category - non-users of the prerequisites view - in cases where students had misconceptions they tended to view them.)

Figure 4 shows differences between the learner model views with reference to the information users focus on. The text and ranked list appear to focus students' attention to a greater extent onto their level of knowledge than do the other views, regardless of whether these are the students' preferred views (40-51% of the time spent inspecting the view). The hierarchy view has a similar effect only for those who would tend not to use that view (50% of inspection time). The concept map focuses attention on knowledge to a lesser extent than the other views for both users and non-users (up to 18% of inspection time), as does the pre-requisites view for non-users, where focus on knowledge was particularly low (5%).

2.3 Discussion

Students generally claimed to find their learner model useful. Viewing the model prompted both selection of areas on which to answer questions, and interactions aimed at changing the learner model more directly. In this paper we are concerned with how students inspect their learner model rather than the resulting choice of task, as task selection may depend on what is found in the model. (Future work will investigate possible differences between browsing the model and using it for a specified purpose.)

When considering only whether students are using a learner model view that they regard as useful according to their individual preferences, there is very little variation in what they attend to - though there is a slightly higher tendency to access descriptions of misconceptions relatively more frequently in a view that they prefer. However, when separating out the data for the individual views it was found that variations between views resulted in gaze being directed towards different information. Using the concept map, regardless of whether participants considered this as one of their preferred views, they focussed less on their knowledge, exploring the areas with insufficient data in more detail. This may be due to the complexity of this view: students can easily see the differences in knowledge level at a glance due to the size of the nodes, but perhaps require more effort to gain an overview of the relationships between the concepts even when already familiar with the layout of the concept map; or, indeed, they may be particularly interested in gaining an understanding of such relationships. Of course, given the level of system usage at the time of the study there were still relatively many uninstantiated nodes in the learner model views, so this factor is likely to also contribute to the amount of time spent investigating this information. Nevertheless, the relative complexity of the model might still result in a broader spread of attention in a more complete model.

In contrast, using the text description and ranked list, although attention is still on the areas with insufficient data, 40-51% of the visual attention is directed at the nodes indicating knowledge level. This is likely to be because both the ranked list and the text summary sequence the information from known, to moderate knowledge, to limited knowledge, with the remainder of the concepts listed as having insufficient data to model them. Because of this sequencing of information this is not a surprising finding; however, we can now suggest that even when students are familiar with a learner model view, they may still follow it sequentially or focus more on the initial information if it is inherently a list format - regardless of their focus of attention in other layouts of the same information about their understanding. (It should be noted that preference for view has not been found to match a user's learning style (see [16]), as measured by Felder and Silverman's learning style classification [21].)

Interestingly, if our comment about ease of noticing knowledge level quickly in the concept map is correct, it is perhaps surprising that the same results were not observed in the pre-requisites structure. Clearly this was the case for the majority claiming to be non-users of this view; however, the 4 who found it a useful presentation format were looking at the nodes representing knowledge level to a greater extent. Perhaps for users who find that a structure showing pre-requisite relationships helps them to more easily identify the most appropriate areas to work on, are less distracted by the overall structure - a finding that did not seem to apply with the concept map.

Conversely, users of the hierarchical relationships structure seem to focus less on the knowledge-related nodes than do the non-users. It may be that users of this view are keen to understand the relationships and work out how their knowledge fits into the overall structure, whereas non-users do not find this helpful.

Although the number of participants is relatively low, there do appear to be some differences between the learner model views in terms of where gaze is directed - this sometimes being related to whether students find the particular view useful. However, it is rather early to be confident of the reasons for this - our suggestions are, at this stage, simply suggestions. But whatever the reasons, there does seem to be something happening. Congruent with one of the reasons suggested for offering multiple external representations in learning environments more generally [22], we have previously recommended that because students have different preferences for views to use when offered a choice, it is useful to offer multiple-view open learner models ([15,16]). Given the above findings we would now argue that consideration should also be given to whether it is important that students focus primarily on their knowledge level - for example to promote reflection and raise their awareness of their knowledge and difficulties, or to facilitate planning of learning episodes within or outside the system. Alternatively, a purpose of opening the model may be to allow the learner to provide information where there is, as yet, insufficient data, where focus specifically on those areas will be necessary - for example, where one of the aims is to use an open learner model to highlight gaps in knowledge to the learner; or if it will be important that the learner can review areas where their knowledge is low, as well as refer to areas with insufficient data in order to distinguish between these two types of information. An open learner model to facilitate navigation may also need to focus attention on both areas with low knowledge and areas with insufficient data - though other issues relating to the structure of the view may also be more relevant (for example, navigation might also be facilitated in particular by inclusion of information about pre-requisite relationships or the overall lecture structure of a course). In an open learner model designed primarily to allow the learner to correct inaccurate model data (or attempt to correct the data, but requiring system approval), it may be useful to use a presentation that encourages broader scanning. Thus, although we still maintain that individual preferences are important both to facilitate students' understanding of their learner model and to motivate them to access their model data, it may also be that different views of the learner model are better suited to different purposes for accessing the model. Students spent up to 30 seconds in their learner model at any one time. Therefore a format that encourages attention to be directed quickly at the components most relevant for the purpose of viewing the model in a particular system, would appear to be useful. This point does, however, need to be judged alongside consideration of a format that is appropriate for the domain. For example, if topics are defined very broadly in a system, it may be harder to design a useful concept map in sufficient detail; or if there is a range of topics and/or concepts that have few pre-requisite relationships, a pre-requisite structure will be less appropriate; or if the learner modelling is very coarse-grained, e.g. with concepts modelled simply as 'known' or 'not known', a ranked list may be less useful. Similarly, if a system expects users to understand relationships between different aspects of the domain, a learner model view that reflects these relationships may be more useful generally.

Of course, if students have only one or two learner model views available, they may focus more on aspects that they neglected in some of the views when they had a greater choice. Thus it may not be the case that a particular learner model view structure will necessarily encourage or inhibit attention to certain components. Nevertheless, given that students were often scanning their learner models quite quickly, it is still likely to be useful to consider what students would naturally attend to when designing an open learner model - if they find a particular structure difficult, they may be less inclined to use it.

Based on the above, our overall recommendation at this stage of the research in open learner modelling is to design open learner models that take into account: (i) the requirements of the domain as represented in the system; (ii) the educational aims of the system and the purpose of opening the model to the user; (iii) the individual preferences of the user; (iv) the user's focus of attention in the learner model.

Clearly there are limitations to this study, the most obvious being that using an eye-tracker may influence the natural choices of the user, given that they are aware that their gaze is being monitored. Furthermore, this was necessarily an experimental, lab-based study. It would obviously be impractical to measure use of Flexi-OLM in this way in a natural setting, where users are accessing the system regularly alongside a lecture course. However, given the results obtained, an interesting next step would be to follow up a set of users later on in a course to see whether their use of the learner model differs when they have had extensive previous interaction with it.

3 Summary

This paper has described an investigation into visual attention in an open learner model. Using an eye-tracker, students' use of a multiple-view open learner model was observed. Results indicate that, although in general students' preferences for learner model view do not affect the information that they visually attend to, some of the individual views do have a tendency to focus attention on information relating to knowledge level more than others. This suggests that, as well as considering individual differences in preference for the presentation of an open learner model, where it is important in a system that the learner model data is used for a particular purpose it may be useful to consider the information that students are likely to visually attend to in different model presentation formats.

References

1. Bull, S., Quigley, S., Mabbott, A.: Computer-Based Formative Assessment to Promote Reflection and Learner Autonomy. Engineering Education: Journal of the Higher Education Academy Engineering Subject Centre 1(1), 8–18 (2006)
2. Corbett, A.T., Anderson, J.: Knowledge Tracing: Modeling the Acquisition of Procedural Knowledge. User Modeling and User-Adapted Interaction 4, 253–278 (1995)
3. Linton, F., Schaefer, H.-P: Recommender Systems for Learning: Building User and Expert Models through Long-Term Observation of Application Use. User Modeling and User-Adapted Interaction 10, 181–207 (2000)
4. Mitrovic, A., Martin, B.: Evaluating the Effects of Open Student Models on Learning, Adaptive Hypermedia and Adaptive Web-Based Systems. In: Proceedings of Second International Conference, pp. 296–305. Springer, Heidelberg (2002)

5. Papanikolaou, K.A., Grigoriadou, M., Kornilakis, H., Magoulas, G.D.: Personalizing the Interaction in a Web-Based Educational Hypermedia System: The Case of INSPIRE. User-Modeling and User-Adapted Interaction 13(3), 213–267 (2003)
6. Weber, G., Brusilovsky, P.: ELM-ART: An Adaptive Versatile System for Web-Based Instruction. Int. Journal of Artificial Intelligence in Education 12(4), 351–384 (2001)
7. Bull, S., Pain, H.: Did I say what I think I said, and do you agree with me? Inspecting and Questioning the Student Model. In: Proceedings of World Conference on Artificial Intelligence in Education, AACE, pp. 501–508 (1995)
8. Mohanarajah, S., Kemp, R., Kemp, E.: Opening a Fuzzy Learner Model. In: Proceedings of Workshop on Learner Modelling for Reflection. In: International Conference on Artificial Intelligence in Education 2005, pp. 62–71 (2005)
9. Kay, J.: Learner Know Thyself: Student Models to Give Learner Control and Responsibility. In: International Conference on Computers in Education, AACE, pp. 17–24 (1997)
10. Dimitrova, V.: StyLE-OLM: Interactive Open Learner Modelling. Int. Journal of Artificial Intelligence in Education 13(1), 35–78 (2003)
11. Zapata-Rivera, J.-D., Greer, J.E.: Externalising Learner Modelling Representations. In: Proceedings of Workshop on External Representations of AIED, International Conference on Artificial Intelligence in Education 2001, pp. 71–76 (2001)
12. Bull, S., Kay, J. (in press). Student Models that Invite the Learner In: The SMILI Open Learner Modelling Framework, Int. Journal of Artificial Intelligence in Education
13. Ainsworth, S., Van Labeke, N.: Using a Multi-Representational Design Framework to Develop and Evaluate a Dynamic Simulation Environment. Dynamic Information and Visualisation Workshop, Tuebingen (July 2002)
14. Cox, R.: Representation Interpretation Versus Representation Construction: An ILE-Based Study Using switchERII. In: Artificial Intelligence in Education (Proceedings), pp. 434–441. IOS Press, Amsterdam (1997)
15. Bull, S., Mabbott, A.: 20000 Inspections of a Domain-Independent Open Learner Model with Individual and Comparison Views. In: International Conference on Intelligent Tutoring Systems, pp. 422–432. Springer-Verlag, Berlin Heidelberg (2006)
16. Mabbott, A., Bull, S.: Alternative Views on Knowledge: Presentation of Open Learner Models. In: Intelligent Tutoring Systems: 7th International Conference, pp. 689–698. Springer-Verlag, Berlin Heidelberg (2004)
17. Qu, L., Wang, N., Johnson, W.L.: Using Learner Focus of Attention to Detect Learner Motivation Factors. In: User Modeling 2005: 10th International Conference, pp. 70–73. Springer-Verlag, Berlin Heidelberg (2005)
18. Wang, H., Chignell, M., Ishizuka, M.: Empathic Tutoring Software Agents Using Real-Time Eye Tracking, Eye Tracking Research and Application. In: Proceedings of Symposium on Eye Tracking Research and Applications, pp. 73–78. ACM Press, New York (2006)
19. Mabbott, A., Bull, S.: Student Preferences for Editing, Persuading and Negotiating the Open Learner Model. In: Intelligent Tutoring Systems: 8th International Conference, pp. 481–490. Springer-Verlag, Berlin Heidelberg (2006)
20. Wood, S., Cox, R., Cheng, P.: Attention Design: Eight Issues to Consider. Computers in Human Behavior 22, 588–602 (2006)
21. Felder, R.M., Silverman, L.K.: Learning and Teaching Styles in Engineering Education. Engineering Education 78(7), 674–681 (1988)
22. Ainsworth, S.: The Functions of Multiple Representations. Computers and Education 33, 131–152 (1999)

EEG-Related Changes in Cognitive Workload, Engagement and Distraction as Students Acquire Problem Solving Skills

Ronald H. Stevens[1], Trysha Galloway[1], and Chris Berka[2]

[1] UCLA IMMEX Project, 5601 W. Slauson Ave. #255, Culver City, CA 90230
immex_ron@hotmail.com,
tryshag@gmail.com
[2] Advanced Brain Monitoring, Inc, Carlsbad, CA 90045
chris@b-alert.com

Abstract. We have begun to model changes in electroencephalography (EEG)-derived measures of cognitive workload, engagement and distraction as individuals developed and refined their problem solving skills in science. For the same problem solving scenario(s) there were significant differences in the levels and dynamics of these three metrics. As expected, workload increased when students were presented with problem sets of greater difficulty. Less expected, however, was the finding that as skills increased, the levels of workload did not decrease accordingly. When these indices were measured across the navigation, decision, and display events within the simulations significant differences in workload and engagement were often observed. Similarly, event-related differences in these categories across a series of the tasks were also often observed, but were highly variable across individuals.

1 Introduction

Skill development has been described as occurring in stages that are characterized by distinctive amounts of time and mental effort required to exercise the skill [1] [10]. Given the complexities of skill acquisition it is not surprising that a variety of approaches have been used to model the process. For instance, some researchers have explored the improved powers of computation in combination with machine learning tools to refine models of skill acquisition and learning behaviors in science and mathematics. Such systems rely on learner models that include continually updated estimates of students' knowledge and misconceptions based on actions such as choosing an incorrect answer or requesting a multimedia hint. Although such learner models are capable of forecasting student difficulties, [12] or identifying when students may require an educational intervention, they still rely on relatively impoverished input due to the limited range of learner actions that can be detected by the tutoring system (e.g., menu choices, mouse clicks) and latency.

Application of neurophysiologic approaches, including the quantification of EEG correlates of workload, attention and task engagement have also been used to provide objective evidence of the progression from stage 2 to stage 3 [2] [3]. There is a large

C. Conati, K. McCoy, and G. Paliouras (Eds.): UM 2007, LNAI 4511, pp. 187–196, 2007.
© Springer-Verlag Berlin Heidelberg 2007

and growing literature on the EEG correlates of attention, memory, and perception [5], although there is a relative dearth of EEG investigations of the process skill acquisition and learning. EEG researchers have generally elected to employ study protocols that utilize training-to-criterion to minimize variability across subjects and to ensure stable EEG parameters could be characterized. In most studies, the EEG data is not even acquired during the training process leaving a potentially rich data source untapped.

Thus, while advanced EEG monitoring is becoming more common in high workload / high stress professions (such as tactical command, air traffic controllers) the ideas have not been comprehensively applied to real-world educational settings, due in part to some obvious challenges. First, the acquisition of problem solving skills is a gradual process and not all novices solve problems in the same way, nor do they follow the same path at the same pace as they develop domain understanding. Next, given the diversity of the student population it is difficult to assess what their relative levels of competence are when performing a task making it difficult to accurately relate EEG measures to other measures of skill. This is further complicated as strategic variability makes analyzing the patterns of students' problem solving record too complicated, costly, and time consuming to be performed routinely by instructors. Nevertheless, there are many aspects of science education that could benefit from deriving data from advanced monitoring devices and combining them with real-time computational models of the tasks and associated outcomes conditions.

This manuscript describes a beginning synthesis of 1) a probabilistic modeling approach where detailed neural network modeling of problem solving at the population level provides estimates of current and future competence, and, 2) a neurophysiologic approach to skill acquisition where real-time measures of attention, engagement and cognitive work load dynamically contribute estimates of allocation of attention resources and working memory demands as skills are acquired and refined.

2   Methods

2.1   The IMMEX™ Problem Solving Environment

The software system used for these studies is termed IMMEX™ whose program structure is based on an extensive literature of how students select and use strategies during scientific problem solving [6] [15].

To illustrate the system, a sample biology task called *Phyto Phyasco* provides evidence of a student's ability to identify why the local potato plants are dying. The problem uses a multimedia presentation to explain the scenario and the student's challenge is to identify the cause. The problem space contains 5 Main Menu items which are used for navigating the problem space, and 38 Sub Menu items describing local weather conditions, soil nutrients, plant appearance, etc. These are decision points, as when the student selects them, s/he confirms that the test was requested and is then presented the data. When students feel they have gathered the information needed to identify the cause they attempt to solve the problem.

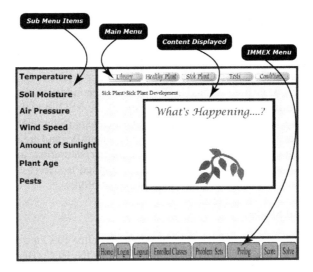

Fig. 1. Sample IMMEX™ simulation. In the Phyto Phyasco simulation, the farmer's potato plants are dying and the challenge for the student is to identify the cause by examining local weather conditions, nutrients, etc. Students navigate throughout the problem space using the Main Menu items and select data resources and make decisions using the Sub Menu Items. The resulting data is shown in the Display.

The IMMEX database serializes timestamps of how students use these items, which are then used to train competitive, self-organizing ANN [11]. As IMMEX problem sets contain many parallel cases learning trajectories can then be developed through Hidden Markov Modeling (HMM) that not only reflect and model students' strategy shifts as they attempt series of cases, but also predict future problem solving performance.

Students often begin by selecting many test items, and consistent with models of skill acquisition [4], refine their strategies with time and select fewer tests, eventually stabilizing with an approach that will be used on subsequent problems. As expected, with practice solve rates increase and time on task decreases. The rate of stabilization, and the strategies stabilized with are influenced by gender, experience [13], and individual or group collaboration. Students often continue to use these stabilized strategies for prolonged periods of time (3-4 months) when serially re-tested [11].

IMMEX problem solving therefore represents a task where it is possible to construct probabilistic models of many different aspects of problem solving skill acquisition. The constraints of working memory are likely to be relevant during such skill acquisition where working memory capacity can become exceeded, and the ability to combine probabilistic performance models with EEG workload metrics could shed light on how different working memory capacities are needed as students gain experience and begin to stabilize their strategies?

2.2 The B-Alert®System

A recently developed commercial wireless EEG sensor headset has combined a battery-powered hardware and sensor placement system to provide a lightweight, easy-to-apply method to acquire and analyze six channels of high-quality EEG (Advanced Brain Monitoring, Inc. Carlsberg, CA). This headset requires no scalp preparation and provides a comfortable and secure sensor-scalp interface for 12 to 24 hours of continuous use. Standardized sensor placements include locations over frontal, central, parietal and occipital regions (sensor sites: F3-F4, C3-C4, Cz-PO, F3-Cz, Fz-C3, Fz-PO). Data are sampled at 256 samples/second with a bandpass from 0.5 Hz and 65Hz (at 3dB attenuation). Quantification of the EEG in real-time, referred to as the B-Alert® system, is achieved using signal analysis techniques to identify and decontaminate fast and slow eye blinks, and identify and reject data points contaminated with excessive muscle activity, amplifier saturation, and/or excursions due to movement artifacts. Wavelet analyses are applied to detect excessive muscle activity (EMG) and to identify and decontaminate eye blinks.

2.3 Subjects and Study

Subjects (n=12) first performed a single 30-minute baseline EEG test session to adjust the software to accommodate individual differences in the EEG (Berka, 2004). They then performed multiple IMMEX problem sets targeted for 8th-10th grade students.

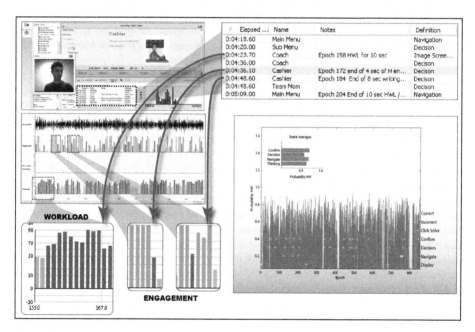

Fig. 2. Relating EEG Workload and Engagement Indexes with Problem Solving Events. The user (not described in the text) is shown engaged in IMMEX problem solving while keyboard and mouse events are simultaneously recorded. Below shows the real-time output of the B-Alert cognitive indexes where workload and engagement data streams were linked with events in the log. In the lower right corner, the timestamps of IMMEX data requests and displays are integrated with the EEG workload indices and then plotted against the one-second epochs of the task. The upper left histograms average the workload indices for each of the IMMEX events including the one second prior to and after the event.

These included *Phyto Pyiasco*, the biology problem described above, *Get Organized* where the goal is to diagnose disorders of organ systems, and a mathematics problem called *Paul's Pepperoni Pizza Palace*.

Subjects generally performed at least 3 cases of each problem set allowing the tracking of strategies and cognitive changes across problem sets as well as cases while students gained experience. Then we aligned the EEG output metrics on a second-by-second basis with the problem solving actions to explore the within-task EEG metric changes. For this alignment, we used software (Morea, Techsmith, Inc.) that captures output from the screen, mouse click and keyboard events as well as video and audio output from the users (Figure 2).

The B-Alert software output includes EEG metrics (from 0.1-1.0) for distraction (DT), engagement (E), and workload (WL) calculated for each 1-second epoch using quadratic and linear discriminant function analyses of model-selected EEG variables derived from power spectral analysis of the 1-Hz bins from 1-40Hz.

These metrics have proven utility in tracking both phasic and tonic changes in cognitive states, and in predicting errors resulting from either fatigue or overload [3]. The cognitive indices are expressed as histograms for each 1-second epoch of the problem solving session and show the probability of WL, E, or DT. By integrating B-Alert and IMMEX data request time stamps, the navigation, decision, and display-related events are then overlaid onto the cognitive indices.

3 Results

3.1 Distributions of Engagement, Distraction and Workload During IMMEX Problem Solving

Figure 3 illustrates the dynamics of the B-Alert EEG measures during IMMEX problem solving for six students over a ten-minute period. In each window, the top display is E, the middle is DT and the bottom is E. Each bar in the histograms represents averaged metrics at 1-second epochs.

Panels A, C and to a lesser extend F most closely represents students who were productively engaged in problem solving; workload levels were moderate and the levels were alternating with cycles of high engagement. Many cycles were associated with navigation and interpretation events (data not shown). Panel B illustrates a student who may be experiencing difficulties and might not be prepared to learn. The workload and engagement levels were low and distraction was consistently high.

The student in Panel D encountered a segment of the simulation that induced 10-15 seconds of distraction (middle row) and decreased workload and engagement. Through the data interleaving process the data that the student was looking at was retrieved, which in this case was an animation of a growing plant. Panel E shows a student who, while not distracted, appeared to be working at beyond optimal capacity with workload levels consistently near 100%. Probabilistic performance models for this student [11] [13] suggested a difficulty in developing efficient strategies on his own.

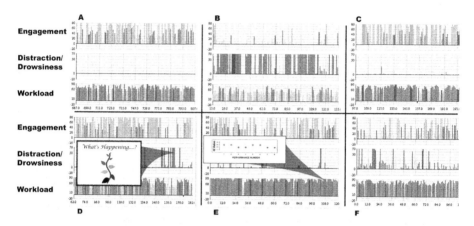

Fig. 3. Dynamics of WL, D and E for Six Students on IMMEX Tasks. This figure shows 10 minute segments of the B-Alert cognitive metrics while students performed IMMEX problems.

3.2 Increases in Problem Solving Skills Are Not Accompanied by Decreases in Cognitive Workload or Engagement

We next measured the seconds needed to solve the first, second and third cases of *Paul's Pepperoni Pizza* (n=7) and calculated the average WL and E across these three performances. As shown in Table 1, while the time needed to complete the task significantly decreased, there were no significant changes in either WL or E.

Table 1. Changes in Time on Task, WL and E With Problem Solving Experience

Performance	Speed (seconds)	WL	E
1	422 ± 234	.629 ± .07	.486 ± .09
2	241 ± 126	.625 ± .08	.469 ± .08
3	136 ± 34	.648 ± .06	.468 ± .09

3.3 Students Apply Similar Workload to Similar Problems and More Workload to More Difficult Problems

Five students also performed 3 cases of *Phyto Phyasco* which is also a middle school IMMEX problem. There were no significant differences between the WL (0.64 ± .05 vs. 0.63 ± .05, p =.42) and E (0.51 ± .07, 0.51 ± .04, p = .92) across the two problem sets. Two individuals also solved the more difficult high school chemistry problem Hazmat. For both of these individuals the WL was significantly greater for the three cases of *Hazmat* than for *Paul's Pepperoni Pizza*. (Subject 103: 0.76 ± .02 vs. 0.71 ± .03, p< 0.001; Subject 247: 0.57 ± .02 vs. 0.49 ± .03, p< 0.005).

Five of the students missed one or more of the cases in the problem set and a paired samples test was performed to determine if, at a performance level, differences existed in WL, E, or DT when the subjects were correctly, or incorrectly, solving a problem. None of these differences were significant.

3.4 The Navigation and Decision-Related Events in IMMEX May Be Behaviorally Relevant

We next increased the granularity of the analysis by dividing performances into segments related to problem framing, test selections, confirmation events where the student decides whether to select data, and closure where the student decides on the problem solution. We then compared the WL and E values across the different events within the different single IMMEX performances. The WL and E values at each subtask boundaries [7] (e.g. Main Menu, Sub Menu, etc.), as well as the epochs immediately before and after the event were averaged across the problem set. As shown in Figure 4 there were often significant differences among these averages at the different events. These differences, however, were neither uniform nor predictable across individuals or tasks.

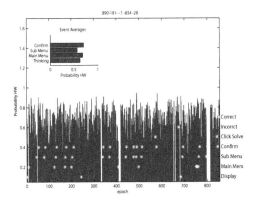

Mean Thinking = 0.628
Mean Main Menu = 0.681
Mean Sub Menu = 0.568
Mean Confirm = 0.699
Significance Thinking vs Main Menu = 0.101
Significance Thinking vs Sub Menu = 0.014
Significance Thinking vs Confirm = 0.003
Significance Main Menu vs Sub Menu = 0.009
Significance Main Menu vs Confirm = 0.571
Significance Sub Menu vs Confirm = 0.000

Fig. 4. Linking Cognitive Workload Indices with IMMEX-related Events. Left: The timestamps of IMMEX data requests and displays are integrated with the EEG workload indices and then plotted against the one-second epochs of the task. The upper left histograms average the workload indices for each of the IMMEX events including the one second prior to and after the event. Right: Table of significant differences between WL events.

We more closely examined events from one student who performed the IMMEX mathematics problem *Paul's Pepperoni Pizza*. The particular student being illustrated missed solving the first case, correctly solved the second case, and then missed the third case indicating that an effective strategy had not yet been formulated.

The problem framing event was defined as the period from when the Prologue first appeared on the screen until the first piece of data information is chosen. For this subject the HWL decreased from the first to the third performance (.72 ± .11 vs. .57 ± .19, t = 28.7, p < .001), and engagement increased .31 ± .30 vs. .49 ±.37, t = 4.3, p <.001). The decreased workload was similar to that observed in other subjects; the increasing E may relate more to the student missing the problem. During the decision-making process, students often demonstrated a cycling of the B-Alert cognitive indexes characterized by relatively high workload and low engagement which then switched to lower workload and higher engagement (Figure 5). The cycle switches were often, but not always, at boundaries associated with the selection of new data.

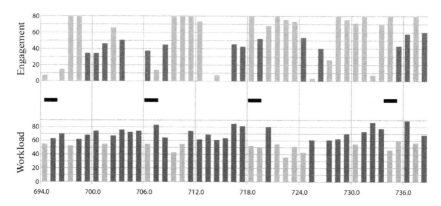

Fig. 5. Fluctuations in WL and E during Problem Solving. The bars indicate the epochs where the student made test selections.

The closing sequences of a problem are complex where the student first makes an irrevocable decision to attempt a solution. Then, the he must make a selection choice from an extensive list of possible solutions. Finally, they must confirm their choice. After that they receive feedback on their success / failure; the students have two such solution attempts. The dynamics of WL and E for one student's first and second solution attempts of *Paul's Pepperoni Pizza* are shown in Fig. 6.

In the 10 seconds before solving the problem (epochs 354 – 364 (I)) there was WL which decreased as the student made his decision (II, III). Two seconds before the student confirmed his choice (epoch 377, IV) there was an increase in engagement which was maintained as the student realized that the answer was incorrect (V).

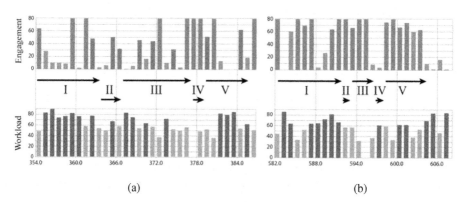

(a)   (b)

Fig. 6. (a) Workload and Engagement Events Related to Problem Closure on the First Attempt. (b) Workload and Engagement Events Related to Problem Closure on the Second Attempt.

The workload and engagement dynamics were different on the second solution attempt. Here there was less WL and more E in the 10 seconds leading up to the decision to solve the problem (Epochs 582- 592, (I, II). At epoch 593 the choice to continue was confirmed, and two seconds before making this decision engagement increased and was maintained during the selection and confirmation process. Between epochs 593 and 596 an incorrect answer was chosen and confirmed (III, IV). At epoch 597 the selection was made and the student learned of the incorrect answer (V).

4 Discussion

We have described a web-based data acquisition architecture and event interleaving process that allows us to begin to map EEG-derived cognitive indices to behaviorally relevant aspects of the students problem solving. An unusual feature of these studies was the application of these technologies to every-day classroom activities that are quite distinct from highly controlled laboratory tasks. In this regard the studies mirrored, and experienced similar challenges of aligning WL measures with subtask boundaries, that were reported by Iqbal et al., [7], and Lee & Tan, [8]

As expected, WL increased when students were presented with problem sets of greater difficulty. Less expected, however, was the finding that as skills increased, the levels of WL did not decrease accordingly; suggesting significant mental commitment may be involved during strategic refinement. Given the anticipated differences between individual students' experience and knowledge we have focused our studies on comparing differences within individuals as skills are developed, rather than extensively compare across individuals.

By restricting the analyses to the seconds surrounding relevant problem solving events such as menu navigation and decision making more refined views of the changing dynamics of WL and E were obtained as skills were refined. Nevertheless, these measurements still accounted for only a small portion of the cognitive workload of the total performance suggesting the need for a finer grained analysis between these events. To this end, we have begun recording videos of the problem solving process as well as of the user on a second by second basis and interleaving them with EEG cognitive indices through log files generated by the problem solving application, the video recording software and the EEG acquisition system. With this more refined system we anticipate being able to link the majority of the WL and E fluctuations to observable events.

Acknowledgment. Supported in part by grants from the National Science Foundation (NSF-ROLE 0231995, DUE Award 0126050, ESE 9453918) and the U.S. Department of Education (R305H050052).

References

[1] Anderson, J.R.: Acquisition of Cognitive Skill. Psychological Review 89, 369–406 (1982)

[2] Berka, C., Levendowski, D.J., Cvetinovic, M.M., Davis, G.F., Lumicao, M.N., Popovic, M.V., Zivkovic, V.T., Olmstead, R.E.: Real-Time Analysis of EEG Indices of Alertness, Cognition and Memory Acquired with a Wireless EEG Headset. International Journal of Human-Computer Interaction 17(2), 151–170 (2004)

[3] Berka, C., Levendowski, D.J., Ramsey, C.K., Davis, G., Lumicao, M.N., Stanney, K., Reeves, L., Harkness, R.S., Tremoulet, P.D., Stibler, K.: Evaluation of an EEG-Workload Model in an Aegis Simulation, Biomonitoring for Physiological and Cognitive Performance during Military Operations, edited by John Caldwell, Nancy Jo Wesentsten. In: Proceddings of SPIE, vol. 5797, pp. 90–99 (2005)

[4] Ericsson, K.A.: Deliberate Practice and the Acquisition and Maintenance of Expert Performance in Medicine and Related Domains. Academic Medicine 79(10), 70–81 (2004)

[5] Fabiani, M., Gratton, G., Coles, M.G.: Event-related Brain Potentials. In: Cacioppo, J.T., Tassinary, L.G., Berntson, G.G. (eds.) Handbook of Psychophysiology, pp. 53–84. Cambridge University Press, Cambridge (2000)

[6] Haider, H., Frensch, P.A.: The Role of Information Reduction in Skill Acquisition. Cognitive Psychology 30, 304–337 (1996)

[7] Igbal, S.T., Adamczyk, P.D., Zheng, X.S., Bailey, B.P.: Towards an Index of Opportunity: Understanding Changes in Mental Workload During Task Execution. In: Proceedings of the ACM Conference on Human Factors in Computing Systems, Portland, Oregon. USA (2005)

[8] Lee, J.C., Tan, D.S.: Using a Low-cost Electroencephalogramph for Task Classification in HCI Research. In: UIST '06. Proceedings of the 19th Annual ACM Symposium on User Interface Software and Technology (Montreux, Switzerland), October 15-18, pp. 81–90. ACM Press, New York, NY (2006)

[9] Poythress, M., Russell, C., Siegel, S., Tremoulet, P.D., Craven, P.L., Berka, C., Levendowski, D.J., Chang, D., Baskin, A., Champney, R., Hale, K., Milham, L.: Correlation between Expected Workload and EEG Indices of Cognitive Workload and Task Engagement. In: Proceedings of 2nd Annual Augmented Cognition International Conference, San Francisco, CA (In press)

[10] Schneider, W., Shiffrin, R.M.: Controlled and Automatic Human Information Processing I: Detection, Search, and Attention. Psychological Reviews 84, 1–66 (1977)

[11] Stevens, R., Casillas, A.: Artificial Neural Networks. In: Mislevy, R.E., Williamson, D.M., Bejar, I. (eds.) Automated Scoring, pp. 259–312. Lawrence Erlbaum, Mahwah (2006)

[12] Stevens, R., Johnson, D.F., Soller, A.: Probabilities and Predictions: Modeling the Development of Scientific Competence. Cell Biology Education, vol. 4(1), pp. 42–57. The American Society for Cell Biology (2005)

[13] Stevens, R., Soller, A., Cooper, M., Sprang, M.: Modeling the Development of Problem Solving Skills in Chemistry with a Web-Based Tutor. In: Lester, J.C., Vicari, R.M., Paraguaca, F. (eds.) Intelligent Tutoring Systems. 7th International Conference Proceedings, pp. 580–591. Springer-Verlag, Berlin Heidelberg, Germany (2004)

[14] Stevens, R., Wang, P., Lopo, A.: Artificial Neural Networks can Distinguish Novice and Expert Strategies during Complex Problem Solving. JAMIA 3(2), 131–138 (1996)

[15] VanLehn, K.: Cognitive Skill Acquisition. Psychology 47, 513–539 (1996)

Eliciting Motivation Knowledge from Log Files Towards Motivation Diagnosis for Adaptive Systems

Mihaela Cocea and Stephan Weibelzahl

National College of Ireland, School of Informatics,
Mayor Street 1, Dublin 1, Ireland
{mcocea,sweibelzahl}@ncirl.ie

Abstract. Motivation is well-known for its importance in learning and its influence on cognitive processes. Adaptive systems would greatly benefit from having a user model of the learner's motivation, especially if integrated with information about knowledge. In this paper a log file analysis for eliciting motivation knowledge is presented, as a first step towards a user model for motivation. Several data mining techniques are used in order to find the best method and the best indicators for disengagement prediction. Results show a very good level of prediction: around 87% correctly predicted instances of all three levels of engagement and 93% correctly predicted instances of disengagement. Data sets with reduced attribute sets show similar results, indicating that engagement level can be predicted from information like reading pages and taking tests, which are common to most e-Learning systems.

Keywords: e-Learning, motivation, log files analysis, data mining, adaptive systems, user modeling.

1 Introduction

Although motivation is a key component of learning, the main focus in adaptive educational systems is on cognitive processes. There is a general agreement about the importance of motivation, but little research is done in this area. Most e-Learning systems, including adaptive systems are focused on cognitive processing and on knowledge acquisition. If motivation is considered when building a system, it only covers aspects of system design, in terms of how the content is structured and presented. Nevertheless, the influence of motivation on cognitive processes explains why some users achieve high performance while others perform poorly or even drop out [18].

Adaptive systems work with user models of goals, knowledge and preferences in order to deliver personalized content and make learning more efficient. Given the close relation between cognitive processes and motivational states, a user model that would integrate information about knowledge and motivational states would lead to a more personalized and more efficient adaptation. Thus, we are interested in motivation diagnosis and in building a user model of the learner's motivation.

In this paper we present the results on the first step of our research project, which is focused on eliciting motivation knowledge from log files. The paper is organized as

C. Conati, K. McCoy, and G. Paliouras (Eds.): UM 2007, LNAI 4511, pp. 197–206, 2007.
© Springer-Verlag Berlin Heidelberg 2007

follows. Section 2 discusses previous work related to motivation in e-Learning; it includes a description of our approach and of the common and the different points in terms of theoretical base and methodology; previous work related to the use of log files analysis in education is also presented, with a particular interest in approaches to motivation. The analysis of log files is discussed in Section 3, and Section 4 concludes the paper with a summary and a brief description of further work.

2 Previous and Current Research

We will refer here only to research on motivation diagnosis, presenting a few relevant works for our approach. We also present our research and stress the communalities and the differences with previous approaches.

2.1 Previous Research on Motivation Diagnosis

Human tutors usually infer motivation from observational cues like mimics, posture, gesture, conversational cues etc. These are difficult to be processed by adaptive systems (e.g. [7], [8], [14]). Moreover, in regards to e-Learning, the amount and type of information that is available to humans and computers is quite limited. Previous approaches have focused on motivation diagnosis from cues that can be easily processed automatically, e.g. learners' interactions with the system, time spent on a task, their statements about their motivation etc.

   Three of these approaches are of particular interest for our research. All of them are related to Keller's ARCS model [16] which stands for Attention, Relevance, Confidence and Satisfaction. First, a rule-based approach has been suggested, inferring motivational states from two sources: the *interactions* of the students with the tutoring system and their *motivational traits* [6]. A second approach infers three aspects of motivation: *confidence*, *confusion* and *effort*, from several sources: the learner's focus of attention, the current task and expected time to perform the task [21]. A third approach used factorial analysis to group user's actions that predict *attention* and *confidence* [29].

2.1.1 Our Perspective on Motivation Diagnosis

These approaches target a motivation diagnosis exclusively from the user's interactions with the systems, without involving him/her in this process. We suggest that a motivational diagnosis based only on the interactions with the system is incomplete despite the obvious advantages of unobtrusive diagnosis.

   Moreover, we based our approach on a different theory of motivation: Social Cognitive Theory (SCT) [2] using concepts like self-efficacy (SE) and self-regulation (SR). SE is generally described by Bandura [2] as the confidence that the individual has in his/her ability to control his/her thoughts, feelings and actions; more specifically, it refers to a person's belief/expectancy in his/her capacity to successfully complete a task. SR refers to a person's ability to control his/her actions, in our case learning [24]. SCT is a sound theoretical base for motivation diagnosis as it is a well established construct in the literature. There is broad evidence that this theory has good application in classroom ([23], [25]), as well as in online learning

([12], [13]) and blended learning ([26]). The theory offers a variety of possibilities to intervene in order to motivate the learner, a framework for influencing the learner's subjective control of the task through *motivational beliefs* (SE) and *cognitive learning strategies* (SR/ self-monitoring) and also fits very well in other current research directions in e-Learning (e.g. personalization, adaptivity, affective computing, collaborative learning) [5].

We propose a two-step approach for diagnosing motivation: First, the system would unobtrusively monitor the learners diagnose their disengagement based on log files. Then, learners identified to be disengaged will be engaged in a dialog in order to assess their self-efficacy, self-regulation and other related motivation concepts. In this paper we present results related only to the first step (i.e., analysis of log files).

2.1.2 Communalities and Differences

Unlike previous works, our approach exploits the interaction log only as a first step towards motivation diagnosis. Our purpose is to distinguish between engaged and disengaged learners in order to focus further on the disengaged. For this purpose we analyse the data from log files.

In order to establish the user's level of engagement we used an approach similar to the one used in [6]. In this study human tutors were asked to rate several motivational characteristics (e.g. confidence, effort, cognitive/sensory interest etc.) from replays of users interactions with a system. In our research, we use the actions and the timestamps registered in log files in order to rate only one motivational aspect: the engagement level of the user.

2.2 Log Files in Research

Logging the users' interactions in educational systems gives the possibility to track their actions at a refined level of detail. Log files are easy to record for a large number of users, they can capture a large variety of information and they can also be presented in an understandable form. Thus, these data are a potentially valuable source of information to be analysed and used in educational settings. Automatic analysis of log data is frequently used to detect regularities and deviations in groups of users, in order to provide more information to tutors about the learners, and to offer suggestions for further actions, in particular for the "deviation" cases.

2.2.1 Log Files in Educational Research

Automatic analysis of interaction data is used in research areas such as educational systems, data mining and machine learning. Educational systems can benefit from data mining and machine learning techniques by giving meaning to click-through data and associating these data with educational information.

Log file analysis has been used for a variety of purposes: provide information to tutors to facilitate and make more accurate the feedback given to learners [19], monitor group activity [15], identify benefits and solve difficulties related to log data analysis [11], use response times to model student disengagement [3], infer attitudes about the system used, attitudes that affect learning [1], developing tools to facilitate interpretation of log files data [20].

2.2.2 Log Files in Motivation Research

Previous research in this area includes a few interesting approaches. A model for detecting learners' engagement [3] was proposed in order to detect whether a student is engaged in answering questions based on item response theory (IRT). The input of the model was: difficulty of the question, how long the student took to respond and whether the response was correct. The output (obtained from the modified IRT formula) was the probability that a student was actively engaged in trying to answer a question. A second approach [9] related to user interests and motivation inferred from server log files, argued that time spent on pages is more important than simple "hits". Usually, the way of determining user's interest is to log the number of "hits" received per page. The author argues that this is inadequate because the browser will log "hits" not only for the page of interest, but also for every page the user visited to get there. He argues that a path independent measure of user interest is needed and that a time-based measure would be such a measure.

3 Log File Analysis

For the analysis presented here, we created several data sets from existing log files. The level of the learner's engagement was rated by an expert. Eight different data mining methods were applied predicting the engagement level from the log data.

3.1 Log File Description

In our analysis we used log files from a system called HTML tutor, which is a web interactive learning environment based on NetCoach [27]. It offers an introduction to HTML and publishing on the Web; it is online and can be accessed freely, based on a login and a password. We don't have any information about the users except the data from the log files. They could be of any age and using the system for different purposes. Table 1 presents the events registered in the log files and the attributes for each event that were included in the log file analysis.

In a previous experiment [4] with a limited number of data, using the total time spent on a session (i.e., between login and logout) as attribute, the analysis showed that it is possible to judge whether a learner was engaged or disengaged only after 45 minutes; the same analysis showed that most of the disengaged users left the system before that time. In order to overcome this problem, we decided to use for the following experiments sequences of 10 minutes instead of complete sessions. Thus, we split the sessions into sequences of 10 minutes; 943 sequences of 10 minutes and 72 sequences varying between 7 and 592 seconds resulted from this process.

Besides the attributes related to events, the data set contains a few more fields: a user ID, a session ID, a sequence ID and total time of the sequence. The number of entries in the data set is 1015, obtained from 48 subjects who spent on HTML tutor between 1 and 7 sessions, each session varying between 1 and 92 sequences. The events/attributes frequencies are displayed in Table 2.

Table 1. Logs events registered and the attributes analysed per session / sequence respectively

Events	Parameters/ Attributes
Goal	The selected goal (from a list of 12 goals)
Preferences	Number; Time spent selecting them
Reading pages	Number of pages; average time reading pages
Pre-tests	Number of pre-tests; average time; number of correct answers; number of incorrect answers
Tests	Number of tests; average time; number of correct answers, number of incorrect answers
Hyperlink, Manual, Help, Glossary, Communication, Search, Remarks, Statistics, Feedback	For each of these: Number of times accessed; average time

Table 2. Frequency of events registered in log files

Events/attributes	Frequency of appearances (in 1015 sequences)
Goal	59
Preferences	7
Reading pages	850
Pre-tests	14
Tests	458
Hyperlinks	245
Manual	7
Help	11
Glossary	76
Communication	6
Search	27
Remarks	6
Statistics	8
Feedback	4

3.2 Expert Ratings on Level of Engagement

For each sequence of 10 minutes a value/code was assigned: engaged (e), neutral (n) and disengaged (d). In the previous experiment [4] we had only 2 categories: engaged and disengaged. Because we introduced the 10 minutes sequences, in some cases it was hard to decide whether overall the learner was engaged or disengaged. Thus, we introduced a third category: neutral. A detailed presentation of the criteria used for this rating is presented in Table 3, which contains the instructions given to a second coder in order to verify the reliability of the ratings.

The investigation conducted in order to verify the coding reliability included two steps: 1) *Informal assessment*, conducted using only 10 sequences; the ratings based on the given instructions were discussed to prevent different results due to instruction vagueness or suggestibility; the percent agreement was 80% (only 2 different ratings from 10); the kappa measurement of agreement was .60 (p=.038) and the Krippendorff's alpha [10] was .60 as well; 2) *Second expert rating*. A second rater coded 100 sequences randomly sampled from the 1015 entries in the data set; the instructions used for the informal assessment were expanded with typical situations/

Table 3. Instructions for level of engagement rating

Timeframes for HTML Tutor
- Necessary time for reading a page: varies from 30 sec. to a maximum of 4-5 minutes.
- Necessary time for a test: varies from just a few seconds to a maximum of 3-4 minutes.

Engaged (e)	Disengaged (d)	Neutral (n)
Spending reasonable time on pages and tests given the characteristics of HTML Tutor	Spending too much time on pages/tests Moving fast through pages/tests	Hard to decide if overall (for the 10 minutes) the person is engages or disengaged
Examples of patters: - people focused reading – spend most of the time reading and less on other tasks - people focused on taking tests - spend most of the time taking tests and less on other tasks - people that read and take tests - spend most of the time reading and taking tests	Automatic logouts Examples of patterns: - spend more than reasonable time on just one or a few tasks - move fast though the same / different tasks	E.g.: for approximately half of the time the person seems engaged and for the other half seems disengaged E.g.: can't decide if overall the person is moving too fast through pages or the amount of time spent on pages is reasonable

patterns for each case. Table 3 includes the instructions given to the second rater (instructions used also for coding all sequences).

The second expert rating resulted in a rater agreement of 92% (only eight different ratings from 100; in further discussion between the raters the eight disagreements were resolved) with a kappa measurement of agreement of .826 (p<.01) and Krippendorff's alpha of .8449. Although the percent agreement is high, we can see that kappa and Krippendorff's alpha have lower values. The percent agreement is not always the best indicator for agreement as it tends to be too liberal, while Cohen's Kappa and Krippendorff's alpha are known to be more conservative [17]. Thus, overall, the values indicate high inter-coder reliability.

3.3 Analysis and Results

In order to perform the analysis, Waikato Environment for Knowledge Analysis (WEKA) [28] was used. Several methods were experimented to find which one is best for our purpose and to see if results are consistent over several methods. We present here trials used only on a reduced data set of 943 entries obtained from the 1015 entries data set by eliminating the entries with time per sequence shorter than 10 minutes. In order to explore the effect of the number of attributes included, we created three different data sets: 1) all 30 attributes except user ID called DS-30; 2) 10 attributes related to the following events: reading pages, tests, hyperlinks and glossary (DS-10) and 3) six attributes related only to reading pages and tests. The experiment was done using 10-fold stratified cross validation iterated 10 times.

The analysis included eight methods [28]: (a) Bayesian Nets with K2 algorithm and maximum 3 parent nodes (BN); (b) Logistic regression (LR); (c) Simple logistic classification (SL); (d) Instance based classification with IBk algorithm (IBk); (e)

Attribute Selected Classification using J48 classifier and Best First search (ASC); (f) Bagging using REP (reduced-error pruning) tree classifier (B); (g) Classification via Regression (CvR) and (h) Decision Trees with J48 classifier based on Quilan's C4.5 algorithm [22] (DT).

The results are displayed in Table 4, which comprises the percentage of correctly classified instances, the true positives (TP) rate, the precision indicator and recall for disengaged class, and the mean absolute error.

Table 4. Experiment results summary

		BN	LR	SL	IBk	ASC	B	CvR	DT
DS-30	%correct	87.07	86.52	87.33	85.62	87.24	87.41	87.64	86.58
	TP rate	0.93	0.93	0.93	0.92	0.93	0.93	0.92	0.93
	Precision	0.91	0.90	0.90	0.91	0.92	0.92	0.92	0.91
	Recall	0.93	0.93	0.93	0.92	0.93	0.93	0.92	0.93
	Error	0.10	0.12	0.12	0.10	0.10	0.12	0.12	0.11
DS-10	%correct	87.18	85.88	85.82	85.13	86.03	86.87	88.07	85.16
	TP rate	0.93	0.93	0.93	0.91	0.92	0.92	0.91	0.91
	Precision	0.91	0.89	0.89	0.92	0.91	0.91	0.92	0.90
	Recall	0.93	0.93	0.93	0.91	0.92	0.92	0.92	0.91
	Error	0.11	0.13	0.14	0.10	0.12	0.13	0.12	0.13
DS-6	%correct	86.68	84.15	84.05	83.18	86.95	86.90	87.21	86.20
	TP rate	0.93	0.93	0.93	0.90	0.92	0.92	0.91	0.92
	Precision	0.90	0.87	0.87	0.90	0.92	0.91	0.92	0.91
	Recall	0.93	0.93	0.93	0.90	0.92	0.92	0.91	0.92
	Error	0.12	0.15	0.15	0.12	0.12	0.13	0.13	0.13

Table 4 shows very good prediction for all methods with a correct prediction varying approximately between 84% and 88%. Even better results are shown by the TP rate, precision and recall indicator for disengaged class: values between 87% and 93%. The mean absolute error varies between 0.10 and 0.15. The very similar results obtained from different methods and trials shows consistency of prediction and of the attributes used for prediction.

The highest percentage of correctly predicted instances was obtained using Classification via Regression (CvR) on all data sets, with a maximum for DS-10. This indicates that the attributes that predict the learner's engagement/ disengagement most accurately are the one related to reading pages, taking tests, following hyperlinks and consulting the glossary. The percentage for DS-6 is slightly lower (87.21%), suggesting that hyperlinks and glossary events do not have a big contribution to the prediction model. The confusion matrix for this result is displayed in Table 5.

Table 5. The confusion matrix for data set DS-6 using CvR

		Predicted		
		Disengaged	Engaged	Neutral
	Disengaged	610	56	0
Actual	Engaged	35	218	0
	Neutral	13	11	0

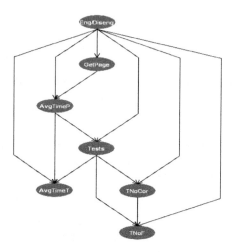

Fig. 1. Bayesian Network from data set DS-6

If we focus on the disengaged learners we see that Bayesian Nets (displayed in Fig. 3) have the best performance on all data sets: 93%, even if the percentage of correctly predicted instances for all three classes varies between data sets.

The Bayesian Network from DS-6 has an interesting structure: Number of False (TNoF) and Correct (TNoCor) Answers to Tests feed into the Number of Tests (Tests). Which itself, together with Average Time on Tests (AvgTimeT) feeds into Average Time spend on Pages (AvrTimeP). All of them also feed directly into the Level of Engagement (Eng/Diseng), i.e., the Bayesian Network structured the attributes in a semantically meaningful way.

As good results were obtained for all trials with small differences between them, considering the MDL (minimum description length) principle we argue for the use of a minimum number of attributes: the six attributes used in DS-6. These attributes were ranked first from all attributes using information gain attribute evaluation. There are no particular attributes that give bad performance, but many of them do not contribute to prediction and thus, removing them does not affect the prediction performance, as we can see from the similarity of results from the three data sets. Thus, the attributes related to reading pages and taking tests are most valuable and as they are common to most e-Learning systems and most frequent actions that occur in using such systems, we argue for a prediction model that includes only these attributes.

4 Summary, Implication and Future Perspectives

We presented results of eliciting motivation knowledge from log files. The analysis showed good overall prediction e.g. 87% using classification via regression and even better value for prediction of disengagement e.g. 93% using Bayesian Nets. The analysis included 943 sequences of 10 minutes from 48 users, showing that a general indicator of the motivational level could be predicted from very basic data commonly recorded in log files, such as events related to reading pages and taking tests. A prediction module could be included in educational systems that log learner's actions. Our research plan includes further elicitation of motivation to be included in a user model in order to have a system that adapts to the motivational level of the learner.

Further work includes an external validation of the expert rating and an analysis of log files from a different system in order to compare the results. We also plan a pilot study in order to compare the dialog responses of learners with their responses on questionnaires, to verify the validity and reliability of the measurement using the dialog.

Acknowledgment. Part of this work was supported by the European Commission through the project "Adaptive Learning Spaces" (229714-CP-1-2006-NL-MINERVA-M).

References

1. Arroyo, I., Murray, T., Woolf, B.P.: Inferring unobservable learning variables from students' help seeking behavior. In: Proceedings of the workshop Analyzing Student-Tutor Interaction Logs to Improve Educational Outcomes at ITS, pp. 29–38 (2004)
2. Bandura, A.: Social foundations of thought and action: A social cognitive theory. Prentice Hall, Englewood Cliffs, NJ (1986)
3. Beck, J.E.: Using response times to model student disengagement. In: Proceedings of the Workshop on Social and Emotional Intelligence in Learning Environments at ITS (2004)
4. Cocea, M., Weibelzahl, S.: Can Log Files Analysis Estimate Learners' Level of Motivation. In: Schaaf, M., Althoff, K.-D.: LWA 2006. Lernen-Wissensentdeckung – Adaptivität. Universität Hildesheim, pp. 32–35 (2006)
5. Cocea, M., Weibelzahl, S.: Motivation–Included or Excluded From E-Learning. In: Kinshuk, Sampson, D.G., Spector, J.M., Isaias, P.: Cognition and Exploratory Learning in Digital Age, pp. 435–437 (2006)
6. De Vicente, A., Pain, H.: Informing the Detection of the Students' Motivational State: an empirical Study. In: Cerri, S.A., Gouarderes, G., Paraguau, F. (eds.) Intelligent Tutoring Systems. 6th International Conference, pp. 933–943. Springer-Verlag, Berlin (2002)
7. D'Mello, S.K., Craig, S.D., Gholson, B., Franklin, S., Picard, R.W., Graesser, A.C.: Integrating Affect Sensors in an Intelligent Tutoring System, In Affective Interactions: The Computer in the Affective Loop Workshop at 2005 International conference on Intelligent User Interfaces, pp. 7–13. AMC Press, New York (2005)
8. Fernandez, R., Picard, R.W.: Classical and Novel Discriminant Features for Affect Recognition from Speech, Interspeech 2005 - Eurospeech 9th European Conference on Speech Communication and Technology, Lisbon Portugal (September 4-8, 2005)
9. Fuller, R., de Graaff, J.J.: Measuring User Motivation from Server Log Files. Retrieved on 14/03/06 from http://www.microsoft.com/usability/webconf/fuller/fuller.htm
10. Hayes, A.F., Krippendorff, K.: Answering the call for a standard reliability measure for coding data. Communication Methods and Measures. (In press) Retrieved on 8/11/2006 from http://www.comm.ohio-state.edu/ahayes/
11. Heiner, C., Beck, J., Mostow, J.: Lessons on Using ITS Data to Answer Educational Research Questions. In: Proceedings of the workshop Analyzing Student-Tutor Interaction Logs to Improve Educational Outcomes at ITS, pp.1–9 (2004)
12. Hodges, C.B.: Designing to Motivate: Motivational Techniques to Incorporate in E-Learning Experiences, The Journal of Interactive Online Learning, vol. 2(3) (2004)

13. Irizarry, R.: Self-Efficacy & Motivation Effects on Online Psychology Student Retention. USDLA Journal, vol. 16(12) (2002)
14. Kapoor, A., Picard, R.W., Ivanov, Y.: Probabilistic Combination of Multiple Modalities to Detect Interest. In: International Conference on Pattern Recognition, Cambridge, U.K (2004)
15. Kay, J., Maisonneuve, N., Yacef, K., Zaïane, O.: Mining patterns of events in students' teamwork data. In: Intelligent Tutoring Systems. Proceedings of the Workshop on Educational Data Mining at the 8th International Conference, pp. 45–52. Jhongli, Taiwan (2006)
16. Keller, J.M.: Development and use of the ARCS model of instructional design. Journal of Instructional Development 10(3), 2–10 (1987)
17. Lombard, M., Snyder-Duch, J., Campanella Bracken, C.: Practical Resources for Assessing and Reporting Intercoder Reliability in Content Analysis Research (2003) Retrieved on 06/11/06 from http://www.temple.edu/mmc/reliability
18. Martinez, M.: High Attrition Rates in e-Learning: Challenges, Predictors, and Solutions. The e-Learning Developers Journal (July 2003) Retrieved on 25/02/2006 from http://www.elearningguild.com
19. Merceron, A., Yacef, K.: A Web-Based Tutoring Tool with Mining Facilities to Improve Learning and Teaching. In: Proceedings of the 11th International Conference on Artificial Intelligence in Education AIED, pp. 201–208. IOS Press, Amsterdam (2003)
20. Mostow, J., Beck, J., Cen, H., Cuneo, A., Gouvea, E., Heiner, C.: An Educational Data Mining Tool to Browse Tutor-Student Interactions: Time Will Tell! In: Educational Data Mining: Papers from the AAAI Workshop, Beck, J.E.(ed.), pp. 15–22 (2005)
21. Qu, L., Wang, N., Johnson, W.L.: Detecting the Learner's Motivational States in an Interactive Learning Environment. In: Looi, C.-K., et al. (eds.) AIED, pp. 547–554. IOS Press, Amsterdam (2005)
22. Quinlan, R.: C4.5: Programs for Machine Learning. Morgan Kaufmann Publishers, San Mateo, CA (1993)
23. Schraw, G., Brooks, D.W.: Helping Students Self-Regulate in Math and Sciences Courses: Improving the Will and the Skill (2000) Retrieved on 14/03/06 from http://dwb.unl.edu /Chau/SR/Self_Reg.html
24. Schunk, D.H., Zimmerman, B.J.: Self-regulation of learning and performance: Issues and educational applications. Lawrence Erlbaum, Hillsdale, NJ (1994)
25. Tuckman, W.B.: A Tripartite Model of Motivation for Achievement: Attitude/Drive/ Strategy (1999) Retrieved on 14/03/06 from http://dwb.unl.edu/Chau/CompMod.html
26. Wang, A.Y., Newlin, M.H.: Predictors of web-student performance: The role of self-efficacy and reasons for taking an on-line class. Computers in Human Behavior 18, 151–163 (2002)
27. Weber, G., Kuhl, H.-C., Weibelzahl, S.: Developing adaptive internet based courses with the authoring system NetCoach. In: Hypermedia: Openness, Structural Awareness, and Adaptivity. LNCS, vol. 2266, pp. 226–238. Springer, Berlin (2002)
28. Witten, I.H., Frank, E.: Data mining. Practical Machine Learning Tools and Techniques. 2nd edn. Morgan Kauffman Publishers, Elsevier (2005)
29. Zhang, G., Cheng, Z., He, A., Huang, T.A: WWW-based Learner's Learning Motivation Detecting System. In: Proceedings of International Workshop on Research Directions and Challenge Problems in Advanced Information Systems Engineering, Honjo City, Japan, (2003) Retrieved on 14/03/06 from http://www.akita-pu.ac.jp/ system/KEST2003

Assessing Learner's Scientific Inquiry Skills Across Time: A Dynamic Bayesian Network Approach

Choo-Yee Ting[1] and Mohammad Reza Beik Zadeh[2]

[1] Faculty of Information Technology, Multimedia University
63100 Cyberjaya, Malaysia
[2] Faculty of Engineering, Multimedia University
63100 Cyberjaya, Malaysia
{cyting, drbeik}@mmu.edu.my

Abstract. In this article, we develop and evaluate three Dynamic Bayesian Network (DBN) models for assessing temporally variable learner scientific inquiry skills (*Hypothesis Generation* and *Variable Identification*) in INQPRO learning environment. Empirical studies were carried out to examine the matching accuracies and identify the models' drawbacks. We demonstrate how the insights gained from a preceding model have eventually led to the improvement of subsequent models. In this study, the entire evaluation process involved 6 domain experts and 61 human learners. The matching accuracies of the models are measured by (1) comparing with the results gathered from the pretest, posttest, and learner's self-rating scores; and (2) comments given by domain experts based on learners' interaction logs and the graph patterns exhibited by the models.

Keywords: Scientific Inquiry Skills, Dynamic Bayesian Networks.

1 Introduction

Recently years have demonstrated the use of scientific-inquiry as an instructional strategy in computer-assisted learning environments such as the *Belvedere* [1], *KIE* [2], *BGuiLE* [3], *SimQuest* [4], *SCI-WISE* [5], *Rashi* [6], and *SmithTown* [7]. However, these systems are not equipped with an inference mechanism that allows modeling of learner's scientific inquiry skills across time. To tackle the challenge with regards to time changes, probabilistic framework particularly the Dynamic Bayesian Network (DBN) approach has been proposed and employed in *DT-Tutor* [8], *Prime Climb* [9], and *i-Tutor* [10]. These systems share the common feature: the DBNs employed are having the nodes identical for all the n time slices. This approach, however, is not applicable to our proposed prototype, INQPRO, as it consists of six Graphical User Interfaces (GUIs). In INQPRO, there is a Bayesian Network (BN) for each GUI. Thus, the main challenge in this study is to identify a sound DBN model that allows different nodes in different time slices without affecting the accuracies in assessing learner's scientific inquiry skills. In the rest of this article, we shall focus our discussion on (1) the characteristics of the three

C. Conati, K. McCoy, and G. Paliouras (Eds.): UM 2007, LNAI 4511, pp. 207–216, 2007.
© Springer-Verlag Berlin Heidelberg 2007

different DBN models; (2) empirical evaluations of the DBN models in assessing learner's scientific inquiry skills.

2   The INQPRO Learning Environment

INQPRO is an intelligent computer-based scientific inquiry exploratory learning environment for scientific inquiry skills acquisition in physics domain. The development of INQPRO is rooted in *Scientific Inquiry Exploratory Learning Model* [11]. It has seven GUIs namely the *Scenario(Sce), Hypothesis Visualization(Vz), Verification(Vf), Formula(Fe), Simulation Experiment(Ex), Data Comparison(Dc),* and *Feedback.* By actively interacting with the GUIs and Intelligent Pedagogical Agent, learners are ultimately expected to command two scientific-inquiry skills: *Hypothesis Generation* $\mathcal{H}$ (node *Hypo* in Fig. 1) and *Variables Identification* $\mathcal{V}$ (node *Var* in Fig. 1). Since $\mathcal{H}$ and $\mathcal{V}$ are interrelated, we introduce $\mathcal{K}$ (node *KnowScientificInquiry* in Fig. 1) to represent the combination of both $\mathcal{H}$ and $\mathcal{V}$.

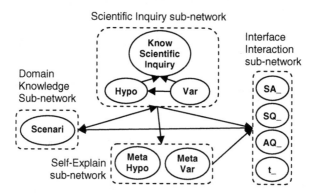

Fig. 1. High-level presentation for a Bayesian network in INQPRO. Each Bayesian network contains 4 subnetworks namely the *Domain Knowledge* subnetwork, *Scientific Inquiry* subnetwork, *Interface Interaction* subnetwork, and *self-Explain* subnetwork.

Fig. 1 depicts the general BN for the INQPRO GUIs. The network is categorized into four sub-networks and each sub-network consists of either *observable* or *non observable* nodes. The *observable* nodes (nodes with prefix of $SA\_$, $SQ\_$, $AQ\_$, $t\_$) are nodes that to be instantiated in light of receiving evidences. Examples of observable nodes are $AQ\_Concept$, $SQ\_Definition$, and $AQ\_Scenario$ in Fig. 2(b). *Non observable* nodes are nodes that cannot be instantiated directly; however, they can be inferred once *observable* nodes are instantiated and BN is updated. Examples of *non observable* nodes in Fig. 2(b) are the nodes *Hypothesis* and *Variable*. To accurately model a learner's $\mathcal{H}$ and $\mathcal{V}$ within a particular GUI, a BN needs to perform both *diagnostic* and *predictive* reasoning. By performing *diagnostic* reasoning, a learner's $\mathcal{H}$ can be inferred from the following evidences: (1) the correctness of hypothesis statement (node *SA_HypoStruct*); (2) the correctness of variable relationships statement (node *SA_HypoRelation*); and (3) whether or not hint is requested from the agent (node *SA_AskHypo*). The *predictive* reasoning, conversely, offers an indirect assessment through the propagation of probability from nodes *Hypothesis* and *Variable* to *KnowScientficInquiry*. Detail explanations regarding the design and integration of nodes into the GUIs can be found in [11]. In the following section, we shall firstly present the general DBN model employed in INQPRO and further on with discussion of how the optimum DBN model is obtained from the empirical study.

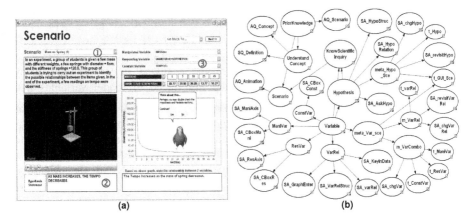

Fig. 2. (a) The *Scenario* GUI (b) Bayesian Network for *Scenario* GUI

3   The Designs and Evaluations of DBN Models

In this study, we employed DBN to tackle the challenges in assessing temporally variable learner's scientific inquiry skills for three main reasons. First, a learner's scientific inquiry skills evolve across time, thus capturing the dependencies between the temporally variable skills is crucial. Second, freedom to navigate from one GUI to another introduces complexity in predetermining a DBN. A predetermined DBN can easily become computationally intractable as it exhibits a 5^n state spaces (combination of different navigation paths) with $n \in \{\text{Integer} > 0\}$. Third, if a *static* BN is employed, the interpretation of new evidences will lead to reinterpretation of previous evidences. In order to overcome this drawback, a DBN must be employed instead of a *static* BN.

Fig. 3 depicts a general three time-slices DBN model employed in INQPRO. The time-slice t_i represents the current INQPRO GUI accessed by a learner while time-slice t_{i-1} describes the immediate previous state. To describe the immediate subsequent interface accessed, the time-slice t_{i+1} is used. These time-slices are interconnected by temporal relations, which are illustrated by the arcs joining variables that evolve over time. In this study, the temporal dependencies between the time-slices are quantified by the Conditional Probability Distribution.

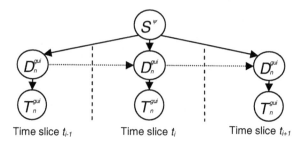

Time slice t_{i-1} Time slice t_i Time slice t_{i+1}

Fig. 3. General DBN model implemented in INQPRO. $D \in \{H,V,K\}$, $gui \in \{INQPRO\ GUIs\}$, $n \in \{0, 1, 2, 3 \ldots\}$, $\psi \in \{H,V,K\}$.

Each time-slice consists of *Dynamic nodes* and *Temporal nodes* summarized by D_n^{gui} and T_n^{gui} respectively. *Dynamic nodes* are introduced to model variables that evolve across over time while the *Temporal nodes* are nodes that exist in a particular time-slice only [12]. Instantiating the *Temporal nodes* to a particular state (e.g. Mastery, non-Mastery) in time *slice* t_{i-1} might not resulting in the similar state instantiation in time slice t_i. *Dynamic nodes* exist in *Scientific Inquiry sub-network*, and *Self-Explain sub-network* while *Temporal nodes* reside in the *Interface Interaction sub-network* (Fig. 1). The *Static nodes* (S^{ψ}) are introduced to model K, H and V that are unknown initially. The *Static nodes* capture the changes in the skills acquisition from one time-slice to another during the learning process and consequently providing the *"local"* (with respect to a particular GUI) mastery level of K, H and V through their classifications. Towards the end of interactions, the ultimate mastery levels of K, H and V are finally revealed through these static nodes.

For ease of explanation, we shall focus our discussion to a three time-slices DBN models $M1$, $M2$, and $M3$. Due to space limitation, we shall only highlight the matching accuracies of $M1$, $M2$, and $M3$ with respect to the results obtained from learner's pretest, posttest, and self-ranking and briefly discuss the comments elicited from domain experts.

3.1 Design and Evaluation of DBN Model $M1$

$M1$ (Fig. 4) depicts the first DBN model that was employed in this study. $M1$ relies solely on the *dynamic nodes* H_n^{gui}, V_n^{gui}, and K_n^{gui} to capture the H, V, and K respectively. The arc directed from V_n^{gui} to H_n^{gui} suggests that the higher the mastery level of V, the more probable it is that a learner's H is at mastery level. Once the posterior probability for V_n^{gui} and H_n^{gui} are known, performing a DBN update algorithm will allow the posterior probability for K to be calculated. $M1$ as our first attempt to model learners' H, V, and K as it resembles the modeling approach implemented by

Intelligent Tutoring Systems researchers [9, 10, 11] to model learners' motivation, concept acquisition, and personality traits that evolve across time.

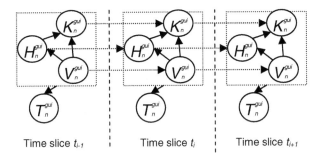

Time slice t_{i-1} Time slice t_i Time slice t_{i+1}

Fig. 4. $\mathcal{M}1$: DBN model with *Dynamic nodes* and *Temporal nodes* only

In this phase of study, we performed a model walk-through with 2 domain experts and conducted a field trial with 30 first-year university learners to evaluate the predictive accuracy of $\mathcal{M}1$. Learners participated in a session that lasted at most 120 minutes consisting of an introduction session to INQPRO environment, a pretest, a session with INQPRO, and a post-test. Both the pretest and posttest consist of 23 multiple choices questions aiming at assessing the $\mathcal{K}$, $\mathcal{H}$ and $\mathcal{V}$. Learners who scored higher than 75% will be graded as "*mastery*" whereas those less than 45% will be regarded as "*non-Mastery*". Before interacting with INQPRO, learners forecast their own rank-how far they understood $\mathcal{K}$, $\mathcal{H}$ and $\mathcal{V}$ (hereafter 'Pre-INQPRO self-ranking'). After the session with INQPRO, the learners again forecast their own rank-how far they have mastered $\mathcal{K}$, $\mathcal{H}$ and $\mathcal{V}$ (hereafter 'Post-INQPRO self-ranking'). A 3-rank scale (*mastery, partial mastery, non-mastery*) was given to help in the self-ranking process. The domain experts were then estimated the accuracies of $\mathcal{M}1$ by studying the interaction logs, videos on the interaction sessions with INQPRO, and patterns of graphs exhibited.

Table 1. Matching accuracies of $\mathcal{M}1$ for $\mathcal{K}$, $\mathcal{H}$ and $\mathcal{V}$

	# and % matched classification			
	Pretest	**Posttest**	**Pre-INQPRO Self-Ranking**	**Post-INQPRO Self-Ranking**
$\mathcal{K}$	24 (80.00%)	25 (83.33%)	18 (60.00%)	11 (36.67%)
$\mathcal{H}$	10 (33.33%)	20 (66.67%)	15 (50.00%)	20 (66.67%)
$\mathcal{V}$	4 (13.33%)	22 (73.33%)	10 (33.33%)	19 (63.33%)

Table 1 depicts matching accuracies of $\mathcal{M}1$ after n GUIs were navigated. The matching accuracies are calculated by comparing the results obtained from pretest, posttest, and self-ranking with the classifications suggested by $\mathcal{M}1$ in time slice t_0

and t_{n-1}. The results indicate that $\mathcal{M}1$ has successfully matched 80% of the pretest while 83.33% matching the post-test. The low accuracy for $\mathcal{V}$ with respect to pretest (13.3%) is mainly due to the misclassification of learners into "*partial-mastery*" while categorized as "*non-mastery*" suggested from pretest. Our further investigation revealed that the learners actually *learned* from the pretest and this *learning* effect has resulting in the mismatch of classifications. We further investigated $\mathcal{M}1$'s behaviour by performing model walk-through with 2 domain experts. The videos containing the interactions process were replayed and the graphs were presented. The experts studied the classification returned by $\mathcal{M}1$ at each GUI and assigned a √ to the classification that matched their judgments while an **x** to those misclassified. Despite the high matching accuracies shown in the post-test section (Table. 1), the experts rejected $\mathcal{M}1$. The experts argued that it is impossible for a learner's acquisition levels of $\mathcal{K}$, $\mathcal{H}$ and $\mathcal{V}$ to differ greatly (fluctuation) from one GUI to another (Fig. 5(a)). Instead, a consistent increment or otherwise (Fig. 5 (b) should be observed. Another argument leads to impracticality of $\mathcal{M}1$ is that the final classification is too much relying on the *nth* GUI visited regardless of *(n-1)th* GUIs visited.

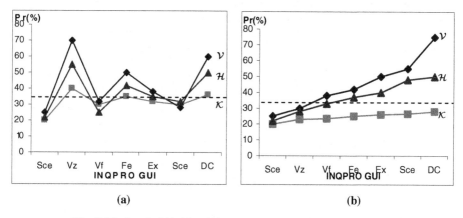

(a)   (b)

Fig. 5. The level of $\mathcal{K}$, $\mathcal{H}$ and $\mathcal{V}$ as modeled by (a) $\mathcal{M}1$, and (b) $\mathcal{M}2$

3.2 Design and Evaluation of DBN Model $\mathcal{M}2$

The varying dependency weights between the *dynamic nodes* and *temporal nodes* at different GUIs have been the main influence for fluctuation patterns in $\mathcal{M}1$. To overcome this drawback, *Static nodes* (nodes S^K, S^H, and S^V) are introduced in $\mathcal{M}2$. The arcs stretching from *static nodes* to *dynamic nodes* suggesting that the *dynamic nodes* are conditioned upon the *static nodes*. This allows a "*global*" rather than "*local*" modeling of $\mathcal{K}$, $\mathcal{H}$ and $\mathcal{V}$ throughout the interaction with INQPRO. The final classifications obtained from the *static nodes* (nodes S^K, S^H, and S^V) would then be the ultimate mastery levels of $\mathcal{K}$, $\mathcal{H}$ and $\mathcal{V}$.

We evaluated $\mathcal{M}2$ by feeding it with the preprocessed dataset obtained from the first experiment (Section 3.1). Doing so would allow us to study and confirm the validity of $\mathcal{M}2$'s behaviour before having it tested with human learners. From Table 2, although there is a slight drop in $\mathcal{K}$, significant increment of the matching accuracies for both $\mathcal{H}$ and $\mathcal{V}$ (Table. 2) is observed. This is mainly because the instantiation of *Temporal nodes* in each GUI is having less probability propagation impact towards the *static nodes* (nodes S^H and S^V) compare to the *dynamic nodes* (nodes H_n^{gui} and V_n^{gui}).

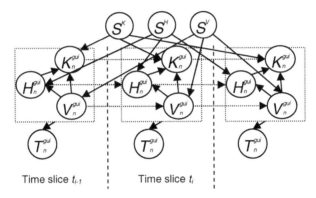

Fig. 6. $\mathcal{M}2$: *Static nodes* are introduced to overcome the drawbacks from $\mathcal{M}1$

The major drawback of this model is that there is a total of $3^5 = 243$ CPT entries for K_n^{gui}. As a result of the huge CPT entries, the probability elicitation becomes intractable. Consequently, the temporal dependency from *n-1* time-slice (node K_{n-1}^{gui}) to *n* time-slice (node K_n^{gui}) becomes insignificant. This drawback is proven from the graph pattern shown in Fig. 5(b). As depicted in the graph, the probability for $\mathcal{K}$ has demonstrated a slow increment depict the significant increment exhibited by both $\mathcal{H}$ and $\mathcal{V}$. Together with negative comments from experts and the low matching accuracy (4%, Table 2) for $\mathcal{K}$ with regard to the post-test and Post-INQPRO self-ranking, we rejected $\mathcal{M}2$ and discontinue with another circle of field trial.

Table 2. Matching accuracy of $\mathcal{M}2$ for $\mathcal{K}$, $\mathcal{H}$ and $\mathcal{V}$ using dataset from first experiment

	# and % correct classification			
	Pretest	**Posttest**	**Pre-INQPRO Self-Ranking**	**Post-INQPRO Self-Ranking**
$\mathcal{K}$	22 (73.33%)	4 (13.33%)	20 (66.67%)	11 (36.67%)
$\mathcal{H}$	17 (56.67%)	20 (66.67%)	19 (63.33%)	21 (70.00%)
$\mathcal{V}$	15 (50.00%)	22 (73.33%)	13 (43.33%)	21 (70.00%)

3.3 Design and Evaluation of DBN Model $\mathcal{M}3$

Fig. 7 depicts the refined DBN Model $\mathcal{M}3$ employed to overcome the intractable CPT for node K_n^{gui}. The key difference between these two models is the arcs that exist between the *static nodes*. We argue that the directions of arcs between the *static nodes* should resemble those *dynamic nodes* as the modeling approach of $\mathcal{K}$, $\mathcal{H}$ and $\mathcal{V}$ should be both "*locally*" and "*globally*" identical. In order to compare $\mathcal{M}2$ and $\mathcal{M}3$ fairly, all the CPTs in $\mathcal{M}3$ remain similar to those in $\mathcal{M}2$ except for the nodes S^H and S^K.

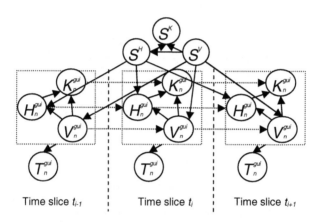

Time slice t_{i-1} Time slice t_i Time slice t_{i+1}

Fig. 7. $\mathcal{M}3$: DBN model with arcs among the *Static nodes*

We evaluated $\mathcal{M}3$ by firstly feeding the model with preprocessed dataset obtained from the first experiment (Section 3.1). As shown in Table 3, the arcs directed among the *static nodes* demonstrated significant improvement to the matching accuracies of $\mathcal{K}$, $\mathcal{H}$ and $\mathcal{V}$. The arc directed from S^V to S^H suggests that reducing the probability of S^H would subsequently causing the probability of S^V to reduce. Thus, due to the large number of learners having "*non-mastery*" for $\mathcal{H}$, the probability for $\mathcal{V}$ drops. Although there is a slight drop in $\mathcal{V}$, the matching accuracies for both $\mathcal{H}$ and $\mathcal{K}$ increase across the pretest, posttest, and self-ranking. The key advantage of this model is its ability to maintain a tractable CPT for S^K while increasing the estimation rate of $\mathcal{K}$.

Table 3. Matching accuracy of $\mathcal{M}3$ for $\mathcal{K}$, $\mathcal{H}$ and $\mathcal{V}$ using dataset from first experiment

	# and % correct classification			
	Pretest	**Posttest**	**Pre-INQPRO Self-Ranking**	**Post-INQPRO Self-Ranking**
$\mathcal{K}$	25 (83.33%)	25 (83.33%)	22 (73.33%)	19 (63.33%)
$\mathcal{H}$	20 (66.67%)	20 (66.67%)	19 (63.33%)	22 (73.33%)
$\mathcal{V}$	13 (43.33%)	22 (73.33%)	13 (43.33%)	21 (70.00%)

We further investigate $\mathcal{M}3$ by presenting learners' interaction logs and the corresponding graphs to the domain experts for verification. By carefully studying the interaction logs and graph patterns for different categories of learners, both the experts came to the conclusion that the estimation of $\mathcal{K}$, $\mathcal{H}$ and $\mathcal{V}$ exhibited by $\mathcal{M}3$ is approximate to domain expert reasoning.

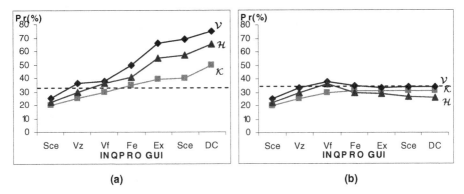

Fig. 8. The level of $\mathcal{K}$, $\mathcal{H}$ and $\mathcal{V}$ as modeled by $\mathcal{M}3$ for (a) *Advance*, and (b) *Moderate* category of learners

Table 4. Matching accuracy of $\mathcal{M}3$ for $\mathcal{K}$, $\mathcal{H}$ and $\mathcal{V}$

		# and % correct classification		
	Pretest	**Posttest**	**Pre-INQPRO Self-Ranking**	**Post-INQPRO Self-Ranking**
$\mathcal{K}$	26 (83.87%)	27 (87.10%)	19 (61.29%)	15 (48.39%)
$\mathcal{H}$	30 (96.77%)	23 (74.19%)	17 (54.84%)	17 (54.84%)
$\mathcal{V}$	20 (64.52%)	25 (80.65%)	18 (58.06%)	29 (93.55%)

We carried out another empirical study to verify the behaviour of $\mathcal{M}3$. A field trial was administered on 31 first-year university learners. Again, the learners went through the experiment procedures exactly described in Section 3.2. The evaluation results show that the matching accuracies of $\mathcal{K}$, $\mathcal{H}$ and $\mathcal{V}$ increase compare to those shown in Table 3. With the consistency demonstrated by $\mathcal{M}3$, we then concluded that $\mathcal{M}3$ is the optimum DBN model for modeling temporally variable $\mathcal{K}$, $\mathcal{H}$ and $\mathcal{V}$.

4   Conclusion and Future Directions

This article aims at highlighting a methodology approach for inferring temporal variable scientific inquiry skills. Three different Dynamic Bayesian Network (DBN) models $\mathcal{M}1$, $\mathcal{M}2$, and $\mathcal{M}3$ were employed to obtain optimum modeling solution to a learner's *Hypothesis Generation* $\mathcal{H}$ and *Variables Identification* $\mathcal{V}$ skills . The evaluations of $\mathcal{M}1$, $\mathcal{M}2$, and $\mathcal{M}3$ were conducted by both human experts and learners. The empirical results indicated that $\mathcal{M}3$ is practically sound as it has achieved the highest matching accuracies for $\mathcal{K}$, $\mathcal{H}$ and $\mathcal{V}$.

The next step of our work involves evaluating and refining the Bayesian networks to achieve higher matching accuracies. These include the integration of metacognition, and implementation of both *soft* and *hard* evidences. The DBN models reported in this article do not take into consideration of differences in CPTs for *dynamic nodes* from one GUI to another. We hypothesize that varying the temporal CPTs would increase the matching accuracies of $\mathcal{M}3$ with respect to the results obtained from pretest, posttest, and self-ranking, and domain experts' judgments.

References

1. Paolucci, M., Suthers, D.D., Weiner, A.: Automated advice-giving strategies for scientific inquiry. In: Frasson, C., Gauthier, G., Lesgold, A. (eds.) Lecture Notes In Computer Science, pp. 372–381. Springer-Verlag, NewYork, NY (1996)
2. Linn, M.C.: Designing the knowledge integration environment. International Journal of Science Education 22, 781–796 (2000)
3. Pryor, A., Soloway, E.: Foundation of Science: Using Technology to Support Authentic Science learning (1997) http://hi-ce.eecs.umich.edu/papers/
4. Veermans, K., van Joolingen, W.R.: Combining Heuristics and Formal Methods in a Tool for Supporting Simulation-Based Discovery Learning. Intelligent Tutoring Systems, pp. 217–226 (2004)
5. Reiser, B.J., Tabak, I., Sandoval, W.A., Smith, B., Steinmuller, F., Leone, T.J.: BGuILE: Stategic and Conceptual Scaffolds for Scientific Inquiry in Biology Classrooms. In: Carver, S.M., Klahr, D.(eds.): Cognition and Instruction: Twenty five years of progress. Erlbaum, Mahvah, NJ.
6. Dragon, T., Woolf, B.P., Marshall, D., Murray, T.: Coaching Within a Domain Independent Inquiry Environment. In: Ikeda, M., Ashley, K.D., Chan, T.-W. (eds.) ITS 2006. LNCS, vol. 4053, pp. 144–153. Springer, Heidelberg (2006)
7. Shute, V.J., Glaser, R.: A large-scale evaluation of an intelligent discovery world: Smithtown. Interative Learning Environments 1, 51–77 (1990)
8. Murray, R.C., VanLehn, K., Mostow, J.: Looking ahead to select tutorial actions: A decision-theoretic approach. International Journal of Artificial Intelligence in Education 14, 235–278 (2004)
9. Conati, C.: Probabilistic Assessment of User's Emotiones in Educational Games. Journal of Applied Artificial Intelligence 16, 555–575 (2002)
10. Pek, P.-K., Poh, K.-L.: Making decisions in an intelligent tutoring system. International Journal of Information Technology and Decision Making 4, 207–233 (2005)
11. Ting, C.Y., Zadeh, M.R.B., Chong, Y.K: A Decision-Theoretic Approach to Scientific Inquiry Exploratory Learning Environment. In: Ikeda, M., Ashley, K.D., Chan, T.-W. (eds.) ITS 2006. LNCS, vol. 4053, pp. 85–94. Springer, Heidelberg (2006)
12. Schafer, R., Weyrath, T.: Assessing Temporally Variable User Properties with Dynamic Bayesian Networks. In: UM97. User Modeling: Proceedings of the Sixth International Conference, Vienna, New York, pp. 377–388. Springer, New York (1997)

From Modelling Domain Knowledge to Metacognitive Skills: Extending a Constraint-Based Tutoring System to Support Collaboration

Nilufar Baghaei and Antonija Mitrovic

Department of Computer Science and Software Engineering
University of Canterbury, Private Bag 4800, Christchurch, New Zealand
nilufar.baghaei@gmail.com, tanja@cosc.canterbury.ac.nz

Abstract. Constraint-based tutors have been shown to increase individual learning in real classroom studies, but would become even more effective if they provided support for collaboration. COLLECT-$\mathcal{UML}$ is a constraint-based intelligent tutoring system that teaches object-oriented analysis and design using Unified Modelling Language. Being one of constraint-based tutors, COLLECT-$\mathcal{UML}$ represents the domain knowledge as a set of constraints. However, it is the first system to also represent a higher-level skill such as collaboration using the same formalism. We started by developing a single-user ITS. The system was evaluated in a real classroom, and the results showed that students' performance increased significantly. In this paper, we present our experiences in extending the system to provide support for collaboration as well as problem-solving. The effectiveness of the system was evaluated in a study conducted at the University of Canterbury in May 2006. In addition to improved problem-solving skills, the participants both acquired declarative knowledge about good collaboration and did collaborate more effectively. The results, therefore, show that Constraint-Based Modelling is an effective technique for modelling and supporting collaboration skills.

1 Introduction

Constraint-based tutors are Intelligent Tutoring Systems (ITS) which use Constraint-Based Modelling (CBM) [15] to represent domain and student models. These tutors have been proven to provide significant learning gains for students in a variety of instructional domains. As is the case with other ITSs [4], constraint-based tutors are problem-solving environments; in order to provide individualized instruction, they diagnose students' actions, and maintain student models, which are then used to provide individualized problem-solving support and generate appropriate pedagogical decisions. Constraint-based tutors have been developed in domains such as SQL (the database query language), database modelling, data normalization [13], punctuation [11] and English vocabulary [10].

All constraint-based tutors developed so far support individual learning. This paper describes extending COLLECT-$\mathcal{UML}$ [1, 3], a constraint-based ITS, to support the

C. Conati, K. McCoy, and G. Paliouras (Eds.): UM 2007, LNAI 4511, pp. 217–227, 2007.
© Springer-Verlag Berlin Heidelberg 2007

acquisition of collaboration skills. COLLECT-*UML* teaches Object-Oriented (OO) analysis and design using Unified Modelling Language (UML). The system provides feedback on both collaboration issues (using the collaboration model, represented as a set of meta-constraints) and task-oriented issues (using the domain model, represented as a set of syntax and semantic constraints).

We start with a brief overview of related work in Section 2. The architecture of COLLECT-*UML* and its interface are discussed in Section 3. Section 4 describes the collaborative model, which has been implemented as a set of meta-constraints. In Section 5, we present the results of an evaluation study conducted recently. Conclusions are given in the last section.

2 Related Work

In the last decade, many researchers have contributed to the development of computer-supported collaborative learning (CSCL) and advantages of collaborative learning over individualised learning have been identified. Some particular benefits of collaborative problem-solving include: encouraging students to verbalise their thinking; encouraging students to work together, ask questions, explain and justify their opinions; increasing students' responsibility for their own learning; increasing the possibility of students solving or examining problems in a variety of ways; and encouraging them to elaborate and reflect upon their knowledge [17]. These benefits, however, are only achieved by well-functioning learning teams [8]. Various strategies for computationally supporting online collaborative learning have been proposed and used, but more studies are needed that test the utility of these techniques [9].

CSCL systems can be classified into three categories based on their collaboration support [9]. The first category includes systems that reflect actions; this basic level of support makes students aware of each others' actions. The systems in the second category monitor the state of interactions; some of them aggregate the interaction data into a set of high-level indicators, and display them to the participants (e.g. Sharlok II [14]), while others internally compare the current state of interaction to a model of ideal interaction, but do not reveal this information to the users (e.g. EPSILON [18]). In the latter case, this information is either intended to be used later by a coaching agent, or analysed by researchers in order to understand the interaction [9]. Finally, the third class of systems offer advice on collaboration. The coach in these systems plays a role similar to that of a teacher. The systems can be distinguished by the nature of the information in their models, and whether they provide feedback on strictly collaboration issues or both social and task-oriented issues. An example of the systems focusing on the social aspects is Group Leader Tutor [12], while COLER [5] addresses both social and task-oriented aspects of group learning.

Although many tutorials, textbooks and other resources on UML are available, we are not aware of any attempt at developing a CSCL environment for UML modelling. However, there has been an attempt [18] at developing a collaborative learning environment for OO design problems using Object Modeling Technique (OMT), a precursor of UML. The system monitors group members' communication patterns and problem solving actions in order to identify situations in which students effectively share new knowledge with their peers while solving problems. The system dynamically assesses a group's interaction, and determines when and why the students are having trouble learning new concepts they share with each other. The system does not evaluate the OMT diagrams and an instructor or intelligent coach's assistance is needed in mediating group knowledge sharing activities. In this regard, even though the system is effective as a collaboration tool, it would probably not be an effective teaching system for a group of novices with the same level of expertise, as the students may agree on the same flawed argument.

3 COLLECT-𝒰𝑀ℒ

COLLECT-𝒰𝑀ℒ is a problem-solving environment implemented in Allegro Common Lisp, in which students construct UML class diagrams that satisfy a given set of requirements. It assists students during problem solving, and guides them towards the correct solution by providing feedback. The system is designed as a complement to classroom teaching and when providing assistance, it assumes that the students are already familiar with the fundamentals of UML.

We started by developing a constraint-based tutoring system which supported students working individually. Being a Web-enabled system, its interface is delivered via a Web browser. The system consists of a session manager that manages sessions and student logs, a student modeller that maintains student models, the constraint set and a pedagogical module. We performed an evaluation study in a real classroom, and

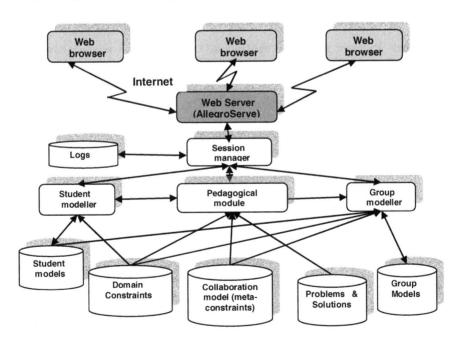

Fig. 1. The architecture of COLLECT-𝒰𝑀ℒ

the results showed that students' performance increased significantly. For details on the functionality and the evaluation studies of this version please refer to [1, 3].

The architecture of the collaborative version of the system (Figure 1) introduces the group modeller, a new component responsible for creating and maintaining group models. The pedagogical module uses both the student model and the group model in order to generate pedagogical actions. The student model records the history of usage for each constraint (both for domain constraints and the constraints from the collaboration model), while the group model records the history of group usage for each domain constraint.

COLLECT-UML contains an ideal solution for each problem, which is compared to the student's solution according to the system's domain knowledge, represented as a set of constraints [15]. The system's domain model contains a set of 133 constraints defining the basic domain principles, a set of problems and their solutions [3]. In order to develop constraints, we studied material in textbooks, such as [7], and also used our own experience in teaching UML and OO analysis and design. Figure 2 illustrates a constraint from the UML domain, which checks whether the student has defined all the methods necessary for the current problem. The relevance condition identifies a method in the ideal solution (IS) and then checks whether the class it belongs to also exists in the student's solution (SS). The student's solution is correct if the satisfaction condition is met, when the matching method also exists in the student's solution. The constraint also contains a message which would be given to the student if the constraint is violated.

```
(54
   "Check whether you have defined all the methods asspecified
   by the problem. You are missing some methods."
(and (match IS METHODS (?* "@" ?tag ?name ?class_tag ?*))
     (match SS CLASSES (?* "@" ?class_tag ?*)))
(match SS METHODS (?* "@" ?tag ?name2 ?class_tag ?*))
"methods"
(?class_tag))
```

Fig. 2. Example of a domain constraint

The student interface is shown in Figure 3. The problem text describes a situation that needs to be modelled by a UML class diagram. Students construct their individual solutions in the private workspace (right). They use the shared workspace (left) to collaboratively construct UML diagrams while communicating via the chat window (bottom). The private workspace enables students to try their own solutions and think about the problem before they start discussing it in the group.

The group diagram is initially disabled. It is activated after a specified amount of time, and the students can start placing components of their solutions in the shared workspace. This may be done by either copying/pasting from private diagram or by drawing new components in the group diagram. The private and shared workspaces can be resized. The students need to select the component names from the problem text by highlighting or double-clicking on the words/phrases. The *Group Members* panel shows the team-mates already connected. Only one student, the one who has the pen, can update the shared workspace at a given time. The control panel provides two buttons to control this workspace: *Get Pen and Leave Pen*, and shows the name of the student who has the control of this area. The chat area enables students to express their opinions by selecting one of the sentence openers, and typing their statement.

While all group members can contribute to the chat area and group solution, only one member of the group (i.e. the group moderator) can submit the group solution (by clicking on the *Submit Group Answer* button). The system provides feedback on the individual solutions, as well as on group solutions and collaboration. All feedback messages will appear in the frame located on the right-hand side of the interface.

The domain-level feedback on both individual and group solutions is offered at four levels of detail: *Simple Feedback*, *Error flag*, *Hint* and *All Hints*. In addition, the group moderator has the option of asking for the complete solution, by clicking on *Show Full Solution* button. The collaboration-based advice is given to individual students based on the content of the chat area (i.e. sentence openers the students used), the student's contributions to the shared diagram and the differences between student's individual solution and the group solution being constructed. The system scales to a large number of participants and to large problem spaces. For more details on the interface and justification of using sentence openers, private workspace and turn taking, please refer to [2].

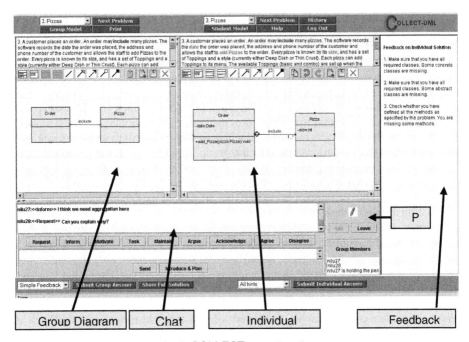

Fig. 3. COLLECT-$\mathcal{UML}$ Interface

4   Modelling Collaboration

Research on learning has demonstrated the usefulness of collaboration for improving student's problem-solving skills. However, simply putting students together and giving them a task does not mean that they will collaborate well. Collaboration is a skill, and, as any other skill, needs to be taught and practised to be acquired. The goal of our research is to support collaboration by modelling collaborative skills. COLLECT-$\mathcal{UML}$ is capable of diagnosing students' collaborative actions, such as contributions to the chat area and contributions to the group diagram, using an explicit model of collaboration. This collaboration model is represented using constraints, the same formalism used to represent domain knowledge. A significant contribution of our work is to show that constraint can be used not only to represent domain-level knowledge, but also higher-order skills such as collaboration.

Our model of collaboration consists of set of 25 meta-constraints representing ideal collaboration. The structure of meta-constraints is identical to that of domain-level constraints: each meta-constraint consists of a relevance condition, a satisfaction condition and a feedback message. The feedback message is presented when the constraint is violated. In order to develop meta-constraints, we studied the existing literature on characteristics of effective collaboration [5, 16, 17, 19], and also used our own experience in collaborative work. The collaborative teaching strategy is based on the socio-cognitive conflict theory [6]. According to this theory, social interaction is constructive only if it creates a confrontation between students' divergent solutions. The meta-constraints are divided into two main groups: constraints that monitor students' contributions to the group diagram (making sure that students remain active, encouraging them to discuss the differences between their individual diagrams and the group diagram, etc.), and constraints that monitor students' contributions to the chat area and the use of sentence openers.

Figure 4 illustrates two meta-constraints. The relevance condition of constraint 223 focuses on aggregation relationships that exist in the student's individual solution between certain classes, when the same classes also exist in the group solution (GS). For this constraint to be satisfied, the corresponding relationships should also appear in the group solution. If that is not the case, the constraint is violated, and the student will be given the feedback message attached to this constraint, which encourages them to discuss those relationships with the group, or add them to the group solution. Constraint 238 is relevant if the student has made a contribution to the chat area, and its satisfaction condition checks whether the student has typed a statement after using any of the available sentence openers. If not, it encourages them to provide more explanation as part of their contribution.

In order to be able to evaluate meta-constraints, the system maintains a rich collection of data about all actions students perform in COLLECT-$\mathcal{UML}$. After each change made to the group diagram, an XML event message containing the update and the id of the student who made that change, is sent to the server. Each chat message will also be sent to the server in the XML format. Histories of all contributions made to the shared diagram as well as the messages posted to the chat area are stored on the server. The meta-constraints are evaluated against these histories, and feedback is given on contributions which involve adding/deleting/updating components in the shared diagram, as well as contributions made to the chat area.

5   Evaluation

An evaluation study was carried out at the University of Canterbury in May 2006. The study involved 48 volunteers enrolled in an introductory Software Engineering

```
(223
  "Some relationship types (aggregations) in your individual
   solution are missing from the group diagram. You may wish to
   share your work by adding those aggregation(s)/discuss it with
   other members."
  (and (match SS RELATIONSHIPS (?* "@" ?rel_tag "aggregation"
         ?c1_tag ?c2_tag ?*))
        (match GS CLASSES (?* "@" ?c1_tag ?*))
        (match GS CLASSES (?* "@" ?c2_tag ?*)))
  (or-p (match GS RELATIONSHIPS (?* "@" ?rel_tag "aggregation"
         ?c1_tag ?c2_tag ?*))
        (match GS RELATIONSHIPS (?* "@" ?rel_tag "aggregation"
         ?c2_tag ?c1_tag ?*)))
  "relationships"
  (?rel_tag ?c1_tag ?c2_tag))

(238
  "Ensure adequate elaboration is provided in explanations."
  (match SC DESC (?* "@" ?tag ?text ?*))
  (not-p (test SC ("null" ?text)))
  "descriptions"
   nil)
```

Fig. 4. Examples of meta-constraints

course. The students learnt UML modelling concepts during two weeks of lectures and had some practice during two weeks of tutorials prior to the study. The study was conducted in two streams of two-hour laboratory sessions over two weeks. In the first week, the students filled out a pre-test and interacted with the single-user version. Doing so gave them a chance to learn the interface and provided us with an opportunity to assess their UML knowledge and decide on the pairs and moderators.

At the beginning of the sessions in the second week, we told students what characteristics we would be looking for in effective collaboration (that was considered as a short training session). The instructions describing the characteristics of good collaboration and the process we expected them to follow were also handed out. The idea of providing students with such a script and therefore supporting instructional learning came from a recent study conducted by Rummel and Spada [16]. The participants were also given a screenshot of the system highlighting the important features of the multi-user interface (Figure 3).

The students were randomly divided into pairs with a pre-specified moderator. The moderator for each pair was the student who had scored higher in the pre-test. The pairs worked on a relatively complex problem individually and joined the group discussion whenever they were ready – the group diagram was activated after 10 minutes. At the end of the session, each participant completed a post-test and a questionnaire commenting on the interface, the impact of the system on their domain knowledge and their collaborative skills, and the quality of the feedback messages on their individual and collaborative activities.

The experimental group consisted of 26 students (13 pairs) who received feedback on their solution as well as their collaborative activities. The control group consisted of 22 students (11 pairs) who only received feedback on their solutions (no feedback on collaboration was provided in this case). All pairs received instructions on characteristics of good collaboration at the beginning of second week.

The total time spent interacting with the system was 1.4 hours for the control and 1.3 hours for the experimental group. The pre-test and post-test each contained four multiple-choice questions, followed by a question where the students were asked to design a simple UML class diagram. The tests included questions of comparable difficulty, dealing with inheritance and association relationships. The post-test also had an extra question, asking the participants to describe the aspects of effective collaborative problem-solving. The mean scores of the pre- and post-test are given in Table 1. The numbers reported for the post-test do not include the collaboration question.

Table 1. Pre- and post-test scores

	Control		Experimental	
	Average	**s. d.**	**Average**	**s. d.**
Collaboration	22%	22%	52%	39%
Pre-test	52%	20%	49%	19%
Post-test	76%	25%	73%	25%
Gain score	17%	28%	21%	31%

There was no significant difference on the pre-test results, meaning that the groups were comparable. The students' performance on the post-test was significantly better for both control group (t = 2.11, p = 0.01) and experimental group (t = 2.06, p = 0.002). The experimental group, who received feedback on their collaboration performed significantly better on the collaboration question (t = 2.02, p = 0.003), showing that they acquired more knowledge on effective collaboration. We also calculated the effect size for the question about collaboration. The common method to calculate it is to subtract the control group's mean score from the experimental group's mean score and divide by the standard deviation of the control group. Using this method, the effect size on student's collaboration knowledge is very high: *(Average collaboration $_{exp}$ – Average collaboration $_{control}$)/ s.d. $_{control}$* = 1.3.

The experimental group students contributed more to the group diagram, with the difference between the average number of individual contribution for control and experimental group being statistically significant (t = 2.03, p = 0.03). The meta-constraints generated collaboration-based feedback 19.4 times on average for the experimental group (for each student).

We have also analyzed the students' individual log files, in order to identify how students learnt the underlying domain concepts in the second week. Figure 5 illustrates the probability of violating a domain constraint plotted against the occasion number for which it was relevant, averaged over all domain constraints and all participants in control and experimental groups. The data points show a regular decrease, which is approximated by a power curve with a close fit of 0.78 and 0.85 for control and experimental groups respectively, thus showing that students do learn constraints over time. The probability of 0.21/0.23 for violating a constraint on the first occasion of application has decreased to 0.09/0.12 at its eleventh occasion, displaying a 61.9%/47.8% decrease in probability for the control/experimental group respectively. Figure 6 illustrates the learning curve for meta-constraints only (for the

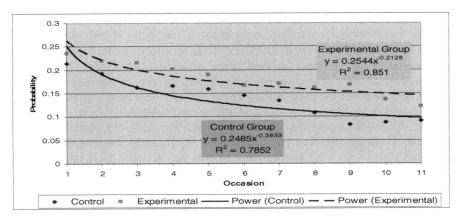

Fig. 5. Probability of domain constraint violation for individuals in control and experimental group

experimental group). There is also a regular decrease, thus showing that students learn meta-constraints over time. Because the students used the system for a short time only, more data is needed to analyze learning of meta-constraints, but the trend identified in this study is encouraging.

The participants were given a questionnaire at the end of the session to determine their perceptions of the system. Most of the participants (61% of control and 78% of experimental group) responded they would recommend the system to other students. The students found the interface easy to learn and use and enjoyed working with a partner. The comments we received on open questions show that the students liked the system and thought it improved their knowledge, and also pointed out several possible improvements.

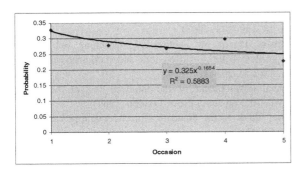

Fig. 6. Probability of meta-constraint violation

6 Conclusions

CBM has previously been used to effectively represent domain knowledge in several ITSs supporting individual learning. The contribution of this research is the use of CBM to model collaboration skills, not only domain knowledge. We described the process of extending COLLECT-$\mathcal{UML}$, an ITS for UML class diagrams, to support collaboration.

The system's effectiveness in teaching good collaboration and UML class diagrams was evaluated in a classroom experiment. The results of both subjective and objective analysis proved that COLLECT-$\mathcal{UML}$ is an effective educational tool. The experimental group students acquired more declarative knowledge on effective collaboration, as they scored significantly higher on the collaboration test. The collaboration skills of the experimental group students were better, as evidenced by these students being more active in collaboration, and contributing more to the group diagram. All students improved their problem-solving skills: the participants from both control and experimental group performed significantly better on the post-test after short sessions with the system, showing that they acquired more knowledge on UML modelling. Finally, the students enjoyed working with the system and found it a valuable asset to their learning.

The results, therefore, show that CBM is an effective technique for modelling and supporting collaboration in CSCL environments.

References

1. Baghaei, N., Mitrovic, A., Irwin, W.: A Constraint-Based Tutor for Learning Object Oriented Analysis and Design using UML. In: Proc. ICCE 2005, pp.11–18 (2005)
2. Baghaei, N., Mitrovic, A.: A Constraint-based Collaborative Environment for Learning UML Class Diagrams. In: Proc. ITS 2006, pp.176–186 (2006)
3. Baghaei, N., Mitrovic, A., Irwin, W.: Problem-Solving Support in a Constraint-based Tutor for UML Class Diagrams, Technology, Instruction, Cognition and Learning Journal, vol. 4(2) (In print) (2006)
4. Brusilovsky, P., Peylo, C.: Adaptive and Intelligent Web-based Educational Systems. Artificial Intelligence in Education 13, 159–172 (2003)
5. Constantino-Gonzalez, M.A., Suthers, D., de los Santos, E.J.: Coaching web- based collaborative learning based on problem solution differences and participation. Int. J. Artificial Intelligence in Education 13(2-4), 263–299 (2003)
6. Doise, W., Mugny, G.: The social development of the intellect. In: Int. Series in Experimental Social Psychology, vol. 10, Pergamon Press, London (1984)
7. Fowler, M.: UML Distilled: a Brief Guide to the Standard Object Modelling Language, 3rd edn. Addison-Wesley, Reading (2004)
8. Jarboe, S.: Procedures for enhancing group decision making. In: Hirokawa, B., Poole, M.(eds.) Communication and Group Decision Making, pp. 345–383 (1996)
9. Jerman, P., Soller, A., Muhlenbrock, M.: From Mirroring to Guiding: A Review of State of the Art Technology for Supporting Collaborative Learning. In: Dillenbourg, P., Eurelings, A.,Hakkarainen, K. (eds.) CSCL 2001, pp. 324–331 (2001)
10. Martin, B., Mitrovic, A.: Domain Modelling: Art or Science? In: Hoppe, U., Verdejo, F., Kay, J.(eds.) Proc. 11th Int. Conference on AIED, pp.183–190 (2003)
11. Mayo, M., Mitrovic, A.: Optimising ITS behaviour with Bayesian networks and decision theory. Artificial Intelligence in Education 12(2), 124–153 (2001)
12. McManus, M., Aiken, R.: Monitoring computer-based problem solving. Int. Journal of Artificial Intelligence in Education 6(4), 307–336 (1995)
13. Mitrovic, A., Suraweera, P., Martin, B., Weerasinghe, A.: DB-suite: Experiences with three Intelligent, Web-based Database Tutors. Journal of Interactive Learning Research 15(4), 409–432 (2004)

14. Ogata, H., Matsuura, K., Yano, Y.: Active Knowledge Awareness Map: Visualizing learners activities in a Web based CSCL environment. Int. Workshop on New Technologies in Collaborative Learning, pp. 89–97 (2000)
15. Ohlsson, S.: Constraint-based Student Modelling. In: Greer, J., McCalla, G. (eds.) Student Modelling: the Key to Individualized Knowledge-based Instruction, pp. 167–189. Springer, Heidelberg (1994)
16. Rummel, N., Spada, H.: Learning to collaborate: An instructional approach to promoting collaborative problem-solving in computer-mediated settings. Journal of the Learning Sciences 14(2), 201–241 (2005)
17. Soller, A.: Supporting Social Interaction in an Intelligent Collaborative Learning System. International Journal of AIED 12, 40–62 (2001)
18. Soller, A., Lesgold, A.: Knowledge acquisition for adaptive collaborative learning environments. AAAI Fall Symposium: Learning How to Do Things (2000)
19. Vizcaino, A.: A Simulated Student Can Improve Collaborative Learning. Int. Journal of Artificial Intelligence in Education 15, 3–40 (2005)

Mobile Opportunistic Planning: Methods and Models

Eric Horvitz, Paul Koch, and Muru Subramani

Microsoft Research, One Microsoft Way
Redmond, Washington USA 98052
{horvitz,paulkoch,murus}@microsoft.com

Abstract. We present a study exploring the promise of developing computational systems to support the discovery and execution of opportunistic activities in mobile settings. We introduce the challenge of mobile opportunistic planning, describe a prototype named *Mobile Commodities*, and focus on the construction and use of probabilistic user models to infer the cost of time required to execute opportunistic plans.

1 Introduction

We believe that computing systems may one day provide great value to people by continuing to identify feasible plans for achieving standing goals in an opportunistic manner—in stream with ongoing activities. We shall explore here the promise of developing methods that can make people aware of opportunities and means for achieving goals in mobile settings. The fundamental idea is straightforward: During the progression of a planned trip, we consider a set of standing goals and preconditions specified by a mobile traveler, perform a search over a space of feasible waypoints for satisfying the goals, and seek to identify and alert the traveler about options for achieving one or more standing goals at minimal cost.

We present a prototype system, named *Mobile Commodities* (MC), which performs a search over the locations of shops, points of interest, and services, and then deliberates about the time and distance added to trips that include waypoints through these locations. MC attempts to minimize the cost of acquiring a product, service, or experience, including a consideration of the cost of time required to include the goal-satisfying waypoint. The MC prototype consists of three programs, one running as a client application on Windows Mobile Pocket PC that accesses GPS information via a Bluetooth puck, the second program running as a desktop companion for assessing preferences, configuring and inspecting policies, and the third, a server-based system that engages in two-way communication with mobile devices via GPRS.

We review the challenge of mobile opportunistic planning, and discuss how distinct subproblems are addressed by different components of MC. We shall focus on the key problem of finding the time to carry out unplanned activities opportunistically, when such activities are overlayed on the execution of existing plans. We present details on the construction and evaluation of probabilistic user models to infer the context-sensitive cost of allocating time to satisfying additional goals, and describe how the models are used in MC to guide the search for opportunistic plans.

C. Conati, K. McCoy, and G. Paliouras (Eds.): UM 2007, LNAI 4511, pp. 228–237, 2007.
© Springer-Verlag Berlin Heidelberg 2007

2   Opportunistic Planning Challenge

Performing background analyses to identify feasible opportunistic plans requires (1) a means for encoding background goals, (2) a method for generating feasible plans for achieving such goals, and (3) a method for evaluating the economic value of alternate plans. A critical aspect of the economic value of opportunistic plans is the context-sensitive cost of the additional time required to satisfy secondary goals. We shall focus on predictive user modeling of the cost of time in Section 3.

Figure 1 displays the main components of mobile opportunistic planning that reflect the core competencies implemented in the MC prototype. The destination analysis component ascertains the intended destination of a user in motion. Methods for identifying a driver's destination includes (1) acquiring the destination from a user, (2) using user-specified rules that identifies a destination from a set of previously encoded set destinations classified by time of day and day of week, (3) use of a location linked to a forthcoming meeting, drawn from an online calendar, and (4) the inference of a probability distribution over forthcoming destination based on a driver's partial trajectory. We have explored the use of all four methods in MC. Space limitations limit our review of probabilistic models of destinations here; we refer readers to detailed discussion in [5]. The current implementation of MC allows users to specify destinations directly, to specify destinations as a function of the time of day and day of week, or to use the locations of forthcoming meetings drawn from an electronic calendar.

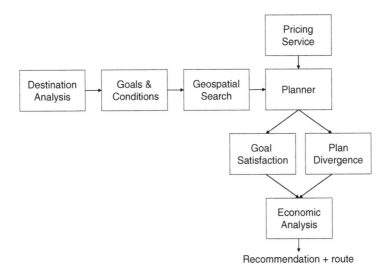

Fig. 1. Flow of analysis for mobile opportunistic planning implemented within the Mobile Commodities (MC) prototype

A second component of MC contains a representation of standing, background goals asserted by users and the preconditions that specify when goals should be activated. We formulated a sample ontology of products and services and we seeded the system with several classes of products, services, and social goals. Products and services encoded in the system include such goals as obtaining groceries, gasoline, meals, haircuts, and oil changes. Users can specify specific retailers or service providers by name. Social goals allow for the specification of locations of friends and family. For each goal, we allow users to specify preconditions on a form that defines when the goal should be activated.

Users can express policies in terms of recurrent needs to acquire items that require cyclic replenishment or satiation. For example, for the goal of refueling their vehicles, users can specify a threshold amount of gasoline remaining in their car's fuel tank. When the amount of gas remaining drops below the threshold level, a background search for opportunities to seek gasoline is triggered. The frame-based specification of a policy for purchasing gasoline allows users to include the capacity of their fuel tank, the average miles per gallon, and the fuel remaining. Figure 2a shows a view of the goals and conditions specification tool for the goal of refueling. For recurrent goals such as replenishing groceries or getting haircuts, users provide a target duration between each purchase or receipt of service. Goals and preferences are specified via the MC desktop program, which synchronizes with a server that communicates with the MC mobile application.

A geospatial search component identifies locations that can satisfy active goals. MC uses the Microsoft MapPoint database to identify locations of shops and services. This subsystem takes the user's current location and target destination, computes an efficient route to the destination, then identifies candidate locations that can satisfy the active goals should they be added as waypoints on the way to the destination. For enhancing the tractability of MC's search, we limit the number of locations of opportunistic waypoints to those within a maximal tolerated distance of locations from points on the expected path that a user will take.

We will highlight the operation of MC with the example of the system computing recommendations for opportunistic gasoline purchases. The MC server has access to all of the gas stations in the Seattle area via the MapPoint database. The system also has access to a gasoline pricing service being developed at our organization. The service provides prices updated daily for all stations in major cities. Figure 2b shows the locations of gas stations in the Greater Seattle region. Figure 2c shows the overlay of prices for different qualities of fuel.

The planning component attempts to satisfy active goals and to minimize the cost of diverging from the efficient path to the primary destination. The planner also performs an economic analysis, seeking to minimize the expected cost of satisfying active goals. The planner first examines the efficient path of the user to their primary destination and considers active goals and their associated candidate locations. It then performs an exhaustive search over alternate routes that include locations that satisfy goals as waypoints on the path to the destination. For each path, it caches the path, the goals satisfied, the available prices of the desired items or services available at the waypoints, a set of directions that routes the driver from the current location through the identified locations, and the total number of miles and time required for each modified route. The economic analysis subsystem provides a context-sensitive *cost of time* for the user, and seeks to minimize the total cost to the user of diverting off of the most efficient path to the primary destination, based on the additional costs of time and of transportation.

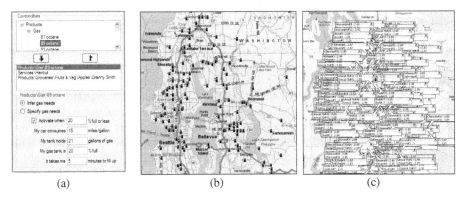

Fig. 2. a: Form within the desktop MC client that allows users to specify goals and preconditions, focused here on the gasoline purchase example; b: view of filling stations for the Seattle
area; c: overlay of current prices for fuel by type of fuel at each location

3 Considering Cost of Divergence

It is not always possible to take time out, even if only a short time, to add a new destination to a trip—especially in opportunistic situations, where time may not have been
allocated ahead of time for making stops. Informal interviews with potential users of
MC highlighted the need for opportunistic planners to represent and reason in a sophisticated manner about the cost of time and other additional travel costs, considering the preferences of the users they support. We pursued the challenge of endowing
the MC with a sense for the cost of time in different contexts.

A user's time is indeed a precious and limited resource—in many cases the most
precious resource handled by the opportunistic planner. Reasoning about the cost of
time is especially important in a system designed to trade off increasing amounts of
distance and time on a trip for accessing increasingly better "deals." We focused on
methods that could allow MC to consider the cost of arriving at a primary destination
later than an initially intended or *target* arrival time.

In the general case, the planner needs to consider multiple properties of a destination and the overall context to assign a cost of delay associated with an unplanned
stop. We explored the use of the Microsoft Outlook calendar as a means for representing and accessing properties of destinations. We view the use of an online calendar as
a transitional representation for context and forthcoming events; we foresee future
versions of MC relying on richer representations of patterns of daily activity. Beyond
using the calendar in a standard way to represent business appointments and special
social events, MC users set up recurrent appointments that capture daily patterns of
activity, such as target times for arriving at work and for returning home. We gave the
MC desktop application the ability to access such daily life events and more traditional appointments via an interface to Microsoft Exchange.

3.1 Assessment of Costs of Time

The computation of the cost of time in MC makes use of several assessments that are
used in conjunction with probabilistic inference to generate the expected costs of time

under uncertainty about context. We found that the assessments and training required approximately a half-hour session of working with forms generated by the MC desktop client. Users first indicate on a seven-day by twenty-four hour spreadsheet-style palette, swaths of time associated with a *low*, *medium*, or *high* cost of arriving at a destination after a target arrival time. Users then directly assess a cost of time in dollars per hour for each of the three states. As we shall see, these background costs are considered by MC when no information is noted on a user's calendar. Users also assess costs of delay for contexts where a calendar is showing a forthcoming appointment. Users are asked to also consider appointments as being associated with low, medium, and high costs contexts, and assess a similar cost of delayed arrival for each of the contexts. Users can optionally enter a *tardy penalty*, a dollar value representing what users would be willing to pay to avoid being late at all. After assessment of background and meeting-centric time costs, the MC desktop application uploads a database of costs by time to the MC server. The server application uses these costs in doing cost analysis during opportunistic planning.

3.2   Learning Predictive Models for the Cost of Time

MC includes a subsystem for constructing probabilistic user models that are used at run time to infer context-sensitive costs of delays. The user models in MC infer (1) the probability that a meeting is associated with a low, medium, or high cost context, and (2) the probability that a target time drawn from a forthcoming appointment on the user's calendar is relevant. The first step in building the predictive models is that extraction of a time-sorted list of appointments from a user's online calendar.

A form displaying the list is composed for user tagging. The form contains two sets of radio selection buttons, adjacent to each appointment item. Users indicate for each meeting whether it is appropriate to consider the start time listed in the appointment as a relevant deadline, and, if so, whether the meeting should be associated with a high, medium, or low cost of being late. Given a database of tagged appointments, the system prepares a training set composed of appointments annotated with tags from the users, and also a set of properties associated with each Outlook appointment. The properties include the day and time of the appointment, meeting duration, strings from the subject and location fields, information about the organizer, the number and nature of the invitees, the response status of the user to an online invitation, whether the meeting is a recurrent meeting or not, and whether the time was marked as busy versus free on the user's calendar. We also include the role of the user, whether the user was the organizer of the meeting versus listed as a required or optional attendee by another organizer. We employ the Microsoft Active Directory service to recognize and annotate organizational relationships among the user, the organizer, and the other attendees. As an example, the system recognizes whether the organizer and attendees are peers, managers, or direct reports. Finally, we note whether the attendees, organizer, or location is "atypical" given the other meetings in the users data base; that is, we identify whether they are present in less than a predefined small fraction of all meetings in the training set.

Given the library of cases, the desktop MC application employs Bayesian structure learning to build Bayesian networks that predict relevancies and cost-of-delay functions. The system constructs models by performing heuristic search over feasible probabilistic dependency models, guided by a *Bayesian score* to rank candidate models. The Bayesian structure search method we use employs both global and local search [2,3]. For each variable, the method creates a tree containing a multinomial distribution at each leaf, exploiting the local structure search methods.

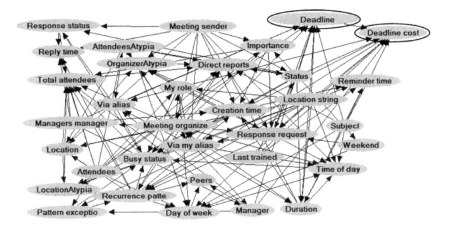

Fig. 3. Bayesian model learned from library of tagged appointments. The model predicts relevancy of target times and the cost function associated with arrival after the specified start time.

A sample predictive model for the cost of time constructed from training data from a subject testing the MC system is displayed in Figure 3. The subject tagged appointments from February 21, 2005 to March 4, 2006, a task which took the subject approximately 45 minutes. We performed a holdout cross validation, using 85 percent of the case library for training the model, and the remaining 15 percent of data to test the predictive accuracy of the models on the remaining 15 percent of holdout data. Target variables for the association of a deadline with the start of an appointment and the cost of being delayed are highlighted as circled nodes. Table 1 displays the accuracies of the inferences about the likelihood of deadlines being associated with calendar items and the probability distribution over the meeting being in the class of low, medium, or high cost of arriving after the target arrival time. The table displays significant predictive lifts over the marginal models for both of these inferences, showing the value of using the model over background statistics.

Table 1. Classification accuracy of predictive model when tested on a holdout set. The accuracy of the respective marginal models are listed beneath the accuracies of the learned models

	Relevant deadline	Cost of delayed arrival
Learned model	0.90	0.88
Marginal model	0.52	0.44

3.3 Integrating Cost of Time into Opportunistic Planning

Adding waypoints to a pre-existing trip in an opportunistic manner adds time and fuel costs to an overall trip. Reasoning about the best options for addressing background goals requires computing the additional costs for each plan option. In the simple, non-probabilistic case, we consider the additional time and miles incurred with the divergence off the most efficient path for each opportunistic plan. We refer to this cost as the cost of divergence (CD) associated with each candidate plan.

MC makes use of the inferences from the predictive model to generate the cost of diverging from the ideal route to the destination. The analysis considers (1) the assessed background default cost of time in different situations, (2) inferences from the predictive model, based on the properties of a forthcoming appointment, about the probability distribution over the cost of arriving at progressively later times after a target start time, and (3) the likelihood that the target start time of an active appointment is relevant. We use these quantities to compute the *expected cost of divergence* (ECD) associated with any amount of time and/or distance added to the trip by considering the costs associated with the deadline relevant and not relevant situations, and combining the two situations together weighted by the likelihood of relevance and its complement.

We focus now on details of how the predictive model is used in MC to compute the cost of divergence. We shall use S^b and S^a to refer to background, non-appointment situations and special appointment contexts, respectively. We use Δd to refer to the additional miles associated with the plan and Δt to refer to the additional time of the trip due to the inclusion of one or more opportunistic waypoints to achieve standing goals, in addition to the estimate of the time required to execute the goal once at the appropriate location. We decompose Δt into the time until a target time, t^b, and the time, t^a, that falls after the target start time. For the case where the time for executing the modified travel plan leads to arrival after the target time, the cost is the sum of the background time cost incurred before the deadline, $C(S^b, t^b)$, the penalty for arriving after the target time, $C^p(S^a, t^a>0)$, and cost of arriving at the primary destination at increasingly later times after the target time has passed, $C(S^a, t^a)$. MC also considers the additional transportation costs (fuel and wear and tear on the vehicle), C^f, associated with the divergence from the efficient path to the primary destination. This transportation cost, $C^f(\Delta d)$ is a function of the difference in distance in miles between the opportunistic plan and the primary trip, Δd, for each plan. S_i^a refers to the cost context (low, medium, and high) for an active target time.

We use $p(A|E)$ to refer to the probability that a deadline for the appointment A is relevant conditioned on evidence E, a set of properties of a forthcoming appointment S^a. The probability that a deadline is not relevant is simply the complement, $1- p(A|E)$. For the case where the deadline is not relevant, the cost of time is just the background default cost based on the default context or situation, $C(S^a, \Delta t)$. For the case where the deadline is active, we have the background time cost incurred before the deadline, $C(S^b, t^b)$, the penalty for being tardy, $C^p(S^a, t^a>0)$, and the growing cost of lateness, capturing the increasing cost with arriving late for the appointment, $C(S^a, t^a)$. MC is uncertain as to the cost functions associated with arriving after the target times associated with specific appointments, so the system computes an expectation by summing over the probability distribution of time cost functions inferred by the predictive model. Putting these terms together, weighting the influences of the appointment and non-appointment scenarios by the appropriate likelihoods, and adding the transportation cost, we compute the ECD for each alternate route as,

$$
\begin{aligned}
ECD = C^f(\Delta d) \\
+ (1 - p(A \mid E))C(S^b, \Delta t) \\
+ p(A \mid E)(\sum_i p(S_i^a \mid E)(C(S_i^a, t^a) + C^p(S_i^a, t^a)) + C(S^b, t^b))
\end{aligned}
\tag{1}
$$

where $p(S_i^a \mid E)$ is the probability that each appointment cost context (low, medium, and high) is active. The costs of divergence described in this section are used to identify the best opportunistic plans in the MC prototype.

4 Operation of MC

When MC users get into their automobiles, the MC mobile client recognizes a Bluetooth puck in the car. A signal is sent from the mobile device to the MC server, identifying the server that the user is beginning a trip. Let us consider the example of opportunistically purchasing gasoline. When MC begins to work to satisfy the goal of identifying a best location to purchase gasoline, the system executes a cycle of analysis on the server every 10 minutes. In each cycle, the system identifies the driver's location. When planning is active, the server component accesses the user's assessments of the cost of time for the default period of time and for appointments. The system also accesses a database of the user's forthcoming appointments and examines the appointment properties. It then computes the cost of time with Equation 1.

For each cycle of opportunistic planning, the server application first computes an ideal path from the user's current location to the assumed destination, using the Map-Point route planner. As an example, when the gasoline goal is active, the application identifies all filling stations within the greater Seattle region and loads current gas prices. The system exhaustively searches through alternative routes from the current location to the destination, going through each candidate waypoint.

For each candidate route and waypoint, a divergence in miles and time for the new route, by taking the difference in miles and in time associated with the new trip and the original trip, as well as the cost assumed for the time required to stop and fill up. An overall dollar value cost of divergence is computed for each candidate trip. This cost is added to the cost of the intended purchase, computed as the price of the gas and the number of gallons required to fill the driver's tank. The system then prioritizes the alternate routes from low net cost to higher costs and sends the top five candidates to the MC mobile client, along with summary information about each candidate, including turn-by-turn directions for each. The directions divert the user off of the current path through the way point and then back to the final destination. Drivers can configure an alerting policy to limit the number of notifications during each trip.

To illustrate how MC operates, we present screens generated by a visualization utility that we created to step through the results of MC's searches. The system displays the original route, as well as candidate routes and locations for purchasing gas

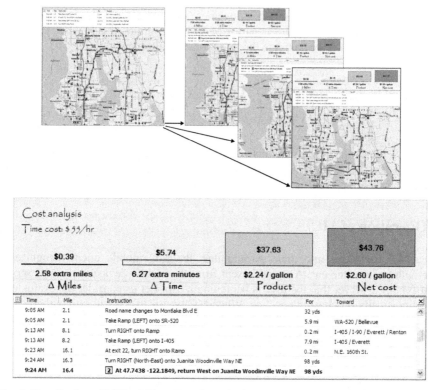

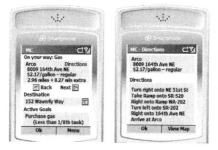

Fig. 4. Top: Portion of MC's deliberation about the best waypoint to stop for fuel. Three alternate plans of the larger search space that satisfy the goal are displayed. Bottom: Economic summary of the cost of diverging from the route to the primary destination for best plan.

Fig. 5. Mobile views of a notification about a best candidate for opportunistic fueling

ordered from lowest cost to highest cost candidates. The top portion of Figure 4 shows a sequence of views displayed by the system. Each view shows a candidate opportunistic plan. A summary of the divergence analysis, including the net cost, as well as breakouts for the cost of time and for the purchase, is displayed for each candidate plan. A summary analysis is displayed in the lower portion of Figure 4. Views rendered on a prototype MC mobile client of a notification about an opportunity, and of the directions for the path including the recommended waypoint, are displayed in Figure 5.

5 Related Work

Several prior studies are relevant to the work on MC. Patterson, *et al.* [6] examined an application that identifies when cognitively compromised people have likely strayed off of expected paths, and that works to route them back to a primary destination. Bohnenberger, *et al.* explored the recommendation of paths through a shopping mall based on representations of shoppers' interests [1]. In other related work, Horvitz, *et al.* [4] described the use of machine learning from tagged case libraries of Outlook appointments to construct probabilistic models to predict whether users will attend meetings or not and models of the cost of interruption for those meetings.

6 Summary and Directions

The Mobile Commodities project has focused on identifying challenges and opportunities for building opportunistic planning systems that work continuously to address goals encoded by people. We presented methods and models used in MC, a prototype that highlights key components and challenges with mobile opportunistic planning. On future directions, we are pursuing four extensions: (1) bundling of opportunities and simultaneous search over multiple goals, coupled with an exploration of more sophisticated planning techniques to address the combinatorial challenges; (2) integration of destination prediction services and the generalization of the methods by considering probability distributions over drivers' destinations, (3) moving to a more comprehensive cost-benefit analysis of opportunities, including the development of the ability to learn over time to recognize special offers and anomalously low prices, and (4) development of pricing systems and mechanisms that allows retailers to post standing and time-limited offers to people in a manner sensitive to preferences and context, potentially negotiating directly with peoples' opportunistic planners. We hope that our initial efforts will stimulate the user modeling community to focus more attention on challenges with mobile opportunistic planning. We see great opportunities ahead.

References

1. Bohnenberger, T., Jameson, A., Kruger, A., Butz, A.: Location-aware shopping assistance: Evaluation of a decision-theoretic approach, Mobile HCI 2002, pp. 155–169 (2002)
2. Chickering, D.M., Heckerman, D., Meek, C.A.: Bayesian approach to learning Bayesian networks with local structure. UAI 1997, pp. 80–89 (1997)
3. Friedman, N., Goldszmidt, M.: Learning Bayesian networks with local structure. UAI 1996, pp. 252–262 (1996)
4. Horvitz, E., Koch, P., Kadie, K., Jacobs, A.: Coordinate: Probabilistic forecasting of presence and availability. UAI 2002, pp. 224–233 (2002)
5. Krumm, J., Horvitz, E.: Predestination: Inferring destinations from partial trajectories, Ubicomp 2006, pp. 243–260 (2006)
6. Patterson, D.J., Liao, L., Gajos, K., Collier, M., Livic, N., Olson, K., Wang, S., Fox, D., Kautz, H.: Opportunity knocks: A system to provide cognitive assistance with transportation services. Ubicomp 2004, pp. 433–450 (2004)

Analyzing Museum Visitors' Behavior Patterns

Massimo Zancanaro[2], Tsvi Kuflik[1], Zvi Boger[3,4], Dina Goren-Bar[1],
and Dan Goldwasser[1]

[1] The University of Haifa, Mount Carmel, Haifa, 31905, Israel
[2] ITC-irst, via Sommarive 18, 38050 Povo, Italy
[3] Ben-Gurion University of the Negev, Beer Sheva,84105, Israel
[4] OPTIMAL – Industrial Neural Systems, Be'er Sheva 84243, Israel
zancana@itc.it;tsvikak@is.haifa.ac.il;zboger@bgu.ac.il;
dgb@univ.haifa.ac.il;dgoldwas@cslx.haifa.ac.il

Abstract. Many studies have investigated personalized information presentation in the context of mobile museum guides. In order to provide such a service, information about museum visitors has to be collected and visitors have to be monitored and modelled in a non-intrusive manner. This can be done by using known museum visiting styles to classify the visiting style of visitors as they start their visit. Past research applied ethnographic observations of the behaviour of visitors and qualitative analysis (mainly site studies and interviews with staff) in several museums to define visiting styles. The current work validates past ethnographic research by applying unsupervised learning approaches to visitors classification. By providing quantitative empirical evidence for a qualitative theory we claim that, from the point of view of assessing the suitability of a qualitative theory in a given scenario, this approach is as valid as a manual annotation of museum visiting styles.

1 Introduction

The museum environment is an attractive arena in which to develop and experiment with ambient intelligence in general and personalized information delivery in particular. Many studies have investigated personalized information presentation in the context of mobile museum guides [1]. Regarding the user characteristics that need to be modelled, most approaches focus on history of interaction and user interests. For example, the GUIDE system presented in [2] adapts web-like presentations by adding information about nearby attractions that might be interesting for the visitor of a city. The HIPPIE system proposes personalized tours in a museum by maintaining a model of user interests and knowledge [3]. The REAL system [4] adapts route descriptions according to the actual user position, the limited technical resources of the device, and the cognitive resources of the user. In the context of the PEACH project [5] a spreading activation technique applied on a domain knowledge-base was implemented to predict the interest in concepts related to those for which the system received explicit feedback from the user.

Knowledge-related features are not, however, the only sources of information that are worth considering for modelling a museum visitor. For example, Petrelli and

C. Conati, K. McCoy, and G. Paliouras (Eds.): UM 2007, LNAI 4511, pp. 238–246, 2007.
© Springer-Verlag Berlin Heidelberg 2007

Not [6] suggest taking into consideration whether the user is visiting the museum alone or with companions, whether she is a first-time or a recurrent visitor, and so on.

Behavioural traits have also been taken into consideration. Sparacino [7] proposed categorization of user types into three main categories: (i) the greedy visitor who wants to know and see as much as possible; (ii) the selective visitor who spends time on artefacts that represent certain concepts only and neglects the others; and (iii) the busy visitor who prefers strolling through the museum in order to get a general idea of the exhibition without spending much time on any exhibits. Her application employs Bayesian networks to model both the user (interest and style) and the appropriateness of the guide's content (length and order).

The same categorization of user types is also used by Hatala and Wakkary [8] together with an ontology-based model of the interests. In both these papers, the validity of such a scheme is justified through qualitative analysis, mainly site studies and interviews with staff at various museums.

In this paper, we will focus on the classification of the visiting style proposed by the ethno methodologists Veron and Levasseur [9]. Starting from ethnographic observations of the behaviour of a number of visitors in several museums, they argued that visitors' movements may be compared to the behaviour of four "typical" animals, and they proposed using this strategy as a way of classifying the "style" of a visitor. Specifically, they suggests that the *ANT* visitor tends to follow a specific path and spends a lot of time observing almost all the exhibits; the *FISH* visitor most of the time moves around in the centre of the room and usually avoids looking at exhibits' details; the *BUTTERFLY* visitor does not follow a specific path but rather is guided by the physical orientation of the exhibits and stops frequently to look for more information; finally, the *GRASSHOPPER* visitor seems to have a specific preference for some preselected exhibits and spends a lot of time observing them while tending to ignore the others. Of course, it might be expected that a given visitor can change her behaviour during a long visit, and it is also possible that the style is affected by the specific interests.

The first attempt to exploit this classification as part of a user model for a mobile guide was in the HIPS project (see mainly [10]) where a Recurrent Artificial Neural Network (ANN) was trained to recognize the visiting style of a visitor given her interaction history. This model was then employed for selecting and tailoring information to the visitor [11]. Although most of the ideas tested experimentally in HIPS underwent user evaluation, the very idea of the existence of visiting styles was taken for granted relying on the qualitative analysis of the original work.

Chittarro and Ieronutti [12] employed Veron and Levasseur's classification in the context of a tool that visualizes users' behaviours in a virtual environment. Their use of the visiting styles was based on qualitative analysis and, again, they did not evaluate the existence of these classes.

In this paper, we are trying to take a step back; we would like to discuss a methodology for validating empirically Veron and Levasseur's model of visiting style. We used log files of 140 visitors exploring a frescoed room with a multimedia museum guide to provide quantitative-based evidence that museum visitors' behavior may effectively be classified according to Veron and Levasseur's model. We used two unsupervised learning techniques (K-means and Auto-Associative ANN) to cluster the visitors' behaviours. The clustering produced by both techniques may be assumed to characterize Veron and Levasseur's four animals. An agreement analysis conducted on the classifications schemes determined by clustering membership revealed a high level of agreement between the two techniques.

This work is intended to complement Veron and Levasseur's ethnographic study by providing empirical evidence for it as well as to provide information in a principled way for further research on user modelling. Our claim, as discussed in the last section, is that this approach may complement—if not replace—reliability analysis of observation schemes derived from qualitative research such as Veron and Levasseur's.

2 Data Collection and Preparation

In the context of a user study of a multimedia mobile guide [13], 143 regular visitors to Torre Aquila[1] in Trento were invited to test the system. Each visitor was requested to visit Torre Aquila with a multimedia guide (although adaptive guides were experimented in Torre Aquila [14], a non-adaptive version was employed for this study). Among the subjects, 61 were males and 82 females. Their age ranged from 20 to 79 years (mean=47, median=50, std.dev=15.9). All were recruited at the entrance of the museum and received a free ticket to visit the castle as a reward for participating in the data collection.

Out of the 143 visit logs, 140 were used for this study; the rest had various errors that prevented their use. The average visit time was 22 minutes, and average time spent in front an exhibit was 4 minutes with standard deviation of 70 seconds. The system automatically logged the visitors' movements in the space (by means of IR sensors) and all their interaction with the museum visitors' guide.

Since we are interested—at this stage—in analyzing the visitors' behavior rather than in predicting the visiting style from the interaction history, we used measures relating to the entire visit rather than temporal-based indices. The measures used for the analysis were the average time spent at each position, the percentage of exhibits visited, a numerical representation between 0 and 1 of the order of the visit (where 1 means that the visitor spent some time on each exhibit and 0 that she did not stop at any exhibit), and a combined description of visitors' behavior, taking into account interaction and whether or not visitors played fully through complete presentations. Further, four cumulative measures were defined considering the percentage of the visit for which the visitor was: (A) interacting with the guide (i.e., asking for more information), but not reaching the conclusion of the presentations; (B) interacting and reaching conclusions; (C) not interacting and not reaching conclusions; and (D) not interacting but reaching conclusions.

Data pre-processing generated 140 7-dimensional vectors including the average time, visit order and completeness, and the percentage of the visit for which the visitor's behavior was according to each of the four types (checking for each and every

---

[1] Torre Aquila is a tower at the Buonconsiglio Castle in Trento, Italy where a fresco called "The Cycle of the Months," a masterpiece of the gothic period, is to be found. This fresco, painted in the Fifteenth Century, covers all fours walls of a room in the tower and illustrates the activities of aristocrats and peasants throughout the year. The museum guide used to collect visitor data is one of the many prototypes developed in the PEACH project; for more details see [14].

position whether the visitor interacted with the system or not and whether he/she viewed complete presentations or not and then calculating the ratios).

3 Analysis of Museum Visitors' Behavior

The visit logs representation was used as an input to an auto-associative ANN and to a K-means clustering algorithm, both of which clustered the data into four clusters in order to validate the Veron and Levasseur classification and see if their visitors' types might be identified.

3.1 Unsupervised Learning with Auto-Associative ANN

Artificial neural networks are used to form data-driven models. In order to perform unsupervised learning, an auto-associative ANN (AA-ANN), in which the "targets" are identical to the inputs, was used. If the trained AA-ANN succeeds in replicating the inputs as outputs, it means that the hidden neurons are encoding the essential information "distilled" from the inputs features. In most cases the outputs of the hidden neurons are close to either one or zero [15]. Thus all examples that generate the same hidden neurons output pattern are deemed to belong to the same cluster.

Table 1. ANN clustering results

Cluster	# of cases	Av T	A	B	C	D	Order	Completeness
1	53	1.22	0.45	**1.81**	0.14	0.24	1.00	1.02
2	36	0.93	0.24	0.42	0.49	**2.97**	1.03	1.02
3	15	0.74	0.77	0.18	**5.68**	1.07	0.99	0.96
4	36	0.84	**2.69**	0.72	0.84	0.14	0.97	0.97

As explained above, the data consisted of 140 visit summary examples with seven visit attributes named: AvT (Average time), A, B, C, D, Order (of the visit) and Completeness (percentage of frescos visited). The AA-ANN used was a fully-connected, feed-forward ANN of two hidden neurons and seven output neurons, each having the sigmoidal transfer function, which was presented with the dataset with the seven input variables and the identical values as targets. The input data were preprocessed by subtracting the mean value of each attribute column, and dividing by the standard deviation of each column. These values were further re-scaled to the 0.1-0.9 range to serve as the AA-ANN targets. The training was done by the Guterman-Boger set of algorithms that starts with non-random connection weights and employs proprietary algorithms for avoiding entering, and escaping from, local minima encountered during the training [16, 17]. The "binary" pattern of the hidden neurons was used for clustering [18]. The average attribute values of the examples in each cluster were divided by the average of the attribute values of the full dataset. The results are shown in Table 1.

The ratios of the attributes that are higher than 1.5 are marked bold, and those with ratios smaller than 0.5 are underlined. It can be seen that cluster # 1 has a high ratio of the B variable, cluster # 2 has a high ratio of variable D, cluster # 4 has a high ratio of variable A, and cluster # 3 has a high ratio of attribute C. The attributes Av T, Order and Completeness apparently do not contribute much to the clusters' formation, although it may be that cluster 1 may have a somewhat higher mean Av T.

Hence Cluster 1 seems to correspond to an *ANT* type (long, ordered and interactive, and gets complete presentations) and cluster 3 corresponds to a *FISH* type (short visit, without getting complete presentations). Cluster 2 corresponds to a *GRASSHOPPER* (tends to get more complete presentations than *BUTTERFLY*) and cluster 4 to a *BUTTERFLY* (less ordered and does not get complete presentations). After the clustering, we also used an ANOVA [19] with the clusters identified as a factor and the cumulative indexes outlined above as dependent variables. Significant differences were found at $p < 0.001$ along all the variables except Order and Completeness. Table 2 summarizes the results.

Table 2. One-way ANOVA on the ANN clusters

		Sum of Squares	df	Mean Squares	F	sig.
Avg Time	Between Groups	282415.70	3	94138.55	30.36	0.00
	Within Groups	421751.20	136	3101.11		
	Total	704166.90	139			
A	Between Groups	6.13	3	2.04	90.50	0.00
	Within Groups	3.07	136	0.02		
	Total	9.19	139			
B	Between Groups	12.55	3	4.18	137.53	0.00
	Within Groups	4.14	136	0.03		
	Total	16.69	139			
C	Between Groups	2.76	3	0.92	68.26	0.00
	Within Groups	1.83	136	0.01		
	Total	4.59	139			
D	Between Groups	11.87	3	3.96	188.04	0.00
	Within Groups	2.84	136	0.02		
	Total	14.70	139			
Order	Between Groups	0.07	3	0.02	1.52	0.21
	Within Groups	1.96	136	0.01		
	Total	2.02	139			
Completeness	Between Groups	0.06	3	0.02	1.55	0.20
	Within Groups	1.87	136	0.01		
	Total	1.93	139			

A Bonferroni [20] post-hoc analysis validated the analysis of the ANN results above and showed that:

- Visitors in cluster 1 take more time than visitors in the other clusters when visiting the exhibits; they are less "A" than 4; they are more "B" than all the others; they are less "C" than 3 and less "D" than 2 and 3. Therefore visitors in clusters 1 exhibit the traits of the visitors' style defined as *ANT*;
- Visitors in cluster 2 take less time than 1 but more than 3; they are less "A" than 4; they are less "B" than 1 and 4; they are less "C" than 3 and more "D" than 1,3 and 4; therefore visitors in cluster 2 may be ascribed to the visitors' style defined as *GRASSHOPER* (i.e., closer to an ant than to a fish)

- Visitors in cluster 3 take less time than 1 and 2; they are less A than 4; they are less "B" than 1 and 4; they are more "C" than all the others and more "D" than 1 and 4 but less than 2; therefore they belong to *FISH*;
- Finally, visitors in cluster 4 take less time than 1; they are more "A" than all the others; they are less "B" than 1 but more than 2 and 3; they are less "C" than 3 and less "D" than 2 and 3; they appear to belong to the style *BUTTERFLY* (i.e., closer to a fish than to an ant).

3.2 Unsupervised Learning with K-Means

As an alternative way of clustering the cumulative measures, we employed the K-means algorithm [21].

In order to reduce the number of variables, we ran a Factor analysis (Principal Components Analysis with varimax rotation). The results showed that 81% of the variance can be explained by 4 factors while Order and Completeness show very low correlation with any factor. Table 3 shows the contribution of the cumulative variables on the four principal factors.

Table 3. Component matrix extracted by the PCA

	Component			
	1	2	3	4
Average Time	0.824	0.143	-0.045	-0.190
A	-0.346	-0.709	0.580	0.046
B	0.918	-0.213	-0.188	0.031
C	-0.541	-0.060	-0.622	0.354
D	-0.405	0.830	0.114	-0.266
Order	0.197	0.452	0.487	0.265
Completeness	0.209	0.225	0.110	0.838

We classify the visitors in 4 clusters using K-means analysis starting from the factors.

A one-way ANOVA [19], using the cumulative indexes as dependent variables and the clusters determined by K-means as a factor, showed that for all the variables there are statistical differences except for Order and Completeness (see Table 4).

A post-hoc analysis using the Bonferroni [20] test showed that:

- Visitors in cluster 1 take less time than visitors in cluster 2 and more than visitors in cluster 4; they are less A than 2; less "B" than 2 and 3; less "C" than 4; and more "D" than all the others; therefore they may be ascribed to the style of *GRASSHOPPER* (closer to an ant than to a fish);
- Visitors in cluster 2 take more time than all the others; are less A than 3; are more "B" than 1 and 3; less "C" than 4; and less "D" than 1 and 4; therefore they share many of the traits of *ANT*;
- Visitors in cluster 3 take less time than 2; they are less A than all the others; more "B" than 1 and less than 2; less "C" than 4; and less "D" than 1 and 4; therefore they resembles visitors belonging to the style of *BUTTERFLY* (closer to a fish than to an ant);

- Finally, visitors in cluster 4 take less time than 1 and 2; they are less "A" than 3; they are less "B" than 2; more "C" than all the others; and less "D" than 1 but more than 2 and 3; therefore they can be classified as *FISH*.

Table 4. One-way ANOVA on the K-means clusters

		Sum of Squares	df	Mean Squares	F	sig.
Avg Time	Between Groups	321775.10	3	107258.35	38.15	0.00
	Within Groups	382391.80	136	2811.71		
	Total	704166.90	139			
A	Between Groups	6.51	3	2.17	109.87	0.00
	Within Groups	2.69	136	0.02		
	Total	9.19	139			
B	Between Groups	11.83	3	3.96	112.47	0.00
	Within Groups	4.79	136	0.04		
	Total	16.69	139			
C	Between Groups	3.42	3	1.14	132.81	0.00
	Within Groups	1.17	136	0.01		
	Total	4.59	139			
D	Between Groups	11.70	3	3.90	175.50	0.00
	Within Groups	3.00	136	0.02		
	Total	14.70	139			
Order	Between Groups	0.08	3	0.03	1.96	0.12
	Within Groups	1.94	136	0.01		
	Total	2.02	139			
Completen	Between Groups	0.04	3	0.01	0.92	0.43
	Within Groups	1.90	136	0.01		
	Total	1.93	139			

3.3 Comparison of the Two Approaches

In order to assess to what extent the two clustering algorithms agree on classification of the visitors into the different visitors styles, we used the κ statistics [22] which provides a better estimation of the bare percentage agreement since it takes into account the possibility of chance agreement.

Table 5 shows the confusion matrix. The value of the κ statistics in our case is 0.860 with a standard error of 0.035 ($p < 0.0001$; N=140). According to Landis and Koch's criteria [23], the agreement is very good (κ > 0.8).

Table 5. Confusion matrix for the classifications based on the ANN and K-means clustering

ANN Labels * Kmean Labels Crosstabulation

Count

		Kmean Labels				Total
		A	B	F	G	
ANN Labels	A	50	1	0	2	53
	B	1	33	2	0	36
	F	0	2	12	1	15
	G	2	0	3	31	36
Total		53	36	17	34	140

4 Discussion, Conclusions and Future Work

Qualitative theories from sociology and other disciplines are often used as a starting point for building computational models of human behavior to be exploited in intelligent systems. Usually, a human expert manually labels a number of examples, and a supervised learning approach is employed to predict in a real situation the behavior of users according to the theory, as modelled (or "learned" by the system). In order to test the objectivity of the observation scheme, reliability analysis is often employed: two or more annotators code a number of sequences, and an agreement analysis is performed by computing Cohen's Kappa (or other similar indexes) and by looking at the confusion matrix. In this paper, we tried to provide quantitative empirical evidence for a qualitative theory. We employed two unsupervised learning techniques for clustering museum visitors' behavior patterns and showed how the clusters obtained from them may be explained in the terms of the theory. We claim that from the point of view of assessing the suitability of a qualitative theory in a given scenario, this approach is as valid as a manual annotation with reliability analysis.

Furthermore, the labels automatically produced may then be used by a supervised learning approach to predict the classes to which visitors belong, as they enter the museum. From a pragmatic point of view, this procedure is cheaper—and less error prone—than manual annotation, especially when a large corpus of data has to be annotated.

Of course, we are not proposing that quantitative approaches may simply substitute qualitative approaches in building computational models of human behavior: the two types of approaches have different strengths and, to some extent, different purposes. Rather, we discussed a technique whose aim is to provide a quantitative validation of a particular qualitative theory.

Future research will focus on predicting visitors' behavior type using information collected during the first period of the visit. We intend to evaluate the correlation between the cumulative data representing the whole visit used for clustering in this work, with partial information available at the beginning of the visit of the same visitors. The results may allow us to use the clustering results as labels for prediction visiting style with partial data.

Additional future research will try to correlate the current clustering results with other notions of visitor's types (such as, for example, Sparacino's [7] and others).

References

1. Baus, J., Kray, C.: A Survey of Mobile Guides. Workshop on Mobile Guides. Mobile Human Computer Interaction '03 (2003)
2. Cheverst, K., Davies, N., Mitchell, K., Friday, A., Efstratiou, C.: Developing a Context-aware Electronic Tourist Guide: Some Issues and Experiences. In: The CHI 2000 Conference on Human factors in Computing Systems, pp. 17–24. The Hague, Netherlands (2000)
3. Oppermann, R., Specht, M.: A Context-Sensitive Nomadic Exhibition Guide. In: proceedings of Handheld and Ubiquitous Computing: Second International Symposium, HUC 2000, Bristol, UK, pp. 127–142 (September 2000)
4. Baus, J., Krüger, A., Wahlster, W.: A Resource-Adaptive Mobile Navigation System. In: Proceedings of the 7th International Conference on Intelligent User Interfaces. San Francisco, CA (2002)

5. Kuflik, T., Callaway, Goren-Bar, Rocchi, C., Stock, O., Zancanaro, M.: Non-Intrusive User Modelling for a Multimedia Museum Visitors Guide System. In: Proceedings of UM 2005, Tenth International Conference on User Modelling, Edinburgh (July 2005)
6. Petrelli, D., Not, E.: User-Centred Design of Flexible Hypermedia for a Mobile Guide: Reflections on the HyperAudio Experience. User Modeling and User-Adapted Interaction: The Journal of Personalization Research 15(3-4), 303–338 (2005) http://dx.doi.org/10.1007/s11257-005-8816-1
7. Sparacino, F.: The Museum Wearable: Real-Time Sensor-Driven Understanding of Visitors Interests for Personalized Visually-Augmented Museum Experiences. Museums and the Web, Boston, Massachusetts (2002)
8. Hatala, M., Wakkary, R.: Ontology-Based User Modeling in an Augmented Audio Reality System for Museums. User Modeling and User-Adapted Interaction. 15, 339–380 (2005)
9. Veron, E., Levasseur, M.: Ethnographie de l'exposition, Paris, Bibliothèque Publique d'Information, Centre Georges Pompidou (1983)
10. Marti, P., Rizzo, A., Petroni, L., Tozzi, G., Diligenti, M.: Adapting the Museum: A Non-intrusive User Modeling Approach. In: Proceedings of User Modeling Conference UM 99 (1999)
11. Not, E., Petrelli, D., Sarini, M., Stock, O., Strapparava, C., Zancanaro, M.: Hypernavigation in the Physical Space: Adapting Presentation to the User and to the Situational Context. The New Review of Hypermedia and Multimedia 4, 33–45 (1998)
12. Chittaro, L., Ieronutti, L.: A Visual Tool for Tracing Users' Behavior in Virtual Environments. In: Proceedings of the Working Conference on Advanced Visual Interfaces, Gallipoli, Italy, pp. 40–47 (2004)
13. Goren-Bar, D., Graziola, I., Pianesi, F., Zancanaro, M., Rocchi, C.: Innovative Approaches for Evaluating Adaptive Mobile Museum Guides. In: Stock, O., Zancanaro, M. (eds.) PEACH: Intelligent Interfaces for Museum Visits. Cognitive Technologies, Springer, Heidelberg (2006)
14. Stock, O., Zancanaro, M.: PEACH: Intelligent Interfaces for Museum Visits. In: Cognitive Technologies Series, Springer, Heidelberg (2006)
15. Boger, Z., Guterman, H.: Knowledge Extraction from Artificial Neural Networks Models. In: Proceedings of the IEEE International Conference on Systems Man and Cybernetics, SMC'97, Orlando, Florida, pp. 3030–3035 (October 1997)
16. Guterman, H.: Application of Principal Component Analysis to the Design of Neural Networks. Neural, Parallel and Scientific Computing 2, 43–54 (1994)
17. Boger, Z.: Who is Afraid of the Big Bad ANN? In: Proceedings of the International Joint Conference on Neural Networks IJCNN'02, Honolulu, pp. 2000–2005 (2002)
18. Boger, Z.: Finding Patients Clusters' Attributes by Auto-associative ANN Modeling. In: Proceedings of the International Joint Conference on Neural Networks IJCNN'03, Portland,OR, pp. 2643–2648 (2003)
19. Rutherford, A.: Introducing Anova and Ancova: A GLM Approach, SAGE (2001)
20. Bonferroni, C.E.: Teoria Statistica Delle Classi e Calcolo delle Probabilità, Pubblicazioni del R Istituto Superiore di Scienze Economiche e Commerciali di Firenze vol. 8, pp. 3–62 (1936)
21. MacQueen, J.: Some Methods for Classification and Analysis of Multivariate Observations. In: Proceedings of the 5th Berkeley Symposium, pp. 281–297 (1967)
22. Cohen, J.: A Coefficient of Agreement for Nominal Scales. Educational and Psychological Measurement 20, 37–46 (1960)
23. Landis, J.R., Koch, G.G.: The Measurement of Observer Agreement for Categorical Data. Biometrics 33, 159–174 (1977)

A Context-Aware Movie Preference Model Using a Bayesian Network for Recommendation and Promotion

Chihiro Ono, Mori Kurokawa, Yoichi Motomura, and Hideki Asoh

KDDI R&D Labs, Inc., Keio University, AIST
ono@kddilabs.jp, mkuro@ae.keio.ac.jp, y.motomura@aist.go.jp,
h.asoh@aist.go.jp

Abstract. This paper proposes a novel approach for constructing users' movie preference models using Bayesian networks. The advantages of the constructed preference models are 1) consideration of users' context in addition to users' personality, 2) multiple applications, such as recommendation and promotion. Data acquisition process through a WWW questionnaire survey and a Bayesian network model construction process using the data are described. The effectiveness of the constructed model in terms of recommendation and promotion is also demonstrated through experiments.

1 Introduction

Modeling user preferences is a key technology in various personalized applications, such as recommendation, intelligent interface, and one-to-one marketing. In this paper, two major issues for constructing preference models are investigated. The first issue is context-awareness. As Internet access via cellular phone becomes more common, diversification of the context in which the user uses the service, e.g. in town, in the home, as well as diversification of the service and item, is also increasing. User preferences may also change, not only according to the users' personality, but also the context such as mood, location, accompanying person, and so forth. Therefore, a user preference model is required that takes account of both the users' personality and the context for various personalized services, such as recommending appropriate items for each user in different situations.

Several approaches for constructing a preference model for recommendation have been developed in research and business fields [1, 17, 20], of which two effective examples include collaborative filtering [3, 7, 18, 19] and the content-based method [13]. Several approaches for integrating both methods have also been investigated in order to combine the merits of each [4, 12, 15]. However, existing approaches cannot handle both users' personality and the situation at the same time.

The second issue is multiple applicability. For example, in addition to the recommendation, a preference model can also be useful for promoting items. Currently, respective preference models for recommendation and promotion are constructed independently, which disturbs efforts to share the data collected by each application. In a preference model that could be used for two or more applications, all collected information, including users' feedback data, could be used to construct and improve the model.

C. Conati, K. McCoy, and G. Paliouras (Eds.): UM 2007, LNAI 4511, pp. 247–257, 2007.
© Springer-Verlag Berlin Heidelberg 2007

In order to solve both issues, we propose a novel way of constructing context-aware and multi-applicable preference models using Bayesian networks. Bayesian networks [9, 16] provide a powerful and flexible method for modeling a complex joint probability distribution of multiple random variables and are applied to various tasks such as printer failure diagnosis, traffic jam prediction, and modeling chemical reactions in body cells [8, 10]. The high flexibility of Bayesian networks is appropriate for representing complex relations between users' preference and contexts. One Bayesian network model can be used for multiple applications that may use different variables as dependent variables, such as recommendation and promotion. Unlike a conventional data analysis model, such as the regression model, Bayesian networks do not specify the direction of inference in advance. Any random variables in the network can be inputs, while any other variables can be the target of prediction by calculating the conditional probabilities.

One of the most difficult problems in using a Bayesian network is the model construction. Although various methods for model construction have been proposed, many are theoretical or only applicable for small scale problems and there remains no established standard for constructing a practically usable Bayesian network model with many variables. In this paper, we propose a novel model construction process and construct a Bayesian network using the data acquired through an original large-scale WWW questionnaire survey. We also show the effectiveness of the model through experiments.

The rest of this paper is organized as follows. Section 2 formulates our movie recommendation and promotion task, while Section 3 describes our approach to model construction and Section 4 explains the data collection process. Section 5 describes the construction process of the Bayesian network model. Evaluation of the model is shown in Section 6, before finally, Section 7 concludes the paper.

2 Preference Model for Movie Recommendation and Promotion

In this paper, we choose movie recommendation and promotion as target applications and constructed a context-aware movie preference model applicable for both applications. In this section, we provide an overview of how a Bayesian network preference model can be used for both recommendation and promotion.

Bayesian networks can be used to model the joint probability distribution of multiple random variables. A random variable is represented as a node of the network, and the links of the network represent dependencies between variables. Conditional independences between variables are represented by the entire structure of the network and used for a more efficient probabilistic inference.

With the Bayesian network, we formulate a movie preference model in the form of a joint probability distribution $P(U, C, S, V)$. Here, U represents a set of users' profile variables, such as age, sex, etc., S represents a set of user situation/context variables such as location, mood, etc., C represents a set of movie attributes, such as genre, director, etc., and V denotes a user's ratings for given movies within a given context.

In the case of movie recommendation, the problem is finding movies that a given user is likely to rate highly. For this purpose, we calculate the conditional probability

P(V |u, s, c) for the target user *U=u*, specific context *S=s*, and the candidate movie *C=c* and then recommend movies in order of probability. Alternatively, we may calculate the conditional probability *P(C| u, s, v)* for the target user *U=u*, context *S=s* and rating *V=positive* to find movies that are highly likely to obtain a positive rating.

Figure 1 shows the flow of the recommender system we are developing (The recommended movies in the figure were blurred to protect copyright). Firstly, a user sends a request for recommendation with his situational data (accompanying person, location, and mood). Subsequently, the recommender system merges the registered user attributes with the input user situational attributes and calculates the probability of the user rating for each candidate movie using the Bayesian network inference engine, before then composing a recommendation list of movies, according to the probability of positive ratings. The recommendation system may receive user feedback, and periodically, the system updates the parameters of the movie preference Bayesian network model using feedback data by using the Bayesian inference engine in order to increase the precision of the recommendation.

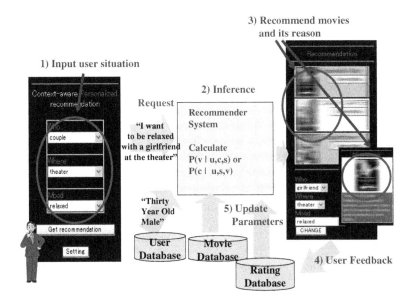

Fig. 1. Flow of the Movie Recommender System

Although the preference model can be used in many ways, here, we explain two typical ways for movie promotion. The first involves finding user segments that may like target movies to be promoted. For this purpose, we calculate the conditional probability *P (U | c, s, v)* for the target movies *C=c*, target context *S=s*, and *V=positive*, whereupon promotional information concerning the target movie is sent to the user segments with high probability.

The second way involves finding solicitation points of the target movie for each user segment. These solicitation points are attractive aspects of the movie to which the target user is likely to react. In this case, prediction of the user impression when a user feels satisfied to see a certain movie in a certain situation could be useful. Our preference model includes impression variables (*I*), such as feeling relaxed or laughter, as an unobservable hidden variable that can be a reason to rate movies. We calculate the conditional probability $P(I \mid u, c, s, v)$ for the target movies $C=c$, $S=s$, and $U=u$. Promotional information concerning the target movie, including personalized solicitation points with a high probability of reacting, are sent to each target user segment.

Figure 2 shows the flow of a promotional assistance system that we are developing. Firstly, an operator sends a request to the system to find candidate target user segments with information concerning a target movie (e.g. comedy, love romance, etc.). Then, after receiving the candidate user segments and choosing the target user segments (e.g. young female, etc.), the operator sends a request to the system to find appropriate solicitation points for each target user segment (e.g. they will be satisfied because they feel relaxed by the movie). Finally, the operator sends personalized promotion information to target user segments (e.g. "This movie makes you feel relaxed!).

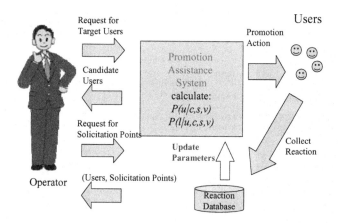

Fig. 2. Flow of the Promotion Assistance System

Here, since a recommendation system and promotion system can use the same movie preference Bayesian network model, feedback and reaction data from users can be commonly used to update the parameters of the model and thus increase the precision of both the recommendation and promotion.

3 Model Construction Strategy

A Bayesian network can be specified with the structure of the network and the conditional probability tables (CPT) attached to each node in the network. There are three major approaches in constructing a network. The first involves specifying both the network structure and the conditional probabilities manually, based on expert domain knowledge, while the second involves estimating both the network structure and the probabilities from the data automatically. There are two ways to follow the second approach. The first is to select variables and a structure from candidates using information criteria such as AIC (Akaike information criteria) or MDL. A typical example is the K2 algorithm proposed by Cooper et al. [6]. The second way is to decide on the existence of links between variables using a statistical test of independence [5]. However, these approaches can handle only small networks. The third approach involves specifying the (rough) network structure manually and estimating the conditional probabilities from the data. This approach is generally used when both learning data and domain knowledge can be obtained. This approach is also the most practical and has been applied to some real-world problems [2, 11]. However, the processes of the model construction used in those examples include various heuristics and no standard process has been established.

Due to the considerable number of random variables in our model, we take the third approach. We initially assume a rough network structure used to predict the user's ratings for movies, which is shown in Fig. 3. This structure means that the overall rating depends on the common variables representing the user's impressions of a movie (feeling excited, feeling scared, feeling sad, feeling relaxed, etc.), and the impressions are based on user attributes, situational attributes, and movie attributes. For the model used in the following experiments, we reverse the direction of links in order to simplify the CPT:

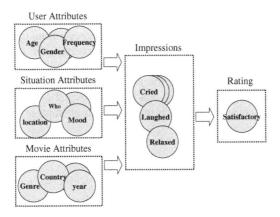

Fig. 3. Model Structure

4   Data Acquisition

The data acquisition procedure was composed of two parts: a small-scale intensive interview and a large-scale questionnaire survey. Firstly, we interviewed a small number of subjects about their movie preferences. In the interview, several movies were presented to a subject and the subject was then asked to classify them into favorite and hated movie groups respectively. The reasons for awarding a favorable rating and their favorite movies were then asked and based on feedback from the interviews, we designed questions for a large-scale questionnaire survey.

The questionnaire survey was conducted in March 2006.

1. Number of subjects: 2153
2. Number of movies: 197
3. Rating condition: Each subject rated 5 to 10 movies that were randomly selected from those he/she had watched.
4. Inquiries:

- User demographic and lifestyle attributes: 30 attributes such as age, gender, and occupation, brand loyalty, time and expenditure on leisure.
- User attributes regarding movie appreciation: 32 attributes such as important factors for selecting movies, and genre preference.(a 7-grade scale for each attribute)
- (For each movie) Situation of watching movie: 43 attributes such as accompanying person, and mood.
- (For each movie) Impression of the movie: 358 attributes such as cried, and laughed. (7-grade scale for each attribute)
- (For each movie) Rating of the movie: 1 attribute (7-grade scale from satisfied very much to not at all satisfied)

In this questionnaire, the number of attributes, such as user situation (43) and user impression (358), is larger when compared to other datasets such as MovieLens.

As for movie attributes, we prepared 26 attributes, such as genre, length, country, and keywords extracted from introductory texts for representing movies.

We divided the data into three parts. For the first part, we extracted rating data for 3 movies as the test data to evaluate the movie promotion, before subsequently extracting 1 rating data from each of the user ratings as the test data to evaluate the recommendation, while the remainder was used for model construction. Here, in the data used for model construction, each user rated an average of 3.26 movies, which was rather sparse.

5 Model Construction Step

Starting from the assumed general structure of the network shown in Fig. 3, we selected effective variables from many observed attributes, determined local network structures that reflect the relationship between selected variables, and estimated the CPTs via a standard maximum likelihood estimation [9], using the questionnaire data. The whole procedure is as follows:

1. Data preprocessing:
- extract keywords from movie introductory texts.
- categorize the extracted keywords into four main categories such as "describing scene," "describing mood," etc.
- further categorize the keywords in each category into three to five sub-categories.

2. Extracting pseudo movie attributes: We introduced pseudo movie attributes to enhance the movie attributes. These pseudo attributes are impressions that are not user specific and can thus be seen as attributes of a movie. The pseudo movie attributes were selected from impression attributes whose scores have little difference within users. Specifically, we calculated:

$$score = I(r, CID)/H(r|CID).$$

Here, $I(r, CID)$ is the mutual information between the attribute value r and the content-ID. $H(r|CID)$ is the conditional entropy of r conditioned by the content-ID. We selected attributes with high scores as pseudo movie attributes because the heavier the relation to the content-ID and the smaller the difference within users, the more the attribute represents the movie characteristics.

3. We grouped all variables into five categories: "user attributes (U)," "user situations (S)," "movie attributes (including pseudo movie attributes)(C)," "impression attributes (excluding pseudo movie attributes)(I)," and "total rating (V)."

4. Clustering attributes in each group: For each group, we calculated the mutual dependency between each attribute and clustered the attributes based on the dependency score using the Ward's clustering method [21]. Subsequently, we extracted a representative attribute that stands for each cluster. The number of clusters (= the number of representing attributes) in each group is shown in Table 1.

Table 1. The number of Clusters for each group

Groups in questionnaire	Number of attributes	Groups after preprocessing	Number of clusters
Demographic and lifestyle attributes	30	Demographic and lifestyle attributes	10
Movie appreciation	32	Movie appreciation	10
Situation	43	Situation	7
Impression	358	Impression	24
		Movie attributes	23
Movie attributes	26		

5. Search structures: In order to find the network structure between groups, we searched the parent child relations between the variables in each group. We then generated candidate structures and selected the one that best fits the data using the AIC. For these processes, BAYONET [12], a tool for constructing a Bayesian network that we developed, was used. When generating the candidate structures, the maximum number of parents was set to 4, while for the comparisons, we constructed 4 types of model as shown in Table 2. The first model includes variables in all groups (V, I, U, C, S), while the second model does not include S. The third model includes S but does not include I and the fourth model does not include S and I.

Table 2. The number of nodes and links in the constructed networks

	Number of nodes	Number of links
UCS-I-V	75	115
UC-I-V	68	107
UCS-V	50	49
UC-V	44	43

6 Evaluation of Models

We evaluated the effectiveness of our movie preference models in terms of the accuracy of rating prediction. Four kinds of constructed models were compared from the viewpoint of the recommendation and promotion performances. In the following evaluations, as described in Section 4, data that is not used in the model construction was used.

6.1 Evaluation of Predicting User Rating

Firstly, the above four types of models were evaluated from the viewpoint of predicting user rating V. As a measure of accuracy, we used the mean absolute error (MAE) of the prediction. When the total number of predicted ratings is N, the number of values of the rating is r, the correct rating value of User i to Movie j in Context k is p_{ijk}, the predicted rating value is v, the MAE can be formulated as:

$$\frac{1}{N}\sum_{ijk} | p_{ijk} - \sum_{v} vP(V = v \mid U = i, C = j, S = k)|.$$

We compared the four types of Bayesian network models, a baseline predictor, and the standard collaborative filtering (CF). As a baseline predictor, we used the predictor that outputs the average rating of each movie and implemented both user-based and item-based collaborative filtering. Pearson correlation is used as the similarity in the CFs[3] .

Table 3. Comparison of Prediction Accuracy

Model	MAE
Baseline	0.927
CF (user-based)	0.975
CF (item-based)	0.930
UC-V	0.887
UCS-V	0.869
UC-I-V	0.862
UCS-I-V	0.854

Table 3 shows the evaluation results. In the experiment, the user-based CF can obtain predictions only for 4.1% (# = 72) of users, while the item-based CF can obtain predictions only for 12.6% (#=221) of users. The MAE values for CFs are also relatively poor, because the number of ratings is rather sparse (only 3.26 movie ratings for each user on average) in our ratings database.

All BN models have a better score than the baseline and CFs. Models with an impression attributes layer (UC-I-V, UCS-I-V) have a better score than the Naïve Bayesian model (UC-V, UCS-V), while models with user situation (UCS-V, UCS-I-V) have a better score than those without (UC-V, UC-I-V). These results demonstrate that the situation attributes work well, and that introducing a hierarchical structure is effective.

6.2 Evaluation of Finding Target User Segments

We evaluated the performance of finding target user segments. We calculated $P(U|C=Ci, S=s, V=positive)$ for 3 movies (C1,C2,C3) that are not used for the model construction, using a model which includes variables in all groups (UCS-I-V). The typical user segment that likes each movie can be characterized by the maximum posterior value (MAP) of user attributes U. Subsequently, we selected users in the typical user segment. As there are many user attributes, some must be selected to obtain the useful user segment. Here, we highlighted three user attributes, namely "gender", "marriage status", and "focus on popularity" because of their strong correlation with overall rating, and selected users with the MAP values of the three attributes. Finally, we compared the ratio of the positive movie ratings for the selected users with that for all users. As shown in Table 4, the ratio of positive ratings for selected users was higher than the equivalent figure for all users and the difference is significant at a 5% level for C1, which demonstrates the effectiveness of the user segmentation based on our preference model. There may be various ways of finding effective target user segments using our user model and exploring better ways remains as a future issue.

Table 4. Comparison of ratio of positive rating among user segments

Movie ID	Target	Number of Users	Ratio of Positive Rating
C1	Whole	1281	36.20%
C1	Segmented	309	42.72%
C2	Whole	1068	32.68%
C2	Segmented	270	36.37%

7 Discussion and Conclusion

This paper proposes a novel approach for constructing a context-aware movie preference model using a Bayesian network and its effectiveness, in terms of recommendation and promotion, is demonstrated through experiments. Although the improvement in prediction accuracy was relatively slight, the results demonstrate that introducing situation attributes and a hierarchical model structure are both effective and promising.

One reason for the modest performance improvement was the sparcity of the data used in the model construction, which compounds the difficulty of the prediction problem. We are now planning a field test of a movie recommender system and a movie promotion assistance system, both of which use the common constructed preference model. In field tests, we aim to conduct additional data acquisition and make an assessment of the improvement in the model performance. Meanwhile, evaluating other aspects, such as subjective impressions of the recommendation results, and the usability of the promotion assistance system should also be conducted.

Acknowledgements. The authors wish to thank, Dr. Shigeyuki Akiba, President and CEO of KDDI R&D Laboratories, Inc. for his continuous support for this study and Ms. Mayomi Haga for her support for data acquisition.

References

1. Adomavicius, G., Tuzhilin, A.: Toward the next generation of recommender systems: a survey of the state-of-the-art and possible extensions. IEEE Trans. on Knowledge and Data Engineering 17(6), 734–749 (2005)
2. Binder, J., Koller, D., Russell, S., Kanazawa, K.: Adaptive probabilistic networks with hidden variables. Machine Learning 29, 213–244 (1997)
3. Breese, J.S., Heckerman, D., Kadie, C.: Empirical analysis of predictive algorithms for collaborative filtering. In: Proceedings of the 14th Annual Conference on Uncertainty in Artificial Intelligence, pp. 43–52 (1998)
4. Burke, R.: Hybrid recommender systems: survey and experiments. User-Modeling and User-Adapted Interactions 12, 331–370 (2002)
5. de Campos, L.M.: Independency relationships and learning algorithms for singly connected networks. Journal of Experimental and Theoretical Artificial Intelligence 10, 511–549 (1998)
6. Cooper, G.F., Herskovits, E.: A Bayesian method for the induction of probabilistic networks from data. Machine Learning 9, 309–347 (2002)
7. Herlocker, J., et al.: Evaluating collaborative filtering recommender systems. ACM Transactions on Information Systems 22(1), 5–53 (2004)
8. Horvitz, E.: Principles of mixed-initiative user interfaces. In: Proc. ACM SIGCHI Conference on Human Factors in Computing Systems (1999)
9. Jensen, F.V.: Bayesian Networks and Decision Graphs. Springer, Heidelberg (2001)
10. Jensen, F.V., et al.: The SACSO methodology for troubleshooting complex systems. Artificial Intelligence for Engineering Design, Analysis and Manufacturing (AIEDAM) 15, 321–333 (2001)
11. Mani, S., McDermott, S., Valtorta, M.: MENTOR: A Bayesian model of prediction of mental retardation in newborns, Research in Developmental Disabilities, vol. 8(5) (1997)
12. Mobasher, B., Jin, X., Zhou, Y.: Semantically enhanced collaborative filtering on the Web. In: Berendt, B., Hotho, A., Mladenić, D., van Someren, M., Spiliopoulou, M., Stumme, G. (eds.) EWMF 2003. LNCS (LNAI), vol. 3209, Springer, Heidelberg (2004)
13. Mooney, R.J., Roy, L.: Content-based book recommending using learning for text categorization. In: Proceedings. of the 5th ACM Conference on Digital Libraries, pp. 195–204 (2000)
14. Motomura, Y.: Bayesian network construction system: BAYONET. In: Proceedings of Tutorial on Bayesian Networks, pp. 54–58 (In Japanese) (2001)

15. Ono, C., Motomura, Y., Asoh, H.: A study of probabilistic models for integrating collaborative and content-based recommendation, Working Notes of IJCAI-05 Workshop on Advances in Preference Handling (2005)
16. Pearl, J.: Probabilistic Reasoning in Intelligent Systems: Networks of Plausible Inference. Morgan Kaufmann Publishers, San Francisco (1988)
17. Resnick, P., Varian, H.R.: Recommender systems. Communications of the ACM 40(3), 56–58 (1997)
18. Resnick, P., Iacovou, N., Suchak, M., Bergstrom, P., Riedl, J.: GroupLens: an open architecture for collaborative filtering of netnews. In: Proceedings of ACM Conference on Computer Supported Cooperative Work, pp. 175–186. ACM Press, New York (1994)
19. Shardanand, U., Maes, P.: Social information filtering: algorithms for automating word of mouth. In: Proceedings of CHI'95 Mosaic of Creativity, pp. 210–217 (1995)
20. Zekerman, I., Alberecht, D.W.: Predictive statistical models for user modeling. User Modeling and User-Adapted Interaction 11(1-2), 5–18 (2001)
21. Ward, J.H.: Hierarchical grouping to optimize an objective function. J. Am. Stat. Assoc. 58, 236–244 (1963)

Intrinsic Motivational Factors for the Intention to Use Adaptive Technology: Validation of a Causal Model

Fabio Pianesi, Ilenia Graziola, and Massimo Zancanaro

ITC-irst, via Sommarie 18, 38050 Povo, Italy
{pianesi,graziola,zancana}@itc.it

Abstract. In this paper, we propose and validate a model of the 'intention to use' adaptive audio-video guides in a museum setting, extending TAM to include intrinsic motivational factors (involvement, attention) and constructs specific to adaptivity (control, personalization). The results of a PLS analysis ran on the data from 115 subjects show that for adaptive museum guides intention to use is not affected by such traditional construct as perceived ease of use, whereas perceived usefulness and enjoyment play an important role. Also, both personalization and control are causally relevant, the former affecting enjoyment and the latter the perceived usefulness.

Keywords: Causal modelling, intention to use, adaptive systems, technology acceptance model, intrinsic motivations, structural equation modelling.

1 Introduction

In this paper, we investigate several constructs that are relevant to model the intention to use adaptive audio-video guides in a museum setting. The general framework we are working within is that of statistical causal (path) modelling, whereby a set of variables are posited along with causal links among them. Most often the variables are latent ones, in that their values are not directly measured but inferred from those of visible, measurable ones. Consistently with the literature, we will refer to the former as factors, latent variables, or constructs, and to the latter as indicators or measurement items.

A well-known example of this approach to modelling people intentions towards technology use is Davis' Technology Acceptance Model (TAM) [9]. [10].; in a simplified form, it hypothesises that the intention to use (IU) a technology (an attitudinal construct) is causally affected by two cognitive beliefs called Perceived Ease of Use (PEU) and Perceived Usefulness (PU), see Fig.1.

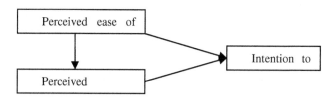

Fig. 1. A simplified version of TAM

C. Conati, K. McCoy, and G. Paliouras (Eds.): UM 2007, LNAI 4511, pp. 258–267, 2007.
© Springer-Verlag Berlin Heidelberg 2007

PEU is concerned with the perceived level of workload the use of the relevant technology requires, while the second measures the degree to which the technology is seen as helpful for the subject in reaching her goals. Moreover, PEU causally affects PU – that is, the more a technology is to use, the more it is perceived as useful.

Models like this are validated on actual data by means of techniques globally referred to as Structural Equation Modelling [15], examples of which are LISREL [18] and the Partial Least Square (PLS) approach [21].

TAM focuses on extrinsic motivations towards intention to use: its constructs refer to beliefs involving concepts such as task execution, performance, goal achievement, etc. Yet, there is growing consensus that intrinsic, emotional factors may, at least in certain cases, play a non-marginal role in determining acceptance and IU (see [Norman 2004] for a general discussion). Arguably, this is the case of museum visits and similar amusement activities, in which people seem more concerned with recreation and engagement than in the pursuance of specific goals.

In this study we propose and investigate an extension of TAM for adaptive audio-video museum guides, including a construct referring to the type of experience people have when visiting museums (involvement), and other constructs related to the nature of the relevant technology (personalization and control). The results show that for adaptive museum guides intention to use is not affected by ease of use, but by the usefulness and enjoyment. Also, both personalization and control are causally relevant, the former affecting enjoyment and the latter the perceived usefulness.

In section 2, we discuss the notion of adaptivity and its application to the museum scenario; in section 3, we introduce the dimensions chosen to model IU for adaptive museum guides, and briefly present the questionnaire used. Section 4 discusses the context of our study: the specific adaptive guide used, and the sample we worked with. The PLS analysis of the data and its results are discussed in section 5, whereas the last section discusses both the results obtained and the limitations of our study.

2 Adaptivity in a Museum Setting

In general terms, adaptivity is the capacity to adjust to changes in the environment. In Information Technology, the term is often intended in a more restricted sense as the capacity of a system to provide users with information in a way that suites better their needs [3]. In this work, we focus on the particular type of adaptation consisting in tailoring information presentation [17].

Several studies have investigated this topic in the context of museum or tourist guides. For example, the GUIDE system [4] provides personalized web-like presentations about nearby attractions that might be interesting for the visitor of a city. The HIPPIE system accompanies visitors on personalized tours in a museum by maintaining a model of user interests and knowledge [24]. The REAL system [2] adapts route descriptions according to the actual user position; it also takes into account the technical limitations of the device chosen by the user so that, for instance, a presentation delivered on a mobile phone would resort more to audio than to graphics. In our own work [27], we experimented with adaptive video presentations dynamically composed by adding or removing detailed descriptions, background information and comparisons according to user's interests and the history of the visit.

The benefits of personalization in such a scenario have been investigated by means of different of approaches, e.g., through observational studies (as in [4]), by using questionnaires to elicit user preferences and attitudes [25; 14] and by interviewing domain experts and educators. None of the studies we are aware of, however, address the more general topic of causally modelling IU by resorting to a mix of intrinsic and extrinsic motivational constructs.

3 The Research Dimensions

Our initial model maintains the basic tenets of TAM; hence it features an IU construct which is directly affected by PU and PEU, with the latter also affecting PU. In order to account for the specificity of adaptive systems, we substituted the usual first order construct of PEU with a second order one, called 'easiness', consisting of three first order factors: ease of use, easy to understand and feedback. The first construct is a general 'ease to use' one, and corresponds to TAM's; 'easy to understand' measures the difficulty/easiness of understanding the guide's behaviour; feedback, in turn, addresses the quality of the feedback provided by the guide.

The importance of intrinsic motivations was already clear to TAM proposers; for example, Davis et al. [10] observed a positive interaction between usefulness and enjoyment. Following these indications, Venkatesh [30] investigated emotional response as a predecessor to acceptance in the context of TAM, and Agarwal and Karahanna [1] combined extrinsic (TAM's) and intrinsic motivational factors, proposing that 'cognitive absorption' is a main determinant of the TAM's beliefs of PU and PEU for web users.

In this work, we exploit a second order construct, called enjoyment, to capture user level of involvement, and posit that it directly affects easiness, PU and IU. Involvement consists of three first order factors: presence, time distortion and flow. The first refers to the compelling sense of being present in a mediated virtual environment [19]; time distortion measures the subjective feeling that time passes rapidly when engaged in an absorbing activity [Novak et al. 2000]; flow is the "holistic sensation that people feel when they act with total involvement" [7], [8].

Drawing on studies on flow, we hypothesise that involvement is affected by the constructs of challenge, skill, and (focused) attention [23], [8]. The underlying idea is that the involvement of an actor in her activity is determined by the balance between the perceived challenge of the interaction and her skills [23] [20], and is manifested in a higher focus on the relevant activity, with little attention left for anything else. To these three construct, we add 'personalization' as another antecedent for involvement, hypothesising that with adaptive technologies, the level of personalization perceived by the user has a causal effect on involvement.

Another important construct we exploit is that of control, which has been shown to contribute to cognitive absorption [1], to affect flow [23], and to play a major role with adaptive systems [16]. Goren-Bar et al. [14] have shown the importance of the location dimension of control (how location awareness impacts on the perception of control) for adaptive guides. Moreover, when a system like the one used in this study (see below) adapts its presentations to the user's level of interest, it is important to understand whether and to what extent such a device impacts on the perceived level of control on the interaction. For these reasons, we modelled control as a second order construct (called 'global control') comprising a dimension of 'location control', one of 'information control' and one of general control. Global control was hypothesised to be causally affected by involvement and to causally affect both easiness and PU.

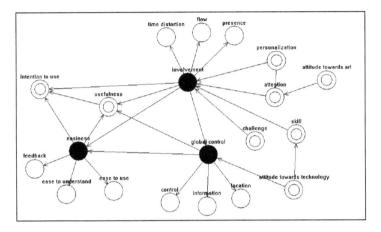

Fig. 2. The theoretical model investigated in this work. Filled circles represent second order constructs. Simple circle represent first order constructs contributing to second order ones.

Table 1. Questionnaire scales, their sources and Cronbach's alpha values

Construct	Reference	Cronbach's alpha
Attitude towards art	Stokmans 1999	0.87
Attitude towards technology	Popovich et al. 1987	
Challenge	Novak et al. 1999	0.88
Control	Novak et al. 1999	0.69
(Control on) information		
Location-based control		
Easy to use	Davis 1989	
Easy to understand		
Feedback		
Flow	Novak et al. 1999	
Focussed attention	Ghani and Deshpande 1994	0.83
Intention to use	Davis 1989	0.88
Personalization		
Presence	Novak et al. 1999	0.70
Skill	Novak et al. 1999	0.86
Time distortion	Novak et al. 1999	
Usefulness	Davis 1989	

Finally, our model exploits two constructs measuring general attitudes towards art and towards technology, meant to control for their possible effects; they were posited to affect attention, and skill and global control, respectively. Figure 2 summarizes the theoretical model in the form of a causal network.

The dimensions described above where operationalized by means of multi-item scales, with the exception of flow, for which a single item was used [23]. Whenever possible – e.g., focused attention – the scales were adapted from already existing scale; when no scales were available, we produced them by our own. Table 1 reports the source of each scale and, when available, the value of Cronbach's alpha found in the original reference. The questionnaire can be found at http:// tcc.itc.it/ i3p/ research/adaptivemodel/.

4   The Study

4.1 The Adaptive System

We used a museum guide providing multimedia presentations of exhibits. A presentation is equivalent to a web page, though it does not consist of text but of verbal comments on a visual animation of parts of the artwork [28].

Fig. 3. A snapshot of the adaptive audio-video guide

The information provided to a visitor is adjusted on the basis of positional information (her actual position, as determined by means of IR) and of the visitor's interests. The latter is expressed by the user through an interface widget called the *like-o-meter*, see Fig. 3: during each presentation, the user may express her interests in the information provided by positioning the needle toward the smiley or the sad face.

The adaptation with respect to the actual location is obtained by automatically triggering a presentation appropriate to the exhibit the user is facing, and by contextualizing it through expressions such as "in front of you", etc. The adaptation with respect to the interests consists in the presentation or more/less additional material according to the visitor's actual expression of interest. The preferences detected are also propagated on a network of related concepts so that presentations of related exhibits may be modified even in the absence of an explicit expression of interest by the visitor [28].

4.2 Procedure and the Sample

One hundred and forty-three (143; 61 males and 82 females; average age=45 years, SD=15.534)) regular visitors of Torre Aquila were invited to test the adaptive multimedia guide. They were recruited at the entrance of the Museo del Buonconsiglio, in Trento; participation in the experiment was rewarded with a free ticket for visiting the whole Museum. Participants were tested individually: at the beginning of the session, they received a short description of the system and were then left free to interact with the system while visiting Torre Aquila. At the end of the visit, subjects were asked to fill the questionnaire. After this, they could continue their (free) visit to the rest of the castle. Participants' age ranged from 20 to 79 years (mean=47, median=50, SD=15.874). The data of 28 visitors were discarded because they failed to complete the questionnaires. The analysis discussed below concerns the data from the remaining 115 visitors.

5   Results

We used PLS to establish the validity of the theoretical model. This technique has minimal demands in terms of sample size and residual distribution [5], [11], hence it is more suited than alternative approaches – e.g., LISREL – for (relatively) small samples as the one used here. The analysis requires that the scales first undergo confirmatory factorial analysis, to determine the validity of the measurement model. Only if this step is successful, it makes sense to proceed to the analysis and validation of the structural model.

5.1 Validation of the Measurement Model

The psychometric properties of the scales that are relevant here refer to their capabilities of actually measuring the constructs they have been purported to measure (convergent validity) and to discriminate one construct from the other (discriminant validity). Convergent and discriminant validity were assessed according to the procedures suggested in [13], [31], and [5]. The data can be found at http:// tcc.itc.it/ i3p/research/adaptivemodel/.

5.2 Assessment of the Structural Model

The results of PLS analysis of the structural model are reproduce in Fig. 4, which reports the path coefficients along with their significance (as computed through t-tests on bootstrap results; 200 iterations), and the explained variance, R^2 (only for constructs with incoming arcs). All first order construct were modelled in the reflective fashion. Similarly, second order constructs were modelled in the molecular fashion [6], and according to the hierarchical component approach described in [21].

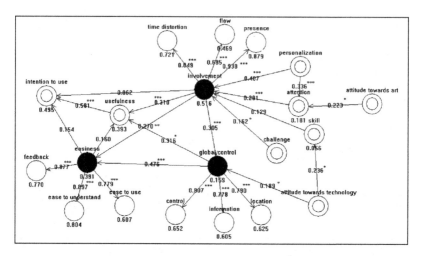

Fig. 4. Results of PLS analysis. Figure close to circles are R^2 values for the corresponding construct. *** p<.001; ** p<.01; * p<.05.

Personalization, attention, skill and challenge together explain 51.6% of the variance in involvement; the latter, together with attitude towards technology, explains 15.9% of the variance of global control. Involvement, global control and easiness explain 39.3% of the variance of usefulness, whereas involvement and global control account for 39.1% of the variance of easiness. Finally, involvement, easiness, and usefulness explain 49.5% of the variance of IU. Table 2 summarizes the status of our initial hypotheses in the light of PLS analysis results.

Table 2. Summary of hypothesis tests. *** p<.001; ** p<.01; * p<.05.

Hypothesis	Supported	Hypothesis	Supported
personalization → involvement	YES***	involvement → global control	YES***
personalization → attention	YES***	involvement → intention to use	NO
attention → involvement	YES***	involvement → usefulness	YES***
attitude towards art → attention	YES*	involvement → easiness	YES**
challenge → involvement	YES*	easiness → usefulness	NO
skill → involvement	NO	easiness → intention to use	NO
attitude towards technology → skill	YES*	usefulness → intention to use	YES***
attitude towards technology → global control	YES*		

Given these results, two important tenets of TAM are not confirmed: in the case of adaptive museum guides, easiness causally affects neither IU nor PU; that is, in our scenario, those beliefs lose much of the explanatory power they have in other domains. At the same time, and again contrary to expectations, involvement does not have a direct effect on IU, but only as mediated through PU, while skill does not appear to causally affect involvement.

As it turns out, the initial model can be simplified. The second order construct of easiness has become irrelevant to model IU, hence it can be dropped along with all the paths it is involved in and its first order constructs, without affecting the explanatory power of the model. Similar considerations apply to skill. Secondly, two of the remaining paths have low parameter values, corresponding to a low (albeit statistically significant) effect of the antecedent on the consequent variable. This is the case of the paths from challenge to involvement, and from attitude towards art to attention. Their contribution to the explained variance of involvement and attention is low: 2.3% and 4.9%, respectively. Little is lost if they are dropped, with an important gain in simplicity. With these modifications, the final model is as reproduced in Fig. 5.

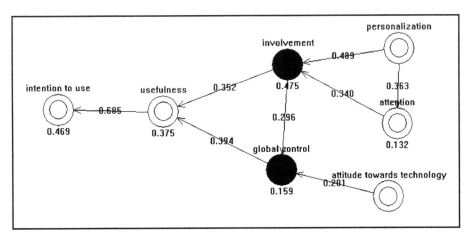

Fig. 5. Final model. First order factors contributing to second order ones are omitted for simplicity.

6 Discussion and Conclusions

In this work we have proposed and validated a causal model of IU for adaptive video guides in a museum setting. The initial model includes both extrinsic motivational constructs (similarly to TAM) and intrinsic ones (involvement), along with others that have been shown to causally affect the latter by earlier studies (skill, challenge, focused attention). It also includes constructs meant to capture some specificities of the interaction with an adaptive guide, such as those attempting to capture the beliefs concerning personalization and control.

The results show that easiness (our version of TAM's PEU) is not causally effective in our scenario, and that involvement affects IU only through the mediation of PU. Control also turned out to play an important role, still mediated by usefulness (tests of a direct connection between our global control and IU yielded non significant results). Of the variables employed here that were shown by other works to significantly affect involvement (challenge, skill and focused attention) only attention turned out to play a relevant role. Finally, personalization is effective in determining the level of involvement.

This study has a number of limitations that must be acknowledged: in the first place, it is based on a single, although realistic and ecological, experience with a specific type of adaptive guide. Conceivably, people' attitudes and beliefs can change after repeated uses of such devices, Finally, the way the adaptive dimensions have been implemented in the guide we used might also have played a role; hence generalization of our results to adaptive guides in general should be pursued with caution.

Despite these limitations, we believe that our study provides important insights on the motivational variables that can determine acceptance of adaptive guides. Besides confirming the crucial role of the global experience and holistic aspects (involvement), it shows that extrinsic variables such as ease of use can play in scenarios like museums a less important than expected role. Finally, it points to the necessity of adapting the theoretical understanding and modelling of IU to the specificities of the scenario, as shown by the role played by constructs such as personalization and control, and by the absence of evidence for a role of challenge and skill.

Acknowledgements. This was partially supported by the Provincia Autonoma di Trento, through a grant to the PEACH project.

References

1. Agarwal, R., Karahanna, E.: Time Flies when You're Having Fun: Cognitive Absorption and Beliefs about Information Technology Usage. MIS Quarterly 24, 665–694 (2000)
2. Baus, J., Krüger, A., Wahlster, W.: A Resource-Adaptive Mobile Navigation System. In: Proceedings of the 7th International Conference on Intelligent User Interfaces (IUI'02), pp.15–22. San Francisco, CA (2002)
3. Brusilovsky, P., Maybury, M.T.: From adaptive hypermedia to the adaptive Web. Communications of the ACM 45, 30–33 (2002)
4. Cheverst, K., Davies, N., Mitchell, K., Friday, A., Efstratiou, C.: Developing a Context-aware Electronic Tourist Guide: Some Issues and Experiences. In: Proceedings of CHI'2000, pp.17–24. The Netherlands (2000)
5. Chin, W.: The Partial Least Square Approach to Structural Equation Modelling. In: Marcoulides, G.A. (ed.) Modern Methods for Business Research, Lawrence Erlbaum Associates, Mahwah, NJ (1998)
6. Chin, W.W., Gopal, A.: Adoption Intention in GSS: Relative Importance of Beliefs. Data Base Advances 26, 42–64 (1995)
7. Csikszentmihalyi, M.: Beyond Boredom and Anxiety. Jossey-Bass, San Francisco (1977)
8. Csikszentmihalyi, M., Csikszentmihalyi, I.: Introduction to Part IV. In: Csikszentmihalyi, M., Csikszentmihalyi, I.S. (eds.) Optimal Experience: Psychological Studies of Flow in Consciousness, Cambridge University Press, Cambridge (1988)
9. Davis, F.D.: Perceived Usefulness, Perceived Ease of Use, and User Acceptance of Information technology. MIS Quarterly 13, 319–340 (1989)
10. Davis, F.D.: User acceptance of information technology: system characteristics, user perceptions and behavioural impacts. International Journal of Man-Machine Studies 38(3), 475–587 (1993)
11. Fornell, C., Bookstein, F.: Two Structural Equation Models: LISREL and PLS Applied to Consumer Exit-Voice Theory. Journal of Marketing Research 19, 440–452 (1982)
12. Ghani, J.A., Deshpande, S.P.: Task Characteristics and the Experience of Optimal Flow in Human-Computer Interaction. The Journal of Psychology 128, 381–391 (1994)

13. Gefen, D., Straub, D.: A Practical Guide to Factorial Validity Using PLS-Graph: Tutorial and Annotated Example. Communications of the Association for Information Systems 16, 91–109 (2005)
14. Goren-Bar, D., Graziola, I., Pianesi, F., Zancanaro, M.: The Influence of Personality Factors on Visitor Attitudes towards Adaptivity Dimensions for Mobile Museum Guides. In User Modelling and User Adapted Interaction: The Journal of Personalization Research 16, 31–62 (2006)
15. Hoyle, R.: Structural equation modeling: concepts, issues and applications. Sage, Thousand Oaks, Ca (1995)
16. Jameson, A., Schwarzkopf, E.: Pros and Cons of Controllability: An Empirical Study. In: Brusilovsky, P., Conejo, E. (eds.) Adaptive Hypermedia and Adaptive Web-based Systems: Proceedings of AH2002, pp. 193–202. Malaga, Spain (2002)
17. Jameson, A.: Adaptive Interfaces and Agents. In: Jacko, J., Sears, A. (eds.) Human-computer interaction handbook, pp. 305–330. Erlbaum, Mahwah, NJ (2003)
18. Kelloway, E.K.: Using LISREL for structural equation modeling: a researcher's guide. Sage, Thousand Oaks, Ca (1998)
19. Kim, T., Biocca, F.: Telepresence via Television: Two Dimensions of Telepresence May Have Different Connections to Memory and Persuasion. Journal of Computer-Mediated Communication, vol. 3(2) (September 1997)
20. LeFevre, J.: Flow and the Quality of Experience During Work and Leisure. In: Csikszentmihalyi, M., Csikszentmihalyi, I. (eds.) Optimal Experience: Psychological Studies of Flow in Consciousness, Cambridge University Press, Cambridge (1988)
21. Lohmöller, J.B.: Latent Variable Path Modelling with Partial Least Squares. Physica-Verlag, Heidelberg (1989)
22. Norman, D.: Emotional Design: Why we love (or hate) everyday things. Basic Books, NY (2004)
23. Novak, T.P., Hoffman, D.L., Yung, Y.F.: Measuring the customer experience in on-line environments: a structural modelling approach. Marketing Science 19, 22–42 (2000)
24. Oppermann, R., Specht, M.: A Context-Sensitive Nomadic Information System as an Exhibition Guide. In: Thomas, P., Gellersen, H.-W. (eds.) HUC 2000. LNCS, vol. 1927, pp. 127–142. Springer, Heidelberg (2000)
25. Petrelli, D., Not, E.: User-centred design of flexible hypermedia for a mobile guide: reflections on the hyperaudio experience. User Modelling and User-Adapted Interaction 15, 303–338 (2005)
26. Popovich, P.M., Hyde, K.R., Zakrajsek, T., Blumer, C.: The development of the Attitudes Toward Computer Usage Scale. Educational and Psychological Measurement 47, 261–269 (1987)
27. Rocchi, C., Zancanaro, M.: Rhetorical Patterns for Adaptive Video Documentaries. In: Proceedings of Adaptive Hypermedia Conference, pp. 324–327. Eindhoven, The Netherlands (2004)
28. Rocchi, C., Graziola, I., Goren-Bar, D., Stock, O.: Adaptive multimedia guide. In: PEACH: Intelligent Interfaces for Museum Visits. Cognitive Technologies Series, Springer, Heidelberg (2006)
29. Stokmans, M.J.W.: Reading attitude and its effect on leisure time reading. Poetics 26, 245–261 (1999)
30. Venkatesh, V.: Creating Favorable User Perceptions: Exploring the Role of Intrinsic Motivations. MIS Quarterly 23, 239–260 (1999)
31. Werts, C.E., Linn, R.L., Jöreskog, K.G.: Intraclass Reliability Estimates: Testing Structural Assumptions. Educational and Psychological Measurement 34, 25–33 (1974)

Improving Social Filtering Techniques Through WordNet-Based User Profiles

Pasquale Lops, Marco Degemmis, and Giovanni Semeraro

Department of Informatics - University of Bari, Italy
{lops,degemmis,semeraro}@di.uniba.it

Abstract. Collaborative filtering algorithms predict the preferences of a user for an item by weighting the contributions of *similar* users, called *neighbors*, for that item. Similarity between users is computed by comparing their rating styles, i.e. the set of ratings given on the *same* items. Unfortunately, similarity between users is computable only if they have common rated items. The main contribution of this paper is a (content-collaborative) hybrid recommender system which overcomes this limitation by computing similarity between users on the ground of their content-based profiles. Traditional keyword-based profiles are unable to capture the *semantics* of user interests, due to the natural language ambiguity. A distinctive feature of the proposed technique is that a statistical model of the user interests is obtained by machine learning techniques integrated with linguistic knowledge contained in the WordNet lexical database. This model, called the *semantic* user profile, is exploited by the hybrid recommender in the neighborhood formation process. The results of an experimental session in a movie recommendation scenario demonstrate the effectiveness of the proposed approach.

1 Background and Motivations

Currently many web sites embody recommender systems as a way of personalizing their content for users. Recommendation algorithms use input about customers' interests to generate a list of recommended items. Among different techniques used to design recommender systems, the *content-based* and the *collaborative filtering* approaches are the most widely adopted to date.

Content-based recommenders analyze a set of objects, usually textual descriptions of the items previously rated by a user, and build a model of user interests based on the features of the objects rated by that user. Thus, the user profile is a structured representation of the user interests which is exploited to recommend new potentially relevant items. Collaborative recommenders differ from content-based ones in that only user opinions are used. They gather user ratings about objects: To provide user X with recommendations, the system computes the *neighborhood* of that user, i.e. the subset of users that have a taste similar to X. Similarity in taste is computed using the similarity of ratings for objects that were rated by *both* users. The system then recommends objects that users in X's neighborhood indicated liking, provided that they have not yet been rated by

C. Conati, K. McCoy, and G. Paliouras (Eds.): UM 2007, LNAI 4511, pp. 268–277, 2007.
© Springer-Verlag Berlin Heidelberg 2007

X. The main advantage of collaborative filtering over content-based methods is that any item can be recommended regardless of its content. On the other hand, one of the main shortcomings is the *sparsity problem*: The number of ratings obtained from users is usually very small compared to the number of ratings that must be predicted. This has a negative effect on the predictions for the *active user* (for which recommendations have to be produced) because it affects the selection of the neighbors. The problem is that the similarity value between users is only computable if users have common rated items: The computation becomes harder in case of extremely sparse user-item matrix [8].

Many researchers have tried to combine different techniques in order to obtain *hybrid recommender systems* able to compensate the drawbacks of each single approach. This paper proposes a *content-based/collaborative feature augmentation hybrid recommender* [4], not yet explored in literature, based on the idea that a potential improvement of collaborative recommendations may come from new strategies exploiting user profiles for neighborhood formation.

In our hybrid recommender, the neighborhood formation process groups together users having *similar* profiles, by computing similarity values *without requiring overlapping ratings*. User profiles are inferred by using machine learning techniques able to analyze both content descriptions of the items and corresponding ratings users provided according to their preferences. The content feeds natural language processing techniques, which rely on the linguistic knowledge stored in the WordNet lexical database [15] in order to detect relevant concepts representing the user interests. The "captured" knowledge is stored in so-called *semantic* user profiles. This approach overcomes the aforementioned limitations of the similarity measures based on co-rated items, such as the Pearson's correlation coefficient, because users might be considered similar not only if they like or dislike the *same* items, but also if they like or dislike *similar* ones, according to the content descriptions of the items (e.g., movies directed by the same director or with similar plot) used to infer user profiles. Finally, collaborative recommendations are produced by a nearest-neighbor algorithm, which predicts scores for the items to be recommended by taking advantage of the output of the profile-based neighborhood formation process.

The paper is organized as follows: After introducing the techniques used for learning WordNet-based user profiles, Section 3 describes the new hybrid recommender system which exploits the knowledge stored in semantic user profiles to improve a classic collaborative filtering method. The effectiveness of the hybrid recommender has been evaluated in experiments reported in Section 4. Related work in the area of content-based/collaborative hybrid recommenders is discussed in Section 5, while conclusions and future work close the paper.

2   Learning User Profiles for the Hybrid Recommender

Our work tries to extend the concept of correlation between users by exploiting a user profile consisting of two parts, one for modeling user *interests* and a separate one for user *disinterests*. In this way, two users turn out *similar* not only if they share preferences, but also if they have *similar* negative tastes, according to the content descriptions of the items.

In our vision, the problem of learning user profiles can be seen as a binary text categorization task: Each document has to be classified as interesting or not interesting compared to the user profile (the induced classifier). A relevant problem is that keywords are rarely an appropriate way of representing the information a user is interested into, because of *polysemy*, the presence of multiple meanings for one word, and *synonymy*, multiple words having the same meaning. We cope with this problem through a relevance feedback method able to learn *semantic* user profiles from documents in which each word is replaced by its correct meaning (sense).

2.1   Document Representation: From Words to Meanings

The task of determining which of the senses of an ambiguous word is invoked in a particular use of that word is known as *word sense disambiguation* (WSD). The goal of a WSD algorithm is to associate the appropriate sense t to a word w_i in document d by exploiting its *context* C (a set of words that precede and follow w_i). The sense t is selected from a predefined set of possibilities, usually known as *sense inventory*. In our system, the sense inventory is obtained from WordNet. The basic building block for WordNet is the SYNSET (SYNonym SET), which represents a specific meaning (sense) of a word. Every synset contains a group of synonymous words that represents a concept. Synsets are organized in a hierarchy through the IS-A relation.

The WSD algorithm takes as input $d = (w_1, w_2, \ldots, w_h)$, the list of all the *nouns* ordered as they appear in a document, and will output a list of synsets $X = (t_1, t_2, \ldots, t_k)$, $(k \leq h)$, in which each t_j is obtained by disambiguating the *target word* w_i based on its context. Noun disambiguation is performed by computing the similarity between each t_{ik} in the sense inventory for the target word w_i and each t_{jh} in the sense inventory for all w_j in its context. The similarity between t_{ik} and t_{jh} is computed by the Leacock-Chodorow measure [10] as a score that is inversely proportional to the length of the path joining t_{ik} with t_{jh}, by traversing their most specific subsumer in the WordNet hierarchy. The sense assigned to w_i is the one with the highest similarity value compared to the context. A detailed version of the algorithm is reported in [19].

The WSD procedure is used to obtain a synset-based vector space representation that we called *bag of synsets* (BOS). In this model, each document is represented by the vector of synsets recognized by the WSD algorithm, rather than a vector of words, as in the classical *bag of words* (BOW) model [18]. Each document is represented by a set of *slots*. Each slot is a textual field corresponding to a specific feature of the document, in an attempt to take into account its structure. In our application scenario, in which documents are movie descriptions, five slots have been selected to represent movies: 1) *title* 2) *cast* 3) *directors* 4) *summary* (text that presents the main parts of the story) 5) *keywords* (words describing the main topics of the movie). The text in each slot is processed differently according to its type of content. Since slots *director* and *cast* contain only proper names, and most of them have no entries in WordNet, we adopted a simplified representation for such entities instead of their WordNet identifier (e.g. *Sean Penn* becomes *sean_penn*). As regards the *title*, the common preprocessing operations performed before WSD produced some unexpected results. For example, slots containing exclusively stopwords, such as "It", became empty, thus we decided to perform WSD only after tokenization. Even though titles may be not very informative in some cases, we finally decided to process them because in other cases they provide evidence of user interests (e.g. "Dracula").

Let D be a collection of N documents, m be the index of the slot. The n-th document in D is reduced to five bags of synsets, one for each slot:

$$d_n^m = \langle t_{n1}^m, t_{n2}^m, \dots, t_{nD_{nm}}^m \rangle, \ \text{m=1}, \dots, 5 \quad n = 1, \dots, N$$

where t_{nk}^m is the k-th synset in slot m of document d_n and D_{nm} is the total number of synsets occurring in the m-th slot of document d_n. For all n, k and m, $t_{nk}^m \in V_m$, which is the vocabulary for the slot m (the set of all different synsets found in slot m). Document d_n is finally represented in the vector space by five synset-frequency vectors:

$$f_n^m = \langle w_{n1}^m, w_{n2}^m, \dots, w_{nD_{nm}}^m \rangle$$

where w_{nk}^m is the weight of the synset t_k in the slot m of document d_n and can be computed in different ways: It can simply be the number of times synset t_k appears in the slot m or a more complex TF-IDF score.

2.2 WordNet-Based User Profiles

A relevance feedback algorithm, adapted for the profiling task, is used to learn *semantic* user profiles from BOS-represented documents [5]. Given a user u and a set of items on which u provided a positive or negative feedback according to his/her interests (positive and negative examples respectively), the relevance feedback method learns a profile p_u structured in two parts. The *positive* part p_u^+ is learned from the content of items judged with positive feedback, while the *negative* one p_u^- is obtained by analyzing items judged with negative feedback. Each part of the profile is structured in five slots, according to the document representation. Each slot contains the synsets (concepts) and the corresponding scores assigned by the learning algorithm representing the degree of interest of the user in that concept. A formal description of p_u follows:

$$p_u^+ = \langle (t_i^m, w_i^m) \rangle, \ \text{m=1}, \dots 5, \quad \text{i=1}, \dots \text{n}$$

where each t_i^m is a synset occurring in slot m of positive examples, w_i^m is the corresponding score assigned to t_i^m, and n is the number of distinct synsets occurring in the set of positive examples.

$$p_u^- = \langle (t_j^m, w_j^m) \rangle, \ \text{m=1}, \dots 5, \quad \text{j=1}, \dots \text{k}$$

where each t_j^m is a synset occurring in slot m of negative examples, w_j^m is the corresponding score assigned to t_i^m, and k is the number of distinct synsets occurring in the set of negative examples.

Results of experiments, performed in order to compare BOS-generated profiles with BOW-generated ones, showed that profile accuracy significantly improved (+2%) when shifting from BOW to BOS [6]. Therefore, we decided to use synset-based profiles in the neighborhood formation process of our hybrid recommender.

3 A Hybrid Recommender System Exploiting WordNet-Based User Profiles

The main steps of the process of producing collaborative recommendations in nearest-neighbor algorithms are:

- *Representation of input data:* the input data is a set of ratings of n users on m items, usually represented as an $n \times m$ user-item matrix, R, such that $r_{i,j}$ represents the rating assigned by the ith user on the jth item.
- *Neighborhood Formation:* it represents the model-building for a collaborative recommender. Users similar to the active user will form a proximity-based neighborhood with him. The main goal of neighborhood formation is to find, for each user a, an ordered list of l users $N_a = (N_1, N_2, \ldots, N_l)$ so that $a \notin N_a$ and $sim(a, N_1)$ is maximum, $sim(a, N_2)$ is the next maximum, $\ldots$.
- *Recommendation Generation:* the final step is to produce a prediction, a numerical value representing the predicted opinion of the active user. It should be based on the neighborhood of users. The classical formula for computing the prediction $p_{a,j}$ for the active user a on item j is reported below and is based on the idea that similarities $w_{a,i}$ among a and his neighbors i are computed over profiles contained in N_a instead of ratings in R:

$$p_{a,j} = \overline{r}_a + \frac{\sum_{i \in N_a} w_{a,i}(r_{i,j} - \overline{r}_i)}{\sum_{i \in N_a} |w_{a,i}|} \tag{1}$$

where $r_{i,j}$ is the rating of the user i on the item j, and $\overline{r}$ is the average rating of a user. If a strategy to determine a subset X of neighbors from N_a is adopted, then similarities $w_{a,i}$ are computed over profiles contained in X rather than profiles in N_a.

In our hybrid recommender, user profiles are partitioned by applying a bisecting k-means clustering algorithm [7] in order to obtain neighborhood N_a. The process is sketched in Fig. 1, and formally described by Algorithm 1. First, a clustering algorithm is applied to the set of user profiles inferred by the content analysis (steps 3 and 4 of Algorithm 1). Then, the neighborhood for the active user is defined as the union of clusters that contain the user profile of the active user. The process of neighborhood selection is applied to both the positive and the negative parts of the user profile (step 5). Clusters obtained by positive parts represent groups of similar users because they share the same interests, while

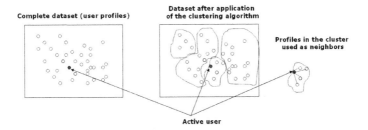

Fig. 1. Neighborhood formation from clustered partitions

Algorithm 1. Neighborhood Formation

1: **Input:** P^+, P^- ▷ $P^+=\{p_1^+,\ldots,p_N^+\}$ is
   the set of positive profiles, $P^-=\{p_1^-,\ldots,p_N^-\}$ is the set of negative profiles, N
   is the number of users in the system.
2: **Output:** N_a ▷ Neighborhood of the active user a.
3: P^+ is partitioned in $P_1^+, P_2^+, \ldots, P_k^+$, where $P_i^+ \cap P_j^+ = \oslash$, for $1 \leq i,j \leq k$, $i \neq j$,
   and $P_1^+ \cup P_2^+ \cup \ldots \cup P_k^+ = P$.   ▷ A clustering algorithm is applied to the
   set of positive profiles representing positive interests in the specific category to
   produce k partitions.
4: P^- is partitioned in $P_1^-, P_2^-, \ldots, P_k^-$, where $P_i^- \cap P_j^- = \oslash$, for $1 \leq i,j \leq k$, $i \neq j$,
   and $P_1^- \cup P_2^- \cup \ldots \cup P_k^- = P$.   ▷ A clustering algorithm is applied to the
   set of negative profiles representing negative interests in the specific category
   to produce k partitions.
5: If $a \in P_i^+$ and $a \in P_j^-$, $N_a = P_i^+ \cup P_j^-$.   ▷ The *neighborhood* N_a for the
   active user a is the union of users contained in the cluster of positive profiles
   (C^+) and the cluster of negative profiles (C^-).

---

clusters obtained by negative parts represent groups of similar users because they share common dislikes. Predictions are then generated using Equation 1.

4   Experimental Evaluation of the Hybrid Recommender

The purpose of the experiments is to validate the hypothesis that the knowledge contained in user profiles is useful to improve the quality of recommendations. The accuracy of a classic collaborative filtering algorithm using the Pearson's correlation coefficient is compared to the accuracy of recommendations generated integrating synset-based user profiles in the phase of neighborhood formation.

The experimental work has been carried out on a collection of $1,628$ textual descriptions of movies rated by $72,916$ real users, the EachMovie dataset[1]. The movies are rated on a 6-point scale that was mapped linearly into the interval $[0,1]$. The original dataset does not contain any information about the content

---

[1] EachMovie dataset no longer available for download: http://www.cs.umn.edu/Research/GroupLens/

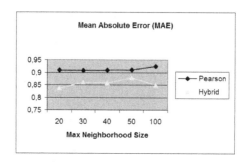

Fig. 2. A comparison of MAE values obtained by two different approaches for the neighborhood formation

of the movies; it was collected from IMDb[2] using a crawler for gathering the *title*, the *director*, the *genre* (the category of the movie), the list of *keywords*, the *summary* and the *cast*. Movies are divided into 10 different genres. The dataset used in the experiment contains 835 distinct users that rated 1,613 movies.

The basic evaluation sequence proceeds as follows. The dataset of users (and their ratings) is divided into a *training set* (the community) and a *test set*. We iterate through the users in the test set, treating each user as the active user. The ratings for the active user are divided into a set of ratings that we treat as observed, I_a, and a set that we will attempt to predict, P_a. The ratings in I_a are used to predict the ratings in P_a. We adopted the *AllBut1* protocol in which the test set P_a for each test user contains a single randomly selected rating and the observed set I_a contains the rest of the ratings. For each user in the test set, predictions were computed for the withheld items by using Equation 1, where neighbors are selected from the community in two different ways.

In the first experiment, neighbors are selected by using the Pearson's correlation coefficient for computing the similarity between users. In the second experiment, the neighborhood of a user is formed by Algorithm 1 by taking as input the set of positive and negative profiles of users.

The technique adopted to compute the neighbors is the best-n-neighbors (n is the neighborhood size), which picks out the best n correlates from N_a. The quality of recommendations is measured in terms of Mean Absolute Error (MAE) [9], that computes the average absolute deviation between a predicted rating and the user's true rating. Lower MAE corresponds to more accurate recommender systems. The procedure was repeated 5 times selecting a different test set. This allows running 5 different trials corresponding to a 5-fold cross validation. Results reported in Fig 2 show that the method using only the Pearson's correlation coefficient for computing users' similarity is fairly accurate. This is not surprising since the EachMovie dataset shows a coverage over ratings (percentage of items for which a filtering algorithm can provide predictions or make recommendations)that tends to be higher than 99,97% [6], and this might not be

---

[2] Internet Movie Database, http://www.imdb.com

representative of real world situations, with very sparse data, with a large portion of cold start users and of items rated just by one user [12].

The second experiment reports results of our hybrid recommender. Even if there is not much room for improvement, results highlight a decrease of MAE values achieved by using clusters of synset-based profiles compared to those obtained using the other technique. Results of the experiments have been compared in order to understand whether the difference between the methods was statistically significant. The comparison of the results obtained for the 10 genre EachMovie datasets has been done by considering the same neighborhood size. Statistical tests were carried out to compare results obtained by systems over the 10 datasets when the neighborhood size is set to 20, 30, 40, 50 and 100. The non-parametric Wilcoxon two-sample paired signed rank test was used ($p < 0.05$). Results showed that the difference between MAE values obtained by the two algorithms for the neighborhood formation process is statistically significant in favor of the technique using synset-based profiles in the neighborhood selection process. These results corroborate the initial hypothesis that a better understanding of users improves recommendations.

5 Related Work

The strategy we adopted to design the hybrid recommender is related to the work of authors who combine collaborative and content-based approaches.

Pazzani [16] proposes the *collaboration via content*, that uses a prediction scheme similar to the standard collaborative filtering, in which similarity among users is computed on the content-based profile of each user, containing weights for the *terms* that indicate that a user will like an object. The similarity between users is computed using Pearson's correlation coefficient between content-based weight vectors. The main limitation of this approach is that due to synonymy, overlap between interests is missed if profiles do not contain exactly the same terms while, due to polysemy, profiles could be incorrectly deemed similar because of ambiguous terms. We try to overcome these problems by using a semantic representation of user profiles in which WordNet concepts (instead of words) are used to represent user interests.

Melville et al. [14] propose the *Content-boosted collaborative filtering*, that deals with the problem of user-item matrix sparsity by using content-based profiles to predict ratings of unrated items. Then, collaborative recommendations are computed over the new "dense" matrix. The problem is that if users rated only a few items, predictions could be inaccurate. In our hybrid recommender, profiles are clustered in order to find neighbors, therefore, if a user profile is inferred from a few ratings, the (reasonable) consequence is only that the user will not be included in the set of neighbors of the active user.

Our work was mainly inspired by: *ifWeb* [1], that supports users in document searching by maintaining user profiles which store both interests and *dis*interests; *SiteIF* [11], which exploits a sense-based representation to build a user profile as a semantic network whose nodes represent senses of the words in documents requested by the user; *Fab* [2], which adopts a relevance feedback method to build user models that are directly compared to determine similar users for collaborative recommendations. According to these works, the content-based part of our hybrid recommender has been conceived as a text classifier able to deal with a sense-based document representation and to distinguish between interests and *dis*interests of users. The strategy we propose to shift from a keyword-based document representation to a sense-based one is *to integrate WordNet lexical knowledge in the WSD process used to provide a semantic representation of training documents* [15]. Recent works [13,3] provided an experimental evidence of the usefulness of embedding WSD in classification tasks, especially when a limited number of labeled examples is given, as in user profiling tasks.

6   Conclusions and Future Work

We have proposed a novel hybrid recommender that implements a neighborhood formation process based on the idea of grouping users by computing similarities between their semantic user profiles instead of their rating style. Our hybrid recommender overcomes some shortcomings of pure collaborative filtering systems: 1) *Sparsity Problem* - we interpreted the MAE improvement as a direct consequence of the proposed neighborhood formation strategy. This improvement is particularly evident in case of data sparsity, when the strategy based on the Pearson's correlation coefficient is more likely to fail. 2) *Lack of Transparency Problem* - the adoption of synset-based profiles to select the neighborhood of users gives the possibility to understand why some users have been selected for producing recommendations. Profiles are represented by senses instead of words, thus a certain level of system transparency has been added. To the best of our knowledge, the clustering of synset-based profiles for the process of neighborhood selection is a novel contribution in the area of collaborative filtering systems, and this approach is significantly different from others presented in literature [17,20].

As a future work we foresee possible improvements for both the content-based and the collaborative parts of the hybrid. The method for selecting like-minded users, described in Algorithm 1, could be modified by introducing a strategy to weigh interests higher than disinterests. People are similar because they like or dislike similar things, but usually the overlap between interests is more informative. The content-based part could be enhanced by learning more accurate profiles, in which entities (e.g. persons, cities, events, etc.) are recognized using the knowledge contained in domain ontologies.

References

1. Asnicar, F., Tasso, C.: ifweb: A Prototype of User Model-based Intelligent Agent for Documentation Filtering and Navigation in the Word Wide Web. In: Tasso, C., Jameson, A., Paris, C.L. (eds.) Proc. of the 1st Int. Workshop on Adaptive Systems and User Modeling on the WWW, pp. 3–12 (1997)
2. Balabanovic, M., Shoham, Y.: Fab: Content-based, Collaborative Recommendation. Communications of the ACM 40(3), 66–72 (1997)

3. Bloedhorn, S., Hotho, A.: Boosting for text classification with semantic features. In: Proc. of the 10th ACM SIGKDD Int. Conf. on Knowledge Discovery and Data Mining, Mining for and from the Semantic Web Workshop, pp. 70–87 (2004)

4. Burke, R.: Hybrid Recommender Systems: Survey and Experiments. User. Modeling and User.-Adapted Interaction 12(4), 331–370 (2002)

5. Degemmis, M., Lops, P., Semeraro, G.: Learning Semantic User Profiles from Text. In: Advanced Data Mining and Applications, Proc. of the 2nd Int. Conf., Xi'an, China, pp. 661–672. Springer, Heidelberg (2006)

6. Degemmis, M., Lops, P., Semeraro, G.: A Content-collaborative Recommender that Exploits Wordnet-based User Profiles for Neighborhood Formation. User Modeling and User-Adapted Interaction, Forthcoming (2007)

7. Hartigan, J.: Clustering Algorithms. John Wiley & Sons, Chichester (1975)

8. Herlocker, J.L., Konstan, J.A., Borchers, A., Riedl, J.: An Algorithmic Framework for Performing Collaborative Filtering. In: Proc. of the 22nd Annual Int. ACM SIGIR Conference on Research and Development in Information Retrieval. Theoretical Models, pp. 230–237. ACM Press, New York (1999)

9. Herlocker, J.L., Konstan, J.A., Terveen, L.G., Riedl, J.T.: Evaluating Collaborative Filtering Recommender Systems. ACM Transactions on Information Systems 22(1), 5–53 (2004)

10. Leacock, C., Chodorow, M.: Combining Local Context and WordNet Similarity for Word Sense Identification. In: Fellbaum, C. (ed.) WordNet: An Electronic Lexical Database, pp. 266–283. MIT Press, Cambridge (1998)

11. Magnini, B., Strapparava, C.: Improving User Modelling with Content-based Techniques. In: Proc. of the 8th Int. Conf. on User Modeling, Sonthofen, Germany, pp. 74–83. Springer, Heidelberg (2001)

12. Massa, P.: Trust-aware Decentralized Recommender Systems. PhD thesis, International Doctorate School in Information and Communication Technologies, University of Trento (2006)

13. Mavroeidis, D., Tsatsaronis, G., Vazirgiannis, M., Theobald, M., Weikum, G.: word sense disambiguation for exploiting hierarchical thesauri in text classification. In: Jorge, A.M., Torgo, L., Brazdil, P.B., Camacho, R., Gama, J. (eds.) PKDD 2005. LNCS (LNAI), vol. 3721, pp. 181–192. Springer, Heidelberg (2005)

14. Melville, P., Mooney, R.J., Nagarajan, R.: Content-boosted Collaborative Filtering for Improved Recommendations. In: Proc. of the 18th National Conf. on Artificial Intelligence and 14th Conf. on Innovative Applications of Artificial Intelligence (AAAI/IAAI-02), Menlo Parc, pp. 187–192. AAAI Press, Stanford, California (2002)

15. Miller, G.: Wordnet: An On-line Lexical Database (Special Issue). International Journal of Lexicography 3(4), 235–312 (1990)

16. Pazzani, M.J.: A Framework for Collaborative, Content-based and Demographic Filtering. Artificial Intelligence Review 13(5-6), 393–408 (1999)

17. Sarwar, B.M., Karypis, G., Konstan, J., Reidl, J.: Recommender Systems for Large-scale e-commerce: Scalable Neighborhood Formation Using Clustering. In: Proc. of the 5th Int. Conf. on Computer and Information Technology (2002)

18. Sebastiani, F.: Machine Learning in Automated Text Categorization. ACM Computing Surveys 34(1), 1–47 (2002)

19. Semeraro, G., Degemmis, M., Lops, P., Basile, P.: Combining Learning and Word Sense Disambiguation for Intelligent User Profiling. In: Proc. of the 20th Int. Joint Conf. on Artificial Intelligence, 2007, Hyderabad, India, pp. 2856–2861 (2007)

20. Ungar, L.H., Foster, D.P.: Clustering Methods for Collaborative Filtering. In: Proc. of the Workshop on Recommendation Systems, AAAI Press, Stanford, California (1998)

Push-Poll Recommender System: Supporting Word of Mouth

Andrew Webster and Julita Vassileva

Department of Computer Science
University of Saskatchewan, Saskatoon SK, S7N 5C9, Canada
asw292@mail.usask.ca, jiv@cs.usask.ca

Abstract. Recommender systems produce social networks as a side effect of predicting what users will like. However, the potential for these social networks to aid in recommending items is largely ignored. We propose a recommender system that works directly with these networks to distribute and recommend items: the informal exchange of information (word of mouth communication) is supported rather than replaced. The paper describes the push-poll approach and evaluates its performance at predicting user ratings for movies against a collaborative filtering algorithm. Overall, the push-poll approach performs significantly better while being computationally efficient and suitable for dynamic domains (e.g. recommending items from RSS feeds).

1 Introduction

The main advantages of recommender systems are that recommendations are supplied *on demand* and are made from *a massive item collection*. For example, Amazon.com can be queried in the middle of the night for book/music recommendations from a list of millions [1]. However, recommending an item and giving a clear explanation of why it was recommended is not forthcoming in these distinctively "black box" systems [2]. We see the lack of believable explanations as a symptom of a wider limitation: the control and execution of a distributed process by a central authority. Recent recommender systems tend to be placed between people as authoritative intermediaries. It appears to the user that she is engaged in a dialog with the system–not her peers–about what to view next, although in fact the system may be associating her with other like-minded users in order to predict items of interest. These user-to-user associations, or *connections*, are left embedded within the system, and their full potential for improving recommendations is largely ignored.

Early recommender systems were said to simulate the informal, verbal exchange of information known as *word of mouth* communication [3]. Revisiting this conceptualization, we propose a recommender system that directly exploits user-to-user connections as the primary method to distribute and recommend information items: word of mouth processes are supported rather than replaced. Our approach models the implicit social networks that normally develop around

C. Conati, K. McCoy, and G. Paliouras (Eds.): UM 2007, LNAI 4511, pp. 278–287, 2007.
© Springer-Verlag Berlin Heidelberg 2007

shared topics of interests, or *channels*. Recommendation is achieved by two interrelated processes: push and poll. *Push* seeds an item into the social network associated with the channel the item is most appropriate for. The item then spreads according to *diffusion of innovation* models [4]. *Poll* queries adjacent users whether the item should be *activated* (i.e. recommended) for the current user, given a certain *activation threshold*. Feedback from users reshapes the network, affecting the spread and activation of subsequent items.

The next section reviews related work on social networks and how information flows in them. The proposed approach, push-poll, is described in Section 4. In Section 5, its performance is evaluated against a common collaborative filtering algorithm (which is reviewed in Section 3). We conclude in Section 6 that there are immediate advantages from directly working with social networks.

2   Related Work

Users' activity within a recommender system has been acknowledged as "inducing an implicit social network and [influences] the connectivities in this network" [5]. *Social networks* [6] are conceptualized as graphs that represent people and the relationships between them as nodes and edges, respectively. Edges, or *connections*, traditionally denote the existence of social relationships (e.g. friendship) but can also indicate more general relationships, e.g. users who have shared interests. Thus, recommender systems produce social networks, i.e. user-to-user connections, *as a consequence* of predicting user-to-item connections.

It has been emphasized that the recommendation process naturally involves bringing people together and how these connections are determined is a significant, but neglected, aspect of recommender systems research [7]. User modeling, either direct (e.g. using explicit input like item ratings) or indirect (e.g. data mining e-mail logs), and the computed similarity between user models was seen as the primary means to obtain social networks that are exploitable by the recommendation process either through structural analysis or by embedding additional information into connections between users. For an example of the former approach, recommender systems in general were evaluated in light of the network structure created between users under certain conditions [5]. One condition that was analyzed was the minimum number of shared items users must rate in order to all be connected together (identifying this number would help strike a balance between ensuring good recommendations and not alienating users with too much work). For an example of the latter approach, explicit indication of trust between users was collected, embedded into the computed social network, and used to generate improved movie recommendations [8].

The study of information propagation through social networks is another related area of research. The spread and adoption of *social innovations* within real-world communities [9] is of particular relevance as ensuing models can be applied to online environments. For example, a model for the spread of discussion topics in *weblogs*, or blogs, is presented in [10] and the identification of a minimal set of people whose adoption of a new product would maximize the spread of that product through the given social network is described in [11].

3   Collaborative Filtering

We begin with a brief overview of the collaborative filtering (CF) algorithm used to evaluate the performance of push-poll in Section 5. CF operates on the *user-item matrix*, R, where entry $r_{c,s}$ indicates the rating score user $c \in \{c_1, c_2, \ldots, c_m\}$ has given item $s \in \{s_1, s_2, \ldots, s_n\}$. Each row represents all ratings a particular user has made, and each column represents all ratings a particular item has collected. Often, rating scores follow a numerical scale (e.g. 1 to 5 stars) and are explicit, but they also may be inferred from item purchases and other implicit user actions [12]. The ultimate goal is to predict the score of empty cells for the *active user*, the user currently requesting recommendations.

CF algorithms are divided into two categories: *memory-based* and *model-based*. We focus on a memory-based algorithm because of its wide use and satisfactory prediction accuracy. For a review of CF, we refer to [13].

3.1   Memory-Based Algorithm

Memory-based CF algorithms rely on exploiting gaps within the user-item matrix. The intuition is that users who have similar preferences will generally rate items in a similar manner. Therefore, if the active user c has not rated item s, but the recommender system can find similar or correlated users (i.e. *neighbours*) who have, then a rating score can be predicted using (1).

$$r_{c,s} = \bar{r}_c + k \sum_{\acute{c} \in \hat{C}} \text{sim}(c, \acute{c}) \times (r_{\acute{c},s} - \bar{r}_{\acute{c}}) \tag{1}$$

$$\text{sim}(c, \acute{c}) = \frac{\sum_{s \in S_{c\acute{c}}} (r_{c,s} - \bar{r}_c)(r_{\acute{c},s} - \bar{r}_{\acute{c}})}{\sqrt{\sum_{s \in S_{c\acute{c}}} (r_{c,s} - \bar{r}_c)^2 \sum_{s \in S_{c\acute{c}}} (r_{\acute{c},s} - \bar{r}_{\acute{c}})^2}} \tag{2}$$

$\hat{C}$ is the set of neighbours for the active user and implies there are some number of rated items in common between the active user and each neighbour. Users tend to use ratings scales differently. For example, on a 1 to 5 rating scale, the active user may seldom rate 1 or 5 while a neighbour only rates 1 and 5. Therefore, the average rating of the active user and current neighbour ($\bar{r}_c$ and $\bar{r}_{\acute{c}}$, respectively) are used to smooth out this inconsistency.

The Pearson coefficient (2) correlates the degree of similarity $\text{sim}(c, \acute{c})$ between two users where $S_{c\acute{c}}$ is the set of items both users have rated in common. The degree of similarity ranges from -1 (perfect negative correlation) to +1 (perfect positive correlation). The similarity value is then used by equation (1) as the impact weight each neighbour has in determining the final predicted value (typically the N most similar neighbours are used). Thus, a neighbour with a similarity value 1 will have a large influence in moving the predicted score towards her (relative) rating. Finally, k is a normalizing factor and is the inverse summation of the absolute similarity values.

An advantage of CF is that nothing needs to be known about the items, for items that are difficult to analyze (e.g. video) this is clearly beneficial. However, CF performs poorly under sparse rating information, especially for new items and users, and does not scale well [14].

4   Push-Poll Approach

Push-poll is envisioned to operate in a massive, highly dynamic environment, and a potential application is recommending items from *Rich Site Summary* (RSS) *feeds* [15]. RSS is a popular method to publish content to the Web and is often used by blogs and news services to alert subscribers to new entries. RSS items follow well-known XML formats and usually include a headline, a short description, and a URL to the full item of interest. The breadth of topics and overwhelming number of feeds presents an exciting challenge for a recommender system that must manage many new and diverse items per day.

Our objective is to treat recommendation as an intuitive process that results from user interaction and follows how information propagates by word of mouth in the real world. We achieve this by modeling (inferring, representing explicitly and maintaining) social networks centred on specific interests and "shepherding" relevant items through these networks.

4.1   Interest-Based Channels

A dedicated process looks for new items by routinely cycling through a list of RSS feeds (determined by developers and/or users). Once detected, new items are analyzed and separated into channels according to their content. Thus, push-poll is a *hybrid recommender system* [16] as it combines CF with *content-based analysis*.

We suggest that RSS items require only a trivial amount of content-based analysis in order to be classified. So-called *collaborative tagging systems* [17] demonstrate successful item classification by having users provide manual classification through a set of freely-chosen keywords, or *tags*, rather than relying on automated analysis or domain experts. The reoccurrence of certain tags points to a consensus regarding the item's content. Term extraction of the RSS item's headline and description would enable a rough guess as to what channel(s) the item initially "fits" into–a channel is simply represented as a unique set of tags. The overlap between the item's tags and the channel's tags defines the potential fit of the item. Later, tagging by users would overrule the system's tag set and trigger a re-examination, possibly causing the item to be introduced into other channels.

The organization of channels inherits the flexibility of collaborative tagging and allows users to freely define their interests and the scope of their interests.

For example, consider a user interested in foreign policy. She may create a channel with a general interpretation using the tag set {*foreign, policy*}. Or, she may desire a narrower focus and conjoin {*American, middleeast*} to the previous set.

4.2   Push (Diffusion)

After a new item has been matched to a channel, it is *seeded* into the corresponding network of users who subscribe to that channel (i.e., one user may create a public channel that is shared with others). For now, we assume this network already exists. Users are represented as nodes and a directed edge between nodes describes that one user *influences* another with a specific strength. Influence strength is the edge weight (ranging from -1 to +1) between a pair of user nodes and is related to the similarity between the users (Section 3.1). It determines how items will propagate through the social networks as explained by the *Independent Cascade* model [18] that captures the probability a person will chose to *adopt* an item depending on how many of her social contacts have already adopted it (note, the item could be a new hairstyle, gadget, etc.).

We use the Independent Cascade model to spread items across the network but modify the terminology to illustrate that users have no voluntary control over whether they adopt an item or not. Instead of "adopting" an item, a user is *infected* with it, and infection is a condition where the item becomes a candidate for activation (Section 4.3). For each new RSS item, some users are targeted to be initial *seeds*, i.e. the nodes that are automatically infected. We suggest some criteria for determining a potential seed: the user provides quick feedback (e.g. rates often) and acts as an authority (i.e., exerts strong, direct influence on many users). However, we leave seed determination as future work.

At the start of the push process, all seed nodes try to infect their "contacts", or neighbour nodes (i.e. the nodes at the end of outgoing edges), with the item. A seed node u infects a neighbour node v with probability $p_{u,v}$–the absolute value of the influence strength from node u to v. Infected nodes have a single attempt that will either succeed or fail at infecting a neighbour node. Success or failure is independent of all previous attempts to infect the node in question. Note, this assumption is relaxed in the *General Cascade* model [11]. After the seed nodes cannot induce any new infections, all newly infected nodes try to infect their neighbours, and this breadth-first cycle repeats until no new infections are possible. Ultimately, depending on their direct/indirect connections to seed users, some users in the network will be infected while others will not.

4.3   Poll (Activation)

If a user is infected with an item, the item is left in the user's respective channel queue. Poll is the process that ultimately activates (i.e. recommends) these queued items, and it is based on the *Threshold Model of Collective Behaviour* [19]. The model is similar to Independent Cascade and describes that node v has an intrinsic threshold level $\theta_{v,s} \in [0, 1]$ for adopting item s and a set of contacts

I that have already adopted. For each node u in I, there is an associated weight $t_{u,v}$ that describes how much "influence" u exerts on v.

Node v will adopt s if (3) holds true, i.e., the influence exerted by v's contacts is greater than v's internal resistance to adopting s. In many models, θ is randomly chosen from a distribution (uniform) to capture various levels of willingness. In our case, I is the set of infected neighbours and θ is computed as a confidence level based on some type of content analysis (e.g. comparing the item's tags against previously liked tag sets). If the system is confident that the item is relevant (e.g. $\theta < 0.25$), then the item is automatically activated. Otherwise, the active user's infected neighbours are polled using (4).

$$\sum_{u \in I} t_{u,v} \geq \theta_{v,s} \tag{3}$$

$$k \sum_{u \in I} t_{u,v} \times r_{u,s} \geq \theta_{v,s} \tag{4}$$

Equation (4) is similar to the CF prediction (1) except rating scale smoothing has been dropped and influence strengths between nodes are used instead of similarity values that are produced by (2) which is an expensive operation. The rating value $r_{u,s} \in [-1, 1]$ captures explicit feedback on the extremes (that u did or did not like the item), and implicit feedback lies on medium values following Nichols' implicit rating strength order [20]. Note, the normalizing factor k allows incoming influence strengths to sum to values greater than 1.

Determination of θ and polling is only performed when needed, i.e. when the user is active and is requesting content for the specific channel(s). While computationally efficient, there is a definite timing issue to this approach as users activating an item early in its lifetime will find infected neighbours have not yet provided feedback. One workaround would be to automatically activate the item for seed nodes, assuming these users will most likely see the item first. Otherwise, an item that failed to be activated could be saved back in the queue for a later activation attempt.

4.4   Network Feedback

Once feedback from a user for an item is recorded, her connections (influence strengths from neighbours who have also provided feedback) are updated. Feedback can be implicit (e.g. following the link of an item to the full story) or explicit (e.g. tagging an item). Note, if feedback is explicitly positive, then a "re-push" could be triggered using the active user as the new seed node. Users in agreement will see their influence strengths move to either positive or negative unity while users with low/noisy agreement will have their connections dropped. Network readjustment will ultimately affect the subsequent spread and activation of later items. In our implementation, a simple pay-off scheme is used to adjust influence strengths. However, more advanced learning algorithms could be used instead.

The question of how these networks are first formed is dependent on the types of modeling and data collection employed by the recommender system. As noted in Section 2, there are a number of means to infer social networks.

5   Evaluation

We compare the performance of a basic implementation of push-poll to the CF algorithm reviewed in Section 3.1 using a simulation. Our goals are to show that the underlying concept of social networks is feasible and to gain insight into its advantages/disadvantages.

We used the well-known *100K MovieLens* data set which contains 100,000 ratings (on a scale of 1 to 5) by 943 users for 1682 movies [21]. Each user is guaranteed to have rated a minimum of 20 movies. Data was captured during a 7 month period from September 1997 to April 1998.

The metric, mean absolute error (MAE), is used to compare performance.

$$\text{MAE} = \frac{\sum_{c=1}^{N} |r_i - \acute{r}_i|}{N} \tag{5}$$

N is the total number of predictions attempted, r_i is the actual rating given by the user, and $\acute{r}_i$ is the predicted rating. Over- and under-estimation of r_i by $\acute{r}_i$ is treated the same by taking the absolute value of the difference between the two. A lower score means more accurate predictions.

Our hypothesis is that push-poll will perform as good as or better than CF at predicting ratings. In a general system, we anticipate the number of users sharing any given channel will be small. Therefore, we wish to investigate how push-poll performs in small vs. large user groups. We also hypothesize that push-poll will do better in narrow content scopes (e.g. American foreign policy vs. foreign policy) with a small group of highly interested users as connections with strong influence strengths are more likely to develop in such situations.

5.1   Simulation

We chose to classify movies by genre due to the lack of additional information in the data set like plot summaries. A general (G) and a narrow (N) genre classification were selected to represent channels a user could "subscribe" to: {*adventure*} with 135 matching *target movies* and {*science-fiction action adventure*} with 27 target movies, respectively. A target movie is a movie that's genre(s) fits those of the genre channel (note, N is a subset of G). For example, The Princess Bride (*action, adventure, children's, romance*) would be a target for G but not N.

A minimum threshold of target movies must be rated by a user before she is selected as a *target user* for the corresponding channel. If this threshold is set low then a large group of target users (~ 200) are captured, and they are conceptualized as "subscribing" to the channel with low interest (LI). If the threshold is relatively high then a small group of target users (~ 25) subscribe with high interest (HI). We assume this threshold is a proxy for interest level as users should have stronger opinions/interest within genres they rate more often.

A number of target movies were then randomly chosen as *test movies* which comprise the trial set of movies that ratings are predicted for. The training set is then comprised of the remaining target movies. Training and trial set sizes were split to capture the situations where rating information is abundant (80/20) or sparse (20/80). Altogether, there were 8 simulation configurations (2 genre channels x 2 interest levels x 2 training/trial combinations) with 5 random test movie sets run 5 times apiece for each configuration. The MAE for each of the 25 runs was averaged and reported in the next section.

For push-poll, seed nodes were randomly selected from target users for each trial movie. System parameters for push-poll were optimally set depending on the interest level: the number of seed nodes was set to ensure the majority of target users were infected ($\sim$ 10 target users for both LI and HI), and the number of infected neighbours polled was 10% of target users for LI and 20% for HI. Push-poll requires initial influence strengths between users to work with. The similarity values (2) calculated from the ratings matrix with non-target users, non-target movies, and trial movies removed were used as initial influence strengths. CF was allowed to use rating information from non-target movies in addition to what push-poll used–significantly more information.

Because an actual rating is being predicted, (1) was used by push-poll with influence strengths substituted for similarity values (activation thresholds were not determined). Each test movie had all its predictions for target users who had rated it performed sequentially (by the rating timestamp) before the next test movie was seeded. Influence strength was updated if it was determined that a pair of users had rated the same test movie. CF performed predictions in the order of the rating timestamp, regardless of the test movie. Finally, after a lapse of 24 hours, CF was allowed to update the similarity values between users using any new rating information introduced between lapses (these re-calculations took the bulk of the simulation time).

5.2   Results

Overall, push-poll significantly outperformed the CF algorithm's MAE score by an average of 1.93% ($p<0.001$). This is an encouraging result, considering the extra rating information used by CF.

The results for LI configurations are presented in the firsthalf of Figure 1. On average, push-poll consistently and significantly outperformed CF by 2.58% in these settings, and both algorithms performed better with the large training set (the 80/20 configuration). However, this intuitive expectation is reversed for CF in HI configurations: we believe correlations for a small group of users are noisy when considering all rating information (target movies and non-target movies) and prediction accuracy is largely dependent on the selected test movies (those that have lots of ratings versus few). Yet, push-poll's behaviour remains consistent for the training/trial splits but experiences increased variance in its scoring. We hypothesize that at the time of rating a user may find only a few neighbours with low influence strength who have already rated. A complete

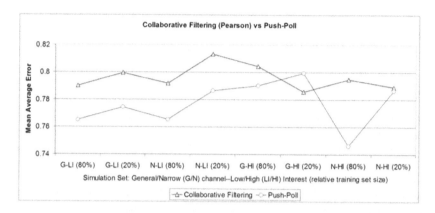

Fig. 1. Mean average error (MAE) results for simulation sets

implementation would leave that movie in the queue, waiting for feedback from stronger connections. However, further testing of this hypothesis is required.

According to our hypothesis, for small user groups (HI), we see push-poll performed better in the narrow genre channel versus the general one (an average of 1.1%). Its best performance (.7462) was in the configuration where a small group of users showed a high level of interest for specific content (with a large training set), indicating that careful selection and development of strong connections between like-minded users for a specific interest will lead to improved prediction accuracy.

6   Conclusions

We presented the design of a push-poll recommender system that supports word of mouth processes by spreading/activating information items through social networks centred on shared interests. A basic implementation of our algorithm significantly outperformed a common CF algorithm. There are a number of advantages to this approach: (1) recommendation is treated as a process and not as an outcome of pre-arranged rules, giving users some intuition over how their interactions affect which items are recommended to them, (2) new items are introduced with a minimum of content analysis; and, (3) the underlying algorithm is computationally efficient since a Pearson coefficient is not computed (we just look up the influence values on demand and do straightforward updates on any feedback). Future work includes developing push-poll into a working system that recommends items of general interest from RSS feeds.

References

1. Linden, G.: Amazon.com Recommendations: Item-to-Item Collaborative Filtering. IEEE Internet Computing 7(1), 76–80 (2003)
2. Herlocker, J.L., Konstan, J., Riedl, J.: Explaining Collaborative Filtering Recommendations. In: Proceedings of the 2000 ACM Conference on Computer Supported Collaborative Work, pp. 241–250. ACM Press, New York (2000)

3. Shardanand, U., Maes, P.: Social Information Filtering: Algorithms for Automating Word of Mouth. In: Proceedings of the ACM Conference on Human Factors in Computing Systems (CHI'95), pp. 210–217. ACM Press, New York (1995)
4. Rogers, E.: Diffusion of Innovations, 5th edn. Free Press, New York (2003)
5. Mirza, B.J., Keller, B.J., Ramakrishnan, N.: Studying Recommendation Algorithms by Graph Analysis. Journal of Intelligent Information Systems 20(2), 131–160 (2003)
6. Wasserman, S., Faust, K.: Social Network Analysis: Methods and Applications. Cambridge University Press, New York (1994)
7. Perugini, S., Gonçalves, M., Fox, E.: Recommender Systems Research: A Connection-Centric Survey. Journal of Intelligent Information Systems 23(2), 107–143 (2004)
8. Golbeck, J.: Generating Predictive Movie Recommendations from Trust in Social Networks. In: Proceedings of the 4th International Conference on Trust Management, Springer, Heidelberg (2006)
9. Valente, T.W.: Network Models and Methods for Studying the Diffusion of Innovations. In: Carrington, P.J., Scott, J., Wasserman, S. (eds.) Models and Methods in Social Network Analysis, New York, pp. 98–116. Cambridge University Press, Cambridge (2005)
10. Gruhl, D., Guha, R., Liben-Nowell, D., Tomkins, A.: Information Diffusion through Blogspace. In: Proceedings of the 13th International Conference on World Wide Web, pp. 491–501. ACM Press, New York (2004)
11. Kempe, D., Kleinberg, J.M., Tardos, É.: Maximizing the Spread of Influence through a Social Network. In: Proceedings KDD, pp. 137–146. ACM Press, New York (2003)
12. Schafer, B., Konstan, J., Riedl, J.: Recommender Systems in E-commerce. In: Proceedings of the 1st ACM Conf. on E-Commerce, pp. 158–166. ACM Press, New York (1999)
13. Adomavicius, G., Tuzhilin, A.: Toward the Next Generation of Recommender Systems: a Survey of the State-of-the-Art and Possible Extensions. IEEE Transactions on Knowledge and Data. Engineering 17(6), 734–749 (2005)
14. Sarwar, B., Karypis, G., Konstan, J., Riedl, J.: Analysis of Recommendation Algorithms for E-Commerce. In: Proceedings of the 2nd ACM Conference on E-Commerce, pp. 158–167. ACM Press, New York (2000)
15. King, A.: The Evolution of RSS (2003) [online] [Accessed 5 November 2006] Available from: http://www.webreference.com/authoring/languages/xml/rss/1/
16. Burke, R.: Hybrid Recommender Systems: Survey and Experiments. User Modeling and User-Adapted Interaction 12(4), 331–370 (2002)
17. Golder, S.A., Huberman, B.A.: Usage Patterns of Collaborative Tagging Systems. Journal of Information Science 32(2), 198–205 (2006)
18. Goldenberg, J., Libai, B., Muller, E.: Talk of the Network: A Complex Systems Look at the Underlying Process of Word-of-Mouth. Marketing Letters 12(3), 209–221 (2001)
19. Granovetter, M.: Threshold Models of Collective Behavior. The American Journal of Sociology 83(6), 1420–1443 (1978)
20. Nichols, D.M.: Implicit Rating and Filtering. In: Proceeding of the 5th DELOS Workshop on Filtering & Collaborative Filtering, Budapest, Hungary, pp. 31–36 (1997)
21. GroupLens Research Project: (2003) GroupLens Home Page [Accessed 5 November 2006] [online] Available from: http://www.grouplens.org

Evaluation of Modeling Music Similarity Perception Via Feature Subset Selection

D.N. Sotiropoulos, A.S. Lampropoulos, and G.A. Tsihrintzis

University of Piraeus, Department of Informatics,
80 Karaoli and Dimitriou St, Piraeus 18534, Greece
dsotirop@students.cs.unipi.gr,
{arislamp,geoatsi}@unipi.gr

Abstract. In this paper, we describe and discuss the evaluation process and results of a content-based music retrieval system that we have developed. In our system, user models embody the ability of evolving and using different music similarity measures for different users. Specifically, a user-supplied relevance feedback and related neural network-based incremental learning procedures allows our system to determine which subset of a set of objective acoustic features approximates more efficiently the subjective music similarity perception of an individual user. The evaluation results verify our hypothesis of a direct relation between subjective music similarity perception and objective acoustic feature subsets. Moreover, it is shown that, after training, retrieved music pieces exhibit significantly improved perceived similarity to user-targeted music pieces.

1 Introduction

Recent advances in digital storage technology and the huge increase in the availability of digital music have led to the creation of large music collections for use by broad classes of computer users. In turn, this fact gives rise to a need for systems that have the ability to manage the content of stored music files. At present, applications that manage music data usually utilize textual meta-information. The best-known example of this textual meta-information organization is probably the ID3 format, an extension to the popular MP3 format. Specifically, the ID3 format allows the user to add tags to the beginning or end of a music file, containing such information as song title, artist, album name, genre, etc. Despite its extended capabilities, ID3-based systems still suffer from serious drawbacks. For example, the textual description of audio content is subjective and the relevant meta-data have to be entered and updated manually, which implies significant effort in both creating and maintaining the music database.

To be able to search through a collection of music pieces and make observations about the similarity between objects that are not directly comparable, we must transform raw data at a certain level of information granularity. Information granules refer to a collection of data that contain only essential information. Such granulation allows more efficient processing for extracting features and computing numerical representations that characterize a music file. As a result, the

C. Conati, K. McCoy, and G. Paliouras (Eds.): UM 2007, LNAI 4511, pp. 288–297, 2007.
© Springer-Verlag Berlin Heidelberg 2007

large amount of detailed information of a song is reduced to a limited set of features. Each feature is a vector of low dimensionality, which captures some aspects of the song and can be used to determine song similarity. An extensive variety of features can be extracted from raw audio data using either their time- or frequency-domain (spectral) representation, [1,5,4,2].

Modern content-based music retrieval (CBMR) systems attempt to retrieve music pieces from a database according to their objective or subjective similarity to the user's query. The most common practice followed in several CBMR systems uses similarity measures that combine a fixed set of objective features and produces a similarity value for two musical pieces. Since the similarity value is produced from objective features, it applies universally (that is, to all users) and, therefore, the procedure is invariant under differences in music similarity perception between different users. However, the proper use of similarity percep-tion information may improve the accuracy and speed of CBMR systems. For example, information about a specific user's music similarity perception could be supplied to the CBMR system through an iterative procedure in which first the CBMR system retrieves music files on the basis of objective features and then the user ranks the retrieved images through a relevance feedback proce-dure. The user-supplied ranking is fed into a learning algorithm which attempts to construct an individualized model of the CBMR system user. This allows the CBMR system to retrieve files for the specific user with higher efficiency, i.e., the system returns a smaller number of files which are perceived by the specific user as more similar.

In this paper, we describe and discuss the evaluation process and results of a content-based music retrieval system that we have developed. In our system, a user-supplied relevance feedback procedure allows our system to determine which subset of a set of objective acoustic features approximates more efficiently the subjective music similarity perception of an individual user. Specifically, the paper is organized as follows: Section 2 provides an overview of previous related work. Section 3 presents the overall architecture of our system. A detailed description of the evaluation process and its results is presented in Section 4. Finally, a summary, conclusions, and suggestions for related future work are given in Section 5.

2   Related Work

Some of the recent works that relate specifically to CBMR with use of user mod-eling and user-supplied relevance feedback and are relevant to the present paper include : (1) A CBMR system that adapts to its user's impressions and resulted from impression-estimation experiments, in which 100 subjects gave their im-pression of 80 music pieces and were, subsequently, clustered into 20 groups [2]. For each unidentified user, the system attempts to identify the most suitable user group. However, no direct relation between user groups and subsets of ob-jective audio features has been explored. (2) A CBMR called MRTB, in which a user-friendly graphical interface in thumbnail form allows easy retrieval result browsing and verification [3]. Again, no direct relation between user models and subsets of objective audio features has been explored. (3) A relevance feedback approach for music retrieval presented in [4] and based on the TreeQ vector quantization process initially proposed by Foote [5]. More specifically relevance feedback was incorporated into the model by modifying the quantization weights of desired vectors. However this method is limited by the need to re-quantize the entire music database for each query. (4) A relevance feedback music retrieval system based on SVM Active Learning which retrieves the desired music piece according to mood and style similarity [6], while our system does not incorporate any prior information concerning the music pieces but relies only the audio signal.

An earlier version of our system was presented in [7], while we have also explored a similar approach in [8] within the framework of content-based *image* retrieval. Our system is a CBMR system, in which user models embody the ability of evolving and using different music similarity measures for different users. Contrary to previous works, *our approach investigates certain subsets in the objective feature set which are able to approximate more efficiently the subjective music similarity perception of an individual user.* Our proposition is based on the fact that each individual conceives differently the information features contained in a music file and assigns different degrees of importance to music features when assessing similarity between two music files. This, in turn, leads to the hypothesis that different individuals possibly assess music similarity via different feature sets and there might even exist certain features that are entirely unidentifiable by certain users. On the basis of this assumption, relevance feedback supplied by an individual user is fed into in an incremental learning process in order to identify that feature subset and the corresponding similarity measure which is in the highest accordance with the user's music similarity perception.

3   Overall System Architecture

Modeling the subjective similarity perception of a certain individual may be computationally realized by the development of an appropriate similarity measure providing the degree of resemblance between two music pieces as a real value in the $[0, 1]$ interval. Thus, the user modeling functionality embedded in our system consists of developing similarity measures which would approximate the similarity values that would be assigned by a specific user to pairs of music pieces. From a mathematical point of view a similarity measure may be interpreted as a continuous non-linear mapping $(F : R^n \rightarrow R, n \leq 30)$ from the space of objective features to the $[0, 1]$ interval of similarity degrees which naturally leads us to the choice of Radial Basis Functions Networks (RBFN's) that are capable of implementing arbitrary nonlinear transformations of the input space. Moreover, the adopted incremental learning procedure lies in the core of the training process where the internal network parameters are modified according to the back propagation rule in response to the user supplied similarity values concerning certain pairs of music pieces.

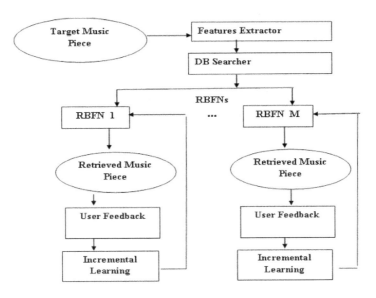

Fig. 1. Incremental Learning Scheme

The overall system architecture is based on the adapted incremental learning technique depicted in Figure 1. Specifically, our scheme consists of the following steps:

1. Seed the search with the *target* music piece corresponding to an existing music piece in the system database. This step uses an *offline process* where the feature extractor extracts the set of values for the complete set of 30 features. Afterwards, a predefined number of subsets from the original feature vectors set, $C_1, \ldots, C_M$, (11 neural networks described in Table 1) are assessed for their ability to capture the subjective music piece similarity perception of a specific user. These subsets of feature vectors are fed into the corresponding neural networks to force them to realize M different similarity measures.
2. Each neural network retrieves the most similar music piece according to the similarity measure it realizes.
3. The user valuates the set of the retrieved music pieces and ranks the degree of similarity between the retrieved music pieces and the target music piece according to his/her own perception.
4. This information is subsequently used by the system in order to adjust the neural networks' parameters. This latter parameter refinement involving the adaptation of the entire neural network parameter set constitutes the fundamental part of the adopted training scheme.
5. The procedure is repeated for a preset number of times, during which the network performance is recorded. In the end, we identify the neural network and the corresponding feature subset that exhibited the most effective performance in modeling the music similarity perception of the specific user.

The objective feature subsets that correspond to each neural network are shown in Table 1. The selection of these subsets has been based on their semantic categorization. In other words, we generated combinations of the objective features to form groups that reflect different semantically meaningful aspects of the music signal. Thus, these feature groups describe not only low-level information captured by statistical properties of the signal, but also high-level information extracted by psychoacoustic algorithms. The user involvement in the feature subsets selection process is indirectly conducted through the incremental learning procedure by providing his/her similarity estimates and thus subsidizing those neural networks whose estimates are closer to those provided by the user. The feature subsets selected (evaluated as more efficient) by a specific user can be identified after the corresponding training session is completed by comparing the relative performance of the converged neural networks.

Table 1. Feature subsets per neural network

Network IDs	Feature Subsets	Feature IDs
1	Complete feature set	$[1 \ldots 30]$
2	All beat-related features	$[20 \ldots 25]$
3	All mean-, standard deviation- and	
	low energy-related features	$[1 \ldots 9]$
4	All MFCC-related features	$[10 \ldots 19]$
5	All pitch-related features	$[26 \ldots 30]$
6	All beat- and pitch-related features	$[20 \ldots 30]$
7	All mean-, standard deviation-, MFCC-	
	and low energy-related features	$[1 \ldots 19]$
8	All MFCC- and pitch-related features	$[10 \ldots 19], [26 \ldots 30]$
9	All mean-, standard deviation-, MFCC-,	
	pitch- and low energy-related features	$[1 \ldots 19], [26 \ldots 30]$
10	All beat-, MFCC- and pitch-related features	$[10 \ldots 30]$
11	Mean and standard deviation of	
	zero-crossings and low energy features	$[4, 8, 9]$

Another point of our investigation concerned the existence of certain feature subsets whose information content might be implicitly characterized as redundant by certain users and thus could be ignored when evaluating similarity of two music pieces. For example, it was observed that when certain users were prompted to give their similarity estimation for a pair of music pieces, with one of them being rock, rhythm related features were evaluated as more efficient in contrast to the pitch related ones. The reason for this fact is that pitch related features contain melody and harmony information which for certain users fail to capture the essence of a rhythm-dominated rock song.

4   Evaluation Process and Results

Our system was evaluated by one hundred (100) users belonging to different age groups and having various music style preferences and related music education levels. As a test database, we used a western music collection of one thousand (1000) music pieces. The evaluation process consisted of three stages: At first, each participant was asked to complete a questionnaire concerning user background information, which was collected for statistical purposes and is summarized in Table 2.

Table 2. Stage I Evaluation Statistics

Overall Favorite Music Genre	Pop 54%
Age Range	21 to 57
CDs Owned	10 to 600
Hours Spent per Week Listening to Music	1 to 70
Where Get Music From	MP3 (47%)
Play Musical Instrument	39%, mostly the guitar
Professionally Involved in Music	3%
Previous Participation in Evaluation	47%

Secondly, each participant was given a predefined set of 11 *pre-trained* neural networks with corresponding subsets of the entire feature set, as in Table 1, in order to finely tune their modifiable parameters by evaluating their music similarity estimation during only 6 training stages (epochs). In the course of each training stage, the user listened to a previously selected music piece which served as the target song of the query and the corresponding most similar music pieces were retrieved from the database according to each neural network. Next, the user was directed to supply his/her own similarity perception estimate for each one of the 11 pairs of songs by typing in a similarity value in the $[0, 1]$ interval. After completing the all six training stages for every RBFN by providing a total of 66 similarity values, each user conducted a save operation in order to update the record of RBFNs' performance history and the newly estimated adjustable parameter values.

Finally, after completing the neural networks training stage each participant was prompted to provide some information concerning the overall training and retrieval performance of the system. Table 3 summarizes the information collected during the third evaluation stage emphasizing the fact that the majority of the users observed the existence of certain neural networks whose retrievals were significantly better than the others. Moreover, most of the participants noticed a gradual improvement of the neural network responses from training stage to training stage.

The second stage of the evaluation process revealed that, during the training session of each user, there were neural networks whose relevant performance in approximating the music similarity perception of that particular user was

Table 3. Stage III Evaluation Statistics

How long (in minutes) did you spent training the system?	27 mins on average
Did you observe a difference in the retrievals returned by the various neural networks during the same training epoch ? 1(minimum difference) to 5(maximum difference)	1 : 2% 2 : 11% 3 : 54% 4 : 24% 5 : 9 %
Did you observe an improvement in the retrievals returned by the various neural networks from training stage to training stage 1(minimum improvement) to 5(maximum improvement)	1 : 3% 2 : 11% 3 : 32% 4 : 46% 5 : 8%
Did you observe any specific neural network that systematically returned better retrievals than the other networks 1 (minimum difference) to 5 (maximum difference)	1 : 2% 2 : 22% 3 : 34% 4 : 36% 5 : 6%
Overall system assessment: 1(Misleading) 2 (Not Helpful) 3 (Good) 4 (Very Good) 5 (Excellent)	2 % 17 % 27 % 32 % 22 %

consistently better than that of the remaining neural networks. Figs. 2 and 3 illustrate typical examples of this fact, as seen from the plots of the time evolution of the error rates of the various networks. In these figures, the horizontal axis counts training epochs (number of relevance feedbacks) and the vertical axis

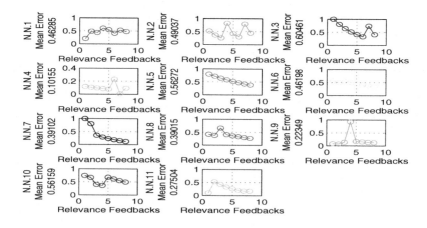

Fig. 2. Typical User Behavior I

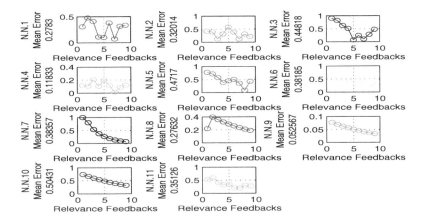

Fig. 3. Typical User Behavior II

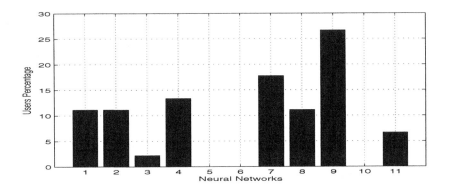

Fig. 4. Preferences Distribution

was corresponds to neural network mean error rate. The neural network with the lowest mean error rate is selected to profile the specific user.

A second justification of the user modeling ability of our system lies in the observation that, even when certain neural network retrievals were assessed as unsatisfactory to the user, the similarity values estimated by the neural networks were quite close to the perceived similarity values provided by the user.

A third observation is that *no* single neural network and corresponding feature subset outperformed all networks in *all* training sessions. On the contrary, the system users are *clustered* by the eleven neural networks into 11 corresponding clusters as in Fig. 4. We observe that the neural networks numbered 5,6 and 10 produce empty user clusters, which implies that the corresponding feature subsets fail to model the music similarity perception of any user. On the other hand, the neural networks numbered 9 and 7 produce clusters containing approximately 27% and 18% of the users. This difference in network performance lies with the qualitative differences of the corresponding feature subsets.

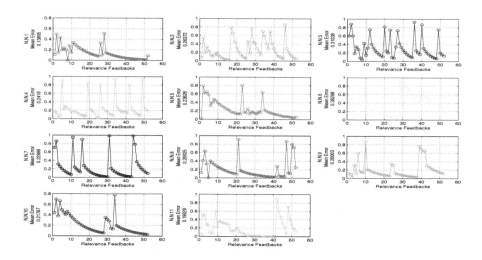

Fig. 5. Error Rate Convergence

Specifically, the feature subsets used by neural networks 9 and 7 describe both acoustic and psychoacoustic music information. This is strong evidence justifying our initial hypothesis that relates feature subsets with the similarity perception of an individual.

Finally, the convergence of the incremental learning process was examined and illustrated in Fig. 5. Specifically, the time evolution of the error rates of all the neural networks is shown over a total of 56 training cycles by the same user. During this training, a total of 8 different target music pieces were given and the system was trained for 7 epochs per given target.

5   Summary, Conclusions and Future Work

In this paper, we described and discussed the evaluation process and results of a content-based music retrieval system that we have developed. Our system constructs music similarity perception models of its users by associating different music similarity measures to different users. This is achieved via a user-supplied relevance feedback procedure and related neural network-based incremental learning which allow the system to determine which subset of a set of objective features approximates more accurately the subjective music similarity perception of an individual user.

The evaluation process involved one hundred (100) users and a western music collection of one thousand (1000) music pieces. The evaluation results lead to two major conclusions. Firstly, it is **verified that exists a relation between subsets of objective features and individualized music similarity perception**. Secondly, **fast convergence was observed, with the error rates converging to low values only within a small number of incremental learning epochs**.

In the future, our system will be expanded further by increasing the number of similarity measures (neural networks) associated with individual users. Further improvements in our system will also be performed in such directions as the use of alternative classifiers or advanced audio signal representation, enhancement and processing techniques that seem to promise higher system efficiency [10,9]. This and other research work is currently in progress and will be reported elsewhere in the near future.

References

1. Tzanetakis, G., Cook, P.: Musical genre classification of audio signals. IEEE Transactions on Speech and Audio Processing 10(5), 293–302 (2002)
2. Kumamoto, T.: Design and evaluation of a music retrieval scheme that adapts to the user's impressions. In: Ardissono, L., Brna, P., Mitrović, A. (eds.) UM 2005. LNCS (LNAI), vol. 3538, pp. 287–296. Springer, Heidelberg (2005)
3. Park, K.S., Yoon, W.J., Lee, K.K., Oh, S.H., Kim, K.M.: MRTB framework: A robust content-based music retrieval and browsing system. IEEE Transactions on Consumer Electronics 51(1), 117–122 (2005)
4. Hoashi, K., Matsumo, K., Inoue, N.: Personalization of user profiles for content-based music retrieval based on relevance feedback. In: Proceedings of ACM International Conference on Multimedia 2003, pp. 110–119. ACM press, New York (2003)
5. Foote, J.T.: Content-based retrieval of music and audio. Procs. Storage and Retrieval for Image and Video Databases (SPIE) 3229, 138–147 (1997)
6. Mandel, M., Poliner, G., Ellis, D.: Support Vector Machine Active Learning for Music Retrieval. ACM Multimedia Systems Journal 12(1), 3–13 (2006)
7. Lampropoulos, A.S., Sotiropoulos, D.N., Tsihrintzis, G.A.: Individualization of music similarity perception via feature subset selection. In: Proceedings of Systems, Man and Cybernetics, 2004 IEEE International Conference, vol. SMC 2004(1), pp. 552–556 (2004)
8. Sotiropoulos, D.N., Tsihrintzis, G.A.: Feature Selection-Based Relevance Feedback In Content-Based Retrieval Systems. In: Proceedings of 5th International Workshop on Image Analysis for Multimedia Interactive Services. WIAMIS (2004)
9. Sotiropoulos, D.N., Lampropoulos, A.S., Tsihrintzis, G.A.: Artificial Immune System-Based Music Piece Similarity Measures and Database Organization. In: Proceedings of 5th EURASIP Conference on Speech and Image Processing, Multimedia Communications and Services. ECSIPM (2005)
10. Lampropoulos, A.S., Lampropoulou, P.S., Tsihrintzis, G.A.: Musical Genre Classification Enhanced by Source Separation Techniques. In: Proceedings of 6th International Conference on Music Information Retrieval. ISMIR (2005)

A Practical Activity Capture Framework for Personal, Lifetime User Modeling

Max Van Kleek and Howard E. Shrobe

MIT Computer Science and
Artificial Intelligence Laboratory (CSAIL),
32 Vassar St.
Cambridge, MA 02139
{emax,hes}@csail.mit.edu

Abstract. This paper addresses the problem of capturing rich, long-term *personal activity logs* of users' interactions with their workstations, for the purpose of deriving predictive, personal user models. Our architecture addresses a number of practical problems with activity capture, including incorporating heterogeneous information from different applications, measuring phenomena with different rates of change, efficiently scheduling knowledge sources, incrementally evolving knowledge representations, and incorporating prior knowledge to combine low-level observations into interpretations better suited for user modeling tasks. We demonstrate that the computational and memory demands of general activity capture are well within reasonable limits even on today's hardware and software platforms.

1 Introduction

Progress in user modeling over recent years has demonstrated that models learned from observing users' actions can boost ease and efficiency of application use, improve interaction quality, and save users time and effort. Yet, despite progress in the field, relatively few applications on the desktop today employ user modelling techniques to adapt to users' needs. The field's most visible successes have instead been in recommender systems for online retailers and content providers, which gain leverage by simultaneously amassing profiles of hundreds, thousands, or millions of users. While this approach has been successful for online businesses and marketplaces, it is not easily applied to desktop applications, which have one primary user, and where information may be much more personal and sensitive in nature. One of the primary obstacles to user modeling on the desktop has been the complexity needed to develop application-specific user modeling systems to learn from user actions. Another is the *bootstrapping problem*, that very little about the user is known when the application is first installed on the user's system.

Our belief is that some of these desktop modeling challenges can be mitigated by decoupling user modeling components from applications, so that models can be shared across applications. In addition to reducing the bootstrapping problem,

C. Conati, K. McCoy, and G. Paliouras (Eds.): UM 2007, LNAI 4511, pp. 298–302, 2007.
© Springer-Verlag Berlin Heidelberg 2007

an advantage to this approach is that it becomes possible to capture task-related contextual connections among applications such as an e-mail client, web browser, and a text editor [3], which would otherwise be missed by application-centered modeling techniques.

This poster focuses on an activity capture framework for building rich logs of a user's activity across his or her desktop applications. This is a first step of a larger project to derive *personal, lifetime user models* (PLUM) that span a user's applications and personal devices. Our paper outlines the challenges we have thus far identified in building long-term logs that are flexible, sustainable, evolvable, and practical using today's hardware and software.

2   Related Work

A number of systems have attempted to fulfill Vannevar Bush's MEMEX vision [4] of building a *personal memory prosthesis* [11] that can capture aspects of everyday life experiences, and archive them for later retrieval [10,1,14]. With respect to this goal, PLUM focuses on monitoring the information-gathering, manipulation, and consumption patterns of the user, in order to collect data needed to build models of a user's information needs. IRIS [5] is another open-source research platform for user modeling and therefore resembles PLUM in intent and purpose, with a wider research scope. Like PLUM, IRIS uses RDF for representing user interaction data. However, IRIS requires users to abandon their existing tools for a specially instrumented desktop environment. PLUM, meanwhile, is comparatively very lightweight, integrates with several existing desktop applications without modification, and may be easily extended to observe activity in new applications. Other systems with similar goals to PLUM include [8] and Slife [16], a new commercial application whose description seems to suggest that it closely mirrors PLUM's technique for interfacing with applications in MacOS X. Neither of these projects appear to be open-source, and details of their implementations are unavailable at time of this publication. Additionally, when details are released, we will investigate integrating PLUM with SUBTLE [9], a new open-source toolkit for constructing statistical models from sensor streams of human activities.

3   Capture Architecture

The system's design goal was to capture user activity in a manner that was both sufficiently general and of high-enough fidelity to eventually accommodate a variety of typical user-modeling purposes. The intended modeling tasks we were targeting include building predictive models of user activity, identifying recurring patterns or routines in user behavior (as in [2]), identifying key collaborators or resources (as [13]), and aiding human memory through reminder and recall [11]. A description of using PLUM's activity logs for latent task analysis be found in [15].

3.1   Activity and Context Observers

Observer modules hold the greatest responsibility of the system – to retrieve information about the user's state and actions from the surrounding computational and physical environment, and transform this information into a representation that can be used by the rest of the system. To accommodate the wide variety of applications just described, we have made it easy for applications to add new observer modules to incorporate new information not previously captured.

Our desktop implementation currently consists of observer modules for Mac-OS X that determine window placement, application focus, actively running processes, nearby WiFi access points, keyboard/mouse idleness, active network connections, and documents being accessed within the user's home directory. Additional application-specific scripts for Acrobat Reader, Safari, Firefox, Apple Mail, Preview, iTunes, iChat and Microsoft Word allow the system to retrieve the contents of open documents, web sites, e-mails and chats. We have short-term plans to develop observers for the Windows platform that employ the .NET Hooks API for instrumentation. [7]

We designed observers to capture as much raw, low-level information in activity logs as possible, rather than summarizing data or deriving higher-level state. This choice made it possible to decouple knowledge sources in the capture framework from activity inference algorithms, enabling us to incrementally add or improve the latter without having to re-build activity logs from scratch. This also allowed us to push probabilistic representations and reasoning out of the capture framework, into the modeling layer. Perhaps most importantly, by avoiding summarizing any data, we minimized the risk of inadvertently losing information that might be of use to applications or activity inference algorithms added later on. However, the biggest drawback with storing raw observations is that it results in the accumulation of a copious amount of data. As we discuss in 3.3, we find that the volume of data is quite manageable for most phenomena.

3.2   Knowledge Representation

Observers encode their observations as temporally-tagged relational graph structures in RDF. [12] We chose RDF for two reasons; first, it allowed us to easily encode rich descriptions of the entities or phenomena that were observed; and second, because it allowed us to incrementally refine our representation as we designed new knowledge sources. Each observation is tagged with a *validity interval*, representing the span of time during which the phenomenon being observed was believed to assume the values in the observation. When each observer is run, it asserts a new observation only if it detects a significant change from the last observation it made; otherwise, it simply extends the last observation's validity interval. Since each observer is designed to sample the environment exactly once every run, the sampling frequency for an observer is determined by the PLUM scheduler. In order to try to capture fast-changing phenomena with as much fidelity as possible, we designed an adaptive, stochastic scheduler that randomly chooses observers with a probability proportional to how frequently (in the past) it observed significant changes. The scheduler can also optionally be made to consider the amount of time observers have taken to execute in the past, to prevent computationally expensive observers from dominating the schedule.

A consequence of having each observer assert low-level observations independently is that we often see a single user action cause several related effects, or take a variety of equivalent forms, arising from the specific way by which that action was taken. Thus, the activity logs reflect a level of abstraction beneath that of user action, and thus beneath that of which our user modeling applications are likely to be interested. To bridge this gap and reduce work required of statistical modeling algorithms, we have made it possible to plug in simple rule-sets during the query process, that derive simple conclusions based on patterns in the data. [15]

3.3   Evaluation and Future Work

To gauge resource consumption, we ran our framework for three weeks on the primary author's laptop[1] with minimally noticeable impact on user application performance. Examining resource utilization while running the set of 10 observers at 2Hz (using the round-robin scheduler) revealed the main observation loop consuming an average of 6 percent of one core and 50MB of RAM, while *mysqld* consumes an additional 0.5 percent CPU and 30MB of RAM. Therefore, during capture, PLUM does not consume significantly more than the typical desktop application (iTunes consumes 5-12 % CPU on the same machine). Randomly querying to the activity log, however, is currently very expensive. We are investigating ways to make tuple query more efficient, including storing individual RDF triples as table rows [17]. The other main concern regarding feasibility besides CPU utilization, is, of course, the space consumed by capture logs. In the three weeks, we accumulated 332MB of data, consisting of approximately 4 million triples. We should note, however, that these observers do not yet capture the full text associated with user actions; for example, observers currently store accessed URLs to documents, instead of their contents. We are currently investigating approaches by which we efficiently store the full text of potentially transient documents, in case this information is needed by modeling applications.

Our final metric for evaluation surrounds the user acceptability of our framework. Regarding information-privacy concerns of storing long-term, high-fidelity logs of user activity, we are hoping to ensure that users maintain total control and ownership of data captured by the system. One way we are starting to achieve this is storing all logs in access-protected databases on the user's own personal devices. A practical issue remaining, however, surrounds whether users can trust applications needing access to their protected activity logs; for this we are currently considering whether OS-kernel level data isolation and labelling approaches (such as those demonstrated in Asbestos [6]) could be applied.[2]

---

[1] A 2Ghz Intel Core Duo Macbook Pro with 2GB of RAM, running MacOS X 10.4.8, Java 1.5, Jena 2.5, mysql 5.0.16.

[2] The PLUM framework may be downloaded at `http://plum.csail.mit.edu`

References

1. Aizawa, K., Tancharoen, D., Kawasaki, S., Yamasaki, T.: Efficient retrieval of life log based on context and content. In: CARPE'04: Proceedings of the the 1st ACM workshop on Continuous archival and retrieval of personal experiences, pp. 22–31. ACM Press, New York (2004)
2. Begole, J.B., Tang, J.C., Hill, R.: Rhythm modeling, visualizations and applications. In: UIST '03: Proceedings of the 16th annual ACM symposium on User interface software and technology, pp. 11–20. ACM Press, New York (2003)
3. Bellotti, V., Dalal, B., Good, N., Flynn, P., Bobrow, D.G., Ducheneaut, N.: What a to-do: studies of task management towards the design of a personal task list manager. In: CHI '04: Proceedings of the SIGCHI conference on Human factors in computing systems, pp. 735–742. ACM Press, New York (2004)
4. Bush, V.: As we may think. The Atlantic Monthly 176(1), 101–108 (1945)
5. Cheyer, A., Park, J., Giuli, R.: Iris: Integrate relate infer share 1st Workshop on The Semantic Desktop 4th International Semantic Web Conference (November 2005)
6. Efstathopoulos, P., Krohn, M., VanDeBogart, S., Frey, C., Ziegler, D., Kohler, E., Mazires, D., Kaashoek, F., Morris, R.: Labels and event processes in the asbestos operating system. In: SOSP '05: Proceedings of the twentieth ACM symposium on Operating systems principles, pp. 17–30. ACM Press, New York (2005)
7. Esposito, D.: Windows hooks in the .net framework. MSDN Magazine (October 2002)
8. Fenstermacher, K.D., Ginsburg, M.: A lightweight framework for cross-application user monitoring. Computer 35(3), 51–59 (2002)
9. Fogarty, J., Hudson, S.E.: Toolkit support for developing and deploying sensor-based statistical models of human situations. In: To appear in CHI '07: Proceedings of the SIGCHI conference on Human factors in computing systems, ACM Press, New York (2007)
10. Gemmell, J., Williams, L., Wood, K., Lueder, R., Bell, G.: Passive capture and ensuing issues for a personal lifetime store. In: CARPE'04: Proceedings of the the 1st ACM workshop on Continuous archival and retrieval of personal experiences, pp. 48–55. ACM Press, New York (2004)
11. Lamming, M., Flynn, M.: Forget-me-not: intimate computing in support of human memory. In: Proceedings FRIEND21 Symposium on Next Generation Human Interfaces (1994)
12. Lassila, O., Swick, R.: Resource description framework RDF model and syntax specification
13. Mitchell, T., Wang, S., Huang, Y., Cheyer, A.: Extracting knowledge about users' activities from raw workstation contents. In: Proceedings of the 21st National Conference on Artificial Intelligence (AAAI-2006), Boston, MA (July 2006)
14. Rhodes, B., Crabtree, I.B.: Wearable computing and the remembrance agent. BT Technology Journal 16(3), 118–124 (1998)
15. van Kleek, M.: Thesis proposal: Proactive support for task and interrupt management (2006)
16. Thomaz, E.: Slife 1.0 (2007) http://www.slifelabs.com
17. Wilkinson, K., Sayers, C., Kuno, H., Reynolds, D.: Efficient RDF storage and retrieval in Jena (2003)

A Probabilistic Relational Student Model for Virtual Laboratories

Julieta Noguez[1], L. Enrique Sucar[2], and Enrique Espinosa[1]

[1] Tecnológico de Monterrey, Campus Ciudad de México,
Calle del Puente 222, Col. Ejidos de Huipulco, Tlalpan
14380 México, D.F., México
{jnoguez,enrique.espinosa}@itesm.mx
[2] Instituto Nacional de Astrofísica, Óptica y Electrónica,
Calle Luis Enrique Erro No, 1, Sta. María Tonantzintla,
72840, Puebla, México
esucar@inaoep.mx

Abstract. We have developed a novel student model based on probabilistic relational models (PRMs). This model combines the advantages of Bayesian networks and object-oriented systems. It facilitates knowledge acquisition and makes it easier to apply the model for different domains. The model is oriented towards virtual laboratories, in which a student interacts by doing experiments in a simulated or remote environment. It represents the students' knowledge at different levels of granularity, combining the performance and exploration behavior in several experiments, to decide the best way to guide the student in the next experiments. Based on this model, we have developed tutors for virtual laboratories in different domains. An evaluation of with a group of students, show a significant improvement in learning when a tutor based on the PRM model is incorporated to a virtual robotics lab.

1 Introduction

An intelligent tutoring system (ITS) tries to emulate a human tutor by adapting itself to the learner. A key element of an intelligent tutor is the student model, that provides knowledge about each student, so the ITS can adapt to the student needs. In the last years, Bayesian networks have become one of the preferred methods for student modeling [1, 2, 4]. However, building a Bayesian network model for a domain is a difficult and time consuming process, and in some cases the model can become too complex, and consequently the inference process could be slow for some applications, in particular those that require a real time response, as virtual laboratories.

Probabilistic relational models [3] (PRM's) provide a new approach to student modeling, integrating the expressive power of Bayesian networks and the facilities of relational models. They provide a more expressive, object-oriented representation that facilitates knowledge acquisition. We have developed a general student model for virtual laboratories based on PRMs, with two main contributions: (i) a generic architecture for incorporating intelligent tutors in virtual laboratories, and (ii) a student

C. Conati, K. McCoy, and G. Paliouras (Eds.): UM 2007, LNAI 4511, pp. 303–308, 2007.
© Springer-Verlag Berlin Heidelberg 2007

model representation based on probabilistic relational model that facilitates the development of ITS for virtual labs in different domains.

2   Probabilistic Relational Models

The basic entities in a PRM [3] are objects or domain entities. Objects in the domain are partitioned into a set of disjoint classes, $X_1, ...,X_n$. Each class is associated with a set of attributes $A(X_i)$. The dependency model is defined at the class level, allowing it to be used for any object in the class. A PRM specifies the probability distribution using the same underlying principles used in Bayesian networks. Each of the random variables in a PRM, the attributes $x.a$ of the individual objects x, is directly influenced by other attributes, which are its parents. A PRM therefore defines for each attribute, a set of parents and a local probabilistic model.

Applying PRMs to ITSs allows for the definition of different structures (*skeletons*) according to the characteristics of different types of students and experiments, which are instantiated as a Bayesian network. This helps to reduce the problem of complexity, because only a partial model is used for a particular student and experiment, avoiding the need to propagate in the whole network. This model also makes knowledge acquisition easier, because the instructor can define the model at a general level in terms of classes and attributes, from which the specific models are derived.

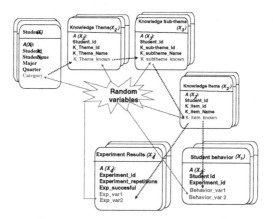

Fig. 1. A general PRM for virtual laboratories. The model specifies the main classes of objects, their attributes and the dependencies between some attributes (random variables).

3   A General Student Model Based on PRMs

In order to apply PRM's to student modeling we have to define the main objects involved in the domain. A general student model oriented to virtual laboratories was designed, starting form a high level structure at the class level, and ending with specific Bayesian networks for different experiments at the lower level. As shown in figure 1, the main classes, related with students and experiments, were defined. Once the model is specified at the class level, including the attributes and their dependencies, we can extract a *skeleton*, that is, a general Bayesian network for a fragment of the model. From the schema in figure 1, a general skeleton for virtual labs was derived, depicted in figure 2. The observations from the students' interactions with a virtual lab are represented by two classes: *experiment performance* and *experiment behavior*, which constitute the lowest level in the hierarchy. The intermediate level represents the different *knowledge items* associated to each experiment, linked to the highest level which groups the items in *sub-themes* and *themes*, and finally into the *students'* general category.

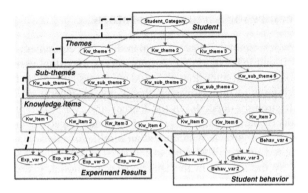

Fig. 2. A general skeleton obtained from the PRM in figure 1. This skeleton specifies a general model for any experiment, which is later instantiated to particular experiments.

From the skeleton, it is possible to define different instances according to the values of specific variables in the model. For example, from the general skeleton for experiments of figure 2, we can define particular instances for each experiment and student level, as it is shown in figure 3 In this case, we illustrate the generation of 9 different networks, for 3 experiments and 3 student levels.

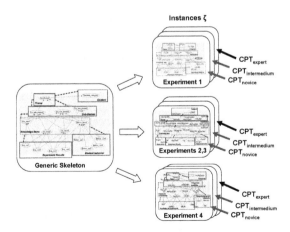

Fig. 3. From a generic skeleton (left), different instances of the student model are obtained, according to the experiment (1, 2 & 3, 4) and the student level (novice, medium, expert)

Once a specific Bayesian network is generated from the skeleton, it can be used to update the student model via standard probability propagation techniques [6]. In this case, it is used to propagate evidence from the experiment evaluation to the knowledge items, and then to the knowledge sub-themes and to the knowledge themes. After each experiment, the knowledge of the student at the different level of granularity is used by the tutor to decide if it should provide help to the student, and at what level of detail. Based on the student category, the tutor decides the difficulty of the next experiments to be presented to the student.

4   An Architecture for Virtual Laboratories

A virtual lab provides remote access to simulated or real equipment, so that students can interact with it and learn by doing. A tutor serves as virtual assistant in this lab. Most virtual laboratories assume that the student learns just by performing experiments and observing the results. However, this is not, in general, an effective and efficient strategy. It strongly depends on the learner ability to explore adequately and interpret the results of the experiments [1]. We have developed a general architecture for virtual laboratories, figure 4. We coupled an *intelligent tutoring system* to the virtual laboratory, based on the PRM student model. The tutor follows the exploration and performance by the student in the lab, updates its model, gives the appropriate help if required, and defines the next experiments.

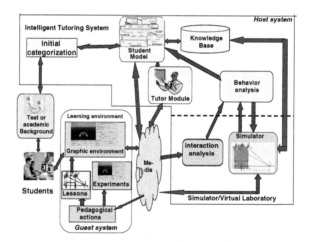

Fig. 4. A generic architecture for virtual laboratories integrating an intelligent tutor. The main elements in this architecture are: (i) a learning environment, (ii) a simulator (virtual laboratory), and (iii) an intelligent tutoring system.

5   Applications and Results

Based on the general architecture and the student model, we develop a virtual laboratory for mobile robotics that incorporates an ITS. To evaluate the impact of the tutor, and in particular the student model on learning, we performed a controlled experiment with a group of 20 students registered in a robotics course at ITESM, México. The class was divided into two groups, 10 students each. The *control group* experimented in the virtual laboratory without the tutor, while the *test group* had the advice of the tutor. A pretest was applied to all students in the concepts related with the experiments. After 2 weeks of experimentation in the virtual lab, a post-test was applied in the same topics. Figure 5 summarizes the results of the post-test for both groups, the pre-test results are also shown for comparison. The results show that the students that explore the virtual environment with the help of the tutor have a better performance [5].

Based on the generic architecture and a set of authoring tools, we have developed other applications: (i) a collaborative robotics laboratory, (ii) a remote lab for learning mobile robotics, and (iii) an introductory physics virtual laboratory. The general model helped to reduce the development time of the ITS for these labs.

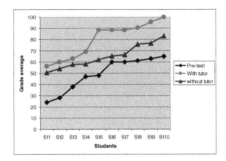

Fig. 5. A comparison of the *test* (with tutor) vs. the *control* (without tutor) groups. The graph shows the students' grade averages per student, in ascending order. The average of pre-test of both groups is included.

6   Conclusions and Future Work

We have developed a generic architecture for integrating intelligent tutoring systems and virtual laboratories. The main element of this architecture is a generic student model based on PRM's. By defining a general framework based on the PRM student model, this can be easily adapted for different experiments, domains and student levels. Based on this generic model we have developed several learning environments. One of them, the virtual robotics laboratory, has been evaluated with a group of students, demonstrating a better learning performance for students with help of the tutor compared to students without help. As future work we plan to integrate our tools in a general authoring tool for ITS for virtual labs.

References

1. Bunt, A., Conati, C.: Probabilistic Student Modelling to Improve Exploratory Behaviour. Journal of User. Modeling and User.-Adapted Interaction 13(3), 269–309 (2003)
2. Conati, C., Gertner, A., VanLehn, K., Druzdel, M.: On line student modeling for coached problem solving using Bayesian networks. In: En Jameson, A., Paris, C., Tasso, C (eds.) Using Modeling: Proceedings of Sixth International Conference. UM97, pp. 231–242. Springer, Heidelberg (1997)

3. Koller, D.: Probabilistic Relational Model. In: Ozevosky, S., Flach, P. (eds.) 9th International Workshop Inductive Logic Programming 1999, pp. 3–13. Springer Verlag, Heidelberg (1999)
4. Mayo, M., Mitrovic, A.: Optimising ITS behaviour with Bayesian networks and decision theory. International Journal of Artificial Intelligence in Education 12(2), 124–153 (2001)
5. Noguez, J., Sucar, L.E.: Intelligent Virtual Laboratory and Project Oriented Learning for Teaching Mobile Robotics. International Journal in Engineering Education, vol. 44(4), pp. 743–757. Tempus Publications (2006) Special Issue on Robotics Education.
6. Pearl, J.: Probabilistic Reasoning in Intelligent Systems. Morgan Kauffman, San Mateo California (1988)

A Semantics-Based Dialogue for Interoperability of User-Adaptive Systems in a Ubiquitous Environment

Federica Cena[1] and Lora M. Aroyo[2]

[1] Department of Computer Science – University of Turin, Italy
{Federica.Cena}@di.unito.it
[2] Department of Computer Science – Free University of Amsterdam, The Netherlands
{l.m.aroyo}@cs.vu.nl

Abstract. In this paper we present an approach to enable interoperability of user-adaptive systems (UASs) in a ubiquitous environment. We model the interactions between systems as a semantics-based dialogue for exchanging user model and context data. We focus on the user data clarification and negotiation tasks, and show how semantics enables, on the one hand, the understanding among user-adaptive systems in a distributed ubiquitous setting, and on the other hand indirectly improves their effectiveness in producing end user results. We deploy and evaluate our approach in the UbiquiTO mobile adaptive tourist guide.

1 Introduction

Adaptation is particularly important for applications in ubiquitous environments, since the variety of users, contexts, and devices implies a huge diversity of user needs to be met [12]. As the users interact with various adaptive systems there are different chunks of user data residing in each of them. There is no common "memory" to keep track of user activities and maintain up-to-date set of user preferences and characteristics. Such a 'memory-bank' would allow for an adequate adaptation to the user and her current context. One way of achieving a rather complete picture of the user's experience is to allow the systems in the ubiquitous setting to share user data and thus provide sufficient information for better adaptation [12]. Systems can share user data by accessing a common storage [9]; alternatively, we can allow direct communication between the applications. In open ubiquitous environment, treating interaction between UASs as a method invocation (as in object-oriented programming) is not appropriate [1]. "These methods assume providing a fixed functionality defined at design time independently of the conditions of their use" [12]. Instead, one of the most important requirements in ubiquitous settings is to gather information at run time about the context in which the interaction occurs (e.g. among users, devices, places, systems involved). At the same time, we need some mechanism for managing critical situations (e.g. clarify or negotiate the data) and being reactive to the context.

C. Conati, K. McCoy, and G. Paliouras (Eds.): UM 2007, LNAI 4511, pp. 309–313, 2007.
© Springer-Verlag Berlin Heidelberg 2007

To address such environment requirements, we propose to model the interaction between UASs as a *semantic dialogue*[1] and in this way to achieve: *user-awareness, semantic-awareness, context-awareness,* and *reactive behaviour* beneficial for the negotiation and clarification of user data in critical situations.

Section 2 sketches a typical interaction scenario to outline the requirements for its realization. In Section 3 we present the semantics-based conversational framework, which deployment is further illustrated in the example presented in Section 4. Finally, Section 5 discusses evaluation aspects within the context of the UbiquiTO test bed.

2   Interoperability Scenario

Mario is an art student at the University of Torino. He has an assignment to write about religious buildings in Torino. He uses his mobile adaptive tourist guide UbiquiTO [6] to gather quickly information about the religious buildings in Torino. To provide this information tailored to Mario's features and context, UbiquiTO needs prior information, i.e. buildings Mario has already seen; what does he so far know about religious art; what is his personal interest in this and related topics. UbiquiTO has already a user profile of Mario but it does not contain all the information necessary to answer those questions. Thus, UbiquiTO searches for other systems (e.g. ARRS [5]) used by Mario and sends them requests for the needed information. UbiquiTO and ARRS first agree on Mario identity. Then, UbiquiTO requests from ARRS the values for Mario's interest in the concept "churches". To provide the correct values, ARRS needs to clarify the request (e.g. churches as sightseeing or as religious objects). UbiquiTO receives the values and the level of certainty for each of them. If this level is not sufficient, it continues the dialogue exploring the domain and Mario's profile for related relevant concepts (e.g. different church styles and religious historical buildings). If, however, it detects that Mario is in a hurry, it uses the values from ARRS despite their low confidence level in order to optimize the response time.

3   Semantics-Based Conversational Framework

In this section, we illustrate our approach for user-adaptive systems interaction in ubiquitous environments. First, we show how we model systems interactions as a dialogue; second, we demonstrate the enriching of this the model with semantics.

Dialogue Games. We base the systems interaction in our scenario on the notion of a dialogue game as introduced by Levin, Moore [10] and Dimitrova [8], "a Dialogue Game (DG) represents an interaction episode concerning a particular goal and discussion topic"[8], and is formally defined as a 5-tuple $<C,P,R,U,S>$ [2], where $C=$ is the *focus*, the set of all possible concepts that can be exchanged during the dialogue; $P =$ the set of *pre-conditions* necessary to trigger the game; $R =$ the actions to perform at the end of the game (*post-conditions*); $U=$ *tactics* is a set of rules to produce speech acts, thus for selecting the moves and the scope of each move, and $S=$

---

[1] A dialogue is a set of Speech Acts [11] performed by actors with the intention to accomplish certain purposes. The basic idea of *dialogue-based* approaches is to represent the interaction process with the conversational conventions used by humans in natural conversation [3].

scopes is the set of the concepts from the focus to be used in speech acts. The systems interact with a set of speech acts (SA), defined by the tactics of the specific game. A statement about the user model is represented as a triple *<concept, value, belief>*. To meet the requirements in section 2, we identify three main games (details in [4]):

i) a *concept-exploratory game* supports *semantic-awareness* by collecting information about the *concepts* and *relations* in the knowledge base. It can be used to negotiate the response, when an exact match is not available; or to clarify the request.
ii) a *value-informative game* supports the *context awareness* and *user awareness* requirements. It informs the actors of the values or beliefs of the other system's knowledge base.
iii) an *explicative game* supports also the *semantics awareness* requirement. It is used when there are a discrepancy in the actors' believes, that needs to be justified.

Semantic-based Dialogue. To address the limitations that emerge in the application of this approach in an ubiquitous environment [4], we express the data model in terms of a common language and shared vocabularies. This provides a common understanding of the exchanged data among the systems and allows them to reason on the semantics of data (on the concepts relations and on the properties value) to decide the next steps of a dialogue.

Reasoning with concepts relations refers to probing for typed properties of a given concept and thus creating the focus of the game and the scope of the next SA. Typed properties are considered here as upper-level concepts (`parents`), low-level concepts (`children`), and directly related concepts at the same level (`siblings`). In our scenario, UbiquiTO requests the concepts `museum` and `historical_building` because they are siblings of the topic (`church`) and they share the property `has_style`. The implication here is that if there is no exact match of the requested concepts, the value of some of the children concepts can be used instead.

Reasoning with properties values refers to considering the property values to select the appropriate scope concepts (S) and to order them according to the game tactics (U). For example, the property `informative factor` expresses the level of usefulness with respect to a specific goal. This allows us to rank the concepts according to their informative factor. In the scenario, UbiquiTO asks ARRS for a username and a birth place, since they are the concepts with the highest informative factors for the goal of user identification.

To conclude, the reasoning with *concept relations* and with *property-values* allows to improve the efficiency of the dialogue, by providing the means to rationally explore a knowledge base and using more efficient tactics for the SAs sequencing.

4 Example: Interoperability Scenario with Semantics Dialogue

Mario selects `visit` → `churches` in UbiquiTO. Since it does not have all the required information to satisfy Mario's request, UbiquiTO initiates a dialog with ARRS[2] to find the missing values. UbiquiTO accesses the public *dialogue API* and implements *strategies rules* to decide which dialogue game to play.

---

[2] The searching of external system does not influence the dialogue management. Thus, we focus only on what happens when the system is found and the interaction starts.

USER IDENTIFICATION - opening a value-informative game

UbiquiTO: Do you have username="Mario"?   *(<inquire move>)*
ARRS: I have username="Mario".   *(<accept move>)*
UbiquiTO: Do you have birthplace="Turin" where username="Mario"?   *(<inquire move>)*
ARRS: I have birthplace ="Turin" and username="Mario"   *(<accept move>)*

UbiquiTO asks ARRS about the `username` of Mario. ARRS confirms and UbiquiTO asks for the next relevant concept for user identification (`birthplace`). The dialogue ends when, according to its identification algorithm, UbiquiTO can reliably assume that they are speaking of the same user. *Scope concepts* in the dialogue are ordered by a *properties-value reasoning* considering the informative factor of each value property. Once the user is identified, the *(<Q, R inquire, user_interest(church)>)* is sent to ARRS. Not having an exact match, ARRS initiates a concepts-explorative game to clarify the request.

QUERY REFINEMENT- starting a concept-explorative game

ARRS: Do you want concept="church" in context = "religious celebration"?   *(<inquire move>)*
UbiquiTO: No, I do not.   *(<deny move>)*
ARRS: Do you want concept="church" in context=" place to visit"?   *(<inquire move>)*
UbiquiTO want information about concept="building".   *(<accept move>)*

ARRS inquires for super-concepts of "church" (e.g. church as religious celebration, or place to visit). The choice of concepts here is done considering the relations among the concepts with *concepts-relation reasoning*. ARRS answers does not satisfy UbiquiTO's request. According to the *strategies rules*, UbiquiTO starts an exploration of related concepts for achieving similar/equivalent results.

RESPONSE NEGOTIATION- starting a concept-explorative game

UbiquiTO: Do you know user interest value in romanic_church?   *(<inquire move>)*
ARRS: yes, value is 0.6   *(<inform move>)*
UbiquiTO: Do you have user interest in gothic_church?   *(<inquire move>)*
ARRS: No, I don't   *(<deny move>)*
UbiquiTO: Do you know user interest in historical_building?   *(<inquire move>)*
ARRS: yes, it is value=0.4   *(<inform move>)*

UbiquiTO inquires the interest values for the *children* of `church`, (e.g. `Romanic`, `Gothic`), and then for its *sibling* `historical_buildings`. Even without an exact interest value, UbiquiTO can infer it as an average of the values of related concepts. At each dialog step, UbiquiTO determines the commitment on the context. If context change occurs UbiquiTO changes the focus, e.g. from *children* to *siblings*. The dialogue ends when UbiquiTO detects a critical context condition.

5   Evaluation and Discussion

Here we discuss the results of the approach evaluation with the UbiquiTO system (for details see [4]). In sec. 4 we saw that, in the interaction with ARRS, UbiquiTO is able to: i) have more reliable user data; and ii) provide the user with better results. We focus only on the first aspect as producing results depends on many additional parameters, besides the input data (e.g. system internal strategies). The test subjects consisted of 15 ARRS's users selected by an availability of sampling strategy. The experimental tasks were organized in three steps. *STEP 1*: users interact with UbiquiTO as a stand-alone system. *STEP 2*: users perform the same tasks as in STEP 1 while UbiquiTO interacts with ARRS. Finally, we compared the results from STEP 1 and STEP 2 with respect to the user model dimensions in order to see *how the user model changes after the interaction dialogue for additional user data.* To estimate in a numerical fashion the changes in the user model, we measured the *Confidence Level* (i.e. a measure of the "subjective validity" of the value, expressed as a system belief in how much the value is reliable). The *Confidence Level* is calculated in the situation i) and ii): the value moved from 0.37 to 0.55 with an average increment of the 17.9 %. We can now conclude from the tests that a dialogue is useful to improve user model data (and as a consequence adaptation results) only if the exchanged data are good. Thus, it needs to be supported by some mechanism for data evaluation [7].

Advantages of the semantic dialogue: it is suitable to model the interaction among UASs in ubiquitous environments since it addresses context requirements; it improves adaptation results, since it allows efficient interoperability interactions for reaching more reliable user data. *Disadvantages of the semantic dialogue*: it can occur only among known systems; it supports only bilateral interactions; it is time consuming and requires lots of computational efforts (to consider all contextual conditions).

References

1. Ardissono, L., Petrone, G., Segnan, M.: A conversational approach to the interaction with web services, Computational intelligence, vol. 20(4) (2004)
2. Aroyo, L., Denaux, R., Dimitrova, V., Pye, M.: Interactive Ontology-Based User Knowledge Acquisition : A Case Study, in the proceedings of UM, workshop (2005)
3. Benatallah, B., Casasti, F., Toumani, F., Hamadi, R.: Conceptual Modeling of web service Conversations. In: Eder, J., Missikoff, M. (eds.) CAiSE 2003. LNCS, vol. 2681, Springer, Heidelberg (2003)
4. Cena, F.: The role of semantic dialogue for adaptation in ubiquitous environment. PhD dissertation, Turin University (2007)
5. Cena, F., Torre, I.: Adapting the Interaction in a Call Centre Interacting with Computers, Interacting with Computers, vol. 18(3). Elsevier, Amsterdam (May 2006)
6. Cena, F., et al. (ed.): Integrating heterogeneous adaptation techniques to build a flexible and usable mobile tourist guide, AICommunication, vol. 19(4), pp. 301–400. IOS Press, Amsterdam (2006)
7. Carmagnola, F., Cena, F.: From Interoperable User Model to Interoperable User Modeling. In: Wade, V., Ashman, H., Smyth, B. (eds.) AH 2006. LNCS, vol. 4018, pp. 20–23. Springer, Heidelberg (2006)
8. Dimitrova, V.: Interactive Open Learner Modelling, Leeds University (2001)
9. Kobsa, A.: Generic user modeling systems. UMUAI 11(1-2), 49–63 (2001)
10. Levin, J., Moore, J.: Dialogue games: meta-communication structures for natural language interaction. Cognitive Science 1(4), 395–420 (2000)
11. Searle, J.: What is a Speech Act. In: Giglioli, P. (ed.) Language and social context, pp. 136–154. Penguin Books Ltd, Harmoudsworth, Middlesex
12. Vassileva, J., McCalla, G., Greer, J.: Multi-Agent Multi-User Modeling. User. Modeling and User.-Adaptive Interaction 13(1), 179–210 (2003)
13. Vassileva, J.: Distributed user modeling for universal information access. HCI (2001)

A User Independent, Biosignal Based, Emotion Recognition Method

G. Rigas[1], C.D. Katsis[1,2], G. Ganiatsas[1], and D.I. Fotiadis[1]

[1] Unit of Medical Technology and Intelligent Information Systems, Dept. of
Computer Science, University of Ioannina, GR 451 10 Ioannina, Greece
[2] Dept. of Medical Physics, Medical School, University of Ioannina, GR 451 10
Ioannina, Greece
{rigas,fotiadis}@cs.uoi.gr, {me00526,gganiats}@cc.uoi.gr

Abstract. A physiological signal based emotion recognition method, for
the assessment of three emotional classes: *happiness, disgust* and *fear*, is
presented. Our approach consists of four steps: (i) biosignal acquisition,
(ii) biosignal preprocessing and feature extraction, (iii) feature selection
and (iv) classification. The input signals are facial electromyograms, the
electrocardiogram, the respiration and the electrodermal skin response.
We have constructed a dataset which consists of 9 healthy subjects. Moreover we present preliminary results which indicate on average, accuracy
rates of $0.48, 0.68$ and 0.69 for recognition of happiness, disgust and fear
emotions, respectively.

Keywords: emotion recognition, biosignals, classification.

1 Introduction

Ongoing research efforts focus on empowering computers to understand human
emotion. A number of findings from neuroscience, physiology and cognitive science, suggests that emotion plays a critical role in rational and intelligent behavior. Apparently, emotion interacts with thinking in ways that are not obvious
but important for intelligent functioning [1]. Furthermore, there are numerous
areas in human computer interaction that could efficiently use the capability
to understand emotion. For example it is accepted that emotional ability is an
essential factor for the next generation of robots [2]. Understanding emotion
can also play a significant role in intelligent rooms [3] and affective computer
tutoring [4]. To our knowledge, only a small number of studies reported in the
literature have demonstrated biosignal based affective recognition that is applicable to multiple users [5]. Apparently, a user independent method is essential
for a practical application, so that the users do not have to be bothered with
training of the system. Furthermore, current systems require 2-5 minutes signal in order to reach to a decision [6,7]. In this paper, we present, a biosignal
based, user independent emotion recognition method. In this paper we propose
a method for emotion recognition, which is fully automated and requires only

C. Conati, K. McCoy, and G. Paliouras (Eds.): UM 2007, LNAI 4511, pp. 314–318, 2007.
© Springer-Verlag Berlin Heidelberg 2007

ten second data acquisition for the signals. The method consists of four steps: (i) biosignal acquisition, (ii) biosignal preprocessing and feature extraction, (iii) feature selection and (iv) classification. The investigated emotional classes are fear, disgust and happiness.

2   Materials and Methods

2.1   Biosignal Acquisition and Dataset

The user's emotional state is defined using information obtained from the following biosignals: facial electromyograms (EMGs), electrocardiogram (ECG), respiration effort and electrodermal activity (EDA). The following set of biosensors are used: (i) for the EMGs signals special thin and flexible surface EMGs grid sensors [8] are placed on the subject's face (a total of 16 EMG channels), (ii) for the ECG, a g.ECG sensor [9] is placed on the subject's thorax, (iii) for the respiration a g.RESP [9] Piezoelectric Respiration Sensor is placed around the subject's thorax and (iv) for the EDA two Ag/AgCl galvanic skin response sensors are attached on the subject's middle and index fingers. We consructed an emotion-specific physiological dataset. We use a set of affective pictures (carefully selected, by an experienced physiologist) drawn from the International Affective Picture System (IAPS) [10], to make the subjects experience the emotional states of interest (fear, disgust and happiness) and simultaneously acquire the various biosignals that accompany them. After being exposed to the outer stimulus the subjects were self annotating their emotional state using the acknowledged technique SAM (Self Assessment Manikin) [11]. SAM has been broadly used for the measurement of the emotional states in a variety of situations including reactions to pictures, images, sounds and advertisements [12]. The obtained dataset consists of 9 subjects and a total number of 118 instances, 30 of them corresponding to happiness, 55 to disgust and 33 to fear.

2.2   Biosignal Pre-processing and Feature Extraction

The acquired raw biosignals are pre-processed using low-pass filters at 500 Hz and 100 Hz for the facial EMGs and ECG respectively, and smoothing (moving average) filters for the respiration and EDA signals. The resolution used for signal digitization is 12 bit. The extracted features from each signal are shown in Table 1, and described in detail in [13].

2.3   Feature Selection

The Simba algorithm [14] is used for feature selection, since it outperforms compared to other well known feature selection algorithms [14]. Having applied the Simba algorithm, from the initial number of 44 features only 9 are selected. These features are shown in Table 2.

Table 1. The features extracted for each of the acquired biosignals (facial EMG, ECG, respiration, and EDA)

EMG	ECG	RESPIRATION	EDA
Mean value	Mean amplitude	Mean amplitude	Mean amplitude
Standard deviation	Rate	Rate	Rate
	Means of absolute values of first differences	Means of absolute values of first differences	Means of absolute values of first differences
	Mean Frequency		Mean rise duration
	Median Frequency		

Table 2. Selected Features ordered by their significance

#	Feature	#	Feature
1	Respiration Rate	6	Left Frontalis Standard Deviation
2	Heart Rate	7	Right Frontalis Standard Deviation
3	Right Masseter Standard Deviation	8	Right Nasalis Standard Deviation
4	Means of absolute of first differences of EDA	9	Left Nasalis Standard Deviation
5	Right Masseter Standard Deviation		

2.4 Classification

In order to exploit the proposed method's potential we have employed the K-NN [15] and the Random Forests [16] classifiers.

3 Results

The method is evaluated using the dataset described in Section 2.1. In order to minimize the bias associated with the random sampling of the training and testing data samples, we use 10 fold cross-validation. For our experiments we use the Weka environment [17]. In Table 3, we present for both classifiers the confusion matrix, the True Positive (TP), False Positive (FP) rates and Precisions for each class. Random Forests and K-NN result in statistically similar performance. However, K-NN performs slightly better. To verify that this slight advantage is not due to the feature selection algorithm, we perform an experiment using the Principal Component Analysis (PCA) [18] instead of the Simba feature selection algorithm. PCA is a well known feature reduction method where the features, using a transformation matrix, are projected into a lower dimension space. The results are shown in Table 4. We notice that there is a significant decrease in performance for both K-NN and Random Forests. Thus, using feature selection in our problem we obtain better performance than feature reduction. Moreover, we notice that K-NN does not outperform Random Forest when PCA is used.

Table 3. Results for (a) K-NN, and (b) Random Forests

Class	Conf. Mat.			TP Rate	FP Rate	Precision
HAPPINESS	14	11	5	0.47	0.19	0.45
DISGUST	10	42	3	0.76	0.32	0.68
FEAR	7	9	17	0.52	0.09	0.68

(a)

Class	Conf. Mat.			TP Rate	FP Rate	Precision
HAPPINESS	13	13	4	0.43	0.16	0.48
DISGUST	10	41	4	0.75	0.38	0.63
FEAR	4	11	18	0.55	0.09	0.69

(b)

Table 4. Results of the K-NN and Random Forest classifiers using the Simba feature selection and PCA approach

	K-NN (K=1)	Random Forests
Simba	**62.70(14.57)**	62.41(12.58)
PCA	50.64(13.92)	**50.81(12.04)**

4   Discussion-Conclusions

In this work, a user independent emotion recognition method is presented. A 10 second period window has been selected based on the fact that there is a time delay between the instance that the subject experienced an emotion and the corresponding response changes in the selected biosignals [19].

Our initial results are promising, indicating the ability to differentiate the three emotional classes. A direct comparison to related approaches, is not feasible since they are applied in different biosignals, number and type of emotional classes.

It must be noticed that we are well aware that the current form and method of application of the biosensors is anything but intuitive and natural. However, considering the current trend towards wearable computing, it can be expected that the biosensors will be sooner tinny enough to be impended into clothing and jewellery [6]. For research purposes we have chosen the aforementioned sensors since they allow a certain flexibility e.g. in terms of placement of the sensors. This flexibility is important given the fact that many aspects of sensor usage are not completely clear, e.g. which facial muscle EMG signals are the most appropriate in order to manifest an emotional state [5]. An important component of our future work is to increase the number of emotions under investigation and to reduce the set of acquired biosignals which may allow for less complicated sensor arrangements to be developed.

Acknowledgments

This work is part funded by the Greek Secretariat for Research and Technology (PENED: project 03ED139, Title: "Intelligent System for monitoring driver's emotional and physical state in real conditions").

References

1. Picard, R.W., Vyzas, E., Healey, J.: Toward machine emotional intelligence: Analysis of affective physiological state. IEEE Transactions Pattern Analysis and Machine Intelligence 23, 1175–1191 (2001)
2. Fujita, M., Takagi, T., Hasegawa, R., Arkin, R.C.: Ethnological modeling and architecture for an entertainment robot. pp. 453–458 (2001)
3. Cohen, M.H., Moser, M.C., Hasha, R., Flanagan, J.L., Hirsh, H.: Room service, al-style. IEEE intelligent systems 14, 8–19 (1999)
4. Picard, R.W.: Affective computing. MIT Press, Cambridge (1995)
5. Goronzy, S., Schaich, P., Williams, J., Haag, A.: Recognition using bio-sensors: First steps towards an automatic system, pp. 36–48. Springer, Heidelberg (2004)
6. Bang, S.W., Kim, S.R., Kim, K.H.: Emotion recognition system using short-term monitoring of physiological signals. Medical Biological Engineering and Computers 42, 419–427 (2004)
7. Dryer, D.C., Lu, D.J., Ark, W.: The emotion mouse. In: 8th International Conference Human Computer interaction, pp. 818–823 (1999)
8. Van Dijk, V., Jonas, I.E., Zwarts, M.J., Stegeman, D.F., Lapatki, B.G.: A thin, flexible multielectrode grid for high-density surface emg. J. Appl Physiol 96, 327–336 (2004)
9. (Last visited 10-11-2006) http://cortechsolutions.com/g.sensors.htm
10. Ghman, A., Vaitl, D., Lang, P.J.: The international affective picture system [photographic slides]. Technical report, Gainesville, The Center for Research in Psychophysiology, University of Florida (1988)
11. Greenwald, M.K., Bradley, M.M., Hamm, A.O., Lang, P.J.: Looking at pictures: evaluative, facial, visceral and behavioral responses. Psychophysiology (1993)
12. Bradley, M., Bowers, D., Lang, P., Heilman, K., Morris, M.: Valence-specific hypoarousal following right temporal lobectomy (1991)
13. Katsis, C.D., Ganiatsas, G., Fotiadis, D.I.: An integrated telemedicine platform for the assessment of affective physiological states. Diagnostic Pathology 1, 1–16 (2006)
14. Navot, A., Tishby, N., Gilad-Bachrach, R.: Margin based feature selection - theory and algorithms. In: Proc. 21International Conference on Machine Learning (ICML) (2004)
15. Darrell, T., Indyk, P., Shakhnarovish, G. (eds.): Nearest-Neighbor Methods in Learning and Vision. MIT Press, Cambridge (2005)
16. Breiman, L.: Random forests. Machine Learning, 45 (2001)
17. Frank, E., Witten, I.H.: Data Mining: Practical machine learning tools and techniques, 2nd edn. San Francisco (2005)
18. Pearson, K.: On lines and planes of closest fit to systems of points in space. Philosophical Magazine 2, 559–572 (1901)
19. Schell, A.M., Filion, D.L., Dawson, M.E.: Handbook of psychophysiology. Cambridge University Press, Cambridge (2000)

A User Model of Psycho-physiological Measure of Emotion

Olivier Villon and Christine Lisetti

Institut Eurécom, 2229 route des crêtes,
F-06904 Sophia Antipolis Cedex, France*
{villon,lisetti}@eurecom.fr

Abstract. The interpretation of physiological signals in terms of emotion requires an appropriate mapping between physiological features and emotion representations. We present a user model associating psychological and physiological representation of emotion in order to bring findings from the psychophysiology domain into User-Modeling computational techniques. We discuss results based on an experiment we performed based on bio-sensors to get physiological measure of emotion, involving 40 subjects.

1 Introduction

Affective computing systems based on psychophysiology aim at interpreting user's physiological activity (e.g. heart rate -HR- and skin conductance -SC-) as discrete emotions or affective dimensions toward near to real time recognition of emotion [1,2,3,4]. Main approaches to perform emotion recognition use user-independent data (with a common training database for different subjects) and enable to build user-models including the user's emotions from that recognition process. Indeed, existing litterature point to the existence of relation between physiological signals and their psychological emotional meaning (e.g. heart rate acceleration and fear are usually positively correlated across subjects [5]. However emotional specificity of subjects [6] suggests that we should take into account in a user model specifity for a particular user. Other existing approaches to emotion recognition are single-subject based and are therefore not fully generalizable but allow precise user's model.

2 Psycho-physiological Emotion Map as a U.M. Representation

Our proposed User Model (UM) aim at mapping physiological emotional measures with associated psychological emotional measures in a emotional given situation, for a specific user (but using both user-dependent and user-independent

---

* The authors would like to acknowledge that this work was partially founded by ST Microelectronics in the framework of the Region Provence-Alpes-Côte-d'Azur (PACA) PACALab.

C. Conati, K. McCoy, and G. Paliouras (Eds.): UM 2007, LNAI 4511, pp. 319–323, 2007.
© Springer-Verlag Berlin Heidelberg 2007

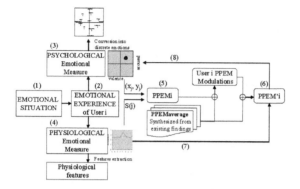

Fig. 1. Psycho Physiological Emotional Map construction and use

data): the Psycho Physiological Emotional Map (**PPEM**, see figure 1) [7]. *In a UM learning phase*, we provide a set of emotional situations to the user (1), which elicit affective experiences (2). We perform psychological (3) and physiological (4) measures associated to the affective experience. The psychological measure can be converted into different representations (discrete and dimensional). A set of features extraction is performed from the physiological measure. Then, the user model called PPEM (single subject form) is built from the association of psycho-physiological measure (5), for the user *i*. Then, from a PPEMaverage (user-independent data : synthesis of existing findings in terms of psycho-physiological maps), we build the modulations from this average for this subject. Finally, by combining these modulations with the PPEMaverage, we build the PPEM'i (parametric form combining user-independent and user-dependent data) which will be used to recognize emotion. *In a UM use phase*, we continuously measure physiological signal from the user and extract features related to emotion (7). By comparing the current features values, with the contents of the PPEM'i, we estimate the emotion representation actually felt by the user (8).

3   Experiment and Results

3.1   Materials and Methods

We performed an experiment to test the possibilities to build the proposed user model. 40 subjects participated (21 men and 19 women, average 32 years old). A set of 61 stimuli (31 images, 5 videos, 25 sounds)was selected to be varied regarding the type of media (audio, visual et video), the contents and the intented emotional characteristic (i.e. pre validated by a population, e.g. 31 images from the International Affective Picture System [8] and 2 videos from [9]), to try to cover the most extended range of emotion. Figure 2 shows the three steps exposure and emotional measure of the same stimuli, performed by each subject. Phase (1) was a slideshow of stimuli and recording of physiological measure (heart rate and skin conductance, using Bodymedia armband used on the left

Fig. 2. The three steps of emotion measures for the experiment

hand and an adapted polar T31 transmitter). Phase (2) was a *static* classification of the same stimuli in the emotional space of expression made of valence*arousal dimensions. Phase (3) was a *dynamic* measure of the valence, during a slideshow of the dynamic stimuli.

3.2 Data Preprocessing and Statistical Analysis

Psychological data. For each subjects, we estimated the position in the valence arousal space as discrete emotion (using the Circumplex model [10] and by dividing the valence and arousal space into five regions), to study the compatibility of both representations into our user model (see figure 3 for an example of clustering).

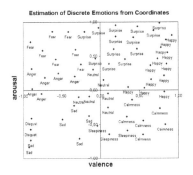

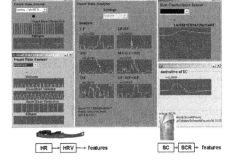

Fig. 3. Estimation of Discrete Emotion from the valence and arousal coordinates expressed by a subject

Fig. 4. Designed Real Time Heart Rate and Skin Conductance Emotional Feature Analyzer

Physiological features. We extracted from the physiological signals 28 features related to emotion (detailed in table 1 with our implementation shown in figure 4). Skin conductance (SC), Skin Conductance level (SCL, the tonic signal in SC), and Skin Conductance Responses (SCRs, the phasic signal in SC, considered as discrete events) were extracted for each stimulus. Heart Rate (HR) and Heart Rate Variablity (the variability in different frequency bands, based on FFTs) were extracted. **Analysis at intra-individual level.** Figure 6 plots the number of subjects which presented a significant linear correlation

Table 1. SC-related and HR-related features calculated for each multimedia stimulus

SC-related Features	Description	HR-related Features	Description
SC (raw)	SCAverage	HR (raw)	HRAverage
	SCMaxAmplitude		HRMin
SCL	SCLOnsetOffsetDiff		HRMax
SCR	SCRsRelativeNb	HRV, in each Freq. bands :	$meanE_i$
	timeStart	with i =LF, MF or HF)	$minE_i$
	meanRiseTime		$maxE_i$
	meanAmplitude		$meanDerivativeE_i$
			sympathovagalBalance
			relativeMFPower
			totalVariability

	a_0	a_1	a_2
PPEMaverage	0.143	0.05	-0.113
subject 1	0.029	-0.128	0.158
dx_1	0.029	0.151	-0.054
subject 2	0.258	0.236	-0.384
dx_2	-0.199	-0.213	0.488

Fig. 5. Built PPEM$'_i$ from PPEMaverage and PPEM$_i$ for two subjects

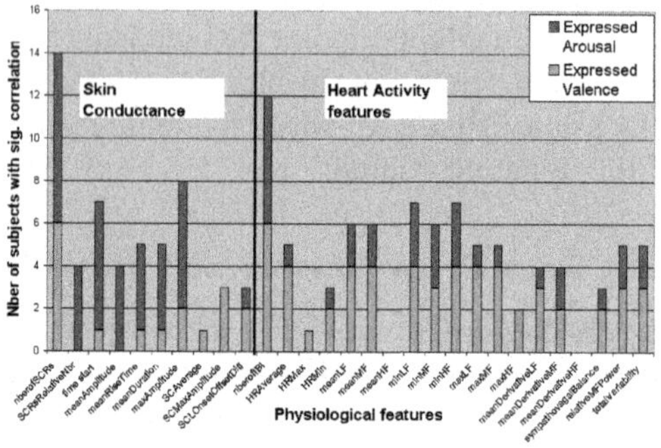

Fig. 6. Number of subjects for which we found a significant linear correlation, for each feature

($p < 0.05$) between physiological features and psychological representation of emotion expressed in the provided valence and arousal space. This results confirm the general population trend that heart rate could be used as an indicator of valence, while skin conductance could be used as an indicator of arousal. Moreover, the different number of significant correlations for each subject is an indicator of inter individual differences.

Using dynamic emotional measure for user modeling. Intra-individual dynamic expression of valence could be considered for a user modeling of psychophysiology. Psychological features performed on the slider values (e.g. averaged rigth derivative of slider movement) analyzed with phyiological features lead in signficant results (a maximum of 63% of significants correlations was found, $p < 0.05$). Thus, the (a_j, b_j) components of PPEM could be taken into consideration. **Combining different emotion representations.** We tested statistically discrete emotion representation with physiological values. Results showed that the mean of 64% of physiological features in each emotion class statistically changes according to classes (One-way ANOVAs with F(1,63) and $p < 0.01$). This validates the possibility to combine dimensional and discrete psychological representations. **Psycho-physiological mappings, from PPEMi to PPEM'i.** We built PPEM'i using multilinear regression model based on least squares method. For example, $valence = a_0 + a_1x_1 + a_2x_2$, with x_1 and x_2 two features values, and a_0, a_1 and a_2 the associated coefficients, could be the model of a subject. Differences between the coefficients provide differences between the psychophysiological mappings. We provide in table 5 an example of models we built for two subjects (PPEMi, user-dependent model) and their equivalent as PPEM'i (combination of user-dependent and user-independent data) using the population average (PPEMaverage, user-independent data) with valence as output. The PPEM$'_i$ combines user-dependent and user-independent data, and allows to compare model among subjects.

4   Discussion

We provided a user model (PPEM) which may help computer sensing of emotion by embedding average psychophysiological rules as well as what we learn from each user. Our results shows that (1) Combining different emotion representations (dimensional and discrete, dynamic and static) into one User Model is suitable ; (2) Considering the average population psychophysiological mappings could be taken into account to facilitate the user modeling. The PPEM$'_i$, which combines user-dependent and user-independent data, may help to model psychophysiological mappings of users, and thus increase the emotion recognition efficiency from physiological signals.

References

1. Picard, R., Healey, J., Vyzas, E.: Toward machine emotional intelligence, analysis of affective physiological signals. IEEE transactions on pattern analysis and machine intelligence, vol. 23(10) (2001)
2. Lisetti, C.L., Nasoz, F.: Using noninvasive wearable computers to recognize human emotions from physiological signals. EURASIP Journal on Applied Signal Processing 11, 1672–1687 (2004)
3. Kim, K.H., Bang, S.W., Kim, S.R.: Emotion recognition system using short-term monitoring of physiological signals. Medical & Biological Engineering & Computing, vol. 42 (2004)
4. Conati, C., Chabbal, R., Maclaren, H.: A study on using biometric sensors for monitoring user emotions in education games. In: Brusilovsky, P., Corbett, A.T., de Rosis, F. (eds.) UM 2003. LNCS, vol. 2702, Springer, Heidelberg (2003)
5. Peter, C., Herbon, A.: Emotion representation and physiology assignments in digital systems. Interacting with Computers 18(2), 139–170 (2006)
6. Fiorito, E., Simons, R.: Emotional imagery and physical anhedonia. Psychophysiology 31, 513–521 (1994)
7. Villon, O., Lisetti, C.: Toward building adaptive user's psycho-physiological maps of emotions using bio-sensors. In: Workshop on Emotion and Computing, KI (2006)
8. Lang, P., Bradley, M., Cuthbert, B.: International affective picture system (iaps): Digitized photographs, instruction manual and affective ratings. Technical report A-6. University of Florida (2005)
9. Rottenberg, J., Ray, R., Gross, J.: Emotion elicitation using films. In: Coan, J., Allen, J. (eds.) The handbook of emotion elicitation and assessment, Oxford University Press, New York (2006)
10. Russell, J.A.: A circumplex model of affect. Journal of Personality and Social Psychology 39(6), 1161–1178 (1980)

A User-Item Predictive Model for Collaborative Filtering Recommendation

Heung-Nam Kim[1], Ae-Ttie Ji[1], Cheol Yeon[1], and Geun-Sik Jo[2]

[1] Intelligent E-Commerce Systems Lab., Dept. of Information Engineering, Inha University
{nami, aerry13, entireboy}@eslab.inha.ac.kr
[2] School of Information Engineering, Inha University, Incheon, Korea
gsjo@inha.ac.kr

Abstract. Collaborative Filtering recommender systems, one of the most representative systems for personalized recommendations in E-commerce, enable users to find the useful information easily. But traditional CF suffers from some weaknesses: scalability and real-time performance. To address these issues, we present a novel model-based CF approach to provide efficient recommendations. In addition, we propose a new method of building a model with dynamic updates, when users present explicit feedback. The experimental evaluation on *MovieLens* datasets shows that our method offers reasonable prediction quality as good as the best of user-based Pearson correlation coefficient algorithm.

1 Introduction

Collaborative filtering is to predict the utility of a certain item for the target user based on the user's previous preferences or the opinions of other similar users, and thereby make proper recommendations [2]. Despite its success and popularity, traditional CF suffers from several problems: sparsity, scalability, and real-time performance. A number of model-based studies have attempted to address these problems [2, 4, 5, 6]. One notable fact in a model-based CF is that model-building can be accomplished offline prior to online recommendation. Thereby, model-based CF is typically faster in terms of recommendation time using the pre-computed model. However, the model-based approach encounters a new limitation: it is difficult to reflect new information instantaneously once the model is built. To solve the limitation, we present a novel model-based approach which supports dynamic updates with reasonable prediction quality. Our approach first determines similarities between the items, and subsequently identifies the confidence of the items, indicating the relevance of prior predictions. Furthermore, this paper presents a method of applying the model to a CF.

2 Building a User-Item Predictive Model

Before describing the algorithm, some definitions of the matrices are introduced.

C. Conati, K. McCoy, and G. Paliouras (Eds.): UM 2007, LNAI 4511, pp. 324–328, 2007.
© Springer-Verlag Berlin Heidelberg 2007

Definition 1 (Rating matrix, R). If there is a list of k users $U=\{u_1,u_2,\ldots,u_k\}$, a list of n items $I=\{i_1,i_2,\ldots i_n\}$, $k \times n$ user-item data can be represented as a *User-item rating matrix, R*. Each $R_{u,j}$ represents the rating of a user u on item i.

Definition 2 (Prediction matrix, P). From matrix R, the system can generate prediction for a target item i that is already rated by a target user u. Each $P_{u,i}$ represents the predicted values of a user u on an item i in a *User-item prediction matrix, P*.

Definition 3 (Absolute Error matrix, AE). From the set of explicit and predicted rating pairs $<R_{u,i}, P_{u,i}>$ for all the data in matrices R and P, a *User-item absolute error matrix, AE*, can be filled as absolute errors, which can be computed as $|R_{u,i} - P_{u,i}|$.

2.1 Item-Based Predictive Model

For constructing P and AE, a user's rating should be predicted for an item that has already been rated. The prediction for a target user u on item i, $P_{u,i}$, is obtained as:

$$P_{u,i} = \overline{R}_i + \frac{\sum_{j \in MSI(u)} (R_{u,j} - \overline{R}_j) \cdot sim(i, j)}{\sum_{j \in MSI(u)} |sim(i, j)|} \tag{1}$$

where $MSI(u)$ is the set of k most similar items to the target item i among items rated by the user u and $R_{u,j}$ is the rating of user u on item j. In addition, $\overline{R}_i$ and $\overline{R}_j$ refer to the average rating of item i and j. $sim(i, j)$ means the similarity between items i and j, which can be calculated using diverse similarity algorithms [2]. We also consider *the inverse item frequency*, which dictates that users rating numerous items present less contribution with regard to similarity than users rating a smaller number of items [6].

As a result of the absolute error matrix, the confidence of an item, which is indicating the relevance of prior predictions for an item, can be computed.

Definition 4 (Item Confidence). Let U_j be a set of users who has already rated for item j in the system and GU^ε_j a set of users whose an absolute error value on item j, $AE_{u,j}$, is less than an predefined error threshold ε, $AE_{u,j} \le \varepsilon$ and $GU^\varepsilon_j \subseteq U_j$. Then, the confidence of item j, $C_\varepsilon(j)$, is defined as

$$C_\varepsilon(j) = \frac{|U_j \cap GU^\varepsilon_j|}{|U_j|}$$

$C_\varepsilon(j)$ is in the interval [0, 1]. If $C_\varepsilon(j) = 0$ then all prior predictions for item j are not relevant whereas if $C_\varepsilon(j) = 1$ then the prior predictions for item j are always relevant.

2.2 Applying the Model to Collaborative Filtering

Our method is divided into an offline phase and an online phase. The former is a model building phase (section 2.1) and the latter is a prediction phase using the pre-computed model. We denominate our approach an *Item Confidence-based CF* (ICCF).

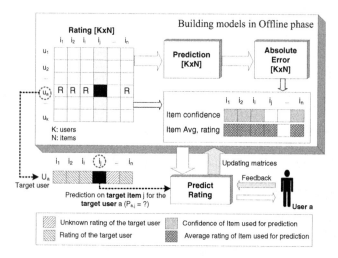

Fig. 1. Applying the model to a collaborative filtering recommendation

In order to compute the predicted rating, each column vector is normalized by subtracting the column average from each rating, and then the item confidence $C_\varepsilon(j)$ is used instead of using item-item similarity. Formally, the prediction $P_{u,i}$ is defined as:

$$P_{u,i} = \overline{R_i} + \frac{\sum_{j \in Item(u)} (R_{u,j} - \overline{R_j}) \cdot c_\varepsilon(j)}{\sum_{j \in Item(u)} c_\varepsilon(j)} \qquad (2)$$

where $Item(u)$ is a set of k highest confidence items which a user u rated and $c_\varepsilon(j)$ is the confidence of item j. In addition, $\overline{R_i}$ and $\overline{R_j}$ refers to the average rating of item i and j. The concept of this prediction is that items of the high confidence present more contribution with regard to prediction than items of the low confidence.

Once the model is built, it is difficult to reflect new information instantaneously despite its significance in the recommender system [3]. To alleviate this weakness, our approach is designed such that the model is updated effectively and users' new opinions are reflected incrementally. From the explicit user feedback, the three user-item matrices; R, P, and AE, can be easily updated. Subsequently item confidence can be re-computed from the updated AE. Therefore, our method can use the update information in the process of new predictions as well as make enhanced predictions.

3   Experimental Evaluation

The data set taken from the well known *MovieLens* contains 100,000 ratings of 1682 movies rated with 1 to 5 by 943 users. For evaluation, the total ratings were divided into two groups: 80% was used as *a training set* and 20% was used as *a test set*. To measure the accuracy of the predictions, *mean absolute error* (MAE), which is widely used for statistical measurements in the diverse algorithms [1, 2, 6] was adopted.

Model Building Experiments. As shown in Table 1, because of better prediction qualities than original similarity algorithms, the models constructed by Inverse item Frequency approaches are taken up in subsequent of experiments.

Table 1. Comparison of the prediction quality achieved by the different similarity measures

	Cos	CosIIF	Corr	CorrIIF	AdCos	AdCosIIF
MAE	0.7482	0.74751	0.75166	0.75124	0.75167	0.75158

3.1 Experiment Results

Experiments with the error threshold. As stated in Section 2.1, the confidence of an item is decided by an error threshold ε, so that the prediction quality is significantly affected by a value of ε. We evaluate a variation of MAE obtained by changing the ε value, when k was set to 30 and k was set to all items rated by the target user. The parameter k means a number of highest confidence items to use in prediction generation. As the ε value increases from 0.2 to 1.2, the prediction quality is improved, and when $\varepsilon=1.2$ was selected, the most accurate results is shown in both cases.

Experiments with k highest confidence items. The following experiments investigate the effect of the parameter k on the performance of CF. Different numbers of k items were selected by highest-confidence order for the prediction generation. Moreover, we selected all items ($k=all$) for the prediction generation process. The error threshold ε for computing item confidence was set to 0.8. Table 2 depicts the variation of an MAE of three methods as the value of k increases from 10 to 80. As the results, according to increment of k value, the prediction quality of three methods is improved.

Table 2. MAE according to variation of k value used in generating the prediction ($\varepsilon = 0.8$)

	10	30	50	70	80	all
ICCF+AdcosIIF	0.7872	0.7641	0.7614	0.7599	0.7589	0.7543
ICCF+CorrIIF	0.786	0.7657	0.7623	0.7594	0.7585	0.7542
ICCF+CosIIF	0.7851	0.7654	0.7620	0.7603	0.7590	0.7542

We conclude from the results that the proposed approaches provide better quality with growth of users opinions and do not consider the sensitivity on the optimal number of neighbors for the prediction generation unlike pure a user-based and an item-based CF.

Comparison to other methods. In order to compare the performance of the item confidence-based approaches, a user-based CF algorithm, wherein the similarity is computed by the Pearson correlation coefficient (denote as *UserCF*) [1], and the item-based CF approach of [2], which employs cosine-based similarity (denote as *ItemCF*), were implemented. And we compare the best result in MAE of each method. As noted a number of previous studies, the size of neighborhood k influences the prediction quality of user-based and item-based CF [2, 4, 6]. Therefore, different numbers of user/item neighbors k were used for the prediction generation in *UserCF* and *ItemCF*. As we can see from table 2, *ICCF+CosIIF* shows considerably improved performance compared to *ItemCF*. In addition, comparing the results achieved by *ICCF+CosIIF* and *UserCF*, our method offers reasonable prediction quality as good as *UserCF*.

Table 3. Comparison of the best results with other approaches

Algorithm	UserCF (k=60)	ItemCF (k=50)	ICCF+CosIIF (ε=0.8, k=all)	ICCF+CosIIF (ε=1.2, k=all)
MAE	0.75340	0.82306	0.75418	0.75386

4   Conclusion

CF for recommendations is a powerful technology for users to find information relevant to their preference. In the present work, we have presented a novel approach to build a model and to provide efficient recommendations. The major advantage of our approach is that it supports updating of the model instantaneously, even when users present explicit feedback. The experimental results demonstrate that the prediction quality improves with growth of items used for the prediction generation. Moreover, our approach offers reasonably good quality although the prediction quality is slightly worse than the best quality of a user-based CF. However, there still remains a defect that our prediction strategy depends on the error threshold. Therefore, we plan to further analyze the model and study a specific method to offer a different optimal value to each user in order to provide more personalized recommendation.

References

1. Resnick, P., Iacovou, N., Suchak, M., Bergstrom, P., Riedl, J.: GroupLens: an open architecture for collaborative filtering of netnews. In: Proc. of the ACM Conf. on Computer supported Cooperative Work, pp. 175–186 (1994)
2. Sarwar, B., Karypis, G., Konstan, J., Reidl, J.: Item-based Collaborative Filtering Recommendation Algorithms. In: Proc. of the 10th Int. Conf. on World Wide Web (2001)
3. Lemire, D., Maclachlan, A.: Slope One Predictors for Online Rating-Based Collaborative Filtering. In: Proc. of SIAM Data Mining (2005)
4. Deshpande, M., Karypis, G.: Item-based top-N recommendation algorithms. ACM Transactions on Information Systems 22, 143–177 (2004)
5. Wang, J., de Vries, A.P., Reinders, M.J.T.: A User-Item Relevance Model for Log-based Collaborative Filtering. In: Lalmas, M., MacFarlane, A., Rüger, S., Tombros, A., Tsikrika, T., Yavlinsky, A. (eds.) Advances in Information Retrieval. LNCS, vol. 3936, pp. 37–48. Springer, Heidelberg (2006)
6. Kim, H.N, Ji, A.T., Jo, G.S.: Enhanced Prediction Algorithm for Item-based Collaborative Filtering Recommendation. In: Bauknecht, K., Pröll, B., Werthner, H. (eds.) EC-Web 2006. LNCS, vol. 4082, pp. 41–50. Springer, Heidelberg (2006)

Automatic Generation of Students' Conceptual Models from Answers in Plain Text*

D. Pérez-Marín[1], E. Alfonseca[1,2], P. Rodríguez[1], and I. Pascual-Nieto[1]

[1] Computer Science Department, Universidad Autonoma de Madrid
[2] Precision and Intelligence Laboratory, Tokyo Institute of Technology
{Diana.Perez,Enrique.Alfonseca,Pilar.Rodriguez,Ismael.Pascual}@uam.es

Abstract. Recently, we have introduced a new procedure to automatically generate students' conceptual models to assist teachers in finding out their students' main misconceptions and lack of concepts, from their interaction with an automatic and adaptive free-text scoring system. In this paper, we present an improvement of this procedure: the models can be built from the students' answers in plain text and they refer not only to one particular student but to the whole class. We also introduce a new tool called COMOV (COnceptual MOdels Viewer) to display the models as concept maps, tables, bar charts or text summaries. Finally, we provide an evaluation of this new approach.

1 Introduction

Conceptual models are knowledge representation formalisms that have been widely applied to e-learning applications. Many systems maintain that keep some kind of student's conceptual model, such as DynMap+ [1], E-TESTER [2] and STyLE-OLM [3]. Other systems represent the structure of a course with conceptual models [4], or use information from the students' assessments to modify the content of the course [5].

In this work, we define a student's conceptual model as a network of interrelated concepts representing what the student has learnt about an area of knowledge. We describe the (to our knowledge) first e-learning system able to fully generate the student's conceptual model. This is done from answers written by the students in plain text using the Willow system [6]. It has been applied to help teachers to identify the main students' misconceptions and concepts to review, with a very good acceptance.

The structure of this paper is as follows: Section 2 describes how to acquire the conceptual models from students' answers written in plain text. Section 3 introduces a new tool called COMOV (Conceptual MOdel Viewer) to display the students' conceptual models to the teacher in different representations. Finally, Section 4 provides the evaluation of the procedure.

---

* This work has been sponsored by Spanish Ministry of Science and Technology, project number TIN2004-03140.

C. Conati, K. McCoy, and G. Paliouras (Eds.): UM 2007, LNAI 4511, pp. 329–333, 2007.
© Springer-Verlag Berlin Heidelberg 2007

2   Conceptual Models and Their Generation

For each area of knowledge, we ask the teachers to provide several questions and to structure them in topics. Also, for each question, we ask at least three different teachers to write one correct answer (reference). In this way, we expect that several paraphrasings of the same content are captured. The teachers are helped in the task of writing the references with automatic procedures such as genetic algorithms to select as references some of the best students' answers of previous years or Anaphora Resolution to automatically generate new references.

We have distinguished three different levels of concepts: **area-of-knowledge concept** (AC) that represents the main domain that the students are learning and is directly taken as the name of the course; **topic concept** (TC) that refers to each topic inside an area-of-knowledge and is taken as the name of each lesson of the course; and **basic concept** (BC), the domain-specific terms relevant to each topic. The BCs are automatically extracted from the references [7].

Each concept has a confidence-value (between 0 and 1) that reflects how well it is understood at the time that the model is shown. Students must use certain concepts in their answers. Thus, a lower confidence-value means that the student does not know the concept as he or she does not use it, while a higher value means that the student confidently uses that concept. The formula applied to calculate the confidence-value, representing the student's knowledge about a term t, given a set of questions $\mathcal{Y}$, is given by Equation (1) [6]. $Freq_{st}(t)$ refers to the frequency of t in the student answer, and $Freq_{ref}(t)$ to its mean frequency in the references.

$$\frac{\sum_{y \in \mathcal{Y}} \frac{Freq_{st}(t)}{Freq_{ref}(t)}}{|\mathcal{Y}|} \tag{1}$$

The confidence-value of a TC is calculated from the confidence values of the BCs that groups and the confidence-value of an AC is calculated from the confidence-values of its TCs. Thus, just by checking if the AC has a high confidence value, it can be seen how well concepts in that area have been understood. The model for the whole class is again estimated by calculating the mean values for each BC, and calculating next the values for TCs and ACs.

Regarding the relationships between the concepts, three kinds of links have been identified: type 1 between ACs and TCs to join the area-of-knowledge to each topic; type 2 between TCs and BCs to join each topic to each concept covered in this topic; and, type 3 between two BCs to join related concepts. Each link has an associated label that indicates the type of link. Type 1 and 2 are given by the structure of the course and thus, the label is fixed, while type 3 links that are extracted from the students' answers are annotated with different labels. The procedure to extract type 3 links is quite simple at the moment: find one BC and mark it as the first BC of the relationship, find another BC in the same sentence and mark it as the second BC of the relationship and extract the words between the first and the second BC and mark them as the linking words of the relationship.

3   Representation

Whenever the teacher wants to review the conceptual model of a student, he or she logs into the conceptual model viewer called COMOV (COnceptual MOdel Viewer). The conceptual model can be represented with COMOV for a particular student or for the whole class as a concept map, a table, a bar chart or a textual summary.

The **concept map** is represented as a spider-like map with the AC in the center and the TCs radially fixed (each of them with its BCs). A color schema has been used so that the background color indicates the type of node and the foreground color indicates the level of knowledge. For the sake of simplicity, the linking words are not explicitly written.

In the **table**, neither the links nor TCs and ACs are captured. Our purpose is to focus the attention of the teacher on just the BCs and how well the students seem to have understood them by looking at the exact confidence-value assigned. In this way, if the table is ordered from higher to lower confidence-value teachers can easily see which are the concepts better understood by the students. Conversely, if the table is ordered from lower to higher confidence-value teachers can see which concepts have still not been assimilated and thus, which concepts should be reviewed.

As in the table, in the **bar chart**, we did not want to represent either links or TCs and ACs instead focussing on the BCs and how well the students have assimilated them. Hence, each BC is represented by a bar and the length of the bar indicates its confidence-value. The resulting bar chart shows in the Y axis the terms and in the X axis their confidence-values.

The system can also generate **text summaries**, one report per student and a class report. Text summaries also focus on the BCs. Each report contains three ordered lists: the confidence-value of the ten most important concepts with the same background color schema as above, the ten worst known concepts and the ten best known concepts.

4   Teachers' and Students' Evaluation of COMOV

In the first term of the academic year 2005-2006, we carried out an experiment in which we applied the new automatic procedure to generate the conceptual models of a group of 31 students of the Telecommunications Engineering degree of the Universidad Autonoma de Madrid from their answers in plain text. After generating the concept maps corresponding to the answers written by each student, a positive correlation is found both between the score given by the teacher to each student's final exam and the number of best-known BCs (46%, statistically significant, p=0.0101), and between the final score and the mean of the confidence-values of the BCs in the map (50%, statistically significant, p = 0.0068). Furthermore, it is very easy for the teacher to observe that students with a high score always have a more complex conceptual model, with more well-known concepts and links between them.

Table 1. Results of the satisfaction survey carried out for six teachers of our home university and their average values in the mean column. The representations are marked as C for concept map, T for table, B for bar chart, and S for text summary.

Feature	T1	T2	T3	T4	T5	T6	Mean
Familiarity with conceptual models	3	2	4	1	4	2	2.7
Intuitiveness of the COMOV's interface	4	4	5	3	3	4	3.8
How informative is the table representation	5	4	3	2	3	5	3.7
How informative is the bar chart representation	2	5	5	4	5	4	4.2
How informative is text summary representation	4	4	5	3	4	5	4.2
How informative is the concept map representation	4	4	5	4	4	5	4.3
Favorite representation	T	B	S/C	B	C	C	C
COMOV usefulness	2	4	5	4	4	5	4.0
Would you use COMOV?	Y	Y	Y	Y	Y	Y	Y
Would you recommend COMOV?	Y	Y	Y	Y	Y	Y	Y

We also asked six teachers of our home university to see the generated conceptual models with COMOV. The goal was to find out how useful they thought that the conceptual model of a student or a group of students was, and which of the four above mentioned representations they considered as the most informative. Teachers filled in a non-anonymous satisfaction questionnaire with some Likert-type items in a scale from 1 (very negative value) up to 5 (very positive value) and some free-text-answer items expressing their opinion. The results of the questionnaire are gathered in Table 1, where each column refers to a teacher.

As it can be seen, most teachers were not very familiar with students' conceptual models. Nevertheless, they considered COMOV useful to identify how well the students have understood the concepts of the lesson. They also thought it was very simple to use and, all of the teachers stated that they would use COMOV in their courses and would recommend its use in other subjects.

Regarding which representation was considered as the most informative, the assigned average values were very similar. It might be because all teachers thought that these representations were quite informative, and in some cases even complementary. Nevertheless, when the teachers were asked to choose one of the several representations, concept maps received more votes.

5 Conclusions and Future Work

We have presented a new procedure for automatically generating students' conceptual models from their answers in plain text. It makes use of a Term Extraction module and syntactic analyzers to produce both the conceptual model of a particular student and the conceptual model of the whole class.

To test the procedure, we performed an experiment in which we generated 31 students' conceptual models and found a positive correlation between the score assigned by the teacher to each student's final exam and the score assigned to each students' generated conceptual model indicating that the concept map is in some way capturing the students' knowledge. Furthermore, we observed that the students whose concept maps are more complex achieved higher scores in the final exam. Teachers also seemed to have found COMOV quite useful and usable. In fact, all of them would use it in their lessons to see how well the students are understanding the concepts exposed in the lectures and they would recommend its use to other colleagues in other subjects. Regarding which representation is their favorite, concept maps were chosen by the majority.

As future work, we plan to improve the extraction of type 3 links and the generation of the group model, continue evaluating the procedure to generate the students' conceptual models in an experiment with more students and, produce templates so the teachers can easily recognize good and bad models at first sight.

References

1. Rueda, U., Larranaga, M., Elorriaga, J., Arruarte, A.: Validating dynmap as a mechanism to visualize the student's evolution through the learning process. LNCS, pp. 864–866. Springer, Heidelberg (2004)
2. Guetl, C., Dreher, H., Williams, R.: E-tester: A computer-based tool for auto-generated question and answer assessment. E-Learn (2005)
3. Dimitrova, V.: Style-olm: Interactive open learner modelling. International Journal of Artificial Intelligence in Education 13, 35–78 (2003)
4. Masthoff, J.: Automatic generation of a navigation structure for adaptive web-based instruction. In: Proceedings of the AH Workshop on Adaptive Systems for Web-based education (2002)
5. Romero, C., Ventura, S., Castro, C., Hall, W., Hg, M.: Using genetic algorithms for data mining in web-based educational hypermedia systems. In: Proceedings of the AH Workshop on Adaptive Systems for Web-based education (2002)
6. Pérez-Marín, D., Alfonseca, E., Freire, M., Rodríguez, P., Guirao, J., Moreno-Sandoval, A.: Automatic generation of students' conceptual models underpinned by free-text adaptive computer assisted assessment. In: Proceedings of the IEEE International Conference on Advanced Learning Techniques (ICALT) (2006)
7. Pérez-Marín, D., Pascual-Nieto, I., Alfonseca, E., Rodríguez, P.: Automatic identification of terms for the generation of students concept maps. In: proceedings of the International Conference on Multimedia and Information Technologies for the Education (MICTE) (2006)

Capturing User Interests by Both Exploitation and Exploration

Ka Cheung Sia[1], Shenghuo Zhu[2], Yun Chi[2], Koji Hino[2], and Belle L. Tseng[2]

[1] University of California, Los Angeles, CA 90095, USA
kcsia@cs.ucla.edu
[2] NEC Laboratories America
10080 N. Wolfe Rd, SW3-350, Cupertino, CA 95014 USA
{zsh,ychi,hino,belle}@sv.nec-labs.com

Abstract. Personalization is one of the important research issues in the areas of information retrieval and Web search. Providing personalized services that are tailored toward the specific preferences and interests of a given user can enhance her experience and satisfaction. However, to effectively capture user interests is a challenging research problem. Some challenges include how to quickly capture user interests in an unobtrusive way, how to provide diversified recommendations, and how to track the drifts of user interests in a timely fashion. In this paper, we propose a model for learning user interests and an algorithm that actively captures user interests through an interactive recommendation process. The key advantage of our algorithm is that it takes into account both *exploitation* (recommending items that belong to users' core interest) and *exploration* (discovering potential interests of users). Extensive experiments using synthetic data and a user study show that our algorithm can quickly capture diversified user interests in an unobtrusive way, even when the user interests may drift along time.

1 Introduction

Personalized recommendation systems that provide users with recommendations on products, news articles, or documents that are tailored toward their personal interests are being used extensively in e-commerce web sites, news portals, and enterprise documentation portals. As pointed out by the research community recently [1], the five major usability goals for user-adaptive systems are: *privacy, controllability, unobtrusiveness, breadth of experience*, and *predictability and comprehensibility*. We are building a prototype of a *Personal Information Manager* that tries to address the above criteria. Such a system runs on a user's personal computer; it collects recent important information that matches the user's personal interests from the Web, the blogosphere, and news sites; it then summarizes the collected information and presents to the user in a succinct form.

To solve the above challenging issues, we use a learning framework and propose an algorithm that actively captures user interests through an *unobtrusive* interactive recommendation process. Unlike a greedy algorithm, which only *exploits* the model of users' interests, the proposed algorithm takes into account *exploration*, i.e., it discovers user potential interests through *topic diversification* [2]. In addition, the exploration nature of this algorithm also makes it adapt quickly to *user interest drift* [3] as well.

C. Conati, K. McCoy, and G. Paliouras (Eds.): UM 2007, LNAI 4511, pp. 334–339, 2007.
© Springer-Verlag Berlin Heidelberg 2007

In the following, we will give an overview of the related work and identify our unique contributions as compared to the literature.

Learning user interests has been studied extensively in the area of information retrieval and Web search&mining. In the information retrieval area, relevance feedback [4,5] has long been used for improving the quality of retrieval. In the Web search and mining area, personalization [6,7] has been one of the most important research topics. Click history [8,9,10,11,12] is one of the commonly used information to learn a search engine user's interests; some other implicit information such as display time [13] and browse history [14] have also been investigated. While these different approaches have proved effective in various areas, a key point that limits their flexibility is that they are all *passive* in nature. That is, all these approaches *exploit* historic data while ignoring *exploring* additional information from users. In comparison, user interests are *actively explored* in our approach. An active feedback framework [15] is recently proposed for probing user preference by presenting documents that are selected based on a statistical decision theory. It is different from our work in the sense that it requires *explicitly* asking users for feedback and it assumes that the ground truth is available.

2   The Learning Framework

Figure 1 illustrates a system that provides a user with personalized recommendation contents. The system observes the user's activities while she browses the web pages, and shows the user a list of Webpage recommendations. Assuming that *clicking* the link of a recommended Webpage after *reading* a short description of the page indicates that she likes the *topic* of the Web page, the system can learn a user model from this observation and, consequently, provides better recommendations.

To model the process of learning user interests, we assume that user interests are represented by a combination of K topics, where K could be a large number. We further assume that each Webpage only belongs to one topic to simplify the model and the anal-

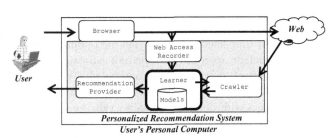

Fig. 1. A diagram of a personalized recommendation system

ysis. When the description of a recommendation of topic i is read by the user, the user clicks the link of the recommended page with probability $\theta_i = \Pr(\text{click}|\text{read}, \text{topic } i)$. Then the user interest model can be represented by the parameter $\Theta = \{\theta_1, \cdots, \theta_K\}$, which is going to be estimated.

When a recommendation item is shown to the user, it has different chances to attract the user's attention depending on its position on the list. In the Web search engine community, it is observed that the position of an entry on the query-result list heavily affects its chance to be clicked by the user[9]. We capture this phenomenon by a probability model; we denote the probability that the user reads a recommendation at the j-th position of the list as $g(j) = \Pr(\text{read}|j)$, for $1 \leq j \leq K$.

Let variable $R = \{r_1, \cdots, r_K\}$ be the ranking order given to the K topics. Then we can express the utility of this ranking order as

$$U(R; \Theta) = \sum_{i=1}^{K} \Pr(\text{click}|\text{read, topic } i; \theta_i) \Pr(\text{read}|r_i) = \sum_{i=1}^{K} \theta_i \cdot g(r_i). \qquad (1)$$

Given a user model, Θ, the goal of the system is to maximize the utility, $U(R, \Theta)$. As a result, we have two problems to solve: 1) we need to estimate the Θ accurately; 2) we need to choose a ranking order R that maximizes the utility.

Learning Θ. We assume the prior of θ_i follows the beta distribution, $B(\theta_i|\alpha_i, \beta_i)$, where α_i and β_i can be initially set to some fixed constants. When the recommendation is ranked at r_i and is not clicked, we have

$$d\Pr(\theta_i|\neg\text{click}, r_i) \propto [1 - \Pr(\text{click}|\theta_i, r_i)] \, d\Pr(\theta_i) = [1 - \theta_i g(r_i)] \, B(\theta_i|\alpha_i, \beta_i)d\theta_i$$
$$\approx [1 - \theta_i]^{g(r_i)} \, B(\theta_i|\alpha_i, \beta_i)d\theta_i \propto B(\theta_i|\alpha_i, \beta_i + g(r_i))d\theta_i,$$
$$(2)$$

in which we used the approximation $(1-x)^y \approx 1-xy$. Since $B(\theta_i|\alpha_i, \beta_i+g(r_i))$ is normalized, we have $d\Pr(\theta_i|\neg\text{click}, r_i) \approx B(\theta_i|\alpha_i, \beta_i + g(r_i))d\theta_i$. That is, the posterior distribution of θ_i follows $B(\theta_i|\alpha_i, \beta_i + g(r_i))$ if the user does not click the recommendation of topic i at position r_i of the list. If the recommendation of topic i is clicked, the posterior distribution of θ_i follows $B(\theta_i|\alpha_i + 1, \beta_i)$. Thus, we have the update formula for the distribution of each θ.

Maximizing Utility. To maximize the one-step expected utility, we may rank topics according to their expected utilities, $\{\theta_i \cdot g(r_i)\}$ This approach is to *exploit* the best estimation of user interests, Θ, to gain the optimal one-step utility. We call it *greedy* approach. Such an approach puts the best estimated θ's on the list, which may deprive the opportunity of showing the *true* optimal θ's. Without being shown, we are unable to get an accurate estimate of the actual best θ's, which lowers the utility gain in later steps. Showing topics with smaller estimated θ values is known as *exploration*. Therefore, we face a trade-off between exploitation and exploration to gain the optimal overall utility. This was also illustrated in the well-known multi-armed bandit problem [16].

To achieve both goals, we rank topics based on their expected utility plus a term related to their variances instead of solely using the expected utility as in the greedy approach. The term related to the variance is known as the *exploration bonus* [17]. In our case, given $\theta_i \sim B(\cdot|\alpha_i, \beta_i)$, the expected utility is $\alpha_i/(\alpha_i + \beta_i)$, and its variance is $\alpha_i\beta_i/[(\alpha_i + \beta_i)^2(\alpha_i + \beta_i + 1)]$. We define the exploration bonus as the variance scaled by a weight parameter λ. Hence, the ranking score, a combination of the expected utility and the exploration bonus, is $\alpha_i/(\alpha_i + \beta_i) \times [1 + \lambda\beta_i/[(\alpha_i + \beta_i)(\alpha_i + \beta_i + 1)]]$. More detail derivations and examples are given in another technical report [18].

3   User Study

We carry out a user study experiment to evaluate the performance of our proposed recommendation strategy, *Exploitation and Exploration* (*E&E* in short), and compare it to two other baselines: *random*, which presents each topic, in a random order, the same number of times on average, and *greedy*, which ranks topics and presents topics based on their learned θ_i' respectively (i.e. $\alpha_i/(\alpha_i + \beta_i)$). The two baselines can be considered as two special cases of *E&E* that each focuses on one aspect respectively. Other than the user study, we do simulations to study the properties of each method. Their performance are similar to the findings from the reinforcement learning literature [16], and the details are described in the technical report [18].

In the user study experiment, we randomly select 45 categories (in level two of the hierarchy) from the Open Directory Project (ODP) [19]. Before each experiment begins, we ask the user to indicate, on a scale of one to nine, her interest level on each topic as the ground truth (θ_i) to measure the estimation accuracy. In each iteration of the experiment, the URL of seven Webpages, each coming from a different category, together with their titles and descriptions, are presented to the user. The user is instructed to click on the URLs that she feels interesting until no more is found to proceed to the next iteration. The click records are then used to update the α_i, β_i values of each topic respectively. We interleave three different strategies randomly throughout 75 iterations without informing the user, while each strategy updates its parameters independently for 25 iterations each. Such settings try to minimize any potential bias by comparing the strategies without dividing users into groups or dividing the test into phases. We have recruited ten users from staff members of NEC Labs and students of UCLA Computer Science department to participate in the experiment.

Click utility. Figure 2(a) shows the click utility (as the fractional improvement of the number of cumulative clicks over *random*) averaged over 10 users. The behavior of each strategy is similar to the simulation, where *E&E* performs noticeably better than *greedy*.

Estimation error of Θ**.** We map the interest levels indicated by users to click probabilities (θ_i) by using $\frac{x-lb}{ub-lb}$, where x is the level selected, lb is the lowest level selected, and ub is the highest level selected by a user. We compute the normalized mean absolute error of the estimated θ_i's at the 25th iteration of the experiment. The error values of *random*, *E&E*, and *greedy* are 21.6, 23.8, and 24.3, respectively. Their relative performance is similar to the prediction from simulation, however, the difference is less noticeable.

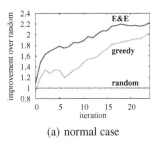

(a) normal case

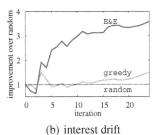

(b) interest drift

Fig. 2. Comparison of click utility of *E&E*, *greedy*, and *random*

Interest drift. We design an experiment in which after a user finishes all iterations of her test, a different user (having different interests) repeats the test using the learned $\alpha'_i s$ and $\beta'_i s$ as initial values. Such a switch of user simulates the scenario when a user has changed her interests at the end of the 25th iteration. Figure 2(b) shows the average click utility (as the fractional improvement of the number of cumulative clicks over *random*) of 5 users, from the 26th to 50th iteration. The result clearly shows that *E&E* adapts to changes faster than *greedy* and improves the click utility towards the end.

From the result of the user study, we conclude that our *E&E* algorithm outperforms the exploitation-only *greedy* algorithm in terms of click utility, parameter estimation error, and the rate of adaptation to user interest drift.

4   Conclusion and Future Directions

In this paper, we study how to effectively capture user interests in a personalized recommendation system. We propose a learning algorithm that uses both exploitation and exploration to captures user interests, represented as a probabilistic model, through an interactive recommendation process. We demonstrate, through simulations and user studies, that our algorithm achieves higher click utility, lower estimation error, and more agile adaptation to user interest drift against a random algorithm and a greedy algorithm. As suggested by the reviewers, two possible future research directions that make the user modelling more realistic include: a more complicated model that assumes a document belongs to multiple topics; introducing dependency and correlation among topics and recommendation items.

References

1. Jameson, A.: User modeling meets usability goals. In: Ardissono, L., Brna, P., Mitrović, A. (eds.) UM 2005. LNCS (LNAI), vol. 3538, Springer, Heidelberg (2005)
2. Ziegler, C.N., McNee, S.M., Konstan, J.A., Lausen, G.: Improving recommendation lists through topic diversification. In: WWW'05 (2005)
3. Webb, G.I., Pazzani, M.J., Billsus, D.: Machine learning for user modeling. User. Modeling and User.-Adapted Interaction 11(1-2), 19–29 (2001)
4. Efthimiadis, E.N.: Interactive query expansion: A user-based evaluation in a relevance feedback environment. Journal of the American Society for Information Science, vol. 51(11) (2000)
5. Kelly, D., Dollu, V.D., Fu, X.: The loquacious user: a document-independent source of terms for query expansion. In: SIGIR (2005)
6. Mobasher, B., Cooley, R., Srivastava, J.: Automatic personalization based on web usage mining. Communications of the ACM, vol. 43(8) (2000)
7. Mobasher, B., Dai, H., Luo, T., Nakagawa, M.: Discovery and evaluation of aggregate usage profiles for web personalization. Data Mining and Knowledge Discovery, vol. 6(1) (2002)
8. Agichtein, E., Brill, E., Dumais, S.: Improving web search ranking by incorporating user behavior information. In: SIGIR (2006)
9. Agichtein, E., Brill, E., Dumais, S., Ragno, R.: Learning user interaction models for predicting web search result preferences. In: SIGIR (2006)
10. Qiu, F., Cho, J.: Automatic identification of user interest for personalized search. In: WWW'06 (2006)

11. Jin, X., Zhou, Y., Mobasher, B.: Task-oriented web user modeling for recommendation. In: Ardissono, L., Brna, P., Mitrović, A. (eds.) UM 2005. LNCS (LNAI), vol. 3538, Springer, Heidelberg (2005)
12. Joachims, T.: Optimizing search engines using clickthrough data. In: SIGKDD (2002)
13. Kelly, D., Belkin, N.J.: Display time as implicit feedback: understanding task effects. In: SIGIR (2004)
14. Sugiyama, K., Hatano, K., Yoshikawa, M.: Adaptive web search based on user profile constructed without any effort from users. In: WWW'04 (2004)
15. Shen, X., Zhai, C.: Active feedback in ad hoc information retrieval. In: SIGIR (2005)
16. Gittins, J.C., Jones, D.M.: A dynamic allocation index for the sequential design of experiments. In: J.G., et al. (ed.) Progress in Statistics, vol. I, pp. 241–266. North-Holland, Amsterdam-London (1974)
17. Sutton, R.S.: Integrated architectures for learning, planning, and reacting based on approximating dynamic programming. In: ICML '90, pp. 216–224. Morgan Kaufman, San Mateo CA (1990)
18. Sia, K.C., Zhu, S., Chi, Y., Hino, K., Tseng, B.L.: Capturing User Interests by Both Exploitation and Exploration. Technical report, NEC Labs America (2006)
19. Netscape: Dmoz open directory project http://www.dmoz.org

Conceptualizing Student Models for ICALL

Luiz Amaral[1] and Detmar Meurers[2]

[1] University of Victoria, Department of Hispanic and Italian Studies
[2] The Ohio State University, Department of Linguistics
{amaral,dm}@ling.osu.edu

Abstract. Student models for Intelligent Computer Assisted Language Learning (ICALL) have largely focused on the acquisition of grammatical structures. In this paper, we motivate a broader perspective of student models for ICALL that incorporates insights from current research on second language acquisition and language testing. We argue for a student model that includes a representation of the learner's ability to use language to perform tasks as well as an explicit activity model that provides information on the language tasks and the inferences for the student model they support.

1 Introduction

In Intelligent Computer-Assisted Language Learning (ICALL), language acquisition has generally been modeled in terms of learning grammatical forms and structures. CASTLE (Murphy and McTear [9]), ICICLE (SLALOM; Michaud, McCoy and Stark [8], and E-tutor (Heift [5]) are examples of ICALL systems which include student models that keep track of students' production in terms of the grammatical accuracy of their performance.

At the same time, research in the field of Second Language Acquisition (cf., e.g., Canale [3], Ellis [4]) has established language acquisition as a process encompassing significantly more than the linguistic knowledge, in particular the ability to use language in a given context to achieve certain goals.

For ICALL systems to include activities that are meaning-based and contextualized, the student model needs to be extended to include the learner's abilities to use language in context for specific goals, such as scanning a text for specific information, describing situations, or using appropriate vocabulary to make requests. Such an extension also makes it possible to model the learners' linguistic abilities relative to particular tasks, such as whether a learner can use proper morpho-syntactic agreement in a simple task or construction only.

Inspired by Bachman (Bachman and Palmer [1]), who refers to the set of non-linguistic properties to be acquired by learners that play a role in their language production as the *strategic competence*, we thus propose to extend ICALL student models with a representation of the relevant aspects of strategic competence. The direction of our approach thus is related to that of Bull et al. ([2]), who argue for extending the scope of student models to incorporate aspects outside the boundary of the domain knowledge. However it is motivated by the specific nature of the language acquisition process we are focusing on.

C. Conati, K. McCoy, and G. Paliouras (Eds.): UM 2007, LNAI 4511, pp. 340–344, 2007.
© Springer-Verlag Berlin Heidelberg 2007

We explore this conceptual issue in the context of developing TAGARELA, an ICALL system for Portuguese designed to be used in the Individualized Instruction Program at the Ohio State University. TAGARELA is an intelligent electronic workbook which analyzes student input for different activities and provides individual feedback. The activity types are similar to the ones found in traditional workbooks: *reading*, *listening*, *description*, *rephrasing*, and *vocabulary*. Crucially, each of the included activities requires the learner to use the foreign language with regards to meaning, as opposed to activities that only require the manipulation of linguistic forms.

2 TAGARELA's Student Model

To extend the student model with the learner's ability to use language in context for specific goals, we propose the architecture in Figure 1.

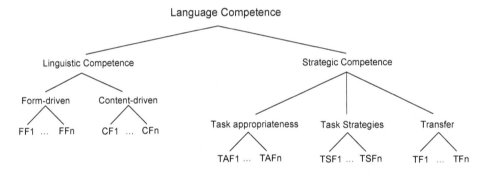

Fig. 1. The TAGARELA student model (domain-knowledge aspects only)

The student model comprises the linguistic and the relevant strategic (non-linguistic) competencies that have to be developed by the learner to use language in order to perform the tasks in TAGARELA.[1] Linguistic competence is divided into *form-driven* and *content-driven*, reflecting two types of linguistic analysis that are performed by the system's natural language processing (NLP) modules: form analysis of spelling and morpho-syntactic errors, and shallow content analysis providing information about the semantic appropriateness of the input. The properties that can be observed and identified by the NLP are represented by the leaves of the linguistic competence tree in the depicted student model. Form features (FF), for example, include spelling, determiner-noun and subject-verb agreement, and word order properties determined by the syntactic processing. Content features (CF) represent, for example, the result of extra/missing content word detection, required concept matching, or synonym identification.

---

[1] In addition to the domain knowledge discussed here, the TAGARELA student model also includes the student's personal information and interaction preferences.

The strategic competence newly added to the model is divided into *task appropriateness*, *task strategies*, and *transfer*. Task appropriateness stores information about the performance of the student relative to the activity classification. Each activity is classified in terms of its type (e.g., listening, reading), level, nature of the input (word, phrase, sentence), and complexity of content manipulation required. Task strategies keeps track of specific abilities students have to use to complete a given activity, e.g., scanning a text to locate specific information or getting the gist of listening passages. Transfer stores information about indicators of structural and lexical transfer from the native language of the student into the second language (cf., e.g., Odlin [10]).

The TF leaves in the student model in Figure 1 are the transfer features which are specified in a separate NLP module that identifies potential instances of negative transfer in the learner input. The TAF and TSF leaves are the relevant features for task appropriateness and task strategies, which are hand-specified in an explicit activity model provided for each exercise. This provides information about the activity and the strategies the student must master to complete it.

2.1   Explicit Activity Models and Assessing Learner Knowledge

An ICALL system architecture including explicit activity models for each exercise is directly relevant for the extension to the student model proposed in this paper. Student models are built and modified based on observations of learner performance (or using information explicitly provided by the learner). The student model does not store properties of the learner input as such, but inferred information about the knowledge the learner used to construct these sentences. Research in ICALL has paid little attention to the validity of the inferences about a student's current state of knowledge. Developers usually take for granted that linguistic errors are caused solely by a lack of linguistic knowledge and do not acknowledge the fact that the task being performed can play a significant role in determining the students' production. To build a model that takes into account the linguistic and the strategic competence of a student, it is necessary to provide mechanisms ensuring that the system's inferences about a student's state of knowledge are valid.

Describing the concept of validity for language tests, Bachman and Palmer ([1], p. 21) state that "construct validity pertains to the meaningfulness and appropriateness of the interpretations that we make on the bases of test scores" and that "in order to justify a particular score interpretation, we need to provide evidence that the test score reflects the area(s) of language ability we want to measure". In the case of ICALL systems that present specific exercises, there are two issues related to the validity of system inferences that we need to pay particular attention to. The first one is known as *content validity*, which McNamara ([7], p. 50) characterizes as the concept that explains the "extent to which the test content forms a satisfactory basis for the inferences to be made from test performance." For ICALL system design, this means that it is important to ensure that the exercise types and contents offered by the system are sufficient to make the necessary inferences about students' state of knowledge.

The second issue on validity of inferences relates to the methods used to obtain information about students' state of knowledge. There are two ways in which properties of exercises affect the result of the system's observations, which we can characterize using notions from assessment theory (cf., e.g., McNamara, [7]). *Construct irrelevant variance* occurs when a given exercise introduces factors that are not relevant to measure the ability we want to observe. *Construct under-representation* occurs when the exercise is too easy for the student, jeopardizing the observation of a given ability. Particular care needs to be taken when the knowledge or skill observed is embedded in contexts that are unfamiliar to the student's experience or irrelevant to what is being assessed. Bachman and Palmer ([1], p. 21) emphasize that the analysis of a student's performance has to be interpreted with respect to a "specific domain of generalization". Thus, when we consider the validity of an interpretation, "we need to consider both the construct definition, and the characteristics of the test tasks".

In sum, in order to guarantee valid interpretations of student performance it is not enough to keep track of students' production; it is vital to have information about the task environment where it occurs. Without a clear description of the exercise items that triggered the student's input, our interpretations about levels of proficiency may not be accurate.

3   Using the Information from the Student Model

As mentioned in the introduction, the TAGARELA system provides individual feedback based on the students' input to an exercise. Feedback is provided on the semantic appropriateness as well as on the grammatical accuracy of the input. The choice of the feedback strategy and contents is based on the student input, the activity model for the exercise the student was dealing with, and the student model. The general feedback strategy uses scaffolding techniques to help the learner develop self-editing skills (cf., e.g., Hyland and Hyland [6]).

Most relevant here is how the content of the scaffolding message is determined. The content depends on identifying the likely source of the error. Based on the learner input annotated by the NLP modules, the student model, and the activity model, the system distinguishes between three possible error sources:

Firstly, an error can result from a student's lack of a specific linguistic ability, e.g., when a given student has not mastered subject verb agreement. This is the classical case handled by ICALL systems, whereas the next two rely on the extensions proposed in Section 2.

Secondly, an error can result from the student's lack of a strategic ability needed for a given task. For example, if the learner has problems scanning a text to locate the relevant concepts, they cannot correctly answer a reading comprehension question asking for those concepts. To diagnose such an error, the system compares the concepts that the activity model identifies for a given text with the corresponding concepts identified in the learner input by the NLP modules. The learner model provides the information whether the learner has been able to pick up the relevant concepts in reading comprehension before.

Thirdly, an error can result from an insufficient mastery of a specific linguistic ability, which allows the student to use it only in certain tasks or constructions. For example, a student may be able to formulate simple sentences with correct subject-verb agreement as part of a picture description task, but fail to use correct agreement forms when answering listening comprehension questions that require more complex content, form, or otherwise increased cognitive load. As in the previous case, the student model and the activity model are essential for determining whether the problem lies in the use of the linguistic forms in general or whether there is a correlation with the use of these linguistic forms only in particular tasks.

4   Conclusion

We motivated the need to extend student models for ICALL to more comprehensively reflect the language acquisition process. To do so, we argued for adding a representation of the strategic competence of a student which represents factors outside of the linguistic competence per se. This makes it possible to model the learner's abilities to use language in context for specific goals and the learner's abilities relative to particular tasks. Updating the model currently requires hand-specification of explicit activity models, which however are well-motivated by the need to support valid inferences about the student's state of knowledge. In future work we intend to explore deriving some of these properties via additional natural language processing and resources.

References

1. Bachman, L.F., Palmer, A.S.: Language Testing in Practice: Designing and Developing Useful Language Tests. Oxford University Press, Oxford (1996)
2. Bull, S., Brna, P., Pain, H.: Extending the scope of the student model. User. Modeling and User.-Adapted interaction 5, 45–65 (1995)
3. Canale, M.: On some dimensions of language proficiency. In: Oller Jr., J. (ed.) Issues in Language Testing Research, Newbury House, Rowley, MA (1983)
4. Ellis, R.: Task-based Language Learning and Teaching. Oxford University Press, Oxford (2003)
5. Heift, T.: Inspectable learner reports for web-based language learning. ReCALL Journal 16(2), 416–431 (2004)
6. Hyland, K., Hyland, F.: Feedback on second language students' writing. Language Teaching 39(2), 1–46 (2006)
7. McNamara, T.: Language Testing. Oxford University Press, Oxford (2000)
8. Michaud, L.N., McCoy, K.F., Stark, L.A.: Modeling the acquisition of english: An intelligent call approach. In: Proceedings of The 8th Int. Confeence on User Modeling, Sonthofen, Germany (July 14–25, 2001)
9. Murphy, M., McTear, M.: Learner modelling for intelligent call. In: Proceedings of the 6th Int. Confernce on User Modeling, Sardinia, Italy (1997)
10. Odlin, T.: Cross-linguistic influence. In: Doughty, C., Long, M. (eds.) Handbook on Second Language Acquisition, pp. 436–486. Blackwell, Oxford (2003)

Context-Dependent User Modelling for Smart Homes

Elena Vildjiounaite[1], Otilia Kocsis[2], Vesa Kyllönen[1], and Basilis Kladis[2]

[1] VTT Technical Research Centre of Finland, Kaytovayla 1, 90580, Oulu, Finland
FirstName.LastName@vtt.fi
[2] LogicDIS, NEO Patron-Athinon 37, 26441 Patras, Greece
okocsis@logicdis.gr, bkladis@logicdis.gr

Abstract. This works presents a user modelling service for a Smart Home – intelligent context-aware environment, providing personalized proactive support to its inhabitants. Diversity of Smart Home applications imposes various technical and implementation requirements, such as the need to model dependency of user preferences on context in a unified and convenient way, both for users and for application developers. This paper introduces the service architecture and currently implemented functionalities: stereotypes-based profiles initialisation; a GUI for acquisition of context-dependent and context-independent preferences, which provides an easy way to create own concepts of context ontology and to map them into already existing concepts; and a method to learn context-dependent user preferences from interaction history.

Keywords: User Model, Context Awareness, Smart Home.

1 Introduction

Context dependency of user preferences is a basis of such applications as location-based services and mobile phone personalisation [1]. Recently, importance of social context was studied in domains of TV [2] and movie recommender systems [3], and the importance of day and time contexts for TV recommendations was proved in the works [4, 5]. However, usually context-dependent model is built specially for each application, and users must learn vocabularies and interfaces of many applications. Configuring context-aware applications usually requires users to describe each context as a set (chain) of appropriate descriptors; and to find all these descriptors in predefined vocabularies. Even if number of predefined context descriptors is fairly small, the effort of finding and chaining them can be a problem [1]. Thus, this effort should be avoided in applications, capable of recognising complex contexts.

Project Amigo [6] aims at developing services for a networked home environment, which offers users intuitive, personalised and unobtrusive interaction. Amigo home recognizes users, their locations, activities and other contexts, which will be used by many applications, e.g., home automation; shopping; support of communications between users; proactive recording of movies and news to users' personal mobile devices and home computers; parental control over what the children watch. Home services need a shared user model, which they would query in a unified way for user

C. Conati, K. McCoy, and G. Paliouras (Eds.): UM 2007, LNAI 4511, pp. 345–349, 2007.
© Springer-Verlag Berlin Heidelberg 2007

preferences in different domains and for user skills, e.g., experience in using speech or graphical interfaces. Furthermore, user model should take into account context-dependency of user preferences. For example, choice of videos to watch depends on who is present in a room, choice of food items to buy depends on future events (parties, trips, public holidays), tastes and diets of family members and guests. Due to the large number and diversity of applications, user effort for system configuration should be reduced as much as possible, but nevertheless the users should be provided with full control over the system when they need it. This work presents first steps towards satisfying the above-listed requirements of a Smart Home.

2 Architecture of the User Modelling and Profiling Service

User Modelling and Profiling Service (UMPS) has an add-on modular architecture, which enables easy plug-in of different user modelling methods. The basic inner shell of the architecture is the Core Profile Service; and its major components are:

(a) The Reasoning Module, responsible for retrieval of different parts of user model (e.g., user age or user preferences) upon other services or applications requests.

(b) The Static Modeller, responsible for creation, removal and modification of user profiles at user's or application's request. It enables user control over the system via GUI, allowing users to edit their personal data and to set directly their preference values. Additionally, users can enable/disable modelling of certain preferences.

(c) The Feedback Analyzer, responsible for detecting and logging of explicit and (mainly) implicit user feedback, thus enabling learning of user preferences.

(d) The Context Module, responsible for accessing context history data, gathered by the Context Management Service. Both asynchronous event-based subscriptions to context data and synchronous context queries are supported by this component.

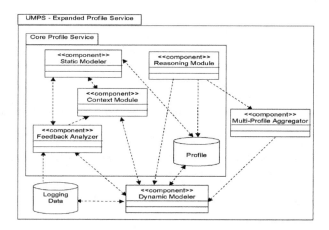

Fig. 1. Architecture of UMPS in Amigo Home

Core Profile Service initiates user modelling, which is based on the common sense knowledge of the system about its potential groups of users (stereotypes) [7] and explicitly acquired user data. In the next step, the user profile is refined based on the knowledge of events and facts of the Amigo system (interaction/context history, user's choice among system's suggestions, user's feedback). This is mainly done by the Expanded Profile Service, the outer shell of UMPS, which includes the following: (a) The Multi-Profile Aggregator, responsible for aggregating profiles in case of multiple users found in the same context (i.e. the same room); and (b) The Dynamic Modeller, responsible for the user profile update based on the interaction/context history, the implicit/explicit feedback received from the user, as well as context changed events received through the Context Module from the Context Management Service.

The proposed client-service architecture (see Fig.1) has many advantages for such complex systems as Amigo home, among them being the reusability of profile data [8]. Each application is an UMPS client, feeding the service with interaction data or using shared profile data, possibly updated by another Amigo application or service.

3 Context-Dependent Static User Modelling

The user profile is a tree-based representation of individual user preferences and personal data, grouped in agreement with user ontology representation in the system, similarly to user characteristics representation in stereotypes. The first step in the generation of a new profile is gathering user's personal data via GUI. The personal data are also used to extract a set of predefined triggers for the initialisation of the profile based on the library of stereotypes. Combination of preference values from different stereotypes is rule-based, and depends on the position of the stereotype in the graph and on the number of contributing stereotypes.

Although stereotypes reduce user effort for system configuration, users need also a means to configure personally important settings. A GUI for explicit acquisition of user preferences (see Fig.2) allows users to specify both context-dependent and independent preferences. GUI shows the ontology-based preference keys in different domains; and users can set their preference values (in a range plus-minus five, where minus denotes dislike) for any key. Users can set as many different values for the same preference key in different contexts as they want, and attach the corresponding context to each value. They can also set a generic preference value for each key, which is context-independent. The Reasoning Module returns the generic preference value when no context-dependent preference value is found, that is, when the degree of similarity between query and stored contexts is less than a predefined threshold.

Instead of requiring users to build descriptions of personally important situations from a set of predefined contexts, the GUI provides an easy way to set preferences for these situations by giving them custom names: the users can add own terms under any concept of context ontology. Mapping of user-defined contexts into designer-defined contexts is fairly easy, because the users only need to edit a set of context types and values, built by the system. The choice of context types in the set depends on a parent of the new term in ontology tree. E.g., when a user adds a term "Dinner with Mother-in-Law" under a "Party" concept, the set of context descriptors to edit contains location and attending persons. Since the users will add own context terms mainly for frequent situations, the "Time" context can be attached separately, if needed (e.g., dinner with mother-in-law is a frequent event, but turkey is a December choice only).

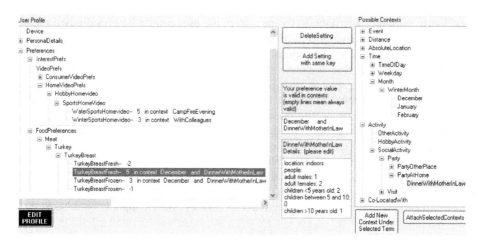

Fig. 2. GUI for acquisition of context-dependent and context-independent user preferences

4   Context-Dependent Dynamic User Modelling

Intelligent user environment should be capable of adjusting to multiple users and of learning users' preferences from interaction history. In Amigo home, interaction history is stored in a form of tuples "context" – "user action", where "context" is a set of descriptors and their values; and "user action" can be IR case, played video, food item added to a shopping list etc. Machine-learning methods are applied to process the history data and to classify items in question as "good" or "bad" for a current context. Since presence of people is a part of context, Dynamic Modeller learns context-dependency of preferences of each user alone and of combinations of multiple users. This way we avoid the need to resolve conflicts between preferences of different users: we just observe the results of how users resolve these conflicts.

For testing the feasibility of the proposed approach, we made initial experiments with Support Vector Machines and Case-Based Reasoning methods on data, collected via user interviews: three persons reported information retrieval cases, TV programs and corresponding contexts during two-four weeks time period. To these cases we added 20% noise (retrieval of similar and arbitrary information in arbitrary contexts), because users might forget to report something. This resulted in approximately 300 IR cases on 55 topics. Among them were several favourite sets of topics for different contexts, such as family favourites on Friday evening; kids' favourites; concerts which mother watches when she is alone; news for workday morning. The data included also four strongly event-related topics: interest in a weather forecast before a business trip; showing of hobby videos to guests; search for toys before a child's birthday. Other cases were occasionally retrieved ones. Thus, we were able to test how the method learns preferences of a single user and of a multi-user environment.

For these experiments we represented context as a list of 48 components, such as time, event, social context etc, and compared performances of context-independent and two context-dependent models, learned by CBR and SVM. Context-independent model recommends topics, if they frequently occur in the history. CBR retrieves cases depending on overall similarity of sets of context descriptors (we calculated it by Cosine measure), whereas SVM considers exact position of each descriptor in a set.

Experimental results have shown, that context-independent model learns favourite topics best of all (average precision and recall were near to 80%); CBR was also good (average precision was 60% and recall was near to 80%), and SVM was the worst (most probably due to the small amount of training data): average precision 40%, average recall 65%. Performance of each context-dependent model for multi-user environment was similar to that for single users. On the other hand, context-independent model was unable to learn any of four event-related topics; CBR learned two topics out of four, and SVM learned all four topics.

5 Conclusions and Future Work

This work presented the user modelling service for Smart Home Environment, which performs both static (via GUI and stereotypes) and dynamic modelling of context-dependent and context-independent user preferences. In a future we plan further data collection and experiments with dynamic modelling and with combining outputs of all components of user modelling service. However, initial results are encouraging: user interviews and experiments suggest that although attempt to learn context-dependency of preferences can hinder learning of favourite (context-independent) topics, it is nevertheless necessary because strong dependency of certain types of user interests on context does exist.

Acknowledgments. This work was done in EU Amigo project (contract IST-004182). We thank all people participated in the data collection.

References

1. Korpipää, P., Häkkilä, J., Kela, J., Ronkainen, S., Känsälä, I.: Utilising Context Ontology in Mobile Device Application Personalisation. In: Proc. MuM, pp. 133–140 (2004)
2. Masthoff, J.: Group Modeling: Selecting a Sequence of Television Items to Suit a Group of Viewers, User Modeling and User-Adapted Interaction 14, pp. 37–85 (2004)
3. Adomavicius, G., Sankaranarayanan, R., Sen, Sh., Tughilin, A.: Incorporating Contextual Information in Recommender Systems Using a Multidimensional Approach. ACM Trans. Inf. Syst. 23(1), 103–145 (2005)
4. Ardissono, L., Gena, C., Torasso, P., Bellifemine, F., Chiarotto, A., Difino, A., Negro, B.: User Modeling and Recommendation Techniques for Personalized electronic Program Guides, Personalization and User Adaptive Interaction in Digital Television, 6, pp. 3–26 (2004)
5. Goren-Bar, D., Glinansky, O.: FIT-recommending TV programs to family members. Computers and Graphics 28, 149–156 (2004)
6. Amigo project. http://www.amigo-project.org
7. Rich, E.: Readings in Intelligent User Interfaces. Springer, Heidelberg (1998)
8. Kobsa, A.: Generic User Modeling Systems. User. Modeling and User.-Adapted Interaction 11, 49–63 (2001)

Conversations Amidst Computing: A Study of Interruptions and Recovery of Task Activity

Shamsi T. Iqbal[1] and Eric Horvitz[2]

[1] Department of Computer Science, University of Illinois, Urbana, IL 61801
[2] Microsoft Research, One Microsoft Way, Redmond, WA 98052
siqbal@uiuc.edu, horvitz@microsoft.com

Abstract. We present results from a field study investigating the influence of conversations on the multitasking behavior of computer users. We report on several findings, including the timing of the resumption of tasks following conversational interruptions and on the nature and rate of computing activities that are performed concurrently with conversation.

Keywords: Interruption, disruption, recovery, conversation, cognitive models.

1 Introduction

Interrupting a task at a computer user's focus of attention often leads to a switching of attention to the source of the interruption [9]. Conversations with other people, including face-to-face conversations, phone calls, and talk through walls have been found to contribute to 15-45% of switches away from the task at a user's focus of attention [2, 3]. Indeed, becoming engaged in conversational dialog may pose greater disruptions to users than alerts delivered within a computing system because social conventions on personal responsiveness may make it difficult to take the time and actions to prepare for the task switch [9, 10].

We report on a study exploring how conversations occurring during computing tasks affect computing activities. We employed a tool with the ability to log computing activities as well as track the occurrence of conversations by noting the acoustical fingerprint of conversations. The tool logged the start and end of conversations as well as sets of activity variables before, during, and after conversations. We describe a field study undertaken with the tool.

2 Logging Computing Activities and Conversations

We developed and fielded a tool named DART (for Disruption Awareness and Recovery Tracker) for studying the influence of interruptions on computing activities. DART was constructed on top of Eve, a set of user and system monitoring components developed at Microsoft Research [4]. DART runs as a background process and logs user activities, including engagement with software applications, switches among windows, and the presence of mouse and keyboard activity. To protect the privacy of study participants, only a subset of keyboard events were recorded. The latter events

C. Conati, K. McCoy, and G. Paliouras (Eds.): UM 2007, LNAI 4511, pp. 350–354, 2007.
© Springer-Verlag Berlin Heidelberg 2007

centered on actions that could provide evidence of attempts to stabilize a task before switching attention to a conversation. These included the typing of periods and the input of carriage returns (evidence of an attempt to complete a sentence or paragraph), the use of shortcuts for saving (intent to save unsaved changes), and shortcuts for cutting and pasting (discharging volatile content stored in human memory).

In a related study [5], we employed DART to investigate disruption and recovery of tasks following email and instant messaging alerts. Here, we focus on conversational disruptions. We integrated into DART a conversation-detection component developed previously at Microsoft Research [4]. The conversation detector recognizes acoustical energy in the audio spectrum in the human-voice range. The component can distinguish live conversation from other acoustical signals, including voices coming from speakers. We note that DART only tracks the occurrence of a conversation; to protect the privacy of subjects, it does not capture conversation audio. Given interim periods of silence that occur naturally during conversations, we employed a heuristic policy for distinguishing a continuation of a conversation from the onset of a new one: quiescence in conversation lasting longer than 15 seconds was considered as indicating a conversation had ended. Similar thresholds have been used to define distinct conversations during instant messaging [1, 6].

A limitation of our study is that the system did not have the ability to distinguish in an explicit manner conversations associated with face-to-face interactions versus phone calls. Also, as the conversation detector simply identified the presence of conversation, we could not disambiguate whether a detected conversation was initiated by the user or by others. Such information would be useful in distinguishing self-interruptions from external interruptions, and for studying how visual cloaking provided by a traditional phone call—and potential reduction in social pressures to attend fully to a conversation—might influence the likelihood and nature of concurrent computing activities.

3   Analysis and Results

We deployed DART for a period of two weeks on the primary machines of 16 people at Microsoft whose job titles included program managers, researchers, and software developers. The participants had microphones installed on their computers as part of their default configuration (largely via embedded laptop microphones). The occurrences of conversations were logged only if the user was active on the computer.

We coarsely classified computing applications into two categories: *task-centric* and *peripheral* applications. We define task-centric applications as the use of software development or productivity applications, used typically within our organization to perform primary job responsibilities, *e.g.*, Visual Studio and Microsoft Office applications. We deemed communication applications, such as Microsoft Outlook for email and calendaring activities, and web search engines as peripheral.

We sought to explore the rate at which a user switched among tasks at different times, as captured by switches among windows of applications open on a user's computer, and the time spent on each application. We also were interested in how often users performed actions that could be characterized as stabilizing the state of a project, *e.g.*, saving files and completing sentences or paragraphs, pasting information that had been previously copied, etc., as it would seem that such actions might be useful to perform so as to leave it in a more recoverable state before turning attention to something else. We were also interested in the influence of visual cues for suspended applications on the efficiency of task recovery; we hypothesized that visible windows could serve to remind users about suspended applications.

We found that computer users spent a mean time of 21 minutes, 49 seconds (s.d. 39m, 59s) per day on conversations that were initiated while they were performing tasks on the computer. Separating the results by job role, the breakdown is 30 minutes 51 seconds (s.d. 26m, 42s) for software developers, 42 minutes 27 seconds (s.d. 47m, 9s) for managers and 2 minutes 1 second (s.d. 2m, 42s) for researchers.

We compared computing activities prior to the conversation (PC) and after the conversation had started (AC). The PC phase was defined as starting 5 minutes prior to the conversation, an observational period enabling us to capture a representative sample of activities before the interruption. Following the initiation of a conversation, users were found to perform the predefined task-state stabilizing activities (saved file, completing sentence, etc.) at a significantly higher rate than during the PC period. These findings are captured as mean rates of task stabilizing activities in Table 1.

48.12% of conversations occurring while users performed computing tasks were associated with inactivity for at least part of the conversation. Out of these, in 0.9% of the cases, users became inactive *after* the conversation started (*i.e.*, activity on the computer persisted for some time into the conversation). In 30.7% of these cases, users were inactive just prior to the conversation and remained inactive throughout the conversation. For the remaining 68.4%, users were temporarily inactive prior to the conversation, but became active as the conversation progressed.

As we could only detect the occurrence of conversations, not the details about the initiating event, we hypothesize that the first breakout is where the user is interrupted by someone else and the second case is where users instigate conversations. For the third case, users decided to continue computing tasks concurrently with the conversation as the conversation progressed, potentially something that could be done more comfortably during telephone conversations than in person. Another explanation for computing activities during conversation is that the conversation somehow caused the user to become active (*e.g.*, check mail). We seek in future work to extend the logging so as to better understand the initiation of conversations.

When conversations led to inactivity for the entire duration of the conversation, 2 tasks (s.d. 1.51) on average were suspended and 16 minutes, 22 seconds (s.d. 14m, 24s) passed before activity was next seen on the computer. We hypothesize that in many of these cases, users left the computer during the conversation, accounting for the rather long break between suspension of and return to the computing tasks, confirmed by later interviews.

Table 1. Task state stabilizing activities/minute

Activity	Pre-Conversation Mean (S.D.)	After Conversation Mean (S.D.)
Save	0.33(0.36)	0.85(1.16)
Paste	0.38(0.36)	1.19(2.63)
Sentence Completion	0.84(0.69)	2.88(4.09)
Paragraph Completion	0.78(0.81)	2.63(4.49)

Table 2. Peripheral activities/minute

Activity	Pre-Conversation	Intra-Conversation
Mail open	0.39 (0.40)	1.13 (2.19)
Mail writes	0.44 (0.36)	1.49 (2.77)
Mail Sends	0.25 (0.14)	0.80 (1.79)
Web mail checks	0.37 (0.29)	1.39 (2.15)
Web searches	0.35 (0.31)	0.77 (1.00)

For cases where users were active on the computer during the conversation, they switched applications at a rate of 0.48/min (s.d. 0.67), significantly lower than the switch rate during the PC period (0.77/min, $t(14)=7.88$, $p<0.001$). Users spent on average 2 minutes and 24 seconds (s.d. 4m, 20s) on each application, significantly higher than during the PC period. Outlook was the most accessed application during this time. Other top applications were Internet Explorer, Visual Studio and Office Communicator. When accessing Outlook, users performed activities at a significantly higher rate ($p<0.0001$ for all actions), as well as higher rates of web mail checks and web search operations, as compared to the PC period (Table 2). This finding may indicate that the disruption of the focused task by the conversation offers users an opportunity to perform less attentionally taxing peripheral tasks, and that these are skimmed during conversation at a higher rate, potentially in a less focused manner. Visual Studio appearing in this list of otherwise peripheral tasks indicates that users were occasionally able to converse and continue working on their ongoing tasks.

Overall, these findings provide evidence that subjects used the break to switch to concurrent peripheral applications. The lower mean switch rate during conversations may be due to crosstalk among related cognitive resources for having conversations and executing computing work, given, *e.g.,* the need to share verbal and other skills simultaneously [7, 8]. It is also possible that users consciously decide to perform only certain tasks (*e.g.*, checking email) in parallel with the conversation as they can effectively share resources without drastic degradation in the performance of either.

Following the completion of a conversation, or becoming active on the computer again if the conversation caused inactivity, users took on average 11 minutes 20 seconds to *resume* their suspended applications. Windows that were less than 25% visible took significantly longer to resume than windows that were more than 75% visible ($t(16)=3.259$, $p<0.005$), suggesting that the visibility of the suspended application windows served as a cue to return to the suspended applications. This observation was validated later through user interviews.

We further explored the relationship between applications that users were focused on before the interruption and the time to resume suspended applications. Our analysis showed that there was a 0.2 probability of not resuming activity on active windows as such within 2 hours of the end of the conversation, which may indicate that users had forgotten about these tasks.

We also explored whether the time spent on active windows before the suspension had an impact on the resumption time. Figure 1 illustrates the findings. Active windows where users spent < 1 minute before suspension, had a 60% probability of being resumed within the first minute of return, but also had a 2.1% probability of not being resumed at all during the session. Windows on which 5-15 minutes were spent before suspension were almost certain to be resumed within 5 minutes.

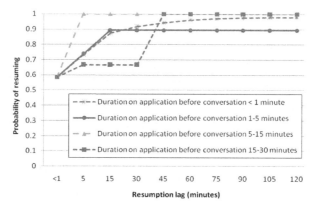

Fig. 1. Cumulative probabilities of resuming work in a suspended active window as a function of resumption lag

4 Conclusion

We performed a field study of user task execution behavior before and following conversational interruptions. We found that, following an interruption of tasks by conversation, users often suspend their ongoing computing tasks to participate in the conversation, may embark on peripheral tasks such as email correspondence and web searches, and show a slowing of computing activities. The time until resuming a task after a conversation was influenced by the duration of activity on the task before the interruption and increased visibility of suspended application windows was associated with faster resumption.

References

1. Avrahami, D., Hudson, S.: Communication characteristics of instant messaging: Effects and predictions of interpersonal relationships. CSCW, pp. 505–514 (2006)
2. Czerwinski, M., Horvitz, E., Wilhite, S.: A diary study of task switching and interruptions. CHI, pp. 175–182 (2004)
3. Gonzalez, V.M., Mark, G.: Constant, multi-tasking craziness: managing multiple working spheres. CHI, pp. 113–120 (2004)
4. Horvitz, E., Apacible, J.: Learning and reasoning about interruption. ICMI, pp. 20–27 (2003)
5. Iqbal, S.T., Horvitz, E.: Disruption and recovery of computing tasks: Field study, analysis, and directions, CHI 2007, (to appear 2007)
6. Isaacs, E., Walendowski, A., Whittaker, S., Schiano, D.J., Kamm, C.: The character, functions, and styles of instant messaging in the workplace. CSCW 2002, pp. 11–20 (2002)
7. Treisman, A.M.: Contextual cues in selective listening. Quarterly Journal of Experimental Psychology, 12, pp. 242–248
8. Wickens, C.D.: Multiple Resources and Performance Prediction. Theoretical Issues in Ergonomic Science, 3 (2), pp. 159–177
9. Wickens, C.D., Hollands, J.: Engineering psychology and human performance, Upper Saddle River, NJ. Prentice-Hall, Englewood Cliffs (2000)
10. Yantis, S.: Stimulus-Driven Attentional capture and attentional control settings. Journal of Experimental Psychology: Human Perception and Performance, vol. 19 (3), pp. 676–681

Cross-Domain Mediation in Collaborative Filtering

Shlomo Berkovsky[1], Tsvi Kuflik[1], and Francesco Ricci[2]

[1] University of Haifa, Haifa
slavax@cs.haifa.ac.il, tsvikak@is.haifa.ac.il
[2] Free University of Bozen-Bolzano, Italy
fricci@unibz.it

Abstract. One of the main problems of collaborative filtering recommenders is the sparsity of the ratings in the users-items matrix, and its negative effect on the prediction accuracy. This paper addresses this issue applying cross-domain mediation of collaborative user models, i.e., importing and aggregating vectors of users' ratings stored by collaborative systems operating in different application domains. The paper presents several mediation approaches and initial experimental evaluation demonstrating that the mediation can improve the accuracy of the generated predictions.

1 Introduction

Nowadays, the overwhelming amounts of information raise a need for intelligent systems providing personalized services tailored to users' needs and interests, represented by their User Models (UMs). Collaborative Filtering (CF) 2 is one of the most popular and widely-used personalization techniques, generating personalized predictions in recommender systems. CF assumes that people with similar tastes, i.e., people who agreed in the past, will also agree in the future. Hence, CF predictions are generated by aggregating the opinions of people with similar tastes.

The input for the CF algorithm is a matrix of users' ratings on items, referred to as the ratings matrix. The CF algorithm is typically decomposed into three stages: (1) similarity computation: weighting all the users with respect to their similarity with the active user, (2) neighborhood formation: selecting K most similar users, i.e., nearest-neighbors for the prediction generation, and (3) prediction generation: computing the prediction by weighting the ratings of the neighbor users on the target item 2.

CF recommender systems suffer from the *new item* and the *new user* bootstrapping problems. The new item problem refers to the fact that if the number of users that rated an item is small, accurate predictions for this item cannot be generated. The new user problem refers to the fact that if the number of items rated by a user is small, it is unlikely that there is an overlap of products rated by this user and other users. Hence, users' similarity cannot be reliably computed and accurate predictions for the user cannot be generated. These problems are referred to as particular cases of a CF *sparsity* problem, where the contents of the ratings matrix are insufficient for generating accurate predictions. To overcome the sparsity, 1 proposed to enrich the UMs of the target recommender system by a mediation (i.e., import and aggregation) of user

C. Conati, K. McCoy, and G. Paliouras (Eds.): UM 2007, LNAI 4511, pp. 355–359, 2007.
© Springer-Verlag Berlin Heidelberg 2007

modeling data from other recommender systems. Mediation enriches the UMs available to the target system and upgrades the accuracy of the generated predictions.

This paper focuses on cross-domain mediation of UMs in CF, which is one of the mediation modes discussed in 1. In cross-domain mediation, the user modeling data is imported from remote systems exploiting the same CF recommendation technique as the target system, in other application domains. Hence, both target and remote systems represent the UMs as a list of ratings provided by a user on the domain items. In this setting, four types of user modeling data can be imported: (1) UMs stored by the remote system, (2) lists of the neighborhood candidates, (3) degrees of similarity between the active user and the other users, computed over the data stored by the remote system, and (4) complete predictions generated by the remote system. This paper elaborates on the last type of cross-domain mediation in CF and presents its implementation and evaluation using the EachMovie dataset 3. Experimental results demonstrate that importing external user modeling data allows achieving higher accuracy of the predictions.

2   Cross-Domain Mediation in Collaborative Filtering

Traditional CF recommender systems store the ratings in a two-dimensional matrix (or map) $M:(user_{id}, item_{id}) \rightarrow rating$, where $user_{id}$ and $item_{id}$ represent the unique identifiers of users and items and *rating* represents the explicit evaluation given by a user $user_{id}$ on an item $item_{id}$. Note that the number of items typically managed by the system is significantly larger than the number of ratings provided by an average user. This leads to a very sparse ratings matrix M and to the sparsity problem of CF.

Conversely, in a domain-distributed setting, the ratings matrix M is split, i.e., every domain d stores a local ratings matrix M_d. The structure of M_d is similar to the structure of M, i.e., it is a two-dimensional matrix of ratings given by a set of users on a set of items. However, this set of items in M_d is restricted to items that belong to a certain application domain d, i.e., $M_d: (user_{id}, item_{id}) \rightarrow rating$, such that $item_{id} \in d$. Hence, this setting can be considered as a vertical partitioning of the ratings matrix M (figure 1).

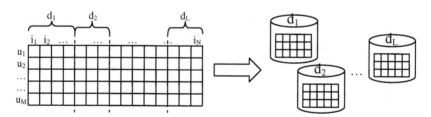

Fig. 1. Domain-related vertical partitioning of the ratings matrix

Note that this is not exactly vertical partitioning of the ratings matrix. In a real vertical partitioning, the partitioned sets of items are disjoint, i.e., every item belongs to a single group of items. In domain-related vertical partitioning, certain items may belong to multiple domains or categories. This setting is not uncommon if the above representation of domains is downscaled to the representation of E-Commerce services. In this case, ambiguous categorization of items may be explained by different classifications of products, their providers, or E-Commerce sites.

Similarly to a centralized CF recommender system, a typical scenario is initiated by a recommendation request issued by a user $user_{id}$ to a CF recommender system R_t in the target application domain t. The target system R_t selects a set of items $\{item_{id}\}$ that can be recommended and initiates a prediction generation process for every $item_{id}$. To enhance the accuracy of the predictions, R_t requests relevant user modeling data from a set of remote CF recommender systems $\{R_d\}$, operating on domains d. The query is formulated as a triple $q=<user_{id}, item_{id}, t>$. In the following discussion, let us assume that the identities of the users and items are unique in all the domains.

According to the first mediation approach, the UMs (i.e., the rating vectors), stored by a remote system R_d, operating in another domain d, are imported. For the sake of simplicity, let us assume that R_d responds to q by sending to R_t the content of the local repository of UMs, i.e., $resp_d=M_d$, where M_d is local ratings matrix containing only the items that belong to domain d. Upon receiving the set of responses $\{resp_d\}$, R_t constructs the unifying ratings matrix M by integrating local and imported data. Over M, traditional CF mechanism is applied. Since the reconstructed matrix M can be considered as the traditional centralized CF matrix, this approach is referred to as **Standard** CF and serves as a baseline for the experimental comparisons.

The second mediation approach is called **Heuristic** and it imports into the target system a list of nearest-neighbors computed by the remote systems R_d. It relies on a heuristic assumption that similarity of users spans across multiple application domains. Hence, if two users are similar in a certain remote application domain d, they may be also similar in the target domain t. Practically, this means that R_d responds to q by sending to R_t the set of K identities of the users most similar to the active user, i.e., $resp_d=\{user_{id}\}$. Upon receiving the set of responses $\{resp_d\}$, R_t aggregates these sets of nearest-neighbors into the overall set of (heuristic) candidates for being the nearest-neighbors, computes their true similarity values according to the local ratings matrix M_t, selects the set of K nearest-neighbors, and generates the predictions.

The third approach is called **Cross-domain** mediation. Here, to compute the overall similarity between users, the target system imports domain-dependent similarity values and aggregates them into an overall similarity value. Upon receiving the request q, every remote system R_d computes locally, i.e., according to the contents of the local ratings matrix M_d, the similarity between the active user and the other users in M_d. A set of K nearest-neighbors is selected, and their $user_{id}$ together with their similarity values are sent to R_t. In other words, $resp_d=\{(user_{id}, sim_d)\}$, where $sim_d=sim(user_{id}, user_{act})$ is the local similarity between a user $user_{id}$ and the active user $user_{act}$, computed using their ratings in the application domain d using a certain similarity metric sim. Upon receiving the set of responses $\{resp_d\}$, R_t aggregates the domain-related similarity values into the overall similarity metric using inter-domain correlation values. As the overall similarity is computed, the K nearest-neighbors are selected and the predictions are generated.

The fourth mediation approach deals with complete CF predictions generated locally by the system R_t from the target domain t and is referred to as **Local**. According to it, the predictions are generated using only the data stored in the ratings matrix M_t of the target system. This is done similarly to the centralized CF, but using a restricted set of ratings on items from t: local similarity values are computed, the set of

K nearest-neighbors is selected and the predictions are generated. However, *Local* CF disregards the fact that the items may belong to several application domains and treats each domain independently. Hence, according to **Remote-Average** variant of *Local* CF, every remote system R_d from another application domain *d*, to which the predicted item belongs, generates a local prediction using the ratings stored in its ratings matrix M_d. The computed predictions are sent to R_t, i.e., $resp_d=pred_d$. Upon receiving the set of responses *{resp_d}* and generating a local prediction using its matrix M_t, R_t aggregates the predictions into a single value by averaging the set of all local predictions.

3   Experimental Evaluation and Conclusions

Experimental evaluation of the proposed mediation approaches involved EachMovie dataset of movie ratings 3. To mimic domain-related vertical partitioning of the ratings matrix, the movies were partitioned according to their genres. Eight genre-related ratings matrices were created: *action, animation, comedy, drama, family, horror, romance,* and *thriller*. In EachMovie, the movies usually belong to multiple (up to *4*) genres. Each movie belongs, on average, to *2.376* genres. Hence the sets of movies in the genre-related matrices were not disjoint. Table 1 summarizes the distribution of movies and ratings among genre-related ratings matrices and sparsity of each matrix.

Table 1. Data Distribution among Genres-Related Matrices

	action	animation	comedy	drama	family	horror	romance	thriller
num. of movies	198	43	400	536	145	87	137	177
num. of ratings	1,166,032	192,769	2,209,218	3,056,203	800,118	432,568	681,409	991,083
sparsity (%)	91.923	93.852	92.425	92.180	92.432	93.181	93.179	92.321

Local and *Remote-Average* CF approaches discussed in previous section were implemented and evaluated. Cosine Similarity was selected as the users' similarity metric, and the minimal number of movies rated by users for the similarity computation was *6* (predictions could not be generated for users that rated below *6* movies). The number of nearest-neighbors used for the prediction generation was *20*.

The experiment evaluated the effect of sparsity of the target user ratings on the accuracy of the predictions. Hence, the users were partitioned to *12* categories, according to the percentage of the rated movies in the target genre: below *3%*, *3%* to *6%*, ..., *30%* to *33%*, and over *33%*. For every group, *1,000* predictions were generated for various combinations of user, movie, and target genre. The predictions' accuracy was measured using the MAE metric 2. The baseline for the comparisons is *Standard* CF, as its results are similar to the results that would have been obtained in traditional centralized CF.

The results show that both *Local* and *Remote-Average* CF outperform *Standard* CF for any percentage of rated movies (statistically significant, *p=2.78E-07* and *p=1.63E-06*, respectively). It can be explained by arguing that the similarity computation over the ratings from the target genre only in *Local* CF (or over the ratings from other movie genres in *Remote-Average*) yields more accurate similarity values than the similarity computation over all the available ratings. This explained by the observation that the ratings from these genres are important for computing the similarity value in the relevant genre, whereas the other ratings may insert noise into the computation. As a result, the predictions are more accurate.

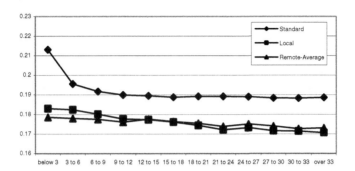

Fig. 2. Local, Remote-Average and Standard CF Approaches

Comparing *Local* and *Remote-Average* CF approaches shows that for a small percentage of rated movies, i.e., sparse ratings matrix, *Remote-Average* CF is slightly more accurate (statistically insignificant). It can be explained by the fact that the predictions are generated using additional knowledge acquired by importing data from other relevant genres and not using the data from the target genre only. For a higher percentage of rated movies, the local data is sufficient and the imported data hampers the accuracy of the predictions.

It should be stressed that in certain conditions *Local* and *Remote-Average* CF approaches are inapplicable. For example, for the group of users that rated less than *3%* of the movies, predictions can be generated only for comedies and dramas, as only in these cases *3%* of the movies is greater than *6*, a minimal number of movies for the similarity computation. Hence, although the accuracy of *Local* and *Remote-Average* CF is higher, they cannot generate predictions for certain movies that will negatively effect on the ability of the system to recommend all the interesting movies.

In summary, the evaluation showed that importing user profile data from other domains yields more accurate predictions. However, this is not applicable for sparse data and aggregating local degrees of similarity (i.e., *Cross-Domain* CF approach) is supposedly a more appropriate solution. In the future, it is planned to implement and evaluate the rest of the proposed cross-domain CF approaches.

References

1. Berkovsky, S.: Decentralized Mediation of User Models for a Better Personalization. In: proc. of the AH Conference (2006)
2. Herlocker, J.L., Konstan, J.A., Borchers, A., Riedl, J.: An Algorithmic Framework for Performing Collaborative Filtering. In: proc. of the SIGIR Conference (1999)
3. McJones, P.: EachMovie Collaborative Filtering Data Set. HP Research (1997)

Driver Destination Models

John Krumm and Eric Horvitz

Microsoft Research
Microsoft Corporation
One Microsoft Way
Redmond, WA 98052 U.S.A.
{jckrumm, horvitz}@microsoft.com

Abstract. Predictive models of destinations represent an opportunity in the context of the increasing availability and sophistication of in-car driving aids. We present analyses of drivers' destinations based on GPS data recorded from 180 volunteer subjects. We focus on the probability of observing drivers visit previously unobserved destinations given time of day and day of week, and the rate of decline of observing such new destinations with time. For the latter, we discover a statistically significant difference based on gender.

Keywords: driving, mobility, destinations, cars, automobiles, navigation.

1   Introduction

Computing is increasingly coming to the aid of drivers, with improved in-car navigation systems, advanced routing services, and comprehensive point-of-interest databases, some with intermittent and ongoing network access. With this sophistication comes the opportunity for developing better models of driver preferences and behavior, to both improve services and decrease unnecessary driving distractions. An understanding of drivers' destinations is one promising direction for improving in-car services. Knowledge of a driver's destination can be used to give anticipatory alerts about traffic and recommendations for re-routing, reminders about location-based tasks, relevant advertising, and useful suggestions for parking, restaurants, and other points of interest. Destination modeling can be especially useful in methods for destination prediction[1, 2]. In [1], we present probabilistic models that predict the destination of drivers as trips progress, based on observational data. In this paper, we review statistics of destinations that support the probabilistic modeling efforts. The analysis is based on logs of trips of 180 drivers. We first show how destinations vary with time of day. Then, we review our research on the scope of destinations for users, exploring how the likelihood of seeing new destinations visited decreases with the observational period.

Our studies are based on GPS data logged from volunteer drivers participating in the Microsoft Multiperson Location Survey (MSMLS), an ongoing study of driving behavior we initiated in early 2004. We recruited employees from our institution and their adult family members by offering participants a 1 in 100 chance of winning a

C. Conati, K. McCoy, and G. Paliouras (Eds.): UM 2007, LNAI 4511, pp. 360–364, 2007.
© Springer-Verlag Berlin Heidelberg 2007

US\$ 200 MP3 player. Each subject was asked to complete a demographic questionnaire. Based on the demographic questionnaire, the average age of our 180 subjects was 36.6 years. 36% of them had non-adult children, 72% were male, and 25% were single.

We ask participants in the MSMLS study to keep the GPS device on the dashboard of their car for two weeks. We modified the GPS devices to allow them to be used without intervention over the observational period; the modified devices turn on when receiving power and retain logs between trips. The devices are set to record time-stamped latitude and longitude coordinates only when the car is moving, reducing the chance of exceeding the GPS's 10,000-point memory over the two-week period. The adaptive recording mode gave points whose median separation distance was 64.4 meters and whose median separation time was 6 seconds. We segmented the GPS data into discrete trips by splitting the sequence at points separated by more than five minutes and eliminating trips under 10 points or one kilometer long. The final point in each trip segment is the trip's destination, which gives us a list of latitude and longitude points, one for each of the 8319 resulting trips.

2 Destinations over Time

We sought to understand how often drivers take trips to different locations and how often they go to places that they have not been observed to visit before, as a function of the length of the observational period. Such data provides prior probability information that can be used within predictive models of destination, which may also consider such factors as time of day and the trajectory of a trip in progress.

In our work on predicting destinations, we explicitly model the likelihood that a driver will visit a destination that they have not been observed to visit over the course of the observational period [1]. The probability of a user visiting a location that has not been observed before is critical in *open-world modeling* of destinations, which admits previously unseen destinations into location prediction, also described in [1]. Prior research on destination prediction has assumed a closed world, limiting the scope of destination prediction to those locations that have been previously visited by drivers. This work includes work by Marmasse and Schmandt[3], Ashbrook and Starner[4], Hariharan and Toyama[5], Liao *et al.*[6], and Gogate *et al.*[7]. All of these studies only consider as candidate destinations those locations that have been extracted from GPS histories, *i.e.* places that subjects have actually visited.

We begin by examining when drivers make trips. Using the time-stamped trips from our MSMLS data, we computed the mean number of trips per week over all our driving subjects for each hour of the day. For each of these trips, we also computed whether or not the destination had been observed before in the study. For a given subject, we defined a location as a *new* destination when no previously observed destination visited by the user had been within a 200 meter radius of that location.

The results are displayed at the top of Fig. 1. The dark curve shows the average number of trips made per week in a given hour of the day over the course of the survey. We see that the number of trips peaks around 5 p.m. – 6 p.m., when the average driver made about 2.66 trips per week. There is another peak around

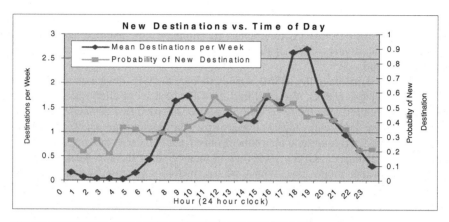

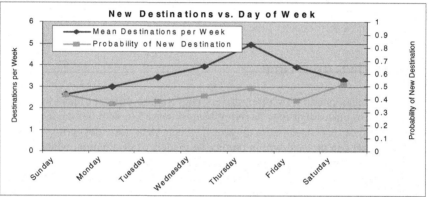

Fig. 1. The number of mean trips in a week and the probability of visiting a previously unobserved destination over the time of day (top graph) and the day of the week (bottom)

8 a.m. – 9 a.m., with about 1.69 trips per week. Both peaks may reflect commuting to and from work. As expected, very few trips are made late at night.

This data can serve as a prior probability distribution in probabilistic models of driving destination and activity. The lighter curve in the graph at the top of Fig. 1 shows the proportion of new destinations, providing the probabilities that destinations reached at different times of the day have been previously visited. The probability of visiting a new destination peaks at 11 a.m. and again at 3 p.m. The data shows that, over the course of the observational period of the study, new destinations are most likely visited in the middle of the day. Such data could help a navigation system automatically determine whether or not to offer driving assistance and information about the predicted destination.

We look at the same data conditioned on the day of the week in the bottom of Fig. 1. Thursday is the peak day for driving trips, after a steady rise in trips starting with Sunday. The plot also shows the probability of visiting a new destination as a function of the day of the week. Saturday slightly beats Thursday as the most probable day to visit a new destination on a given trip.

3   Falloff in Observing New Destinations

As we mentioned, most destination prediction algorithms limit their predictions about future destinations to previously observed destinations [2]. Clearly, the rate of seeing previously unobserved destinations is highest at the outset of the observation period. We would expect to see the rate of observing such new destinations decrease with ongoing observation, given drivers' habitual patterns of visiting locations, based on recurrent activities. We now focus on our studies of the change in rate of seeing new locations with observation period for all participants as well as breakouts for people with different demographical attributes.

The black squares in Fig. 2 show how the number of new destinations decreases significantly with the number of days into the MSMLS survey. The average number of new destinations over all subjects on the first day is 3.6, dropping to 1.6 on the second day and 1.34 on the third day. To avoid edge effects, we ignore the first day of the study. The drop in new destinations is well modeled by an exponential decay of the form $d(t) = ae^{-bt}$, where t is the number of days into the survey and $d(t)$ is the number of destinations on day t that have not been visited on any previous day. We performed a least squares fit of this equation to the measured average of new destinations and found $d(t) = 2.142e^{-0.134t}$.

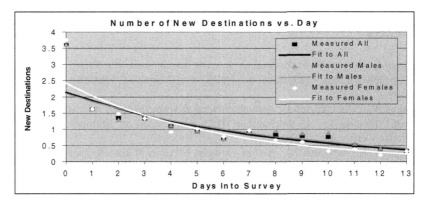

Fig. 2. Number of new destinations visited over duration of observation period for all participants and for groups conditioned on gender

We now explore how new destinations decrease over time based on drivers' demographics. For each subject, we computed parameters a and b of the exponential model describing decay in seeing new destinations using least squares. We examined splits along gender, single versus partnered, children at home, and the existence of extended family within a 50 mile radius. For each category, we removed all b exponents beyond the category's 3-sigma points to eliminate the effect of outliers. We also removed subjects whose least squares fit was degenerate due to a lack of data, *e.g.* only one day of available data. We performed a t-test on the b values to compare the decay rate for each pair of categories. Of the four splits, we found a statistically significant difference in decay rates only along gender lines. For men, the mean decay rate is $b = 0.0695$, and for women $b = 0.1960$, implying that women's rate of visiting new destinations falls off faster than men's ($t(35) = 2.03$, $p < 0.026$). The aggregate fits for men and women are shown in Fig. 2.

The analysis shows that, in aggregate, drivers quickly approach a steady state where visiting new destinations is relatively rare. After 14 days of observation, for example, drivers are visiting an average of 0.33 new destinations per day. Since the median number of trips per day for all our subjects was 3.53, this implies that after two weeks, the probability of a driver going to a new destination per trip is approximately $0.33/3.53 \approx 0.09$.

4 Conclusions

We reviewed the MSMLS dataset and presented several analyses of the data in support of ongoing efforts to construct probabilistic models of destination. We showed how the number of trips and visits to previously unobserved destinations varies with the time of day and day of week. We described how quickly drivers tend to reach a steady state in visiting new destinations over an observation horizon. Finally, we explored the influence of demographic attributes on the rate of visiting previously unobserved destinations and identified an influence of gender.

References

1. Krumm, J., Horvitz, E.: Predestination: Inferring Destinations from Partial Trajectories. In: Eighth International Conference on Ubiquitous Computing UbiComp, 2006. Orange County, CA (2006)
2. Kostov, V., et al.: Travel Destination Prediction Using Frequent Crossing Pattern from Driving History. In: 8th International IEEE Conference on Intelligent Transportation Systems, Vienna, Austria (2005)
3. Marmasse, N., Schmandt, C.: A User-Centered Location Model. Personal and Ubiquitous Computing (6), 318–321 (2002)
4. Ashbrook, D., Starner, T.: Using GPS To Learn Significant Locations and Predict Movement Across Multiple Users. Personal and Ubiquitous Computing 7(5), 275–286 (2003)
5. Hariharan, R., Toyama, K.: Project Lachesis: Parsing and Modeling Location Histories. In: GIScience 2004, Springer, Heidelberg (2004)
6. Liao, L., Fox, D., Kautz, H.: Learning and Inferring Transportation Routines. In Proceedings of the 19th National Conference on Artificial Intelligence (AAAI 2004). San Jose, CA, USA (2004)
7. Gogate, V., et al.: Modeling Transportation Routines using Hybrid Dynamic Mixed Networks. In: Uncertainty in Artificial Intelligence (UAI 2005) (2005)

Enabling Efficient Real Time User Modeling in On-Line Campus

Santi Caballé, Fatos Xhafa, Thanasis Daradoumis, and Raul Fernandez

Open University of Catalonia, Department of Computer Science and Multimedia
Av. Tibidabo, 39-43, 08035 Barcelona, Spain
{scaballe,fxhafa,adaradoumis,rfernandezco}@uoc.edu

Abstract. User modelling in on-line distance learning is an important research field focusing on two important aspects: describing and predicting students' actions and intentions as well as adapting the learning process to students' features, habits, interests, preferences, and so on. The aim is to greatly stimulate and improve the learning experience. In this context, user modeling implies a constant processing and analysis of user interaction data during long-term learning activities, which produces large and considerably complex information. As a consequence, processing this information is costly and requires computational capacity beyond that of a single computer. In order to overcome this obstacle, in this paper we show how a parallel processing approach can considerably decrease the time of processing log data that come from on-line distance educational web-based systems. The results of our study show the feasibility of using Grid middleware to speed and scale up the processing of log data and thus achieving an efficient and dynamic user modeling in on-line distance learning.

1 Introduction

User modeling [1] is a mature research field mostly involved in the information technology context. It is mainly utilized in software systems for inferring the users' goals, skills, knowledge, needs and preferences and thus achieving more adequate adaptation and personalization on the basis of the user activity pattern built. This inference process relies in turn on being able to track the users' actions when interacting with the application such as the users' choice of buttons and menu items [2].

In this paper, we focus on and are interested in web-based applications that support on-line distance learning. These applications, due to the high degree of user interaction, take great advantage of the tracking-based techniques of user modeling such as providing broader and better support for the users of Web-based educational systems [2]. Indeed, the data analysis of the information captured from the actions performed by learners is a core function for the modeling of the learner's behavior during the learning process and of the learning process itself as well. In addition, the building of learner models may help identify navigation patterns and adapt the system's usability to the actual learners' needs resulting in a great stimulation of the learning experience. However, the information generated in web-based learning applications can be of a great variety of type and formats [3]. Moreover, these applications are characterized

C. Conati, K. McCoy, and G. Paliouras (Eds.): UM 2007, LNAI 4511, pp. 365–369, 2007.
© Springer-Verlag Berlin Heidelberg 2007

by a high degree of user-user and user-system interaction which stresses the amount of interaction data generated. Therefore, there is a strong need for powerful solutions that record the large volume of interaction data and can be used to perform an efficient interaction analysis and knowledge extraction.

Based on this vision, a preliminary study was conducted [3] to show that a Grid [4] approach might increase the efficiency of processing a large amount of information from user activity log files. In order to show the feasibility of our approach, we used the log data from the internal campus of the Open University of Catalonia though it can be applied for reducing the processing time of log data from web-based application in general. Our ultimate objective is to make it possible to continuously monitor and adapt the learning process and objects to the actual students' learning needs as well as to validate the campus' usability by analyzing and evaluating its actual usage.

2 Modeling Students' Behavior in Web-Based Distance Learning Settings: The Case of the Open University of Catalonia

Our real web-based learning context is the Open University of Catalonia (UOC) [5] which offers distance education through the Internet in different languages. As of this writing, about 40,000 students, lectures and tutors from everywhere participate in some of the 23 official degrees and other PhD and post-graduate programs resulting in more than 600 official courses.

From our experience at the UOC, the description and prediction of our students' behavior and navigation patterns when interacting with the virtual campus is a first issue. Indeed, a well-designed system's usability is a key point to stimulate and satisfy the students' learning experience. In addition, the monitoring and evaluation of real, long-term, complex, problem-solving situations is a must in our context. The aim is to adapt the learning process and objects to the actual students' learning needs as well as to validate the campus' usability by monitoring and evaluating its actual usage.

In order to achieve these goals, the analysis of the campus activity and specifically the users' traces captured while browsing the campus is essential in this context. The collection of this information in log files and the later analysis and interpretations of this information provide the means to model the actual user's behavior and activity patterns. However, in the context of the UOC, the whole user interaction generates a great amount of information a day (about 10 GB) which is filtered and collected in large daily log files. Furthermore, this large information is found in an ill-structured highly redundant form needing a great amount of computational power to constantly process log data [5]. As a matter of fact, the computational cost is the main obstacle to processing this data in real time [3] and hence in our real situation this processing tends to be done offline in order to avoid harming the performance of the logging application, but as it takes place after the completion of the learning activity it has less impact on it.

3 An Efficient Processing of Log Data

In order to deal with the above mentioned problems and inconvenients, we have developed a simple application in Java, called *UOCLogsProcessing* that processes log files of the UOC. However, as the processing is done sequentially, it takes too long to complete the work and it has to be done after the completion of the learning activity, which makes the construction of effective real-time user models not possible.

The distributed platform has been developed using the JXTA [7] protocols and offers a shared Grid where client peers can submit their tasks in the form of Java programs stored on signed jar files and are remotely solved on the nodes of the platform. The architecture of the JXTA platform is made up of two types of peers: *common client peers* and *broker peers*. The former can create and submit their requests while the later are the administrators of the Grid, which are in charge of efficiently assigning client requests to the Grid nodes and notify the results to the owner's requests. To assure an efficient use of resources, brokers use different allocation algorithms, which can be viewed as economic models, to determine the best candidate node to process each new received request. The implementation and design of peers, groups, job and presence discovery, pipe-based messaging, etc. are developed using the latest updated JXTA libraries [7]. This distributed platform has been deployed in a large-scale, distributed and heterogeneous P2P network using nodes from PlanetLab[1] platform.

3.1 Parallelizing the Processing of Log Files

The parallel implementation follows the Master-Worker (MW) [8] paradigm. In a nutshell, the log file is split off into a certain number of parts, which can be exactly equal to the number of grid nodes (slaves) that will participate in the processing or can be larger. In this later case some peer nodes could receive more than one part for processing. By splitting the original file into more parts than peer slave candidates for processing, we can achieve different degrees of granularity of the parallel processing. Achieving different degrees of granularity is very desirable in Grid environments given the high heterogeneity of computing resources. Note that we have a perfect split of the problem in many independent parts. In the end, the master node just needs to append to a unique file the arriving of partial solutions (partial result files after processing). The main steps of the MW parallel algorithm to process a log file in the JXTA platform are as follows:

1. [**Pre-processing phase**]: *UOCLogsProcessing* counts the total number of lines of the log file, totalNbLines, and knowing the total number of parts to split the file off, nbParts, each peer node will receive and process a totalNbLines/nbParts of lines from the file.
2. [**Master Loop**]: Repeat
    a. Read totalNbLines/nbParts lines from the original file and create a file with them.
    b. Create a request and submit it to JXTA platform
    c. [**Juxta-cat processing**]:
        i.   The request is received by a broker of JXTA platform and it is assigned to a peer node of the platform.
        ii. The peer node, upon receiving and accepting the request, notifies it to the Broker node.

---

[1] http://www.planet-lab.org. As of Feb. 24, 2007, PlanetLab consists of 755 nodes at 363 sites.

iii.   The peer node receives the corresponding part of the file to process by direct JXTA transfer from the Master node.

iv.   The peer runs *UOCLogProcessing* functionality for processing the lines of the file, one at a time, and stores the results of the processing in a buffer.

v.   The peer node, once the processing of the request is done, sends back to the master node the content of the buffer.

Until the original log file has been completely scanned.

3.   [**Master's final phase**]: Receive messages (partial files) from peers and append in the correct order the newly received resulting file to the final file containing the information extracted from the original log file.

3.2 Experimental Results

In this section we present the experimental results from measuring the speedup obtained by the grid processing. Battery test involved both large amounts of log information (i.e. daily log files) and well-stratified short samples consisting of representative daily periods with different activity degrees. In addition, other tests included a few log files with selected file size forming a sample of each representative stratum. This allowed us to obtain reliable statistical results using an input data size easy to use.

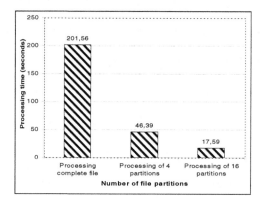

Fig. 1. Processing times of a log file of 100Mb for the case of processing without partitions and by partitioning into 4 and 16 parts, respectively, resulting in a speed-up of 0,543 and 0,71 respectively

The battery test was processed by the *UOCLogsProcessing* application executed on single-processor machines involving usual configurations. Moreover, it was executed several times with different workload in order to have more reliable results in statistical terms involving file size, number of log entries processed and execution time along with other basic statistics. The same battery test was processed by JXTA platform using 8 peer nodes and by considering 4, 8 and 16 parts of the original file.

Parallel efficiency and speed up are then computed involving the number of grid nodes and the time needed by the grid to process each log file. Fig. 1 shows the considerable decrease in execution time we achieved using the JXTA platform.

4 Conclusions and Further Work

In this paper, we have shown how to model the learner's behavior and activity pattern by using user modeling tracking-based techniques. However, the information generated from tracking the learners is usually very large, tedious, and ill-formatted and as a result processing this information is time-consuming. In order to overcome this problem, we have proposed a Grid-aware implementation that considerably reduces the processing time of log data and allow us to build and constantly maintain user models.

Further work will include the implementation of a more thorough mining process of the log files, which due to the nature of the log files of our virtual campus will require more processing time in comparison to the log processor used in this work.

Acknowledgements. This work has been partially supported by the Spanish MCYT project TSI2005-08225-C07-05.

References

1. Bushey, R., Mauney, JM., Deelman, T.: The Development of Behaviour-Based User Models for a Computer System. In: Kay, J. (ed.) User Modeling: Proceedings of the UM99, pp. 109–118. Springer, Heidelberg (1999)
2. Gaudioso, E., Boticario, J.G.: Towards web-based adaptive learning communities. In: Proceedings of Artificial Intelligence in Education 2003, Sydney, Australia, IOS Press, Amsterdam, Trento, Italy (2003)
3. Xhafa, F., Caballé, S.: Daradoumis, Th., Zhou, N.: A Grid-Based Approach for Processing Group Activity Log Files. In: proc. of the GADA'04, Cyprus (2004)
4. Foster, I., Kesselman, C.: The Grid: Blueprint for a Future Computing Infrastructure, pp. 15–52. Morgan Kaufmann, San Francisco (1998)
5. Open University of Catalonia web page as of (February 2007), http://www.uoc.edu
6. Carbó, J., Mor, E., Minguillón, J.: User Navigational Behavior in e-Learning Virtual Environments. The 2005 IEEE/WIC/ACM International Conference on Web Intelligence (WI'05), pp. 243–249 (2005)
7. JXTA: web page as of (February 2007), http://www.jxta.org/
8. Master-Worker: web page as of (February 2007), http://www.cs.wisc.edu/condor/mw/

Eliciting Adaptation Knowledge from On-Line Tutors to Increase Motivation

Teresa Hurley and Stephan Weibelzahl

National College of Ireland, School of Informatics,
Mayor Street 1,
Dublin 1, Ireland
{thurley,sweibelzahl}@ncirl.ie

Abstract. In the classroom, teachers know how to motivate their students and how to exploit this knowledge to adapt or optimize their instruction when a student shows signs of demotivation. In on-line learning environments it is much more difficult to assess a learner's motivation and to have adaptive intervention strategies and rules of application to help prevent attrition or drop-out. In this paper, we present results from a survey of on-line tutors on how they motivate their learners. These results will inform the development of an adaptation engine by extracting and validating selection rules for strategies to increase motivation depending on the learner's self-efficacy, goal orientation, locus of control and perceived task difficulty in adaptive Intelligent Tutoring Systems.

1 Introduction

On-line learning is a dynamic and potentially enriching forms of learning but attrition remains a serious problem [4]. Motivation to learn is affected by the learner's self-efficacy, goal orientation, locus of control and perceived task difficulty. In the traditional classroom tutors infer learners' levels of motivation from several cues, including speech, behavior, attendance, body language or feedback, and offer interventional strategies aimed at increasing motivation. Intelligent Tutoring Systems (ITS) need to be able to recognize when the learner is becoming demotivated and to intervene with effective motivational strategies. Such an ITS would comprise two main components, an assessment mechanism that infers the learner's level of motivation from observing the learner's behaviour, and an adaptation component that selects the most appropriate intervention strategy to increase motivation. This paper presents the results of a survey of on-line tutors on how they motivate their learners. These results will inform the development of the adaptation component by extracting and validating selection rules for strategies to increase motivation.

The focus of this research is intervention strategies which can be implemented and validated in an Intelligent Tutoring System to increase motivation and reduce attrition. Previous approaches in this field were mainly based on the ARCS model, which is an instructional design model ([3][9][12]). In contrast, the approach being taken in this research is based on Social Cognitive Theory (SCT) [1], particularly on

C. Conati, K. McCoy, and G. Paliouras (Eds.): UM 2007, LNAI 4511, pp. 370–374, 2007.
© Springer-Verlag Berlin Heidelberg 2007

self-efficacy, locus of control, perceived task difficulty and goal orientation. Self-efficacy is the individuals' confidence in their ability to control their thoughts, feelings, and actions, and therefore influence an outcome. Individuals with an external locus of control believe that factors such as luck, task difficulty, or other people's actions, cause success or failure [10]. Individuals with an internal locus of control believe that success is due to their own efforts. Perception of task difficulty will affect the expectancy for success, and it has a strong influence on both instigation of a learning activity as well as persistence. Goals enhance self-regulation through their effects on motivation, learning, self-efficacy and self-evaluations of progress [1]. Individuals with a learning goal orientation strive to master the task and are more likely to engage in self-regulatory activities such as monitoring, planning, and deep-level cognitive strategies. Individuals orientated towards performance approach goals are concerned with positive evaluations of their abilities in comparison to others and focus on how they are judged by parents, teachers or peers. Individuals with performance avoidance goals want to look smart and not appear incompetent and so may avoid challenging tasks, or exhibit low persistence, when encountering difficulties [8]. Individuals may have both mastery and performance goals [7]. Disengaged orientation is displayed by students who "do not really care about doing well in school or learning the material; their goal is simply to get through the activity" [2]. As learners differ widely, intervention strategies must be adapted to suit the individual and the task, thereby focusing the attention on the learner rather than on instructional design.

2   Eliciting Intervention Strategies from On-Line Tutors

A learner model was created based on the SCT constructs of Self-Efficacy, Goal Orientation, Locus of Control and Perceived Task Difficulty, as these are the four most important factors contributing to self-regulation. Research has shown that self regulatory behavior can account for academic achievement [8]. The model contained 21 learner profiles which were systematically developed using the above constructs (see Table 1). The profiles were selected from a possible 48 as the most likely to experience demotivation. For example, a person with the profile of Persona 1 is likely to become demotivated when not sufficiently challenged.

Based on the model personas (i.e., short textual descriptions) were then developed, e.g. Persona 1: "Chris is an intelligent student who enjoys learning for its own sake. She is motivated to learn new things and enjoys being challenged *(GO:Mastery)*. She believes she can do very well in her studies as she has a very good understanding of her subject *(SE:High)*. Chris believes hard work will conquer almost any problem and lead to success *(LOC: Internal)*. However, she finds that she becomes bored when she has to work on a concept which she already understands well *(PTD:Low)*."

From the literature on motivation and an initial pilot questionnaire, completed by classroom tutors, a list of intervention strategies was compiled (see Table 2). In order to identify rules to determine which intervention strategy is the most appropriate for each learner's persona, on-line tutors were surveyed. If, for example, a learner had low self-efficacy and external locus of control, tutors might indicate that reviewing progress with the student at regular intervals would be a strategy to adopt. In this way the relationship between motivational states and intervention strategies was elicited with the assistance of the on-line tutors.

Participants were randomly assigned to one of six online surveys containing either three or four personas. The same 14 intervention strategies were presented in the same order under each persona. The tutors were asked to select the strategies they would *Highly Recommend, Recommend* or considered *Not Applicable* for each persona. They were also asked to suggest any further strategies that they find particularly useful in the case of each persona type. The tutors were required to have at least two years experience teaching on-line. The survey could be completed anonymously or the participants could enter their email address if they wished to get feedback on the results. Sixty participants completed the surveys which resulted in each persona getting a minimum of six and a maximum of fourteen responses.

Table 1. Profile of personas. Self Efficacy (SE) [High (H) / Medium (M) / Low (L)]; Goal Orientation (GO) [Mastery (M) / Performance Avoidance (Pa) / Performance Approach (PA) / Disengagement (D)]; Locus of Control (LOC) [Internal (I) / External (E)]; Perceived Task Difficulty (PTD) [Low (L) / High (H)]

Persona	1	2	3	4	5	6	7	8	9	10	11	12	13	14	15	16	17	18	19	20	21
SE	H	H	M	M	M	M	L	L	M	H	L	L	M	M	M	M	H	L	L	M	M
GO	M	M	M	M	M	M	M	Pa	Pa	Pa	PA	PA	PA	PA	PA	PA	PA	D	D	D	D
LOC	I	E	I	I	E	E	E	E	E	E	I	E	I	E	I	E	I	I	E	E	I
PTD	L	L	L	H	L	H	H	H	H	H	H	H	L	L	H	H	L	H	H	H	H

3 Results

The participants varied widely in the number of years' of experience they had as on-line tutors. The least experienced participants had tutored on-line for two years, and the most experienced had tutored for eighteen years. The average was five years.

For the purpose of this paper, we merged *Highly Recommended* and *Recommended* strategies into one category, which is the subject of this paper.

Using the Weka data mining tool set [11], five different algorithms were applied to predict whether a strategy was marked as recommended by the tutors or not. These algorithms included the following classifiers: 1) Bayesian Networks. 2) IBk, an instance-based k-nearest neighbours classifier. 3) J48, generating pruned C4.5 decision trees. 4) PART, a classifier based on partial C4.5 decision trees and rules. 5) Naïve Bayes as a standard baseline. All experiments were run with a 10-fold cross validation. Table 3 provides an overview of the results.

Both, Bayesian Networks and J48 are able to predict the recommendations very well, with correct prediction rates from at least 66% and up to 93%. Strategy 4, *Encourage the student to use on-line quizzes*, seems to be harder to predict. This strategy has also been recommended less often than most other strategies. The fact that results across methods are similar means that the pattern in the data is pretty obvious.

Table 2. Intervention strategies

1	Review progress with student at regular intervals
2	Provide regular positive and specific feedback to student
3	Encourage student to clearly define his/her academic goals
4	Encourage the student to use on-line quizzes
5	Remind student of the student support services
6	Encourage student to use the chat room/discussion forums
7	Help student to develop a study plan/timetable
8	Explain importance of and encourage student to maintain contact with tutor
9	Encourage peer to peer contact
10	Encourage student to base self-evaluation on personal improvement/mastery when possible, rather than grades
11	Encourage the student to reflect on and evaluate his/her learning
12	Explain why learning a particular content is important
13	Provide guidance to extra learning resources
14	No intervention required

Table 3. Correct predictions (%) of the five algorithms separated by the 13 intervention strategies

	BayNet	IBk	J48	PART	NaïveBayes
Strategy 1	89.86	89.86	89.86	89.86	89.86
Strategy 2	93.26	93.26	93.26	93.26	93.26
Strategy 3	84.55	80.78	84.55	82.03	84.55
Strategy 4	66.09	58.88	66.58	63.11	65.23
Strategy 5	74.04	74.80	77.31	77.12	74.33
Strategy 6	86.50	85.71	86.50	86.50	86.50
Strategy 7	70.92	67.59	68.83	70.23	69.81
Strategy 8	83.60	82.64	83.60	83.60	83.50
Strategy 9	88.90	88.22	88.90	88.90	88.90
Strategy 10	82.64	80.66	82.64	82.25	82.64
Strategy 11	88.90	88.90	88.90	88.90	88.90
Strategy 12	79.24	74.86	79.24	78.57	78.47
Strategy 13	80.67	79.66	80.67	80.67	80.67

4   Discussion

We demonstrated that knowledge about appropriate motivation intervention strategies can be elicited from tutors by prompting them with systematically constructed personas. While the relationship between parameters of the personas and intervention strategies are not obvious and cannot be explained directly by the tutors, we were able to demonstrate that standard machine learning algorithms can learn to predict this relationship well.

An assessment component that creates an accurate model of the motivational states of the learner is currently being developed in a related project being carried out by a fellow researcher and it is planned to use this assessment component in the validation stage of this study. The fact that this automatic assessment component has not yet been developed is currently a limitation for us, but once it exists, appropriate intervention strategies can be inferred. Future work will focus on an empirical validation of the predictions in a real learning environment to see if the intervention strategies adopted actually increase the motivation of the learner.

References

1. Bandura, A.: Social foundations of thought and action: A social cognitive theory. Prentice-Hall, Englewood Cliffs, NJ (1986)
2. Beal, C.R., Lee, H.: Creating a pedagogical model that uses student self reports of motivation and mood to adapt ITS instruction. Workshop on motivation and affect in educational software, July 18-22, Amsterdam, Netherlands. Retrieved on 23 March 2006 (2005), from http://www.wayangoutpost.net/paper/Beal&LeeCRC.pdf
3. De Vicente, A., Pain, H.: Validating the Detection of a student's Motivational State. In: Mendez Vilas, A., Mesa Gonzalez, J. A., Mesa Gonzalez, J. (eds.) Proceedings of the Second International Conference on Multimedia Information and Communication Technologies in Education m-ICTE (2003)
4. Dille, B., Mezack, M.: Identifying predictors of high risk among community college telecourse students. The. American Journal of Distance Education 5(1), 24–35 (1991)
5. Pajares, F., Schunk, D.H.: Self-Beliefs and School Success: Self-Efficacy, Self-Concept, and School Achievement. In: Riding, R., Rayner, S. (eds.) Perception, pp. 239–266. Ablex Publishing, London (2001)
6. Pintrich, P.R., De Groot, E.V.: Motivational and self-regulated learning components of classroom academic performance. Journal of Educational Psychology 82(1), 33–40 (1990)
7. Pintrich, P.R., Garcia, T.: Student goal orientation and self-regulation in the college classroom. In: Maehr, M.L., Pintrich, P.R. (eds.) Advances in motivation and achievement: Goals and self-regulatory processes, vol. 7, pp. 371–402. JAI Press, Greenwich, CT (1991)
8. Pintrich, P.R., Schunk, D.H.: Motivation in education: Theory, research, and practice. Prentice Hall, Englewood Cliffs, NJ (1996)
9. Qu, L., Wang, N., Johnson, W.L.: Detecting the Learner's Motivational States in an Interactive Learning Environment. In: Looi, C.-K., et al. (ed.) Artificial Intelligence in Education. pp. 547–554. IOS Press, Amsterdam, Trento, Italy (2005)
10. Rotter, J.B.: Generalized expectancies for internal versus external control of reinforcement. Psychological Monographs, 80(Whole No. 609) (1966)
11. Witten, I.H., Frank, E., Trigg, L.E., Hall, M., Holmes, G., Cunningham, S.J: Weka: Practical machine learning tools and techniques with Java implementations. In: Proc ICONIP/ ANZIIS/ANNES99 Future Directions for Intelligent Systems and Information Sciences, Dunedin, New Zealand, pp. 192–196 (November 1999)
12. Zhang, G., Cheng, Z., He, A., Huang, T.: A WWW-based Learner's Learning Motivation Detecting System. In: Proceedings of International Workshop on Research Directions and Challenge Problems in Advanced Information Systems Engineering, Honjo City, Japan, (September 16–19, 2003), http://www.akita-pu.ac.jp/system/KEST2003/

Improving User Taught Task Models*

Phillip Michalak and James Allen

University of Rochester
Rochester, New York

Abstract. Task models are essential components in many approaches to user modelling because they provide the context with which to interpret, predict, and respond to user behavior. The quality of such models is critical to their ability to support these functions. This paper describes work on improving task models that are automatically acquired from demonstration. Modifications to a standard planning algorithm are described and applied to an example learned task model, showing the utility of incorporating plan-based reasoning into task learning systems.

1 Introduction and Related Work

Task models are essential components in many approaches to user modelling because they provide the context with which to interpret, predict, and respond to user behavior. Intelligent tutoring systems (e.g. [1]) need to model the tasks that trainees will perform so that they can determine flawed behavior in order to offer timely and appropriate remediation. Systems that adapt content to users (e.g. [2]) must understand the tasks that the user is trying to perform in order to provide appropriate content when it is needed. Plan recognition approaches (e.g. [3]) attempt to explain and predict behavior by constructing explanations that are consistent with task models and prior observation. The quality of the underlying task models determines their ability to support the interpretation, prediction, and response functions mentioned above. This paper describes work that improves the detail and accuracy of task models that have been learned from demonstration.

Typically task models are painstakingly constructed by hand for each domain, a difficult task in its own right and one complicated by the fact that domains are often incompletely or inaccurately specified through knowledge engineering. This paper describes work based on the Procedure Learning On the Web (PLOW) system ([4]), which continues a recent trend of automatic task model acquisition. Some previous machine learning methods (e.g. [5]) use version spaces to represent demonstration ambiguity and require multiple training examples to eliminate it.

---

* This material is based upon work supported by National Science Foundation, grant #IIS-0328811, DARPA, sub-contract from West Florida, grant #IHMC-UR-07-01 and support from DARPA with a subaward from SRI International. Any opinions, findings, and conclusions or recommendations expressed in this material are those of the authors and do not necessarily reflect the views of above named organizations.

C. Conati, K. McCoy, and G. Paliouras (Eds.): UM 2007, LNAI 4511, pp. 375–379, 2007.
© Springer-Verlag Berlin Heidelberg 2007

Non-version space approaches (e.g. [6]) face similar difficulties; multiple examples are required to generalize from specific examples to a level that captures the essence of the training examples. In contrast, the PLOW system requires only a single demonstration to learn a task model because it leverages natural language. A play by play task description given as it is demonstrated provides three key types of information unrecoverable by observation alone: task parameterization information, sub-task structure, and semantic annotation for observed action.

In addition to their primary role in task execution, PLOW's task models can also serve as the basis for various user modelling techniques. This paper describes a mechanism for improving task models to better support those roles. Specifically, this mechanism discovers missing precondition and effect information in the task representations and relaxes the implicit total order on task steps that arises from a sequential demonstration. The Diligent system ([7]) recovered similar information through a simulated experimentation approach, but the plan based approach yields finer grained detail when primitive task models are known a priori. Section 2 describes the method by which missing information is recovered from models learned by PLOW, and Sect. 3 provides a brief example of this method.

2   Improving Learned Task Models

This section describes a mechanism for improving task model quality and thus ability to support user modelling functions. Each PLOW task model is translated into a specially crafted planning domain and then analyzed by a modified Graphplan [8] algorithm which recovers missing information about necessary task preconditions, effects, and order constraints. This process is a recursive one; improved task models are used in the analysis of higher level task models.

The constants, initial facts, goals, and operators of a specially crafted planning domain are extracted from each (sub-)task model. The planning domain constants come from a task model's constants and parameters. Task model parameters are treated as constants because this analysis never considers a particular parameterized instance; no values are ever assigned to the parameters during reasoning. Task model constants and parameters typically result from spoken and web browser interaction (e.g. typing "http://www.nytimes.com/" into an instrumented web browser or saying "Put the title of the book here").

The planning domain initial facts come from task model preconditions. Essentially, the reasoning algorithm assumes that the task model preconditions are true, and attempts to construct plans that achieve its goals by using the steps specified in the task. Accordingly, the effects and the steps of a task model are formulated as planning domain goals. Treating the steps as goals forces the planner to consider only plans that include those steps.

The operators of the planning domain are summaries of the task models that the system knows about. Specifically, those task models that achieve one or more steps of the task being analyzed are included as domain operators. Operator definitions take task parameters, preconditions, and effects to be their variables, preconditions, and effects, respectively.

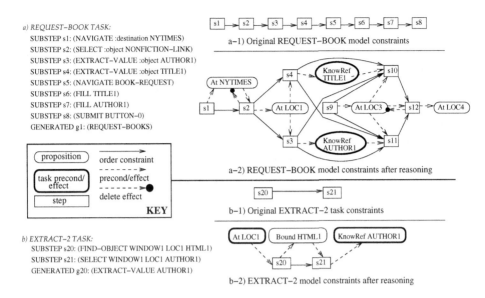

a) REQUEST–BOOK TASK:
SUBSTEP s1: (NAVIGATE :destination NYTIMES)
SUBSTEP s2: (SELECT :object NONFICTION–LINK)
SUBSTEP s3: (EXTRACT–VALUE :object AUTHOR1)
SUBSTEP s4: (EXTRACT–VALUE :object TITLE1)
SUBSTEP s5: (NAVIGATE BOOK–REQUEST)
SUBSTEP s6: (FILL TITLE1)
SUBSTEP s7: (FILL AUTHOR1)
SUBSTEP s8: (SUBMIT BUTTON–0)
GENERATED g1: (REQUEST–BOOKS)

a–1) Original REQUEST–BOOK model constraints

a–2) REQUEST–BOOK model constraints after reasoning

b–1) Original EXTRACT–2 task constraints

KEY
proposition — order constraint
task precond/effect — precond/effect
step — delete effect

b) EXTRACT–2 TASK:
SUBSTEP s20: (FIND–OBJECT WINDOW1 LOC1 HTML1)
SUBSTEP s21: (SELECT WINDOW1 LOC1 AUTHOR1)
GENERATED g20: (EXTRACT–VALUE AUTHOR1)

b–2) EXTRACT–2 model constraints after reasoning

Fig. 1. Task models for (a) requesting the purchase of a best-selling non-fiction book and its sub-task (b) extracting the author name from a web page, before and after analysis

The resulting planning domain represents the basic constraints of the task model: that the specified steps occur and that the necessary effects hold after task completion when the task preconditions are assumed to be true.

The planning algorithm takes as input standard type, initial condition, goal, and operator descriptions derived from task models as described above. Extensions to the original Graphplan algorithm infer missing information about preconditions, effects, and operator order, as well as rate the quality of each solution. The plan graph of Fig. 2 depicts the minimum cost solution for the author name extraction sub-task of Fig. 1-b; it will be used to illustrate the extensions described below.

The algorithm first augments the planning domain's initial facts to include all facts that enable sub-step achieving operators. This operation guarantees that all of the task sub-steps are achievable, but possibly at the expense of domain integrity. For example, Fig. 2 shows that the additional preconditions (shaded) enable a text selection action in the first time step, despite the fact that it should occur *after* the object finding action.

The second extension modifies the search algorithm to terminate once an acceptable *set* of solutions has been found or it can be guaranteed that none will ever be found. Intuitively, invalid solutions that are enabled by augmenting the initial preconditions should be pruned; the search algorithm assigns a cost to each solution based on the number of *abductive* preconditions that it uses, and

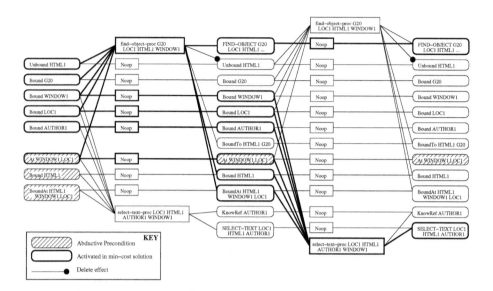

Fig. 2. A plan graph corresponding to the planning domain of the sub-task depicted in Fig. 1-b. The minimum cost solution is accented in bold.

accepts only minimum cost solutions. The incorrect solution described above is pruned because it must assume more facts than the bold-faced minimum cost solution of Fig. 2.

The third extension to the basic Graphplan algorithm computes the consistent characteristics of the minimal cost solutions: binary order constraints, assumed preconditions, and effects. The resulting sets are those elements that are present in every valid minimal cost solution. Since the example of Fig. 2 has just a single minimum cost solution, its preconditions and effects are taken to be necessary. These sets are output by the planning algorithm, and can be contrasted with the declared preconditions, effects, and order constraints of the original task.

3   Example

This section briefly describes the algorithm as it operates on the book request task model depicted in Fig. 1-a. The algorithm first decomposes the task model into its constituent sub-steps and recursively analyzes them. The author extraction sub-task, for example, is translated into a planning domain and analyzed as depicted in Fig. 2. An additional precondition (**At WINDOW1 LOC1**) and effect (**KnowRef AUTHOR1**) are recovered from the minimal cost solution. The other sub-steps of the book request task are likewise translated to planning domains and analyzed. Specifically, predicates of the form (**KnowRef <ITEM>**) are recovered as effects of the selection actions and as preconditions for the form filling actions. Analysis of the high level task resumes with updated planning operators reflecting these discoveries. The algorithm determines that:

the extract sequences precede the fill sequences, the extract steps can occur in either order, and the field filling steps can occur in either order. These refinements are shown graphically in Fig. 1-a.

The refined model more precisely characterizes the task. For example, a plan recognizer using the improved task model can, among other things, recognize task instances in which sub-tasks are performed in different orders. Additionally, the augmented precondition and effect detail of the improved model can be used to infer reasons why each individual action might be taken, allowing novel plans to be attributed to the user.

4   Conclusion

This paper presents a novel use of planning to recover missing information in task models, and describes its operation on a simple task model learned from a single demonstration with the PLOW system. The improved task models that result from this analysis are useful for understanding and reasoning about user behavior. Though this treatment analyzes procedures after they have been learned in their entirety, it is a straightforward modification to analyze procedures incrementally as new information is learned (e.g. additional sub-task specifications, preconditions, effects, etc.).

References

1. Litman, D.J., Silliman, S.: Itspoke: An intelligent tutoring spoken dialogue system. In: Proceedings of the Human Language Technology Conference: 4th Meeting of the North American Chapter of the Association for Computational Linguistics (HLT/NAACL), Boston, MA (2004)
2. Rich, C., Sidner, C.: Collagen: A collaboration manager for software interface agents. User. Modeling and User. Adapted Interaction 8(3/4), 315–350 (1998)
3. Carberry, S.: Plan Recognition in Natural Language Dialogue. MIT Press, Cambridge (1990)
4. Jung, H., Allen, J., Chambers, N., Galescu, L., Swift, M., Taysom, W.: One-shot procedure learning from instruction and observation. In: Proceedings of the International FLAIRS Conference (FLAIRS-2006): Special Track on Natural Language and Knowledge Representation, AAAI Press, Stanford, California, USA (2006)
5. Lau, T., Domingos, P., Weld, D.: Learning programs from traces using version space algebra. In: Proceedings of the 2nd International Conference on Knowledge Capture (K-CAP) (2003)
6. Bauer, M.: Towards the automatic acquisition of plan libraries. In: European Conference on Artificial Intelligence, pp. 484–488 (1998)
7. Angros, R., Johnson, W.L., Rickel, J., Scholer, A.: Learning domain knowledge for teaching procedural skills. In: AAMAS, pp. 1372–1378. ACM Press, New York (2002)
8. Blum, A., Furst, M.: Fast planning through planning graph analysis. Artificial Intelligence 90, 281–300 (1997)

Inducing User Affect Recognition Models for Task-Oriented Environments

Sunyoung Lee, Scott W. McQuiggan, and James C. Lester

Department of Computer Science, North Carolina State University, Raleigh, NC 27695
{slee7,swmcquig,lester}@ncsu.edu

Abstract. Accurately recognizing users' affective states could contribute to more productive and enjoyable interactions, particularly for task-oriented learning environments. In addition to using physiological data, affect recognition models can leverage knowledge of task structure and user goals to effectively reason about users' affective states. In this paper we present an inductive approach to recognizing users' affective states based on appraisal theory, a motivational-affect account of cognition in which individuals' emotions are generated in response to their assessment of how their actions and events in the environment relate to their goals. Rather than manually creating the models, the models are learned from training sessions in which (1) physiological data, (2) information about users' goals and actions, and (3) environmental information are recorded from traces produced by users performing a range of tasks in a virtual environment. An empirical evaluation with a task-oriented learning environment testbed suggests that an inductive approach can learn accurate models and that appraisal-based models exploiting knowledge of task structure and user goals can outperform purely physiologically-based models.

1 Introduction

Affect recognition is the task of identifying the emotional state of an individual from a variety of physical cues, which are produced in response to affective changes in the individual. These include visually observable cues such as body and head posture, facial expressions, and posture, and changes in physiological signals such as heart rate, skin conductivity, temperature, and respiration. Affect recognition work has explored emotion classification from self reports [1], post-hoc reports [9], physiological signals [3], [7], [8], combinations of visual cues and physiological signals [2], and from world state feature representations of temporal, locational and intentional information [6]. This body of research serves as the springboard for the work described in this paper, which reports on techniques for recognizing users' affective states from both physiological and task structure information. Because affect is fundamentally a cognitive process in which the user appraises the relationship between herself and her environment [4], affect recognition models should take into account both physiological and environmental information. For task-oriented environments, affect recognition models can leverage knowledge of task structure and user goals to effectively reason about users' affective states. In particular, for

C. Conati, K. McCoy, and G. Paliouras (Eds.): UM 2007, LNAI 4511, pp. 380–384, 2007.
© Springer-Verlag Berlin Heidelberg 2007

task-oriented environments, affect recognition models can use appraisal theory [5] to recognize users' emotions generated in response to their assessment of how their actions and events in the environment relate to their goals.

In this paper, we present an inductive approach to recognizing users' affective states in task-oriented virtual environments by learning affect recognition models. The models, which exploit task structure as well as physiological and environmental information, are induced from training data acquired from traces of users performing tasks in rich virtual environments. Experimental results suggest that induced models can accurately predict users' affect states, and they are sufficiently efficient to meet the real-time performance requirements of interactive task-oriented environments.

2 Affect Recognition Models

The prospect of creating affect recognition model learners that can induce empirically grounded models of affect to recognize users' emotional states from a combination of physiological data and a representation of environmental information holds much appeal. To this end, this paper proposes an inductive approach to generating affect recognition models trained to recognize user affect in runtime task-oriented environments.

2.1 The Crystal Island Testbed

To serve as an effective "laboratory" for studying user affect recognition in an interactive task-oriented environment, a testbed should pose the same kinds of challenges that affect recognition modelers are likely to encounter in future runtime environments. It should offer users a broad range of actions to perform and provide a rich set of tasks and goals in a nontrivial task-oriented virtual environment. The goals should exhibit some complexity, and the environment should be populated by manipulable artifacts and be inhabited by multiple characters. To this end, we have devised Crystal Island, a task-oriented learning environment testbed featuring a science mystery. The mystery is set on a recently discovered volcanic island where a research station has been established to study the unique flora and fauna. In the current testbed, there are twenty goals that users can achieve, three hundred unique actions that users can carry out, and over fifty unique locations in which the actions can be performed.

2.2 Model Induction

In a formal evaluation, data was gathered from thirty-six subjects. There were 5 female and 31 male participants varying in age, ethnic group, and marriage status.[1] After filling out a consent form and demographic survey, participants began training sessions. The training testbed provided them with specific goals and guided them through the solution to the mystery. Periodically a "self-report emotion dialog" box would appear requesting input from them about their affective state. Participants were

---

[1] Approximately 44% of the participants were Asian, 50% were Caucasian, and 6% were of other ethnicities. Participants' average age was 26.0 (SD=5.4).

asked to select one emotion from a set of six emotions (*excitement, fear, frustration, happiness, relaxation,* and *sadness*) that was most closely related to their feelings at that particular juncture. After solving the science mystery, participants completed a post-experiment survey before exiting the training session. During the user interaction, the following observable attributes were logged:

- *User Actions*: Affect recognition models can observe users' actions in the world and their relationship to achieving particular goals; affect recognition models also have access to auxiliary information about the interactions, e.g., any artifacts manipulated such as which objects have been picked up or which doors have been opened, as well as the characters with whom users have interacted.
- *User Locations*: Affect recognition models have access to a variety of information about the user's precise location in the environment and the location's relationship to achieving particular goals.
- *Temporal Information*: Affect recognition models can observe the time user's spend on a task, the time spent in particular abstract locations (e.g., particular rooms of the environment), and the time carrying out particular actions.
- *Task Structure*: Affect recognition models can observe the user's task progression, i.e., whether the user is completing actions that will or will not help achieve certain goals. The affect recognition model also has access to knowledge of the explicitly stated goal in the training environment.
- *Physiological Response*: Affect recognition models can observe users' physiological changes (blood volume pulse and galvanic skin response) in response to events in the environment, such as carrying out an action, goal achievement, or interacting with a particular agent in the environment.
- *Self-report Affective States:* A set of six self-report emotions (excitement, fear, frustration, happiness, relaxation, and sadness) were used as class labels during training the affect recognition models.

Each training log was first translated into a full observational attribute vector. Attributes observed directly from the environment were combined with physiological response attributes and self-reported affective states. Once the dataset was prepared, it was passed to the learning systems. The affect data were loaded into the WEKA machine learning tool [10], a naïve Bayes classifier and decision tree were learned, and tenfold cross-validation analyses were run on the resulting models. The entire dataset was used to generate several types of affect recognition models. These included models that considered different sets of observed attributes, e.g., datasets with and without goal knowledge.

2.3 Results

Table 1 below reports the overall results of naïve Bayes and decision tree affect recognition models. The percentages refer to correctly classified instances. The highest performing model is a decision tree affect recognition model induced from representations of user actions, locations, task structure, and temporal information.

Table 1. Classification results for decision tree and naive Bayes models with specified datasets

Classifier	Physiological Data Only	Goals, Actions, Locations
Naïve Bayes	56.72%	62.94%
Decision Tree	71.34%	95.23%

Because participants choose from a selection of six affective states, chance is 16.7%. An additional baseline to consider is selecting the most common affective state, frustration, which appeared in 34.4% of self-reported affective states.

The results suggest that an approach to affect recognition based on appraisal theory can be effective in task-oriented environments, and that representations of user action, location, task structure and temporal information can be used to realize it in a computational model. The affect recognition models reported on here appear to capture the relationship between user actions and goals that are assessed during users' appraisal periods.

3   Conclusion

Recent advances in affective reasoning have demonstrated that emotion plays a central role in human cognition and should therefore play an equally important role in human-computer interaction. This paper has introduced an inductive approach to generating affect recognition models. In this approach, affect recognition model-learners observe training users in a task-oriented environment in which user actions, locations, goals, and temporal information are monitored. After problem-solving traces have been recorded, affect recognition models are induced that are both accurate and efficient.

In the future, it will be important to investigate affect recognition models that will enable affect-informed systems to make "early" predictions of user affect, perhaps informing runtime components of possible undesired user emotions. Early detection would allow systems adequate time to prepare for particular affective states or to take action in an effort to ward off states such as high levels of frustration.

Acknowledgements

The authors would like to thank the members of the IntelliMedia Center for Intelligent Systems at North Carolina State University for their contributions to the implementation of Crystal Island. The authors also wish to thank Valve Software for authorizing the use of their Source™ engine and SDK. This research was supported by the National Science Foundation under Grant REC-0632450. Any opinions, findings, and conclusions or recommendations expressed in this material are those of the authors and do not necessarily reflect the views of the National Science Foundation.

References

1. Beal, C., Lee, H.: Creating a pedagogical model that uses student self reports of motivation and mood to adapt ITS instruction. In: AIED Workshop on Motivation and Affect in Educational Software (2005)
2. Burleson, W., Picard, R.: Affective agents: Sustaining motivation to learn through failure and a state of stuck. In: Workshop of Social and Emotional Intelligence in Learning Environments, with the 7th Intl. Conf. on Intelligent Tutoring Systems (2004)
3. Conati, C., Mclaren, H.: Data-driven refinement of a probabilistic model of user affect. In: Proc. of the 10th Intl. Conf. on User Modeling, pp. 40–49. Springer, Heidelberg (2005)
4. Gratch, J., Marsella, S.: A domain-independent framework for modeling emotion. Journal of Cognitive Systems Research 5(4), 269–306 (2004)
5. Lazarus, R.: Emotion and Adaptation. Oxford University Press, New York (1991)
6. McQuiggan, S., Lee, S., Lester, J.: Predicting user physiological response for interactive environments: an inductive approach. In: Proc. of the 2nd Conf. on Artificial Intelligence and Interactive Digital Entertainment, pp. 60–65. AAAI Press, Stanford, California, USA (2006)
7. Picard, R., Vyzas, E., Healey, J.: Toward machine emotional intelligence: analysis of affective physiological state. IEEE Transactions Pattern Analysis and Machine Intelligence 23(10), 1185–1191 (2001)
8. Prendinger, H., Ishizuka, M.: The empathic companion: A character-based interface that addresses users' affective states. Applied Artificial Intelligence 19, 267–285 (2005)
9. de Vicente, A., Pain, H.: Informing the detection of the students' motivational state: an empirical study. In: Proc. of the 6th Intl. Conf. on Intelligent Tutoring Systems. pp. 933–943. Springer, New York (2002)
10. Witten, I., Frank, E.: Data Mining: Practical Machine Learning Tools and Techniques, 2nd edn. Morgan Kaufman, San Francisco (2005)

Interactive User Modeling for Personalized Access to Museum Collections: The Rijksmuseum Case Study

Yiwen Wang[1], Lora M. Aroyo[2], Natalia Stash[1], and Lloyd Rutledge[3]

[1] Eindhoven University of Technology, The Netherlands
{y.wang,n.v.stash}@tue.nl
[2] Free University Amsterdam, The Netherlands
l.m.aroyo@cs.vu.nl
3 Telematica Institute, Enschede, The Netherlands
CWI Amsterdam, The Netherlands
Lloyd.Rutledge@cwi.nl

Abstract. In this paper we present an approach for personalized access to museum collections. We use a RDF/OWL specification of the Rijksmuseum Amsterdam collections as a driver for an interactive dialog. The user gives his/her judgment on the artefacts, indicating likes or dislikes. The elicited user model is further used for generating recommendations of artefacts and topics. In this way we support exploration and discovery of information in museum collections. A user study provided insights in characteristics of our target user group, and showed how novice and expert users employ their background knowledge and implicit interest in order to elicit their art preference in the museum collections.

Keywords: CHIP (Cultural Heritage Information Presentation), user study, adaptive system, personalization, RDF/OWL, recommendations, user modeling.

1 Introduction

The CHIP[1] project is part of the Dutch Science Foundation funded program CATCH for Continuous Access to Cultural Heritage. Since early 2005 the CHIP research team has been working at the Rijksmuseum Amsterdam and interviewed curators and collection managers in order to perform detailed analysis of the museum domain, target users and museum web applications. As a result of this extensive domain and context analysis requirements were obtained for the development of several low-fidelity prototypes [1]. The prototypes focused on eliciting information from domain experts about novel personalization functions for the visitors on the museum web site. We proposed an approach based on an interactive semantics-driven dialog for eliciting user knowledge, inspired from previous work on the adaptive learning content management system SWALE [2].

---

[1] CHIP project: http://www.chip-project.org

C. Conati, K. McCoy, and G. Paliouras (Eds.): UM 2007, LNAI 4511, pp. 385–389, 2007.
© Springer-Verlag Berlin Heidelberg 2007

In this paper, we present the results of a user study with real users evaluating our first functional prototype. The results show that novices need support in externalizing their implicit art preferences and thus profit from the CHIP adaptive dialog. The experts, on the other hand, have prior knowledge and use the interactive dialog in order to discover new insights and semantic relationships in particular collections. The ultimate goal for our research is to realize 'the Virtual New Rijksmuseum" where different types of users can easily find their ways in the Rijksmuseum and access information which is tailored to their needs, personal interests and competency level.

2   Personalization in Museum Collections

In the last few years, dedicated recommender systems have gained popularity and become more and more established practice in online commerce, like purchasing of books, music, and organizing a travel. Museums also direct their efforts to provide personalized services to the general audience via their websites. There are various examples of museum websites attempting to meet the needs of individual users. A key problem here is the semantic vocabulary gap between the experts-created descriptions and the implicit and often not domain-related art preferences of end users. Moreover, museum collections maintain multiple perspectives for their information disclosure. These challenges lend themselves well to the application of recommender technology as explored in this work. Our goal is to bridge the vocabulary gap and provide a user-driven approach for eliciting user's preferences and characteristics, and recommend known/new information from the collection in a coherent and comprehensive way. Studies show that understanding is stimulated when the systems use concepts familiar to the user (considering interests and knowledge level) [3]. In this paper, we capitalize on the non-obtrusive collection of users data as part of an active interaction with the museum collection (versus filling in static isolated preference forms).

3   Cultural Heritage Information Presentation

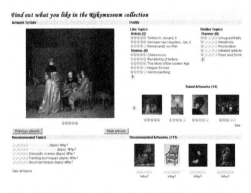

Fig. 1. CHIP interactive user modeling interface

We developed an interactive quiz to help users find artefacts and topics of their interests in the Rijksmuseum collection. Figure 1 gives a snapshot of its user interface. On the top-left artefacts to rate are presented as an interactive dialog. The ratings are stored in a user profile (top-right) and are used to filter the relevant artefacts (bottom-right) and topics (bottom-left). Each recommendation is accompanied with an explanation ('why?' option). The demo collects feedback about the recommended items by allowing users to rate also recommendations. In this way the system gradually builds the user profile to be used for personalized tours generation. The user profile we build is an extended overlay of the CHIP domain model depicted in Figure 2. It contains topics and artefacts of interest assessed in a five-star scale (respectively -1, -0.5, 0, 0.5 1), where 1 is maximum interest, -1 is maximum distaste and 0 is neutral. The topics are grouped in four main categories, i.e. artist, theme, period-location and style.

The rich semantic modeling of the domain with mappings to common vocabularies (Getty vocabularies[2] and Iconclass thesaurus[3]) and use of open standards (e.g. VRA, SKOS and OWL/RDF), allows us to maintain a light-weight user profile and efficiently perform the reasoning over the domain model. This allows for a dynamic and run-time calculation of the user's interest, as well as a high-level of serendipity of the suggested items and explanations. We also store the skipped (not rated, but presented items), in order to optimize the presentation sequence. We use XSLT to convert the XML of the Rijksmuseum database into the RDF scheme we developed. Much of this transformation derives from the taxonomical merging resulting in two types of new triples: (1) equivalence - identifies concepts across taxonomies that are the same; (2) narrower and broader terms - defines local extensions within hierarchical taxonomies.

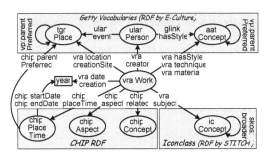

Fig. 2. CHIP RDF data model

Figure 2 shows our current RDF data model, representing these vocabularies/thesauruses. The initial RDF representation was provided by the E-Culture project (for Getty) [4] and the STITCH project (for IconClass) [5].

4   User Study at the Rijksmuseum Amsterdam

Based on our first recommender prototype, we did a first formative user study with two-fold focus: (1) to test with real users the effectiveness of the demo with respect to novices and experts; and (2) to gain insight in characteristics of the target group in order to elicit requirements for the user modeling scheme and approach. The rationale of this study[4] is illustrated in Figure 3. It contains five steps: Step 2–4 focus on testing the effectiveness of CHIP demo. Step 1 and 5 are two additional questionnaires about users' background and usability issues of the CHIP demo.

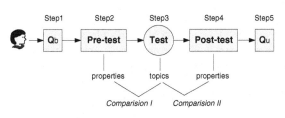

Fig. 3. Rationale of the user study

[2] Getty vocabularies: http://www.getty.edu/research/conducting_research/vocabularies/
[3] Iconclass thesauru: http://www.iconclass.nl/libertas/ic?style=index.xsl
[4] CHIP user study: http://www.chip-project.org:8091/demoUserStudy/

To test the demo, we designed a novel method to compare the process of rating and recommendation of experts and novices while using the demo. We claim that the CHIP recommender helps novices to elicit art preferences from their implicit knowledge/interest in museum collections. To test it, we let users rate their interest in art-related properties before and after using the demo. Here, it is called 'pre-test', 'test' and 'post-test', which refer to step 2 to 4 in Figure 3. In consultation with the Rijksmuseum domain experts, the demo used a selected data source which covered 37 properties from 4 popular artefacts. These properties are randomly divided into two questionnaires, pre-test and post-test, in a non-overlapping way. Users assess each property on a five-degree scale from 'not interested at all' to 'very interested'. The main idea was to measure whether the properties generated as recommended topics from the demo match the properties positively rated by the users in the pre-test and post-test questionnaires. This measure of discrepance is expressed in Comparision I and Comparision II, see buttom Figure 3.

To gain insight in our target users, we designed two additional questionnaires, one about the users' background (e.g. age, education, interest in art, etc.) and another about usability issues of the demo, see Qb and Qu in step 1 and 5 in Figure 3.

In total 39 users participated in this study that was held in a period of two weeks in August 2006 at the Rijksmuseum Amsterdam. 33 users were randomly selected from the actual visitors of the museum. In addition, we also asked 6 employees (no domain experts) of the Rijksmuseum to take part in the study.

5   Results and Analysis of the User Study

In the questionnaires, we collected user characteristics (e.g. age, gender, profession) and comments on the demo usability. Some dominant factors appeared as characteristics of the users:

- Small group with 2-4 persons and a male took the leading role (67%)
- Mid-age people in 30-60 years old and well educated (62%)
- No prior knowledge about the Rijksmuseum collections (62%)
- Visit the museum for education (98%) and strong interest in art (92%)
- Recommendations are useful (82%) and explanations is helpful (57%)

These findings guide our subsequent user-centered design of personalized adaptive systems: (1) consider community/social aspects in the user model, (2) enable collaborative tasks among users, (3) not explicitly test user's pre-knowledge, and (4) no need to motivate users but focus on providing art education in a pleasant way.

To distinguish within these 39 participants between novices and experts, we roughly defined an expert-value as a weighted sum of five factors: prior knowledge of the Rijksmuseum collection (v1), visiting frequency of Rijksmuseum (v2) and other museums (v3), interest in art (v4) and history (v5), calculated by:

$$expert\text{-}value = V1*0.5 + (V2+V3)*0.15 + (V4+V5)*0.1$$

If the user's expert-value is higher than a particular threshold (2.5), then she will be idenitfied as an expert, otherwise as a novice. However, there is no sharp distinction between them. To establish the correspondence of properties collected from pre/post-test (Pp) and the actual test (Tp), we use a valuation function V to obtain values in the range of -1, 0 and 1, that we can compare (when both values have a similar sign there is a positive correspondence), as expressed in the formula: $Cp = V(Pp)*V(Tp)$. For a particular user, we derive a combined positive correspondence, over all properties P, by applying: $\Sigma C = \Sigma Cp$. At this point, we do not consider negative correspondences, as they seemed not to contain valuable information. By using this interpretation model, all data from the pre/post-test and test were processed.

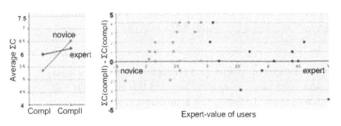

Fig. 4. ΣC in Comparison I and II according to user expert-value

In Figure 4 (left part), we show the comparison of ΣC based on two groups: novices and experts. A significant increase, 1.18, was found for novices when relating Comparison I and II. Besides, we found a very slight increase, 0.23, for the experts. Secondly, when we plot the difference of ΣC between comparison I and II on a continuous range of the expert-value, we may observe (right part, Figure 4), ignoring extreme values, a convergence as expert level increases. These results confirmed our hypothesis that the novices indeed profit from using demo to elicit their art preferences in the Rijksmuseum collections.

6 Conclusion

In this paper we have presented a user study of the CHIP demo, indicating that personalized adaptive systems have the potential to benefit users in various contexts. It is well integrated in the tasks users expect to perform on a museum website, and in the same time gathers necessary data about the users in order to provide personalized information access and presentation. It is geared towards user's characteristics and behaviors, and it can make the active interaction more effective and fruitful.

References

1. Rutledge, L., Aroyo, L., Stash, N.: Determining User Interests About Museum Collections. In: Proceedings of WWW'06 International Conference (poster) (2006)
2. Denaux, R., Dimitrova, D., Aroyo, L.: Integrating Open User Modeling and Learning Content Management for the Semantic Web. In: Proceedings of User Modeling Conference (2005)
3. Bowen, J., Filippini-Fantoni, S.: Personalization and the web from a museum perspective. In: Proceedings of Museums on the Web Conference (2004)
4. Schreiber, G., Amin, A., van Assem, M., de Boer, V., Hardman, L., Hildebrand, M., Hollink, L., Huang, Z., van Kersen, J., de Niet, M., Omelayenko, B., van Ossenbruggen, J., Siebes, R., Taekema, J., Wielemaker, J., Wielinga, B.: MultimediaN E-Culture demonstrator. In: Cruz, I., Decker, S., Allemang, D., Preist, C., Schwabe, D., Mika, P., Uschold, M., Aroyo, L. (eds.) ISWC 2006. LNCS, vol. 4273, Springer, Heidelberg (2006)
5. van Gendt, M., Isaac, A., van der Meij, L., Schloback, S.: Semantic Web Techniques for Multiple Views on Heterogeneous Collections: A Case Study. In: Gonzalo, J., Thanos, C., Verdejo, M.F., Carrasco, R.C. (eds.) ECDL 2006. LNCS, vol. 4172, Springer, Heidelberg (2006)

Kansei Processing Agent for Personalizing Retrieval

Sunkyoung Baek, Myunggwon Hwang, and Pankoo Kim[*]

Dept. of Computer Science, Chosun University, Gwangju 501-759 Korea
{zamilla100,mghwang,pkkim}@chosun.ac.kr

Abstract. In the present, methods of creating and processing a profile are insufficient for achieving personalization information retrieval that reflects the subjective Kansei preference of users. To rectify this insufficiency, we have created a Kansei information processing agent. Our study proposes a Kansei agent for the creation, accumulation and renewal of profiles in personalized retrieval and explores possible contributions to the development of a Kansei-based recommendation system and personalizing service.

Keywords: Kansei, Kansei Processing, Personalizing Retrieval.

1 Introduction

Personalization is defined as a type of processing that provides appropriate and timely service by utilizing the profile information of a user [1]. When a user offers information to website the web-engine provides the user with the most appropriate information based on user's basic profile [2][3]. However, the existing methods of information retrieval do not consider semantic content, such as a user's Kansei and preference [4][5][6][7]. To rectify this insufficiency, we have created a Kansei information processing agent. Our study proposes a Kansei agent for the creation, accumulation and renewal of profiles in personalized retrieval and explores possible contributions to the development of a Kansei-based recommendation system and personalizing service.

2 Kansei Processing Agent

We reveal the full architecture of personalization image retrieval and propose a Kansei processing agent. And the final purpose of this study is to realize Kansei adaptive personalization image retrieval according to a user's Kansei preference. We define a number of standard Kansei among the many Kansei of individuals. First, we use the Kansei of color and shape of representative visual information and vocabulary as high-level information for the expression of Kansei. For our purposes, we choose Kansei-words that express both properties as color and shape, and named the selections the Kansei-key. We use the 'Meaning of color' as defined by Hewlett-Packard to determine a color's Kansei [8]. To define the Kansei of shape, we consulted the Kansei-vocabulary scale created in our previous study [9][10][11].

---

[*] Corresponding author.

C. Conati, K. McCoy, and G. Paliouras (Eds.): UM 2007, LNAI 4511, pp. 390–394, 2007.
© Springer-Verlag Berlin Heidelberg 2007

From the above contents we select the common Kansei vocabularies of color and shape. All of the selected 21 Kansei-key have two properties (color and shape) that are use representatively. When the Kansei-key has several color properties, the case has no priority order; however, it is considered a priority order in the case of shape. The reason is that the priority order of shape considers distances between each vocabulary as well as vocabulary and shape. For the selection of shape's property, we set a range of shape. The range is a group that includes Kansei-key by clustering the result of the Kansei-vocabulary scale [12]. Table 1 presents the some Kansei-key and properties.

Table 1. Kansei-key and Properties

Kansei-key	Color	Shape
pure(Key 1)	light blue	rounded triangle, rounded polygon
aggressive(Key 21)	bright red	sector, isosceles right triangle

Next, almost images contain a variety of visual information such as color, shape and so on. Defining and processing the Kansei related to a particular image is difficult and ambiguous because, in most cases, the image is a mixture of visual information. So we were faced problems that are Kansei processing of the images.

To overcome these problems, we indicate a method of personal Kansei processing using Kansei-weight. Kansei-weight is defined using each property of the Kansei-key. We indicate the matter that expresses the Kansei-weight for the properties of the Kansei-key in order to measure a user's Kansei information. The properties defined by the Kansei-key have an initial Kansei-weight. Each key has 40 weight spaces consisting of the 20 color weights and the 20 shape weights.

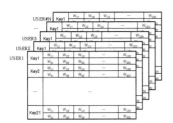

Fig. 1. Weight Space about Kansei-key

Table 2. Initial Kansei-weight about Kansei-key

Kansei key	C_1 S_1	C_2 S_2	~ ~	C_{11} S_{11}	C_{12} S_{12}	C_{13} S_{13}	C_{14} S_{14}	C_{15} S_{15}	C_{16} S_{16}	C_{16} S_{16}	C_{17} S_{17}	C_{18} S_{18}	C_{19} C_{19}	C_{20} S_{20}
soft	0 19	7 2	~ ~	7 0	0 0	0 0	0 0	0 0	0 0	0 0	0 0	7 0	0 0	0 0

Figure 1 is the table of weight space according to the Kansei-key. The Kansei-key contains the weight of the identical rate in each property as well as the fixed sum of the weight. The sum of the weight of each property is defined to the invariable 21, and it is possible for each weight to change according to the taste of an individual's Kansei. The scope of the key-weight of each property is defined from 0 to 21 and the sum of all key-weights is limited to 21.

And then, we consider the general Kansei of a category for recommending a product's images. This study considered the Kansei-rate of the product categories to achieve a higher level of satisfaction through applying individual Kansei. We selected five categories from a web shopping mall to define the common Kansei-rate of

Table 3. The Kansei-rate of Each Category

Category	Kansei-rate	Category	Kansei-rate
Kitchen utensils	$R_{category\_c}=0.2, R_{category\_s}=0.7$	Clothes	$R_{category\_c}=0.65, R_{category\_s}=0.21$
Electronic products	$R_{category\_c}=0.25, R_{category\_s}=0.56$	Furniture	$R_{category\_c}=0.2, R_{category\_s}=0.8$
Car	$R_{category\_c}=0.43, R_{category\_s}=0.49$		

individuals. Using the sample images from each category, we acquired the Kansei-rate (color:shape) influencing the Kansei of an individual.

Based on the previous definitions of the Kansei-key, initial Kansei-weight and Kansei-rate of each category, we propose a measure of the Kansei information content of each image. For retrieving the image queried by the user's Kansei, the Kansei content of all the images in the database is measured. It is necessary to process the low-level features of both color and shape. From this, we get a rate of 20 predefined colors using a color histogram. Shape, on the other hand, is measured according to its similarity to the 20 shape models using the adaptive-TSR (Tangent Space Representation) [13]. After receiving a measure of the low-level information, the Kansei information content measures the image's Kansei using formula (1). The greater the measure of the Kansei information content, the more appropriate the result to the user's Kansei.

$$K_{image} = \sum_{i=1}^{20}\{H_{color\_i}W_{color\_i}R_{category\_c} + S_{a-TSR\_i}W_{shape\_i}R_{category\_s}\} \qquad (1)$$

K_{image} : Kansei information content by image H_{color} : Rate of each color using color histogram

W_{color} : Kansei-weight of color according to Kansei-key $R_{ategory\_c}$: Kansei-rate of colors by category

S_{a-TSR} : Similarity of shape using Adaptive-TSR W_{shape} : Kansei-weight of shape according to Kansei-key

$R_{ategory\_s}$: Kansei-rate of shapes by category

The previous contents process enables us to recommend the results of the appropriate product image. Sometimes the results produced by our defined property Kansei-key fell short of achieving full user satisfaction. Therefore, it needs modification according to the user's preference and the Kansei differences. In other words, we propose the modification of the individual Kansei information through an adaptive individual renewing the property of the Kansei-key and weighting the property for the product retrieval according to individual tastes based on visual information.

$$W_{color\_i} = (W_{color\_i} + H_{color\_i})\frac{\sum W_{color\_i}}{\sum W_{color\_i}+1} \qquad (2)$$

$$W_{shape\_i} = (W_{shape\_i} + S_{a-TSR\_i})\frac{\sum W_{shape\_i}}{\sum W_{shape\_i}+1} \qquad (3)$$

Fig. 2. Interface for Evaluation

To accomplish this, we use the user's evaluation of the result. It is possible to retrieve a more suitable product for users by accommodating and renewing the Kansei-key's weight. Following the user's evaluation, the accuracy of the Kansei information increases through the renewing of the Kansei-weight. The formulas (2) and (3) are used to renew the Kansei-weight of color and shape. These formulas are only applied to the color and (or) the shape of the image, when users agree.

3   Experimental Results and Evaluation

For the experiment of the agent indicated in section 2, we construct the Kansei adaptive personalization image retrieval system. We use 250 images in total (five product categories each containing 50 images) and update the Kansei-weight according to individual preference on the personal Kansei database.

The sample subject groups composed of ten people, retrieved images for the evaluation of our methods. When users first connect to the system, they query the system using Kansei-vocabulary and then choose a category. The user receives results from the system and evaluates them. It is possible for users to retrieve a more suitable product by accumulating and renewing the Kansei-weight. If the same user continually retrieves a product's image, the Kansei-weight will correspond with the user's Kansei and preference for the product's image. We present the experimental results in figure 3. In figure 3, the second weight-table presents the results of the updated and accumulated Kansei-weight according to the user's evaluated feedback.

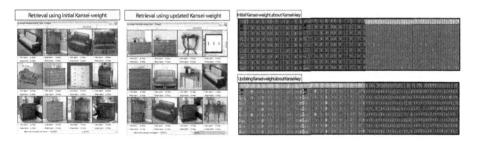

Fig. 3. Experimental Results and Table of Updated Kansei-weight

And then we evaluate the Kansei processing agent by asking ten people to repeatedly approach the system and evaluate the results by selecting 'agree' and 'deny.' When the agent is applying initial Kansei-weight, the user's satisfaction is 58%. However, when applying personalization, satisfaction increases to 79%. In the first evaluation, the level of user satisfaction is not so high. However, the more personalization increases, the higher the level of satisfaction. Therefore, we can see that our proposed agent applies effective methods for personalizing Kansei information retrieval, and that our agent is able to process Kansei.

4   Conclusions

In this study, we suggest a Kansei processing agent according to individual Kansei. For our proposed method, we defined individual Kansei and Kansei-key according to visual information of a product's image. Then we proposed the measuring method of the Kansei information content. Furthermore, the study offered an indicative method that is able to renew personal Kansei information using the user's evaluation. For experimentation and evaluation of these methods, we constructed the Kansei adaptive personalization image retrieval system and evaluated the Kansei processing agent according to the user's feedback. All of this has demonstrated that we are able to get suitable results for personal service based on Kansei. Our proposed methods would be applicable in the fields of Kansei-based personalizing service, information retrieval, Kansei engineering and so on.

Acknowledgments. This research was supported by the MIC(Ministry of Information and Communication), Korea, under the ITRC(Information Technology Research Center) support program supervised by the IITA(Institute of Information Technology Advancement (IITA-2006-C1090-0603-0040).

References

1. Yussupova, N.I., Konig-Ries, B., Popov, D.V., Vaynerman, I.A.: Personalizing the Usage of Complex Services. CSIT'2005, Ufa, Russia (2005)
2. Coutand, O., Sutterer, M., Lau, S., Droegehorn, O., David, K.: User Profile Management for Personalizing Services in Pervasive Computing. ASWN (2006)
3. Ligas, M., Charles, F.: Personalizing Services Encounters-The Role of Service Provider Actions in Developing Consumer Trust. Journal of Services Marketing Quarterly, vol. 25(4) (2004)
4. Yamazaki, H., Kondo, K.: A Method of Changing a Color Scheme with KANSEI Scales. Journal for Geometry and Graphics 3(1), 77–84 (1999)
5. Murai, S., Ono, K., Tanaka, N.: KANSEI-based Color Design for City Map. ARSRIN 2001, vol. 1(3) (2001)
6. Nagamachi, M.: The Story of Kansei Engineering. Tokyo: JSA, vol. 6 (2003)
7. Lee, S.H., Harada, A., Stappers, P.J.: Pleasure with Products-Design based on Kansei. In: Proceedings of the Pleasure-based Human Factors Seminar (2000)
8. Baek, S.K., Cho, M.Y., Kim, P.K.: Matching Colors with KANSEI Vocabulary using Similarity Measure based on WordNet. In: Gervasi, O., Gavrilova, M., Kumar, V., Laganà, A., Lee, H.P., Mun, Y., Taniar, D., Tan, C.J.K. (eds.) ICCSA 2005. LNCS, vol. 3480, pp. 37–45. Springer, Heidelberg (2005)
9. Baek, S.K., Ko, K.P., Jeong, H.Y., Lee, N.G., You, S., Ch., K.P.K.: The Creation of KANSEI-Vocabulary Scale by Shape. Petra Pernaer (Ed.). In: Proceeding of Industrial Conference on Data Mining, 258–268 (2006)
10. Osgood, C.E., Suci, G.J., Tannenbaum, P.H.: The Measurement of Meaning. Univ. of Illinois Press, Urbana, IL (1957)
11. Baek, S.K., Hwang, M.G., Cho, M.Y., Choi, Ch., Kim, P.K.: Object Retrieval by Query with Sensibility Based on The KANSEI-Vocabulary Scale. In: Huang, T.S., Sebe, N., Lew, M.S., Pavlović, V., Kölsch, M., Galata, A., Kisačanin, B. (eds.) Computer Vision in Human-Computer Interaction. LNCS, vol. 3979, pp. 109–119. Springer, Heidelberg (2006)
12. Baek, S.K., Hwang, K.S., Kim, P.K.: Classification of KANSEI Vocabulary according to Visual Shape Information. In: Proceeding of Korea Computer Congress vol. 33(1B), pp. 76–78 (2006)
13. Hwang, M.G., Baek, S.K., Kong, H.J., Shin, J.H., Kim, W.P., Kim, S.H., Kim, P.K.: Adaptive-Tangent Space Representation for Image Retrieval Based on Kansei. In: Gelbukh, A., Reyes-Garcia, C.A. (eds.) MICAI 2006. LNCS (LNAI), vol. 4293, pp. 828–837. Springer, Heidelberg (2006)

Maximizing the Utility of Situated Public Displays

Jörg Müller[1], Antonio Krüger[1], and Tsvi Kuflik[2]

[1] Institute for Geoinformatics, University of Münster, Germany
[2] MIS department, University of Haifa, Israel

Abstract. Situated public displays are intended to convey important information to a large and heterogeneous population. Because of the heterogeneity of the population, they may risk providing a lot of irrelevant information. Many such important information items presented on public displays are actionables, items that are intended to trigger specific actions. The expected utility that such actionables have for a user depend on the value of the action for the user. A goal should be to provide for each user the actionables with highest utility. This can be achieved by adapting the information presentation to the users currently in front of the display. Adaptation can take place either by identifying individual users, by using statistics about the user groups usually in front of the display or by a combination of both. We present a formal framework based on decision theory that enables the integration of sensor data and statistics and allows to choose the optimal actionable to present based on this data.

1 Introduction

The falling costs of large displays and their potential usefulness increases the numbers of available public displays and they are starting to appear in many public places. Situated Public Displays (SPD) [5] are intended to convey useful information to large and heterogeneous populations, assuming that even though the characteristics of the users are partially unknown, the information provided on the SPD may be useful in a given context. Obvious examples are dynamic timetables at train/bus stations that present the planned timetable and any relevant updated information such as changes of platforms and delays. This information may be augmented by weather information at various destinations and even by the list of open coffee shops for passengers of delayed trains. Our previous research on traditional public displays such as paper-based pinboards and placards, has shown that most of the information presented to the public are actionables, which are intended to cause people to act. In the context of an university examples for actionables are talk announcements, open positions or special bargains for students. The associated actions can only be taken within a certain window of space and time, as for example talks take place in a certain room at a certain time and job postings are outdated after a while. In this work we are primarily concentrating on the presentation of actionables through

C. Conati, K. McCoy, and G. Paliouras (Eds.): UM 2007, LNAI 4511, pp. 395–399, 2007.
© Springer-Verlag Berlin Heidelberg 2007

SPD. Even though the basic nature of SPD is to provide public information to large and highly heterogeneous populations, the basic assumption of complete anonymity may not be true. The user population in different places might be well known. For instance at universities there may be students, faculty and administrative staff with their particular interests and information needs. Hence actionables presented on public displays may be adapted to the interests of the current viewers and by that try to maximize their value for the users in question. The goal of this research is to establish a formal framework that will help estimating the expected utility of an actionable for users and groups alike. We are investigating the interesting question how to make use of different types of information about viewers and their interests, to finally decide which actionable to present on a SPD at a given moment in time.

2   Related and Prior Work

Research on various aspects of SPD has received considerable attention recently. SPD have been used to enhance the access for members of an organization to personal information anywhere within the organization, such as the BlueBoard system from IBM [7]. Additional work has been done to support spontaneous interaction between members of an organization, e.g. in the context of Group-Cast [4], which aimed at improving interaction not directly related to the usual office work and supported social interaction by displaying mutual interests and hobbies on nearby large displays. Research on the CWall System [3] revealed the relevance to support groups of peers or Communities of Practice within organizations. Related to our work is also the Plasma Poster Network [2]. Here, the displays resemble real poster boards where anyone could post items to distribute information to people within the organization. The Lancaster ecampus project [9] is a campus wide installation of networked displays where several experiences have been made with displays at various locations in different contexts. Because of the more public nature of the installation, one important observation that has been made, is that the quality of content is very important and that deployment and maintenance costs should not be underestimated. A few longitudinal studies have looked at social and technical requirements of semi-public displays in organizations, such as door displays [1] or conference room reservation and notification tools [6].

In our department we have installed a system of five SPD presenting relevant information for students and faculty. The displays mainly show actionables and changes to actionables. The question that we will discuss in the following, is how to decide which actionable to present to which users, depending on the characteristics of the actionable and the interests of the users.

3   Deciding Which Actionables to Advertise

Assuming the user in front of the SPD is identified (by a personal Bluetooth device for instance), the SPD content can be personalized by taking into account personal characteristics of the user (by having access to an individual user profile and schedule). As an example, the system may decide to remind an interesting talk given to a specific audience that seems to be of interest to the user even though he is not officially part of the target audience. Let us formalize the decision of selecting a single actionable to advertise.

We assume that there is a set of actionables $\mathcal{A} = \{a_1, \ldots, a_n\}$ that can be advertised and a set of users $\mathcal{U} = \{u_1, \ldots, u_p\}$ that can act upon these actionables. We have some evidence $\mathcal{E}$ that describes the situation that we can base our decision on, like sensor data, time, location etc. Then for each user u and each actionable a_k there is a utility $U_u(actupon(u, a_k))$ describing how useful it would be for that user to do the action, for example attend the talk.

An algorithm for finding the optimal actionable to advertise would now calculate the expected utility for each available actionable and choose the one that achieves the maximum expected utility. The expected utility for the user u $EU_u(advertise(a_i)|\mathcal{E})$ of advertising the actionable a_i given evidence $\mathcal{E}$ is what we expect to be the total utility for the user if we advertise this actionable. Following decision theory [8], we define

$$EU_u(advertise(a_i)|\mathcal{E}) =$$
$$\sum_{a_k \in \mathcal{A}} P(actupon(u, a_k)|advertise(a_i), \mathcal{E})U_u(actupon(u, a_k))$$

Where, $P(actupon(u, a_k)|advertise(a_k), \mathcal{E})$ is the probability that user u takes the action a_k given that we advertise a_i and evidence $\mathcal{E}$. $U(actupon(u, a_k))$ again is the utility for the user u of taking the action a_k.

In reality, we may have more than one user in front of the display. Then we will have to maximize the expected utility $EU_\mathcal{D}$ for the whole group $\mathcal{D} \subseteq \mathcal{U}$ of users that are in front of the display. We assume that the probabilities of users taking an action are pairwise independent, and that the utility for the group is the sum of the utilities of the users. Thus, we can state:

$$EU_\mathcal{D}(advertise(a_i)|\mathcal{E}) =$$
$$\sum_{a_k \in \mathcal{A}} \sum_{u_l \in \mathcal{D}} P(actupon(u_l, a_k)|advertise(a_i), \mathcal{E})U_{u_l}(actupon(u_l, a_k))$$

In a real-world setting, having all users identified may not be realistic. However, it could be possible to gather some statistics about which user groups usually pass the display at certain times. In our department for example, SPD are located at the entrances of and throughout the building. There are four different institutes each with three to seven groups of researchers. Each institute has students from five different years. In addition, there is administrative staff. Altogether there are more than forty different groups of users (with varying sizes) in that building. Information delivered over the public displays may be relevant to all (a change in the opening hours of the cafeteria) or parts of group members (a talk scheduled in one of the research groups). The different groups usually stay within certain regions of the building, and do so at different times. Students show up before first class starts, so no point in displaying schedule changes at

08:00 am when administrative staff arrives etc. Based on this idea, instead of dealing with individual users, we may take a stereotypic user modeling approach based on the characteristics of the groups (thus, we do not need to know the individual utilities $U_u(actupon(u, a_k))$). Let us suppose that there is a number of groups $\mathcal{G}$ such that each user is a member of one group. For each group $g \in \mathcal{G}$ we have an estimation $U_g(actupon(g, a_k))$ of how useful that action would be for members of the group. Then, we only need for each user u_l in front of the display and each group $g_m \in \mathcal{G}$, some estimation $P(u_l \in g_m | \mathcal{E})$ of the probability that the user belongs to this group, for example based on the current time, location of the display or sensor data. With this approach, the expected utility for the group would be

$$EU_{\mathcal{D}}(advertise(a_i)|\mathcal{E}) =$$

$$\sum_{a_k \in \mathcal{A}} \sum_{u_l \in \mathcal{D}} \sum_{g_m \in \mathcal{G}} P(u_l \in g_m | \mathcal{E}) P(actupon(g_m, a_k)|advertise(a_i), \mathcal{E}) U_g(actupon(g_m, a_k))$$

Thus, we have presented a formula that calculates the expected utility of advertising an actionable given that we know a number of parameters.

4   Discussion

In the above we introduced the need for adaptation of public displays, the information sources that may be available for that and a formal definition that allows the selection of the best actionables to advertise, in order to optimize the users utilities. Two main issues become now the focus of our interest. The individual utilities $U_u(actupon(u, a_k))$ and the probability that a user will act upon an advertised actionable $P(actupon(u_l, a_k)|advertise(a_i), \mathcal{E})$. The utility of the action itself can be modeled as $benefit(u, a_k) - cost(u, a_k)$. The individual benefits are highly user dependent and should be estimated based on a user model. A user model may be represented in different ways: one way is a user model composed of weights assigned to concepts drawn from an organizational ontology (so every user has his/her own personal preference with respect to the common ontology). Another approach may be by a weighted vector of terms drawn from a domain vocabulary (or several domains). Other relevant aspects may be organizational role, education, marital status, age, preferences with respect to leisure activities and more. The "cost" side of the utility is less user depended and can be calculated e.g., considering time required, budget to be spent, and traveling distance. Assuming that we have the models for dealing with individual users, then group models can be calculated as an average of the individual models of the users that are members in these groups. The other way around, individual user models could be bootstrapped by group models if available. In addition to the individual utilities, we need an estimate of the probability of users acting upon the information. This may be impacted by the overall utility value, the time left until the deadline, the possible alternatives, the need to change existing plans and so on. A strength of our approach is that some of the parameters can be estimated online from sensor data, while others can be obtained from statistics. So it adapts easily to different situations where different sensors and amounts of a priori knowledge are available, and it is does not matter that some users are identified and while others are not. A weakness of our formalism is that each user can be member of only one group, but this can easily be circumvented by modeling intersections of groups as additional groups. A different aspect to be dealt with is the optimization of the limited space and time that is available for all possible information items on a SPD. Of course we only take into account the utility for users, so we do not look at the particular needs of other stakeholders like information providers or display owners, who themselves might have their particular interests and want the information to be presented only to certain groups of individuals.

Acknowledgements. We would like to thank Oliver Paczkowski and our team for all the work on the display environment and Martin Mühlenbrock for hints on advertising.

References

1. Cheverst, K., Fitton, D., Dix, A.: Exploring the evolution of office door displays. In: O'Hara, K., Perry, M., Churchill, E., Russell, D. (eds.) Public and Situated Displays: Social and Interactional Aspects of Shared Display Technologies, Kluwer International, Dordrecht (2003)
2. Churchill, E., Nelson, L., Denoue, L., Girgensohn, A.: The plasma poster network: Posting multimedia content in public places. In: Human-Computer Interaction INTERACT 03, IOS Press, Amsterdam (2003)
3. Grasso, A., Mühlenbrock, M., Roulland, F., Snowdon, D.: Supporting communities of practice with large screen displays. In: O'Hara, K., Perry, M., Churchill, E., Russell, D. (eds.) Public and Situated Displays: Social and Interactional Aspects of Shared Display Technologies, Kluwer International, Dordrecht (2003)
4. Mccarthy, J.F., Costa, T.J., Liongosari, E.S.: Unicast, outcast and groupcast: Three steps toward ubiquitous, peripheral displays. In: Abowd, G.D., Brumitt, B., Shafer, S. (eds.) Ubicomp 2001: Ubiquitous Computing. LNCS, vol. 2201, p. 332. Springer, Heidelberg (2001)
5. Müller, J., Krüger, A.: Towards situated public displays as multicast systems. In: UbiqUM 2006 Workshop on Ubiquitous User Modeling, The 17th European Conference on Artificial Intelligence (2006)
6. O'Hara, K., Perry, M., Lewis, S.: Situated web signs and the ordering of social action. In: O'Hara, K., Perry, M., Churchill, E., Russell, D. (eds.) Public and Situated Displays: Social and Interactional Aspects of Shared Display Technologies, Kluwer International, Dordrecht (2003)
7. Russel, D.M., Sue, A.: Large interactive public displays: Use patterns, support patterns, community patterns. In: O'Hara, K., Perry, M., Churchill, E., Russell, D. (eds.) Public and Situated Displays: Social and Interactional Aspects of Shared Display Technologies, Kluwer International, Dordrecht (2003)
8. Russell, S.J., Norvig, P.: Artificial Intelligence: A Modern Approach, 2nd edn. Prentice Hall, Englewood Cliffs (2002)
9. Storz, O., Friday, A., Davies, N., Finney, J., Sas, C., Sheridan, J.: Public ubiquitous computing systems: Lessons from the e-campus display deployments. IEEE Pervasive Computing 5(3), 40–47 (2006)

Modeling Preferences in a Distributed Recommender System

Sylvain Castagnos and Anne Boyer

LORIA - Université Nancy 2, Campus Scientifique - B.P.239
54506 Vandoeuvre-lès-Nancy Cedex, France
{sylvain.castagnos,anne.boyer}@loria.fr

Abstract. A good way to help users finding relevant items on document platforms consists in suggesting content in accordance with their preferences. When implementing such a recommender system, the number of potential users and the confidential nature of some data should be taken into account. This paper introduces a new P2P recommender system which models individual preferences and exploits them through a user-centered filtering algorithm. The latter has been designed to deal with problems of scalability, reactivity, and privacy.

1 Introduction

Usual search engines provide too many results to ensure that the active user will identify the most relevant items in a reasonable time. As a result, the scientific community is rethinking the existing services of searching and accessing information under the designation "Web 2.0".

A solution consists in providing each user with items that are likely to interest him/her. To do this, we first build his/her model by collecting his/her preferences. Our approach is based on an analysis of usages. Nevertheless, it is not always possible to collect data about the active user quickly enough. Collaborative filtering techniques [1] are a good way to cope with this difficulty. There are several fundamental problems when implementing a collaborative filtering algorithm. In this paper, we pay attention to significant problems such as scalability, reactivity, and respect of privacy.

Our algorithm relies on a distributed user-based collaborative filtering technique. It has been integrated in our document sharing system called "SofoS".[1] We state the hypothesis that documents are transient on the platform, whereas human-computer interactions are long-standing. We assume that, in this case, a user-based approach may be more appropriate than an item-based one. If a significant proportion of resources is constantly removed or added, correlations between users will potentially need fewer updates than an item correlation model.

Our P2P model offers the advantage of being fully distributed. It collects data about the preferences of users, and takes advantage of an "Adaptive User-centered Recommender Algorithm" called AURA. The latter provides a service

---

[1] SofoS is the acronym for "Sharing Our Files On the System".

C. Conati, K. McCoy, and G. Paliouras (Eds.): UM 2007, LNAI 4511, pp. 400–404, 2007.
© Springer-Verlag Berlin Heidelberg 2007

which builds a virtual community of interests, centered on the active user by selecting his/her nearest neighbors. AURA is an anytime algorithm which furthermore requires very little computation time and memory space.

2   Related Work

A way to classify collaborative filtering techniques is to consider user-based methods in opposition to item-based algorithms. For example, Miller *et al.*[3] show the great potential of distributed item-based algorithms. They propose a P2P version of the item-item algorithm, and thus address the problems of portability (even on mobile devices), privacy, and security with a high quality of recommendations. On the contrary, we explored a distributed user-based approach within a client/server context in [2]. In this model, implicit criteria are used to generate explicit ratings. These votes are anonymously sent to the server. An offline clustering algorithm is then applied, and group profiles are sent to clients. The identification phase is done on the client side in order to cope with privacy. This model also deals with sparsity and scalability. We highlighted the added value of a user-based approach in the situation where users are relatively stable, whereas the set of items may often vary considerably.

In this paper, we introduce a new user-based collaborative filtering technique (AURA), distributing profiles and computations. It has been integrated in the SofoS platform and relies on a P2P architecture.

3   SofoS

3.1   Construction of Preference Models

SofoS is our new document platform, using a recommender system to provide users with content. Once it is installed, users can share and/or search documents, as they do on P2P applications like Napster. The goal of SofoS is also to assist users to find the most relevant sources of information in the most efficient way. In order to reach this objective, the platform exploits the AURA recommender module. The performance of this module crucially depends on the accuracy of the individual user preference models.

The first step when modeling preferences of users consists in choosing an efficient way to collect data. Proposing a series of questions to users is an efficient way to do accurate preference elicitation. Such an approach however would require asking hundreds of questions, and most users are generally not willing to take enough time to carry through such a lengthy process. This is why we prefer to let users explicitly rate the items they want, without order constraints.

However, an explicit data collection may be insufficient. Psychological studies [4] have shown that people construct their preferences while learning about the available items. This means that *a priori* ratings are not necessarily relevant. Unfortunately, few users provide a feedback about their consultations. We assume that, despite the explicit voluntary completion of profiles, there are a lot of missing data.

We consequently add a user modeling function based on the Chan formula [2]. This function relies on an analysis of usages. It temporarily collects information about the action of the active user (frequency and duration of consultations for each item, etc.) and transforms them into numerical votes. In order to preserve privacy, all data related to the user's actions remain on his/her peer. The explicit ratings and the estimated numerical votes constitute the active user's personal profile.

3.2   The AURA Algorithm

The personal preference-based profiles are used by AURA, in order to provide each user with the content that most likely interests him/her. AURA relies on a Peer-to-Peer architecture.

Each user on a given peer of the system has his/her own profile and a single ID. The session data remain on the local machine in order to enhance privacy. There is no central server required since sessions are only used to distinguish users on a given peer.

For each user, we use a hash function requiring the IP address and the login in order to generate his/her ID on his/her computer. In this way, an ID does not allow identification of the name or IP address of the corresponding user. The communication module uses an IP multicast address to broadcast the packets containing addressees' IDs.

Users can both share items on the platform and integrate a feedback about their preferences. Each item has a profile on the platform. In addition to the available documents, each peer owns 7 pieces of information: a personal profile (cf. section 3.1), a public profile, a group profile and 4 lists of IDs (list "A" for IDs of peers belonging to its group, list "B" for those which exceed the minimum-correlation threshold as explained below, list "C" for the black-listed IDs and list "O" for IDs of peers which have added the active user to their group profile).

The public profile is the part of the personal profile that the active user u_a accepts to share with others. The algorithm also has to build a group profile. It represents the preferences of a virtual community of interests, and has been especially designed to be as close as possible to the active user's expectations. In order to do that, the peer of the active user asks for the public profiles of all the peers it can reach through the platform. Then, for each of these profiles, it computes a similarity measure with the personal profile of the active user. The active user can indirectly define a minimum-correlation threshold which corresponds to the radius of his/her trust circle.

If the similarity is lower than this fixed threshold, which is specific to each user, the ID of the peer is added to the list "A" and the corresponding profile is included in the group profile of the active user, using the procedure of table 1.

We used the Pearson correlation coefficient to establish a similarity measure. Of course, if this similarity measure is higher than the threshold, we add the ID of the peer to the list "B". The list "C" is used to systematically ignore some peers. It enables to improve trust – i.e. confidence that users have in the recommendations – by identifying malicious users. The trust increasing process will not be considered here.

When his/her personal profile changes, the active user has the possibility to update his/her public profile p_a. In this case, the active peer has to contact every peer[2] whose ID is in the list "O". Each of these peers re-computes the similarity measure. If it exceeds the threshold, the profile p_a has to be removed from the group profile, using the procedure of table 1. Otherwise, p_a has to be updated in the group profile, that is to say the peer must remove the old profile and add the new one.

Table 1. Add or remove a public profile

Proc AddToGroupProfile(profile of u_n)	**Proc** RemoveToGroupProfile(old profile)
$W = W + |w(u_a, u_n)|$	$W = W - |w(u_a, u_n)|$
for each item i **do**	**for** each item i **do**
$(u_{l,i}) = (u_{l,i}) * (W - |w(u_a, u_n)|)$	$(u_{l,i}) = (u_{l,i}) * (W + |w(u_a, u_n)|)$
$(u_{l,i}) = ((u_{l,i}) + w(u_a, u_n) * (u_{n,i}))/W$	$(u_{l,i}) = ((u_{l,i}) - w(u_a, u_n) * (u_{n,i}))/W$
end for	**end for**

$(u_{l,i})$ the rating for item i in the group profile;
$(u_{n,i})$ the rating of user n for item i;
W the sum of $|w(u_a, u_i)|$, which is stored;
$w(u_a, u_n)$ the correlation coefficient between the active user u_a and u_n.

4 Discussion

In our system, the users have complete access to their preferences. They have an effect on what and when to share with others. Only numerical votes are exchanged and the logs of user actions are transient. Even when the active user does not want to share his/her preferences, it is possible to do predictions, since public profiles of other peers are temporarily available on the active user device. Each user has a single ID, but the anonymity is ensured by the fact that there is no table linking IDs and identities.

As regards scalability, our model no longer suffers from limitations since the algorithms used to compute group profiles and predictions are in $o(b)$, where b is the number of commonly valuated items between two users, since computations are made incrementally in a dynamic context. In return, AURA requires quite a lot of network traffic. This is particularly true if we use a random discovery architecture. Other P2P structures can improve communications [3].

We evaluated our model in terms of prediction relevancy by computing the *Mean Absolute Error* (MAE) on the GroupLens test set[3]. We simulated arrivals of peers by progressively adding new profiles. As shown on figure 1, we got predictions as good as using the PocketLens algorithm [3]. PocketLens relies on a distributed item-based approach. This comparison demonstrates that AURA provides as relevant results as an efficient item-based collaborative filtering.

---

[2] A packet is broadcasted with an heading containing peers' IDs, the old profile and the new public profile.

[3] http://www.grouplens.org/

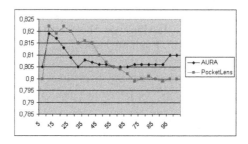

Fig. 1. MAE as neighborhood size grows

We also conducted some tests in order to measure computation time. They highlight the fact that AURA allows to do real-time predictions. It does not need to do offline computations, since we can take into account 10,000 profiles with 150 items in less than 0.5 second. For 100,000 users, we need about 3 seconds. The system does not have to wait until all similarity measures end. As the algorithm is incremental, we can stop considering other peers at any moment.

5   Conclusion

SofoS is a new document sharing platform including a recommender system. To cope with numerous problems specific to information retrieval, we proposed a Peer-to-Peer collaborative filtering model which is totally distributed. It allows real-time personalization. We show in this paper that AURA can deal with important problems such as scalability, privacy, and quality.

Our algorithm is anytime and incremental. Contrary to PocketLens, our model is user-based because we consider that the set of items can change. Even if an item is deleted, we can continue to exploit its ratings in the computation of predictions. Moreover, the dynamic context of our model allows the system to update the modified profiles instead of resetting all the knowledge about neighbors. At last, our model has very low memory requirements because it does not need to store any neighbors' ratings, similarity matrix, dot product matrix, etc. It only requires the sum of the Pearson coefficients and four lists of user IDs.

References

1. Breese, J.S., Heckerman, D., Kadie, C.: Empirical Analysis of Predictive Algorithms for Collaborative Filtering. In: Proceedings of UAI-98. San Francisco, CA (July (1998)
2. Castagnos, S., Boyer, A.: A Client/Server User-Based Collaborative Filtering Algorithm: Model and Implementation. In: Proceedings of the 17th European Conference on Artificial Intelligence (ECAI2006). Riva del Garda, Italy (August 2006)
3. Bradley, N., Miller, J.A., Konstan, J.R.: PocketLens: Toward a Personal Recommender System. ACM Transactions on Information Systems 22 (July 2004)
4. Payne, J.W., Bettman, J.R., Johnson, E.J.: The Adaptive Decision Maker. Cambridge University Press, Cambridge (1993)

Multiple Evidence Combination in Web Site Search Based on Users' Access Histories

Chen Ding[1,*] and Jin Zhou[2]

[1] Department of Computer Science, Ryerson University, Canada
[2] DB2 Information Management, IBM, Canada
cding@ryerson.ca, jinzhou@ca.ibm.com

Abstract. Despite the success of global search engines, web site search is still problematic in its retrieval accuracy. In this study, we propose to extract terms based on users' access histories to build web page representations, and then use multiple evidence combination to combine these log-based terms with text-based and anchor-based terms. We test different combination approaches and baseline retrieval models. Our experimental results show that the server log, when used in multiple evidence combination, can improve the effectiveness of the web site search, whereas the impact on different models is different.

1 Introduction

The basic idea of multiple evidence combination [3] is that by combining multiple sources of evidence we can compensate for the weakness of a single source. Many studies have achieved a positive result [5] [7]. In this paper, we investigate using different combination models in the web site search. The server log has been used a lot in the web usage mining area [8]. Here we use it in the site search. Log-based index [4] is one of the sources of evidence we consider, and the other two sources include the original text information and the anchor text information.

We test the performance of two combination approaches – the combination of representations, and of ranking scores, using linear combination [5] and inference network models [7]. We also consider three different baseline information retrieval (IR) models – Dot-product with TFIDF weighting schemes (TFIDF) [6], Cosine Similarity [1] and Okapi [1]. The experiment results show that the texts extracted from server logs are able to improve the retrieval effectiveness. Among these approaches, the combination of representations using the inference network model achieves the best performance, whereas the biggest improvement is from the combination of scores using the TFIDF model. We find that server log analysis has different impact on different combination and retrieval models.

The rest of the paper is organized as follows. Section 2 describes how we build index based on users' access histories. Section 3 shows how we do the multiple evidence combination and the experiment results. Section 4 concludes the paper.

---

* This work is sponsored by Natural Science & Engineering Research Council of Canada (grant 299021-04).

C. Conati, K. McCoy, and G. Paliouras (Eds.): UM 2007, LNAI 4511, pp. 405–409, 2007.
© Springer-Verlag Berlin Heidelberg 2007

2 Evidence Based on Users' Access Histories

When a user accesses a sequence of web pages, he usually has a particular information-seeking task in mind. For instance, a student wants to find out information on the database course at university A, he submits the query "university A database course" to Google, after reviewing the result list, he clicks on a professor's homepage p_0, then from there, he goes to the course web page p_1, and follows a link to the course outline page p_2. Or, he might find a link to the professor's homepage from the department web site, and then just follow the links to the course page. In both cases, the initial query terms or anchor terms on the link are representative of this user's information task. As long as the user does not deviate from this initial task, these terms could represent topics of all three pages p_0, p_1, and p_2. The idea of using query terms in the search is also presented in [2] although they used it for web search.

When a user follows hyperlinks to view more pages, there are two possibilities. One is that he changes his initial information task and wants to find something else. The other is that he continues on his initial task, but narrow down or generalize it a little bit. In the latter case, the entry terms can still represent the topics of other pages in the session, whereas the generalization or specialization of the initial information task could be reflected in anchor texts along the access path.

Based on these observations, we proposed a novel approach of representing a web page based on users' access histories [4]. The following formulas show how we propagate entry terms and extract more terms along the access path k.

$$\vec{V}_{ki} = \alpha_1 \cdot s(p_0, p_i) \cdot rl_k(p_0, p_i) \cdot \vec{V}_{k0} + \beta_1 \cdot \sum_{j=1}^{i-1} s(p_j, p_i) \cdot rl_k(p_j, p_i) \cdot \vec{V}_{k, j-1 \to j} + \gamma_1 \cdot \vec{V}_{k, i-1 \to i} \cdot \quad (1)$$

$$s(p_i, p_j) = \cos(p_i, p_j) = \frac{\vec{V}_{ti} \cdot \vec{V}_{tj}}{\left|\vec{V}_{ti}\right|\left|\vec{V}_{tj}\right|} \cdot \quad (2)$$

$$rl_k(p_i, p_j) = \frac{1}{dist_k(p_i, p_j) + 1} \cdot \quad (3)$$

Where $s(p_j, p_i)$ calculates the cosine similarity score between the page p_i and p_j, $\vec{V}_{ti}$ is the term vector of the page p_i based on the text analysis, $dist_k(p_i, p_j)$ measures the distance between the page p_i and p_j along the path k, $\vec{V}_{k0}$ is the entry term vector for the path k, $\vec{V}_{ki}$ is the vector of the page p_i based on analysis on the path k, $\vec{V}_{k, j-1 \to j}$ is the vector of anchor texts from the page p_{j-1} to p_j, α_1, β_1, and γ_1 is the weighting factor for each part and the sum of them is equal to 1. Although the cosine similarity score can be affected by the size of the term space, we chose it mainly for the simplicity reason and the toolset we used [6].

In order to avoid that people might repeatedly access the same page with the same entry terms to impact the scoring, the same session from one user is only counted once. The propagation is stopped after a certain level if it is not on the initial task any more. Since one page might have multiple representations calculated from different sessions, we need to combine them to have a single representation [4].

3 Experiment

In the experiment, we collected web server logs from a computer science departmental web site (www.scs.ryerson.ca) during the period of Jan 2005 to Dec 2005, and downloaded web pages during the month of Oct 2005 for the text analysis and the anchor extraction.

The main purpose of the experiment is to compare different combination models, to see which one is the most effective, and which one can gain the most from combining the log-based evidence. We used the Lemur Toolkit [6] to implement three baseline IR models. We implemented the linear combination model to combine document representations and ranking scores, and Indri [6] implementation for the inference network model. The text-based retrieval is taken as the baseline run. In each combination model, we chose different values of α, β, γ to test the performance. Since we are not aimed at finding an optimal set of parameters in this study, we chose a representative sample of parameter combinations. The lower bound of α is set as 0.3 because we believe that the portion from the text index should not be too low, especially in our data set, many web pages are not in the anchor or log index.

We selected 24 queries [9]. 15 of them are extracted from queries recorded in server logs, and others are randomly chosen from a list of relevant topics. We use three metrics to measure the effectiveness of the algorithm, the top 10 precision (P@10), which is the precision at 10 answers, the R-precision (RP), which is the precision at the point where the number of answers is equal to the number of relevant documents, and the average precision (AP), which is the average of precision values at every seen relevant document. In order to measure how well is our algorithm to put the most relevant pages in top positions, we calculate another metric, the top 10 precision for the highly relevant pages (HP@10).

In the results shown in Table 1-3, TXT means the retrieval based on the text-based index, LOG means the log-based retrieval, CALL means combining all three representations, CXYZ means the retrieval based on the score combination where X:Y:Z is the ratio between α, β, and γ. For CXYZ, we chose 22 combinations of parameters in the experiment [9], although we only list 4 representative ones here to analyze the results. In Table 4, since Indri is the representation combination model, CXYZ means the weight is assigned to different representations, and CALL means all three representations are combined as a single one without any weighting factor. The best result for each metric is highlighted in the table.

Table 1, 2 and 3 show four metrics averaged on all queries for the linear combination model that takes TFIDF, Cosine Similarity and Okapi respectively as the baseline model. Table 4 shows four metrics averaged on all queries for Indri model.

A general conclusion from these results is that the combination of the log-based evidence can improve the effectiveness of the text-based retrieval. Depending on the baseline IR model, the degree of improvement is different. Depending on the baseline IR model, sometimes the score combination is better, or the representation combination is better. Combination models are especially effective in promoting highly relevant results to top 10 positions.

Table 1. Four performance metrics averaged on 24 queries (TFIDF model)

	P@10	RP	AP	HP@10
TXT	0.200	0.187	0.176	0.079
LOG	0.273	0.226	0.177	0.108
CALL	0.224	0.236	0.227	0.09
C334	**0.290**	**0.282**	**0.265**	**0.115**
C433	0.257	0.271	0.248	0.101
C460	0.261	0.263	0.251	0.099
C640	0.224	0.250	0.228	0.084

Table 2. Four performance metrics averaged on 24 queries (Cosine Similarity model)

	P@10	RP	AP	HP@10
TXT	0.289	0.280	0.276	0.105
LOG	0.317	0.266	0.228	0.133
CALL	0.318	0.331	0.325	0.12
C334	**0.353**	**0.392**	**0.375**	**0.155**
C433	0.348	0.389	**0.376**	0.15
C460	0.286	0.327	0.322	0.146
C640	0.329	0.350	0.346	0.13

Table 3. Four performance metrics averaged on 24 queries (Okapi model)

	P@10	RP	AP	HP@10
TXT	0.407	0.402	0.389	0.159
LOG	0.314	0.235	0.197	0.13
CALL	**0.450**	**0.448**	**0.453**	**0.191**
C334	0.341	0.342	0.344	0.136
C433	0.393	0.396	0.372	0.158
C460	0.395	0.412	0.413	0.171
C640	0.435	0.448	0.443	0.185

Table 4. Four performance metrics averaged on 24 queries (Indri model)

	P@10	RP	AP	HP@10
TXT	0.422	0.399	0.378	0.175
LOG	0.275	0.264	0.235	0.105
CALL	**0.456**	**0.469**	**0.469**	**0.201**
C334	0.373	0.380	0.363	0.162
C433	0.347	0.354	0.346	0.145
C460	0.447	0.466	0.449	0.193
C640	0.457	0.445	0.418	0.189

There are some limitations of the current experiment. First, the experiment on only one web site might not be very convincing. The second limitation of the current experiment design is that most of the queries are extracted from the web server log, which favors the log-based index more. For the new queries or unpopular queries, the weight on the log part should be decreased. Thirdly, it is worthy of the further investigation on the impact of the query set on the result and also the correlation between the choice of α, β, γ and the final precision results. In the next stage of the experiment, we would like to do the same experiment on another web site to make our conclusion more generalized, and it is also necessary to compare with some existing systems.

4 Conclusions

The web server log is a unique source for web site search, if we can use it wisely, we should be able to find a solution that can improve the current web site search engines. In this study, we test and compare different combination approaches. The experiment results are positive. Generally, multiple evidence combination with the texts extracted from users' access histories can improve the retrieval effectiveness of the web site search. Its impact on different baseline IR models and combination models are different. This work can be extended in several directions such as those listed in the discussion part.

References

1. Baeza-Yates, R., Ribeiro-Neto, B.: Modern Information Retrieval. Addison-Wesley, New York (1999)
2. Balfe, E., Smyth, B.: Improving Web Search through Collaborative Query Recommendation. In: Proceedings of the 16th European Conference on Artificial Intelligence, pp. 268–272 (2004)
3. Croft, W.B.: Combining Approaches to Information Retrieval. In: Croft, W. B (Ed.), Advances in Information Retrieval: Recent Research from the Center for Intelligent Information Retrieval, pp. 1–36 (2000)
4. Ding, C., Zhou, J.: Log-based Indexing to Improve Web Site Search. Accepted by the 22nd Annual ACM Symposium on Applied Computing – Information Access and Retrieval Track (2007)
5. Lee, J.H.: Analyses of Multiple Evidence Combination. Proceedings of the 20th Annual International ACM SIGIR Conference on Research and Development in Information Retrieval, pp. 267–276 (1997)
6. Lemur Project, http://www.lemurproject.org/
7. Metzler, D., Croft, W.B.: Combining the Language Model and Inference Network Approaches to Retrieval. Information Processing and Management 40, 735–750 (2004)
8. Pierrakos, D., Paliouras, G., Papatheodorou, C., Spyropoulos, C.D.: Web Usage Mining as a Tool for Personalization: A Survey. User. Modeling and User.-Adapted Interaction 13, 311–372 (2003)
9. Zhou, J.: Web Site Search: Rank Combination with Supporting Evidence, Master's Thesis, Ryerson University (2006)

MyPlace Locator: Flexible Sharing of Location Information

Mark Assad, David J. Carmichael, Judy Kay, and Bob Kummerfeld*

The University of Sydney, Sydney, Australia
{massad,dcarmich,judy,bob}@it.usyd.edu.au

Abstract. As location information plays such an important role in pervasive and context-aware computing, location modelling can be cast as a particularly important user modelling problem. Moreover, given the potential sensitivity of personal information about location, it is critical to ensure adequate user control over the use of the location user modelling information. This paper describes MyPlace Locator, a system for modelling people's location, based upon a range of pervasive sensors. A critical feature, the focus of this paper, is the user model control: users can determine the granularity in space and time of the location information released from their model. Users can do this on the level of a single user or a group of users. We describe the interface and report its qualitative evaluation.

Keywords: location modelling, pervasive computing, user control, scrutability.

1 Introduction

The vision of pervasive computing is based upon the availability of information as it is needed, in the form that meets the needs and preferences of the individual. To date, one of the dominant themes of pervasive computing research has concerned modelling of location, largely dealing with the technical issues of collecting sensor and other information that can contribute to modelling a person's location.

Privacy and user control are also critical in this context. As location data can be particularly sensitive, some systems keep personal information only on the user's device [1]. There is also a developing set of privacy principles for managing personal data in ubiquitous computing contexts [2]. Good interfaces are essential if these principles are to be put into effect: previous research indicates it will be challenging to create such interfaces, for example, in relation to P3P [3] and Lederer et al [4]. Iachello et al. [5] conducted a study which indicated that people valued control over the release of their location information, including being able to give inaccurate information. Lederer et al. [6] studied user's preferences on location disclosure and found that the recipient was more important than the

---

* This research was part funded by the Smart Internet Technology CRC Australia.

C. Conati, K. McCoy, and G. Paliouras (Eds.): UM 2007, LNAI 4511, pp. 410–414, 2007.
© Springer-Verlag Berlin Heidelberg 2007

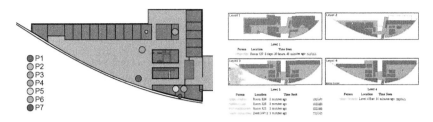

(a) Detailed view of a single wing   (b) Screen shot of the web interface

Fig. 1. An example MyPlace Locator display based on a floor plan of our building

situation when controlling disclosure. Patil and Lai [7] found that people tend to define privacy preferences in terms of groups, such as "family" or work "team". Significantly, these studies involved hypothetical preferences as the participants had not actually used a real system.

Our MyPlace Locator service has been in use for four months. Its location modelling is based on Bluetooth proximity sensors and system activity sensors. It has been restricted to a small community of users. An important aspect of our recent work, as we prepare for broader use of the system, is user model control. Users can control the spatial accuracy and longevity of the location data released from their model. The interface allows control of these for individuals or groups of users. The paper describes the system, its privacy preference options and a qualitative evaluation.

2   System Overview

The main interface to MyPlace Locator is a web page that allow users to view their own and other people's location. MyPlace Locator uses two forms of evidence about people's location: Bluetooth Phones and Computer Activity Sensors. This means it is straightforward for people to join the system by registering their Bluetooth-enabled phone, or installing a small sensor program on their computer. We have Bluetooth sensors in 16 locations within our building. Each of these constantly scans for any Bluetooth devices within the coverage area of a few nearby rooms. Computer system activity sensors bleep out how long it has been since the user last used the mouse or keyboard.

The reasoning about location is based on accretion/resolution [8]: this allows a system to *accrete* arbitrary information about users and then, when asked, to apply one of a selection of *resolvers* to interpret it. If there is conflicting evidence about the user's location, the *resolver* deals with this to determine a location value. In the current implementation, we use a Point resolver [8].

The MyPlace Locator interface is shown in Figure 1. This displays the four floors of a building, with a list of the registered users either in the building or elsewhere. The enlarged display of a single wing at the left shows that the display includes a list of the people whose last location was determined to be on that

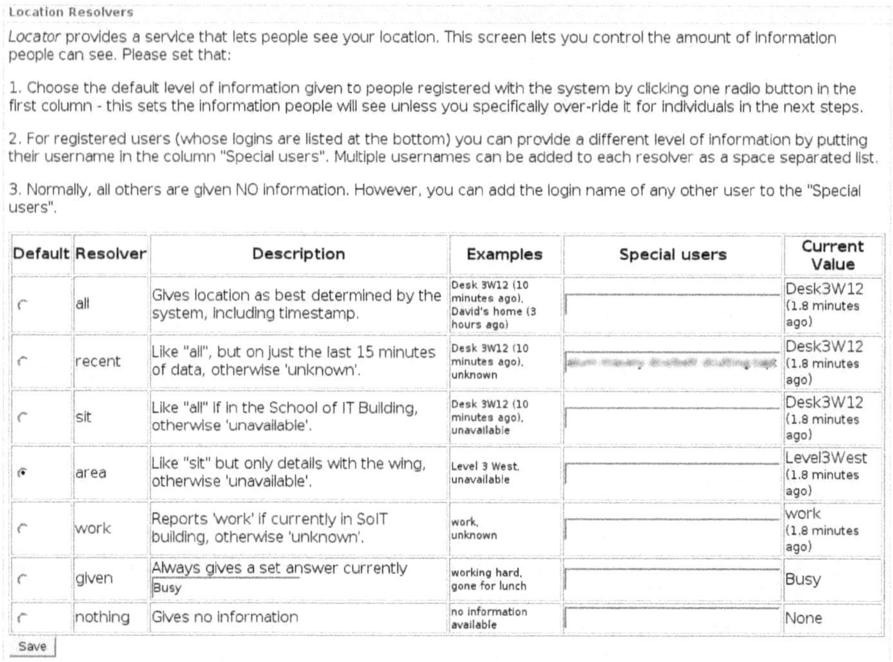

Location Resolvers

Locator provides a service that lets people see your location. This screen lets you control the amount of information people can see. Please set that:

1. Choose the default level of information given to people registered with the system by clicking one radio button in the first column - this sets the information people will see unless you specifically over-ride it for individuals in the next steps.

2. For registered users (whose logins are listed at the bottom) you can provide a different level of information by putting their username in the column "Special users". Multiple usernames can be added to each resolver as a space separated list.

3. Normally, all others are given NO information. However, you can add the login name of any other user to the "Special users".

Default	Resolver	Description	Examples	Special users	Current Value
○	all	Gives location as best determined by the system, including timestamp.	Desk 3W12 (10 minutes ago), David's home (3 hours ago)		Desk3W12 (1.8 minutes ago)
○	recent	Like "all", but on just the last 15 minutes of data, otherwise 'unknown'.	Desk 3W12 (10 minutes ago), unknown	▓▓▓▓▓▓▓▓	Desk3W12 (1.8 minutes ago)
○	sit	Like "all" if in the School of IT Building, otherwise 'unavailable'.	Desk 3W12 (10 minutes ago), unavailable		Desk3W12 (1.8 minutes ago)
⦿	area	Like "sit" but only details with the wing, otherwise 'unavailable'.	Level 3 West, unavailable		Level3West (1.8 minutes ago)
○	work	Reports 'work' if currently in SoIT building, otherwise 'unknown'.	work, unknown		work (1.8 minutes ago)
○	given	Always gives a set answer currently Busy	working hard, gone for lunch		Busy
○	nothing	Gives no information	no information available		None

Save

Fig. 2. Interface for selecting the resolver to be applied to each person

wing. This is the anonymised list associating people's names with a coloured dot. That dot appears also on the map at the last location for that person. The size of the dot indicates the freshness of the data: so if there is recent evidence that the person was at this location, the dot is larger.

The blurred location data at the right of the figure has four pieces of information for each person: their name, their most recent location, the freshness of the information and a link to an explanation. The link labelled *explain* takes the user to a page with the full details - type, source, time and location - of the last ten pieces of location evidence. If a person saw that their location was incorrect, they could use this information to check why.

3   User Model Control Interface

Figure 2 shows the control interface for disclosure of location information from a user's model. As the instructions at the top of the screen indicate, preferences are defined in three stages. First, the user chooses the default level of information by clicking a button in the left column. In the figure, the third option "area" has been selected. In Step 2, the user can specify people who should be provided with a different level of information, by listing their logins under "Special users". In the figure, this has been blurred to obscure the names of the actual people selected. Finally, users can add other people, beyond the registered users: this enables access to the location information from this model for people who are not already registered with the system.

Each row has a short description of that option. There are also some illustrative examples and, in the rightmost column, the current value for this user is shown, following guidelines suggested in [7]. The amount of information release decreases as the rows go down the screen, The top row "all" releases all location information, while the bottom "nothing" releases none. Not shown in the figure, there is also a column at the right with a list of all the registered users.

4   Evaluation

We designed a qualitative evaluation to assess how people would user the interface in Figure 2 to control the release of their location user model. We recruited twenty-four users. Ten had been active users of the system over two months. The other fourteen were registered with the system, shown the location display then immediately asked to configure their disclosure settings.

Participants were invited to use the interface. They were given no training. They were asked to think-aloud as they used the interface: this provided us with insights about usability problems as well as participant responses to the broad ideas of controlling a user model.

We discuss the results from the experienced users first. All these people registered with the system when there was no choice about the information disclosed. They generally had more sensors than the other participants: a Bluetooth mobile phone and system sensors at both work and home. Five chose 'all' as the default and two each chose 'recent' and 'area'. Notably, two participants chose a more restricted default and then listed most of the currently registered users for *all* information. They explained that they were happy to release their location to the current users who they knew: however, they were concerned about new people joining the system.

The new users had a somewhat more diverse set of choices. Four chose 'all' and four more chose 'recent', with two choosing to restrict location to the building and two restricting it to the area in the building. One chose the restrictive 'work' and one chose to reveal no information, because they saw no benefit. Users in this group generally had less sensors: normally either a Bluetooth phone, or system sensors, but seldom both.

The results for the participants who had substantial experience of the system were qualitatively different from the others. This may be partly due to the fact that these users had chosen to make use of the location system when all available information was made available to all registered users: had anyone been unwilling to allow their location information to be available, they would not have joined the system. The more experienced participants may also differ from the others because they had stronger links with the other people who had registered with the system: this would alter their willingness to share their location information. However, there also appears to be an effect due to the greater understanding of the system, its benefits and how it operates in practice. They were the only users to apply more subtle schemes, such as those accounting for the possibility of new people joining the system.

5   Conclusions

We have described our MyPlace Locator system which has been used for four months by twelve registered users who work together. We conducted a study of the personalisation preferences for both our existing users and potential new users. Only one of the potential new users opted for releasing no location information and only one selected to merely be shown as *at work* when at work and *unknown* otherwise.

There are limitations in our study. It concerned one workplace and the use-study involved one cohesive work group. In addition, all the participants in the studies are computer scientists. This work makes a new contribution in reporting the choices people made for user model privacy preferences, both in the case of users of the existing system and others, who have not had experience in using MyPlace Locator. A notable aspect of the study is the diversity in participant responses: different people elected for different approaches to specifying their preferences for release of their own location information to others.

References

1. Hazas, M., Ward, A.: A high performance privacy-oriented location system. In: Proceedings of the First IEEE International Conference on Pervasive Computing and Communications (PerCom), pp. 216–233. IEEE Computer Society Press, Los Alamitos (2003)
2. Langheinrich, M.: Privacy by design - principles of privacy-aware ubiquitous systems. In: UbiComp, 3rd Intl. Conf. on Ubiquitous Computing, pp. 273–291 (2001)
3. Ackerman, M.S., Cranor, L.: Privacy critics: UI components to safeguard user' privacy. In: CHI '99 extended abstracts, pp. 258–259. ACM Press, New York (1999)
4. Lederer, S., Hong, J., Jiang, X., Dey, A., Landay, J., Mankoff, J.: Towards everyday privacy for ubiquitous computing. Technical Report Technical Report UCBCSD -03-1283, Computer Science Division, University of California, Berkeley (2003)
5. Iachello, G., Smith, I.E., Consolvo, S., Abowd, G.D., Hughes, J., Howard, J., Potter, F., Scott, J., Sohn, T., Hightower, J., LaMarca, A.: Control, deception, and communication: Evaluating the deployment of a location-enhanced messaging service. In: Beigl, M., Intille, S.S., Rekimoto, J., Tokuda, H. (eds.) UbiComp 2005. LNCS, vol. 3660, pp. 213–231. Springer, Heidelberg (2005)
6. Lederer, S., Mankoff, J., Dey, A.K.: Who wants to know what when? privacy preference determinants in ubiquitous computing. In: CHI '03 extended abstracts on Human factors in computing systems, pp. 724–725. ACM Press, New York (2003)
7. Patil, S., Lai, J.: Who gets to know what when: configuring privacy permissions in an awareness application. In: Proceedings of CHI '05, pp. 101–110. ACM Press, New York (2005)
8. Carmichael, D., Kay, J., Kummerfeld, R.: Consistent modeling of users, devices and environments in a ubiquitous computing environment. User. Modeling and User.-Adapted Interaction 15, 197–234 (2005)

Personalised Mashups: Opportunities and Challenges for User Modelling

Minh Dang Thang, Vania Dimitrova, and Karim Djemame

School of Computing, University of Leeds,
Leeds LS2 9JT, UK
m.t.dang@leeds.ac.uk, {karim,vania}@comp.leeds.ac.uk
http://www.comp.leeds.ac.uk

Abstract. Web 2.0 has emerged as the business ideology and development paradigm for the next generation of web applications. This paper proposes the use of personalisation techniques to enhance the functionality of web mashups, one of the most popular Web 2.0 applications. A prototype of a personalised travel assistant which combines interactive maps with public data pulled from the Internet is presented. An experimental study with the prototype points at opportunities and challenges mashups bring to personalisation research.

Keywords: Web 2.0, mashups, application of user modelling.

1 Introduction

Coined as an attempt to describe a new trend of innovation-driven and user-centric web development, Web 2.0 receives strong industrial support and is influencing the way Internet technologies are being produced and deployed [1]. The time appears ripe for the user modelling community to start looking at how the Web 2.0 paradigm will affect research on personalisation and adaptation. Mashups, which collect and integrate information and services from several sources on the web, are emerging as compelling Web 2.0 applications [2]. Recognising the emerging potential of mashups, various initiatives have been established to facilitate mashup development [5] and to standardise their architectures in certain domains [3]. However, there is no systematic study of opportunities and challenges to employing personalisation functionality in mashups.

This paper will illustrate the use of personalisation techniques to enhance the functionality of web mashups. We will present a mashup application of a travel assistant which integrates interactive maps with user-tailored access to data from both a public resource directory and a socially constructed content. Based on the findings of an evaluation study, we will discuss opportunities and challenges for personalised mashups.

---

[1] http://www.web2con.com/web2006/

[2] http://www.programmableweb.com maintains a comprehensive list of mashups

C. Conati, K. McCoy, and G. Paliouras (Eds.): UM 2007, LNAI 4511, pp. 415–419, 2007.
© Springer-Verlag Berlin Heidelberg 2007

2   Case Study: Personalised Travel Assistant

The first step in designing a personalised mashup is to choose an appropriate domain, for which two factors are critical: (a) availability of free access to appropriate data, and (b) potential for personalisation to add value to the application. Consequently, we identified access to geographic data as a suitable domain.

Geographic mashups are among the most popular mashup categories. Commonly, these applications use interactive maps for access to public data. The following data and APIs were chosen for our case study: (a) `Google Maps` [3] (a Javascript library enabling web developers to integrate interactive maps in their applications); (b) `Yahoo! Local Search` [4] (enables search for places, e.g. businesses, parks, shops, through the `Yahoo!` directory); and (c) `Upcoming` [5] (searches through a social database with descriptions of events, e.g. concerts, exhibitions, and sport activities). These sources cover the main types of data in geographic mashups - maps, public directories, and social content.

There are strong reasons to believe that personalisation can add value to geographic mashups where users come from the general public (hence, differ significantly in their preferences, tasks, interests, and capabilities), and finding information in vast repositories of data can be a tedious task. A number of user-adaptive applications for access to geographic data have been implemented [4]. The case study presented here was inspired by the work on adaptive tourist guides which provide user-tailored information about weather, points of interest, accommodation, dining, etc. [6]. A distinctive characteristic of the travel assistant mashup presented here is that it pulls data from open repositories and dynamic, community-created databases.

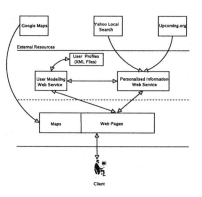

Fig. 1. Architecture of the personalised travel assistant

3   System Architecture

A Service Oriented Architecture (SOA) has been used for the design of a personalised mashup in our case study. The travel assistant has three main components (Fig. 1): external data sources, a set of web services which maintain access to external databases and implement the system's personalisation functionality, and a client web page manager which integrates interactive maps with data provided

---

[3] http://www.google.com/apis/maps/
[4] http://developer.yahoo.com/search/local/
[5] http://www.upcoming.org

from the web services. Fig. 2 shows a screenshot with places list tailored to a user's personal interests.

Web services implement the main personalisation components of the system, i.e. user modelling and adaptation. The separation of these components into different Web services enables reuse and integration of personalisation functionality across applications. A *user modelling web service* (UM-WS) is responsible for maintaining a model of each user registered with the system. User models are built from explicit information entered by users. A *personalised information web service* (PI-WS) retrieves user profiles from UM-WS, uses them to compose appropriate queries to the external APIs, and filters and orders the information returned according to its relevance to the user's profile by using heuristic

Fig. 2. Suggested places in New York, filtered and re-ordered according to the user's profile

rules, e.g. give priority to most recently added interests or consider existing ranking.

4 Evaluation

An experimental study was conducted to: (a) test the robustness of the architecture and examine the system's performance; (b) assess the users' satisfaction with the system; (c) determine what benefits, if any, can be added by personalisation; and (d) identify future improvements.

32 people (students, lecturers, and professionals) took part in the study. 18 of them (Group 1) interacted with the personalised version presented above, while 14 users (Group 2) interacted with a non-personalised version where UM-WS and PI-WS were replaced with a simple web information service that pulled data from the external resources and showed the results without any filtering or re-ordering. The groups had a similar distribution with regard to gender/occupation/age.

The users were asked to imagine the planning a short trip to New York and to use the travel assistant to find five interesting places or events, as well as to identify two other cities to visit with three interesting places or events for each city. The participants were asked to record their time for each task and filled in an electronic questionnaire with their feedback. Next we outline the main problems experienced by the users, see [1] for a detailed description.

Several problems were **common for both groups**: (a) Quality of information: insufficient detail, lack of pictures, unclear descriptions; (b) Incomplete data: missing information about cities; (c) Peculiarities: wrong locations (e.g. London, Kentucky versus London UK), strange places/events (e.g. New York police department); (d) Interface problems: the map window was too small, map navigation was cumbersome, items should be grouped in categories. While (d) can be fixed easily, (a)-(b) are typical for Web 2.0 applications which provide access to dynamic collections with user-created web content, and (c) directs to the need of semantic approaches to enhance geographic search.

Certain problems were pointed **only by Group1**: (a) Recommendations limited the choices; (b) Recommendations did not correspond to the user's profile; (c) Users did not have control over the adaptation; (d) There were no explanations why recommendations were given; (e) Group recommendations were needed for planing a joint trip. While (a) points at typical limitations of content-based filtering which can be addressed with collaborative filtering, (b) directs to the need of enhanced algorithms for comparing similarities between user profiles and open, community-created categories in Web 2.0 applications, (c)-(d) refer to usability problems brought by personalisation [2], and (e) points out that group recommendations can be beneficial in mashups.

Problems experienced **only by Group2** included: (a) Irrelevant recommendations (e.g. a charity organisation, a parking authority); and (b) Difficulty to find places related to the user's interests. These problems point at opportunities for personalisation to enhanced the users' experiences with intelligent mashups.

Most participants from Group1 (78%) found the recommended information relevant to their interests, as opposed to less than half of the participants from Group2 (43%) with the same opinion. Contrary to our initial expectations, the users with the personalised system did not perform the tasks quicker. We expect the benefits of personalisation to be stronger when more data sources are integrated and advanced personalisation techniques added.

The users pointed at future improvements which could be grouped in three categories: (a) Searching through more data sources: include information about places and events from other data repositories and add relevant information about flights and public transport; (b) Expanding the functionality: add route planning and driving directions, suggest optimal path between locations in terms of distance and time, compare place/event location with accommodation address, search for locations within convenient distance; (c) Improving the personalisation algorithms: integrate collaborative filtering, add web services that dynamically refine the user's profile, employ semantic-enhanced services to find relevant information (e.g. some users pointed that an ontology would be helpful).

5   Discussion: Opportunities and Challenges

Although the case study was limited to a particular domain, the domain selection criteria followed can be applied to other subject areas where free data is available and personalisation can add value to the applications. We believe that, at present, personalised mashups should easily be implemented for news and online shopping applications. With more and more data made available, we will see personalised mashups combining several types of media (e.g text, pictures, videos) in applications that provide web as well as mobile access. With more user modelling services being available, we expect to see creative applications which take advantage of advanced personalisation techniques. Opportunities include integrating collaborative filtering services (such as those offered by Amazon) in a shopping assistant mashup, adding group recommendations for trip planning, or using presentation adaptation techniques to combine data from several media. We believe that personalised mashups will offer exciting opportunities for the deployment of user modelling techniques.

The case study highlighted several challenges that mashups bring to personalisation research. The moving from central databases with relatively stable data fields and controlled information quality to open, dynamic, and community-driven heterogeneous collections imposes major challenges to web applications in general, and to personalisation research in particular. One of the most critical problems is the diversity of semantics and XML Schemas across data repositories accessed in a mashup application. The openness of the Web requires tolerance of different viewpoints, especially when community-driven content is employed. Although collaborative filtering provides techniques for accommodating community opinions, it requires availability of rankings, which may come from several sources and can have different range and semantics.

Another fundamental challenge to personalisation, particularly relevant for mashups, is dealing with incomplete and noisy data. This can lead to offering inappropriate or insufficient information and thus can reduce the users' satisfaction and trust in the system. There can be quick partial solutions, e.g. including *default* or *popular* data, and integrating descriptions from several places by employing some techniques from adaptive hypermedia. However, in order to fully address this challenge, more sophisticated approaches would be needed. For example, taking into account users' opinions about quality and relevance of data and incorporating an appropriate trust model.

References

1. Thang Dang, M.: Personalisation meets web 2.0 through web services: A case study in GIS. Technical report, MSc Dissertation, School of Computing, Leeds University, UK (2006)
2. Jameson, A.: The Human-Computer Interaction Handbook. Fundamentals, Evolving Technologies and Emerging Applications, chapter Adaptive Interfaces and Agents. Lawrence Erlbaum Associates, Publishers (2003)
3. Jhingran, A.: Enterprise information mashups: integrating information, simply. In: VLDB '06: Proceedings of the 32nd international conference on Very large data bases, pp. 3–4, VLDB Endowment (2006)
4. Krueger, A., Baus, J., Heckmann, D., Kruppa, M., Wasinger, R.: The adaptive web: Methods and strategies of web personalization. In: chapter Web-based mobile guides, Springer, Heidelberg (2006)
5. Murthy, S., Maier, D., Delcambre, L.: Mash-o-matic. In: DocEng '06: Proceedings of the 2006 ACM symposium on Document engineering, pp. 205–214. ACM Press, New York (2006)
6. Rinner, C., Raubal, M.: Personalized multi-criteria decision strategies in location-based decision support. Journal of Geographic Information Sciences 2, 149–156 (2004)

Personalized Control of Smart Environments

Giovanni Cozzolongo, Berardina De Carolis, and Sebastiano Pizzutilo

Dipartimento di Informatica – University of Bari
www.di.uniba.it

Abstract. Interaction with smart environments, to be effective, should be easy, natural and should be proactively adapted to users needs. In this paper we propose the use of a butler agent acting as a mediator between environment devices and users. As any good butler, it is able to observe and learn about users preferences but it leaves to its "owner" the last word on decisions. This is possible by employing user and context modeling techniques in order to provide a dynamic adaptation of the interaction with the environment according to the vision of ambient intelligence.

1 Introduction

Interaction with smart environments should be easy, natural and, by applying Ambient Intelligence (AmI) solutions, should be proactively adapted to the users' needs [1]. According to several research works, common approaches to handle personal interaction with a smart environment consist in using user-driven *predefined* configuration of *scenario* or *proactive adaptation.* This second approach consists mainly in observing the lifestyle and desires of the inhabitants and in learning how to anticipate and accommodate their needs [2]. For achieving this aim, we propose the use of a "butler" agent able to proactively adapt the interaction between the environment services and users. We have adopted the butler character, with its typical features, such as loyalty, discretion and general helpfulness, because it has often been considered a symbol for cooperation. It should be always present when needed but not too intrusive, it should be able to learn about users preferences and habits but leaving the last word on critical decisions to its users [3]. This agent employs user and context modeling for proactive adapting the interaction with the environment services, and it is able to adapt its autonomy on the basis of the user authorization level. As far as user modeling is concerned, the *butler* agent takes into account elements of uncertainty and the possibility to deal with incomplete information typical of an intelligent environment. By taking into account users' feedback actions in the environment, the agents learns variation in the model allowing a continuous refinement and tuning.

In this paper we present an extension of the C@sa a multiagent system [4]. In particular the system architecture has been extended to handle the automated control of a smart environment such as a laboratory, a meeting room, etc.

Next Section focusses on the description of the butler agent user modeling capabilities and how the autonomy is managed. Then, Section 3 describes how the feedback can be used to learn and update the model. Finally conclusions are illustrated in Section 4.

C. Conati, K. McCoy, and G. Paliouras (Eds.): UM 2007, LNAI 4511, pp. 420–424, 2007.
© Springer-Verlag Berlin Heidelberg 2007

2   Agent Based User Modeling

User modeling is a crucial task for the effectiveness and efficacy of the butler agent decisions. In particular, when modeling the user in a dynamic context it is important to update the default model dynamically and consistently according to the actions performed by the environment inhabitants. These actions may be interpreted as positive or negative feedback toward the decisions taken by the agent. If we reason in agent-related terms, we should define its *percepts*, its *reasoning* and its *effectors* [5]. In the considered domain, the agent's perceptual inputs are the context features and the user feedback actions. Obviously, the effectors are the messages addressed to the agents controlling the devices in order to execute the decided actions.

The reasoning behavior will include two aspects: an **engine to reason on user** preferences and needs in the current context and a **learning** technique to maintain the intrinsic variability of this type of domain.

Several techniques can be used to reason about the user. In our case, we have to address two main issues: i) building a statistical model of the preferences of the environment inhabitants and ii) handling imprecise and sometimes conflicting data typical of this domain. Bayesian Networks (BNs) are a way to deal with these requirements since they are a powerful way of handling uncertainty, especially when there are causal relationships between various events.

Starting from collected data about users typical behaviors in the environment, it is possible to learn the BN structure of the initial model. Then, the agent instantiates this model for the specific setting by copying it as the usage profile of an influence sphere. During the interaction the agent observes the users behavior overtime and learns variations in the model in order to adjust the dynamic adaptation of the environment. Moreover, it is necessary to take into account that users may change their behavior, therefore by interpreting users' feedback it is possible to update the model. As we will see later on, this decisional behavior is related to the agent level of autonomy for fulfilling a goal. In fact the butler agent may ask for confirmation to the user or perform automatically the decided action accordingly.

In order to test and validate our approach, we decided to focus on the modeling of the environment comfort. Working on the modeling of this type of service seems appropriate for testing our approach since comfort involves several devices and, according to several definitions, its perception is highly individual and involves different human senses (temperature, light, intimacy, sounds, level of noise, smell, etc.)[6]. Contextual factors to be considered in the experiment are internal and external temperature, humidity, the status of environment (devices, windows, air conditioning, heating system) and thermic situation of people in the environment.

2.1   Building the Initial Model

We selected as "smart environment" our research laboratory equipped with air conditioning, heating and windows. Since we do not have biosensors for collecting thermic user data, the initial model of the group of inhabitants has been built collecting the daily diaries of 25 subjects attending the laboratory, aging between 20 and 40 equally distributed in gender, belonging to the following categories: researchers, undergraduate and Ph.D students. We asked these people to contextualize their needs and preferences to their activity, daytime, humidity, temperature, wind, etc.. The dataset was used as input to a bayesian network structure learning tool. An example of diary entry is the following:

Monday, 3.00 p.m , spring, working on the computer for writing a paper, inside is getting hot, I'm feeling a bit hot, outside is cooler and slightly windy, I open the window.

During the period of data collection we monitored and stored automatically timestamped values of the internal and external temperature, the level of humidity and the direction and speed of the wind. Then we coupled these data with the information collected into the diary in order to structure them and to relate subjective perceptions to sensor data. Then, from the collected dataset, we learned the structure of a BN using the NPC algorithm of Hugin 6.5 [7]. This structure has been manually revised and the resulting network is shown in Figure 1.

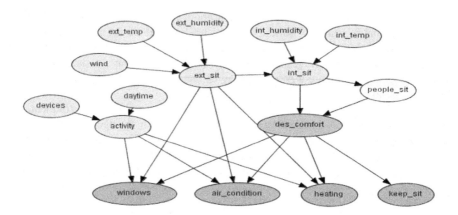

Fig. 1. The BN representing the initial user model

Root nodes are mainly related to context factors such as external and internal temperature and humidity, wind, active devices and daytime. Then we have a set of **intermediate** nodes that are used to infer information about the user or the context, for instance the internal and external climatic situation, presumed goal about thermic comfort, the main group activity, etc. The **leaves** nodes correspond to variables that are used to infer which are the most probable actions that the environment should perform.

2.2 Autonomy

Another important issue regards the level of autonomy that a personal agent has in making its decision and performing automatically the related actions without human intervention [8,9]. A possible trade-off between human control and agent autonomy can be achieved by i) adjusting the level of autonomy according to a fixed user authorization level and ii) learning from user feedback on the agent decisions [10].

In our case, the autonomy of the butler agent regards two dimensions: i) the **Execution Level**: which handle the autonomy related to execution of actions (tasks, subtasks, request of services, and so on), ii) the **Communication Level**: which is related to the degree of intrusiveness in communicating to the user [11]. The Execution Autonomy is inversely proportional to the Communication one. Each dimension has an associated value in a 3 values scale: "null", "medium" and "high".

As far as the execution autonomy is concerned, each level is associated to a probability threshold for an action to be executed. When the autonomy level is high the inferred action is executed anyway since the threshold in this case is 0. When the autonomy is medium only the actions having a probability higher than 0.5 will be executed. The null value of the autonomy level implies that the threshold is 1, so that the agent has to ask for confirmation of every action.

As we will see this approach allows us to modulate the level of agent's autonomy/intrusiveness since autonomy values are revised as a consequence to the type of feedback the user provides to the agent: *positive* feedback enforces the autonomy on that category of task, *negative* one reduces it. Initially, the user sets explicitly the autonomy level for a task and can always revise it.

3 Learning from User's Feedback

In this type of application, we consider the following types of user's feedback:

1. **positive feedback:** the user accepts the action executed by the agent.
2. **contrast feedback:** the user executes an action different from the one proposed by the agent but achieving the same goal.
3. **negative feedback:** the user undoes the action executed by the agent but he/she does not execute any other action.

In case a positive or a contrast feedback is provided, the data related to this experience will be considered to update the model by using this contextual change for learning variation in the probability distribution of the network. In particular, the agent, using the EM algorithm, will enforce (in case of positive feedback) or weak (in case of contrast feedback) the causal relations between the context nodes, the goal and the action. All the collected data will be also added to the log for offline revision of the model and for investigating the motivation for the errors. This analysis could help in further refining the model by finding out new behavior patterns in which the user does something completely unexpected by the system.

Feedback has also an impact on the agent's autonomy. In fact, in case of positive feedback, if it possible, the execution autonomy increases and consequently the communication autonomy decreases. On the contrary, when a contrast feedback is provided, the execution autonomy decreases and the communication one increases.

The interpretation of negative feedback is more difficult. In this case, no other actions are performed in order to achieve the presumed comfort goal. This behavior could then be interpreted in two ways by the agent: i) the model failed in inferring the presumed comfort goal (i.e. users are comfortable in the current situation); ii) there is a context feature that is not represented in the model and the agent cannot take it into account. In the first case it is possible to learn the new experience data with difference evidence on the goal state and update the probability tables accordingly. In the second case the problem is more difficult to be solved automatically and it is indeed part of our future work in which we are giving to the agent a "body" and clarification dialog capabilities.

4   Conclusions and Future Work Directions

We performed an evaluation study aiming at testing the model accuracy and understanding which was the impact of the initial level of autonomy on the system behavior. The results show that introducing autonomy variation improves the accuracy of the model realizing a tradeoff between control and intelligent behavior of the agent. As pointed out in the paper, some context factors could be not foreseen in the model causing prediction errors. In this case the analysis of the context log could be used to find out problems in the initial structure of the model. In the near future, we intend to investigate on this issue and also on the implications of giving a "body" to the butler agent in order to engage the user in a direct interaction with the environment.

References

1. Shadbolt, N.: Ambient Intelligence. IEEE Intelligent Systems. vol. 18(4) (2003)
2. Byun, H.E., Cheverst, K.: Exploiting User Models and Context-Awareness to Support Personal Daily Activities, Workshop in UM2001 on User Modelling for Context-AwareApplications, Sonthofen, Germany (2001)
3. Maes, P.: Agents that Reduce Work and Information Overload. In: Communications of the ACM, vol. 37(7), pp. 31–40, 146. ACM Press, New York (July 1994)
4. De Carolis, B., Cozzolongo, G., Pizzutilo, S., Plantamura, V.L.: Agent-Based Home Simulation and Control. In: Hacid, M.-S., Murray, N.V., Raś, Z.W., Tsumoto, S. (eds.) ISMIS 2005. LNCS (LNAI), vol. 3488, pp. 404–412. Springer, Heidelberg (2005)
5. Russell, S.J., Norvig, P.: Artificial Intelligence: a Modern Approach. Prentice-Hall, Englewood Cliffs (1998)
6. Spronk, B.A: House is not a Home: Witold Rybczynski Explores the History of Domestic Comfort. Aurora Online (2001)
7. http://www.hugin.com
8. Falcone, R., Castelfranchi, C.: Tuning the collaboration level with autonomous agents: A principled theory. In: Esposito, F. (ed.) AI*IA 2001: Advances in Artificial Intelligence. LNCS (LNAI), vol. 2175, pp. 212–224. Springer, Heidelberg (2001)
9. Dastani, M., Dignum, F., Meyer, J.J.: Autonomy and agent deliberation. In: Proceedings of The First International Workshop on Computational Autonomy - Potential, Risks, Solutions (2003)
10. Scerri, P., Tambe, M., Lee, H., Pynadath, D., et al.: Don't cancel my Barcelona trip: Adjusting the autonomy of agent proxies in human organizations. In: Proceedings of the AAAI Fall Symposium on Socially Intelligent Agents - the human in the loop (2000)
11. Horvitz, E.: Principles of Mixed-Initiative User Interfaces. In: Proceedings of CHI '99, ACM SIGCHI Conference on Human Factors in Computing Systems, Pittsburgh, PA, (May 1999)

Studying Model Ambiguity in a Language ITS

Brent Martin and Amanda Nicholas

Intelligent Computer Tutoring Group
Department of Computer Science and Software Engineering
University of Canterbury
Private Bag 4800, Christchurch, New Zealand
{brent,amn39}@cosc.canterbury.ac.nz

Abstract. Ambiguity is a well-known problem in student modelling, and in user modelling in general. In this paper we present the results of an experiment in the domain of German adjectives. We trialled a modified student interface that gathers more data during problem solving by requiring the student to perform a related subtask. There is evidence that the students who performed the subtask outperformed the control group on a post-test despite the extra task slowing them down, suggesting the extra effort required by the students to overcome ambiguity was worth the intervention.

Keywords: Student Modelling, Language learning, ITS.

1 Introduction

Dealing with ambiguity is a serious problem in developing Intelligent Tutoring Systems for foreign languages [1]. Although the system can detect that the student has made an error, the source of this error may be difficult to determine. Menzel defines four sources of ambiguity: limited observability, polysemy, alternative conceptualisations of domain knowledge and structural uncertainty. In a domain with high ambiguity feedback messages can be difficult to determine. Good feedback should refer the student to the underlying domain principle. If it is not possible to determine which domain principle has been broken, correctly targeted feedback cannot be given. One approach to avoid ambiguity is to require the student to specify the intermediate steps they carry out mentally, however this may reduce transference [1] [2]. This research compares two constraint-based (CBM) tutors: one that matches the real world more closely, and one that decreases ambiguity as much as possible.

German adjective endings are a difficult topic for students to master. This is due to the number of endings that must be memorised, and the amount of knowledge required of the sentence to get the ending correct. Rogers studied the main areas of weakness in students with more than four years of experience learning German [3]. She states "...much anecdotal 'evidence' from teachers of German as a foreign language emphasises morphology as a major area of weakness (e.g. adjective endings...)". Her study showed that approximately 5% of errors made by advanced learners of German were errors in adjective endings.

C. Conati, K. McCoy, and G. Paliouras (Eds.): UM 2007, LNAI 4511, pp. 425–429, 2007.
© Springer-Verlag Berlin Heidelberg 2007

Table 1. Adjective endings when preceded by the definite article

Case	Masculine	Feminine	Neuter	Plural
Nominative	e	e	e	en
Accusative	en	e	e	en
Genative	en	en	en	en
Dative	en	en	en	en

German adjectives must agree with the nouns they modify. This means that the ending of an adjective varies based on the gender and case of the noun, and whether the noun is preceded by a definite article, indefinite article, or no article. For example, Table 1 lists the endings for the case where an adjective is preceded by an indefinite article. For example, take the sentence "Das graue Haus ist neu". (The grey house is new). Here "Haus" is the noun, and its gender is neuter. The house is the subject of the sentence, and so it is in the nominative case. Das is the article, and it is the direct article. The adjective is "grau", and it takes the ending "e" because, by consulting table 1, we see that adjectives preceding a neuter noun in the nominative case must end in "e". It is important to note that the endings are not unique; the ending "e" appears in a number of situations, as does "en". This is one reason why these endings are ambiguous.

Menzel identified four major sources of ambiguity that should be considered when creating CBM tutors, particularly for foreign languages [1]. These are: limited observability of internal variables of the problem domain; polysemy (multiple meanings) of symbols used in the problem domain; alternative conceptualisations of domain knowledge; uncertainty about the intended structure of the student's solution. German adjective endings suffer from three of the four defined sources of ambiguity. Limited observability and polysemy are both present in the multiple possible meanings of a single ending. When the student incorrectly gives an adjective ending, it could be due to either a *rule* error or a *fact* error. If the student does not know the gender or the case of the noun, they have made a fact error. If the student has correctly determined the case, gender and article, and still gives the adjective ending incorrectly, they have made a rule error; they do not know the underlying grammatical principle that determines the adjective ending.

In the next section we summarise how constraint-based modelling was applied to the domain of German adjectives. Section 3 describes the experiment and presents the results. Finally, we conclude in Section 4.

2   Constraint-Based Modelling

CBM[4] is a modelling approach based on the theory of learning from performance errors [5]. It models the domain as a set of state constraints, where each constraint represents a declarative concept that must be learned and internalised before the student can achieve mastery of the domain. Constraints represent restrictions on solution *states,* and take the form:

If   <relevance condition> is true for the student's solution,
THEN   <satisfaction condition> must also be true

The following is an example of a constraint from the German adjectives domain (*IS* and *SS* refer to the ideal and student solutions, respectively):

```
(21 "When the article is an 'ein-word', the only possible
endings are -e, -en, -er and -es."

(and (match *IS* ("I"))(match *SS* (?anything ?*)))

(or (match *SS* (?* "e"))       (match *SS* (?* "e" "n"))
    (match *SS* (?* "e" "r")) (match *SS* (?* "e" "s")))))
```

This constraint checks that the student has used an appropriate ending for an "ein-word". The relevance condition first checks that the article for this problem is indefinite ("I"), and that the student has attempted an answer. The satisfaction condition then checks that the adjective the student typed ends with one of the valid endings. If this is not true, the feedback message is given. The student model consists of the set of constraints, along with information about whether or not each has been successfully applied, for each attempt where it was relevant.

3 Experiment

We hypothesised that forcing the students to supply information about their problem-solving process and providing feedback based on that information would enable the system to give them better instruction, and thus they would be better able to learn the domain. We tested this hypothesis by building two versions of an ITS for German adjectives, where the two systems differed in the interface used and the underlying domain/student model (constraints).

The tutors were developed using the WETAS tutoring shell [6]. The problem set comprised of 55 problems, which was identical for both tutors. Some were obtained from existing sources [7, 8], however, most problems were written especially for this ITS. An example of one of the problems in the tutor is

Die ? Blumen gefallen mir. (bunt) (*I like the colourful flowers*)

The two tutors shared a very similar interface. In the centre of the screen was an area for the student to answer the question. The problem was displayed in the form of a sentence with a gap left where the adjective should be, and the adjective to be inserted was given in brackets at the end of the sentence. Below there was a selection box that allowed the student to choose the desired feedback level, and a button to submit their answer for evaluation. Feedback messages appeared at the bottom of the screen.

Students using the experimental system were asked to fill in the gender and case of the noun, the article type, and the adjective with its ending. The possible answers for gender, case and article were all given in combo boxes. This ensured that there would not be problems with students referring to the same concept by a different name, or misspelling names. Below the combo boxes there was a text field for the student to fill in the appropriate form of the adjective. Students using the control were asked to fill in the correct adjective form only. Domain constraints were sourced from a number of German textbooks (e.g. [8]), which contain advice on how students can remember the endings more easily.

An evaluation study of the two tutors was conducted on the 6th of September 2006 at the University of Canterbury, Christchurch. Students enrolled in a beginning German course used one of the two systems over one 50-minute period. The students had been taught adjective endings previously in class. The class was divided randomly into two even groups, and the students were first asked to complete a pre-test. They then used the tutoring system for as long as time permitted, or until they finished all 55 questions. Afterwards they completed a post-test. Each test contained six questions in the same format as described previously. The final three questions also asked the student to specify the gender and case of the noun present in the sentence, and the type of article preceding the noun. The experiment was carried out in two streams. To allow for any difference in the difficulty of the pre- and post-tests, Test 1 was used as the pre-test for Stream A, and the post-test for Stream B; Test 2 was used as the post-test for Stream A and pre-test for Stream B.

23 students took part in the evaluation. 12 students used the experimental tutor and 11 students used the control. Students using the control system solved more problems with fewer attempts than those using the experimental tutor. This result is unsurprising, because students using the control only had to fill in one value correctly, whereas students using the experimental tutor had to supply four values. Students using the experimental tutor also saw more feedback messages. This is also unsurprising; their task was larger so there were more opportunities to make mistakes.

Unfortunately, the study revealed the pre- and post-tests were not of comparable difficulty. To overcome this, we compared the results for test 1 only, and compared the outcome for pre- and post-test regardless of which stream the students belonged to. This is not strictly valid because the samples are different; it relies on the assumption that the students in the two streams (and using the same tutor) were comparable, and this cannot be easily measured. Using this assumption, a t-test of the score for producing the correct adjective ending showed no significant difference between the test 1 pre-test scores for the two tutors (mean = 4.8 and 4.6 for the control and experimental groups respectively, SD = 0.8 and 1.6, $p > 0.7$). When test 1 is used as a post-test however, there is a larger difference between the two groups, with the experimental tutor achieving a score of 5.7 compared to 5.0 for the experimental group, although the result is not statistically significant ($p = 0.15$).

We also compared the performance of the two groups in terms of their ability to perform the subtask (determine case and gender). Again there was no significant difference on pre-test score between the control and experimental groups (5.0 versus 4.9). For the post-test, the experimental group again outperformed the control group, scoring an average of 5.7 compared to 4.8 for the control group. The result was statistically significant ($p < 0.05$). This is what we would expect, given that the experimental group practised this specific task. An analysis of learning curves [9] also showed a better "power curve" for the subtask constraints.

Finally, the students were asked to fill in a subjective survey at the end of the study. Responses from were overwhelmingly positive to both versions of the tutor. Further, the staff from the German department indicated they would like to pursue this technology further, because the students had reacted so positively. They also commented that the results for the formal adjectives test were considerably higher than in previous years, which they attributed to the tutoring systems.

4 Conclusions

Tutoring systems that teach natural languages are susceptible to the problem of ambiguity in student answers, making it difficult to apportion blame appropriately and thus provide effective feedback. Even a highly constrained domain such as German adjectives exhibits this problem. Requiring the student to supply additional information is often frowned upon because it reduces the similarity with "real world" problems and may thus negatively affect transfer.

We examined this problem in the domain of German adjectives by providing two versions of a simple ITS; the control required the students to complete the original task only (and thus suffered from ambiguity) while the experimental group forced them to also complete a subtask that disambiguated their response. The results were not conclusive because of problems with the pre- and post-test difficulties. However, there was evidence from these tests that the experimental group performed better on both the original task and the subtask despite having solved considerably fewer problems because of the additional time needed to complete the subtask. This suggests that far from detracting from the students' ability to complete the main task, the extra disambiguation benefited their learning. Further, when the domain models were analysed (via learning curves), the additional constraints required for the subtask appeared to enhance the performance of the model in capturing what was learned, suggesting that the subtask was an integral part of the main task.

This study has shown that adding extra task requirements to overcome ambiguity in language learning is not always a bad thing, and can in fact be advantageous. This is a positive outcome that encourages us to further explore how constraint-based models may support language learning.

References

1. Menzel, W.: Constraint-based modeling and ambiguity. International Journal of Artificial Intelligence in Education 16(1), 29–63 (2006)
2. Anderson, J.R., Corbett, A.T., Koedinger, K.R., Pelletier, R.: Cognitive Tutors: Lessons Learned. Journal of the Learning Sciences 4(2), 167–207 (1995)
3. Rogers, M.: On major types of written error in advanced students of german. International Review of Applied Linguistics in Language Teaching 22(1), 1–39 (1984)
4. Ohlsson, S.: Constraint-Based Student Modeling. In: Greer, J., McCalla, G. (eds.) Student Modeling: The Key to Individualized Knowledge-Based Instruction, pp. 167–189. Springer, Heidelberg (1994)
5. Ohlsson, S.: Learning from Performance Errors. Psychological Review 3(2), 241–262 (1996)
6. Martin, B., Mitrovic, A.: Authoring web-based tutoring systems with WETAS. In: International conference on computers in education, Auckland. pp. 183-187 (2002)
7. Werner, G.: Langenscheidts Grammatik-training Deutsch, Langenscheidt KG (2001)
8. Kahlen, L.: Interactive German Made Easy. McGraw-Hill, New York (2006)
9. Newell, A., Rosenbloom, P.S.: Mechanisms of skill acquisition and the law of practice. In: Cognitive skills and their acquisition, Anderson, J.R., (ed.), Lawrence Erlbaum Associates: Hillsdale, NJ. pp. 1–56 (1981)

Tailoring and the Efficiency of Information Seeking

Nathalie Colineau and Cécile Paris

CSIRO - ICT Centre
Locked Bag 17, North Ryde NSW 1670, Australia
{nathalie.colineau,cecile.paris}@csiro.au

Abstract. We present an empirical study assessing the impact of tailoring on information seeking tasks. Our aim was to evaluate whether providing tailored information would help people find the information they need more quickly and more accurately. Our results show that tailored documents have an impact on information seeking, at least when the information to be found is spread over a number of sources and needs to be synthesised.

1 Introduction

With the increasing amount of available information, finding what one needs is not an easy task. Tailoring information to people's needs seems like an effective way to deliver information to people (e.g., [4], [3], [1], [5]). There have been experiments to test whether users prefer information customisation over generic information (e.g., [6], [7]), or whether tailored information leads to more behavioural changes when information is meant to influence behaviour (e.g., [2]). However, the impact of tailoring on the efficiency of information seeking has not been tested.

This is the specific question we addressed in this work: Is tailoring effective in an information seeking task? Our aim was to evaluate whether providing tailored information would help people find the information they needed, allowing them to find the information more quickly and more accurately than when using generic information. We exploited one of our applications, SciFly [8], a system that automatically generates brochures tailored to the user's stated interests (i.e., their query). The availability of both the generic (existing) brochures and the SciFly tailored brochures allowed us to compare the effectiveness of tailored brochures over generic brochures in information seeking tasks. We describe our experimental setting and our results.

2 Impact of Tailoring Content on an Information Seeking Task

The objective was to assess the usefulness of tailoring in answering people's information needs, especially in situations when the topic of interest is spread over multiple documents, necessitating users to consult more than one document to get the information. (Note that this is what currently happens when someone asks for a brochure about one or more topics, at least at CSIRO, as there cannot be a brochure for every possible combination of topics a customer may have.) We wanted to assess whether

C. Conati, K. McCoy, and G. Paliouras (Eds.): UM 2007, LNAI 4511, pp. 430–434, 2007.
© Springer-Verlag Berlin Heidelberg 2007

producing a tailored brochure would help people get to the information they needed more quickly and more accurately.

2.1 Experimental Design

We did a two-group post-test only randomised experiment. Subjects were given brochures about a topic of research undertaken at CSIRO and asked to answer a set of factoid questions[1] (e.g., who is the project leader of T1?). Some questions required browsing the entire document to find the answers, others looking for a specific paragraph. There were 4 questions and 12 facts to be found. The design (illustrated in Table 1) was done such that each group (of 12 subjects) performed the task twice: once with a tailored brochure and once with a set of non-tailored brochures.

Table 1. Experiment setup

	Non-tailored	Tailored
Topic1: Image Analysis	Group A	Group B
Topic2: Environmental Informatics	Group B	Group A

For repeatability purposes, we chose two different topics with two sets of similar questions. This allowed us to verify that the results observed in the first task were not due to a group but to the type of brochure (i.e., tailored *vs.* non-tailored). In the group performing the task with the tailored material (our treatment group), subjects were given only one brochure, a brochure generated by Scifly, tailored to the chosen topic. In the group performing the task with the generic material, subjects were given the set of existing (generic) brochures that covered the topic. As a result, there was additional content, in particular, content related to other projects carried out in the division's laboratories. It is important to note, however, that the text fragments (paragraphs) used in the tailored brochures were the same as those used in the generic brochures; both were manually written by the communicators.

Our aim was to find out whether one group would perform the task better (more correct answers, fewer incorrect answers) and whether one group would complete the task faster. Our hypotheses were that the group with the tailored brochures would perform better and faster, as the other group had to search for the relevant facts in more material and had irrelevant information, and that the group with the generic brochures would retrieve more incorrect answers. We used the following measures:

– *Time performance*: We recorded the time spent to complete the task.
– *Recall of correct items of information*: We counted for each subject the number of correct items of information retrieved out of the 12 items to be found. We calculated the mean of correct items for each group and computed a t-Test. We calculated the recall rate by computing the proportion of correct answers retrieved by the subjects out of the 144 correct answers (12 correct answers for 12 subjects).
– *Precision of information retrieved*: We counted for each subject the number of incorrect items of information brought back instead of (or in addition to) the

---

[1] The questions had clear factual answers to avoid ambiguity in the judgment of correctness.

correct answers. (Sometimes, the subjects answered the question correctly but included additional irrelevant and thus incorrect information.) We calculated the mean of incorrect items of information retrieved for each group and computed a t-Test. We calculated the precision rate by taking the proportion of correct answers retrieved by the subjects (a maximum of 144) to all answers retrieved by the subjects (which could be more than 144, if they retrieved incorrect items as well as correct ones).

2.2 Results

We used the tools available at http://faculty.vassar.edu/lowry/VassarStats.html. Table 2 shows the results on time performance. They confirm the direction of our hypothesis: for both topics, the group performing with the non-tailored brochures took more time to perform the task than the group with the tailored brochures: most subjects needed between 400 and 600 seconds to complete the task with the tailored brochure, while they needed between 100 and 200 seconds more with the non-tailored brochures. The difference observed is statistically significant.

Table 2. t-Test results for the time performance (mean time for each group, in seconds)

	Non-tailored brochures		Tailored brochures	
	Group A	**626.5**	Group B	**409.75**
Topic 1	t	**+3.83**	df	22
	P one-tailed		**0.000456**	

	Group B	**602.08**	Group A	**483.5**
Topic 2	t	**+1.76**	df	22
	P one-tailed		**0.0461535**	

Table 3. t-Test results for the number of correct items of information retrieved (mean)

	Non-tailored brochures		Tailored brochures	
Topic 1	Group A	**10.5**	Group B	**10.41**

	Group B	**8.16**	Group A	**10.5**
Topic 2	t	**+2.85**	df	22
	P one-tailed		**0.0046565**	

As shown in Table 3, when the task was performed the first time (i.e., on topic 1), there was hardly any difference on the number of correct items of information retrieved. The difference in mean did not confirm the direction of our hypothesis, as group A (with generic brochures) retrieved more correct items on average than group B (with tailored brochure). The difference is tiny (overall, one more correct item was found), but enough to reject our hypothesis. Thus, there was no need to perform the t-Test to determine the level of confidence. Considering their closeness in performance, we consider that the two groups performed equally on that measure.

When performing the task for the second time (i.e., on topic 2), however, the difference was statistically significant (at and beyond 0.005). Considering that the subjects were less familiar with topic 2 (which we know from a questionnaire), the customised brochure may have provided a real difference here, reducing considerably the search space and facilitating the retrieval of information. Note that the recall performance for the group working with the tailored brochure is constant across topics, averaging the retrieval of 10 items out of 12. In contrast, the recall performance for the group working with the non-tailored brochures dropped significantly from an average of 10 to 8 correct items retrieved. (See Table 5.)

Table 4 shows the number of incorrect items of information retrieved[2]. In both tasks, the group performing with the tailored brochure performed better, bringing back less irrelevant content. However, this is statistically significant in the first case only. We have no explanation as to why this is the case. We did notice that, in most cases, it was not so much people answering the questions wrongly, but more people including additional (irrelevant) information.

Table 4. t-Test results for the number of incorrect items (mean)

	Non-tailored brochures		Tailored brochures	
	Group A	1.75	Group B	0
Topic 1	t	+3.78	df	22
	P one-tailed		0.000515	

	Group B	2.91	Group A	1.83
Topic 2	t	+1.05	df	22
	P one-tailed		0.152558	

Table 5. Recall rates, precision rates and F-measures

	Non-tailored brochures		Tailored brochures	
	Recall	87.5%	Recall	86.7%
Topic 1	Precision	85.7%	Precision	100%
	F-measure	0.86	F-measure	0.92

	Recall	68%	Recall	87.5%
Topic 2	Precision	73.6%	Precision	85.1%
	F-measure	0.70	F-measure	0.86

Putting these results in perspective using the F-measure (see Table 5), we observe that, in terms of overall performance, the group with the tailored brochures did better.

Referring back to our original hypotheses, we can conclude that we have shown that the results observed were not due to the performance of a specific group, but due to the tailoring. With content tailored to their needs, people can find the information they are looking for more quickly, more accurately, and thus, overall, demonstrate better performance.

---

[2] For example, for the question about naming the divisions carrying out some research on topic 1, if the names given were incorrect, we counted 1 point by incorrect name.

3   Conclusion

Our aim was to understand the impact of tailoring on information seeking tasks. We presented an experiment and its results, showing that tailored documents have an impact on information seeking, at least when the information to be found is spread over a number of sources. With documents tailored to their needs, people find the information they seek more quickly, and overall, more accurately. We can conclude that tailoring is indeed useful in information seeking tasks.

Acknowledgement

We want to thank all members of our team for their contribution to the development of SciFly and all the people who participated in our experiment.

References

1. André, E., Müller, J., Rist, T.: WIP/PPP: automatic generation of personalized multimedia presentations. In: Proc. of ACM Multimedia, pp. 407–408 (1996)
2. Campbell, M.K., DeVellis, B.M., Strecher, V.J., Ammerman, A.S., DeVellis, R.F., Sandler, R.S.: Improving dietary behavior: The effectiveness of tailored messages in primary care settings. American Journal of Public Health 84, 783–787 (1994)
3. Chedrawy, Z., Sibte, S., Abidi, R.: An Adaptive Personalized Recommendation Strategy Featuring Context Sensitive Content Adaptation. In: Wade, V., Ashman, H., Smyth, B. (eds.) AH 2006. LNCS, vol. 4018, pp. 61–70. Springer, Heidelberg (2006)
4. De Carolis, B., De Rosis, F., Andreoli, C., Cavallo, V., De Cicco, M.L.: The dynamic generation of hypertext presentations of medical guidelines. The New Review of Hypermedia and Multimedia 4, 67–88 (1998)
5. Elhadad, N., McKeown, K., Kaufman, D., Jordan, D.: Facilitating physicians' access to information via tailored text summarization. In: AMIA Annual Symposium, 2005, Washington DC (2005)
6. Kaplan, C., Fenwick, J., Chen, J.: Adaptive Hypertext Navigation Based on User Goals and Context. In: User Modelling and User Adapted Interaction, 3, pp. 193–220 (1993)
7. Paris, C., Wu, M., Vercoustre, A-M., Wan, S., Wilkins, P., Wilkinson, R.: An Empirical Study of the Effect of Coherent and Tailored Document Delivery as an Interface to Organizational Websites". In: Brusilovsky, P., Corbett, A.T., de Rosis, F. (eds.) UM 2003. LNCS, vol. 2702, pp. 133–144. Springer, Heidelberg (2003)
8. Paris, C., Colineau, N.: Scifly: Tailored Corporate Brochures on Demand. CSIRO Technical Report 06/268 (2006)

The Effect of Model Granularity on Student Performance Prediction Using Bayesian Networks

Zachary A. Pardos, Neil T. Heffernan, Brigham Anderson, and Cristina L. Heffernan

Worcester Polytechnic Institute, Carnegie Mellon University, Worcester Public Schools
{zpardos,nth}@wpi.edu

Abstract. A standing question in the field of Intelligent Tutoring Systems and User Modeling in general is what is the appropriate level of model granularity (how many skills to model) and how is that granularity derived? In this paper we will explore models with varying levels of skill generality (1, 5, 39 and 106 skill models) and measure the accuracy of these models by predicting student performance within our tutoring system called ASSISTment as well as their performance on a state standardized test. We employ the use of Bayes nets to model user knowledge and to use for prediction of student responses. Our results show that the finer the granularity of the skill model, the better we can predict student performance for our online data. However, for the standardized test data we received, it was the 39 skill model that performed the best. We view this as support for fine-grained skill models despite the finest grain model not predicting the state test scores the best.

1 Introduction

There are many researches in the user modeling community working with Intelligent Tutoring Systems and using Bayesian networks to model user knowledge [3, 4, 7]. Greer and colleagues [6] have investigated methods for using different levels of granularity and ways to conceptualize student knowledge. We seek to address the question of what is the right level of granularly to track student knowledge. Essentially this means how many skills should we attempt to track? We will call a set of skills (and their tagging to questions) a skill model. We will compare different skill models that differ in the number of skills and see how well the different models can fit a data set of student responses collected via the ASSISTment system [8].

1.1 Background on the MCAS State Test and ASSISTment Project

We will be evaluating our models by using the 8th grade 2005 Massachusetts Comprehensive Assessment System (MCAS) mathematics test which was taken after the online data being used was collected. The ASSISTment system is an e-learning and e-assessing system [8]. In the 2004-2005 school year, 600+ students used the system about once every two weeks. Eight math teachers from two schools would bring their students to the computer lab, at which time students would be presented

C. Conati, K. McCoy, and G. Paliouras (Eds.): UM 2007, LNAI 4511, pp. 435–439, 2007.
© Springer-Verlag Berlin Heidelberg 2007

with randomly selected MCAS test items. Each tutoring item, which we call an ASSISTment, is based upon a publicly released MCAS item which we have added "tutoring" to. We believe that the ASSISTment system has a better chance of showing the utility of fine-grained skill modeling due to the fact that we can ask scaffolding questions that break the problem down in to parts and allow us to tell if the student got the item wrong because they did not know one skill versus another. As a matter of logging, the student is only marked as getting the item correct if they answer the question correctly on the first attempt without assistance from the system.

2   Model Creation and Prediction

In April of 2005, a 7 hour "coding session" was staged where our subject-matter expert, Cristina Heffernan, with the assistance of the 2nd author, set out to make up skills and tag all of the 300 existing 8th grade MCAS items with these skills. Because we wanted to be able to track learning between items, we wanted to come up with a number of skills that were somewhat fine-grained but not too fine-grained such that each item had a different skill. We imposed upon our subject-matter expert that no one item would be tagged with more than 3 skills. She gave the skills names, but the real essence of a skill was what items it was tagged to. This model is referred to as the 'April' model or the WPI-106. The National Council of Teachers of Mathematics and the Massachusetts Department of Education use broad classifications of 5 and 39 skill sets. The 39 and 5 skill classifications were not tagged to the questions. Instead, the skills in the coarse-grained models were mapped to the finer-grained models in a "is a part of" type of hierarchy, as opposed to a prerequisite hierarchy [3]. The appropriate question-skill tagging for the WPI-5 and WPI-39 models could therefore be derived from this hierarchy.

2.1   How the Skill Mapping Is Used to Create a Bayes Net

Our Bayes nets consist of 3 layers of binomial random variable nodes. The top layer nodes represent knowledge of a skill set with a background probability of 0.50, while the bottom layer nodes are the actual question nodes with conditional probabilities set to 0.10 for guess and 0.05 for slip. The intermediary 2nd layer consists of ALL[1] gates that, in part, allow us to only specify a guess and slip parameter for the question nodes regardless of how many skills are tagged to it. The guess and slip parameters were not learned but instead set ad hoc. When we later try to predict MCAS questions, a guess value of 0.25 will be used to reflect the fact that the MCAS items being predicted are all multiple choice, while the online ASSISTment items have mostly been converted from multiple-choice to text-input fields. Future research will explore learning the parameters from data.

---

[1] An 'ALL' gate is equivalent to a logical AND. The Bayes Net Toolkit (BNT) we use evaluates Matlab's ALL function to represent the Boolean node. This function takes a vector of values as opposed to only 2 values if using the AND function. Since a question node may have more than 2 skills tagged to it, the ALL function is used.

2.2 Model Prediction Procedure

A prediction evaluation is run for each model one student at a time. The student's responses are presented to the Bayes net as evidence and inference (exact join-tree) is made on the skills to attain knowledge probabilities. To predict each of the 29 questions we used the inferred skill probabilities to ask the Bayes Net what the probability is that the student will get the question correct. We get a *predicted score* by taking the sum of the probabilities for all questions. Finally, we find the percent error by taking the absolute value of the difference between predicted and actual score and dividing that by 29. The *Average Error* of a skill model is the average error across the 600 students.

3 Results

An early version of the results in this section (using approximate inference instead of exact inference and without Section 3.1) appears in a workshop paper [8]. The MAD score is the mean absolute difference between predicted and actual score. The under/over prediction is our predicted average score minus the actual average score on the test. The centering is a result of offsetting every user's predicted score by the average under/over prediction amount for that model and recalculating MAD and error percentage.

Table 1. Model prediction performance results for the MCAS test. All models' non-centered error rates are statistically significantly different at the p<.05 level.

Model	Error	MAD	Under/Over	Cent. Error	Cent. MAD
WPI-39	13.40%	3.89	↓ 1.9	12.28%	3.56
WPI-106	14.88%	4.31	↓ 1.7	14.12%	4.10
WPI-5	18.60%	5.39	↓ 4.2	13.98%	4.06
WPI-1	23.77%	6.90	↓ 5.0	18.70%	5.42

3.1 Internal/Online Data Prediction Results

To answer the research question of how well these skill sets model student performance *within the system* we measure the internal fit. The internal fit is how accurately we can predict student answers to our online question items. If we are able to accurately predict a student's response to a given question, this brings us closer to a computer adaptive tutoring application of being able to intelligently select the appropriate next questions for learning and or assessing purposes. Results are shown bellow.

Table 2. Model prediction performance results for internal fit

Model	Error	MAD	Under/Over	Cent. Error	Cent. MAD
WPI-106	5.50%	15.25	↓ 12.31	4.74%	12.70
WPI-39	9.56%	26.70	↓ 20.14	8.01%	22.10
WPI-5	17.04%	45.15	↓ 31.60	12.94%	34.64
WPI-1	26.86%	69.92	↓ 42.17	19.57%	51.50

The internal fit prediction was run similar to an N-fold cross validation where N is the number of question responses for that student. The network was presented with evidence minus the question being predicted. One point was added to the internal total score if the probability of correct was greater than 0.50 for that question. This was repeated for each question answered by the student. The mean absolute difference between predicted total and actual total score was tabulated in the same fashion as the section above. All the differences between the models in Table 2 were statistically significantly different at the p < .05 level.

4   Discussion and Conclusions

The results we present seem mixed on first blush. The internal fit showed that the finer grained the model, the better the fit to the data collected from the ASSISTment system. This result is in accord with some other work we have done using mixed-effect-modeling rather than Bayes nets [5]. Somewhat surprising, at least to us, is that this same trend did not continue as we expected in the result shown in Table 1. In hindsight, we think we have an explanation. When we try to predict the MCAS test, we are predicting only 29 questions, but they represent a subset of the 109 skills that we are tracking. So the WPI-106, which tries to track all 106 skills, is left at a disadvantage since only 27% of the skills it is tracking appear on the 2005 MCAS test. Essentially ¾ of the data that the WPI-106 collects is practically thrown out and never used. Whereas the WPI-39 can benefit from its fine-grained tracking and 46% of its skills are sampled on the 29 item MCAS test.

As a field we want to be able to build good fitting models that track many skills. Interestingly, item response theory, the dominate methodology used in assessing student performance on most state tests, tends to model knowledge as a unidimensional construct by allowing the items themselves to vary in difficulty (and other properties of items like discrimination and the probability of guessing). Some of our colleagues are pursuing item response models for this very dataset [1, 2] with considerable success, but we think that item response models don't help teachers identify what skills a students should work on, so even though it might be very good predictor of students, it seems to suffer in other ways.

5 Future Work

Our results suggest the 106 skill model as being best for internal fit while the 39 skill model is best for the MCAS test, however, a combination of models may be optimal. Building a hierarchy in an aggregate or prerequisite way [3] will likely best represent the various granularities of student understanding and comprehension. These levels of understanding may change over time, so a dynamic Bayes approach will be needed to model these changes as well as model the important variable of learning.

Acknowledgments. This research was made possible by the US Dept of Education, Institute of Education Science, "Effective Mathematics Education Research" program grant #R305K03140, the Office of Naval Research grant #N00014-03-1-0221, NSF CAREER award to Neil Heffernan, and the Spencer Foundation. All of the opinions in this article are those of the authors, and not those of any of the funders. This work would not have been possible without the assistance of the 2004-2005 WPI/CMU ASSISTment Team that helped make possible this dataset.

References

1. Anozie, N., Junker, B.W.: Predicting end-of-year accountability assessment scores from monthly student records in an online tutoring system. In: Beck, J., Aimeur, E., Barnes, T. (eds.) Educational Data Mining: Papers from the AAAI Workshop, Technical Report WS-06-05, Menlo Park, pp. 1–6. AAAI Press, Stanford, California, USA (2006)
2. Ayers, E., Junker, B.W.: Do skills combine additively to predict task difficulty in eighth grade mathematics? In: Beck, J., Aimeur, E., Barnes, T. (eds.) Educational Data Mining: Papers from the AAAI Workshop, Technical Report WS-06-05, Menlo Park, pp. 14–20. AAAI Press, Stanford, California, USA (2006)
3. Carmona1, C., Millán, E., Pérez-de-la-Cruz, J.L., Trella1, M., Conejo, R.: Introducing Prerequisite Relations in a Multi-layered Bayesian Student Model. In: Ardissono, B., Mitrovic (eds.) User Modeling 2005. 10th International Conference, pp. 347–356. Springer, Heidelberg (2005)
4. Conati, C., Gertner, A., VanLehn, K.: Using bayesian networks to manage uncertainty in student modeling. User. Modeling and User.-Adapted Interaction 12(4), 371–417 (2002)
5. Feng, M., Heffernan, N.T., Mani, M., Heffernan, C.: Using Mixed-Effects Modeling to Compare Different Grain-Sized Skill Models. In: Beck, J., Aimeur, E., & Barnes, T (Eds). Educational Data Mining: Papers from the AAAI Workshop. Menlo Park, CA: AAAI Press. pp. 57-66. Technical Report WS-06-05. ISBN 978-1-57735-287-7 (2006)
6. McCalla, G.I., Greer, J.E.: Granularity– based reasoning and belief revision in student models. In: Greer, J.E., McCalla, G.I. (eds.) Student Modelling: The Key to Individualized Knowledge–Based Instruction, pages, pp. 39–62. Springer, Berlin (1994)
7. Mislevy, R.J., Gitomer, D.H.: The role of probability-based inference in an intelligent tutoring system. User.-Modeling and User. Adapted Interaction 5, 253–282 (1996)
8. Pardos, Z.A., Heffernan, N.T., Anderson, B., Heffernan, C.L.: Using Fine-Grained Skill Models to Fit Student Performance with Bayesian Networks. Workshop in Educational Data Mining held at the Eight International Conference on Intelligent Tutoring Systems. Taiwan (2006)

To Share or Not to Share: Supporting the User Decision in Mobile Social Software Applications

Giuseppe Lugano and Pertti Saariluoma

Social ICT – Human Dimensions Research Group,
University of Jyväskylä, Finland
gilugano@cc.jyu.fi, psa@it.jyu.fi

Abstract. User's privacy concerns represent one of the most serious obstacles to the wide adoption of mobile social software applications. In this paper, we introduce a conceptual model which tackles the problem from the perspective of trade-off between privacy and trust, where the user takes the decision with minimal privacy loss. To support the user decision, we introduce the Mobile Access Control List (Macl), a privacy management mechanism which takes into account the user attitude towards mobile sharing, his communication history and social network relationships.

Keywords: Privacy, Sharing, Trust, Mobile Social Software.

1 Introduction

Today, more than two billion people daily use mobile phones to communicate, mostly calling or sending text messages. The shift from second to third generation (3G) has transformed mobile phones into mobile multimedia computers, which are able to connect to the Internet, take pictures, record clips or watch movies, just to mention some of the features not available a few years ago. Although they are not yet widely spread, mobile data services are expected to grow in the coming years, while voice call revenues decrease. In particular, successful social web paradigms, like blogs and media sharing Internet services, will be accessible and integrated with mobile devices through mobile social software applications (MoSoSo), typically running on Smartphones and PDAs. Extending Shirky's definition of social software MoSoSo has been previously defined as a *kind of software that supports interaction among networked mobile users* [10]. Thus, it is a class of mobile applications whose scope is to support social interaction among interconnected users, with the emphasis of collaboration and data sharing. In some cases, MoSoSo is implemented by the vendor, as in the case of Nokia [13] or developed by third parties [6]. Being personalization through contextual data one of the salient characteristics of MoSoSo, one of the most serious obstacles to their adoption is represented by users' privacy concerns. Hence, there is need of providing effective mechanisms for privacy management of personal data.

C. Conati, K. McCoy, and G. Paliouras (Eds.): UM 2007, LNAI 4511, pp. 440–444, 2007.
© Springer-Verlag Berlin Heidelberg 2007

2 Theoretical Background

2.1 Mobile Privacy Management

Social interaction is a complex phenomenon; although a lot of research and theories have been proposed, there is not a single framework to explain human social behavior. A classic framework, very influential in HCI, although originally developed for face-to-face settings, has been introduced by Erving Goffman [8]. More recently, researchers have studied how individuals perceive their status in social groups [2]. Human social behavior has been studied also from other perspectives; for example, marketing literature suggests that it is motivated mainly by value, which is shaped by both economic (utility related) and psychological (needs related) factors [3]. Benefits can be either extrinsic or intrinsic [5].

Theories of human social behavior have been utilized in mobile and ubiquitous computing environments to investigate privacy concerns [1,4,9,16] and they typically take into account not only individual needs, but also recurrent patterns of social roles and relationships. An important aspect of the problem concerns the identification of the parameters to consider when designing for privacy in the mobile context. One of them is certainly privacy harm, defined also as user's global privacy sensitivity [14]. This parameter has been studied as an individual utility maximization problem from the user - service provider perspective, making a distinction between general and individualized privacy policies. When considering the trade of personal data between end users, such policies do not exist and are often agreed time by time. As Raento observes [15], "*the privacy of a piece of data is approximately equal to the expected benefit you can gain from disclosing it, minus the expected harm that may come from disclosing it*". Analyzing the problem from the perspective of the trade-off between privacy and trust [17], the user choice follows a process which consists of the following steps:

1   Decide whether to trade trust for privacy or not
2   Determine minimal privacy damage
3   Compute trust gain
4   Trade privacy for trust if trust gain is greater than minimal privacy damage
5   Selection: user selects the set with minimal privacy loss

3 Mobile Privacy Management Design

3.1 General Approach

Observing the model suggested in [17], there are two core elements needed to let the user make a selection: the computation of trust gain and estimation of minimal privacy damage. Here, we assess such attributes on the basis of three dimensions: the user, the recipient and the data. From the system perspective, users are represented by their profile, containing not only data which is visible to others (name, phone number, date of birth, photo…), but also an hidden section, which consists of mobile usage patterns, attitudes towards sharing and history of social behavior, expressed by communication logs of past interaction with his social network. Communication history and system usage patterns can support the user in a number of ways; for instance, to automatically infer and measure his social network [7]. Here, user's communication logs, together with information present in the user profile, are used to assess the level of acquaintance with a certain contact. With appropriate algorithms, such as the ones suggested in [11], it is possible, making some simplifications, to translate the data logs, which represent the network distance, into social distance. This process has its roots in Moreno's sociometric measurement [12], which has been very influential in the field of Social Network Analysis.

3.2 Minimal Privacy Damage

Although one of the steps of the privacy-trust trade-off problem is the computation of privacy damage, we consider here the privacy sensitivity perceived by the user for any kind of information that can be shared. Obviously, there is a relation between the two parameters: for low sensitivity items, the potential privacy damage is small. On the contrary, for very sensitive items, the value of privacy damage is high.

The easiest way to assess the privacy sensitivity associated with sharable items is to ask the user his opinion about them. This strategy is used when configuring Internet firewalls; for example, in ZoneAlarm, the default configuration is obtained by analyzing the user answers to a few questions concerning Internet security, connection type and surfing habits. In a similar way, the user is asked to express a value for the privacy sensitivity of each item that could be shared with his mobile, including location, status and mood, address-book, calendar, ring-tones, applications and personal media (photos, videos). User's answers will be encoded as default rule in the Mobile Access Control List (Macl), introduced in the next section. A range of values is used to express how sensitive a piece of information is, including "Highest sensitivity", "High sensitivity", "Medium sensitivity", "Low sensitivity", "No sensitivity". Textual labels are easy to choose for the user, but have a corresponding numerical value used by device. A possible mapping assigns "1" to the "Highest sensitivity and "0" to "No sensitivity", with the other labels having intermediate values in this range.

3.3 User Profile and Mobile Access Control List (Macl)

Once the user has compiled the survey, the application generates the user profile, which consists of public and private sections. The former is a section that can be disclosed to others, while the latter is either hidden or used only by the user for personalization of the application. The most important structure present in the user profile is the Mobile Access Control List (Macl), private table which expresses associations of sharable items (columns) and rules connected to perceived privacy sensitivity values (rows). As the access control list (Acl) used in computer systems, it maintains and controls access privileges to certain actions. In this case, the actions are related to sharing contents between end users in mobile context.

A Macl (Fig.1) consists of three types of rules: default, contact and context. Only the first one, which is created with the user's answers to the survey, is mandatory. In that case, the same privacy settings are applied to all users and in any context. To achieve higher personalization, additional lines can be added for each of the contacts present in the address-book or for specific contexts. As logical expressions, rules might become very complex when more parameters are involved.

Rule Type	Label	Location	Status	Mood	...	Personal Media
Default	Default	Highest.	Low	Low	...	Medium
Contact	Name1	High	High	High	...	High
...					...	
Context	AtWork	Highest	Low	Low	...	High

Fig.1. Example of Mobile Access Control List (Macl)

A Macl is updated either by manual user interventions or automatically by the system, by using probabilistic models based on user communication and history of past interactions with the system. As one of our initial goals was to reduce the time and effort required to the user when granting sharing permissions, one might observe that the specification of context rules and privacy sensitivity values for each contact present in the address-book might even require a higher workload for the user. Once again, it is a matter of finding a good compromise between quality of results and user intervention. Of course, manual specification of rules and settings requires additional work, but also produces more reliable results. However, average users are usually happy with the default configuration, which requires only the initial effort of answering to a short survey. One additional means for improving trust would require that each time a person is using somebody else trusted information, the original owner should be notified or asked for permission to use that information. This kind of disclosure policy would create symmetric privacy situations, similar to the ones often happening in face-to-face communication.

4   Conclusion

In this article, we introduced a conceptual model for dealing with privacy in MoSoSo applications. Even if human social behavior and mobile context are complex phenomena, automatic support of the user decision making is in some cases a desirable feature. Already today, the need of privacy management mechanisms is perceived as important, but in the near future it will become essential. Through agent technology, ubiquitous services will access and exchange personal data on behalf of the user. Mobile access control lists and privacy management mechanisms could become a key component of ubiquitous services, leaving the control and decision to the user. Without that kind of support, the number of daily decisions could easily become unmanageable for the average user. For example, let us consider the problem of spam emails; in the early days of the Internet, users were not worried about spam, although it existed in several forms. After a few years, it became one of the most serious Internet problems. Today, a full solution to the problem has not been found, but spam filters have become an essential feature of email systems. In a similar way, privacy management mechanisms could ensure a wider adoption of mobile social software. Future work includes the design of the optimal survey for the generation of the user profile and an evaluation of the proposed approach.

References

1. Agre, P.: Changing Places: Contexts of Awareness in Computing. Human-Computer Interaction 16(2-4), 177–192 (2001)
2. Anderson, C., Srivastasva, S., Beer, J., Spataro, S., Chatman, J.: Knowing your place: Self perceptions of status in face-to-face groups. Journal of personality and social psychology, pp. 1094–1110 (2006)
3. Babin, B.J., Darben, W.R., Griffin, M.: Work and/or Fun: Measuring Hedonic and Utilitarian shopping value. Journal of Consumer Research 20(1), 644–656 (1994)
4. Bellotti, V., Sellen, A.: Design for Privacy in Ubiquitous Computing Environments. In: Proc. ECSCW'93, pp. 77–92 (1993)
5. Davis, F.D., Bagozzi, R.P., Warshaw, P.R.: Extrinsic and Intrinsic Motivation to Use Computers in the Workplace. Applied Social Psychology 22(14), 1111–1132 (1992)
6. Eagle, N., Pentland, A.: Social Serendipity: Mobilizing Social Software. IEEE Pervasive Computing, Special Issue: The Smart Phone, pp. 28–34 (2005)
7. Farnham, S., Portnoy, W., Turski, A., Cheng, L., Vronay, D.: Personal Map: Automatically Modeling the User's Online Social Network. Interact '03, pp. 567–574 (2003)
8. Goffman, E.: The Presentation of Self in Everyday Life. Doubleday, Garden City, New York (1959)
9. Langheinrich, M.: Personal Privacy in Ubiquitous Computing. Ph.d. Thesis (2005)
10. Lugano, G.: Understanding Mobile Relationships, Workshop on Human-Centered Technology (2006)
11. Lugano, G., Kyppö, J., Saariluoma, P.: Designing People's Interconnections in Mobile Social Networks. In: I International Conference on Multidisciplinary Information Sciences and Technologies (2006)
12. Moreno, J.L.: Who Shall Survive? Fundations of Sociometry, Group Psychotherapy, and Sociodrama. Beacon House (1977)
13. Persson, P., Younghee, J.: Nokia sensor: from research to product. Designing for User eXperience, San Francisco, California (2005)
14. Preibusch, S.: Personalized Services with Negotiable Privacy Policies. CHI 2006 Workshop on Privacy-Enhanced personalization, Montréal, Canada (2006)
15. Raento, M.: Kill your personal data dead. MobileHCI 04 Workshop on Location Systems Privacy and Control (2004)
16. Raento, M., Oulasvirta, A.: Privacy Management for social awareness applications. Context Awareness for Proactive Systems (CAPS), pp. 105–114 (2005)
17. Seigneur, J.-M., Jensen, C.: Trading Privacy for Trust. 2nd International Conference on Trust Management (2004)

Towards a Tag-Based User Model: How Can User Model Benefit from Tags?

Francesca Carmagnola, Federica Cena, Omar Cortassa, Cristina Gena, and Ilaria Torre

Dipartimento di Informatica, Università di Torino, Italy
{carmagnola,cena,cortassa,cgena,torre}@di.unito.it

Abstract. Social tagging is a kind of social annotation by which users label resources, typically web objects, by means of keywords with the goal of sharing, discovering and recovering them. In this paper we investigate the possibility of exploiting the user tagging activity in order to infer knowledge about the user. Up to now the relation between tagging and user modeling seems not to have been investigated in depth. Given the widespread diffusion of web tools for collaborative tagging, it is interesting to understand how user modeling can benefit from this feedback.

1 Introduction and State of the Art

With the beginning of the new millennium, the Web has seen a big transformation which led to the explosion of the so-called "social software" and to the definition of a new paradigm of the Web, the Web 2.0[1]. This new paradigm offers users several ways to participate in the creation of web content: it makes easy and stimulating the process of tagging (labeling resources by means of keywords), inserting new contents, sharing objects, providing comments and so on. These activities are typically defined as "social" or "collaborative" annotations. In the last two years several projects have been developed in the field of adaptive systems. For example, Ahn et al. [1] use social annotation to improve information visualization by presenting visual indicators that provide information about user and group annotations to resources; Bateman et al. [3] propose a framework for integrating social tagging into a natural language ontology. Finally some works make tags themselves the object of adaptation, e.g. Xu et al. [8].

Up to now nobody seems to have exploited tag annotation in order to enrich and extend the user model. van Setten [7] provide some ideas about how information systems can adapt themselves using annotations to support users in finding the information they need. Moreover, they indicate that this profile can then be used for recommendation, using techniques as collaborative filtering or case based reasoning. This is indeed a way of tags, but it would be even more interesting to semantically analyze tags and reason on them in order to infer new knowledge about a specific user.

---

[1] http://www.oreillynet.com/pub/a/oreilly/tim/news/2005/09/30/what-is-web-20.html

C. Conati, K. McCoy, and G. Paliouras (Eds.): UM 2007, LNAI 4511, pp. 445–449, 2007.
© Springer-Verlag Berlin Heidelberg 2007

The aim of our work is quite to understand *how tags can be used for user modeling,* and specifically how tags can be useful to *increase* and *improve* the *knowledge* of an adaptive system about users. This work moves from a recommender system, iCITY [4], a web-based multi-device application that provides suggestions on cultural events in the city of Turin, and allows users to tag the events. Events are classified on the basis of a domain ontology, and suggestions are based on user model and user location, and the user interface is adapted to the device being used.

The paper is structured as follows. In Sec. 2 we analyze reasoning on the action of tagging, and on the content of tags. We also present a test we carried out to support our analysis. Finally Sec. 3 concludes the paper and presents some open issues.

2   Reasoning on Tags

Tags can be useful in increasing and optimizing the knowledge of an adaptive system about a user. What we want to investigate in this first part of the section is the relevance of *tagging* (meant as the *action* led by a user when adding tags), showing *how* and *why* this action could represent an important feedback for user profiling. Thus, we start analyzing the user model of iCITY and, in particular, the user dimensions that could be inferred from the **action of tagging**:

i) **user's interactivity level,** namely the measure of how much the user interacts with the system. It is related, on the one hand, with the willingness of the user to interact with the application, and, on the other hand, with the real possibility of the user to interact with it. The action of tagging seems to be a relevant indicator of the user interactivity level, since it requires some effort to accomplish it, compared to the other user actions;

ii) **user's organization level,** which identifies the attitude of the user in organizing and categorizing things. In all the tagging services available on the web, the main motivation for user to tag is to satisfy the need of organizing resources in a personal way in order to better visualize, store and retrieve them later;

iii) **user's interest in a content,** if a user spends time in selecting or inserting tags on a specific item she is probably interested in the item.

Now, we want to investigate the chance to reason on the **semantics of specific tags** inserted by the user in order to enrich the user model by refining the value of existing user features and inferring new user features. To accomplish such a goal, the following three main tasks seem to be necessary.

1) Categorization of tags. In order to explore how iCITY users tag events and, consequently, how this knowledge can be exploited for user modeling, we carried out an initial evaluation. We selected a list of events from the RSS channel that feeds iCITY[2], to simulate the tagging activity on the web site. We chose 15 events belonging to different categories (art, theatre, cinema, music, books), and then we set the items in three homogeneous groups to be presented to three different groups of users. We selected 39 users choosing them between students (23 subjects), researchers working in our departments (10 s.), relatives and friends (6 s.). We organized the

---

[2] http://www.torinocultura.it/

experimental tasks as follows: we showed each user a printed list containing 5 events and their description, and we asked them to tag them. They could freely write their own tags (up to 5 tags for event) or choose them from the words contained in the event description (the reason of this second option is that iCITY suggests also the tags automatically extracted from the event description). We collected 217 tags and we analyzed them in an inductive way, following the principles of the Grounded Theory [6]. The main two categories emerged from our analysis are the following: *proposed tags* (tags derived from the event description): 76% of tags and *free tags* (not derived from the description): 24% of tags.

We then analyzed tags taking also into account other properties related to the tagged event. Thus other categories emerged: *specific tags* (tags that add some specification about the event): 61.19%; *generic tags* (tags that classify the event in a more general dimension): 22.37%; *contextual tags* (tags about the context of the event: location, time, etc.): 13.24%; *synonym tags* (tags that are synonyms of terms in the event description): 2.74%; *invented tags* (e.g. unhyphenated compound words like "PicassoExhibition"): 2.17%. Considering the gap between our test and the real online service iCITY provides, the next step of our analysis has been to integrate the classification obtained by our test with the categories that could not be detected with it. Thus, first of all we included the categories *Subjective tags* (tags that express user's opinion and emotion) and *Organizational tags* (tags that identify personal stuff).

Then, we took into account the types of tags suggested by iCITY, which suggests tags on the basis of i) the most popular tags in the community; ii) the most used tags previously inserted by the user, and iii) the tags recommended on the basis of the user model features combined with the event description. As a consequence, our classification is extended with the following three categories: *Most popular tags*, *Most used tags* and *Recommended tags*. These categories will be taken into account as subclasses of the general class *Proposed tags*.

2) How to automatically analyse tags. At this point of our analysis, the main problem to face with is how to transform all the above categories into information processable by machine in order to reason on them. According to the above tags classification, some tags can be analyzed exploiting the iCITY events ontology, other categories of tags can be detected on the basis of the user behaviour, but a better solution might be analyzing tags by mean of a natural language ontology, such as WordNet[3].

In the following we provide, for each category of our classification, some ideas of how to analyze them:

- *proposed tags/free tags*: this is the easiest category to detect, since the categories are based on the user selections and the proposed selections are controlled by the system. Thus, it is possible to check if the tags come from the system's inference (*recommended tags*), if they come from the *most used tags* of the user, if they belong to other users (*most popular tags*), if they are inserted for the first time from the user (*free tags*), and in this specific case also if they do not belong to the WordNet dictionary (*invented tags*);

---

[3] http://wordnet.princeton.edu/

- *generic/specific tags*: for each event, tags are recognized as "general" if they are mapped on the upper categories of the iCITY ontology; "specific" if they are mapped on instances or lower concepts of WordNet related to the categories of the ontology;
- *synonym tags*: inserted tags are compared with WordNet vocabulary in order to identify synonyms of the word used in the description of the specific event;
- *contextual tag*: by means of the WordNet vocabulary, iCITY tries to discover whether the tag is related to the context of the event. It is possible only for tags with a well-defined format (e.g. time) or tags which represent instances of previously identified as contextual concepts in WordNet (e.g. location-based concepts);
- *subjective tags*: these tags express user's opinion and emotion, and, again, they can be identified by means of WordNet.
- *organizational tags*: these tags can be used to organize events and thus it is difficult to recognize them by using WordNet. Tags can be assumed to be *organizational* if the same user uses them with a high frequency.

Finally, we also consider the *meaning* of the tag: WordNet can return the category to which the tag belongs and this could be useful in order to discover whether the tag pertains to the same category of the event. E.g., a user could tag a movie like "Ray", about the Ray Charles' life, with the tag "jazz", which is a lower concept of WordNet category three. A final remark to this section regards a big problem we have not taken into account up to now. It is the possible polysemy of tags, which can make difficult the use of WordNet. For discussions about that see Dix, Levialdi and Malizia [5].

3) Matching between tags and user model dimensions: starting from the above described classification of tags, we then analyzed how each tag category can be relevant for user modeling dimensions. In the following we provide a description of it.

If the user selects one of the *proposed tags*, we can infer a medium level of **participation** in the tagging activity; we can also assume a low level of **knowledge** on the content and a medium level of **organization** (maybe she could be not so interested in well categorizing the events). All these inferences are weak since the user behaviour could be due as well to slackness or to the fact that she simply found the right tag among those ones suggested by the system. Analyzing more specifically the type of the proposed tags, if the user selects the *most popular tags* we can weakly infer that she *trusts the other people* of the community and that she conforms herself to the general thought (*conformism*). While if she always uses the same tags after some interactions, we could infer a propensity to regular habits (*orderliness*). Finally, if the user selects tags recommended by the system, we could infer a high level of *trust in the system*. On the contrary, if the user uses a lot of *free tags*, we can make other assumptions. Her **knowledge** in the topic is probably medium-high, because inserting free tags requires a specific knowledge in the area. It could also mean a high **creativity**, a great **participation** in the tagging activity (because using personal words requires more effort than to simply selecting from suggested tags) and a high level of organization. The last three values are even higher when the *free tag* is an *invented* one. If the user uses *specific* words, this could indicate a great **knowledge** in the topic; but, on the contrary, if she uses *generic words,* this does not necessarily imply a low knowledge. In fact, if the generic words are appropriate, it could mean a high knowledge that allows using high abstract concepts. The use of *synonyms* could imply again a good **knowledge** in the topic and a high level of **creativity**; while *contextual tags* could mean that the user has high **practical knowledge** probably derived from a direct participation at event, and thus a high **interest** in it. The *meaning* of the tag could reveal some cross-categorization, that could reveal a high **knowledge** in the event. Finally, *organizational tags* express a high attitude to **organization** and **creativity** and *subjective tags* reveal a tendency to *personalize* the interaction.

3 Conclusion and Future Work

In this paper we have analyzed the possible contribution that the analysis of tagging activity can bring to user modeling. The next step is to verify these hypotheses with a deep evaluation. At the same time we are investigating the possibility of exploiting the list of tags publicly available in the accounts (express through URLs) of the web communities the user belongs to, since most of them make the list publicly available in some xml-based syntax. By importing such tags (and to map them onto the domain ontology) it would be possible to enrich and extend the user model and consequently improve and refine recommendations.

References

1. Ahn, J., Farzan, R., Brusilovsky, P.A: Two-Level Adaptive Visualization for Information Access to Open-Corpus Educational Resources, Workshop on Social Navigation and Community-Based Adaptation Technologies (AH 06), Dublin, Ireland (June 20th, 2006)
2. Allport, G.W.: Pattern and growth in personality.Rinehart and Winston, Holt, NY (1965)
3. Bateman, S., Brooks, C., McCalla, G.: Collaborative Tagging Approaches for Onto-logical Metadata in Adaptive E-Learning Systems, Workshop on Applications of Semantic Web Technologies for E-Learning (AH 06), Dublin, Ireland (June 20th, 2006)
4. Carmagnola, F., Cena, F., Console, L., Cortassa, O., Ferri, M., Gena, C., Goy, A., Parena, M., Torre, I., Toso, A., Vernero, F., Vellar, A.: iCITY – an adaptive social mobile guide for cultural events, Workshop on Mobile Guide, Italy (October 18th, 2006)
5. Dix, A., Levialdi, S., Malizia, A.: Semantic Halo for Collaboration Tagging, Systems, Workshop on Social Navigation and Community-Based Adaptation Tech-nologies (AH 06), Dublin, Ireland (June 20th, 2006)
6. Strauss, A.L., Corbin, J.M.: Basics of qualitative research: techniques and procedures for developing grounded theory. SAGE, Thousand Oaks (1998)
7. van Setten, M., Brussee, R., van Vliet, H., Gazendam, L., van H uten Y., Veenstra M.: On the Importance of Who Tagged What, Workshop on Social Navigation and Community-Based Adaptation Technologies (AH 06), Dub-lin, Ireland (June 20th, 2006)
8. Xu, Z., Fu, Y., Mao, J., Su, D.: Towards the Semantic Web: Collaborative Tag Suggestions, Workshop on Collaborative Web Tagging (WWW06), Edinburgh, Scotland (May 22nd, 2006)

Web Customer Modeling for Automated Session Prioritization on High Traffic Sites

Nicolas Poggi[1], Toni Moreno[2,3], Josep Lluis Berral[1], Ricard Gavaldà[4], and Jordi Torres[1,2]

[1] Computer Architecture Department, U. Politècnica de Catalunya, Barcelona, Spain
[2] Barcelona Supercomputing Center, Barcelona, Spain
[3] Department of Management, U. Politècnica de Catalunya, Barcelona, Spain
[4] Department of Software, U. Politècnica de Catalunya, Barcelona, Spain

Abstract. In the Web environment, user identification is becoming a major challenge for admission control systems on high traffic sites. When a web server is overloaded there is a significant loss of throughput when we compare finished sessions and the number of responses per second; longer sessions are usually the ones ending in sales but also the most sensitive to load failures. Session-based admission control systems maintain a high QoS for a limited number of sessions, but does not maximize revenue as it treats all non-logged sessions the same. We present a novel method for learning to assign priorities to sessions according to the revenue that will generate. For this, we use traditional machine learning techniques and Markov-chain models. We are able to train a system to estimate the probability of the user's purchasing intentions according to its early navigation clicks and other static information. The predictions can be used by admission control systems to prioritize sessions or deny them if no resources are available, thus improving sales throughput per unit of time for a given infrastructure. We test our approach on access logs obtained from a high-traffic online travel agency, with promising results.

Keywords: Web prediction, navigation patterns, machine learning, data mining, admission control, resource management, autonomic computing, e-commerce.

1   Introduction

During the recent years there have been important changes in web technologies. There has been a shift from originally serving mainly static pages to fully dynamic sites. Dynamic applications have a huge demand on CPU power, opposed to network bandwidth that has been the traditional bottleneck of the web. Websites now make the use of fully featured programming languages, implementing XML-based web services for B2B communication, SSL for security, on-the-fly generated media, and technologies such as AJAX and for interactivity. While these technologies improve the user experience and privacy, they also increase the demand for CPU power [2].

C. Conati, K. McCoy, and G. Paliouras (Eds.): UM 2007, LNAI 4511, pp. 450–454, 2007.
© Springer-Verlag Berlin Heidelberg 2007

With the increase of dynamic websites, system overload is becoming a common situation and its incidence is growing along. Improving the infrastructure of a website might not be simple; for cost reasons, scalability problems or because some peaks are infrequent, websites might not be able to adapt rapidly in hardware to user fluctuations. When a server is overloaded, it will typically refuse to serve any connections, as resources get locked and a race condition occurs. Session-based admission control systems [3] allow to maintain QoS on overloads by keeping a high throughput in terms of properly finished sessions for a limited number of users. However, by denying access to exceeding users, the website looses potential customers.

This paper proposes a novel approach consisting of generating a model for web user behavior in a real, complex website and using it to support decisions regarding the allocation of the available resources, based on a revenue-related metrics. In our user models, we try to understand how to best capture the features that make a customer more likely to make a purchase, and therefore more attractive — from the point of view of maximizing revenues — to maintain in the system even in the case of a severe overload. In this sense, we are proposing a per user-adaptive policy for admission control and session prioritization. Details on related work are given in the extended version [1].

2   Our Approach

Our approach consists in using web dynamic application log files to learn models that make predictions about each class of user future behavior, with the objective of assigning a priority value to every customer based on the expected revenue that s/he will generate, which in our case essentially depends on whether s/he will make a purchase. For this we have developed the AUGURES architecture, a prototype which currently implements: an access log preprocessor, to remove non-user generated actions and rewrite the log in a more convenient format; a module generating two high-order Markov chains, one for purchasing users and another for non-purchasing users; and an offline learning module (the predictor) running chosen classifiers form the WEKA machine learning package [4].

AUGURES is first trained by preprocessing a training log file, then the buying and non-buying Markov models are generated from it. Subsequently, each transaction on the training log is passed through both Markov models and their resulting probabilities added as static variables on the training log file. We then build the predictor from the training data; from this point, we can run incoming sessions from a new log file against the predictor, which will produce a probability on the users' purchasing intentions. In our generic approach we assume that from the log files we can extract at least the following information for each user transaction:

1. Date and time of transaction (discretized to a few categories).
2. Session identifier
3. "Tag", identifying the type of transaction performed by the page.

4. Whether the user is logged in at this moment.
5. Whether s/he is a returning customer, and whether s/he bought in the past.
6. Length of the current session, in number of transactions.
7. The "class", that is, the behavior we want to predict. This information is computed by looking "forward" in the logfile, so it can only be computed for the training set.

We call the previous information *static* because it reflects little information about the navigation path of the user in this session. On the other hand, it is reasonable to believe that the sequence of requests made by the user should help in predicting his/her future behavior. We call this sequence the *dynamic information* of the session; it can be identified by the sequence of tags (user clicks) in the associated transactions.

Unfortunately, most machine learning algorithms are not well adapted to dealing with variables that are themselves sequences, and some ad-hoc mechanism has to be designed. We propose to use higher-order Markov chains to obtain the extra information. More precisely, we model separately the navigation patterns of buyers and non-buyers with two order-k Markov chains (we use $k = 2$). These Markov chains let us assign probabilities $\Pr[buyer|p]$ and $\Pr[nonbuyer|p]$ given that the last k tags in the session are those described by the path p, see the extended version for details [1].

3   Experiments

The data for the experiment was provided by Atrapalo.com, a high traffic Spanish online travel agency, that makes use of the above mentioned state-of-the-art web technologies. It consisted of about 112,000 transactions collected over approximately one day. The data was preprocessed to remove erroneous entries, transactions clearly corresponding to automated bots and crawlers, and one-click sessions corresponding to banners. The resulting data contained 42 different tags or "pages" accessed by the users in their navigation.

An important feature of the data is that only about 2% of the sessions end in purchase; since buying sessions are longer in average than non-buying ones, this means about 6.6% of transactions have "buying" label. We prepared a training dataset of about 7,000 transactions. These were chosen randomly, except that we forced that about 50% were buying ones so that these were sufficiently represented. Another dataset was prepared for testing, containing the rest of the buying transactions plus a sufficient number of non-buying ones not appearing in the training dataset, so that the proportion of buyers was the original 6.6%.

After building a classifier using the training dataset, we can compute for each transaction in the testing set a "true" buying/nonbuying label and a "predicted" label. Thus, we can divide them into the 4 typical categories of true positives (tp), false positives (fp), true negatives (tn), and false negatives (fn). For example, false positives are the transactions that are predicted to be followed by purchase but that in fact did not.

	j48 classifier	NB classifier	Logistic
%recall	78.1	68.5	72.4
%precision	9.8	8.4	9.0

Fig. 1. Models built by different classifiers admitting N=30,000 transactions

The measures we are interested in this study are the classical *recall* and *precision*, as well as one that is specific to our setting, which we call *%admitted*.

- %admitted is (tp+fp)/(tp+fp+tn+fn), or the fraction of incoming transactions that would be admitted into the system. The number if allowed transactions is the one that may be limited by the available infrastructure.
- the recall is tp/(tp+fn), the fraction of real buyers that are admitted.
- the precision is tp/(tp+fp), the fraction of admitted transactions that really end up in purchase.

For the time being, we control the %admitted quantity by the ad-hoc but simple method of assigning different weights to buyers and nonbuyers when training. In a first set of experiments, we wanted to compare different learning methods. We used the 50%buyers-50%non-buyers training dataset to train a logistic linear regression (WEKA's `Logistic` method), a decision tree (WEKA's j48 method), and a Naive Bayes classifier.

We also fixed %admitted to about 28.5%, so that 30,000 transactions in the test dataset are admitted. The results are given in Figure 1. One can see that there are noticeable, but not drastic, differences in recall and precision among the methods. An important implication can be drawn from the recall figures, which reaches 78% for the j48 method: in an overload situation where less than 30% of the transactions can be admitted, a system admitting transactions at random, also a 30% of all buying transactions would be admitted, and 70% of buyers would be unserved; by using our mechanism, we would instead accept 78% of the buying transactions and leave only 22% buyers unserved.

In a second set of experiments we wanted to simulate the effect of different infrastructure capacity. We repeated the experiment above for different values of %admitted or, equivalently, for different numbers of admitted transactions N. We present the results (for the j48 method only) on Figure 2.

One can observe that as admission is made harder (N decreases), both recall and precision strictly grow. In other words, when less resources are available our system tends to let in only the most promising transactions.

	N=5,000	N=10,000	N=30,000	N=50,000
%admitted	4.2	10.5	28.2	42.4
%recall	40.6	54.41	78.1	85.8
%precision	34.5	18.3	9.8	7.0

Fig. 2. Models built by the j48 classifier forcing %admitted to different values

4   Conclusions

Websites might become overloaded by certain events such as news events or promotions, as they can potentially reach millions of users. When a peak situation occurs most infrastructures become stalled and throughput is reduced even though there are more users. To prevent this, load admission control mechanisms are used to allow only a certain number of sessions, however current session based admission systems don't differentiate between users and might be denying access to users with the intention to purchase. As a proof of concept, we have taken a dataset from high traffic online travel agency to perform experiments to approximate users purchasing intentions from their navigational patterns.

In our experiments, we are able to train a model from previously recorded navigational information that can be used to tell apart, with nontrivial probability, whether a session will lead to purchase after a few clicks. From the results, in a situation where less than 30% of the transactions can be admitted, AUGURES would admit 78% of buying customers opposed to 30% from a random strategy. By assigning different weights to false positives and false negatives, the model can adapt itself dynamically maintaining a reasonable precision. As future work we plan to investigate other models to improve predictions, classification criteria, and at the same time test the applicability of the predictor models for a production environment. For further details please refer to the extended version or research group site [1].

Acknowledgements

This work is supported by the Ministry of Science and Technology of Spain and the European Union under contract TIN2004-07739-C02-01. R. Gavaldà is partially supported by the 6th Framework Program of EU through the integrated project DELIS (#001907), by the EU PASCAL Network of Excellence, IST-2002-506778, and by the DGICYT MOISES-BAR project, TIN2005-08832-C03-03. Experiments data and domain knowledge provided by Atrapalo.com

References

1. Poggi, N., Moreno, T., Berral, J., Gavalda, R., Torres, J.: Web customer modeling for automated session prioritization on high traffic sites. Technical Report, UPC, Group site (2006) at `http://research.ac.upc.edu/eDragon`
2. Guitart, J., Beltran, V., Carrera, D., Torres, J., Ayguadé, E.: Characterizing secure dynamic web applications scalability. In: 19th International Parallel and Distributed Processing Symposium, pp. 166–176. Denver, Colorado, USA (2005)
3. Guitart, J., Carrera, D., Beltran, V., Torres, J., Ayguadé, E.: Session-Based Adaptive Overload Control for Secure Dynamic Web Applications. In: 34th International Conference on Parallel Processing (ICPP'05), pp. 341–349. Oslo, Norway (2005)
4. Witten, I.H., Frank, E.: Data Mining: Practical Machine Learning Tools and Techniques 2nd edn. Morgan Kaufmann, San Francisco (2005) `http://www.cs.waikato.ac.nz/~ml/weka`

What's in a Step? Toward General, Abstract Representations of Tutoring System Log Data

Kurt VanLehn[1], Kenneth R. Koedinger[2], Alida Skogsholm[2], Adaeze Nwaigwe[2], Robert G.M. Hausmann[1], Anders Weinstein[1], and Benjamin Billings[2]

[1] LRDC, University of Pittsburgh, Pittsburgh, PA, USA
{vanlehn,andersw,bobhaus}@pitt.edu
[2] HCII, Carnegie-Mellon University, Pittsburgh, PA, USA
{koedinger,alida,anwaigwe,bkb}@cmu.edu

Abstract. The Pittsburgh Science of Learning Center (PSLC) is developing a data storage and analysis facility, called DataShop. It currently handles log data from 6 full-year tutoring systems and dozens of smaller, experimental tutoring systems. DataShop requires a representation of log data that supports a variety of tutoring systems, atheoretical analyses and theoretical analyses. The theory-based analyses are strongly related to student modeling, so the lessons learned in developing the DataShop's representation may apply to student modeling in general. This report discusses the representation originally used by the DataShop, the problems encountered, and how the key concept of "step" evolved to meet these challenges.

Keywords: Student modeling, educational data mining, tutoring systems.

1 The Pittsburgh Science of Learning Center DataShop

The PSLC DataShop (http://learnlab.web.cmu.edu/datashop/) provides the following functions: (1) Data security with appropriate anonymity; (2) A standard, extensible representation; (3) Easy export to standard tools, such as spreadsheets and statistical packages; (4) Analytic tools specific to log data; and (5) Reification of the PSLC theoretical framework. This last goal is explained below.

The DataShop grew out of Ritter and Koedinger's [1] standard framework for representing log data. Its analysis tools, which are described below, evolved from Anderson and Koedinger's early work on learning curves [2].

The DataShop is part of the PSLC LearnLab—an internationally shared facility for doing *in vivo* experimentation (http://www.learnlab.org). Although the DataShop is in daily operation supporting thousands of students, teachers and researchers around the world, it is still developing in order to incorporate new kinds of student-tutor interactivity. We report on the representational challenges that have been faced.

C. Conati, K. McCoy, and G. Paliouras (Eds.): UM 2007, LNAI 4511, pp. 455–459, 2007.
© Springer-Verlag Berlin Heidelberg 2007

2   Three Levels of Description

The log data are a chronological record of all the student's interactions with a tutoring system. These interactions are described at three levels: transactions, step histories and knowledge component applications. Each level is described below.

The lowest level is the *transaction* [1], which is a communication between the student and the system. For instance, the following is a sequence of transactions in an algebra tutor:

1. The tool displays "2x(3-4x)-13 =__x^2 + __x + __ = (__x + __)(__x + __)".
2. The student puts the cursor in the first blank and enters "8".
   The tutor tells the student that the entry is incorrect.
3. The student asks for a hint.
   The tutor tells the student "Check your signs."
4. The student replaces the "8" with "-8".
   The tutor tells the student that the entry is correct.
5. The student puts the cursor in the next blank and enters "6".
   The tutor tells the student that the entry is correct.

The next level represents the log data as a sequence of episodes, called *step-attempt histories* [3]. Each episode is terminated by a *step,* which is a user interface action that is correct and advances the solution of the problem. The *history* of that step consists of the student's incorrect attempts at entering that step, help requests, hints, and any other transactions that might aid the student to make the step. For instance, in the list above, transactions 2 through 4 comprise the first step-attempt history; transaction 5 is the second one. This level of description assumes that only some user interface actions are steps, and that the correct/incorrect distinction makes sense for them. Thus, this level of representation has some theoretical commitments, but fairly weak ones.

The third level of description is based on the PSLC theoretical framework, which assumes that domain knowledge can be usefully decomposed into *knowledge components* [4]. This is intended to be a generic, neutral term that covers many kinds of knowledge: procedural, conceptual, perceptual, etc. For example, in learning Chinese as a second language, a single knowledge component (KC) might represent a word's phonological, orthographic, and semantic representations, as well as the associations between them. In physics, Newton's third law might be represented as a single knowledge component. Most PSLC tutoring systems represent domain knowledge as KCs, and they label every step with the KCs that must be applied to generate that step. For instance, the step entered at line 7 above results from applying two KCs: the Distributive Law and Simplification. Thus, at this level of description, the log data are viewed as a sequence of *knowledge component applications*.

3   The DataShop's Analytical Tools

We discuss only two tools, the Error Report and the Learning Curve generator, that illustrate the need for the three levels of log data description.

In its simplest usage, the Error Report is given a problem and prints a table that lists each step in the problem along with a summary of the students' step-attempt histories. For instance, the error report for filling in the first blank of "2x(-4x+3)-13= __x^2+...", might state that: 69% of the students entered the correct response on the first attempt, 12% asked for a hint, 10% entered "8" and got the hint "Check your signs," and 9% entered "-4" and got the hint "Hmm; not what I got. Please try again." Such error reports are useful for determining which common errors are not receiving pedagogically useful feedback. The Error Report uses only the step level of description. KC applications play no role in its reports, so a tutoring system that does not use KCs can still get Error Reports for its log data.

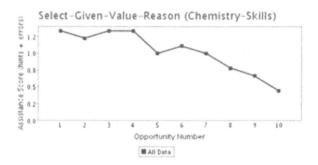

Fig. 1. Learning Curve for the KC Select-Given-Value-Reason

In our usage, a *learning curve* displays the students' increasing mastery of a knowledge component over time [2, 5]. As a simple illustration, suppose we want a learning curve for a particular KC for a particular student. The tool first locates all the step-attempt histories corresponding to applications of that KC. For each history, it calculates the *assistance score*, which is simply the number of help requests plus the number of errors in that episode. For instance, for the first step-attempt history mentioned above (transactions 2 through 4), the assistance score is 2; for the second step-attempt history, the assistance score is 0. Then the Learning Curve generator plots a graph (see Fig. 1) where the points correspond to step-attempt histories, the y-axis is the assistance score, and the x-axis is ordinal and chronological (i.e., the Nth KC application is at $x = N$ on the graph.) Theory suggests that the learning curve should start with large amounts of assistance on the first KC application, less on the second, and so on. Often the learning curve for a single student is too noisy to see such a pattern, so it is common to aggregate over all the students. In Fig. 1, for instance, the point at $x = 1$ has a y-value that is the average over all students' assistance scores for their first application of the KC.

4   Representational Lessons Learned

This section discusses representational lessons learned while trying to accommodate an increasing set of tutoring systems. When log data from VLAB, a simulated chemistry laboratory with a direct-manipulation interface (www.chemcollective.org), were added to the DataShop, we had to allow multiple transactions to be associated with a single step. For instance, a single step "heat beaker A" should be associated with the three transactions: (1) removing a Bunsen burner from storage, (2) placing it under the beaker and (3) turning on the flame.

More recently, we added the inverse capability: a single student transaction may be associated with multiple steps. When log data from Andes, a physics tutoring system (www.andes.pitt.edu) were first added to the DataShop, each correct equation entered by the student was treated as a step. However, this made the error reports nearly useless because few students entered the same steps. For instance, one student might enter "W_y = -W" as one step and "W = m*g" as another. A second student might enter their algebraic combination, "W_y = -m*g". Even if a problem needs only N primitive equations to solve it, most subsets of the set of N equations correspond to a possible compound equation. Thus, the error report for a problem with 10 primitive equations may have as many as $N^2 = 1028$ steps. Moreover, each would probably have just one or two step-attempt histories because only one or two students happened to enter exactly that algebraic combination of primitive equations. Fortunately, Andes decomposes a student equation into the primitive equations that comprise it. Each such primitive equation became a step in the DataShop representation. Thus, if the student entered "W_y = -m*g", then this student action is associated with two steps, "W_y = -W" and "W = m*g". That is, a single student transaction may be associated with multiple steps.

The third major issue involves partitioning the transactions into step-attempt histories. We implied earlier that all the errors, help requests, and other non-step transactions that occurred between two steps became the step-attempt history for the second step. That is, the partitions were chronological. This does not make sense in some cases. For instance, suppose the student makes the error mentioned earlier by entering "8" in the first blank of "2x(-4x+3)-13 = __x^2 + __x + __". The tutor gives the hint "Check your signs," but the student does not fix the error. Instead, the student puts the cursor in the second blank and enters "6" which is correct. If we used only the chronological scheme, the error and the hint would become part of the step-attempt history for "6." This is wrong because the student actually didn't have any trouble entering the "6." An Error Report that showed "-8" and "Check your signs" associated with the "6" step would be very confusing. On the other hand, a partition based on the location of the cursor at the time of the entry would assign the appropriate step-attempt histories to the steps of this problem.

Chronology and location are just two cues that can be used for deciding how to partition the log data into step-attempt history. The situation becomes more complex when dealing with natural language tutoring systems. A single transaction, such as a student saying "The block moves downward, speeding up," might be analyzed as two steps: "The block moves downward" and "The block speeds up". We are currently evaluating multiple heuristics by comparing their performance with human coders [6]. These explorations should be useful not only to the DataShop, but also to other applications that do student modeling (e.g., [3]).

5 Conclusions

The central concept in the DataShop log data representation has turned out to be the step. It connects the transaction-level representation to the theoretically-derived KC level. The step level also provides a way for tutoring systems that do not have KC-level analyses to still get some use of the DataShop.

However, the concepts of "step" and "step-attempt history" have evolved in subtle ways. Several years ago, "step" meant an actual student transaction that was a correct part of the solution to the problem, and "step-attempt history" meant all the non-step transactions that immediately preceded the step. Now there is no longer a one-to-one relationship between steps and transactions, and the transactions that comprise a step-attempt history need not immediately precede the step.

A *step* is now defined as the smallest possible correct entry that a student can make. By "smallest", we mean that the step cannot be re-expressed as two or more steps.

Although the KC applications required to solve a problem are determined solely by the problem and the KC-level analysis of the task domain, the steps required to solve a problem are also a function of the user interface. For instance, in a natural language interface, when the student enters "the baseball's velocity is 10 m/s at 30°," it corresponds to two steps: "the baseball's velocity is 10 m/s" and "the baseball's velocity is 30°" However, if the user interface were graphical instead, so that the student specifies the baseball's velocity by clicking and dragging out a vector, what was once a compound of two steps now becomes one, because in the graphical user interface, the vector drawing step cannot be decomposed.

References

1. Ritter, S., Koedinger, K.: Towards lightweight tutoring agents, in Artificial Intelligence in Education. In: Greer, J. (ed.) Association for Advancement of Computers in Education, pp. 91–98. Charlottesville, NC (1995)
2. Anderson, J.R., et al.: Cognitive Tutors: Lessons Learned. The. Journal of the Learning Sciences 4(2), 167–207 (1995)
3. VanLehn, K.: Intelligent tutoring systems for continuous, embedded assessment, in The future of assessment: Shaping teaching and learning. Dwyer, C.A. (ed.) (In press) Erbaum: Mahwah, NJ
4. VanLehn, K.: The behavior of tutoring systems. International Journal of Artificial Intelligence and Education, vol.16, (2006)
5. Cen, H., Koedinger, K.R., Junker, B.: Learning Factors Analysis – A general method for cognitive model evaluation and improvement, in Intelligent Tutoring Systems: In: 8th International Conferenc. Ikeda, M., Ashley, K., Chan,T.-W. (eds.) pp. 164–175 Springer, Berlin (2006)
6. Nwaigwe, A., et al.: Exploring alternative methods for error attribution in learning curve analysis in intelligent tutoring systems. In: Proceedings of AI in Education, IOS Press, Amsterdam (In Press) (2007)

Encouraging Contributions to Online Communities with Personalization and Incentives

F. Maxwell Harper

GroupLens Research, University of Minnesota
Minneapolis, MN 55455, USA
harper@cs.umn.edu

Abstract. Increasingly, online systems depend on user contributions such as posts, ratings, tags, and comments. Many of these systems wish to encourage broader participation or the contribution of higher quality content. In this doctoral consortium paper, I present past work and propose future work on understanding user motivations to contribute online and on the use of personalization technology and incentives to shape participation.

Keywords: Incentives, personalization, online communities.

1 Promoting Contributions with Incentives

As of December, 2006, six of the ten most popular Web sites in the United States[1] simply could not exist without user-contributed content. These sites – Myspace, EBay, YouTube, Craigslist, Wikipedia, and Facebook – leverage content created by users to create fantastically large and varied social spaces, marketplaces, and repositories of information. Amazon, also in the top ten sites, relies on user reviews, lists, ratings, and tags to enrich the site and help users make purchase decisions. User contributions also are driving the proliferation of online discussions, wikis, and blogs.

The user-centric paradigm of content creation on the Internet (a major component of what is sometimes called Web 2.0) makes new, powerful types of content possible, but also leaves sites vulnerable to the whims of their users. Successful sites manage to attract diverse, committed, or many users. The content these users create cannot be replicated by marketing departments or editorial staff. But success is far from guaranteed. Sites must now compete for users' time and effort. As a result, some communities that rely on user contributions simply die from lack of participation.

Sites' success also depends on the quality of what users contribute. The online encyclopedia Wikipedia is an example of a site that maintains high quality standards. One study found that science articles in the free Wikipedia and the commercially produced Encyclopaedia Britannica contain similar numbers of errors [8]. Other sites struggle with quality. For example, both Yahoo! Answers and Slashdot have worked to elevate the quality of discourse through the design of incentives that reward high-quality contributions.

---

[1] Top sites as measured in terms of total traffic by alexa.com.

C. Conati, K. McCoy, and G. Paliouras (Eds.): UM 2007, LNAI 4511, pp. 460–464, 2007.
© Springer-Verlag Berlin Heidelberg 2007

Because of online systems' dependence on user contributions, it has become useful to develop tools that encourage users to participate in particular ways. Increasingly, Web sites are using one class of tools, *designed incentives*, to this end. Designed incentives are mechanisms built into a software interface that encourage, reward, or persuade users. An example of a designed incentive is the awarding of "points" and "levels" to users who participate in Yahoo! Answers.

Designed incentives are a manifestation of Web sites' desire to shape user contributions – often to encourage members to contribute, or to discourage low-quality content. What sorts of designed incentives are there in online systems? Which incentives work, and why? Can we exploit personalization technology to offer different incentives to different individuals for greater overall effect? In this paper, I report on related work and a research agenda to begin to answer these questions.

2 Related Work on Incentives

There is a substantial amount of work from the social sciences on the use and effectiveness of incentives for encouraging workers to be more productive. Clark and Wilson defined incentives, saying "organizations distribute incentives to individuals in order to induce them to contribute activity" and classified incentives as material, solidary, status, and purposive [4][14]. While their work examined incentives in the context of organizations, their taxonomy can be mapped to incentives in online systems to provide an analytic framework for examining system designs. Other work has looked at the effect of monetary incentives (e.g. [5]), finding that they tend to dampen people's intrinsic motivations to act. Systems such as Google Answers and MetaCafe have tied financial incentives to user contributions, and it is an open research question whether these financial rewards in fact lead to greater contributions. Oliver [12] argues that rewards and punishments have fundamental differences not just in how they motivate users, but in the resulting effects on people's propensity towards collective action. It is an interesting question whether her thesis holds when collective action consists of contributions to an online system.

To date, little work has been done on understanding online incentives in practice. An ACM GROUP 2005 workshop ("Sustaining Community: The role and design of incentive mechanisms in online systems") produced a report [7] on the role of incentives in eight online systems, and proposed a tentative framework for understanding these incentives. This work provides a nice start to understanding online incentives, but could be broadened by looking at sites across the Internet.

More work has been done to understand the effect of designed incentives on user behavior in online systems. Cheng and Vassileva conducted a series of studies in Comtella, a system built for sharing links to research papers. Comtella offers a distributed moderation interface, and allows users to receive explicit status points in the community. They found that many users acted to check their status in the system, and that users who checked their status more frequently were more inclined to act to increase their status [3]. They also found that a combination of persuasive messages and reputation-based incentives increased the amount of work users would contribute, and caused users to use the system more extensively and log in more frequently with no apparent downturn in overall system quality [2]. Beenen et al. found that goal-setting and reminding users of their uniqueness in an email message helped them to rate more movies in an online recommendation system [1]. Rashid et al. found that users are more likely to provide ratings when they can see their potential for improving recommendation quality [13].

3 Research Directions

In this section, I lay out my past and future research agenda. To date, I have studied user motivations to contribute to online communities, and I have evaluated several personalized interfaces designed to promote participation. I propose to carry this work forward by examining the use of designed incentives such as leaderboards or user status displays. I am interested in understanding whether (and why) designed incentives work, and evaluating the potential for improving these incentives through the use of personalization algorithms.

3.1 Completed Work and Work in Progress

A user must have some intrinsic or extrinsic motivation to contribute content to an online community; designed incentives may capitalize on this motivation. For example, if a user tags articles in order to help other users, an effective incentive might provide a display of how many times that user's tags have been viewed or clicked by others. To investigate user motivations to contribute to MovieLens (www.movielens.org), an online movie recommendation system, we built an economic model of the costs and benefits of rating movies [10]. Based on a survey we conducted, we found that users differ greatly in their motivations to contribute to the system. Some respondents indicated that they contribute because of the fun of rating movies, some contribute to help the system, and others contribute to get better movie recommendations. Thus, we believe that user preferences could be modeled to build interfaces or incentives that are personalized for greater effectiveness.

We followed this work by testing the idea that personalization can increase user motivation to contribute. As an experimental platform, we introduced online discussion forums into MovieLens, augmented with an entity recognition system that allows us to track which movies are mentioned in which conversational threads [6]. The augmented discussion forums allowed us to build and test a number personalization algorithms based on users' histories of movie ratings and forum use. The goal of these algorithms was to entice members to read or write forum messages. We found that some personalization algorithms had strong positive effects, while others did not. For example, compared with baseline algorithms, an algorithm displaying the presence of a potentially contentious message nearly tripled user interest, while an algorithm designed to display familiar member names or movie names had little effect [9].

We have also investigated the use of social comparisons to motivate participation in MovieLens. Just as sites like Amazon display a list of "Top Reviewers", or discussion forums display the number of posts an author has contributed, we showed members how many movies they had rated compared with others in the system. To deliver this information, we sent email messages to members with personalized information about how many movies they had rated compared with other members. We found that these messages did boost ratings activity, but potentially at the cost of lowering activity in other areas of the system [11]. Members who were below average rated the most to catch up to the norm; we speculate that interfaces that continue to show users that they have the potential for improvement may be very successful at eliciting contributions.

Finally, we have begun a study of member contributions in question and answer sites such as Google Answers, Yahoo! Answers, and AllExperts. These sites vary in their incentives to ask or answer questions, which has led to very different patterns of use. In this research, we hope to determine how well the different sites provide answers to different types of questions (e.g. questions seeking advice vs. questions seeking facts), and how the design of the site's incentives plays into their success or failure.

3.2 Future Work

In future work, I hope to continue to study interfaces that broaden participation or improve the quality of user contributions to online communities. I am especially interested in studying the use of designed incentives such as leaderboards, user status indicators, or mechanisms that allow members to earn access to system privileges. Designed incentives such as these are built purely to shape user contributions, and are becoming increasingly important in the design of online communities.

There are many aspects of designed incentives that remain poorly understood. One of my goals is to analyze and taxonomize incentives in practice and in theory. I think that understanding incentives in practice will provide researchers with a useful context for developing new types of incentives and for building personalization algorithms that adapt incentives to particular people or groups of people. This research can and should build on the extensive background in understanding organizational incentives (e.g. [4]), and the work from the ACM GROUP 2005 workshop on incentives [7]. I imagine building a framework based on social science theory relevant to the study of online incentives, then filling the framework with case studies found in practice. I am interested in receiving feedback on the appropriate scope of this work, and on the most interesting dimensions for analysis.

Another of my research goals is to develop personalization algorithms that improve the effectiveness of online incentives to participate. In MovieLens, we might develop algorithms based on users' preferences and familiarity with various system features and entities. We can use these data to infer which aspects of the system are important for the user, or to compute a user's similarity to other users in the system in terms of feature use, social interaction, and movie preferences. For example, we might compare a "standard" leaderboard to one that displays the contributions of others in a user's social network. I imagine testing these ideas in one or more controlled field studies in MovieLens. I am interested in receiving feedback from the research community on the design of such an experiment.

4 Conclusion

Designed incentives are widely used in online systems, but not well understood. I am interested in pursuing research to better understand how incentives can be used to promote positive discourse on the Internet. I believe that personalization techniques that understand user motivations and preferences can be used to improve the persuasiveness of incentives, and I am interested in investigating these techniques.

Acknowledgments. This work was made better and more fun thanks to Joe Konstan and my colleagues in GroupLens. Funding is thanks to NSF, grant IIS 03-24851.

References

1. Beenen, G., Ling, K., Wang, X., Chang, K., Frankowski, D., Resnick, P., Kraut, R.: Using social psychology to motivate contributions to online communities. CSCW (2004)
2. Cheng, R., Vassileva, J.: Design and evaluation of an adaptive incentive mechanism for sustained educational online communities. UMUAI, vol. 16(3) (2006)
3. Cheng, R., Vassileva, J.: User Motivation and Persuasion Strategy for Peer-to-Peer Communities. HICSS (2005)
4. Clark, P., Wilson, J.: Incentive Systems: A. Theory of Organizations. Administrative Science Quarterly, vol. 6(2) (1961)
5. Deci, E., Koestner, R., Ryan, R.: A Meta-Analytic Review of Experiments Examining the Effects of Extrinsic Rewards on Intrinsic Motivation. Psychological Bulletin, vol. 125(6) (1999)
6. Drenner, S., Harper, F., Frankowski, D., Riedl, J., Terveen, L.: Insert Movie Reference Here: A System to Bridge Conversation and Item-Oriented Web Sites. CHI (2006)
7. Erickson, T.: Sustaining Community – Incentive Mechanisms in Online Systems: Final Report of the Group 2005 Workshop. Unpublished (2006) http://www.visi.com/~snowfall/Group05IncentivesReport.pdf
8. Giles, J.: Internet encyclopaedias go head to head. Nature, 438 (2005)
9. Harper, F., Frankowski, D., Drenner, S., Ren, Y., Kiesler, S., Terveen, L., Kraut, R., Riedl, J.: Talk Amongst Yourselves: Inviting Users To Participat. In: Online Conversations. IUI (2007)
10. Harper, F., Li, X., Chen, Y., Konstan, J.: An Economic Model of User Rating in an Online Recommender System. UM (2005)
11. Harper, F., Li, X., Chen, Y., Konstan, J.: Social Comparisons to Motivate Contributions to an Online Community. To appear in Persuasive (2007)
12. Oliver, P.: Rewards and Punishments as Selective Incentives for Collective Action: Theoretical Investigations. The American Journal of Sociology, vol. 85(6) (1980)
13. Rashid, A., Ling, K., Tassone, R., Resnick, P., Kraut, R., Riedl, J.: Motivating Participation by Displaying the Value of Contribution. CHI (2006)
14. Wilson, J.B.: What government agencies do and why they do it. Basic Books (1989)

Semantic-Enhanced Personalised Support for Knowledge Sharing in Virtual Communities

Styliani Kleanthous

School of Computing, University of Leeds, UK
stellak@comp.leeds.ac.uk

Abstract. Virtual communities are currently one of the fastest growing applications on the web. In this research, we argue that personalised support should be tailored to the needs of the community as a whole, as opposed to adapting only to individuals. Based on *4 processes* identified as important, we propose a computational framework that includes the extraction of a comprehensive *community model* and the deployment of that model to provide *support* adapted to the effective functioning of a community.

1 Introduction

Virtual communities (VCs), where people with common interests and goals communicate, share resources, and construct knowledge, are currently one of the fastest growing web environments [9]. In this research, we consider closely-knit communities[1] that may exist in either organisational or educational context and have the following characteristics: common purpose, identified by the participants or a facilitator; commitment to the sharing of information and generation of new knowledge; shared resources; high level of dialogue, interaction and collaboration; equal membership inside the community. A common misconception is to believe that a virtual community will be effective when people and technology are present [3]. Appropriate support for the effective functioning of online communities is paramount. In this line, personalisation and adaptation can play a crucial role, as illustrated by recent user modelling approaches that support social web-groups (e.g. [2, 11]).

However, personalisation research has mainly focused on adapting to the needs of individual members, as opposed to supporting communities to function as a whole [8]. We argue that effective support tailored to VCs requires considering the wholeness of the community and facilitating the processes that influence the success of knowledge sharing and collaboration. Although initial attempts show applicability of user modelling approaches to provide personalised support to a VC by encouraging participation [1, 2], participation per se cannot guarantee the success of knowledge sharing. To the best of our knowledge, there is no holistic community adaptation framework that aims at supporting the key processes of effective knowledge sharing.

---

[1] To keep this research focused, we exclude loosely structured communities, such as de Del.icio.us or CiteUlike.com, although some of the approaches discussed here can be applicable to such communities.

C. Conati, K. McCoy, and G. Paliouras (Eds.): UM 2007, LNAI 4511, pp. 465–469, 2007.
© Springer-Verlag Berlin Heidelberg 2007

Research in organisational psychology [10] has identified that effective teams and groups operating in the boundaries of an organisation build *transactive memory*, develop *shared mental models*, establish *cognitive consensus*, and become aware of who their *cognitively central* and *peripheral* members are . Since we are dealing with closely-knit communities with characteristics similar to those of groups and teams, the above processes can also be applied to a broader context to inform what support should be provided to a VC.

- **Transactive Memory (TM)** deals with the relationship between the memory system of individuals and the communication that occurs between them.
- **Shared Mental Models (SMM)** is all members' shared understanding of the key elements and processes of the community's relevant environment.
- **Cognitive consensus (CCs)** deals with shared conceptualisations between members and shared understanding of the meaning concepts encapsulate.
- **Cognitive Centrality (CCen)** considers the importance of the contribution of individual members with regard to the community's context.

Our review of computational methods that address TM, SMM, CCen, and CCs considering several representative systems[2], revealed that although the four processes have been partially supported, the absence of a complete community model, the personalisation and adaptation to the individual rather than the community, and the ignorance or partial use of tracking data, compose the main obstacles to their holistic success [8]. The majority of the studies undertaken so far lack a purpose built framework which will enable holistic personalisation to VC. This research aims at filling that gap with the development of a rigorous framework based on a comprehensive community model and using that model to support the building of TM, SMM, CCs and identification of CCen inside a VC.

2   Aims and Objectives of This Research

Our research is based on the following assumptions: (a) providing adaptation tailored to the community as a whole will help the community perform better; and (b) facilitating the building of TM, development of SMM, establishment of CCs and identifying CCen inside VC, will improve the functioning of the community.

Based on these assumptions, the following research questions have been derived:

- How to extract a computational model to represent the functioning and evolution of VC as a whole, using semantically enhanced tracking data?
- Using that model, how to provide personalised functionality to support the development of TM, building of SMM, establishment of CCs and identification of CCen?
- How can personalised support of the above processes affect the functioning of the community?

To deal with the above questions, we propose a computational framework, which consists of two major parts. The first deals with the development of a community model that represents the whole community and is informed by the 4 processes. The

[2] References are provided through [8].

second deals with the application of the model to offer adaptive support to improve the functioning of the community. Fig.1 illustrates the architecture of the framework following the general architecture of user-adaptive systems defined in [7].

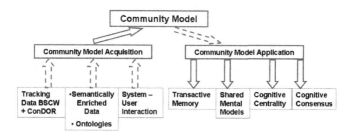

Fig. 1. Computational Framework for holistic personalised support to VC

3 Methodology and Progress to Date

We will outline the steps being undertaken in this research and will point at the progress to date (this PhD project is approaching the end of year one):

Formalisation of the input: This is the initial stage which includes: specifying the format of the tracking data, choosing appropriate metadata fields, and identifying the role of ontology. We have two years' tracking data from an existing VC of some 25 researchers with common interests working together and sharing documents with the BSCW[3] system. Information held concerns *Hierarchies of Folders (H_F), Folders (F), Resources (R), Members (M)* and *Actions (A)* that can affect the community *Environment (E)*. We also have data from ConDOR[4] [6] which provides us with the structure of *Discussions (D)*. In the *Resource* element we store data created by users (*RCreatedData*), and formal metadata (*RMetadata[5]*). The input formalisation stage has been completed and the data is prepared for processing in the next stage. Metadata extraction from the uploaded resources is being performed.

An existing ontology will be imported and used in this research to extend our knowledge upon the data we are dealing with. It is envisaged that the ontology will be in RDF or OWL, and an appropriate reasoner for extracting knowledge will be used.

Definition and validation of the community model: At this stage, the structure of the community model is defined, algorithms to extract this model from the input data are implemented, and the model is appropriately validated. Currently, the structure of the community model has been defined. To represent the whole community we consider: *individual user models*, a *relationships model*, *community context* represented by an *ontology*, lists of the *popular* and *peripheral topics*, and a list of the *cognitively central members*.

---

[3] BSCW (Basic Support for Cooperative Work) is a popular robust tool for knowledge sharing, which has been developed at Fraunhofer Institute of Technology, Germany.

[4] ConDOR (Construction of Dynamic Open Resources) is a tool to support collaborative writing and knowledge sharing, which has been developed at the University of Leeds.

[5] The metadata follows Dublin Core Education http://dublincore.org/groups/education/

An individual user model represents a single member and includes user interests, type of participation (e.g. uploading resources, initiating discussions), level of the user's cognitive centrality, relationships the user has with other members in the community, and personal hierarchies of folders and resources created by this member.

Relationships within VC are important. We have identified four types of relationships which can exist between two users: *ReadRes(A,B)* – member *A* reads resources uploaded by member *B*, *ReadDisc(A,B)* – *A* reads discussions initiated by *B*, *UploadSim(A,B)* - *A* and *B* upload similar resources, *InterestSim(A,B)* - *A* and *B* have similar interests, and *ReadSim(A,B)* – *A* and *B* read similar resources. We have defined simple statistical measures for *ReadRes* and *ReadDisc*. To identify the *UploadSim* and *ReadSim* similarities, association rule mining algorithms will be used. A classification algorithm can be adopted for the *InterestSim* type of relationship to be derived, where user interests can be classified under the ontology classes in order to identify similar user interests. Definition of these algorithms is under development.

Relationships are also important to define a person's position in the community. Graph centrality, as studied in social networks research [4], can define a member's centrality due to his relationships and can be distinguished in three types. *Degree Centrality* represents the relationships a person has with others in the community, *Centrality of Betweeness* represents the ability of a person to control the communication between two other people in the community, and finally *Closeness Centrality* can be related to the peripherality of a person (e.g how distant he/she is from the other VC members). The edge on the graph represents the total relationship between two people. We have derived formulas to calculate relationships as a sum of all the relationships. This approach extends the algorithms in [1].

Changes of members' interests or participation can be captured to model the *evolution of the community*. This is a crucial point in the community extraction algorithms we are developing, and is being dealt with at the moment. Currently, we examine the applicability of approaches that measure graph changes, e.g. [11].

Following the layered evaluation methodology of adaptive applications [5], appropriate evaluation is needed to assess whether the model is complete and how well the elements included reflect the characteristics of the community. In this preliminary evaluation phase, the existing data of the BSCW community will be used to check if the model can detect user's characteristics and relationships and the community's characteristics and maintained those in a comprehensive model.

Application of the community model for the generation of community-tailored support: The third step is to define how the community model can be used in a VC in order to decide what activities will be needed to support the 4 processes. This will lead to the implementation of push factors and will be tailored to both newly joining members (newcomers) and existing members (oldtimers) along with the community evolution and resource organisation. This stage has not commenced yet, we have currently identified basic level of support based on literature review [8].

Support to *newcomers* and *oldtimers* can be in the form of pop-up messages with useful information for the member. Use of different colour or size of letters can be used to emphasise relevant topics in the community's common interface. Useful information about the task at hand, along with information to promote awareness in the community, can help members to integrate and motivate them to contribute to the community.

Following the second phase of the layered evaluation of adaptive applications [5], the adaptation decisions will be evaluated prior to the complete system integration.

Framework deployment: This step includes extending a traditional VC system with the algorithms for community model extraction and adaptation developed in the second and third part of the methodology. The demonstrator will validate the framework. At this stage, appropriate tests of the system will be carried out.

Evaluation with users: Formative and summative evaluation techniques [5] will be used for system evaluation. A form of formative evaluation will take place in the second, third and fourth part of the methodology. Summative evaluation will be performed after the system is extended with the adaptive functionality and we ensure that it works properly.

4 Expected Contribution to Knowledge

The novelty of this research lays primarily in the development of the community model based on the 4 processes, and the exploitation of that model to provide personalised support to the whole community. With this PhD project, we expect to contribute to the user modelling and adaptive learning systems research communities with: (a) a novel framework for holistic personalised support in VC, (b) a mechanism for extracting and maintaining a community model based on the 4 processes, and (c) deployment of the community model to provide holistic support to a VC.

References

1. Bretzke, H., Vassileva, J.: Motivating Cooperation on Peer to Peer Networks. In: Brusilovsky, P., Corbett, A.T., de Rosis, F. (eds.) UM 2003. LNCS, vol. 2702, Springer, Heidelberg (2003)
2. Cheng, R., Vassileva, J.: Design and Evaluation of an Adaptive Incentive Mechanism for Sustained Educational Online Communities. UMUAI journal 16(3), 348 (2006)
3. Fischer, G., Ostwald, J.: Knowledge Management: Problems, Promises, Realities, and Challenges. IEEE Intelligent Systems 16(1), 60–72 (2001)
4. Freeman, L.: Centrality in social networks conceptual clarification. Social Networks 1(3), 239 (1979)
5. Gena, C., Weibelzahl, S.: Usability Engineering for the Adaptive Web. In: P. Brusilovsky, et al. (eds.): The Adaptive Web: Methods and Strategies of Web Personalization, Springer (To appear)
6. Gonzalez-Barahona, J., et al.: Towards Community-Driven Development of Educational Materials: The Edukalibre Approach. In: Proceedings of 1st, ECTEL06. LNCS, Springer, Heidelberg (2006)
7. Jameson, A.: Adaptive Interfaces and Agents. In: Jacko, J.A., Sears, A. (eds.) Human-Computer Interaction Handbook, Erlbaum, Mahwah, NJ (2003)
8. Kleanthous, S., Dimitrova, V.: Towards a Holistic Personalised Support for Knowledge Sharing in Virtual Learning Communities. Workshop on TEL CoP, Crete, Greece (2006)
9. Lazar, J., Preece, J.: Social Considerations in Online Communities: Usability, Sociability, and Success Factors. In: Cognition in the Digital World, Lawrence Erlbaum, Mahwah, NJ (2002)
10. Mohammed, S., Dumville, B.C.: Team mental models in a team knowledge framework: expanding theory and measurement across disciplinary boundaries. Journal of Organizational Behavior 22(2), 89–106 (2001)
11. Song, X.: ExpertiseNet: Relational and Evolutionary Expert Modeling. In: Ardissono, L., Brna, P., Mitrović, A. (eds.) UM 2005. LNCS (LNAI), vol. 3538, Springer, Heidelberg (2005)

Explaining Recommendations

Nava Tintarev

Department of Computing Science, University of Aberdeen, UK
ntintare@csd.abdn.ac.uk

Abstract. This thesis investigates the properties of a good explanation in a movie recommender system. Beginning with a summarized literature review, we suggest seven criteria for evaluation of explanations in recommender systems. This is followed by an attempt to define the properties of a useful explanation, using a movie review corpus and focus groups. We conclude with planned experiments and evaluation.

1 Research Area

Explanations in intelligent systems began with expert systems which were predominantly based on heuristics [1], but also on case-based reasoning (CBR) [2], and model based approaches [3]. In recent years more commercial or entertainment inclined expert systems called recommender systems have begun to offer explanations as well [4,5,6]. These systems represent user preferences for the purpose of suggesting items to purchase or examine, i.e. recommendations. An explanation in this type of system is formulated along the lines of *"Item A is recommended to you because..."*. The justification following may depend on the underlying recommendation algorithm (e.g. content-based, collaborative-based). Explanations are also intrinsically linked to the way recommendations are presented and the degree of interactivity, see [7] for an in-depth discussion.

The recommender systems community is reaching a consensus that accuracy metrics such as mean average error (MAE), precision and recall, can only partially evaluate a recommender system [8]. User satisfaction, and derivatives thereof such as serendipity [8], diversity [9] and trust [10] are increasingly seen as important. The definition of a *good* explanation is still largely open, and the ways in which explanations can contribute to a recommender system will be the topic of my thesis.

2 Aims and Objectives

The aim of our research is to provide explanations that are optimal for a given user and given criterion (e.g. Trust, see Section 3.1). Our objectives are, for a selection of criteria, to:

C. Conati, K. McCoy, and G. Paliouras (Eds.): UM 2007, LNAI 4511, pp. 470–474, 2007.
© Springer-Verlag Berlin Heidelberg 2007

Table 1. Criteria

Criteria	Definition
Transparency	Explain how the system works
Scrutability	Allow users to tell the system it is wrong
Trust	Increase users' confidence in the system
Effectiveness	Help users make good decisions
Persuasiveness	Convince users to try or buy (also called conversion)
Efficiency	Help users make decisions faster
Satisfaction	Increase the ease of usability or enjoyment

- decide upon metrics; *e.g. Trust - increased usage, users return to system.*
- investigate what constitutes optimal content; *what content optimizes Trust?*
- investigate what constitutes optimal length; *which length optimizes Trust?*
- build and evaluate an explanation generation system.

We believe that explanations should take into consideration which properties are important for each user. For instance, [5] showed poor acceptance for explanations using information about the user's favorite actor or actress. It would seem plausible that this property (actor/actress) is more important to some users than others. In fact, this is likely to be the case, given that the variance in acceptance for this type of explanations was exceptionally high. Also, we would like to follow in the footsteps of [11,10] who suggest that concise explanations may be more persuasive and trust inducing respectively.

In later stages of our work we plan to evaluate our conclusions by incorporating explanations into a movie recommender system, using the Duine toolkit[1].

3   Work Done So Far

3.1   Criteria

To determine what makes a good explanation, it is first necessary to consider the ways in which explanations can be evaluated. In a literature survey (see [7] for details) we have identified seven different criteria by which explanations for single recommendations have been evaluated with users in the past: transparency [12], scrutability [13], trust [10,14], effectiveness [1], persuasiveness [5], efficiency [15], and satisfaction [16]. We describe each criteria briefly in Table 1. A tentative definition of metrics can be found in [7].

3.2   Analysis of Review Corpus

Having determined the possible advantages of explanations as criteria, we chose to investigate if there is a difference between explanations that were considered useful for deciding whether or not to watch a movie, i.e. *Effective* explanations.

---

[1] Telematica Instituut: http://duine.sf.net

Table 2. Properties with frequency counts

Cast (28)	Good in its genre (26)	Initial expectations (22)	Script (19)
Visuals and atmosphere (18)	Suites mood (18)	Realistic (15)	Director (12)
Subject matter (12)	Easy viewing (8)	Repulsive or violent (7)	Kids (7)
Dialogs (6)	Pace (5)	Soundtrack (5)	Original (5)
Studio (2)	Sex (1)		

For this purpose we analyzed 74 user reviews [2] of DVD movies on the British Amazon website [3]. Amazon's reviews are particularly suitable for analysis. The reviews themselves are rated by other users as useful or not. This function may reflect not only what kind of reviews people write, but also what kind of reviews people like to *read*. The corpus referred to 37 movies, each with one useful and one non-useful review. Each review was voted useful/non-useful by at least half, but not less than five of the voters.

In a parallel study of 49 reviews, for 49 different movies, we investigated which properties were mentioned the most often (see Table 2). These properties were based on an informal exploration of reviews on the MovieLens [4] website . For each review, we recorded the frequency of mentioned properties. A property was awarded a point for each mention, regardless of whether it was in favor or disfavor of the movie.

Results: Table 3 summarizes the general properties of useful and non-useful reviews. Useful reviews were longer ($p < 0.01$), and included (a longer) synopsis ($p<0.01$). We also found that useful reviews were more linguistically complex, with a higher Flesch-Kincaid Grade Level ($p<0.01$). The difference for the percentage of passive sentences was not significant however.

Table 3. Mean values for amazon reviews

	total length (words)	synopsis length (words)	% Passive	Grade level
Useful	294.3	87.6	10.6	9.9
Non-Useful	102	3.0	6.1	8.0

We found that reviewers referenced a particular character, rather than the actor or actress. Often, users mentioned that the type of movie was what they would or would not expect in the genre, such as *"the best comedy that I have ever seen"*. Initial expectations were often influenced by adaptations from books, previous releases, awards, and previous reviews.

---

[2] Although reviews are not identical to explanations within a recommender system, we believe that they are sufficiently similar to deduce properties of a useful explanation.

[3] http://amazon.co.uk

[4] http://movielens.umn.edu/

3.3   Focus Groups

To investigate how these properties could be applied to explanations, two focus groups with a total of 11 participants were conducted. In these focus groups the participants described movies they had seen; their initial expectations, their reactions after seeing the movie, what it was that formed their opinion of the movie and what kind of explanation they would like to receive. A limited summary follows below.

- The decisive properties for seeing a movie varied between users e.g. director, script complexity, dialogs, genre, and subject matter.
- Movies seen with groups of friends were often "light, easy viewing", with simpler scripts than those viewed in more intimate company or alone. Light movies were also preferred before a mentally demanding activity such as an exam.
- Participants did not want to be dissuaded from watching movies, even if it would have helped them avoid watching a movie they had not enjoyed in the past. Social effects such as movie popularity and an outing with friends were often in play.
- Some properties were more descriptive, such as cast, filming location, and black and white. This became particularly clear when participants attempted to clarify the identity of a movie.
- Reviews may help users enjoy movies more, rather than serve merely as decision aids. Participants believed that correcting faulty expectations of a movie would not influence whether or not they saw it. Rather, it could increase their acceptance upon viewing, and save potential disappointment.

4   Planned Work and Conclusion

We plan to conduct a number of experiments in order to refine our idea of how explanations should be presented in natural language. In one study participants will be asked to compare sets of reviews controlled for scenario, and type of movie properties. They will be asked to edit these reviews as well as to specify which of the properties from a list should be mentioned in a review of this movie. A second study will target the question of balancing the number of properties to mention versus the amount of detail. We will also compare different interfaces, and user preferences for text versus graphics.

The final model of explanations will be implemented in a movie recommender system. Our aim is to evaluate the system with users, according to several of the criteria mentioned in Section 3.1. For example a likely metric for *Effectiveness* is the difference in rating for a movie upon recommendation, and after viewing [4]. We plan to compare the system with and without explanations for each criterion, and also measure criteria against each other (e.g. longer explanations inspire *Trust* but decrease *Efficiency*).

We hope that our work on explanations will contribute to the field of recommender systems, via an understanding of how to personalize explanations, and how much content to present.

References

1. Buchanan, B.G., Shortliffe, E.H. (eds.): 30-35. In: The Rule-Based Expert Systems: The MYCIN Experiments of the Stanford Heuristic Programming Project, pp. 571–665 Addison-Wesley Publishing Company (1985)
2. Doyle, D., Tsymbal, A., Cunningham, P.: A review of explanation and explanation in case-based reasoning. Technical report, Department of Computer Science, Trinity College, Dublin (2003)
3. Druzdzel, M.J.: Qualitative verbal explanations in bayesian belief networks. Artificial Intelligence and Simulation of Behaviour Quarterly, special issue on Bayesian networks, pp. 43–54 (1996)
4. Bilgic, M., Mooney, R.J.: Explaining recommendations: Satisfaction vs. promotion. In: Beyond Personalization Workshop, IUI (2005)
5. Herlocker, J.L., Konstan, J.A., Riedl, J.: Explaining collaborative filtering recommendations. In: Computer Supported Cooperative Work (2000)
6. Mcsherry, D.: Explanation in recommender systems. Artificial Intelligence Review 24(2), 179–197 (2005)
7. Tintarev, N., Masthoff, J.: A survey of explanations in recommender systems. In: WPRSIUI associated with ICDE (2007)
8. McNee, S.M., Riedl, J., Konstan, J.A.: Being accurate is not enough: How accuracy metrics have hurt recommender systems. In: Extended Abstracts of CHI (2006)
9. Ziegler, C.N., McNee, S.M., Konstan, J.A., Lausen, G.: Improving recommendation lists through topic diversification. In: WWW'05 (2005)
10. Chen, L., Pu, P.: Trust building in recommender agents. In: WPRSIU'02 (2002)
11. Carenini, G.J., Moore, J.: An empirical study of the influence of argument conciseness on argument effectiveness. In: Proceedings of the 38th Annual Meeting of the Association for Computational Linguistics (2000)
12. Sinha, R., Swearingen, K.: The role of transparency in recommender systems. In: Conference on Human Factors in Computing Systems (2002)
13. Czarkowski, M.: Evaluating scrutable adaptive hypertext. In: 10th International Conference on User Modeling, Workshop 3: Evaluation of Adaptive Systems (2005)
14. Swearingen, K., Sinha, R.: Interaction design for recommender systems. In: Designing Interactive Systems (2002)
15. Thompson, C.A., Göker, M.H., Langley, P.: A personalized system for conversational recommendations. J. Artif. Intell. Res (JAIR) 21, 393–428 (2004)
16. Sinha, R., Swearingen, K.: Comparing recommendations made by online systems and friends. In: DELOS-NSF Workshop on Personalization and Recommender Systems in Digital Libraries (2001)

Designing Persuasive Health Behaviour Change Dialogs

Hien Nguyen

hnguyen@csd.abdn.ac.uk

Abstract. Using theories of behaviour change, argumentation theory, and findings in social psychology, our research explores new methods to raise the persuasiveness of adaptive dialog-based systems using tailored arguments and onscreen characters to enhance the system's credibility and trustworthiness. Initial results revealed the existence of individual preferences for arguments, types of communication, and appearance of onscreen characters. In the future, we will explore methods to learn these preferences through interactions with the user, and to utilize them to maximize the persuasion effect of the system. The final outcome of the research will be a persuasion model that is capable of modelling the user's cognitive and affective state and generating tailored arguments to move the user in the desired direction.

1 Introduction

More and more people use the Internet to seek out health related information [1]. Thus, Internet-based automated systems have the potential to provide users with an equivalence of the "ideal" one-on-one, tailored interaction with an expert to adopt health promoting behaviour more economically and conveniently. Even if these systems are less effective than actual one-on-one counselling, they still result in a greater impact due to their ability to reach more users (impact = efficacy x reach) [2].

Among automated content generation systems, dialog-based systems are argued to be particularly effective for providing health education and affecting health behaviour change [2]. By adding speech and nonverbal conversational modalities (e.g., facial expressions), such systems can also convey social cues and emotions to enhance their trustworthiness and credibility, thereby their persuasiveness [3].

Our research explores new methods to raise the persuasiveness of adaptive dialog-based systems using tailored arguments (section 2) and onscreen characters (section 3). This paper discusses our underlying theoretical framework, goals and some preliminary results.

2 Generating Persuasive Arguments

Most effective health behaviour change programs implement interventions based on theories of behaviour change, which suggest *why* and *how* people change their habits (see [4]). Among them, the Transtheoretical Model of Behaviour Change (TTM) [5] is the most widely used and has proven to have reasonable success in a variety of

C. Conati, K. McCoy, and G. Paliouras (Eds.): UM 2007, LNAI 4511, pp. 475–479, 2007.
© Springer-Verlag Berlin Heidelberg 2007

contexts such as: smoking cessation, low fat diets, etc. The theory has been argued the most suitable for dialog-based systems [4], and applied in a number of scenarios [6,7]. It proposes that individuals go through five *stages of change* before change is actually achieved. Each stage is accompanied by a *set of signs* explaining why they are in such a stage. To move to the next stage, an individual usually applies a number of overt and covert activities, or *processes of change*. Different processes are differentially effective in each stage (see [5] for details).

While TTM can help to define the high-level communicative goals of a dialog (e.g. to move an individual from "thinking about changing" to "planning to take actions" by recommending appropriate action plans), argumentation theories provide strategies to express these goals in the most effective way. Firstly, argumentation schemas provide a way to connect premises and conclusions to make arguments (more) acceptable (e.g. argument from expert opinion) [8,9]. A number of guidelines is also provided for selecting, ordering the conclusions, supporting and opposing evidence of an argument as summarized in [10]. Finally, Rhetorical Structure Theory (RST) [11] helps to enhance the coherence of an argument.

Social psychology also suggests characteristics of the audience that can affect an argument's acceptability. The two most mentioned are: *message discrepancy* and *receiver involvement*. On any given topic, there are likely to be a variety of points of view, or positions (e.g., extremely against, extremely supportive, or neutral). *Message discrepancy* refers to the difference between the audience's existing position and that advocated in a message. Research (see [3] for a full review) has shown that while discrepancy enhances persuasiveness, extremely discrepant messages that fall in the audience's *latitude of rejection* (positions that they find unacceptable) may be discounted, counter-argued against, or perceived as more discrepant than they objectively are. Any of these outcomes could impair their persuasiveness. *Receiver involvement* reflects what outcomes are important to the audience (e.g. parents whose children are about to go to college may have more involvement with proposals to increase tuition fees), and also affects persuasion. It enhances the efficacy of strong messages and limits that of weak messages.

Persuasion can be enhanced at every aspect mentioned above. One common suggestion of all these theories is that to enhance persuasion, arguments should be tailored to the user's knowledge, values and preferences. However, regardless of the considerable amount of research in this field, persuasive argument generation systems [6,7,10,12,13] mostly use hard-coded rules that utilise no or very little background of the users. Hence, using theories mentioned above as our theoretical framework, our research aims to develop a *persuasion model* that can represent:

1. The reasons why the user does not want to or cannot move to the next stage.
2. Strategies (processes of change) that can help the user to overcome obstacles.
3. A repertoire of arguments expressing these strategies.

The model enables us to generate arguments that: (1) represent the most beneficial processes of change for the current state of the user, (2) are constructed from schemas found acceptable the user, (3) consist of evidence found convincing by the user, (4) have not been defeated before, (5) are relevant, (6) and do not fall into his/her latitude of rejection. This leads to the following research questions:

- **RQ1:** How to learn the user's preferences for arguments based on past interactions (e.g., which sources (expert, similar individuals/groups), or types of evidence (statistical data, concrete examples) he/she find more convincing)?
- **RQ2:** How to select the most persuasive argument based on the user's preferences (e.g., is the source more important than the strength of the argument)?
- **RQ3:** How to classify arguments according to their corresponding process of change, relevance, and their discrepancy with the user's current position?

3   Designing Persuasive User Interfaces with Onscreen Characters

In persuasive communication, social psychology suggests that the source itself can also influence the persuasiveness of the message. The three most recognized characteristics of the source that influence its persuasiveness are *perceived credibility*, *likeability* and *similarity* [3]. *Appearance cues* of the source (e.g. a white lab coat can make one a doctor or a scientist), as well as *physical attractiveness* have been shown to affect perceived credibility. Furthermore, onscreen characters have been acknowledged to have positive effects on the users' attitudes and experience of interaction (see [14,15] for a literature review).

This has inspired us to investigate more effective ways to utilize onscreen characters to enhance the system's trustworthiness and credibility, and reduce users' boredom when using the system. Currently, we explore a number of issues including:

- **RQ4:** Whether social appearance of a highly credible source enhances persuasion. If so, how we can design onscreen characters that can be perceived highly credible.
- **RQ5:** Which type of interaction is more appropriate when using a team of animated agents to present information: *indirect interaction* (where the user listens to a conversation among the agents) or *direct interaction* (where the user converses with the agents)?

4   Work Done So Far

With respect to the effect of onscreen characters on users' perception, we have set up a series of experiments to explore whether showing the source visually in the form of a static image increases the perceived credibility of the message [14]. Our results suggest that adding an image of a highly credible source (regarding the topic discussed in the message) can increase the message's perceived credibility, but that of a lowly credible source can damage it. The source's perceived credibility regarding a topic can be influenced by his/her appearance. In our experiments, appearance influences the most likely profession of the source perceived by the participants, which influences their perceived expertness on a topic. For instance, if a source is perceived as a doctor, it is perceived to have higher credibility if talking about the health benefits of exercise, but lower credibility when talking about fitness programs. The opposite holds for a source perceived as a sport instructor (see [14] for details).

The above experiments were followed by two experiments investigating the persuasive effects on the audience's attitudes of direct versus indirect communication, one-sided versus two-sided messages, and one agent versus a team presenting the message [15]. Our second experiment suggests that dialog-based systems with the visual appearance of a conversational agent(s) are preferred over systems that use text only, as they are perceived to be more personal and caring, less boring, and to some extent easier to follow. When comparing our four dialog-based systems, we found somewhat conflicting results. Experiment 1 suggested a clear trend in which a two-sided message presented in an indirect communication was the most persuasive, followed by a two-sided message presented in a direct communication, a one-sided message presented by one agent, and a one-sided message presented by a team of agents (see [15] for details).

With respect to the effect of the receiver on persuasion, in three experiments, we have explored how the receiver's position can be modelled computationally, as a function of the strength, involvement, and position of arguments in a set [16]. An accurate prediction of a receiver's position after hearing one or more arguments may help a persuasive system to select the next argument to present (e.g. by choosing one that is sufficiently discrepant to maximize its effect, but does not fall in the latitude of rejection). In the first experiment, subjects rated the position and strength of 56 arguments on nuclear power. Subjects were more consistent in rating position than strength. With regards to position, the most variation seems to arise when an argument contains elements that can be seen as against nuclear power as well as elements that can be seen as in favour. This can be explained by the concept of receiver involvement discussed in section 2. With regards to strength, there was a lot of variation in the subjects' rationale. Some subjects mentioned the credibility of the source, some did not trust percentage data while others saw it as evidence, some subjects regarded an argument stronger if it was two-sided. This confirmed that there is a need to learn the user's argument preferences. More work is needed to determine how to model individual user differences in the judgement of strength. In the second and the third experiments, participants were asked to judge a fictional character's reaction after hearing a single argument or set of arguments given a specific scenario. The arguments differed with respect to strength, position, and involvement. We found that a strong, highly discrepant argument has more persuasive effect than a weak, less discrepant argument ($p<.05$). A strong argument was found to have more impact than a weak argument, given that the two argument are roughly equally lowly discrepant ($p<.005$). A strong, but less discrepant argument was found to have significantly more effect than a weak, but more discrepant argument ($p<.05$). While people definitely consider argument strength when perceiving arguments, we could not conclude whether the argument's position is taken into account (see [16] for details).

5   Conclusions

This paper discusses two branches of our research: (1) generating tailored arguments using TTM, argumentation theories, and findings in social psychology on persuasion as our theoretical framework, and (2) utilizing onscreen characters to enhance the system's credibility and trustworthiness.

The first phase of the research focuses on studying individual preferences people might have for arguments, types of communication, appearance of onscreen characters. The second phase of the research explores new methods to learn these preferences through interactions with the user, and to utilize them to maximise the persuasion effect of the system. The final outcome is a persuasion model that is capable of modelling the user's cognitive and affective state and generating tailored arguments to move the user in the desired direction. All findings will be incorporated into a proof-of-concept system in the domain of promoting healthy behaviour.

References

1. Pew: Internet health resources, Washington, DC, Pew Internet & American Life Project (2003)
2. Bickmore, T.: Methodological review: Health dialog systems for patients and consumers. Journal of Biomedical Informatics 39(5), 556–571 (2006)
3. Stiff, J.B., Mongeau, P.A.: Persuasive Communication, 2nd edn. The Guilford Press (2002)
4. Migneault, J.P., Farzanfar, R., Wright, J.A., Friedman, R.H.: How to write health dialog for a talking computer. Journal of Biomedical Informatics 39(5), 468–481 (2006)
5. Prochaska, J.O., Norcross, J.C.: Stages of change. Psychotherapy 38(4), 443–448 (2001)
6. Cavalluzzi, A., Carofiglio, V., de Rosis, F.: Affective Advice Giving Dialogs, Tutorial and Research Workshop on Affective Dialogue Systems (2004)
7. Grasso, F., Cawsey, A., Jones, R.: Dialectical argumentation to solve conflicts in advice giving: a case study in the promotion of healthy nutrition. Journal of Human-Computer Studies 53, 1077–1115 (2000)
8. Perelman, C., Olbrechts-Tyteca, L.: The New Rhetoric: a Treatise on Argumentation, University of Notre Dame, Notre Dame Press (1969)
9. Walton, D.: Argumentation Schemes for Presumptive Reasoning. Erlbaum, Mahwah, N.J (1996)
10. Carenini, G., Moore, J.: A strategy for generating evaluative arguments. In: Proceedings of the Fisrt International Conference on Natural Language Generation, pp. 47–54 (2000)
11. Mann, W., Thompson, S.: Rhetorical structure theory: toward a functional theory of text organization. Text. 8, 243–281 (1988)
12. Reiter, E., Robertson, R., Osman, L.: Lessons from a failure: generating tailored smoking cessation letters. Artificial Intelligence 144, 41–58 (2003)
13. Guerini, M.: Persuasion Models for Multimodal Message Generation, PhD thesis (2006)
14. Nguyen, H., Masthoff, J.: Is it me or is it what I say? Source image and persuasion. In: Proceedings of the 2nd International Conference on Persuasive Technology (Palo Alto, California) (In press) (2007)
15. Nguyen, H., Masthoff, J., Edwards, P.: Persuasive effects of embodied conversational agent teams. In: Proceedings of 12th International Conference on Human-Computer Interaction (Beijing, China) (In press) (2007)
16. Nguyen, H., Masthoff, J., Edwards, P.: Modelling a receiver's position to persuasive arguments. In: Proceedings of the 2nd International Conference on Persuasive Technology (Palo Alto, California) (In press) (2007)

User-Centered Design for Personalized Access to Cultural Heritage

Yiwen Wang

Eindhoven University of Technology
P.O. Box 513, 5600 MB Eindhoven, The Netherlands
y.wang@tue.nl

Abstract. The volume of digital cultural heritage is huge and rapidly growing. The overload of art information has created the need to help people find out what they like in the enormous museum collections and provide them with the most convenient access point. In this paper, we present a research plan to address these issues. Our approach involves: (1) use of ontologies as shared vocabularies and thesauri to model the domain of art; (2) an interactive ontology-based elicitation of user interests and preferences in art to be stored as an extended overlay user model; (3) RDF/OWL reasoning strategies for predicting users' interests and generating recommendations; and (4) The Rijksmuseum Amsterdam use case for a personalized museum tour combining both the virtual Web space and the physical museum space to enhance the users' experience. We follow a user-centered design for collecting requirements, testing out design choices and evaluating stages of our prototypes.

Keywords: CHIP (Cultural Heritage Information Presentation), user-centered design, user modeling, personalization, Semantic Web, RDF, recommendations.

1 Introduction

Since early 2005 the CHIP research team has been working at the Rijksmuseum Amsterdam within the context of the Cultural Heritage Information Personalization project, part of the Dutch Science Foundation funded program CATCH [1] for Continuous Access to Cultural Heritage in the Netherlands. CHIP is a collaborative project of the Rijksmuseum Amsterdam, the Technische Universiteit Eindhoven and the Telematica Instituut. As a PhD student, I joined this project in July, 2006 when it has already been running for a year. As mediators between the technical and the art worlds, working inside the museum allowed us to realize a real application-driven approach by performing frequent interviews with curators and collection managers as well as having a close contact with real museum visitors to extract realistic use cases and requirements. CHIP aims to provide personalized experience for various visitors to allow for the disclosure of the rich Rijksmuseum collection. In this

---

[1] CATCH project: http://www.now.nl/catch

C. Conati, K. McCoy, and G. Paliouras (Eds.): UM 2007, LNAI 4511, pp. 480–484, 2007.
© Springer-Verlag Berlin Heidelberg 2007

context, my PhD research goal is to explore the following: (1) an ontology-based domain model to bridge the visitor-expert vocabulary gap; (2) interactive user modeling to collect user characteristics and preferences; (3) providing optimal response with regard to the computational complexity of adaptive recommender systems and; (4) designing use cases for adaptive recommender systems, e.g. a personalized museum tour.

The rest of this paper is organized as follows: Section 2 describes the background and research problems. In section 3, we present a brief description of the state of the CHIP project, focusing on personalization in museum collections, the CHIP recommender system and the RDF/OWL domain model. Section 4 discusses the main research questions, the approach and evaluation study results. Finally, section 5 presents a work plan of the PhD project.

2 Background and Problem Statement

Since Picard outlined the need for personalization of online museum collections in 1997 [1], there have been various examples of museums directing their efforts to provide personalized services to users. The CHIP project is now in the process of exploring various tours from famous museums inside/outside the Netherlands (e.g. Multimedia/PDA tour[2] at Van Gogh museum, Online tour at Tate Modern[3] and Guided/Audio tour at the Rijksmuseum Amsterdam) in order to extract requirements to build personalized museum tours on mobile devices. In this area, the PEACH project[4] shows that creating an interactive and personalized guide can enhance the cultural heritage appreciation of the individual users. Other studies show that personalization enables the change of the museum mass communication paradigm into a user-centered interactive information exchange, where the 'museum monologue turns into a dialogue', and becomes 'a new communication stratagem based on a continuous process of collaboration, learning and adaptation between the museum and its visitors' [2].

However, despite large investments and efforts, the cultural heritage/museum domain encounters a number of obstacles/problems, as illustrated in Figure 1. Problems 5-6 are the core problems in this research. A main bottleneck here is the vocabulary gap between descriptions of the collections created by domain experts, which do not align with the implicit and often not domain related preferences of the end users. Moreover, there is a vast space of possibilities and perspectives in which museum collections can be presented to the end users.

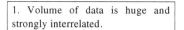

1. Volume of data is huge and strongly interrelated.

2. Digitization progress is slow.

3. Databases are disconnected.

4. Objects are described differently in different schemes and systems.

5. It is difficult to find new user information from existing data.

6. Presentation does not suit the need of individual users.

Fig. 1. Problems bundle

---

[2] Van Gogh museum Multimedia PDA tour, 2005 Muse SILVER Award of Educational/ Interpretive http://www.mediaandtechnology.org/muse/2005muse_art.html
[3] Tate Modern online tour: http://www.tate.org.uk/modern/multimediatour/
[4] PEACH (Personal Experience with Active Cultural Heritage): http://peach.itc.it/home.html

To solve these problems, our current approach is to collect user preference data to use in a recommender system of artworks and to provide dynamic generation of personalized presentations depending on the user, his/her current task and final goal. In the last decade, dedicated recommender systems have gained popularity and become more and more established practice in online commerce. Amazon recommends books to users based on the feedback of similar users. Considering that explicit feedback is the most reliable source of information for personalization [3], in our system, we let the users rate artefacts to get recommendations. In such a way, we collect user preference data and minimize disturbing them to the extent possible.

3   Overview of the CHIP Demonstrator

The CHIP functional prototype provides recommendations of artefacts and art-related topics based on user's ratings of artifacts in a five-point scale. Additionally, it allows users to rate the recommended items as well. In this way, the system gradually builds a profile of the user, which can be further used for generating personalized museum tours. Figure 2 depicts the process of interactive user modeling and generating of recommendations, with corresponding CHIP demonstrator screenshots.

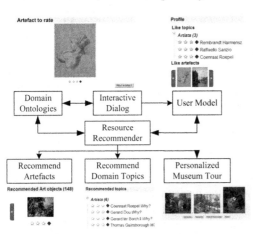

Fig. 2. Interactive UM & Recommendation

The user model (profile) is an extended overlay of the CHIP RDF/OWL domain model. To process RDF data, we use the Sesame[5] semantic repository and the SeRQL[6] query language. The initial RDF/OWL model is provided by the MultimediaN N9C E-Culture project [7] and is extended with IconClass mappings done by the STITCH project[8]. The data model contains mappings to the common vocabularies (Getty [9], Inconclass [10] and ARIA [11]) and uses open standards, like VRA, SKOS and OWL/RDF.

This rich semantic modeling of the Rijksmuseum collection allows us to maintain a lightweight user profile and perform a dynamic, real-time calculation of the user's interest. We also store the presented but non-rated items, so that we can use this information for optimization of the presentation sequence. The system

---

[5] Sesame: open source Java framework for storing, querying and reasoning with RDF (schema).

[6] SeRQL: Sesame RDF Query Language, http://www.openrdf.org/doc/sesame/users/

[7] MultimediaN N9C Eculture project http://e-culture.multimedian.nl/

[8] STITCH project: http://www.cs.vu.nl/STITCH/

[9] Getty vocabulary http://www.getty.edu/research/conducting_research/vocabularies/

[10] Iconclass thesaurus http://www.iconclass.nl/libertas/ic?style=index.xsl

[11] ARIA vocabulary http://www.rijksmuseum.nl/collectie/ontdekdecollectie?lang=en

calculates the likelihood of preference based on the user's ratings and it directly links to a given node in the semantic domain network. We use these links as properties of nodes in applying content-based recommendation techniques [4].

4 Research Questions and Approach

The main research question is: How can we develop methods and tools for generating personalized presentations of cultural-heritage objects both in the virtual (Web) and physical (museum) spaces? We identify here four main issues:

- Vocabulary gap. How to bridge the discrepancy between the descriptions of cultural heritage collections defined by domain experts and the implicit and often not domain related preference of end users?
- Serendipity of discovering new user information. How to acquire unknown/new user information based on the users interactive behavior and similarities to other users for which a user profile is available?
- Unobtrusive information gathering. What is the best way to minimize the amount of information a user must provide explicitly, in favor of information obtained (incrementally) by inducing user preference from ratings of a limited subset of artefact collections? In this way, will the system gather enough information for the user model?
- Avoid the cold-start problem. How to allow the user to profit immediately from the recommender system, without forcing the user to engage in the tedious task of providing a lot of information beforehand?

To bridge the vocabulary gap, we deploy a domain model based on existing ontology-based thesauri that allows for mappings to the Rijksmuseum collection model concepts. This model may be extended to capture additional information needed for a full user profile.

In the CHIP prototype recommender, the rating of recommendations provides a first means of incrementally rating preferences generated from rating a minimal subset of artefacts. When applying recommendations to the construction of personalized tours, we will analyze the user's navigation behavior in order to incrementally refine the user model and provide better recommendations. To avoid bothering the user, we minimize the explicit preference statements by providing users with a small set of artefacts, for which an explicit rating is required. To the extent possible we derive a user model from the initial ratings as an overlay of the domain data model. By providing a small set of samples, we minimize the amount of information the user must provide. Initial recommendations can then later be improved by incremental refining preference ratings. An interesting research issue here is what is the minimal subset of artefacts sufficiently covering all potential topics of interest and allowing for a proper overlap among user profiles?

Following a user-centered design cycle, we have so far reached two steps: (1) collect, analyze and structure the domain data model, and (2) perform a first evaluation based on our first prototype of the recommender system. After collecting data and feedback from real users, as a next step, we will revise/improve the design of the CHIP system, preparing for the next design cycle, such as creating and testing the personalized museum tours.

During August to October 2006, a first user study of the CHIP demonstrator was performed at the Rijksmuseum Amsterdam. Our goal was: (1) to test the effectiveness of the CHIP recommender system with real users; (2) to gain insight in user characteristics of our target group. In total 39 users participated in this study, including actual visitors and museum employees. The empirical results confirmed our hypothesis that the CHIP recommender indeed helps novice users elicit art preferences from their implicit knowledge/interest in museum collection. Additionally, we generated some main user characteristics, like small groups with 2-4 persons, well educated people in mid-age, no prior knowledge of the museum collections. For more details about the user study, please see our paper of the Rijksmuseum case study [5].

5 Work Plan

In the first year of my PhD project I have performed an initial domain analysis and worked on requirements extraction and assessment of the CHIP recommender prototype. The goal is to continue with the user-centered process of design, improve and apply recommendations in the construction of personalized tours, both virtual and physical, through the museum's collections. To achieve this goal, we now use a small scale user model that captures user preferences as an overlay of the domain collection model (e.g. artists, artefacts, styles). Based on our initial assessment and further user studies, we target to extend the user model with explicit characteristics, such as level of expertise and group characteristics derived from the ontological modeling of the collection. In this way, we aim at a user profile enriched with semantics and a rich set of characteristics, to allow for more advanced applications of recommendation systems, yet is minimal with respect to the effort required of the individual user.

Acknowledgments. I would like to thank my supervisor Lora Aroyo for her valuable comments on this paper.

References

1. Picard, R.W.: Affective Computing. MIT Press, Cambridge (1997)
2. Bowen, J., Filippini-Fantoni, S.: Personalization and the web from a museum perspective. In: Proc. Museums on the Web Conference (2004)
3. Farzan, R., Brusilovsky, P.: Social Navigation Support in a Course Recommendation System. In: Proc. 4th International Conference on Adaptive Hypermedia and Adaptive Web-based Systems (2006)
4. Balabanovic, M., Shoham, Y.: Fab: Content-Based, Collaborative Recommendation. In: Comm. ACM, vol. 40(3), pp. 66–72 (1997)
5. Wang, Y., Aroyo, L., Stash, N., Rutledge, L.: Interactive User Modeling for Personalized Access to Museum Collections: The Rijksmuseum Case Study. To be presented at the 11th International Conference on User Modeling, UM 2007 (June 2007)

Author Index

Lecture Notes in Artificial Intelligence (LNAI)

Vol. 4274: Q. Huo, B. Ma, E.-S. Chng, H. Li (Eds.), Chinese Spoken Language Processing. XXIV, 805 pages. 2006.

Vol. 4265: L. Todorovski, N. Lavrač, K.P. Jantke (Eds.), Discovery Science. XIV, 384 pages. 2006.

Vol. 4264: J.L. Balcázar, P.M. Long, F. Stephan (Eds.), Algorithmic Learning Theory. XIII, 393 pages. 2006.

Vol. 4259: S. Greco, Y. Hata, S. Hirano, M. Inuiguchi, S. Miyamoto, H.S. Nguyen, R. Słowiński (Eds.), Rough Sets and Current Trends in Computing. XXII, 951 pages. 2006.

Vol. 4253: B. Gabrys, R.J. Howlett, L.C. Jain (Eds.), Knowledge-Based Intelligent Information and Engineering Systems, Part III. XXXII, 1301 pages. 2006.

Vol. 4252: B. Gabrys, R.J. Howlett, L.C. Jain (Eds.), Knowledge-Based Intelligent Information and Engineering Systems, Part II. XXXIII, 1335 pages. 2006.

Vol. 4251: B. Gabrys, R.J. Howlett, L.C. Jain (Eds.), Knowledge-Based Intelligent Information and Engineering Systems, Part I. LXVI, 1297 pages. 2006.

Vol. 4248: S. Staab, V. Svátek (Eds.), Managing Knowledge in a World of Networks. XIV, 400 pages. 2006.

Vol. 4246: M. Hermann, A. Voronkov (Eds.), Logic for Programming, Artificial Intelligence, and Reasoning. XIII, 588 pages. 2006.

Vol. 4223: L. Wang, L. Jiao, G. Shi, X. Li, J. Liu (Eds.), Fuzzy Systems and Knowledge Discovery. XXVIII, 1335 pages. 2006.

Vol. 4213: J. Fürnkranz, T. Scheffer, M. Spiliopoulou (Eds.), Knowledge Discovery in Databases: PKDD 2006. XXII, 660 pages. 2006.

Vol. 4212: J. Fürnkranz, T. Scheffer, M. Spiliopoulou (Eds.), Machine Learning: ECML 2006. XXIII, 851 pages. 2006.

Vol. 4211: P. Vogt, Y. Sugita, E. Tuci, C.L. Nehaniv (Eds.), Symbol Grounding and Beyond. VIII, 237 pages. 2006.

Vol. 4203: F. Esposito, Z.W. Raś, D. Malerba, G. Semeraro (Eds.), Foundations of Intelligent Systems. XVIII, 767 pages. 2006.

Vol. 4201: Y. Sakakibara, S. Kobayashi, K. Sato, T. Nishino, E. Tomita (Eds.), Grammatical Inference: Algorithms and Applications. XII, 359 pages. 2006.

Vol. 4200: I.F.C. Smith (Ed.), Intelligent Computing in Engineering and Architecture. XIII, 692 pages. 2006.

Vol. 4198: O. Nasraoui, O. Zaïane, M. Spiliopoulou, B. Mobasher, B. Masand, P.S. Yu (Eds.), Advances in Web Mining and Web Usage Analysis. IX, 177 pages. 2006.

Vol. 4196: K. Fischer, I.J. Timm, E. André, N. Zhong (Eds.), Multiagent System Technologies. X, 185 pages. 2006.

Vol. 4188: P. Sojka, I. Kopeček, K. Pala (Eds.), Text, Speech and Dialogue. XV, 721 pages. 2006.

Vol. 4183: J. Euzenat, J. Domingue (Eds.), Artificial Intelligence: Methodology, Systems, and Applications. XIII, 291 pages. 2006.

Vol. 4180: M. Kohlhase, OMDoc – An Open Markup Format for Mathematical Documents [version 1.2]. XIX, 428 pages. 2006.

Vol. 4177: R. Marín, E. Onaindía, A. Bugarín, J. Santos (Eds.), Current Topics in Artificial Intelligence. XV, 482 pages. 2006.

Vol. 4160: M. Fisher, W. van der Hoek, B. Konev, A. Lisitsa (Eds.), Logics in Artificial Intelligence. XII, 516 pages. 2006.

Vol. 4155: O. Stock, M. Schaerf (Eds.), Reasoning, Action and Interaction in AI Theories and Systems. XVIII, 343 pages. 2006.

Vol. 4149: M. Klusch, M. Rovatsos, T.R. Payne (Eds.), Cooperative Information Agents X. XII, 477 pages. 2006.

Vol. 4140: J.S. Sichman, H. Coelho, S.O. Rezende (Eds.), Advances in Artificial Intelligence - IBERAMIA-SBIA 2006. XXIII, 635 pages. 2006.

Vol. 4139: T. Salakoski, F. Ginter, S. Pyysalo, T. Pahikkala (Eds.), Advances in Natural Language Processing. XVI, 771 pages. 2006.

Vol. 4133: J. Gratch, M. Young, R. Aylett, D. Ballin, P. Olivier (Eds.), Intelligent Virtual Agents. XIV, 472 pages. 2006.

Vol. 4130: U. Furbach, N. Shankar (Eds.), Automated Reasoning. XV, 680 pages. 2006.

Vol. 4120: J. Calmet, T. Ida, D. Wang (Eds.), Artificial Intelligence and Symbolic Computation. XIII, 269 pages. 2006.

Vol. 4118: Z. Despotovic, S. Joseph, C. Sartori (Eds.), Agents and Peer-to-Peer Computing. XIV, 173 pages. 2006.

Vol. 4114: D.-S. Huang, K. Li, G.W. Irwin (Eds.), Computational Intelligence, Part II. XXVII, 1337 pages. 2006.

Vol. 4108: J.M. Borwein, W.M. Farmer (Eds.), Mathematical Knowledge Management. VIII, 295 pages. 2006.

Vol. 4106: T.R. Roth-Berghofer, M.H. Göker, H.A. Güvenir (Eds.), Advances in Case-Based Reasoning. XIV, 566 pages. 2006.

Vol. 4099: Q. Yang, G. Webb (Eds.), PRICAI 2006: Trends in Artificial Intelligence. XXVIII, 1263 pages. 2006.

Vol. 4095: S. Nolfi, G. Baldassarre, R. Calabretta, J.C.T. Hallam, D. Marocco, J.-A. Meyer, O. Miglino, D. Parisi (Eds.), From Animals to Animats 9. XV, 869 pages. 2006.

Vol. 4093: X. Li, O.R. Zaïane, Z. Li (Eds.), Advanced Data Mining and Applications. XXI, 1110 pages. 2006.

Vol. 4092: J. Lang, F. Lin, J. Wang (Eds.), Knowledge Science, Engineering and Management. XV, 664 pages. 2006.

Vol. 4088: Z.-Z. Shi, R. Sadananda (Eds.), Agent Computing and Multi-Agent Systems. XVII, 827 pages. 2006.

Vol. 4087: F. Schwenker, S. Marinai (Eds.), Artificial Neural Networks in Pattern Recognition. IX, 299 pages. 2006.

Vol. 4068: H. Schärfe, P. Hitzler, P. Øhrstrøm (Eds.), Conceptual Structures: Inspiration and Application. XI, 455 pages. 2006.

Vol. 4065: P. Perner (Ed.), Advances in Data Mining. XI, 592 pages. 2006.